This is a global equity **Social and Economic Developmen[t]**
After the costs of the development and production of eac[h]
"Our Musical World" are met, all profits from your purchas[e]
distributed to the project participants or to create other such for-edu-
cation materials globally.

Thank you for your patronage!

About This Project:

Each of the themes and topics of **"Our Musical World"** is designed
to facilitate critical thinking and when possible, group or community
discussion skills in addressing many of the most enlightening cultural
phenomenon or pressing mis-perceptions in our world today.

Although *music* is clearly the more pronounced window through
which we will address life-related topics, it should be clear that in no
way are the topics of this project music specific, nor is the focus and
goal of this book, music exclusive. Rather, we have taken great care
to extract from the musicians comments, photographs, interviews, and
musical performances, critical socio-cultural issues that may have a
direct bearing on any area of study including (but not limited to): education, languages, counseling, the arts, philosophy, social studies/so-
ciology, religion, and history, as well as upon any individual or group
who may wish to create a stronger sense of community and well-being
across our collective cultural diversity. *Note:* The *Discussion/Reflec-
tion* activities spread throughout each Unit or the activities in the back
of each Unit (*Unit Activities*) are designed to more easily facilitate
group interaction.

Be a Part of Our Global Community:

We especially invite you to *dialogue* with others around the world on
our websites:

www.visionsandvibrations.com
or www.ourmusicalworld.com.

Instructions: You will be prompted to log-on to your respective forum
using your unique code below, to acknowledge perimeters of respectful
discussion, and to file a "bio" (at your discretion) that will help other's
know you or to better interpret your postings. You will then have in-
stant portal access to much of the world!

Your Unique Reader/Student Code is:

REA4-0GG4-5EJ7-N7JR

Our Musical World

Creative Insights into a Planet's Cultural Diversity

Léonie E. Naylor
Michael L. Naylor

with contributions from many of our world's creative artists

Visions & Vibrations International, LLC
Ann Arbor, Michigan

VISIONS & VIBRATIONS
INTERNATIONAL

Printed in the United States of America. Globally distributed.
Second Edition

Book formatting, graphic design, and text setting: Kazuko Sacks and Brandon Naylor
Music editor: Robert Martens, Solid Sound Studios, Ann Arbor, MI
Culture author and editor: Leonie E. Naylor
Interior graphic design assistance: Brandon B. Naylor, Kazuko Sacks, Clara Trent
Text editing/proofing: Tom Zimmerman, Joan Hutchinson
Cover concept: Brandon B. Naylor,
Cover fulfillment: Kazuko Sacks
Front cover photos: Courtesy of (clockwise/upper left) Kevin Locke (Photo: Bruce Wendt), Chinese Opera (Photo: P. Wei), J.M. Volcy, young girl (Photo: nikada33), Mady Kouyate.
Back cover photo: (right) Cuban musicians, (Photo: "Faut," 1961).

Library of Congress Cataloging-in-Publication Data

Naylor, Léonie E., Michael L.
    Our Musical World: Creative Insights into a Planet's Cultural Diversity
    Includes bibliographical references and indexes.
    1. Music appreciation. 2. World music—appreciation. 3. World culture—Studies, appreciation.
    4. Ethnomusicology—Multi-cultural studies.

ISBN: 978-0-9816609-0-5

Published by: Visions & Vibrations International
    P.O. Box 130830 / Ann Arbor, MI 48113-0830, U.S.A.
    Reader Support: www.visionsandvibrations.com or www.ourmusicalworld.com

Naylor 2134-8 W07

10 9 8 7 6 5 4 3 2 1

"Musik er liv, som dette uudslukkelig"

"Music is life, and like it, is inextinguishable."

Carl Nielsen, 4th Symphony preface, 1916

"Music is your own experience,
your thoughts, your wisdom.

If you don't live it, it won't
come out of your horn."

Charlie Parker, 1955

Table of Contents

List of CD tracks and Recording Information viii

Acknowledgments xiii

Preface xiv

Unit I: Introduction: Envisioning a Single Humanity Through Music 1
    Why Study Creativity? 2
    The Journey 3
    The Nature(s) of Music Composition 9
    Listening to Music: Hearing vs. Listening 10
    Change and Time: Concepts in Motion 14
    Musical Terms and Concepts 19
    Unit I: Activities 21

Unit II: Human Universals 25
    Building the "Mind's Files" 27
    Music: the Universal—*Not* the Universal Language 29
    The Life Cycle: Stories and Rituals 30
    The Influence of "Culture" (Super & Sub) 33
    The Value of a "Multi-Culture" Vision...37
    Families, Communities, and Subcultures 40
    Media and Technology: and the Influence on Musical Affinity 46
    Musical Terms and Concepts 45/49
    Unit II: Activities 51

Unit III: Native America: The Spirit in Symbolism 57
    Perceptual Tools for Decoding Symbolism 58
    Exercising Our Intuition 60
    Native American Symbolism: The World of the Circle 62
    Honoring the Gift 64
    Songkeepers: Music as a Way of Life 74
    Respecting the Circle: Culture Balancing 77
    The Talking Circle: Listening below the Surface 82
    Cultural Healing: The Role of Education 87
    Musical Terms and Concepts (the Sonograph) 88
    Unit III: Activities 92

Unit IV: Africa–America: Tales and Visions of a Racial Legacy 97
    The Legacy of "Culture Bias" 99
    Recognizing Biases toward Music 101
    R.E.S.P.E.C.T. and the Human Condition 105
    Understanding Racial Barriers and Biases 106
    Assimilation and Fusion: Spirituals and Gospel Music 108
    Communication from the Heart: Blues to Hip-hop 116
    Hip-hop: Today's Voice of Truth 124
    Encoding and Signifying: Reclaiming the Voice 127
    Pan "African-American" 130
    Pan Have We DNA: Calypso and the Calypsonian of Trinidad 133
    Seeing The History of Racial Unity 137
    Unit IV: Activities 140

Unit V: The Middle East (and Southern Asia): Religion and Music **145**
    Categorization vs Stereotyping 149
    Music and Religion: Reconciling Belief Systems 151
    Counterculture Music 155
    Intoning the Verses: Chant, Melody of the Spirit 157
    When Is It Culture? When Nation? When Religion? 166
    Overcoming Stereotypes: Melodies of the Islamic World..........................168
    Pillars and Practices of Islam 170
    Islamic Chant 172
    The Diversity of Musical Practices 176
    Instrumental Music 181
    Persian Poetry and Music 187
    Overcoming Religious and Cultural Separation 189
    "Sacred" Spaces & The Classroom 194
    Religion, Youth, and Media Today 195
    Unit V: Activities 201

Unit VI: Europe: The Influence of Ancestry and Imperialism **209**
    European "Classical," or "Art," Music in Perspective 212
    Respecting and Understanding History and Ancestry 214
    Respecting the Life Cycle 217
    The Impact of the "Empire" Mindset 218
    The Renaissance and Harmony 219
    More on Harmony 224
    Musical Terms and Concepts 226
    Baroque: The Reformation to Bach 229
    Classicism Personified 236
    Artistry and Humanness: Mozart and Beethoven 237
    Romanticism and Nationalism: The Culmination of Empire 243
    Italian Opera 245
    Programmatic Music and the Tone Poem 247
    "Classical" Music Today 249
    Unit VI Activities 252

Unit VII: Jewish and Romani: Stories of Creativity and Influence **258**
    Under the Radar: The Jewish Diaspora 259
    Sephardic and Ashkenazi Music 261
    Jewish Music and Influences Today 265
    Under the Radar (Part II): The Creativity of the "Romani" 270
    Poetry in Motion – Romani Dance Traditions 277
    Jewish-Rom Connection 280
    The Trans-/Intercontinental Musician: "Harmonia" 282
    Beyond Nation: Spain 286
    Musical Terms and Concepts 289
    Flamenco: Anthem of Spanish Fusion 291
    The Guitar – Ancestors and Descendants 293
    Greece – The "Cradle" of Western Civilization? 295
    When History is Distorted 299
    Unit VII Activities 300

Unit VIII: Africa and Latin America: Rites, Rituals, and Community Life **305**
    Rituals – Community Rites of Passage 307
    Rites of Passage Rituals 310
    Africa: Respecting Ancestry / Protecting the Community 314
    The Griot – The Ancestry of Storytelling 315
    Growing up with Music: Congolese Drums, Dance, and Community 318

Highlife – A Fusion of Functions and Cultures 323
Process, Not Goal 328
Struggles in Africa – Balancing the Equation 329
Today's Africa 332
Fluidity in Latin American Communities 335
Salsa: The Sauce of Life 343
Mexican Hospitality 347
South American Fusion 352
Samba: Music of, and for, Community 353
Colombian Cumbia 356
Dance and Music – Unit Postscript 359
Unit VIII Activities 364

Unit IX: Asia: Seeking Balance (and Healing) Through Music 369
Understanding the "Healing" Powers of Music 371
The Healing Power in Musical Storytelling 376
Out of India – History and Music Across Generations 377
The Role of the Teacher 381
Indian Instrumental Music 385
Rasa and the Rasika 386
The Ancient and the Modern 389
China: Spirit Greater Than Reality? 390
Chinese Opera – Dynamic Stories of a Complex History 393
Chinese Music Today 400
Korea and Japan – Cultures of Contrast 404
Korean Pansori – A Study of Time and Order 405
Telling Stories of "Others" – Seeking a Balance in Presentation 408
Japanese Storytelling – Contrasts in Time and Space 410
Coming to Know "Noh" (or Kabuki) 412
Modeling Cultural Motion: Indonesian Gamelan "Outside – In" 421
Summary: Music and the Power of Balance 428
Unit IX Activities 435

Unit X: Creolization: Creating Community Beyond Race and Nation 441
Music in the United States: "Take Two" 445
Toward a "Just" Perception 447
Creolization: Acceptance of the Human Condition 449
Heeding the Creole Voice 455
Ethnicity (Identity) Today 463
Jazz: An Embodiment of the American Creole 464
An Evolving Creole Art 466
Early Jazz – and the Legacy of New Orleans 468
Jazz – From Mainstream to Backroom 473
Other "Visions" of Creolization 478
Celtic Connections 480
Our World Today 483
The "Jazz" Experience 488
Unit X Activities: Creative Collaboration 504

Appendix:
Further Exploration: Websites 513
Glossary 519
Index 531

Pic. #1A What is art? What makes art "worthy" of our time to stop and hear, see, or absorb its influence? Perhaps one of art's greatest values is to simply cause us to pause and reflect or ask, *Why is this here? What can I learn from this?* This was the general reaction to these figures mounted high above a strolling population in a trendy shopping district of south-central Paris, France. Photo: Authors.

Pic #1B *The Vlatava River in the summertime and this overexposed photo – almost seem to suggest a painting. This is also a re-minder – that it is the jour-ney of humans through life – and life itself that is the inspiration of ALL art. Therefore, as all humans go through this journey, we can – with time, effort, and motivation – find respect for any artwork as well.* Photo: Authors.

Our Musical World
CD Track Listing and Recording Information

Unit I

1.1 "Images of Mogador," from the CD: <u>An Affair of the Harp,</u> by James Hartway. Harp performed by Kerstin Allvin. c. 2003, High Heel Records. Contact: webmaster@highheelrecords.com*

1.2 "Musique Arabo," from the CD: <u>Andalusian Music of Morocco</u>, performed by the Orchestre Chabab Al Andalous. c. 2004, Rabat, Morocco. Contact: www.minculture.gov.ma

Unit II

1.3 "Tsukuyomi," from the CD: <u>Karasu Randa</u>, by Karasu Randa, c. 2004, Mie, Japan.

1.4 "Kanté no Kanto," from the CD: <u>Mali Jazz</u>, composed by A.Biswane, featuring Vieux Kanté. Performed by Fra Fra Sound, c. 2002, Pramisi Records, the Netherlands. Contact: www.frafra-sound.com.

1.5 "Pueblo Andino" ("Andean Village"), from the CD: <u>Inca Son</u>, by César Villalobos, c. 2003, Inca Son Music. Contact: www.incason.com or www.ixtlanartists.com

Unit III

1.6 "Grand Entry," by Jeremy "Worm" Dearly, Jr., from the CD: <u>Midnite Express: Live in Cali</u>, c. 2005, Midnite Express Productions. Contact: midniteexpress@msn.com

1.7 "Itancanyapi" and "Midnight Strong Heart," performed by Kevin Locke, from the CD: <u>Midnight Strong Heart</u>, c.2003, Red Feather Music. Contact: www.kevinlocke.com or www.ixtlanartists.com

1.8 "Ecuador San Juanito / Sera," performed by Ecuador Manta, from the CD: <u>Alegrando el Alma</u>, c.2000, Ecuador Manta. Contact: www.ecuadormanta.com

1.9 "We'll Be Here," performed by Tiger/Tiger (Lee and Stephen Tiger), from the CD: <u>Space Age Indian</u>, c.1994, Stinger/Hopanke Music, A Tribal Experience/Soar. Contact: www.tigertigermusic.com

1.10 "Babylon World," performed by Casper Lomayesva, from the CD: <u>Honor the People</u>, c.2004, Third Mesa Publishing. Contact: www.3rdmesa.com

Unit IV

1.11 "Freedom," conducted by Dr. Augustus Hill with the Brazeal Dennard Community Chorus, from the CD: <u>Spring Concert, 2003</u>, c. 2003.

1.12 "Son, Sing the Blues," by Robert Penn, from the CD: <u>Live and Mighty</u>, c. 2004, Kimi Records.

1.13 Part I: "Pow-Wow Blues," by Joe Reilly, from the CD: <u>Mothers and Daughters</u>, c. 2001, Semper Records. Contact: www.sempermediagroup.com

Part II: "You Used to Call Me Mama," by Shari Kane, from the CD: <u>Madcat and Kane: Up against the Wall</u>, c. 2005, Hit Records.

---

* All Internet contact information is subject to change by the artist. The information provided was accurate at the publication of this edition. If you are unable to reach the artist at this address, please do a general search.

1.14 "Spare Change," by S.K.L.F.L. (Anthony Morgan), from the CD: <u>A Poet's Theme</u>, c. 2003, Brown Bomber Records.

1.15 "Berimbau," by Preston Vismale, from his personal recorded archives: c. 2004.

1.16 "Pan Have We DNA," by Chalkdust, from the CD: <u>Pan Have We DNA</u>, c. 2004, Juba Productions.

Unit V

1.17 "Muni" (believed to be from the Atharvareda-R Vlasinvictor), by Mrinalini Arkatkar, from her personal recorded archives, c.2005.

1.18 "Shema – Kiddusha"(from Jewish daily prayers), by Herman Slomovits, from the CD: <u>Herman Slomovits, Cantor</u>, c. 1958.

1.19 "Yebul – Homage to the Three Jewels," by the Ven. Samu Sunim, from the CD: <u>Moon Journeying through Clouds</u>, c. 1995, BSC.

1.20 "Madh" ("Praise Song"), from the Orchestra Chabab al Andalouss, from the CD: <u>Musique Arabo Andalouse Du Maroc</u>, c. 2004.

2.1 "Aminti Billah," written by Laure Dakkash, performed by Zein Al-Jundi, from the CD: <u>Traditional Songs from Syria</u>, c. 2004, ARC Music International. Contact: www.arcmusic.co.uk*

2.2 "Celestial Lover," by Mehri Vaghei, lyrics by Moayeri, music composed by Reza Babakhanlou, arranged by Millad Omranlou, from the CD: <u>Music of the Persian Symphony Orchestra</u>, c. 2000.

2.3 Part I: "Hidden Words of Baha'u'llah" (Persian: 38 & 40), by F. Enayati, from the CD: <u>Naghmeha I</u>, c. 1990.

Part II: "Is There Any Remover of Difficulties," a prayer by the "Bab" (Gate), recited by Lorintha Umtuch (Yakama Nation), from the CD: <u>Native American Style Bahá'í Songs</u>, c. 2004.

Part III: "Guide Me," prayer by Abdu'l-Bahá, composed by Kosta Kontos, recited by Helen and Kim Kontos, from the CD: <u>To the Eternal I Call Thee</u>, c. 2005. Contact: www.bahai.org.

2.4 "Mecca to Medina," by Euphrates, from the CD: <u>Stereotypes Incorporated</u>, c. 2004, Ilm Productions. Contact: www.euphrates.ca

Unit VI

2.5 "Cantate Domine," by Claudio Monteverdi, from the CD: <u>Glory to God</u>, by the Wayne State Concert Chorale, Dennis Tini, conductor, c. 1998.

2.6 "Christ lag in Todesbanden," from Bach Cantata No. 4, by J.S. Bach, transcribed and conducted by Leopold Stokowski, from the CD: <u>Leopold Stokowski: Bach-Stokowski Transcriptions</u>, c. 2001, by Fono Enterprises & Allegro Music.

2.7 "Fugue," from the Prelude and Fugue in G minor by J.S. Bach, performed by Elaine Bovender, c. 2005, from a personal recording.

2.8 "Lacrymosa" from the <u>Requiem</u> by Wolfgang Amadeus Mozart, performed by the Wayne State University Concert Chorale, from the CD: <u>Glory to God</u>, c. 1998.

---

* Use www.arcmusic.co.uk for all Arc Music International artists.

2.9　Middle section of fourth movement – Symphony No. 9: <u>Choral</u>, by Ludwig van Beethoven, conducted by Wilhelm Furtwängler with the Berlin Philharmonic Orchestra (live recording), from the CD: <u>Wilhelm Furtwängler, Beethoven Symphony No. 9,</u> c. 2001, Allergro/Fono Enterprise.

2.10　"Va Pensiero," by Giuseppe Verdi, from the opera: <u>Nabucco</u>, from the CD: <u>Nabucco</u>, c. 2000, Fono Enterprises, Italy.

2.11　"Basho: Yellow Rose Petals," by James Hartway, based upon "haikai" by Basho, performed by Kerstin Allvin, harp, from the CD: <u>An Affair of the Harp</u>, c. 2003, High Heel Records. Contact: webmaster@highheelrecords.com

Unit VII

2.12　A medley of Sephardic music in three parts. Part I: "Quando el rey Nimrod," Part II: "Arvoles lloran por lluvias," and Part III: "Yendome para Marsilia," performed by The Burning Bush, from the CD: <u>Best of Yiddish, Klezmer, and Sephardic Music</u>, c. 1996, Arc Music International.

2.13　A medley of Ashkenazi music in three parts. Part I: "Sirba mit Harbster Bletlekh," Part II: "Una noche al borde de la mar," and Part III: "Hey Zhankoye!" by The Burning Bush, from the CD: <u>Best of Yiddish, Klezmer, and Sephardic Music</u>, c. 1996, Arc Music International.

2.14　"The Deli Song," by Sandor and Lazlo Slomovits, from the CD: <u>The Best of Gemini</u>, c. 1999, Gemini. Contact: www.geminichildrensmusic.com

2.15　"Madrid," composed by Avishai Cohen, from the CD: <u>Avishai Cohen: At Home</u>, c. 1999, Razdaz Records. Contact: www.avishaimusic.com

2.16　A medley of three pieces. Part I: "Banatana," Part II: "Doina lui Cozma," and Part III: "Trec Tiganii," by Taraful din Baia, from the CD: <u>Gypsies of Romania</u>, c. 2000, Arc Music International.

2.17　"Melodies from Bukovina," by Harmonia, from the CD: <u>Harmonia: Music of Eastern Europe</u>, c. 2003, Traditional Crossroads. Contact: www.ixtlanartists.com

2.18　"Muñeira de Coia," by the Workshop-School for Galician Folk Instruments, from the CD: <u>Cantes del Pueblo,: Traditional Music of Spain</u>, c. 2002, Arc Music International.

2.19　"Asturias (Leyenda)," from the <u>Suite Española</u>, Op. 47*, by Isaac Albeniz, from a live recording by Lee Dyament, c. 2005.

2.20　"Kleftikos," from <u>Five Greek Dances</u>, for String Orchestra, by Nikos Skalkottas (1904-1949), Publisher, Universal Edition, Wien. Recording copyright: Apollo Classics, performed by the Sinfonietta Cracovia (from Kraków, Poland), Kypros Markou, Conductor.

Unit VIII

3.1　"Kumbuna," by Mady Kouyate, from the CD: <u>Kelemagni</u>, c. 2004.

3.2　"Sava Maiyaka," by Jean-Claude Biza Sompa and Bichini Bia Congo, from the DVD <u>Bichini Bia Congo</u>, c. 2004, Contact: www.mbongivillage.org

3.3　"Bjrj Ka Mbjrj (Live and Let Live)," by Oliver De Coque, from the CD: <u>Live and Let Live</u>, c. 2004.

3.4　"Mvidi Mukulu," by Mulopo Mulomede, from the CD: <u>My Hope</u>, c. 2004.

---

* These numbers "Opus 47," etc., are notations of classification, used to distinguish and codify a composer's work by sequence, order, or genre.

3.5 "No Quiero Nada Mas," by Trío los Favoritos, from the CD: <u>Trío los Favoritos</u>, c. 2004.

3.6 A Medley of Mexican music, including: "La Negra (The Black Woman)," "El Pastor (The Pastor)," and "El Arrancazacate," by Mariachi Sol, from the CD: <u>Mexico Lindo</u>, c. 1999, Arc Music International.

3.7 "Candela y Tumbao," by Arc Studio Band (featuring Gastón de Avila, vocals), from the CD: <u>Salsa Tumbao</u>, Arc Music International c. 2002.

3.8 "Brisa Marina," by Arc Studio Ensemble, from the CD: <u>Samba Bossa do Brazil</u>, c. 1999, Arc Music International.

3.9 "Cumbia Cienagüera," by Istvan Dely & Millero Congo, from the CD: <u>Millero Congo</u>, c. 1996, Insignia Records, Contact: www.insigniarecords.com

Unit IX

3.10 "Song by Saint Eknath," by Mrinalini Arkatkar, from a personal recording, c. 2005.

3.11 "Raga Shuddha Sarang," by Baluji Shrivastav, from the CD: <u>Classical Indian Sitar and Surbahar Ragas</u>, c. 1999, Arc Music International.

3.12 "Die Lian Hua," by Wei Li, from the CD: <u>Classical Chinese Folksongs and Opera</u>, c. 1997, Arc Music International.

3.13 "Sorrow of Separation," by Xiao Dong Wei, from the CD: <u>Sorrow of Separation,</u> c. 2005. Contact: xdwei@aol.com

3.14 "Shimch'ong'ga," (famous Korean traditional song), by Min-Su Kim, (P'ansori solo), from the CD: <u>Traditional Music from Korea</u>, c.1999, Arc Music International.

3.15 "Raijo & Ranjo," two versions: Noh and Kabuki comparisons (Japanese theater) from the recording: <u>Six Hidden Views of Japanese Music</u>, compiled by William Malm, c. 1981.

3.16 "Takaramono (Treasure)/Sabani wo Koide," by Painu Kajipito Marchan, from the CDs: <u>Takaramono/Iriomote</u>, c. 2001, Painukaji.

3.17 "Excerpt – 'Early Krishna,'" from Mahabharata, University of Michigan Gamelan, with Wasi Bantolo and Pak Parmardi, c. 2005, Univ. of Michigan.

3.18 "Tongkuilangji" by Sipakatau, from the CD: <u>New Experiment of Percussion</u>, c. 2004.

3.19 "The Fourth Valley/with Faces Beaming," by Ben Koen, from the CD: <u>Songs from the Green Mountain</u>, c. 1998, Qing Shan Music.

CD #4

Unit X

4.1 "Kil Pake/Selo," by Jean-Marc Volsy, a medley from the CD: <u>Bel Koud Kannon</u>, c. 2002.

4.2 "High Society" and "That's a Plenty," by Charlie Gabriel, from the CD: <u>Gabriel Traditional Jazz Band & Friends,</u> (featuring: Marcus Belgrave), c. 1993.

4.3 "The 12th Step," by Michael Zaporski, from the CD: <u>Insight</u>, c. 2003, Daddy Z.

4.4 "Reel des éboulements," by Mackinaw, from the CD: <u>Folk Music from Quebec</u>, c. 2001, Arc Music International.

4.5 "Muirruhgachs, Mermaids, and Mamiwata," by Chris Collins, from the CD: <u>Shamrock Shore</u>, c. 2005.

4.6 "Les Yeux de la Jeunesse" (The Eyes of Youth), by Dennis Tini, from the CD: <u>The Eyes of Youth</u>, c. 2004, Nicole Tini Music.

4.7 "Let Them See Jesus," by Carl Phillips and the PAB Singers, Detroit, Michigan, from the CD: <u>Let Them See Jesus</u>, c. 2005 .

4.8 "O Son of Spirit," by Ben Koen, from the CD: <u>Reliance</u>, c. 1997, Qing Shan Music.

4.9   "Esh Hal Qadny," composed by Hossam Ramzy, performed by Dalinda, from the CD: <u>Turquoise</u>, c. 2002, Arc Music International.

4.10   "Â Bientot," by Michael Zaporski, from the CD: <u>Insight</u>, c. 2003, Daddy Z.

4.11   "Doroogh Go" (Dishonest), by Arash, from the CD: <u>Doroogh Goo</u>, c. 2005

4.12   "Bachbatá" <u>Brandenburg Concertos</u>, Concerto Nº 3 in G Major, Allegro, by Johann Sebastian Bach, with the Capella Istropolitana (Slovak Philharmonic Chamber Orchestra) and Istvan and Shangó Dely, c. 2002.

Note: All of these musicians give their music and comments solely as included or stated on their behalf in the text. They do not necessarily concur, agree, or disagree with the opinions and perspectives of the authors as represented in other portions of this text project.

Pic. #1C *All the musicians on the CDs above and any CD you will ever purchase (with few exceptions) have logged thousands of hours learning their instrument, and – if they begin to master the inter-connection of the physical with the emotional or spiritual that makes music attractive to us – performing on their instruments. This is of course true of every art and craft. Yet, for musicians to speak their language or "art" – they must also log thousands of miles to rehearsals and "gigs" to master the vocabulary of music.* Photo: Authors.

Acknowledgments

We cannot fittingly acknowledge the contributions of so many musicians, teachers, family, friends, colleagues, and students over decades. We will attempt to partially recognize some of the contributors to this work and then remind the reader that there are so many others for whose contributions we are equally grateful.

We begin by thanking all the artists mentioned in the text or included on the CDs. They clearly represent the creativity in our world with class and honor. Their experiences and perceptions both through their music and in their comments will expose us to new possibilities. Additionally, the visions of many of the students and instructors, past and present, with whom we've been able to learn, question, and discuss life and music…are included in this text as well.

We also want to acknowledge all our past teachers, colleagues, and musician friends in the countries we've lived or worked, most notably those in the U.S.A., Germany, France, Switzerland, the U.K., and the Seychelles Islands. We especially wish to acknowledge all the folks at ARC Music International (especially Caren-Alexandra and Jon Entwistle), Bill Wilson at Lark in the Morning (San Francisco, CA), the Departments of Music at Wayne State University (Detroit, Michigan – USA) and Ethnomusicology and Romance Languages at the University of Michigan (Ann Arbor, Michigan – USA), the Department of Professional Counseling at Eastern Michigan University, Wikipedia.org, and the photographers cited in the text for assistance in locating images to connect to the text, and all of our family members for their support.

Above all, we must acknowledge with enormous parents' pride our son, Brandon, for his creativity not only in his graphic design ideas, but in the special manner by which he inspires us with his life.

Finally, we owe whatever global vision we've been able to acquire and pass on to the reader to our discovery of the Bahá'í Faith and the teachings of Bahá'u'lláh. It is from these experiences that we've learned to see all cultures as part of one world, all religions as a continuous chain of inspiration, and all races as simply— the human race.

May you, the reader, find the vision of a single world, the beauty of all cultures, and the magnificence of the enormous creativity in *Our Musical World*.

Pic.#2 *The collage (right) represents some of the most powerful influences in the author's lives. The collage generally is also a visual metaphor for the nature of life and the natural process of cultural fusion and intercultural exchange discussed throughout this text. This is the process by which all music comes into existence. In the collage there are distinct images representing unique cultural contributions across the spectrum of time. However, the entire picture is much more fluid, representative of its multiple influences, and as a whole is likely to be interpreted substantially differently from the single influences of any of the contributing sources. This is a visual metaphor of cultural fusion, arguably the process by which every cultural expression develops over time.* Graphic design: Brandon Naylor, 2005.

Preface

Perhaps, in one sense, the essence of life is perpetual growth in the acquisition of positive human qualities and the development of our capacity to interact respectfully with others for the betterment our varied human communities. If so, then each of us is on a journey, which, if we are lucky, will lead to the fulfillment of our individual human potential, whatever that is and however we believe it is acquired.

    The following is a bit about the authors' paths, and ultimately, the manner by which they acquired their cultural/musical tastes or affinities. Most of our tastes, musical or otherwise, and certainly those of the musicians represented in this text, are intensely personal. Therefore, we offer many of these stories and experiences in a personal way to you, the reader, that you may also reflect upon your own insights, tastes, creative capacities, and their relationship to—*Our (Musical) World.*

Pic. 2A *Pictures of a father and son* (Morocco – Photo: Terry Abrams)

Authors' Stories

Note: We offer these stories of our experiences for two reasons only. One, that you might see how we evolved to the perceptions and experiences from which this text is born, including: our own misunderstandings, biases, or strengths. And two, that you might similarly reflect and, when possible, survey the evolution of your own experiences, tastes, and values.

Léonie's Story

"The integrity of life is in sacrificing for others." These words, which were told to me as a child by my dear mother and father now departed from this world, still resonate within me. Many of my greatest capacities and sensitivities must be accredited largely to the values that my parents instilled in me. At the age of nine, I remember my parents took my siblings and me on one of our adventures in the forests and mountains. On the way they would ask us to listen to the sounds of nature and to pick up something that we found special. It was usually a leaf, a flower, a colored stone, a peacock feather, or a pitcher plant. On our "snack" break, they would ask us what made the item we picked special to us. After hearing our limited responses, they told us what each of the item represented to them. They used many deeply symbolic references that personified the items in order to show us how each of them was just as precious, valuable, and, therefore, each in their own unique and different ways, important. My mother would then ask us to sit quietly on the mountain top and observe and listen to the different birds, insects, trees, wild flowers, the sound of the river the wind, and all the other natural beauties and how they each assisted and enhanced each other.

    I cite the experience above for only one reason. I hope that it facilitates a small insight into who I am, and how experiences such as this one, and each challenge in one's life, give us the opportunity to see the world through a unique and fresh perspective, while simultaneously learning to honor human "oneness" and the manner by which each of us can profoundly enhance, learn from, and assist others over the life experience.

    As to my path… I was born the daughter of Noé and Sabine Isaac and grew up on the other side of the world in the Seychelles Islands (located in the Indian Ocean), in a culture of multiple races, cultural backgrounds, and languages. I first worked as a World Tourism and International Relations Officer, interacting with dignitaries from most of the European countries on a weekly basis. I was later educated and worked in Austria in International Relations and Tourism Management, France (languages), and Germany (languages), where I worked in the Seychelles International Tourism Office and organized or participated in multi-cultural conferences and seminars throughout Europe. I further extended my desire for acquiring additional international and cultural knowledge by traveling to Czech Republic, Hungary, Kenya, Saudi Arabia, India, Honduras, Mexico, Canada, Jamaica, Bermuda, Puerto Rico, and the Bahamas, prior to and after coming to the United States with my American husband in 1983. It was during these initial experiences that I was first able to liken the human world to that world of nature shown me by my parents.

As I continued on my path of learning, I served as a multi-lingual supervisor for Delta Airlines in Coral Gables, Florida (where I first learned to what extent "racism" existed in our world), had a child who was born premature (1.5 lbs.) and whom I (with the assistance of doctors and nurses) raised to be a strong and successful student (where I first learned how being "gifted" can take so many forms), worked through numerous health problems of my own (where I learned how grateful we can become for the smallest things in life), and later pursued a B.A. in French and Spanish and an M.A. in French and Comparative Literature at the University of Michigan (where I learned a deeper gratitude for life and how hard I was capable of working despite discomfort and pain).

All of these experiences further prepared me to work for nearly a decade with adults and students from alternative populations. I began to see the manner by which we stereotype and classify diversity, which, in turn, fueled my thirst for justice and equity generally, and set me on a path to becoming an advisor, advocate, and counselor of international students and individuals expelled from the mainstream population.

As a result, not long ago I completed a Master's degree from Eastern Michigan University as a Limited License Professional Counselor (L.L.P.C.). My areas of specialty include multi-cultural counseling, substance abuse, domestic violence, depression, building rapport and relationships with resistant, low self-esteem clients faced with acculturation issues, and in creating alternatives for clients based on a realistic understanding of the impact each of our cultural histories has on the development of our life perspectives and life choices. It is through observation, experience, and training that I have increasingly sought to better understand the diverse manner by which we share our common human experiences. Over time, I've come to understand the benefit in *seeing* cultural diversity, *practicing* cultural appreciation, and *advocating* cultural healing, which infers a simultaneous desire to see our history accurately, balanced by an understanding that others have evolved and possess a different balance of cultural strengths and liabilities. But in the end, it has been my experience, as I learn more about myself and others, that there is little fruit that can come from the past, if we do not have the strongest motivation to plant and cultivate it by taking action.

I've further witnessed that much of what we teach in our schools, experience in our media, and consume en route to the establishment of our per-

Pic. 2BC *We learn primarily by example and experience. So many of our values, likes, and dislikes are passed to us from prior generations. Yet only when we are aware of these connections can we either appreciate or, often, change or enhance them. Authors' Léonie's parents, Michael's parents, authors, and son. Collage: B Naylor.*

ceptions of our world vision is inadequately informed as concerns the real nature of human cultural exchange (the transference of ideas, traits, and values between culture groups), and thus, this misinformation is subject to distorting a healthy perspective of our ever-emerging (global) human community.

Concerning this work, my husband and I come from nearly opposite worlds, and now, in our second quarter-century of marriage, we have shared much. He is a musician; I, someone who has sung, danced, and enjoyed music my whole life. He, someone intimately acquainted with the ways of the Western, fast-paced, and highly individualistic world; I, from an island culture that places enormous importance on community-life. He from a culture that sees and speaks "difference" (of race, nationality, and culture); I, from one that has learned about differences—but lives more from a creative "creole" perspective and a unified culture-system, necessarily demanding an intimate acceptance of diversity and relative ambiguity about "race." For these reasons, we have combined our perspectives and knowledge. My husband's… the knowledge of human creativity through music; my own… the knowledge of both our diverse and yet common human experiences—mentally, emotionally, and culturally.

Like most, our path as a family has not always been smooth, without conflict, or grave challenges. Why then, would a path to an accurate and harmonious vision of humanity require any less work or be accomplished without trials, discomfort, and challenges? In all cases, I sincerely hope that you will enjoy our work, and will share your perspectives with us at our website: **www.visionsandvibrations.com**.

Michael's Story:

I have a Ph.D. in **Ethnomusicology** (study of ethnic [from ethnos = people] music) from the University of Michigan, and degrees in film and media composition and performance from the University of Miami (Florida, U.S.A.), and it is the world's music through which we will be examining our planet's diverse cultures. But I defer to Léonie's story—as the source for the shape and scope of this text—to not merely focus on musical discussions and analysis (otherwise, my inclination). If anything valuable lies in this text, it is more likely because of our collaboration as well as the contact and insight we've gathered from numerous folks (musicians or not) across many countries, and finally, the result of all of the mistakes we've made and the bumps and bruises we've acquired along the way in attempting to understand others, experiences which have forced us to relinquish any allegiance to a superior or inferior culture or musical system.

Personally, I was born the son of a band director (Roger Naylor) and a loving mother (Dorothy Naylor-Marks). I am, furthermore, the grandson of a musician and furniture salesman, Earl Hunt—who was an enormously colorful figure and a band leader (early jazz), and I grew up in the Midwest of the United States with music all around me. The primary sounds in my musical environment, besides popular radio, which I listened to regularly (especially while doing odd jobs), were symphonic band music, classical orchestral music, church choir music, and big band jazz. So along with other teenage concerns, I had what "I believed to be" an extremely diversified musical upbringing, and, I began to play the music of my experience on the trombone, the same instrument my father had played.

My first awareness on any personal level of the many types of music available to me outside of my prior experiences occurred in high school. I frequently said, "I'm into all kinds of music," which I learned really meant I was into a fair amount of music from the narrow experiences of "my world." My last year in high school I attended the Interlochen Arts Academy in Michigan, where I was paired with a roommate from the south side of Chicago, Mathew.

I remember going to the practice room with Matt and hearing him sing gospel songs he had learned as a part of his path, from his family and a result of American history. He sang these songs with his eyes closed, the music coming from deep inside his soul. He told me stories about his family's traditions, introducing me to a whole new world. From this vantage point, I began to realize there was a world of possibilities awaiting me. The question was simply: *What would I do with this knowledge?*

Answer: Initially, nothing! The pre-requisite for change is a certain measure of willingness to be uncomfortable, maybe even periodically miserable. Who would choose such an option?

In my case, however, a hunger for adventure drove me over time to start looking beyond my narrow world. I transferred to the University of Miami (Florida), where I began to play as a professional studio musician in orchestras and bands that backed up celebrities such as Frank Sinatra, Debbie Reynolds, Julio Iglesias, Raphael, the Four Tops, the Stylistics, and others. [Note: a studio musician is a musician for hire, a *sideman*, or part of an orchestra].

While I was in Miami, I was also exposed to salsa (Latin-Caribbean), samba (Brazilian), and Haitian music and was able to tour the Caribbean a few times with groups from these cultures. I was still playing my father's trombone, but now—not like it had ever been played before! During this time I also came into contact with the "fusion" music of Africa and Europe, styles of music that further influenced my musical curiosity. Most importantly, I also began a spiritual search, which led me to the discovery of the Baha'i Faith. This was the outcome of a search for "purpose" and an explanation for why or how a single Creator could have given our world so many diverse religions. In any event, these experiences would all have major influences on my future life choices.

Later, I made my first musical tour to Europe and then to Cyprus, Syria, Jordan, Egypt, Israel, Tunisia, and I had opportunities to play with the late, great Celia Cruz in a salsa band, to travel through Europe with jazz bands, and tour much of South America (Uruguay, Argentina, Paraguay, Bolivia, Peru, Ecuador, Colombia, and Venezuela) with a folk music group representing the Baha'i Faith. These experiences really opened my eyes to our world's wealth of cultural expressions (See Unit V—Religion and Music in the Middle East). I was frequently surprised by many aspects of these cultures' music, and I found I could often directly connect them to my own ancestry and experiences.

Later, I met Léonie, from the Seychelles Islands, who eventually consented to be my wife. Subsequent visits to Léonie's culture would prove to be among the most life-changing experiences of all. Through Léonie and her family, I experienced an island culture that was enormously creative and virtually devoid of an entrenched perception of "race." I would eventually explore these concepts further in my doctoral research on her culture's music (Unit X) and would also begin to learn the merits of large, extended family and community structures, as well as the importance music plays in marking the life cycle or in healing cultural imbalances (Units VIII and IX). I also began to realize that the more we see and experience, the more we will become comfortable in embracing change, which then cycles back and strengthens our desire to learn more.

Summary:

Through our lives as a multicultural, multiracial, (and numerous other *multi*) family, we are learning to engage in the struggle of reeducating, rethinking, and reevaluating our perceptions of the world.

By virtue of—not in spite of—both failures and successes in contending with illnesses, addictions, and personal imbalances, struggling to make livings as teachers, musicians, or counselors, and later teaching in universities and colleges (educational corporations), counseling clients of the greatest possible cultural diversity, learning from people's paths, concerns, and life experiences, continuing to travel and research in remote corners of the earth, and, making friends with people from many cultural or religious backgrounds and from so-called *races or nations* (Units III, IV, VI, VII, & X), we have come to believe in a few important principles upon which this project is built:

- There is no contradiction in liking who we are and in simultaneously loving what we can become.

- There is no intelligence in remaining small and confined, when the world is designed for our exploration.

- There is not a single person—much less a single music—in this world from whom we cannot learn numerous positive ideas and values. We simply have to try to be open to it, to approach each new experience with some degree of humility, and to attempt to focus not on the results, but on the process of learning.

We sincerely hope you, the reader, will find value in the conversations with your ancestors, brothers, sisters, and elders on this planet. We also hope that, while you read and listen, you will formulate new visions, questions, and a hunger to acquire a fair and just vision of our human family.

> *"Acquiring an affinity for justice allows one to see the world of cultures and music as equally valid, and the world of humanity as a single community. The potential for growth now becomes enormous. To believe otherwise assumes there is a superior culture, race, or musical style, which is counter-intuitive."* Naylor & Naylor, "Caught between Race and Racelessness," The Center for Cultural Healing, 2003, p. iv.

About This Text

This text, its CDs, and instructional materials are all created to honor you and your time by emphasizing the perceptual skills and creative qualities you might find practical and relevant to your own lives and careers. Whether you are reading this for your own growth and enjoyment or are using this program as part of a course or study circle, we hope that it will enhance the quality and enjoyment of your life experience.

Most of us are inundated with facts and information. Although we will provide some information and facts here, we hope to provide only what is essential to enhance the cultural and musical experiences that may impact your life. We will, therefore, place a much higher importance on the insights, options, alternatives, and overall perceptual tools that encourage each of us to grow in our understanding of such qualities as humility, honesty, creativity, and, above all, flexibility in embracing change.

Pic #3 *Robert Martin, from Virginia, sees musical instruments not just as sound- or music-makers, not as a means for making money or playing music, but as works of art in their own right. Our perceptions of everything in this world are directly the result of our experiences.* Photo: Copyright, R. Martin, (see also 6.24, p.247.)

The themes in this text that we hope will assist this process include the following:

- Cultural "justice" is essential to a balanced and open perspective of our world. This text assumes there is no superior or inferior culture or music. Rather, all music is expressive of human experience and worthy of appreciation, which we equate with respect. To achieve this perspective, we will place a greater emphasis upon the culture groups that are under- or misrepresented in mainstream Western education and media. We will not assume that Western European or Euro-American music or culture is superior or worthy of greater attention simply because it has received greater attention in the past or is more akin to the affinities (perceptions of value) to which many of us are accustomed. That said, we also will not exclude European or "art" music; it has undeniably enhanced our world's cultural systems and provided us with creative masterpieces.

- The manner in which cultures fuse, exchange, transfer their thoughts, and *"creolize"* (i.e., manifest qualities of "creolité," or human creativity) will be given far greater emphasis than categorization and labeling in this text.

- Most of our *mind's files* about "others" (information we have about culture groups that are not a part of our personal life experiences) have been acquired through filtered or interpretive sources, unless we have both traveled and *lived* extensively elsewhere. That is, media, textbooks, or lessons are frequently not presented by the culture-bearers (representatives from those cultures) themselves. Rather, such information comes through media productions or sources that have spoken (however respectfully) for the cultures being portrayed. In music textbooks, this method of informing means that the author provides the voice of the culture's musicians. Regardless of the writer's maturity and respect for each culture, we are left wondering, "What would the musicians themselves have said?"

Although we have been forced to make decisions about what should be included or omitted, we have tried to collect the voices of the musicians and culture-bearers themselves. Whenever possible we have asked each contributor, "Given limited parameters (one to two pages, or one to two musical examples), what would you like to say to a predominantly Western (European/American) audience?" We, in turn, have taken the predominant themes and topics from their comments, and prefaced each unit with a discussion of these themes and topics. The final result is this text and CD project.

Finding Diversity in Our Own Communities

When we speak of *traveling* in this text, we mean the growth that occurs with learning about the world around us. Music is a valuable and accessible tool for learning about others whose language we do not speak or whose lands we may never be able to visit physically. However, venturing into the worlds of others is not the only means by which we can develop the experiences, flexibility, and disciplines necessary to more fully appreciate the diversity of the world's cultures.

The world has been in a process of exchange and cross-cultural communication for so long that we can find reflections of our world and nearly every culture and musical style, right within our own community. To illustrate this, we have selected much of the music for this text from a single region (Detroit/ Southern Michigan, United States) or have augmented it with contributions from musicians the authors have known through their contacts in this region. As we explore the many options available in our immediate world, we can also find every variety of cultural possibility to expand our experiences. Add to this the Internet, video, and the multitude of other technological innovations, and it is virtually impossible not to become a citizen of the world if one finds that a desirable goal.

In our case, although many of the musicians in this text live (or have lived) around the world, our personal contacts with them occurred within a few miles' radius of our own home. We take this approach to magnify the reality of our world today. Wherever we live, whatever the circumstances of our upbringing, the world and all of its cultures and music are accessible to us, if we just take the time to listen!

Challenges and Rewards

Is it reasonable or beneficial to claim one's lifestyle, culture, or community superior to another? If not, then how could we claim that one style of music is superior to another?

We may not like all music; we may not agree with all lyrics, symbols, rituals, or belief systems. The premise of this text is that we honor ourselves by respecting or appreciating the expressions of others. We

accomplish this by seeking to understand the deepest and most heartfelt levels of each culture's value systems through their music. Every musical expression is simultaneously a link to a culture's past … and to our future. If this project does its job correctly, you will come to understand ultimately that "they" (other cultures) are a part of you and your past, and your link to being comfortable with the inevitable vision of a singular human race. Regardless, we will attempt to distinguish "tolerance" and respect.

Scope of Representation

Historically, many of our music, art, or literature courses have been taught with a focus on the work or product itself, and much less on the manner in which the work reflects the people who created it. In a music class, for example, we would discuss the musical structure, the form, the sounds, the instruments, or the musicmakers, but not emphasize as much, the context or social relevance of the work (i.e., the function or purpose of the music's existence). Until the last few decades, this was the academic model for teaching most branches of cultural expression (language, art, music, dance, culinary arts, etc.). Then came interdisciplinary movements to combine the "ologies" ("studies of"). This meant that the study of "anthrop" (human), "socio" (social), and, in our case, musical concepts and perceptual tools was reconnected to present the entire experience of a culture.

Among these "ologies" was **ethnomusicology:** the study of "people's" music. This new field of study began to provide equal but different respect to folk, ethnic, popular, classical, and religious music of all cultures.

Increasingly now, we are beginning to understand that, if all human beings are worthy of equal respect, then exploring their music, however different from our tastes and experiences, can be a valuable experience as well. This simply means if I don't like something largely because it reflects qualities different from those in my own world, it is to my advantage to ask more and deeper questions and to assume I will benefit from the exchange.

Unfortunately, we cannot claim that we have picked all of the best topics, the most representational pieces, or even the most representative examples of each artist, genre, or culture. What we do hope, however, is that this text will in some way act as a bridge to your own further investigation of other cultural and creative possibilities.

Pic #4 *Around virtually every corner is a cultural and, very frequently, a musical surprise. Some, when they come across the new experience, just keep walking and never really observe the potential in the new experience. Others will stop and take in the beauty of human art, as was the case on this corner in San Francisco. Here, a group of exceptional break-dancers told us they were the "posse" and that they've been working together for nearly two years.* Photo: Authors.

We say these things to place our efforts in proper perspective and, above all, to caution the reader against planting our perspectives too firmly in their minds. Any attempt to reconnect humanity and its music can, at best, only provide examples and snapshots of possibilities. Imagine the uproar in a Western university if a music department were forced to gather the entire evolution of Western European music history within a single semester's class. And yet we are attempting to represent the entire world over a much longer period of time within the confines of a single text. Our challenge: how can we do this respectfully?

Pic.#4A *If we view this picture of jazz musicians playing an older "traditional" style jazz, then do we also have room in our perceptual files to accommodate the myriad of other— perhaps more modern—styles of jazz as well?* Photo: courtesy Joe Gough

We might wish to keep three pertinent points in mind:

1) **Human cultures** are constantly in flux. What represents the "tradition" today will likely be very different tomorrow.

2) The only way to continually **update our mind's files** on the cultures of the world is to remain constantly **questioning** and in a state of perpetual *creative investigation* concerning the "world."

3) **Anything** that keeps us from being **interested** in another culture's music is generally the result of perceptual/cultural **baggage** that we have acquired along our own life journey thus far. Because we share the life-journey with every human on the planet, there are far more ways in which we are similar in our diversity than strongly diverse in our similarities.

With regard to chapter topics, we will explore how we arrive at our tastes and distastes for music over the life-cycle, i.e., the influences of families, cultures, and subcultures on our values, and the impact of media on our perceptions (Unit II). Through the samples from Native American cultures (Unit III), we will examine symbolism in music and the various ways in which we can improve our depth of listening and perception. In Unit IV, we will confront barriers and biases and examine how they developed historically and how they can be overcome as well as analyze how our African Diaspora cultures created fusions of influence, developed signified or encoded meaning, and used (and continue to use) music to heal from the impact of racism. We will look at the influence of the world's religions on music and, through the music of the Middle Eastern and North African cultures (Unit V), explore the difference between categorizing and stereotyping others.

The influence of European culture on the world's values and certainly on its music has been profound, and we will look at the concept of "nation," the attributes of the music of European culture, and the strong influence of European history and music on how we live today (Unit VI). Then, in Unit VII, will look at two culture groups (Jewish and Romani [Gypsy]) that have had enormous impact on Europe's and, ultimately, the world's culture and music. We will also explore why some cultures are virtually absent from our music history books. Through examples of musical and cultural expressions of Africa and Latin America (Unit VIII), we will examine the nature of rituals and rites that mark the life cycle and

help us to forge community. We will also examine various ways of achieving balance as expressed through the storytelling musical genres of India, China, Japan, Korea, and Indonesia (Unit IX). As a summary, we will look at the phenomenon of creolization, or creative cultural fusion, in American jazz and popular music as it is embodied in the cultural dynamics and music of much of the world today.

And finally, we will offer some perceptions that may guide readers to incorporate their own creativity in the context of building ever stronger and more diverse communities over time. To facilitate this, we hope you will choose to take advantage of the opportunity to expand your community-building skills by engaging with others in the "**Discussion/Reflections**" activities throughout the text. In all instances, personalizing or sharing within a group of diverse individuals maximizes the impact of the topics and themes included in this text.

Although to some degree we have opted to connect topics of universal interest to the world's musical cultures by regions (Native American, African, European) or by *genre* (rock 'n' roll, "classical," ritual or dance music of Mexico or the Middle East), we urge the reader to remember these are only handles for discussion. We hope that you will consistently remember that *every* culture's music reflects the topics and dynamics we are using to frame the other musical cultures. Whether storytelling through music, representation, and symbolism in celebrating community or the cycle of life, or other means by which we can examine music, each topic is likely to bear as much significance to Beethoven, as to the blues, Bob Dylan, or the music of Brazil, Bulgaria, or Bangladesh.

Activities for Further Growth

We have included a range of questions or possible activities at the end of each Unit as well. It is our belief that these activities can reinforce the concepts of the text and CDs for both the student and the casual reader. Within the units, you will find **Discussion/Reflections** sections to reinforce concepts and listening (these may be used in group discussion or for individual reflection). The *activities* will be divided into four orientations that should accommodate a diversity of learning styles:

#1 *Understanding Concepts:* These are basic questions worded to encourage further thought or investigation of your own understanding of the more important terms or concepts in the Unit. This activity is also a means by which we can check our own files and demonstrate our capacity for a more flexible and deeper reflection on diverse cultures and music.

#2 *Listening Deeper:* If you listened to the pieces while reading the text, this is by far the best approach! If not, you now have another chance to both listen and contemplate some of the values or possible interpretations of the music. More than anything, we hope that you will take the opportunity to isolate the music experience from the flow of your daily lives (i.e., not play it in the car, while studying, etc.) and thus give yourself a chance at a deeper, more thoughtful appreciation for the music and musicians/composers who created it.

#3 *Developing Passion:* Many among us will find that, for nearly every topic or music discussed, we will have either a burning passion or perhaps subtle interest to learn more. Because information is, for most of us, enormously accessible, we may wish to research, contact musicians or culture-bearers familiar with the music, or directly and personally increase our contact with music. The suggestions in this section are designed to increase our understanding of the culture and music in a more intimate or personal manner.

#4 *Exercising Our <u>Own</u> Creativity:* The ultimate way in which we honor others is to implement what we have learned from them into our own lives. If we truly have benefited from hearing the music and reading the comments of the musicians, the ultimate honor is to then "compose" our own work based on what we've learned. So, what do *you* have as an instrument? How do you prefer to express your creativity? This section will point out some possibilities for the inclusion or *fusion* of some of the ideas of the Unit into your own creative skills. Feel free

to create a work of your own imagination. This exercise might enhance your own creative confidence and perhaps assist you to be less critical or judgmental of your own artistic capacity.

We hope that you will not only find these activities helpful but also share your successes, thoughts, or discoveries and investigate our other products and services at our website: **www.visionsandvibrations.com**.

An Invitation to Dialogue

We will continue to invite input from the reader, from other musicians, and from those who live among or have affinity for the diversity of the world's peoples and cultures. Consider this text not as a definitive representation on *anything*, but simply as an initiator of dialogue. We, the authors, our teachers, mentors, and musician friends, as well as our beneficiary organization, *Visions and Vibrations International, LLC*, hope to facilitate a dialogue with individuals from the rest of our planet. Please feel free to give feedback at our website address to help us increase the effectiveness of our dialogue: **www.visionsandvibrations.com.**

It is with greatest respect for your experience and perspectives that we hope to learn of your successes, struggles, and challenges in your exploration of *Our Musical World*.

Pic. 6A & 6B *A group of young adults play (above) and dance (below) with parents and grandparents in a street festival in Malaga, Spain. The degree to which a community makes it "fashionable" for young people to honor their ancestry and older traditions will determine the extent to which they exert energy toward these traditions. In this case, young and old enjoy performing traditions of previous generations, although it is expected by all that the young will also manifest the "modern" changes in their world as well.* Photos: Authors.

Personal Meditation: Preface

Every one of us develops our values and tastes by virtue of the sum total of our experiences in life. You may wish to make a survey of your experiences over time. For each phase of life, list your major influences from parents, siblings, peers, and/or major events (happy memories, trips, trauma, and losses). Then try to. recall your musical experiences and contacts. Finally, can you see any impact on your life or musical tastes today that resulted from these events and experiences?

Childhood:

Major events/influences:

Musical contacts:

Influence still visible or felt today:

* * *

Late Primary/early Secondary:

Major events/influences:

Musical contacts:

Influence still visible or felt today:

* * *

Secondary/College:

Major events/influences:

Musical contacts:

Influence still visible or felt today:

* * *

Later Adult years:

Major events/influences:

Musical contacts:

Influence still visible or felt today: </bI>

What are your hopes/goals/dreams—for the fullest (most satisfying or complete) utilization of your creative skills or abilities for the betterment of our world?

Introduction:
Envisioning a Single Humanity Through Music

UNIT

I

Topics to Consider in Unit I

➤ *How might we define creativity, "culture," or the art of "appreciating" others?*

➤ *In what way can understanding musical creativity enhance our own creative development?*

➤ *What are some "universals" we share with everyone on the planet?*

➤ *What are some of the challenges to deepening our listening and appreciation skills of other cultures' music (or their values)?*

➤ *What are some of the steps through which composers go to create interesting "compositions"? How does this relate to our own creative potentials?*

➤ *What are some ways to improve our listening (vs. hearing) abilities?*

➤ *What are some of the means by which "traditions" change over time? (and what is the "real" definition of "tradition"?)*

➤ *What does a composition by an American composer share with that of a praise song from Morocco?*

UNIT I

Introduction:
Envisioning a Single Humanity Through Music

Throughout the course of human evolution, each of us in our time creates our world of values based primarily upon the strategies and perceptions we acquire from our immediate environment and community. As our needs and goals evolve, we increasingly will come into contact with "new" or different options. We reject or accept the opportunity to learn from these options based upon their proximity to our values, or upon the depth and degree to which we've been trained to be flexible or value others. Our preferences for art, food, or music are to a great degree, therefore, the result of these experiences more than any inherent degree of superiority. The more keenly we internalize this fact, the more quickly we will see 'justice' "with our own eyes and not the eyes of our neighbors." [1.1] Naylor and Naylor, 2003, P.14.

Some "Workable" Definitions

(These are in the authors' words. It is suggested that readers re-formulate them into their own.)

Creativity: The capacity to adapt, to enjoy change, to problem-solve, and to manifest personal or community flexibility and capacities in our lives. In music, creativity includes the mastering of skill sets for the purpose of reflecting personal experiences into a unique blend or fusion of sounds. To some degree, creativity also demands a willingness to take chances, to make mistakes, and both to take criticism (constructive suggestions/external input) and to trust one's intuition and personal insights without judging them.

Music: Sounds organized in time, which have emotional and cultural significance to their creators. Most music additionally serves the purpose of connecting individuals to a sense of community and to the life cycle, or of expressing the thoughts and emotions of the musicians to a constituency of "appreciators" who have generally similar tastes (affinities) or experiences.

Culture: A term used to loosely categorize for discussion the sum total of all expressions, language, art, ideals, artifacts, values, and, of course, music of humans of similar origin or geographical location, or more frequently with similar tastes, who share meanings, values, or affinities, regardless of the superficial appearance of race, nationality, gender, or other determinants. The term *culture groups* will be used interchangeably with *culture* to denote common subcategories or more firmly identifiable cultures, whenever possible, as determined or communicated of by the people (culture groups) themselves.

General note: *Whatever the terms used to denote a group of humans, they are more frequently convenient than accurate.*

Appreciation: *Respecting* something or someone and his or her ideals and expressions, usually through the exertion of some personal effort. Appreciation need not include "liking" (though one may find it easier to respect something having reached the state of liking it), but it does demand more effort and sacrifice than "tolerance" or any other form of passive and dispassionate co-existence.

Why Study Creativity?

> *"We must remember that the psychology of the creative person is the psychology of a person who walks around in life, who looks, and sees, and feels, who takes into account what life is and, somehow or other, wants to get out something he/she has within him(her)self."* Zilboorg, Creativity, "The Psychology of the Creative Personality", Hastings House, 1959, p. 25

Today, regardless of one's culture of origin, most individuals will need to acquire some degree of flexibility in communication with those whose experiences are considerably different from their own. At the core of the flexibility required for the journey into the cultures, lives, and musical genius of others is our understanding and capacity to be *creative*. In its root form, creativity is the ability to be spontaneous and willing to take chances, possibly at the risk of making mistakes or being criticized by those around us.

Of course, it is creativity that has given us electricity, air travel, computers, and most certainly, classical symphonies, hip-hop, and rock 'n' roll. To draw from the depths of our intuition (spirit, soul, etc.) something that at first may seem strange to others and possibly even to ourselves is nonetheless a critical component of the creative spirit. In many instances, the world's most creative music was initially rejected or spurned by the societies in which it appeared, only later to be embraced or to make a significant impact on the culture or the lives of its culture's descendants. But what is the greatest advantage of the study of the world's musical creativity? What do we learn from the insights of other culture systems as they are reflected in their music that we can practically apply to our lives?

At the pace at which many of us are actively moving, we may find it difficult to invest energy in activities we cannot justify as relevant to our immediate goals or career advancement. In many cases, if we do not see material, physical, or financial gain in an activity, the prospects of our investing passion or energy into it are slim. Therefore, we may want to be aware of possible motives as to why appreciating music, and, more importantly, respecting the people who make it, might prove valuable.

Music as a Tool for Enhancing Our Own Creativity

To begin, we might recognize that every time we come to a deeper understanding of another human's **values** (the traits, human qualities, and aesthetics they prefer to emphasize)[1,2] through any form of expression (music included) we advance our own vocabulary for "creating" solutions to problems or challenges. That this is so can be clearly seen as we contemplate any of our heroes thus far in our lives. They may be teachers, pastors, priests, or rabbis, coaches or mentors, actors or musicians, or just as likely, parents, grandparents, or other family members. In most cases, somewhere in their rising to the status of hero in our eyes, they performed an act or multiple acts of incredible creativity. They solved a problem, presented a thought or idea, or spoke of life's experiences in a manner that touched us, honored us, and left us, in some ways, wanting to be like them.

Pic1.1 *The colors and images in these paintings by Nancy Eckels reflect the parallel world's of art and music. In all art, image and, colors (whether visual or audio) blend together to induce thought and emotion, and to nudge us from our everyday world into the world of the passion, emotion, and experience of the author or artist.* Copyright: Nancy Eckels, 2004.

Impactful experiences and events, or heroic and inspirational insights eventually combine to motivate our choices of hobbies, professions, and, ultimately, our own unique creative outlook on life. In this sense we are a "fusion,"[1.3] or combination, of all the influences. This is what made Mozart, Duke Ellington, Charlie Pride, James Brown, Jimi Hendrix… or the "Mozarts" from any culture… *creative heroes* in their own right.

The Journey

Whether in school, in the workplace, or in decoding the representations of media or film presentations about *others,* each of us must constantly make decisions about what we will let into our world, or in what manner we will remember each image or event for the future. Yet, how adept are we at seeing the diversity of human cultures with the same level of passion and respect we might demonstrate to those of our own cultural backgrounds? And, assuming we desire to be comfortable in this relatively "new" world environment, how do we develop the skills and perceptual tools to accomplish this?

How We Got Here

Historically, as our planet evolved, an individual may have been defined solely by the goals or perceptions of value of his/her kin-structure, family, or clan. As culture structures enlarged, he or she may have been born into a village or tribal system (Ex: Uruba, Igbo, Diné, Lakota, Celtic, or Saxon). As culture systems enlarged further, regional identifiers would give way to identification by nation (Ex: French, American, Iranian, Japanese), linguistic groupings (Ex: German-speaking, Russian-speaking, Creole-speaking), continent (Ex: in the "West," Asian, African), or even the creation of systems of human racial designations which bequeathed to us the lasting image of "difference" by virtue of appearance. How human beings have defined themselves is, therefore, a combination of historical reference and the creation of terms and concepts used by our collective ancestries (often based upon very primitive or even fear-based initiatives) to describe "otherness."

We have all been brought up with centuries of terms and categories to define ourselves and others as different: "them" and "us." Most often, these terms do not resemble who *they* are or, for that matter, who we are. For instance, we now know that, regardless of the political or strategic circumstances under which culture groups or systems meet, even in war or under hierarchically suppressive or divided human socio-systems, each culture system will exchange language, material, and creative expressions with the other. Frequently, without conscious awareness, the *creativity* of our human nature will insure the mutual and unilateral exchange of ideas and expressions across even the most substantial "human-made" borders or barriers. What is difficult to understand, however, is that the culture's awareness of the exchange of expressions and traits may pass for centuries unnoticed. Generations of *culture-bearers*[1.4] may be educated to believe (as we will see in subsequent units) one thing about their identity or the origin of their culture's values and expressions, when another *reality* may be simultaneously more relevant yet beyond their scope of perception.

Musical Universals

When we say "appreciation" of the music of other cultures, we mean to imply "respecting" the music to the best of our abilities, as the culture desires us to respect it, on their terms—not ours. Whatever our individual tastes and trained perspectives of "us" and "them" (or "our music" and "their music") may be, a just, fair, or balanced perspective will call for us to keep the following in the forefront of our minds:

Pic. 1.1B *Oguz (playing the dulcimer – left) and Mario (playing the Dombek – right) reflect the complete mixture of our world – of Czech, German, Italian, Greek, and Romani descent – playing instruments and music of even further fusion, might give us a glimpse into the sort of "flexible minds" and perceptions youth will need as our planet continues to evolve.* Photo: Authors.

•All music genres (styles of music) are ethnic. Whether the music of the Ba-Benzele (Central African Republic) or that of Beethoven (Austria/Germany), all music is the result of cultural values and ethnicity. Therefore, all music is equally "ethnic" or "folk." Only the relative values, aesthetics (perceptions of what is beautiful), instruments, and means of expression of the "folk" change. To somehow believe that our music, or music of a specific culture, is less ethnic than that of some other culture is a form of cultural arrogance and an impediment to a balanced vision.

•Music, much more than the sounds, the elements, or even the feelings or entertainment value it provides, is a profound representation of the people who create it. Their values, their beliefs, and their "purpose for living," whether we agree with them or not, are imbedded in the musical symbols, if we take time to read them.

•We must also remember that each piece is a sonograph, or sound picture, of only one aspect of the culture at one moment in time. It is very human to hear small samples of music from one time period and assume it to be the whole picture. The challenge is to become comfortable with knowing that, as soon as we have an image or perspective on another culture, it is likely already out-of-date with their new and evolving reality. This is a mindset essential to living in our current century.

•   Music is universal, but it is not a universal language!! All cultures have music. And all music has value. However, just as with any language, value is seldom recognized and respected without investigating and attempting to understand how the people who create it feel about it themselves. To accomplish this, we may learn to ask: "What would you wish us to know about yourself?" The humility (willingness to put others in front of ourselves or be teachable) required to ask such a question is the centerpiece of respecting others.

•   The variations in the manner in which music is used around the world can be put into a few broad-stroke categories. Although these categories should never be seen as exclusive of each other and are perpetually changing, they can be helpful in developing a more inclusive attitude toward others. Among these categories:

Story-telling: Music expresses and articulates the process of life over time. It reflects the values of the people in their time and space. It is both a documentary of life and a reflection of the dreams and creative potential of the people. Most story-telling music, however, is reflected through deep symbolism and not in graphic or easily comprehensible narrative. The musical representation of each generation's stories will also evolve over time and be congruent with the evolution of technology and the experiences of the storyteller.

Community Ritual: Since all humans share the connection to the "cycle of life" and the natural processes of personal growth from birth to death, music (and usually religion and dance as well) has enormous impact in reconciling, marking, and celebrating these natural processes... and almost always in a community environment. Community rites and rituals marked by music are, therefore, some of the most important events in our lives, regardless of the time in which we appear on this earth.

Balancing Ourselves and Entertainment: Music as a means for creating a sense of balance, as a way to stabilize ourselves physically, mentally, or emotionally – or as an outlet for expressing frustration, anxiety, or emotional release – has a corresponding importance to our lifestyles and levels of stress. Though we may not look at the music we play in the car, while cleaning the house, while studying, or as background for a dinner party as "balancing" or "healing," much of the use of music today is, as it has been historically, for precisely that purpose. This includes movies, concerts, and television, where the elaborate productions, visual effects, and creative use of technology with music provide us escapes from the tensions and concerns in our lives.

Although nearly all music can be channeled into the above categories, some of the storytelling may be instructional (educational), some of the rituals may be for entertainment or for creating personal and community balance, and some of our entertainment may also have a spiritual/life-connecting impact, possibly expressed through some form of storytelling. Regardless, it is critical to our well-being that we attempt to see the commonality in our human experience through the manner in which we create and express ourselves through music. With this vision, we may counter the efforts of our ancestors to separate themselves from each other or to believe in human labels and outmoded values that are impotent to reflect human reality.

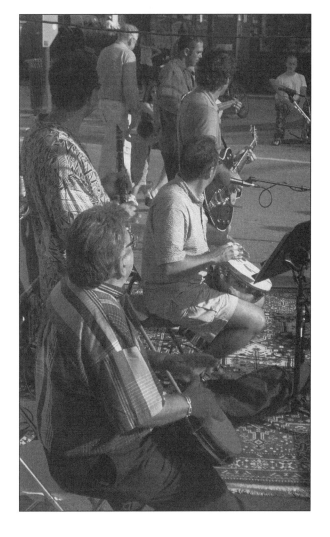

Pic 1.2 *If you ask someone from a culture that has not created the specialization and separation of human learning valued in Western academic traditions to speak of a musical event – that includes music, dance, theater, religion, community interaction, and an ancestry of evolution that has spanned two thousand years – do you think he or she will talk about the musical notes?*

This Armenian band is playing for a street dance at the Chicago Armenian festival. They are far less interested in what we think of their music, than in our dancing and enjoying their music by virtue of our participation. Photo: Authors.

Keeping the aforementioned points in mind, we may attempt to see all musical forms (and cultures) much like fruit in a bowl. Though each type of fruit possesses the characteristics of fruit and is therefore called "fruit," each also has unique qualities and unique applications. We may prefer one variety of fruit to another for pie, or may prefer one type or another to eat raw or cooked. It would be more than foolish, however, to say, *"The apple is good, but the banana is 'bad' fruit."* Each has its applications, and we have come to recognize our tastes for fruit as simply our tastes, not as a reference to the validity of the fruit itself. Yet, do we speak about music, food, clothing, or art with the same objectivity? If not, this might be something to consider as a first approach to appreciation. More often than not, we like what we like not because it is superior, but rather because it is what we have come to know the best. The ridiculousness of labeling a culture mentally or verbally as "bad" or inferior should eventually become as embarrassing as believing a pineapple to be bad because it doesn't appeal to our taste.

To address the daunting task of inciting perceptual change through a single text, we will cross the line from music to *anthropology* (the study of human culture), to *philosophy* (the study of human thought), to *history* (the study of past human events), to *theology* (the study of human belief in a Higher Power). We may also need to address the *drama* or theater of the event, the *dance* or movement of the ritual, or the purpose of the expression beyond the sounds and their organization.

But through all these different slants on music, we will never actually be off the topic. Instead, we will just be creatively experimenting with the de-categorization and reintegration of perceptions, and the flexibility that each culture may require of us in respecting their musical ideas on their terms, not merely the ones we have been trained to value.

Re-education

What we know today should obviously not be considered inadequate or in any way inferior or superior to the knowledge of any other human being. We are all the product of our experiences, and there is a fairly good likelihood, had anyone else had our life, they would also have many of our tastes, values, or problems. This is the universal nature of life experiences. Though each individual may also have "free will" to choose his or her influences and an element of autonomy in decision making, experiences and environment play a huge part in our tastes and preferences. Yet, in a very simple way, we usually know on some inner level every time we come into contact with some new and refreshing experience that there is *more* that we can learn or that, from an alternative perspective, we could relearn much of what we have learned.

Stories from the Human Family

"Okay, honesty time. I wish I could say that I always liked discovering that I've been wrong about something, or that I have prejudices and biases, or that I've mishandled or disrespected someone or their culture.

"Truthfully, I've always thought that others would see me as being wiser and more educated if I masked my faults. I can also honestly say that I have seldom in the past enjoyed being uncomfortable, as I might be when I hear some new or exceedingly different music, eat some weird food, or seek to communicate with someone whose language and values are different than mine.

"But I have also realized that each time I encounter something I didn't know, something I had incorrectly learned, or a new way to know something, a sort of 'ah-ha' effect (I know this isn't terribly scientific) goes off in my mind. Each 'ah-ha' or 'I didn't know that he/she/it was so good, represents a shift or potential for a shift in my system of values. At such moments, information or insight has come to me that might broaden my world. I guess I'm starting to get to like this."
[By permission: John Peterson., USA male, university graduate student, 34 yrs.]

Note: All personal student or reader comments used throughout the text are collected and used by permission of the individual, in some cases on the condition of anonymity (unless names are included). Culture or age demographics will be included when available or relevant to the interpretation of the comments.

To illustrate the above comments by musical example, we might hear a song or CD by an artist who, although perhaps not a part of our world, we still admit we like. Perhaps later, we are told that the music or artist is "rock, jazz, country, R&B" or something that previously we thought *we couldn't stand.* At that moment, we are faced with a decision. We have experienced the "ah-hah" effect, but that doesn't imply we'll learn or grow from it. Either we must admit that we might actually like that music after all, dwelling enough upon this observation to *upload* new information on that musical genre into our mind's files, or we may quickly revert to our previous perceptions, creating a type of cultural amnesia that dismisses the validity of the experience in favor of our previous thoughts or ideas. That is, the student's comments above are more significantly relevant to his growth in applying the knowledge of the "ah-hah" moment to his files than in the observation alone.

Whatever the case, it is supremely critical to look at education, and specifically culture "re-education" (learning of new ways to consider "old" experiences, to re-think history, and to find new ways of seeing our world), as a process and not a destination. To de-emphasize the attainment of *goals* in regard to becoming "educated" is an important adjustment. As an example, we will often misperceive, over-generalize, and trivialize or patronize other cultures. To believe otherwise is contradictory to the humility and awareness that are most critical to increasing the accuracy and justice of our perceptions. Knowledge is not now, nor has it ever been, stationary.

Very frequently, as soon as we load information about the music or its relationship to the people who make it into our mind's files,[1.5] there is a distinct likelihood that some creative individual in that culture is already creating a new fusion of ideas that will change or influence that tradition forever. Any attachment to the belief that we can "arrive" at a point where we have a permanent and valid understanding of a culture group or expression is as invalid as it is futile.

Cultural Justice

Embedded in an ancient history of human cultures seeking power and position over others or in building institutions and systems of administration predicated upon cultural-centricity, imbalance, hierarchy, or entitlement (i.e., resources, titles, spaces, and places) is the simple, albeit intuitive perception that we must come to value and respect each other, if for no other reason than for our survival.

Regrettably, what has often been passed off as "education" is often culturally-centric and, therefore, partial and unfulfilling in its capacity to create a just or equitable vision of our planet's diverse cultures. What often is equated to "respecting" others or helping us to become educated about others is often a degeneration to *tolerating* or, just as often, patronizing others with gestures that neither fully acknowledge the injustices of the past nor equally value culture groups that are not our own.

Working on behalf of *cultural justice*, therefore, is an active lifestyle through which we seek to uncover and acknowledge the full nature of social, economic, and cultural injustice historically; assess our role and place in the hierarchy of power and control that has resulted from this history; and begin to seek to optimize our personal and professional energy on behalf of healing our cultures—not merely for others, but especially for our own happiness and well-being.

Questions

- *What is the difference between "patronizing," "tolerating," and" respecting" an individual or a cultural system?*
- *Can you think of a manner in which you may be "tolerating" or have been tolerated by another culture, rather than respected equally?*
- *How might you exert effort that makes the injustice known in a helpful manner, rather than perpetuating it?*

Packing Our Bags

Beyond the tools of this text/CD, the following thoughts may also benefit the reader somewhere along the journey:

- Most people reading this text are living in Western cultures (European or American) or are from larger cities elsewhere on the planet. These cultural environments represent some of the most competitive and fast-paced societies in the world. Being "quick," "right," or "on top of things" is critical to survival in condensed, fast-paced, or highly competitive environments. Most appreciation skills are learned slowly, over time, and through a wide variety of stages and growth periods that require "being wrong" or "not knowing."

- Many of us do not like to hear criticism or discover shortcomings, even though they are *human* and *natural* and their discovery is *essential to our growth*. There are a multitude of historical reasons (see Units IV through X) that have led to the placement of "demonstrating what we know," empiricism, and the orientation toward "correctness or perfection" over the process orientation of questioning, discovery, and, above all… humility. But *humility*[1.6] might need to be placed at the top of the list for anyone who wishes to comprehend the depth and diversity of the world's music.

- If we feel apathetic about exploring something outside our experience, we might wish to look at our schedule, life-pace, or activity level. We may have much more packed into our schedule than we can humanly accomplish and have any room left for creative new experiences. It's hard to be motivated when we're exhausted, overworked, and without time to feel, think, contemplate, listen, and experience creativity (ours or others') at a deeper level. Once we are aware of this, we can make choices and adjust our lives.

- If you ever feel irritated at the thought of being asked to further consider other musics, specific cultures, or ways of living, and you have never reserved time for such encounters, then you may be experiencing the natural result of having been segregated or isolated within a restricted culture system. Even when we believe that we are already open-minded and knowledgeable, in the face of the multitude of myths and mis-information that has been passed to us as cultural documentary (mostly unintentionally) through media, history and culture studies in schools, it is natural to feel irritation. After all, our intentions were to be sensitive to others, to learn about others, and yet we still ended up with partially or fully biased information. We may in time come to understand that this is just part of the re-education experience.

- From wherever we approach a new or different experience, becoming engaged and, if possible, passionately motivated to experience or learn from it should precede any acquisition of information. Information (like most material learned for exams) becomes increasingly pointless over time if we are not motivated to use it, mold it, and creatively work it into our lives. Are becoming passionate, excited, and engaged—skills that can be learned and enhanced? We cetainly hope so.

Pic. 1.2A *At first glance this collage may seem to have very little to "say" beyond being a fascinating blend of images, textures, and design. But if you look closely, you'll see the images of Elvis Presley and B.B. King imbedded in the dense texture of images. Although many in America may think of rock 'n' roll or rhythm and blues (R&B) as essentially "black" or "white," investigation of the music will extend our perceptions way beyond the simplistic questions of race. Most clearly, American history, like that of much of the world, needs some rewriting and reinvestigation from the perspective of equity and balance across cultures. As concerns the music itself, both Elvis's and B.B.'s music is the result of numerous fusions of all of America's cultures and component parts. Robert Bartley's collage captures this "fusion" of American music and culture.* Photo and collage: Courtesy and copyright, Robert Bartley, 2005.

"A teacher who can arouse a feeling for one single good action, for one single good poem, accomplishes more than he who fills our memory with rows and rows of natural objects, classified with name and form." Goethe, *Elective Affinities*, 1809

The Nature(s) of Music Composition

A Vehicle for the Human <u>Tradition</u> of <u>Change</u>

Tradition: From *traditio*, or *traditionis*: originally meant a delivery or surrender of something to someone or something else. Although frequently traditions are held to a mythical cultural foundation or a fixed standard advocating a lack of change or flexibility, they are anything but "un-flexible." Though the degree of change will vary across cultures and generations, traditions are, like the original meaning itself, as flexible and prone to change as the human beings that create them.

As our society or cultural structures change and evolve, so do our values and our perceptions of what we consider to be either traditional or modern. How we see and call ourselves is not as important as who we really are. Although many of us may still use terms like Italian-American, African-American, Hispanic-American, Korean, etc., the tradition of our times (and, arguably, that of our planet over the entire history of its evolution) has been that of perpetual change. Therefore, what was once modern is now traditional. And what is now traditional will likely not be around in its exact form or perceived in the same manner tomorrow. Human culture groups are by nature fluid, multifaceted, and highly creative organisms whose borders are now, and always have been, much more flexible than we are prone to imagining.

When any culture group is presented with new information, technology, and insights, according to the strategies and value systems of their time, they will transfer, fuse, and appropriately take on or reject these new characteristics and expressions. Each generation of each culture-group will make hundreds and thousands of alterations in the determination and expression of their values and needs through language, music, art, science, religion, etc. It is human nature to select the combination of activities, language, and artistic expressions according to what we believe will bring us respect and integrity or enhance our lives and self-worth. In short, we strategize the activities, associations, and advancements (or, conversely, create limitations), that eventually evolve to make up our world.

Understanding the Creativity of Composition

A **composition** of any variety—literary, culinary, or musical—is a creative "invention" of the sum total of experiences, techniques, and available resources of the composer at a particular moment in time. Whether designed to remain spontaneous (improvised) and not written or repeated in its original format, or spontaneously created (improvised) and then manipulated, worked, and recorded or written for posterity (composed), compositions will be channeled into service in the categories of human expression mentioned earlier. How, then, can we understand the composition process a bit more tangibly?

Creative artists and composers generally follow a simple progression of steps in creating their art (Note: many may be simultaneous or unconscious):

Observation/Inspiration: Making an observation in life, having an inspiration from a particular event or experience, or completing a commission, as in "write a song about _____."

Reflection/Meditation: Converting the inspiration into a formula for expression. This includes contemplating the form, techniques, market (audience), and, frequently, research about a "new" vocabulary or instrument.

Improvisation: All compositions begin as "improvisations." The act of composition is a refinement of initial ideas and settling on the "best" of those possibilities.

Refinement: Very few artworks do not also include a refinement or "re-working" process. To refine is to seek betterment and completion to the artist's satisfaction.

Presentation: Once the art is completed, the artist must now make sure that there is a suitable venue for it. Fulfillment of an artwork is generally accomplished through sharing it with the world. However, even art that is not performed might still be therapeutic to the artist.

Artists draw their inspiration from multiple sources and dimensions. We can call these dimensions, broadly, the *spiritual* (something beyond the self), the *cognitive* (one's thoughts, reflections, and conscious insights), the *emotional,* and the *temporal* (time and culture or environment). Whatever comes into the artist's paths, however far it may be from their culture of origin, is open to fusion and incorporation into their world. They will naturally not play the song, the instrument, or the elements of the new influence or music the way the initial culture's musicians played them. But they will grasp the spirit, the sounds, and the energy from the music and, using their own already established vocabulary, incorporate these new inspirations into a fresh and unique configuration, a *composition* varying in part from prior creations and unique to the new source of inspiration.

Although there may or may not be an external motive for a composition (as in a commission for a specific function or purpose), there is always a motive in the composer's mind. Even if the motive is to compose something that appears to have no purpose or that is designed to befuddle our imaginations, this still is a motive or purpose.

We will soon make the first of over sixty journeys into the visions and creative thoughts of musicians and musical composers. Before we do, however, let's examine some important tips for increasing the depth and impact of the musical experience. Try to keep in mind that practicing these suggestions without a preconceived notion of a goal or result is in itself a demonstration of respect and honor (appreciation) to the musicians and the music.

Listening to Music: *Hearing vs. Listening*

The satisfaction that comes from having someone really *listen* to us, when we are speaking, comes from that person's undivided attention. We know for a fact that when someone is truly listening to us, we feel respected and in touch with that person. Of course, music is not a person, but it is *always* the expression of people.

A high percentage of the music most of us hear during the course of our day is a background to our "life-scape." We consume music daily while driving, cooking, studying, and moving from place to place. But even for those of us who are musicians, much of what we hear we may not actually listen to.

We suggest (unless otherwise indicated) that you read the information about the piece in the text before listening. An even more beneficial process, but one which takes more time, is to listen first, observe and record your observations or thoughts about the music (a reflection of your mind's files), read the material in the text, and then listen once more. Regardless, you will learn more and acquire a broader perspective of the world (music or otherwise) if you try to adhere to the following proven techniques in listening for deepest appreciation (respect):

1) Listen to the music (person) in isolation from other activities. Try to isolate the music from studying or other activities such as watching the television, housecleaning, and even driving a car.

2) When possible, listen to new music or influences in a positive or encouraging environment. You will be amazed how much growth is possible if you surround yourself with encouraging influences or you do not surround yourself with discouraging influences.

3) You may find it helpful to repeat or record your observations (This can be done mentally or physically. When physical, we call it a "sonograph" or sound picture – see Unit III). The point of note-taking is that we are less likely to drift away from the musical experience if we try to write about it. Here are additional suggestions to help keep focused:

   • Get comfortable but maintain sufficient body tension (sitting upright, etc.) to avoid dozing or losing concentration.

   • Catch yourself if you drift from the musical experience and pull yourself back to the experience.

   • Don't be anxious about drifting. Even the most trained listeners drift occasionally. Also remember, for the majority of us, music is an accompaniment to our lives requiring only partial concentration. Therefore this discipline may feel foreign at first.

- Remember that learning to concentrate on music attentively will improve our listening concentration overall. This is one skill (concentrated listening) that has been proven to have transferable qualities to our relationships with other people.

4) Finally, for each musical example, there will be comments from the musician or culture bearer concerning the music, the culture, and possibly the individual piece ("Inside the Musician's World"). We may also include more specific information about the piece, its musical vocabulary, and the elements of the composition itself ("The Recipe of Sound"). Depending upon your interests, the exercise of learning the elements and vocablary of the music is a way of showing respect for the musician.

What Is a "Good" Listener?

Léonie's Perspective

Dr. Van der Kolk* believes that nonverbal behaviors (actions) make up more than fifty percent of the messages that are communicated in social relationships and are usually perceived as honest and less subject to manipulation than verbal behaviors. Furthermore, Karl Rogers** believed that, in order to be considered a skilled counselor and listener, one must have "unconditional positive regard" or be accepting of an individual unconditionally and non-judgmentally, allowing the person to explore all thoughts and feelings, positive or negative, without danger of judging or condemnation. The combination of perceiving actions and having an "empathetic understanding" helps us comprehend the person's (culture's) thoughts, feelings, and expressions more accurately and from their own perspective. Finally, having "congruence" means to be authentic and genuine, thus, having no aloof façade. Instead, the listener is honestly and humbly present and transparent with no hidden or preconceived agenda or air of authority.

Based on this information…

- Can you think of someone whom you feel is a "good listener?" What makes the person come to mind?
- How does the person sit, look at you, or hold him or herself when you are struggling to understand or express something personal or intimate?
- Do you feel that you often listen to others with empathy?
- In your own thoughts, how does incorporating the three core conditions above provide respect, value, and understanding to both the individual and the listener?

Questions: Examining Our "Listening Skills"

- *Considering the "good listener" habits, in what areas could you stand to improve?*
- *What do you feel are the greatest personal challenges to your becoming a better listener? (i.e., Were you listened to well as a child or young adult yourself? Is your schedule packed with activities? etc.)*
- *What sort of "listening" practice habits could you implement into your life at present?*

    * Van der Kolk, Bessel, Psychological Trauma, American Psychiatric Publications, 1987.

    **Rogers, Karl, The Carl Rogers Reader, edited by Kirschenbaum and Henderson, 1989.

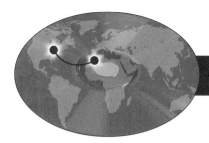

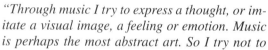

James Hartway

Note: James Hartway is a composer of numerous styles, from pieces for orchestra to small ensemble works such as those featured in this project. Although he has received numerous awards for his own works, he is also a professor of music theory (the language of music) and creative composition at Wayne State University in Detroit, Michigan (U.S.A.), where he annually nurtures and encourages the creativity and musical thoughtfulness of numerous students to find their own creative voices as well. As you will see, he is a strong advocate of creativity and of experimenting with sound to create emotions and imagery from an ever-expanding array of personal experiences. This is what he had to tell us about the composition process:

> *"Through music I try to express a thought, or imitate a visual image, a feeling or emotion. Music is perhaps the most abstract art. So I try not to use the tried and true path … and I tell this to my students: 'Forget major or minor scales or the tools they've already used.' In order to get deeply into the core of oneself, it's important to start with a clean slate, if possible. When I teach composition, I try to teach students to find their own voice, and of course that's what I've been trying to do in my composition… through experimentation. I try to give a perspective, which is really what art is, a perspective done through the medium of the artist.*

Dr. Hartway was asked what he felt were the largest blocks or impediments to creativity in modern Western cultures. He responded:

> *"I've been very disappointed in our culture for the most part in that we have interchanged and mixed up entertainment and entertainers with art and artists. A lot of musicians are really entertainers. They are there to make an entertaining product… what sells, or to imitate what has already sold. That has a place. But I really wish our culture could learn to distinguish between this, and what is created as an extension of the artist.*

> *"Our society has put so much emphasis on making a living, making the almighty buck… but there are a lot of ways to live. A sense of self-fulfillment is for me more of a sign of a successful human being than millions of dollars in the bank. I think we need to get back in touch with a certain sort of spirituality that goes with life, one that involves thinking and creativity… things which much of the society-at-large does not hold in very high esteem."*

CD 1.1

"Trance Music," from **"Images of Mogador,"** for flute, viola, and harp, CD: <u>**An Affair of the Harp**</u>, copyright 2003, James Hartway, featuring Kerstin Allvin on harp.

> Dr. Hartway spoke of this piece as follows: *"'Images of Mogador' was commissioned by virtue of someone having heard another piece of mine. I was accepting applause on stage, and the economic advisor to the King of Morocco appeared on stage as if by magic, and said in front of everyone, he'd like me to write a work for next year's festival. Of course I was excited and immediately knew what I would write.*
>
> *"The first night in Morocco, I was in a small hotel and they had brought in some Moroccan musicians that performed for us. The music that they played was unfamiliar to me, but it was Goanuan music... trance music. This music epitomized the sort of creative and spiritual music that I aspire to in my own works. It was a natural fit. It was improvisatory, rhapsodic, expressive, it was sensual, it was rhythmic—it had all the elements you would want of great music. These incredible artists from Africa, singing, playing and dancing... it was spectacular."*

The Recipe of Sound

"Trance music" is the opening *movement* (one of three sections to the piece), which demonstrates Dr. Hartway's recollections of the spectacular event he experienced through use of tone, combining of instruments (orchestration), rhythmic variation (varied duration of sounds), and expressive dynamics (changes in speed and volume).

After a strong and dynamic start (accented by the harp) with quick scalier (stepwise motion) of the flute and viola, there is an immediate, calm return to the sensual, spiritual feeling and a slow evolution of rhythm and melodic exchange between instruments. Then (pause), the viola speaks by itself (cadenza-like), eliciting the free or improvisatory aspect of the music, followed again by multiple other variations: flute and harp interaction, increase in rhythmic flow, return to quick movements of melodic exchange between the flute and viola, the harp acting almost as the large "tar" (tambourine-like drum), which builds to the conclusion.

Now, all that being said, put Dr. Hartway's experience back into your mind, become him for a minute, close your eyes if you wish, and listen again to the music. You should find yourself transported back to the magic he experienced in that small hotel in Morocco.

"Education is not merely a means for earning a living or an instrument for the acquisition of wealth. It is an initiation into the life of spirit, a training of the human soul in the pursuit of truth and the practice of virtue." Vijaya Lakshmi Pandit

"Change" and "Time": Concepts in Motion

We've probably all heard it said that change is inevitable. Yet at times, we all feel threatened by change. It's not uncommon, as we progress through the life cycle, to lament the fact that things have changed so much. The awareness that one of the only constants in life is *change* is reflected in every place and in every generation of every culture. Although change varies in degree and scope according to the evolution of the culture's values or belief systems and its history of contact with outside culture groups, cultures can no more remain stagnant than can the living component parts from which cultures are derived – human beings.

Still, even in the fastest-changing cultures, we can see so many ways in which we carry on the older traditions, but in new or altered forms. And, in the most ancient of traditions, we may see a multitude of ways that even they have been changed or altered.

Even when appearing to be the same, an ancient musical tradition will carry a familiar message or story, but in a variety of different ways. Although there is merit for those who feel compelled to preserve the older or more ancient traditions because they are a part of human history, it is probably not beneficial to exert too much energy lamenting change. In fact, the oldest of the items or traditions we seek to preserve were probably, not all that long ago, the result of creative new changes.

In some ways, the nature and inevitability of growth and evolution in human cultures is exactly parallel to the growth of a child to an adult. However much we enjoyed childhood, lamenting the transition to adulthood is futile. In terms of music, time is better spent seeing the connections of the music to

Pic. 1.4A *Perhaps nowhere in the world are there more profound examples of cultures that adapt and become adept at change than Diapsora groups (cultures widely dispersed by the events of history). Among such groups are the communities and families of the Jewish Diaspora. Ari Gradus, originally from Israel, also spends some of his time in New York City. He says: "The inspiration for my work is from my background growing up in Israel. I am the first generation of Jewish people that grew up with Israel as a Jewish state. My grandfather was a philosopher and an observant Jew, and he taught me the beauty of the religion and culture. My work is not the heavy or dark material common with Jewish artists. It reflects the happy, colorful, and there is a lot of music; this is about rejoicing. This painting: The History of My People, shows the whole movement of the Jewish people: from Abraham, to Mt. Sinai, Moses taking the tablets to Israel, the destruction of Jerusalem, to the people being led into exile, then 2,000 years in the Diapsora, the Holocaust, and finally coming back through the gates back to Israel." Mr. Gradus's works are marked by enormous spirit, humor, color, creativity, and the spirit of change.* Photo: Author, copyright, Ari Gradus, www.arigradus.com, 2005.

its past, observing the way in which it has changed (the result of the new fusions of influences), and looking for connections between what we know or understand and its parallel to the music we are studying. To assist with the first of these, the following are some ways in which musical traditions might change over time:

Changing Traditions

*   The technology of the instrumentation or the means of performance may change. Common devices for change are the use of modern instruments (not the older ancestral models), the use of traditional instruments either combined with electronic or synthesized ones or digitally sampled and performed by these instruments, and lighting or visual representation through media technology. In a very real sense, media and recording have permanently changed and altered every single performance or musical genre on the face of the planet. Because of media technology, it is virtually impossible for any musician not to become aware of other musical performance and presentation formats elsewhere on the planet.

*   The performance context will change. This is something that may go unnoticed much of the time, but even in the most "ancient" of traditions, we will likely see what used to be a closed group event or ritual, or one that would be done within the confinement of the community, now "re-created" in a performance environment (e.g., on a stage). That is, what used to be an activity wherein everyone who witnessed it was also a participant is likely to become a *representation* or performance before a group of observers. Many times these observers will include "outsiders" to the culture. As generations pass, it is likely that people within the culture will be nearly as fascinated or unfamiliar with the presentation as those from outside the culture.

*   One of the most unnoticed forces in the changing traditions of musical genres is the way in which cultures influence each other. As long as we perceive our music to be truly "our music," we will not be able to see how the entire evolution of humankind, its instruments, expressive features, language, and symbols have been perpetually passed or exchanged from culture to culture. Once each new experience is in our world, we often perceive it as having been created there. Generally, music (and all cultural expressions) will prosper and infiltrate any imposed perception of "otherness" if the creative instincts of the artist are so inspired.

Similarly, our perceptions of time are as much human inventions as those of most of the labels we use to designate branches of humanity. Time, as the saying goes, is "relative"! To what? To the expressed values we acquire as we go through the life experience, to the rhythm of our society and cultural environment, and to the values and pace at which we choose to live our lives. In the case of learning to listen effectively or appreciatively to music, we will need as much time as it takes… no more, no less. The time needed will be different for each of us.

Pic. 1.4B *It might serve us well to know that not only will traditions change, evidenced by the fusion of this Gothic cathedral and modern building, but that "change" itself may be the oldest and most profound tradition in human history.* Photo: Köln, Germany, Author.

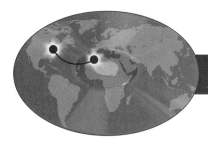

Orchestra Chabab Al Andalous de Rabat

Note: After hearing Dr. Hartway's piece, one may become more interested in the exciting musical heritage of Moroccan music and its vibrant cultural history. By chance, as is usually the case whenever we desire new knowledge, someone/thing will then come into our lives, as did a Moroccan student, whom we then asked to help us with a class discussion. This we did not only to encourage the student to share but also to enhance our own growth. He brought CDs and videos, and clearly was excited to be involved. We, in turn, were treated to an amazing array of Moroccan musical styles and incredible cultural and musical passion on the student's part.

The next semester we received an email from the student (Soufiane Hjiyej Andaloussi), informing us that he would be visiting his home and asking us if we wanted anything. This project was mentioned, and we asked if he thought anyone would like to be a part of it. He replied: *"I'm certain there are very good musicians who might want to participate."*

What follows is a small sampling of the jewels of Moroccan culture which Soufiane was able to secure, in particular the work of Orchestra Chabab Al Andalouss from Rabat, Morocco, and its director, Mohamed Debby, to whom we are indebted. Both the music and its story represent a graphic display of the natural process of cultural fusion over time.

Mr. Debby writes: *"The Arabo Andalusian music is originally from Al-Andalus, the name given by the Arabic or Muslim inhabitants to the Iberian peninsula (Spain), which was occupied by the dynasty of the Ommeyades for seven centuries. The people of this region developed numerous art and cultural forms while in this province. Most notably, architecture, poetry, and musical forms. Over time, the influence of this music, and such masters as Niryab,[1,7] have instilled the singing of noubas (vocalized poetry in dialogue with instrumentation), praise songs (see Madh in Unit V), and Sanaâ, (classical Arabic poetry) as part of a dialogue between instrumentalists and vocalists. Although performance of the noubas is performed differently by each practitioner, the poems of divine love, human love, beauty, and awe of nature and 'God's' world are all designed to be played at precise moments of the day."*

The Orchestra Chabab Al Andalous de Rabat was created in 1987 by *"young music lovers from different horizons"* (M. Debby). Although all of the musicians in the orchestra have their own jobs, Mr. Debby writes, *"The association of Chabab Al Andalouss has an objective of promoting this worldwide heritage— to the world. That's really a big part of what we do."*

When asked to participate in this project by Soufiane, Mr. Debby replied, *"I am more than happy for what you are doing. It is a pleasure for us to share our modest knowledge. Personally, I am a banker, and the orchestra is, for each of us, a part-time occupation. We are a group of semi-professional amateurs... all of us are still learning as we practice. But our principle notion is to foster a rebirth of this phenomenal heritage, perhaps to evolve to the level of creativity that existed at the time of its creation. We get a lot of encouragement from family and friends.*

"Using today's technology, we are developing and recording it step by step. This way, more youth of today will have the chance to listen to the music, and perhaps learn the poems."

What we will hear is a musical style that is a fusion of influences incorporating the music of the Arab world (see Unit V), most importantly that of Islamic poetry; numerous influences from the Jewish and Gypsy communities (see Unit VII); the eventual fusion over time of all cultural influences both in Morocco and Spain; and, finally, the incorporation of musical instruments and technology from Western Europe.

"Musique Arabo," from the CD: **Andalusian Music of Morocco,** performed by the Orchestre Chabab Al Andalous. c. 2004, Rabat, Morocco.

Mohamed Debby writes: *"The Andalusian music is close to the western 'indoor' (classical) music. It does not have a four-beat meter like most popular Arabic music today. One basic rule to create a good sound is to have a proportional distribution between the instruments. For example, you must have four violins for every ud (oud). Another rule is to give a good (fair) representation of all the instruments."*

This recording is a condensed version of the entire work, which runs 15 minutes. One may at first be surprised by the appearance of the piano, which plays a combination of *phrygian* and *harmonic minor* **scales** (menus of pitches or tones that exist in Western music) that are most similar to a couple of ***magamat*** (Arabic scales). The piano section is followed by a section played by the violin (the descendant of the ***r'bab, rababa(h), rebaba,*** still used by some Moroccan or Arabic orchestras).

The quality of meditation and trance, spoken of earlier, are imbued in the music, which, as it progresses, evolves to "praise" poetry and eventually to the inclusion of the full orchestra and chorus. Although we will address musical styles from this region in later units (Units V, X), the style of melodic singing is greatly influenced by the style used in the chanting of the Quran (Koran).

Pic. 1.5-1 *The "rebec" evolved from the "rababah" to become the violin.* Painting: Gerard David, 1509.

The Recipe of Sound

Mr. Debby indicated how important the unity and collective harmony of the musicians are in performing the music you will hear. Balance is also essential in the blending of the instruments.

Mr. Debby writes, *"Basically, the minimum group we can have is four violins, one ud (oud), one cello, one darbouga, one tar (a large-frame tambourine-like instrument), and two to four singers. To create really good music, we also like to have the rebab, a kanoun (qanun – a zither instrument with strings laid out flat, plucked by a large pick, or plectrum), and an alto or double bass."*

If we were to make a *sonograph* (sound picture or graph of the musical instruments) over a time line, it might look as follows:

Piano solo – free rhythm	Violin solo – free rhythm	Full orchestra with poetic chant & chorus
:40 sec	2:14	2:00

"Composing" i.e., Creative Discipline

The "creative" process in all mediums or professions, despite the differences in the instruments used or the function of the creation, is remarkably similar.

First, we all must be exposed to, and in some manner encouraged or learn to be confident in the utilization of skills, "talents," or tools over the course of our lives—whether writing creatively, singing, playing an instrument, drawing, studying mechanics, or engaging in some other activity. In most cases, in whatever area(s) of human expression we have been exposed and given positive reinforcement (from someone/somewhere)—we will likely continue to pursue to the point of acquiring a level of comfort or confidence.

Second, we all acquire beliefs, values, and preferences in life (the way we choose to see the world, how we utilize our skills, and ultimately, the type of "song" we prefer "singing"). Our values will determine the areas of comfort and preference or the places we are more likely to direct our abilities. Needless to say, the wider our experiences, the wider the potential application of our skills.

Next, in whichever areas we learn the confidence to be creative, we go through the phases of "composition" outlined in pages 9-10 with varying degrees of intensity and awareness, including (but not limited to) *Observations and Reflection, Improvisation, Refinement, and Presentation.* Of all these stages, there are two that are the most likely to be derailed by self-doubt, self-judgment, insecurity, or fear of the criticism of others.

Improvisation: This is the art of spontaneously taking our inspiration and the sum total of skills and experience on our "instruments" acquired by the specific moment in time of our creating, and *throwing them* into the world. That is, NO composition can be "good" before it "IS" (comes into existence).

Refinement (Discipline): Once our ideas have reached the light, they must now be refined. This is actually the art of "composing." It is a process of disciplined decision-making about what will stay, what will go (be cut), and what should be altered or "bettered." Here we must have the confidence to complete the project (take the creative process to a "resting point"). Whether or not we will present or perform our creation is arguably a lesser issue in the development of our creativity. (However, "creative works" around much of the world are generally believed to reach their fulfillment only after being shared with others).

Exercise: You may wish to do this in a group or alone. (Group work is always encouraged).

- *Pick a thought, a topic, or an instrument. Now, "freestyle" a creation (poem, song, drawing, photo) right where you are, using whatever you have available to express yourself.*

- *Observe: How comfortable were you? Did you complete a statement or creative thought, or did you often stop in embarrassment or self-critique your work? How can your comfort with being spontaneously creative be enhanced? What are the forces that infringe upon comfort with spontaneous "improvisation"?*

Musical Terms and Concepts

Trance music: Nearly all cultures or culture groups have some form of music known as *trance music*. The general purpose of the music is to employ an overwhelming connection of repetitive rhythm and vibrant emotion to elicit a state of "trance" from the listener. The state of trance is achieved by the listener being extremely involved with the music physically, emotionally, and spiritually, and thus being transported beyond consciousness of time and place in this world. Most trance pieces are attached to religious ritual, as is the case with Moroccan Goanuan music.

Movement: Many forms of European art or "classical" music have multiple sections within a single piece. We call these sections movements. Although there will be a break between each movement, the listener should consider the movements to be similar to paragraphs in a single essay. All the movements go together to make up the composition.

Scales (scalier motion): Scales are menus of pitches (singable sounds or recognizable frequencies) that are used throughout a particular piece. All culture systems have specific "menus" that are important. Some are seven-note systems (diatonic), some are five-note systems (pentatonic), but all have a unique spacing and quality defined by the distance between the steps (intervals in the scale) of the pitches in the menu.

Meter: Beats or pulses in most of the world's music are organized into more manageable groups or cycles. The *meter* is, therefore, the number of beats in the beat group or cycle of a particular piece. The vast majority of our Western[1.8] music is organized in beat or pulse patterns of two beats, three beats, and four beats; that is, we count: 1, 2, 3, 4 – and then start again with beat one. Many non-Western culture systems have traditional or standard meters that exceed four-beat cycles. However, today's media is influencing much of the modern music of nearly all cultures toward four-beat meters, which have a wider international appeal.

Ud (Oud): This is the ancestor or precursor to the guitar. We say this instrument is from the *lute* family, but it actually predates the lute (the European ancestor of the guitar) and is, by recorded accounts, the first and most prolifically used *guitar* still used in varied forms through much of the world. (We will discuss the *ud* in Unit V)

Sonograph: Literally a "sound picture," the *sonograph* is a means of taking *musical notes* while the music is in progress. We will use this technique over the course of the text to increase our concentration and understanding of the "recipe" or musical elements in each piece.

Texture: All music derives its unique beauty from its specific combinations of instruments. How each instrument enters, is layered with others, or is withdrawn helps build or reduce tension in the music (see Unit II). Texture is, therefore, the *density* of musical layering or activity.

Pic. 1.5A Interdisciplinary "thought" --- is becoming ever-increasingly emphasized in education and in promoting an accurate means for viewing our world. In the simplest sense, interdisciplinary work seeks to find parallels or connections between the various disciplines or modes of human perception (seeking to integrate human disciplines over excessive specialization). In this picture, the work and endeavors in a professional kitchen is nearly identical to those in the professions of the performing arts. 1) the recipe in creating food and the outcome -- "the dish" is identical to the many elements in music, theater, or dance that result in the composition; 2) the preparation of food in a busy kitchen requires finally-tuned communication and teamwork, essential ingredients in all the performing arts; 3) and the satisfaction of the staff – is derived from their collaborative creativity, consistency, and ability to sustain both for as long as they seek to remain "artists." Photo: Courtesy Susanna Naranjo

Pic. 1.5B, C, & D *The "creativity process" for all creations is essentially identical. A "motivation" or need sparks an idea. The idea sparks an action based upon the individual's experiences (and learned techniques). And, the application of materials and techniques produces a product. In all cases, "improvisation" or a creative and spontaneous fusion of inspiration and techniques produces something "unique" as in: a magnificent building (B), and a rather unusual décor (and use of human bones) of a cathedral in the Czech Republic (C), and a unique spin on "puppetry" before a stage of jazz musicians playing compositions of their own "fusion" of interests and experiences (D).* Photos: Courtesy Brandon Naylor.

Unit I Activities

Note: The activities provided at the close of each Unit are designed to give each of us more opportunity to explore the music, cultures, perceptual tools, or concepts within the Unit. If you are reading and listening for personal enhancement, feel free to choose whichever activities you wish. If you are using this text for a university or college course, you will likely be given directions by your instructor as to which options are more applicable to the scope and nature of your course.

Activity #1: Understanding Concepts

Based upon your perception of the reading, answer the following questions:

1) *Cultures or Culture Groups:* What are they? How are they determined?

2) *Creativity:* What is it? Are you creative? If so, how? If not, why not? Is it possible that one truly is *not creative?* Why or why not?

3) Since we have only begun to discuss music as a creative expression, it might be a good time to contemplate what we think music should or should not be.

   - Must music be pleasing?

   - Should music make us feel good?

   - Could the sound of the birds or the wind through the trees be considered music? Why or why not?

   - If I hit a garbage can or throw rocks down some stairs, could I be making music? Why or why not?

4) The musical composition process was discussed in Unit I. Answer the following in your own words:

   - How do you think music is composed?

   - Is a musical composition ever *completely original?* If so, how is this? If not, why not?

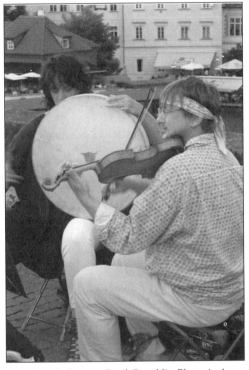

Musicians in Prague, Czech Republic. Photo Authors.

Activity #2: Listening Deeper

Read the composer's/musician's comments for CD selections 1.1 and 1.2. Listen again to these selections. For each, answer the following:

1) In what way is this "creative" music?

2) What do you think the organizer (composer) intended for us, in creating this music?

3) If you don't "like" the music (which you may not at first), can you at least respect the composer's "organization of sound in time" or imagine what he/she may wish to teach us? Or, if you find the music interesting or "like it," do you know why? In both instances, what experiences in your life would lead you to like or not like it? If you listened to the piece for a second time, or after you read the notes, did your perception of the piece change? If you didn't listen to the piece all the way to its conclusion or would not listen to it again, do you know why?

4) Do you hear any similarities between the two musical selections? Is there, in your opinion, a "fusion" of music (and cultural) sounds between the two pieces? If so, how or in what way?

Activity #3: **Exercising Passion**

Did you feel excitement or *passion* (intense enthusiasm or interest) for anything that you read or heard in Unit I? If so, you might wish to further investigate and document one or more of the following:

1) You might find a composer or songwriter to interview concerning his or her perspectives of the creative process. Why does he or she *compose music?* What are the challenges or obstacles? What are the benefits?

2) Have you met anyone from Spain or Morocco? Do you have any means of contacting someone from these cultures? What could you ask them? How would they describe their culture, their food, their art, or their music? Try to conduct an interview with someone. Try simply to be respectful to his or her concerns, and you will likely have a very positive experience.

3) Are you aware of a film about a famous composer or, perhaps, about Morocco? You might check out the film to see whether it gives you better insight into the world of the composer or the culture-bearers (people) of Morocco. You may wish to write some notes as you are watching so that you don't forget your thoughts over time.

4) The Internet is always available. Who is your favorite composer or songwriter? What can we learn about the composition process from his or her comments or perspectives? What else can we find out about Morocco? About the fusion of Spanish and "Moorish" or North African (Moroccan) cultures? Pick a topic of interest – and let it fly!

Note: Make sure, whenever possible, that you screen your Web sites. Questions we might ask: Is the person who is posting the information a member of the culture group or someone very knowledgeable or passionate about the culture? If so, the information you glean from the site will likely be beneficial to you. If not, you may wish to look elsewhere.

Pic. 1.5E *The parallel between texture in visual art and texture in sound is strong. In visual art, the various textures and dimensions provide the viewer with all the concepts of motion as well as emotion through manipulation of space and contrast of materials. In music, the layering of instruments provides a thicker or thinner texture as well; thus, emotions and the aural spectrum are manipulated, and motion and emotion are again affected.* Image: "Tango" by Laurie Fowler and Bill Thelen, Michigan, Copyright: 2004.

Activity #4: **Exercising Our Own Creativity**

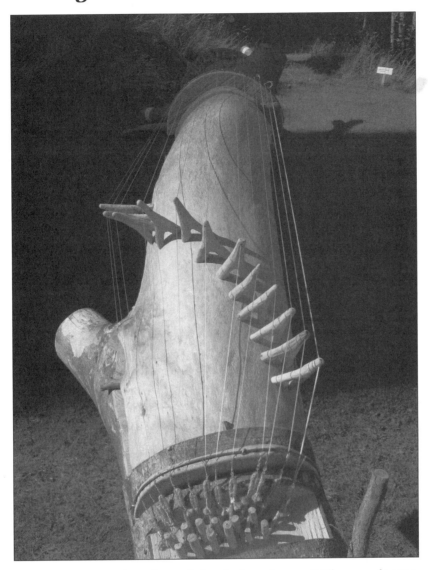

Pic. 1.6 *The key to any form of appreciation of others – is respect! When we make something inspired by another culture we might ask ourselves, would "they" – the people of the other culture, the musicians, even people of a different time period – would they respect my reaction? Would this fallen tree respect the fact that it is now an incredible fusion of instrument and nature (kayageum/koto fusion – see zithers of Eastern Asia)?* Photo: istock.

What do you love to use as your "instrument" of creativity... poetry, writing, cooking, scrap-booking, decorating, fashion, dance, music, working on cars, carpentry, party-planning? However you prefer to express yourself, there is not a human being on the planet who is *not* creative.

In its most basic form, creativity is also problem-solving. Is it possible to be a human being and not have problems that need solving? However *routine, mundane, or normal* our creative skills may seem to us, however outside the perception of *art* our skills may appear to us, being creative is an essential part of life and equally essential in appreciating the creativity of others. All most of us require to boost our perceptions of our own creativity is the simple investment of energy to nurture that creativity. One manner of creative expression is to take a concept, a thought, an idea, or a fact, and reflect on its form, texture, or qualities. We try to look for a parallel in the medium of our "instrument."

Then we see if we can express that concept through our own being and talents. This is the basis of the creative process in brief.

1) Read Dr. Hartway's comments about creativity. What in the two pieces represents something you might imitate through your instruments? [Perhaps trying to understand trance as a form of meditation – getting lost in a passion or expression of something "higher" than ourselves. Or the process of creating without any expectation of how it might "turn out."] How can this be applied to your creative skills? Give it a try!

2) Take the time to find out a bit more about Morocco. Examine a painting or the architecture of a building. Listen again to the piece by *Orchestre Chabab*. Find a recipe or clothing style. How could this be incorporated into your own creative skills? What might you be able to create? Try to "make" (or create) anything that you would give as a gift to someone – in the manner that these musicians/composers gave you their gifts? Finally, do you think someone from Morocco would be honored by the sincerity of your efforts?

Unit I: Endnotes

1.1   The last line is from the writings of Baha'u'llah and is an admonition to "justice" as the greatest of all human virtues. If emphasized, it becomes the pathway to an independent and clear vision.

1.2   The terms "cultural traits" or "values" will be used throughout this text to imply the following: all culture groups, regions, or groupings of humans with similar affinities have predominant strategies and belief systems. The more emphasized and predominant of these traits or systems are their "values." Although we generalize severely in attempting to describe entire culture systems within a few pages or musical examples, it does help to ask culture-bearers "what they feel is important" and, when the responses frequently indicate one or more prevalent traits, to isolate and discuss those traits as values important to the understanding of the culture's identity and self-vision.

1.3   The term "fusion," though more frequently used in science, will be used to indicate the age-old and natural process of two or more cultures or culturally expressive traits coming together to form another expression unique to either or all of the contributing sources.

1.4   The term "culture-bearer" is a frequently used term in anthropology to indicate those who bear allegiance and familiarity through birth and the largest portion of their lives to specific culture groups. The assumption is generally that birth and the abundance of life's experiences within the realm of a specific culture system will lead that individual to possess more of the traits or values of that system. The extension of this is that representation of culture bearers' thoughts will lead the outsider to a better understanding of the culture or the culture's expressions … e.g., music.

1.5   We have found it enormously helpful to make the analogy of the acquisition of experiential information in life to the loading of a filing system in our mind, since verbal communication of any topic will use words that bring up particular files and each file can have only the sum total of information of our life's experiences and education. See Unit III for more information on this topic.

1.6   "Humility" will be discussed more later. Briefly, we will define humility as an attitude or quality of putting others and their knowledge in a place of respect, being teachable and desiring to see ourselves not as better, and in some cases submitting ourselves to the knowledge and experiences of others, for the sake of our own growth.

1.7   Ziryab is considered the master of the Arabo Andalusian school and father of its importation to Morocco. Born in Baghdad, he is credited with bringing the Udistes—a type of poetic chant which evolved into the Noubas used today—into a "conservatory" style of instruction which, through his ten children and disciples, was able to find its way back to Morocco and into the musical systems of both Spain and North Africa to the present day.

1.8   The term "Western" will be used frequently throughout the text to refer to predominant characteristics that have evolved from European culture and its satellite or affiliate culture systems. This includes America and all cultures heavily influenced by the values, perceptions, and cultural structures of Europe. It also includes, of course, the main doctrines and methods of communication emphasized by Europe's most prolific tool of proclamation: the university systems of education.

Graphic Design Endnotes, courtesy:
Slavojub Pantelic, 2005.

Human Universals

UNIT

II

Topics to Consider in Unit II

➤ *How do we acquire our values and tastes (mind files)?*

➤ *What are some of the more "motivating" reasons for learning about other cultures?*

➤ *What are some of the greatest challenges to the Western appreciator of other cultures' music (and values)?*

➤ *What are the influences of our "larger" or "sub" cultures on our values? Which are easier to see or detect? Which are more difficult?*

➤ *What are some of the universals of the life cycle – and how are they reflected in music?*

➤ *What are some of the ways in which our family backgrounds shape both our tastes and distastes in music?*

➤ *How does the music of a Japanese student, jazz musicians from the Netherlands mixed with the experiences of musicians from Mali, and the composition from a musician from Peru reflect those musicians' comments and life experiences?*

➤ *What is rhythm? What is texture, melody, orchestration, or a "rhythm section"?*

➤ *What are some of the influences of media in shaping our tastes, living patterns, and values?*

UNIT II

Human Universals

Learning More about Our Values and Tastes—and How They Were Established

"One should guard against preaching to young people success in the customary form as the main aim in life. The most important motive for work in school and in life is pleasure in the work, pleasure in its result, and the knowledge of the value of the result to community." Albert Einstein (1879-1955), On Education

An important prerequisite for learning anything new, perhaps more than any single other perceptual tool, is having first a solid knowledge of ourselves. That is, before learning about new music or people, it is helpful to know what is or isn't part of our acquired system of values. Further, we might also consider where these values evolved, as well as whether they actually are the values we wish to continue to pursue. It is also generally helpful to know what we like or dislike and *how we acquired these tastes*. The paradox of life is that in order to move effectively forward, we are perpetually called to look *backwards* over our life experiences and question whether what we hear or perceive is accurate, of benefit, or perhaps the result of some poorly loaded files.

Knowing ourselves means knowing what we have in our *mind's files* and how and from where that information was *loaded into those files*. This may sound simple, but as we advance in our pursuit of knowledge, especially as we continue to reassess our place in the context of a single planet, we amass a human library composed of the sum total of our experiences and education. We will find many files in this library that are well loaded (accurate and respectful information), but we might also find many more that have been loaded with only partial or even completely inaccurate or *biased* information.

Growth in all things is a process over time. Most of us have been trained to see growth in phases or categories (1st grade, 2nd grade, or 20s, 30s, 40s). Some may see things more organically, perhaps as a perpetual process of fusion and change. Still, as Einstein suggests, when we find pleasure in the process, when we contemplate the possibility that success may be better defined as the impact our lives and efforts have upon those around us, we may wish to assess the means by which a lasting growth can be accomplished and enjoyed. Our awareness of ourselves and of our values in general is the focus of this Unit.

How Motivated Are We to Learn about Others?

Our motivation will determine the energy we will invest (or choose *not* to invest) in the learning process. We might ask a rather simple question: How interested are we in the lives of people in China, Ghana, or Russia? Or those in Lakota cultures? What about Chinese opera, country music from the '50s, Bob Marley, or the music for a specific film? We might have a strong *affinity*[2.1] for some of these cultures or musical genres. In such cases, we are likely to find quicker access and deeper appreciation for whatever comes from the people or is associated with the music. In other instances, we may have passive or even negative feelings concerning a culture group or musical genre. In either case, we grow or will remain as limited in our tastes and perceptions as the level of our motivation. In fact, the degree or level of motivation we have is precisely due to our experiences and education as well. Therefore, our motivation is a good place to start in assessing our file system.

We may begin by contemplating the following, because so much of the music and art we enjoy has been created by individuals who have both asked and attempted to answer these questions:

- *What is most important to us in life?*
- *What truly brings us lasting enjoyment and pleasure?*
- *What makes us truly (and lastingly) happy?*

Most of these questions are answered against the standards and values we have set for "success" or fulfillment in life. When we feel (intuitively have passion) or see (consciously understand) in what way the exertion of our effort will increase the quality of our lives, we are much more likely to invest energy in new experiences.

Pic. 2.1 *A line dance at Chicago's Latin American Festival attracts everyone regardless of ethnicity. Participation in community dance events is common in nearly every culture, particularly in celebrating or marking events in the life cycle.* Photo: Authors.

Recognizing the Content in Our Mind's Files

Most of us have heard: *"He got that from his dad,"* or *"She takes after her mother."* There is no question in most of our minds that we acquire the vast majority of our training and many of our values, tastes, and qualities initially through combinations of genetic transference (physical inheritance) and clan and family relations (contact with our family of origin or replacement families). We may also be aware at some level of how much our peers, colleagues, the media, and education during our growth years have affected what we know and *what we value.*

With the cultural expressions or music we already like—much of which has been influenced by the close bonds we have with family, friends, and relatives—not much examination is required. We like "rock"—they like "rock"; we like "opera"—they like "opera"; or we have an affinity for Polish sausage, polka, or the speeches of the late Pope John Paul—a quick look and we see they have the same tastes and values. What oftentimes is not asked is how we have acquired this information and values, and, if by chance, along with those values, we have also inherited negative biases.

Since it doesn't appear that many of us have the opportunity of choosing our family of origin, our race, or the location for the acquisition of our early values in life, it's pointless to question this process or lament our powerlessness in its regard. What is completely relevant, however, is learning to recognize what we know, what we don't know, and how we acquired both. In this manner, we become increasingly aware of both who we are (to value and embrace it) and what possible alternatives we have to those of our upbringing. Asking hard questions that make us conscious of our values and biases is the manifestation of *humility,* compassion, and a critically thinking, questioning mind.

Building the "Mind's Files"

Whenever we hear a piece of music, we will automatically react to it by virtue of our experiences and affinities at the point in time when the contact occurs. As before, if we like the music or have had extensive contact with it, the experience will likely prompt the "pulling" of the files in our mind that are quite adequately loaded with information. Each of our musical files is "bookmarked" by experiences of varying degrees of intimacy and usually labeled according to these experiences as well. Concerts, our CD collection, the CDs or music of those we love or admire, the radio stations we or others we admire play—in most cases, there is little effort required on our part to appreciate much of the music we derive from these sources.

Finding the motivation to examine, load, or re-load the files that have insufficient or inaccurate information, or for which we are required to physically, mentally, or emotionally exert energy, is a bit trickier. One of the most helpful tools to overcoming the barriers of apathy or cool motivation (often expressed as "I don't have the time") is the recognition that the bulk of our human training historically has been to focus on the points of distinction and separation rather than on the consideration that music is a neither inflexible nor immobile expression devoid of alteration.[2.2] As a result, whatever the experience, artist, or genre, the reality of most cultures or their music is seldom that which is encapsulated in our memory. There will seldom be a single musical culture or artist we currently find distasteful that will not have since generated a piece or a number of pieces we *might* now enjoy. The issue is not one of the music's potential, but of our potential to remain or become flexible and open.

When all is said and done, if we remember that growth is a process, education is a process, and acquiring new or alternative affinities for the world of music is most certainly a process, we will also learn to have compassion for ourselves as we struggle. Knowing that struggle is a requirement in any area of life if we are to experience long and lasting satisfaction or happiness may help us through the transitions we will inevitably encounter as we open up to new cultures or music.

Concerning the challenges in respecting the world's music, here are some other points in our collective history we might wish to consider:

- Time in music: The standard airplay of most radio stations' music in the United States and much of Europe is 3.5 to 4.5 minutes.[2.3] This means that many of us have been raised with a very limited exposure to music of longer duration. In prior generations, as well as in other parts of the world today, airplay is not limited by commercial concerns or to such condensed timeframes. This means that for listeners in many Western cultures, music of longer duration will be a challenge in terms of patience and duration of concentrated listening skills required.

Motivation: Patience in listening to music has a direct application to our capacity to be patient and listen to other human beings in general. Deeper listening skills and the human qualities required to nurture these skills transfer well to the arena of human relationships.

- Radio stations: In the United States and, to a lesser degree, European or world markets, music formats and radio play are "market" driven. This means each station is funded by advertising dollars and, as such, it is beneficial for stations to play the most narrow and exclusive musical styles in order to attract a narrow market from advertisers. As a result, exposure to musical diversity is greatly limited, and many of us must search a variety of stations or sources to find exposure to varied musical styles.

Motivation: The CDs with this text, satellite radio, MP3 players, and Internet downloads give us the capacity to find any music in the world in little or no time should we choose to do so. More importantly, the excitement we get by turning to the colleague at work, school, or wherever to ask simply, "What do you listen to …?" may open up a relationship and avenue for learning that will change our lives.

- Pace of life: Since success in many urban or technologically "advanced" cultures is defined by what we do, not necessarily *who we are,* many of us may find we have completely loaded or filled schedules. The more condensed our schedule, the more likely we will have little time for artistic, reflective, or creative pursuits. It also means much of our musical exposure will be in the context of activities which force musical or cultural reflections into the background.

Motivation: Over the course of this text, we will come into contact with numerous cultures and perspectives that will either encourage us to consider alternatives to "how" we might live, or at least ask questions about how we currently live. If we desire growth, we will learn to recognize the alternatives when they brush our world. Much of this awareness will come from slowing down—taking moments to observe things around us.

Stories from the Human Family

Michael's Experience:

I've realized over the years that I think and do so much without considering alternatives, without asking the question, "What else could I be doing?" In addition, I've had so many situations over the years where I was certain I understood what was occurring or what was best, only to find later that I was not even close. I've also learned, fortunately, that much of learning requires a bit (or a lot) of discomfort before I become resolved, patient, or willing to add the new information to my bank of experiences.

For example: I had a music composition teacher who was teaching us to write film music. When we were given our first project to write music for an orchestra, I knew that I'd be fine. After all, I'd written music for orchestras in Europe and had played in orchestras for some time. I spent a great deal of effort creating something quite interesting, intending to "show off" a lot of what I knew. "This should impress Professor _____," I thought to myself.

When I handed the score[2.4] to my instructor, he did not smile or congratulate me as I anticipated. Instead, he folded the score in half, handed it to me, and said, "You write what you know— and in this case to impress others, but it is so sloppy. Did you care that someone needs to read this?" Then he walked away before I could react.

After an emotional roller coaster ride which took me from horror to anger, hurt to confusion, I went back to him and asked, "Why did you hand back my score? Wasn't it good?"

He replied, "I don't know about the music you wrote, but the score was sloppy and hard to read. If you can't communicate so that others can understand you, then you can only write music for yourself... and that wouldn't make for a very good career, would it?"

To this day, despite the agony of the lesson, I'm grateful to this teacher for helping me learn, first, that we can only communicate that which we know or are aware of. But more importantly, that what we communicate has benefit only if we do it in a manner that is meaningful to others.

If we want our communications to be meaningful only to ourselves or those very much like us, then we need not expand our knowledge of other communication options. But if we wish to communicate to the many who are outside of our experiences, then we might remember what I learned that day:

Since I had put so much energy into trying to impress or to assert my prowess, values I had learned early as part of my cultural experience, I had forgotten to learn to write neatly and take care in the manner of presentation so that others would feel valued by my communication. Experience in Miami, Florida, 1985.

Therefore:

It is not what we think we are communicating to others—but how others *perceive* our communication, as well as how respected and honored they feel by the sincerity of our interest in them that ultimately matters. Any mistakes we make after this are likely to be as quickly forgotten as the material we studied for an exam the night before.

Music: The Universal—Not the Universal Language

"Real education should educate us out of self into something far finer; into a selflessness which links us with all humanity." Nancy Astor, (1879-1964) *"Viscountess Astor" (Quotations).*

As we began to construct this text, the highly respected actor and equally regarded activist Mr. Edward James Olmos wrote to us concerning music and its impact on both himself personally and Latino cultures generally: *"The combinations of cultures and their rhythms have shown me how beautifully we as a human race can come together. Music is much like a universal language which brings all of the human race together."*

It is very true that music is *universal*. Unlike much of spoken language, it can be understood emotionally, spiritually, or intuitively, even when we don't understand all of the symbols or the lyrics and stories in their entirety. For this reason perhaps more than any other, music is an excellent tool for acquainting ourselves with human diversity and for developing the necessary skills to respect the multiple possibilities within our human family.

Mr. Olmos has traveled around the world, worked extensively for civil and cultural rights, and spent a lifetime in the arts. He has acquired the necessary experiences to question his perceptions, to look more deeply into the possibilities behind the musical symbols, and to patiently and methodically seek the meaning in a given musical and cultural expression. That is, the universality of music (music exists in every culture in the world) does not necessarily imply we will have a universally *deep and engaged* understanding without considerable effort.

Pic 2.2 *Edward James Olmos with university students.* Photo: courtesy Edward James Olmos

To assist us in our efforts, we should look at some of the means by which we acquire our musical tastes through contact with layers of cultural groups at *larger* or *subcultural* levels. We can then more aptly apply the following human universals to the musical expressions of others:

- All culture groups tell stories of their past, their present, and reflect upon their hopes for the future. These stories are laden with symbolism according to the experiences of the storytellers over the culture's history. Although the vocabulary of the music may not always be familiar, the human experience relative to the universal nature of the *life cycle*[2.5] has always applied and will ever apply equally to every human being. Somewhere in every story is a link to our own.

- All human beings will acquire tastes and values by virtue of the contacts they have with other humans. For convenience or clarity, we can divide these contacts into two categories:

    Subcultures: Our families, religious groups, career colleagues, school friends, or any group with whom we have a strong affiliation. We change our sub-cultural affiliations as we go through life. A single event, such as an illness, a new job, or a birth or death can change our affinities permanently, but observing our *subculture's* impact on our tastes and affiliations is essential to knowing what we have in our mind's files.

    Larger culture (Superculture): This might include the most generalized affiliation by continent ("African" or "Western" cultures) or be more specific to a country or region ("American," "French," "Jamaican"). However, to greater or lesser degrees, the influence of the economic, political, or educational values of the larger culture (which also impact the lives of all the members of our sub-cultures, including our friends and family) have enormous impact on the acquisition of affinities and tastes in all things.

- Without question, many of the values of the larger cultures and subcultures are now acquired (or at least heavily influenced) by media. As such, the cultures with the "loudest" media voices are likely to have the greatest impact globally on our affinities and values. For example, we see much of the world being heavily influenced by American movies and music, not because the movies and music are necessarily "better" or more valuable, but because they are disseminated more prolifically.

We will take a look at each of the phenomena above, in order to better understand how we acquire not only our musical tastes, but our values and tastes overall.

The Life Cycle: Stories and Rituals

> *"The good neighbor looks beyond the external accidents and discerns those inner qualities that make all men human and, therefore, brothers."* Martin Luther King, Jr., *Strength to Love*, 1963

The passage of life, from whatever corner of the globe we may traverse it, *will* be told through music. Music is like a diamond ring: its tones and rhythms provide the setting for the loose diamonds of human experience. The majority of the world's music tells stories. Many of these stories are about the things we as humans share with everyone on the planet: growing up, loving, losing a loved one, the joys and trials of family, birth, marriage, death—all of the experiences that are part of the human journey. Since these subjects are the subjects addressed in every language and style of music, we can assume with increasing accuracy that nearly every story told will have some connection to the issues and concerns of our universal progression through the life cycle.

What storytelling provides is a connection between generations and a connection to the passage of life generally. Bereft of a record of the connection we share with our passage through life's pain, joy, and confusion, we'd be isolated within our own experience and have less record of our ancestry. Naturally, each generation of each culture will clothe the universal in the language and symbols of the temporal.

Even when the connection of a story to us or our lives is vague by virtue of its textual content or foreignness to our cultural experiences (different languages, instruments, or sounds), because it is being created by a human being, it must have some connection to our human experience and our journey through the life cycle.

Universals of the Life Cycle (Expressed Differently)

Although all musicians express their stories through the languages, instruments, technology, and history of their evolution and unique cultural perspectives, we can expect that:

• *Most* music will reflect the experience and location in the life cycle of the musician (child, youth, young adult, mature adult, elder, etc.).

• *Much* music will be created to speak to members of the culture[2.6] either about the phase currently experienced by the musician or one through which the musician has passed.

• *Seldom* is music created to speak about a portion of the life cycle through which the musician has not passed. Simply put, it is difficult to create an expression about something we have not lived.

• *Never* will we hear a piece that is devoid of some connection to the life cycle. That is, however remote or symbolic, the art or music we create is always connected to the human experience. Although the degree of immediacy or graphic connection to the life cycle may be different for each piece, understanding and seeing connections based upon this fundamental knowledge is very helpful, if not essential.

Léonie's Perspectives on the Life Cycle

Discussion Reflection II-A

"Elders" in my culture (as in many others) have traditionally been viewed in a positive light, as repositories of information and wisdom, as the cornerstones of our being, our history, and our heritage. Those living and those who are no longer with us have inspired us with their lessons, their experience, and, often, the maturity and tolerance they have for our impatience or inexperience. Conversely, youth have a voice, but only in so far as they respect their elders, honor their elders, and don't exalt themselves or their ideas disproportionately beyond their age and experience.

In my culture, or in what many still erroneously call "third world cultures," counseling does exist, but primarily in the context of grounded, intuitive, and experienced elders. Throughout my upbringing, if we had concerns, we would go to our mother, father, grandmother, grandfather, or other elders and we would seek their wisdom, as the life-cycle would naturally dictate. They did not often have the intelligence born from books. In fact, several of them did not go to school at all. But their personal maturity, intuition, and general experiential wisdom had greater influence on many of us than a majority of the theories born from education that a modern counselor or educator might feel inclined to use.

I've always found it interesting how different cultures give weight to different portions of the life cycle. It seems that in most Western cultures much power is given to the young adult stage of the life cycle. Youthfulness, looking young, acting young, and being young are given so much weight. We can see it in advertising, in the cosmetic industry, and in so many other reflections of Western cultural values. But what is the message we send to our elders? Or perhaps more importantly, how might this influence the manner in which we listen (or do not listen) to them?

Questions
• *Why do you suppose that listening to and caring for the elderly is given so much emphasis in non-Western cultures? How does this compare to your experiences?*
• *To what degree do you feel that your culture, school, or family discusses or understands the life cycle? To what degree do they support or not support respecting and caring for elders?*
• *If you perceive an imbalance, how might this affect your life? The lives of your children? What could be done to correct life-cycle imbalances?*

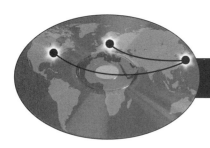

Inside the Musician's World

Karasu Randa,
Japanese "Local" Musician

Note: If notoriety or *fame* is the basis upon which we become informed, respect, and appreciate creativity in music, we will miss many wonderfully creative expressions and will likely frequently be disappointed by much of the more famous music along the way. Although media can play a wonderful role in exposing us to the creative works of artists, it is just as capable of being used to select and screen sincere and insightful works which do not fit commercial formulas or are not competitive with costly and often "glitzy" productions from our sound worlds. The following piece is an example of the creativity in a non-commercial/non-famous work.

A Japanese student who plays the **shamisen** as a hobby, but who also has a very strong appreciation of her ancient heritage, mentioned she knew of some artists she thought might be good for this project. One of them, Karasu Randa, is a 24-year-old street-musician who is currently studying freezer-equipment design while working in a factory. Fairly well known by the youth in Mie (a district of Honshu, the largest Japanese island), Karasu doesn't know exactly why he likes music so much, but he passionately pursues it in his own way. When we asked for a picture, he replied: *"I don't want my picture in the text; I just play what I've grown to know. I'm not famous, but I love music."*

Perhaps it is the love for music and the creative spirit, or perhaps it is the musician's connection to ancient traditions of storytelling and his elders whom he said inspired his musical interests that makes his songs enjoyable (Unit IX). Regardless, the lyrics, his goals in life and for his music, and his sense of connectivity to seeking purpose in life (a primary concern of his age and place in the life-cycle), though possibly atypical compared to the perceptions of *success* held by many youth even in his own country, are refreshing and worthy of thought. We might also note how critical social ties to peers and career in community-building is to the young-adult phase of the life-cycle. These universal concerns of a young adult are vivid in both Karasu's music and comments.

CD 1.3

"Tsukuyomi," copyright 2004, Karasu Randa, Mie, Japan

Karasu Randa plays guitar and writes his own songs, about which he says, *"I create songs because I like people to utilize my music for relaxation or to extend their passion and love of life."* He goes on to say, *"I believe music is for creating strong emotions … not for adding to our problems or causing conflict."* When we asked him which of the selections of his CD he preferred, he told us "Shaka-bana" (which refers to the flower of *Shakyamuni* or the Buddha), a song about beauty and devotion; and "Tsukuyomi," which translates to "moon" in an old Japanese dialect. The connection of life and the life cycle to metaphors of nature is part of an ancient tradition in art, poetry, and music throughout Asia, especially in the songs, theater, and meditative music of Japan.

"What I wanted to say by this song is that the person telling the story has lost one of the most important things in life: his innocence, honesty, and qualities of childhood. This is a part of what happens as we become adults and move out of the cycle of childhood. Now, he knows… the world is not perfect, beautiful, or kind to him. In addition, he also knows he will never be able to return to his childhood.

"But deep inside, he would love to return to that time that he didn't know anything about this world and was just an innocent child. This is something any sensitive or feeling adult must wish for at times when he confronts the harshness of adult life."

The Recipe of Sound

The piece starts and ends with two young adults discussing "young adult topics" over the sound of waves. The introduction contrasts the pure voice of Mr. Karasu and the lyrics, which speak to the innocence of childhood, in much the same manner that adult responsibilities in the material world contrast with the innocence of childhood.

When the guitar and rhythm enter, the simple layers (texture) of guitar with the occasional thumping of the guitar are the only accompaniment to the melody. This is a perfect setting, in its *lack of density,* to complement the innocence spoken of in the song.

The **timbre** (sound quality) of the voice is equally clear and personifies childhood and innocence as well. Historically, much of early Japanese music blended silence and sparse texture with topics that connect the life cycle to nature; this song exemplifies this connection.

The Influence of "Culture": Super and Subculture Influences

"Human culture groups are by nature fluid, multifaceted, and highly creative organisms whose borders are much more flexible than we are prone to imagining. When these groups are presented with new information, technology, and insights, they will, according to strategies of their own design, transfer, fuse, and appropriate ('take them on') at will." Author, (Léonie N.), "The Creativity in Culture," 1997.

One of the most elusive concepts in our vocabulary is embodied in the word *culture*. Many have argued that, because the term brings up notions of a fixed set of values, it should not be used at all to discuss human communities, regardless of how traditional they may seem. This argument holds a lot of value, particularly as communication, media, and travel allow for intensive contact between cultures on a daily basis.

Although *cultures* or *culture groups*[2.7] are traditionally defined as the beliefs, customs, and social behavior shared by a particular nation or people according to their place, class, or time period, this definition certainly held much more weight in times when inter-cultural contact (contact between diverse cultural groups) was less frequent or less sustained. But in truth, it would be difficult to find a time in recorded history in which inter-/intra-cultural contact was not an important if not essential concern.

Still, in order to summarize cultural or artistic characteristics, we need to find a handle for discussion. Therefore, we deploy culture as a means of characterizing tendencies, speaking of history, and summarizing values and expressive traits if for no other reason than to advance our knowledge about human evolution. We will, however, also perpetually remind the reader to keep a flexible and fluid perception of cultures and their music, in order to accommodate the cultures' consistently updating visions of themselves and the sound-world as they are today and as they will evolve tomorrow.

On one hand, it would be convenient if the racial, national, or other identifiers we use to denote a person's culture could accurately define that person or culture. However, people do not usually belong to a single culture or culture group when it comes to how they live or what music they prefer. The multitude

Pic.2.3A *In a Las Vegas entertainment spot, Debra (violinist) says she's fond of classical music and Celtic music – the music she's playing here. Rob (bass) is most fond of jazz and classical music, but has taken the job of learning to play Celtic music with Debra. Rob has, in essence, taken on a new "sub-cultural" influence. His opportunities for growth are therefore greater than Debra's – for now.* Photo: Author.

of options any individual may experience during a typical life-span necessitates the moving about and association in numerous sub-cultures or culture groups. Each of these culture groups—family, peers, colleagues at work, religious groups, hobbies, and any one of a million other possibilities—contribute to the individual's personality and perceptions of value. What further complicates the matter is that there are also the aforementioned *larger culture systems* or supercultures (the country, continent, or larger systems) which greatly influence every individual within them. These "larger" cultures, for better or worse, impose laws, create doctrines, and broadcast values through education, politics, economics, and media that, based on their history, affect any and all within their jurisdiction.

Therefore, the music we love is the combination of the evolution of the super culture (its history in all facets) and its intersection with and impact upon the subculture groups: family, friends, and associates. To understand how culture groups influence our personal evolution and, ultimately, our musical value systems, consider these points:

Pic. 2.4 *What we perceive in life may be a distortion of reality. Culture systems overlap, integrate, repel, attract, and, ultimately, influence our perception of the world. Though we may see something as insignificant in our world, it may be momentous in the world of another. For these reasons, we are better off learning to state our tastes and values with "humility qualifiers": "I think – it is my experience – I feel – It might be—" all are preferable ways of stating our beliefs and tastes. Such qualifiers leave the door open for alternative expressions which we will inevitably encounter later in life.* Photo: Navy Pier sculpture, Chicago, IL, Author.

- Each generation of each culture group will make hundreds and thousands of alterations and determinations in the creation and expression of values through language and music. Therefore, we should use cultural labels only in so far as they assist us in upgrading voids in our knowledge, but not as fixed or inflexible entities.

- In addition to our cultures of origin (place/groups from birth to adulthood), each of us, depending upon our generation and influences, selects the combination of activities, language, and musical expressions which we believe will bring us respect and integrity, enhance our lives, make us feel good, or simply bring us enjoyment. In turn, these activities, changes, and new associations or expressions evolve to make up not only *our world* but also the standards by which we assess the worlds of others.

- Are we comfortable asking pointed questions of ourselves without feeling bad, guilty, or placing blame on ourselves, our country, or family of origin? That is, if we operate by the belief system that there are not superior or inferior cultures, but rather superior or inferior traits within cultures (generally, equally distributed), it will be much easier for us to see both the positives and negatives in our own system of values. To ask hard and candid questions of our culturally learned perspectives facilitates quicker and more profound growth in our awareness and in the expansion of our mind's files.

- All human expressions bear resemblance or owe their existence to something previously in existence. Our tastes, likes, dislikes, and musical expressions are not entirely "original"—but are reconfigurations of preexisting thought.

Stories from the Human Family

"Everyone in America likes that song (patriotic popular song). How could you be American and not like it? I think that we are "proud to be American" because of our freedom … that's what makes the song so appealing." (Eighteen-year-old American female student)

Interpretation: Certainly, not *everyone* in America likes the song. The concept of "freedom," though embraced by perhaps *nearly* all Americans, is likely to have diverse interpretations. To some, patriotism might be complete acceptance of the policies of government or the belief in American dominance and supremacy in world affairs. To others, it might be the license to question and protest those very values. Regardless, one cannot dispute that American history, its Constitution, and its policies (including the emphasis on "freedom" and its multiple possible interpretations) directly affects <u>all</u> American citizens and their musical choices. This is what is meant by *"larger (super) culture" influence.*

"Oops, there it goes …"

Michael's Experience:
I can't help but recall my first trip to the Seychelles Islands (in the Indian Ocean). My family and I were to take a boat from the main island of Mahé to the island of La Digue. The journey was to last about an hour, and the sea was extremely rough. I'd been on ships many times before, so I promptly nudged myself to the bow of the ship on the top deck. I loved the feel of the sea-water as it splashed onto my face. I felt like a modern-day Robinson Crusoe.

I failed to notice that all of the locals, my wife included (who had warned me about the intensity of the Seychelles' sun), were going down into the lower levels of the ship to lie down for the duration of the trip. In time, one of the shipmates came to me, advising me to join the Seychellois (people of Seychelles) in the lower level "so that you won't get sick — really sick." I thanked him... but said I'd be all right. Then I laughed to myself, thinking that he probably took me for a soft tourist. "I've been on lots of ships before," I thought. "I certainly can handle these waves. Obviously, this guy doesn't know me very well." What I failed to consider was that in the world of my experience, boats are either smaller boats on lakes or big cruise ships on the ocean. Those were my experiences, the basis for my perceptions, my judgments, and my reality.

Needless to say, in time I became extremely ill. More importantly, I dearly regretted my arrogance. In fact, I regretted it for about three days. I had mistakenly made my world—the world." in the Seychelles Islands, 1987.

Interpretation: In both instances above, the tendency to trust or rely exclusively upon our world of perceptions, our experiences, or our interpretation creates a conflict with the possibility of alternate interpretations. When we become aware of the influences of culture systems, as well as the reality that there are multiple other truths that may not be manifest within our culture groups, we begin to question perceptions while seeking to expose ourselves to the values others hold in high esteem. We may never like the music of South Korea or Ghana as well as that of our own country, but knowing that we have only a piece of the entire truth, in time, becomes a great motivator for acquiring new knowledge or, minimally, qualifying what we do know with humility modifiers.

Larger culture systems/supercultures (country, continent, Eastern vs. Western, etc.) and their influence on our tastes and values may be hard to see. At times vague, opaque, or completely obscure, these larger value systems often go unnoticed because the greatest percentage of those people in our world are a part of the same system. When we have no mode of comparison, it is very difficult to see what we like, much less how we acquired those tastes. For example, in American music, the system of capitalism, the manner in which radio, TV, or films are funded, the extent to which media makes the artists "famous," and, to a large extent, the fact that the music to which we have access is selected and marketed usually by large corporations, are important considerations to the musical worlds of *all* Americans. Yes, even those who choose to resist or rebel against these cultural operatives. Additionally, the *freedom* for anyone to pursue a career in music or not to pursue music, the systems of racial separation and integration that are part of America's racial perception and vocabulary, and a host of other possibilities too numerous to mention all affect each American's vision in one manner or another. Though variable in outcome as a result of subculture (family, religion, peers, etc.), larger culture values, such as "capitalism," will impact the vision of every person brought up under their influence.

Pic.2.4A *"All too commonly, we find our men of affairs facing revolutionary situations with a philosophy that is outmoded ... (they) tend to lay stratagems in terms of the conflict that is over, and not the one ahead. We have left behind a multi-cultural world where only a small segment of the people inhabiting it really counted; we are living in the same multi-cultural world, but one in which people with the most diverse modes of thought and behavior are in continuous interaction."* Melville Herskovits, "Cultural Relativism," 1972. Photo: Courtesy Lisa Gagne.

To extend this even further, the system of values that evolves to become one's *country, nation,* or the source of the *larger cultural* traits will have already greatly influenced our grandparents and our parents before we even arrive on this earth. We will spend our first couple of decades being raised by these individuals, exposed to their tastes in music, until we are adults and can begin to independently investigate the musical worlds of others. So pervasive is the historical influence of politics, economics, wars and conflicts, cultural perceptions, and biases of a larger culture on the education, the media, and the generations of people who grow up under their influence that only an extremely intense focus on seeking to understand their influence can help us understand their impact on our tastes, values, and biases.

It is not unusual for a visitor from another country to have a more objective perspective on the values and cultural traits of the host country than the natives will. Only when we know of other options or have experienced other possibilities do we have a means of comparison with which to differentiate the absolutes of the human condition (things all humans experience or value) from behaviors and attitudes which are influenced by the evolution of the larger culture systems and, thus, may be experienced alternatively elsewhere.

The Value of a "Multi-Cultural" Vision

Discussion Reflection II-B

Léonie's Experience

From my experience, in each of my sojourns to a new country or culture, my patience, listening skills, and perceptions were challenged during the first hours, days, or months in the new surroundings. Confusion and self-doubt at some point replaced much of the excitement I had experienced in the months of planning for the trip.

The emotional roller-coaster of my first encounters in a new culture (often referred to as "culture shock") was at first unsettling. I frequently lamented the fact that cultural education was not provided by the host country or community to help me feel more comfortable, safe, and welcome during the difficult periods of adjustment. However, over time, I came to realize that the struggles and difficulties I faced in making a "home" of each new culture presented me with opportunities to expand my own cultural values while obtaining an understanding of my host country. In turn, I was enabled to share my own cultural values, which at times may have helped balance or enhance the lives of those in my host country. In all cases, however, I obtained a more objective perspective of myself and both my culture and upbringing.

Learning in or about other cultures, is essential to nurturing a culturally equitable vision of humanity. And, we can obtain an objective vision of our place in the world only by having some diversity in our experiences… as a means of comparison.

What is the advantage of a comprehensive "multicultural" view of our world?

The saying that we cannot teach what we do not have could equally be applied to our understanding of our own lives and cultures. We cannot advocate change, recognize imbalances, or seek to alter or balance anything that is beyond our perception. Having contact with the widest of experiences or cultural views provides us alternatives. We may later choose our initial way of living or perceiving, but now it's a choice and not simply a habit or the result of not knowing alternatives.

Questions

- Have you ever experienced the discomfort of being in a "foreign" or unfamiliar culture? If so, how did you respond? Have you had a fairly prolonged contact (months or years of visiting or living, perhaps) with a culture other than your own? If so, what was that like? If not, why do you think you haven't chosen that path?

- If you have been able to experience another culture, did you learn to see or appreciate anything with greater clarity about your own culture from the experience?

- If you have not had such an experience, or, in order to have another such experience, how might you make it happen with your current resources and lifestyle?

- Is there a way to have intimate contact with other cultures even while living in your current homeland? How might you do this?

Inside the Musician's World

Fra Fra Sound
with Musicians from Mali

Note: What occured in the evolution of the national heritage of the Netherlands that led to an educational system and a people that, to a large extent is accepting of cultural exchange, learning languages, and creating liaisons with people of many nations? How was this achieved despite having been engaged in both the intense nationalism and colonization which swept most of Europe?

National influence on our affinities and values is, to a large degree, the result of evolution, history, geographic location, and the traits and qualities that result from all these factors. The Netherlands (or Holland) was passed from the Romans (as a province of lower Germany) to the Franks, to the Holy Roman Empire, to the Dukes of Burgundy, and to Phillip II of Spain. After numerous struggles as well as changes in religious orientation and political leadership, the Dutch found their way, through the leadership of and influences from France, Austria, and Germany, through WWI (the Netherlands was neutral), and finally, the occupation of Nazi Germany in WWII, to the multilingual, multicultural society of today.

What influence does such an evolution have on the people? What impact does such a history have on the music? Bordered by France, Belgium, Germany, and England, many Dutch speak from two to five languages. Multiple languages, histories, and forms of expression are an integral part of Dutch education, linking young Dutch students from very early ages to much of the rest of the world.

In coming across the group "Fra Fra Sound" by reference from a fellow local musician, we wrote the group's director, Vincent Henar, to ask for a sample of their music. The CD we received was a collaboration that the primarily Dutch group had made with musicians from Mali (Northwest Africa). Although it may not seem that such a collaboration is of a *nationalist* influence, given the heritage and diversity of the "Dutch" experience and their current multicultural reality, this is exactly what you might expect from the musicians of the Netherlands today. [Note: We will see, in Unit X, why jazz is also an excellent vehicle for such collaborations, as it is a fusion art in all its aspects.]

The CD "Mali Jazz" Liner Notes:

> *"Fra Fra Sound 1997 tour of West Africa led to a concert in Mali. There, three Malian musicians joined the group spontaneously. Without planning, jazz (U.S., Europe) and the music of Mali, innovation and traditions, modern Western and traditional African instruments were soon blended in communicating with one another.*

> *"This memorable concert resulted in several joint performances, close friendships and the "Mali Jazz" project, a CD with intriguing improvisations, spiritually dynamic vocals, and a universal kind of swing."* (Notes by Frits Lagerwerff)

Although we will spend more time breaking down some of the influences of African cultures and African musicians on the rest of the world (Unit VIII), this collaboration clearly shows the importance of not only seeing global fusion as a tradition and not a phase but also recognizing the influence of the larger culture system on the affinities, tastes, and values of its people.

"Kanté no Kanto," from the CD: <u>**Mali Jazz,**</u> composed by A.Biswane, featuring Vieux Kanté. Performed by Fra Fra Sound, c. 2002, Pramisi Records, the Netherlands.

Vincent Henar, the founder and leader of *Fra Fra Sound,* wrote to us concerning his perspectives on music and this collaboration: *"The art of music might be equally seen as an instrument or vehicle for both personal development and community purposes. If we have a true love and understanding of music, it will teach us about the history of mankind and civilization. It will awaken awareness, contribute to updating geographics, and inform us about other people, their languages, customs, and lifestyle. Music is a true way to cultivate and enrich people's everyday lives. Music awakens understanding, love, and harmony. It is a world language beyond the spoken word.*

"Fra Fra Sound feels that its music is a reflection of here and now. A reflection of our own lives and times with respect for the past and with an openness to the future. (This CD) is connected with the great wealth of African cultures and the African Diaspora throughout the rest of the world.

"The music industry has robbed music away from ordinary people; it's been transformed into a commercial item lacking responsibility towards the youth, towards education, and towards the dignity in human creativity. Not enough children and youngsters have the possibility to experience diverse live (or recorded) music. There are many mysteries in human history. Music can guide and reveal some of these mysteries ..."

Although we are free to agree or disagree with what musicians such as Mr. Henar have to say, we can hear much of the passion he articulates in the musical arrangement of "Kanté no Kanto"—in this case, a completely natural (unforced) fusion of music that melds the multiple influences of Malian, Dutch, and the African Diaspora (blues, R & B, jazz, calypso, rumba, samba, salsa, soul, fusion, hip hop, or drum & bass) with some melodic and rhythmic elements of their origin. The music of Moussa 'Vieux' Kanté, the young master of the 8-stringed *kamal ngoni* (likely a relative of the ud and the modern guitar) will lend his instrumental and vocal chant-like melodic ornamentation to modern Western instrumentation. This sort of fusion exemplifies many of the elements of the current traditions in Afro-Beat or modern African music. It is also a tribute to the respect and interest shown by many young European and American jazz artists toward the music of the African continent.

The Recipe of Sound

The piece begins with the initial scat-style singing (improvised singing of syllables) and the repetition of a melody on the string instrument (*kamal ngoni*) that will become the drone or mantra (repetitive backbone) of the piece. When the other instruments enter, there is an immediate infusion musically and instrumentally of hundreds of years of change and modernization. Modern harmonies, melodic lines, and most certainly syncopated drum patterns with the accented beats on 2 and (nearly) 4 bring ancient African, modern jazz, and current R&B/funk into harmony.

Perhaps more important to the value of this piece are the subtle improvisations of Vieux Kanté's *kamal ngoni* and the percussion, as well as the pronounced improvised piano solo by Mark Milan over the repetitive structure, tight *rhythm section,* and orchestrated *horn lines.* It is the contrast in *planned or orchestrated composition,* including the melodies and accents in the rhythmic flow, together with the unplanned or spontaneous collaborations that give this piece its energy and, ultimately, define its character.

This being said, you may also wish to listen to this piece again with your eyes closed and reflect upon the words of Mr. Henar: *"If we have a true love and understanding of music, it will teach us about the history of mankind and civilization. It will awaken awareness....Music awakens understanding, love, and harmony. It is a world language beyond the spoken word."* Do you hear what he feels?

Families, Communities, and the Impact of Subculture Groups

Although it would be much simpler for each of us to consider ourselves solely in terms of the larger cultural influences (as in "I'm French, that's why I do such and such"), most of us have an entire network of *subcultures* through which we pass over the course of our lives. Moreover, as we will discuss throughout this text, "larger" cultures are also seldom the way we perceive them but instead the result of perceptual exchange with other culture systems over time. When these facts are not acknowledged, there can be an incredible strain between people's reality and their *perception* of their reality, or between self-awareness and self-perception.

For example, one might say: "I'm Italian" or "Polish," while living outside of Italy or Poland, thereby latching onto the belief in ethnic origins and pride in ancestry. But if that person lives, works, and values most of the influences of African-American, Latin, or other culture systems, then there may be as much or more affinity for those culture groups or a host of others as there is any real knowledge or influence of Italian or Polish ancestry.

We may feel consciously compelled to express ourselves in accordance with our perceptions of the larger culture group, but most of us have as many if not more characteristics which resemble the groups of more prolonged contact, interest, or affinity. This simply means that, beyond the enormous impact of our parents and immediate family, becoming aware of the network of subcultures through which we pass will help us understand why we like what we like or, perhaps more importantly, why we have aversions to or biases against other expressions.

In truth, most of us are living in the age of emerging awareness of the *global cultural exchange*— or, as some have said, our "global village": I may be a "white"/Caucasian-American, but have a greater affinity for Greek or Mexican music. Or I may be an "African-American," a Baptist, and an opera-fan as well. In all cases, I will have a collection of affinities and tastes which move fluidly over a number of supposed boundaries.

The Influence of Family and Community

As we mentioned, we do not choose many of the subcultures into which we are born, and hopefully we will not spend a second regretting who or what we are. Yet we also have the option of choosing other culture groups, and we will, as a necessary product of life's requirement for change and evolution, likely adopt many expressions and values that are not a part of our original family or community. Before we examine many of the world's musical styles and the cultures that create them, and before we hopefully embrace much of the world's wisdom and values as part of our own, we might look carefully at some of the ways our musical tastes can be affected by our immediate family, our parents, brothers and sisters, uncles, grandparents, and most intimate or immediate community structures.

Pic. 2.5A *Mother and children playing music. The act of creating music or dancing as families creates a bond or releases tensions.* Photo: Marcel Mooij.

Pic. 2.6 *These ones will grow up in Montreal far from the roots of their Caribbean ancestry. Just as little "Canadians" will become their friends, learn their dances, and wear the costumes or eat their Caribbean food, they too will fuse the dialects and expressions of Canadian culture into their Caribbean ancestry.* Photo: Authors.

- The sound world of our family (especially that of our parents' determination) will mold our initial musical experiences. What they listen to, allow us to listen to or watch on TV, and the radio stations they play will be our first contact with music.

- As we grow and establish contact with friends outside the family, we will be increasingly exposed to alternatives. Some we will embrace; others we will reject or remain indifferent to. But we will now begin to become more involved in the selection and exchange of musical influences.

- Depending upon our relationships with our parents, our siblings, or our family generally, we will begin to embrace as *ours* or reject as *theirs* the music of our family. In cases where the parents are not particularly engaged (or are detached) or are disrespectful or abusive of our growth and potential, we will rebel against their tastes in music. In other instances, where involvement and sacrifice are made on our behalf by family members, we are likely to embrace their musical affinities as part of us. In any instance, we will have deeply imbedded associations from our childhood that will be directly attached to the music that was playing as we grew up.

- The influence of peers on most of us, especially over the course of our adolescent and young adult years, will also have a profound effect on our later musical values. Since these years have the greatest impact in the shaping of our adult personalities and the initial choices we make in the directions of our careers and life-pursuits, the musical associations we build during this time will have enormous impact on our musical world for the rest of our lives. It is not unusual for young adults to carry the music of these years well into their adult lives. This is why we frequently see "revivals" of artists or bands which may have disappeared for decades, when the teenagers of a few decades earlier reach the age of financial prominence (late 30s to 50s) and the music of their young adult years is missed and can now be subsidized.

Of course, our religions, our hobbies, the languages we learn, or the places to which we travel will all influence our musical tastes. It's generally helpful to remember that though we may call ourselves one thing by virtue of strong affinities or biases learned primarily during our formative years, we may in reality be influenced by a combination of traits and qualities which are quite different from these perceptions.

Music, as Mr. Henar mentions, is a language that frequently communicates without words. This is why it is such a profound gateway to the lives and thoughts of other cultures with which we share few apparent commonalities. Once we have the motivation to listen to those outside of the realm of our cultural experiences, which in all honesty may require considerable effort at the onset, we may be able to learn to continue to respect our past, family, peer, and community values in music while adding the alternatives expressed by others. We may also begin to see the other musical scenes as being just one more subculture to experience. That is, I can claim to be Latino, or any other identifier I may choose, but if I don't give too much credence to these titles, I will likely increase the degree to which I have as much (or more) affection for other cultures as I have for my own.

> *"History has thus far recorded principally the experience of tribes, cultures, classes, and nations. With the physical unification of the planet in this century and acknowledgement of the interdependence of all who live on it, the history of humanity as one people is now beginning. The long, slow civilizing of human character has been a sporadic development, uneven and admittedly inequitable in the material advantages it has conferred.*
>
> *"Nevertheless, endowed with the wealth of all the genetic and cultural diversity that has evolved through past ages, the earth's inhabitants are now challenged to draw on their collective inheritance to take up, consciously and systematically, the responsibility for the design of their future."* The Prosperity of Humankind," Bahá'í Office for Social and Economic Development, Haifa, Israel, Readings: p.54.

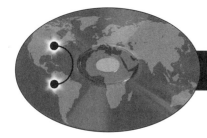

Inside the Musician's World

César Villalobos
and "Inca Son"

Note: As discussed earlier, one of the more subtly profound benefits of experiencing other culture groups is the depth of perspective they provide us about our own culture(s) by comparison. Especially in what are erroneously termed "third world" or indigenous cultures throughout the world, the prolific images of Western media often lure individuals into also believing that their own cultures are inferior or "less than" those of the technology-based cultures. In time, and with maturity, an individual who travels will see that each culture may be *sophisticated* in different ways. What tends to be true is that many of the cultures bereft of the in-

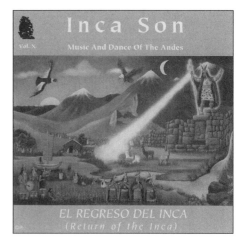

tensity of focus on materialism or technology to the degree that parallels many Western cultures have a more heightened sense of community and potentially a better balance in their daily lives with the natural cycle of life (see Unit VIII).

César Villalobos is originally from the Andes highlands of Peru, where various indigenous groups live, regularly exchanging cultural traits with Afro-Latino or Spanish populations. Upon coming to North America, he founded *Inca Son,* a music and dance performance ensemble that performs over much of North America. Although it has been prestigiously recognized and honored in America and Europe, the group is very popular in Peru as well. One of the reasons for this is that, by virtue of the work and travels outside their community, they have come to value their origins to an even greater degree. Mr. Villalobos, the group's founder and primary composer, makes it clear what he values in the acknowledgement section of the CD *Inca Son*:

> *"I want to thank the Great Spirit, then my family, especially my sister Maria-Teo, the world's greatest Peruvian cook! Thanks also to the great musicians and dancers that make up Inca Son… and finally to those of you that support Inca Son. I promise to give my heart and soul wherever Inca Son may perform, leaving each audience with a feeling for the richness of Andean culture."*

"Pueblo Andino," ("Andean Village") from the CD: **Inca Son,** by César Villalobos, c. 2003, Inca Son Music.

> Mr. Villalobos told us: *"When I started making this album, I wrote the song "Andean Village" with the idea of going back to my country for good. I reconsidered when I thought of having to leave behind my kids, and also a beautiful person who had entered my life … my son Conor.*
>
> *You ask about music … it is a part of the daily life of an Andean village. It's our form of entertainment, and it's the way we connect as a community, to each other, and to our cultural past. In my village there were no television, computers, cinema, video games. I learned songs as a little boy from my family and from the other people in the village who I saw at work in the fields, at church, at celebrations, festivals, births, funerals, and rituals. Music is present at all of these activities. The elders pass on their musical traditions to the younger generation.*
>
> *As I look at the lifestyles of American children, I sometimes feel sad about their lack of a real musical tradition. I didn't have the material comforts that most kids here enjoy, but I had something maybe more important: a connection to my community and an ancient culture, largely through a musical legacy. We learned at an early age to make flutes and to play them by ear. We not only learned the songs of our ancestors, we learned the dances as well. This is the tradition I carry on through Inca Son, Music and Dance of the Andes."*

The lyrics of "Pueblo Andino" articulate the conflicts and challenges, as well as the benefits, of experiencing life outside of our culture. We learn new things, some of them about how not to live life, but in César's case, they brought new meaning and love for his home, and also eventually pointed out a path he would need to take as an educator of the children of his new culture. The lyrics (translated from Spanish) are:

> *The time has come for me to leave*
> *I return to the village*
> *The one I maybe never should have left*
> *My luggage is full*
> *Of the things I learned*
> *Of different types of cultures*
> *In which I've lived*

Pic. 2.7A *A small city (Cuzco, Peru) is seen through ancient Incan ruins.* Photo: Dustin Brunson

Coro (Chorus):

> *I left young to fulfill my yearnings*
> *Andean village so close to heaven*
> *The most beautiful thing of all in this world*
> *I never left I was always there.*
> *Girl of the village, I come back to find you*
> *Forgive me for being gone*
> *In my heart you were always there*
> *Today I return to you until I die*
>
> *I found racism but I overcame it*
> *Proud of my race*
> *Inca blood within me*
> *My hair is long, with coppery skin*
> *But white are my bones*
> *And great my heart*
> *Coro – 2nd time*

In response to the question "How do you generate ideas for your songs?" Mr. Villalobos commented: *"In the Andes, people look at music as a constant companion. A shepherd who spends lonely hours guarding flocks on a mountainside takes out his flutes and plays. The music makes him happier and keeps him company in his solitude. People often tell me that my music, which is so specific to a place, is also universal. I've played across the U.S., Canada, Europe, and Latin America, to people of all ages, from all walks of life: from presidents to the humblest of village people. And everyone responds to the music and to the message I try to communicate through it. I think that this is because Andean music has an eternal quality and because it's a musical form that comes from the heart of the people. It's been here for centuries, and I hope that it's here for centuries to come.*

The music I play is a combination of ancient and modern traditions. I might play a well-known song like "My Heart Will Go On" from the movie "Titanic," but I play it on the panpipes, or siku, in my native Quechua language. These Andean pipes are thousands of years old. They have been found in the tombs and on the pottery of the Moche, who lived in the north of my country centuries before the Inca. The Andean people have used these flutes for centuries to express their deepest feelings: happiness, grief, pride, and victory. People make sikus today just as their ancestors did: by binding two rows of cane that comes from highland bamboo, with braided straps."

This is an embodiment of *fusion* or the creative gesture of taking parts of our past and combining them in some unique fashion with the sound world of our twenty-first-century present.

The indigenous peoples of the Andes have had an extraordinary history. A significant part of their culture and history is tied to their music. Music is considered to have both a spiritual and communal capacity. Many of the melodies and rhythms are intended to represent the different aspects of their lives and their relationship to Mother Earth, or "Pacha Mama." [2.8]

The Recipe of Sound

The music of Quichua Mashis (pronounced: kechewah mashees) is the traditional music from the Andes mountains. Better known as the Inca Empire, this region of South America covers Ecuador, Peru and Bolivia.

The fusion of Spanish and indigenous cultures is very apparent in the instrumentation and lyrics of this song. The Spanish acoustic guitar combines with its smaller brother, the **charango,** a small mandolin-like 10-string instrument with higher pitches. The *pan-flutes* or **zampoña** (of various sizes) are, however, distinctly of indigenous cultures in the Andes, as are the drums and, of course, the topic of the song.

Musical Terms and Concepts

Much Andean music today is a fusion of influences deeply rooted in the past but set in the modern. The musical elements include:

Rhythms: (*the way the music flows over time*) – A drum rhythm pattern based upon a dance rhythm that pits a four-note subdivision per beat (dividing each beat into four pieces, which in Western music is called *sixteenth-note* sub-

division [four beats times four subdivisions per beat]) against a three-note-per-beat subdivision (called a "triplet" subdivision). The music uses both devices in the layers of instruments, which include (from top to bottom):

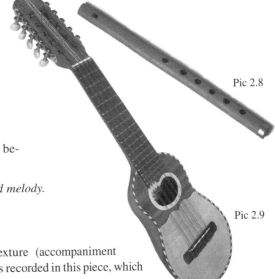

Pic 2.8

Melody layers: Melodies are notes or pitches which are played one after the other. They are generally singable musical lines.

Voice – Harmonized.

Quena – Wood or bamboo flute, which plays the answers between phrases sung by the vocalist (in the chorus). Pic 2.8.

The *charango* and guitar function in two roles: *rhythm and melody.* Pic.2.9.

Pic 2.9

Rhythmic Layers (Texture):

Charango and guitar – provide the basic rhythmic texture (accompaniment rhythms). Note: There are multiple charango and guitar lines recorded in this piece, which add to its density of texture and energy.

The bass melody – The lowest-pitched melody of the piece, played by both a bass guitar and an acoustic[2.9] guitar, although a melody functions more as an element or contributor to the way the music flows over time (rhythm).

The percussion (non-pitched) rhythm instruments – which include a large "tom-tom"-shaped drum (*Bombo*) and shakers (*Chakchas*) made traditionally from the hooves of goats.

We might also acknowledge the **production** of the piece. By *production in music,* we refer to the manner in which the instruments are *arranged* (pieced together in the composition) and *recorded* (the art of preserving and presenting music through technology). In today's world, certainly during the last century, and, arguably, throughout human history, technology has played an ever-increasing role in music. Although we will examine the role of media and technology below, listen carefully to the precise blend of instruments, voices, and even talking and laughing in this piece. Do you get the feeling of a balanced community? Can you feel César's affection for his village? In this piece, does the equity or balance of the piece's *arrangement* and *production* support the story that is being told?

Media, Technology, and the Influence on Musical Affinity

Inevitably, the more we inquire about how our music files are built, the more we will come to recognize the influence of media on almost all of our perceptions. But just how enormous is the influence of radio, television, films, and recording technology on the establishment of our musical tastes and values? Answer: very!

Looking Back: An Overview of the Evolution of Media Technology

The information and experiences we have in our memory determine what we *like* and value and, consequently, what we also find foreign or not enjoyable. Although technology has always been a part of the evolution of the world's music, it is really only in the last century that *mass media* —radio, recording technology, television, and film—have played major roles in both the exposure and exclusion of the world's music from our soundscape.

So what influence has the manner of delivery of information or the choices made by those who produce, record, or broadcast the music and information through media had on our files? Let's consider the following:

Pic. 2.7D *This radio D.J. may be young and "mixing" the music of his peers, but over a few decades the music will nearly inevitably disappear and then re-surface as "oldies."* Photo: Courtesy Benoit Faure.

• From the very onset of radio and television, American/European media ("voices" of the larger culture systems) have been funded by advertising or government and have been partially or entirely subjected to the concerns of the corporations/governments that funded the programming. This includes both the scope and nature of their content. Does this impact what we will have access to in music? All radio, television, and recorded media are subject to "market" philosophies that, in simplest terms, say one of two things:

1) The more appealing (entertaining or accessible) the program to the masses, the more widespread will be the viewing/listening audience or the market, or 2) in other instances, such as radio, the narrower the radio station's format[2.10] (which style of music or talk programs will be aired),[2.11] the better (more specifically) advertisers can target the most narrow markets with their products. This dictates the narrowing of the music to very specific genres, artists, and selections, and in turn determines what record companies will produce, what we will hear, and, ultimately, what we won't hear.

Pic. 2.8 *If you've never thought about the role that media plays in projecting images and sounds into our world, go listen to a band or musicians practice their craft before the amplification, sound, signal processing (alteration of the sound quality), or other electronic devices are employed. Or watch a scene from a movie before the special effects and music are added. Seeking a balance in our use and exposure to media technology is important. Media technology might be viewed as just another sort of instrument. In the hands of a thoughtful, sensitive artist, it can produce wonderful results. In the hands of greed, it might produce what greedy minds imagine.* Photo: Authors.

- "Capitalism"[2.12] is to a large degree the system most Western cultures and especially American society use to determine the value of something. In *The Mystery of Capital* Hernando de Soto describes capitalism and its influence on Western cultures as follows: *"In the West ... every parcel of land, every building, every piece of equipment, or store of inventories is represented in a property document that is the visible sign of the vast hidden process that connects all these assets to the rest of economy."* He goes on to say that through capital value is given to the entity of most things in Western culture. This includes music as well. The value of most artists and their music today is based primarily upon their capacity to generate capital. Underground or alternative markets exist, as their names suggest, to counter or run alternatively to mainstream culture, but even these markets are affected by capitalism and the influence of the market system. Although it may be tempting to look at *capitalism* as either "good" or "bad," this is really not the issue at all. In terms of creativity, however, many artists feel that the stronger the influence of the market or capital systems as the defining force of compensation for their work, the more the creativity of the artists' visions may be prone to restriction. When this occurs, artists can take fewer risks or are forced to subjugate much of their creativity to accommodate support for their livelihood.

- Technology—especially the development of recording technology—is the primary means by which we've been able to retain, solidify, and disseminate the music of the world's musicians. Without recording technology, we'd have little or no sound record of much of the world's popular or folk music. Print technology provides documentation of the approximate sounds (notation of music), but cannot actually provide us documentation of the sounds themselves. Obviously, the benefit of digital and computer technology in recording today is that increasingly artists need not be attached to the corporate or market systems to create and record their works. On average, an instructor of musical composition in a university or college may receive four to ten CDs of student musical groups or creative projects annually. The relationship of media to technology is primarily in how many of those works the masses (i.e., the rest of us) will hear.

So how does the media determine the market or *capital* of a musical piece? Is it the creativity or *freshness* of the music? Sometimes media can project a musical expression or artist that, were it not for its influence, we'd never have had the pleasure of hearing. At other times media will perpetuate the careers, and the music, of artists we probably wish we'd never had the pleasure of hearing. But what is indisputable is that the media creates "star" images and popularizes music by virtue of the exposure it provides to artists and the communication of their music to the masses. Therefore, those who direct or control the programming in the media—from advertisers, to corporations, to record company executives—have enormous impact over our sound world.

Since the beginning of the Dodge "Victory Hour," the first musical radio program to be broadcast nationally (in 1928), to the "Ed Sullivan Show" (television's first successful variety show, in 1948), to the *"make-a-star shows"* of whatever generation we may be a part of, media is the primary tool by which we gain exposure to much of our musical world, and incidentally, was how every one of our ancestors over the past few generations became acquainted with much of their music as well.

We cannot overestimate the impact of media, even though we may vary in our perception of its value or benefit. What is important, however, is that we contemplate its influence and possibly consider the music in cultures or markets that are not as narrowly constricted by the parameters imposed by market and capital considerations.

Media...Materialism... & Finding "Value"

Discussion Reflection II-C

As mass media technology continually increases its prolific influence on the world's peoples (often combined with an insatiable striving for "market" or economic value), every one of us is called upon to increase our rigor in evaluating individually what we will let into our lives and how often.

Because much media is impacted by a multi-billion dollar advertising industry, movies, video games, and musical artists are perpetually thrust into our vision, many becoming megahits, superstars, and household names, not always because of their creative or life-enhancing merit or message.

You may wish to read again the following two statements by Mr. Henar and Mr. Villalobos, and reflect upon each while listening to their music (CD 1.4 and CD 1.5). You may also wish to pay close attention to the comments of the other artists in relation to their "creative" expressions.

"The music industry has robbed music away from ordinary people; it's been transformed into a commercial item lacking responsibility towards the youth, towards education, and towards the dignity in human creativity. Not enough children and youngsters have the possibility to experience diverse life (or recorded) music. There are many mysteries in human history. Music can guide and reveal some of these mysteries . . ." - Mr. Henar.

"As I look at the lifestyles of American children, I sometimes feel sad about their lack of a real musical tradition. I didn't have the material comforts that most kids here enjoy, but I had something maybe more important: a connection to my community and an ancient culture, largely through a musical legacy. We learned at an early age to make flutes and to play them by ear. We not only learned the songs of our ancestors, we learned the dances as well. This is the tradition I carry on through Inca Son, Music and Dance of the Andes." - Mr. Villalobos

Questions

- *Replacing "music industry" with mass media (e.g., movies, video games, computer games, music, etc.) what percentage of what you see or hear is educational, transformational, or reflective of human dignity or creativity? Should it be? (Can you support your thoughts?)*

- *What role might media consumerism play in the development of our capacity to be creative? What about in assisting us to connect deeply to our families and communities?*

Musical Terms and Concepts

Shamisen: The shamisen is a three-stringed, fretless (no bars to divide pitches) lute (guitar-like instrument). It is used primarily in Japan as an accompaniment instrument for story-telling genres, specifically, in Noh or Kabuki theater pieces (Japanese musical theater from the 12th to 19th centuries). Pic 2.8A.

Timbre: The quality of the sound. "Bright," "mellow," "airy," or "harsh,"—these are the words we use to describe how we perceive sound quality. Timbre or sound quality is determined by the shape of the wave-form or sound frequency. A rounded wave-form (sine wave) is similar to sound produced by the flute (mellow). A square wave (pulse or square) is similar to the sound produced by an electric guitar (harsh or distorted).

Pic 2.8A Dabisen
(like a Shamisen)

Improvisation: *All* musical composition begins as "improvisation" (spontaneous composition). However, improvisation in musical performances or recordings is spontaneous ideas or composition "on the spot."

All improvisations, however, are still based upon formulas and patterns known to the musicians through their experiences and prior practice, though they may be re-arranged or altered in a fresh or new manner.

Scat-singing: Singing without text or lyrics. Most forms of scat-singing sound like the vocalist is imitating a saxophone or piano. In jazz, scat-singing is improvisation by the vocalist.

Rhythm section: Is an extension of "traditional" jazz (New Orleans jazz—frequently called "Dixieland" jazz). The rhythm section consists of drums, a bass instrument, piano, guitar, or synthesizer. The instruments create the rhythmic feeling or "groove," often erroneously referred to as "the beat" in music.

Pic. 2.9 *A standard rhythm section includes: guitar (and/or piano), bass, and drums. Other instruments such as congas or hand percussion, banjo, or synthesizers could be added.* Photo: Authors.

Pic. 2.9A *The process of composition for multiple instruments begins with musical ideas that are created and then "thick-ened" by adding multiple other musical events to the texture. This is also called "arranging" or "orchestration."* Photo: Nicholas Sutcliffe.

Orchestration: To orchestrate a piece is to take a kernel of an idea—a melody or two, a rhythm, or an entire song or composition—and spread the idea amongst a number of instruments. Frequently in "classi-cal" or Western art music, compositions are designed on piano and then later are *orchestrated* for the symphony orchestra.

Horn lines: This is a generic term used in popular music for trumpet, saxophone, and trombone melodies or lines in popular or jazz music.

Arrangement: As the term suggests, a musical arrangement is a re-ordering or re-orchestration, usually of an existing piece. Most arrangements are *covers,* or the re-arranging of already recorded or performed music.

Rhythm: How music *flows over time.* Since all music happens over time, we speak of the manner in which it moves over time as the rhythm. Most music in the world uses *beats or pulses* to regulate its flow at a certain *tempo* (the rate or speed of the music). In these cases, as in most popular or dance music throughout the world, the manner in which the music moves over these beats is the rhythm. Sometimes we may say, "I like the beat," but what we are really saying is, "I like the rhythm or flow of music *over the beat.* "

Subdivision: A dividing of the beats into smaller elements, usually two, three, or four. Subdivisions aid in giving us changes in the feel or flow of the music. If you have a steady beat and divide it into two piec-es, the music feels faster though the beat is still the same. Dividing the beat into three or four increases the speed at which the notes or sounds are flowing up against the beat.

Melody: One of the elements in nearly all of the world's music, the melody is the primary carrier of the story or focus in most musical pieces. Series of recognizable or singable frequencies, pitches, or notes that are organized *one after the other,* melodies are "singable" for the most part. Since all cultures have story-telling music with lyrics or words, in most cases the stories are attached to melodies capable of being pro-duced by the human voice – one note at a time.

Unit II Activities

Activity #1: Understanding Concepts

Based upon your perception of the reading, describe in your own words the impact you see in your own musical tastes or "mind files" of the following:

1) Larger culture: How do the values and principles you see being most stressed in your country of origin (country which formulated the greatest part of your experiences) affect the way you live your life (i.e., the things you most stress or that occupy the greatest part of your time and energy, etc.)?

    a. Select one pervasive trait of your larger culture system (in America, for example, the emphasis of finance or "capital" as a symbol of one's success). In what way does this trait or emphasis affect you? Where does this trait get most of its power, or in what manner is it *broadcast* or disseminated to you (via family, education, media, etc.)?

    b. How does this trait influence what you hear in music, where you hear music, or, ultimately, how you have formulated your tastes and distastes in music?

2) Subculture: Let's start with family. In what manner do the tastes in music of your parents or siblings impact your tastes? If your tastes are the same as theirs (or similar), why? If they are different, can you trace or express why you think this is so?

    a. What about your peers? Have they influenced your tastes in music? What is your relationship to your parents and does that influence your choice and relationships with peers?

    b. Now to further extend this exercise: How does the larger culture influence your parents', your peers', and, subsequently, your relationship with music?

3) Media: What percentage of the world's music (the music currently being listened to around the world) do you think you've heard or have access to in your sound world? How have you come to this conclusion? To what extent do you think the media influences this exposure or lack of exposure?

    a. How do you understand the relationship of "capitalism" or a market-driven system to the music that is broadcast or disseminated through media and marketing?

    b. What would one need to do to sidestep (slightly) the influence of media and develop a pattern of soliciting new or more diverse music from the world's cultures? Would it require a life-style adjustment?

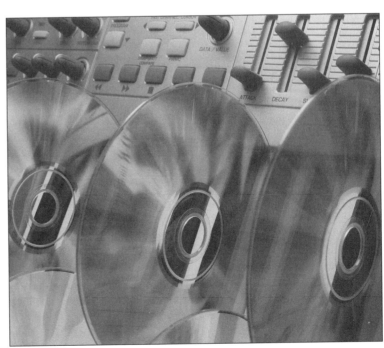

Today nearly anyone can create high-quality music with use of digital recording computer technology. Photo: istockphoto.

Activity #2: Listening Deeper

Read the composer's/musician's comments for CDs 1.3, 1.4, and 1.5. Read the questions below for each example. Then, listen again to CD selections 1.3, 1.4, and 1.5. Now, answer the questions to the best of your ability.

CD 1.3 Artist: Karasu Randa

1) What in the music do you hear that reflects the passion of the artist for music and his vision of music according to his comments? (It might be in the *timbre* or style of the singing or playing, in the *rhythm*, or in the *arrangement*.)

2) Can you hear a reflection of the meaning of the song in the style of its performance? What are the musical elements that contribute to this connection?

CD 1.4 Artist: Fra Fra Sound

1) Mr. Henar writes, *"If we have a true love and understanding of music ... it will awaken awareness, it will contribute to updating geographics, and it will inform us about other people, their languages, customs, and lifestyle."* In what manner can you hear these comments in the music? Do you feel the respect of the group's musicians (Fra Fra Sound) for the musicians from Mali in the music? If so, how?

2) Mr. Henar goes on to say, *"The music industry has robbed music away from ordinary people, it's been transformed into a commercial item lacking responsibility towards the youth, towards education, and towards the dignity in human creativity. Not enough children and youngsters have the possibility to experience diverse live (or recorded) music."* Do you agree with this statement? If so, why? If not, why not? If we assume that media and commerce are not inherently "bad," but that such influences can be restrictive of the musical creativity to which we have access, what might you do to expand the range of musical creativity in your world?

Activity #3: Exercising Passion

Did you find any one of the pieces, interviews, or concepts of Unit II intriguing? If so, you might consider the following activities to further your interests and ignite your passion for learning:

1) Do you know any people from Japan, the Netherlands, Mali, or South America? Could you talk to them and ask them questions about their world? How does what they say about the way they live compare to what you know or to the way you were raised?

2) What do you know about the Inca or Quechua Indians of the Andes mountain regions? You may wish to look up these magnificent culture groups on the Internet. What do you find most fascinating about their history? Can you find a website where the indigenous people themselves talk about their world or their music?

3) Is there any music you've heard (i.e., music in your world) that has some qualities or characteristics of any of the music in Unit II? Where do you think those musicians got that influence? Are there any elements in the music of Unit II that you think may have come from your world to theirs? Where or how do you think this exchange took place?

Activity #4: Exercising Our Own Creativity

What about your own creativity? As always, the most critical aspect of creativity—whether culinary, verbal, aural, or visual—is that we develop our skills. A couple of pre-requisites are essential, however, until we feel completely comfortable with our creativity in any area.

Pick the tool or skill you wish to use to exercise your creativity (even if it's one you've hardly ever used before or aren't enormously confident to use—be brave!). Then pick a "market" or a person to whom you'd like to communicate (a friend or a family member). This is who will be sitting on your shoulder or be in your mind as you create your work.

Possible topics:

1) What would you like to tell someone about the most profound influence or experience of your childhood? How could you express that through your creative skills?

2) What would you like to tell someone about your nation (it could be positive or constructive criticism)? How can you express these thoughts through your creative skills?

3) The song "Andean Village" speaks of the longing and love Mr. Villalobos has for his village and how he longs to return. Where is the place or location in your past that you'd most like to *return* to? How would you say that through your creative skills?

Important creative mindset: When we exercise our own creativity, we should attempt not to judge ourselves too harshly. We will, over the course of this text, place an enormous emphasis on *postponing judgment*. What we mean by this is that, whenever we are creating (or looking to appreciate the creativity of others), there is a human tendency to question the beauty, validity, and worth of our efforts *while we are creating!* This is poison to the creative process.

Try as best you can to create without judgment or critiquing your efforts. You can and will do better each time, but the process of creativity does not tolerate too much self-judgment until you've been exercising your skills for some time. Just try to create with little or no concern for the outcome; enjoy the process as best you can!

Pic. 2.9B *There is no question that this little "princess" in the south of Spain will be nurtured into the traditions of her ancestry and with much attention given to her from the elders. Assuming that the elders also accept that she will in some ways change and alter (creatively adapt) these traditions as she becomes an adult, little or no "generation gap" will arise. The natural cycle of life accommodates both the respect of elders and ancestry and the modernization or adaptation of change.* Photo: Authors.

When we see or hear something in someone else's country – immediately our own files and experiences "pop" to the surface. This sign in Münster, Germany – appears to be the sign of a pub (which it is), and little more. But in asking the owner for permission to photograph for this text – we received a nearly 20-minute explanation of the origin of German family names and their "link" to professions or occupations. "Stuhlmacher" literally means: the "furniture (stool) makers." This location was (for centuries) their gathering place both before and after work. Photo: Authors.

When we consider most arts or crafts, our focus is on the appearance of the final production or product: in opera, the fully costumed "stars"; in movies, the fully costumed and special effect-enhanced actors; and in music, those on stage or the CD cover. What seldom is visible (and usually sufficiently acknowledged), are the enormous efforts of stage-hands, gaffers, set builders, and, in this case, audio engineers. These individuals must be content with the respect given from within their own profession. Photo: in Hungary, Authors.

The technology that makes concerts, recordings, and festivals possible, includes rows of speakers for performers (monitors located in the front of the stage) and audience; dozens of microphones, amplifiers, and a few mixer-boards, lighting (used even in the daytime to give accents to performers); and, in most cases, recording and video technology to document the event (such as this video camera located on a crane ("boom"). Photo: Artist Ilona Knopfler band, Author.

Unit II: Endnotes

2.1 *Affinities* are inclinations toward, tastes for, or feelings of identification with some thing, quality, or manner of expression. Most of us will find that affinities can transfer from something that we already like to something that we don't know—if it possesses those same qualities (we'll call this process *affinity transfer*). The more we expand our affinities, the quicker and more in-depth our appreciation for others and their music.

2.2 Although we will address the multitude of variations in affinity for change in subsequent chapters, and do not disallow that some traditions will change more slowly than others, we will operate from the perspective that even the smallest changes—the fabric of an Orthodox priest's ancient garb, the strings manufactured to be attached to a three-hundred-year-old instrument—are still changes.

2.3 The length of the standard commercial radio song is 3.5 minutes, dating back to the length of the original 75 rpm recordings. Since only that amount of music could be put on the original records, and early in the history of radio, the stations were funded by advertising dollars (market-driven), recordings have been maintained at the very short and narrow time span of 3.5 - 4.5 minutes.

2.4 A *score* in music is the notation for all the instruments of the ensemble or orchestra on a single page. Most scores have multiple pages (depending on the length and speed of the piece). Scores are created first; then the individual notes or "parts" are written for each instrumentalist.

2.5 We will speak of the *life cycle* throughout this text. When we spend time traveling, researching, or just having contact with the world's cultures, we begin to see that the universal human experience from birth to death, the concerns of being human, having family, and all the community rites and rituals give us immediate access to the expressions of every human culture group. The differences in the manner in which each human experience is celebrated or marked generally pales in comparison to the similarities of the experiences themselves.

2.6 We will use "culture" and "culture group" interchangeably in the text. The purpose is to facilitate discussion of cultural characteristics by setting up files, but we will hope to balance these generalizations with consistent and thorough discussions of fusion and exchange of values between cultures.

2.7 See 2.6 above.

2.8 You may wish to check www. Incasite.com or www.incason.com for more information on either "Inca Son" or Andes culture and music. For more information on Inca son, you may also contact www.ixlanArtists.com.

2.9 The term *acoustic* refers to any instrument that does not have an amplification system (electronic amplification sound "pick-up" system) built into it.

2.10 A radio format, or programming format, or programming genre refers to the overall content broadcasting over a radio station. Over the years, formats have evolved and new ones have been introduced. Today, many radio formats are designed to reach a specifically defined segment or niche of the listening population, based on such demographic criteria as age, ethnicity, background, etc.

2.11 The following are some of the more common radio "formats" or restrictive markets in radio stations today. The advent of satellite radio and digital radio formats, however, may expand or further contract the listener's sound-world.

* Country music
* Contemporary hit radio (CHR) music
* Adult contemporary music
* Rock and alternative music
* Urban music formats
* Jazz and classical music
* Oldies and nostalgia music
* Spanish and Latin music
* World music

Pic. 2.9B *In every major city around the world, subculture groups will congregate, re-creating the cultural dances, concerts, food, clothing, and music of their homeland. In Chicago, for example, the Latino festival (line dance), an Armenian festival in Evanston, as well as a Caribbean festival and a large Chinese concert all occurred on one weekend in August. However, these groups now function as subculture systems, since participants are just as influenced by American culture and values. Visitors will take home and take on small or large pieces of the culture as well.*

In this photo of the Latino Festival (Grant Park, Chicago, Illinois – USA), you will also see the enormous impact of media. Do you think these artists look or feel "larger than life" off the stage, without the lights, without the sound system, or away from the hundreds of seats set up in an "audience" fashion? Photo: Authors.

* Religious programming
* Public, government, community radio
* College, student
* News, talk, sports
* Other (children's, ethnic, brokered)

2.12 An economic system based on the private ownership of the means of production and distribution of goods, characterized by a "free" and competitive market and motivated by profit.

Native America: The Spirit in Symbolism

UNIT

III

Topics to Consider in Unit III

➤ *How might we understand "symbolism" in general? As relates to the meaning of vocabulary? And, specifically in musical expressions?*

➤ *What are some of the main tools and considerations in "de-coding" symbols of culture or music?*

➤ *What is "intuition"? What are the blocks to developing and trusting intuition? And – how can we better develop it?*

➤ *What are some of the most important and pervasive symbols in Native American culture systems? And – how might we benefit personally from a better (deeper) understanding of Native symbolism?*

➤ *What is a "pow-wow" and what does it represent to Native Americans?*

➤ *What is the significance of the "drum," dance, and the circle in the pow-wow experience?*

➤ *What is the significance of the pow-wow, flute music, and specific rituals, ancestry, history in general to Mr. Bedeau, Mr. Locke, Mr. Burga, Tiger/Tiger, and Casper respectively?*

➤ *How important are "songkeepers" to Native traditions?*

➤ *What is "culture balancing" and how might it be important, if not essential, to improving the quality of our lives?*

➤ *How can we manifest in our lives – through such tools as the "talking circle" — deeper listening skills as manifest in many Native cultures?*

➤ *What sort of music or messages do young Native musicians have for us today?*

UNIT III

Native America:
The Spirit in Symbolism

"There is only one thing which can master the perplexed stuff of epic material into unity; and that is an ability to see in particular human experience some significant symbolism of man's general destiny." Lascelles Abercrombie, *British Poet Quotes*, 1881-1938.

"When a man does a piece of work which is admired by all we say that it is wonderful; but when we see the changes of day and night, the sun, the moon, and the stars in the sky, and the changing seasons upon the earth, with their ripening fruits, anyone must realize that it is the work of someone more powerful than man." Chased-by-Bears (1843-1915) Santee-Yanktonai[3.0]

"If we knew the extent to which Indian ideas have shaped American culture, the United States might recognize Native American societies as cultural assets from which we could continue to learn. Indian history is the antidote to pious ethnocentrism of American exceptionalism, the notion that European Americans are God's chosen people. We must temper our national pride with critical self-knowledge." James Loewen, *Lies My Teacher Told Me*, Touchstone, 1995, p.136.

Understanding the Aesthetics of a Culture ... Through Its Symbolism

Perhaps you've had the experience where someone said or did something that you were certain you understood, only to find out later you had completely misunderstood the person's intentions. Maybe you were even a little offended, only to find out that the person's actions had, for this person, a completely opposite meaning from that of your initial interpretation. If meaning in expressions is *not universal* in communications within our own languages or cultures, then it must be even less so in languages or cultures in which we are uninitiated. In fact, all communication is *symbolic* in its nature. Words, facial expressions, body language, colors, movement, and sounds all require reading and interpretation before they take on meaning.

What comes into your mind (which files "surface") when you see the words:

HUMILITY

RELIGION

ROCK 'N' ROLL

Is **humility** embarrassment (to humiliate)—or is it putting others' lives or opinions ahead of our own?

Is **religion** your church or synagogue, mosque or temple? Is it your beliefs or a particular orientation or the beliefs of others? Or is it "re-connection" to a higher purpose in life (the original meaning from the Latin pre (re) and suffix (ligion see Unit V)?

And is **rock 'n' roll** heavy metal, or is it the music of Elvis, Kiss, or Jimi Hendrix? Or perhaps the music of Chuck Berry, Ray Charles, or the Chinese artist Cui Jian?

Human expressions and communications are filled with imagery, are constantly changing, and are subject to the creative nature of each culture group in each generation. In general, understanding what sounds and words *mean* requires deep reading into their *symbolism*.[3.1] In most music, an appeal is made to our emotions and senses, frequently without a concrete *factual,* or verbalized, communication. For these reasons, a music appreciator must learn to become a deeper listener or reader of symbolism.

Music is oftentimes defined as *sounds and pitches organized in time,* which have meaning to those who create them. Music is a combining of vibrations (sounds) that frequently have both pitched (recognizable frequencies) and un-pitched sounds and, however organized, have at least some intention or purpose behind them. The question for us is: what is the purpose or meaning? That is, if those who make the music create their organization of sounds with an intent foreign to our experience, what tools can we use to understand its meaning?

If we can accept the simple premise that music, even more than words, is laden with symbolic meaning, just as we accept that words do not have inherent meaning but are given meaning according to our personal experiences and acquired values, then our goal becomes more defined. If we strive to postpone judgment or opinions, put a blanket on our biases or prejudgments, and *listen* more *deeply* to what is *symbolized* by the sounds, then we ask of the music: What is really being "said" (communicated)?

Perceptual "Tools" for Decoding Symbolism in Music

Motivation is the ever-reoccurring partner in the acquisition of skills and knowledge. One motivation for "decoding" the symbolism in the expressions of others may be that this skill is as helpful in understanding the meaning in simple conversations with friends and family as it is in understanding the expressive nature of Chinese opera. After motivation it is then essential to learn the skills that can help us question the meaning of human expression, whether in the world of words, the world of images, or the world of sound.

Verbal and Nonverbal

Most songs that are instructional, factual, or literal are generally not created as "art," nor are they generally designed to communicate as deeply to the emotion or spirit as to the intellect. In the majority of music with poetic lyrics, however, we are both required to explore nonverbal communication and to understand the depth of the intent or meaning of the text. We generally do not know, unless we read the musicians' or composer's intent for the composition, the exact or literal intent of the artists themselves. So we must be content to infer our own meaning from the organization of sounds. This is where we come back to our own file systems.

How we might use or perceive one piece of music, how we might interpret a song or musical piece in our world, might be completely different from the world behind the musical piece. Each culture has a wide diversity of skills and *aesthetics* in human expression. Among the expressive variations in music is the depth to which culture groups use nonverbal communication—body posture, eye contact, hand gestures, and a host of other nonverbal means including pitches and vibrations, to express themselves. Following is a partial list of considerations to help us better perceive nonverbal communication in order to grasp larger portions of the *symbolic* meaning in music. Note: Some of these assume we have access to persons from the culture in some form or another (email, in-person, telephone, oral histories, or documentation from within the culture through film, photography, or art).

Pic. 3.1 *Kevin Locke playing a flute in the Dakotas.* Photo: Courtesy of Mr. Locke and Bruce Wendt.

- The duration of a culture's history will greatly impact the "symbols" in its music. The older the culture, the longer the traditions and depth of interconnection to ancestry and to the symbolism of various phases in the culture's evolution. This means that, with cultures that have a history spanning millennia, we must be prepared to read multiple symbols within a singular expression that could reflect numerous generations, past to present.

Suggestions: We can *practice*—by reading transcriptions of oral histories or texts, or by having discussions with the culture-bearers. We can keep our questions open and remember that whatever may sound "primitive," "ancient," or "foreign" to our ears *will unquestionably* still relate to the commonality of our mutual human experience and have a parallel in some fashion to our world. Additionally, we must always be prepared to change and update our perceptions. Especially today, the *tradition* (in a fixed sense) of yesteryear is not likely to be the *tradition* (as in something giving way to something else) of today. Even when we have an accurate perception of symbols based upon an interpretation of the past, it is not likely to be the same interpretation as that of the culture's representatives today.

- If there is text or storytelling in the music, unless we know the language of the culture very well, we must be prepared to simply not know and to look for "clues" in the music or nonverbal messaging. Even if we gain access to the culture-bearers, it can still be complex to decode the symbolism of their responses. The answers we receive will directly correlate to the degree of trust the culture-bearers feel for our motives and the depth of sensitivity or respect of our questions—and will still be encoded with meaning based upon the culture-bearers' history.

If there is no text, or we cannot ask questions to gain access to the inner circle of the symbols, we must always assume that there is meaning beyond or deeper than any meaning we can immediately perceive. This simply means we assume greater depth and value as a habit. If we find out later that the piece was simply a "joke," a party tune, or a piece of simple entertainment, we have at least not underestimated its value.

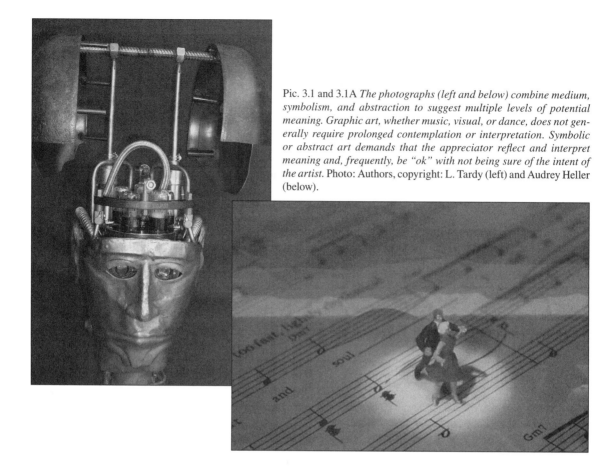

Pic. 3.1 and 3.1A *The photographs (left and below) combine medium, symbolism, and abstraction to suggest multiple levels of potential meaning. Graphic art, whether music, visual, or dance, does not generally require prolonged contemplation or interpretation. Symbolic or abstract art demands that the appreciator reflect and interpret meaning and, frequently, be "ok" with not being sure of the intent of the artist.* Photo: Authors, copyright: L. Tardy (left) and Audrey Heller (below).

Suggestion: We try whenever possible to pay attention to the communication styles of the culture-bearers, verbally and especially non-verbally. If visual (live meeting, performance, or video/DVD): Do they bow? How do they hold their eyes? Where are we in age relation to them, and how would someone of our age act in their culture? Can we read facial or body expressions or emotions? If aural: Do we get an emotion from their vocal quality, from the quality of the sound or layering of musical layers? Is there a parallel in our sound-world?

We can never be 100% certain of our interpretations of symbolism. The absolute best friend of an appreciative "art decoder" is simple patience and the willingness not to draw conclusions too quickly or, if possible, at all. Beyond this, we must rely upon a tool that we may not often be called upon to use, one essential to the interpretation of art and music—*intuition*.[3.2]

Exercising Our Intuition

What takes place from the first encounter with a new person, culture, or music is that the files of our experiences immediately surface and are compared against the new experience. That this cognitive processing is instinctive and a basic part of human nature is supported by generations of psychological, anthropological, and multiple other derivations of human learning across the centuries. In simplest terms, we talk or write about others according to our experiences.

However, when the interpretation is void of respect or a depth of reading of the culture's symbolism, or if one culture assumes superiority over another by virtue of its strength in arms or technology, then respect for a culture or its art or symbols can be absent and remain so for centuries.

As an essential part of the remainder of this unit, we will be discussing the wealth and incredible depth of symbolism in the world of our Native American music, past and present. But for most non-Natives and many Natives brought up in European-based schools and culture groups, there was until very recently an enormous void between what Europeans perceived and wrote of Native culture's symbolism and the culture's perceptions themselves.

Because of the fact that Western films, books, and documentaries of a high percentage of the world's cultures—and especially those cultures that do not value making films, writing books, and documenting their lives—are based on insufficient information or are grossly lacking in the acquisition of the voices *of the cultures themselves*, we must defer to human intuition as our perceptual and decoding device.

Intuition and the Art of Symbolic Interpretation

We've all heard of *women's intuition*, but is there really such a thing as individuals becoming acutely aware of truth from the perspective of a "gut" feeling (or hunch)? If so, can human beings have such instincts about each other or about each other's music, even if we actually know very little about either the people or the musical piece?

Although human **intuition** is generally seen as *knowing something without experience or conscious knowledge,* its essence is to rely upon an inner sense (emotional/spiritual hunch) rather than upon our experiences. The use of intuition is essential in combination with our experiences to decode musical or cultural expressions outside of our primary cultures. We cannot often rely upon facts or experience, especially if the facts we have or experiences we are using to decode the meaning of a musical work are based upon information that is outdated, uninformed, or without merit.

Frequently in music, because of the multiple layers of textual, instrumental, and even visual, kinetic, or other expressive media, *truth* or a deeper level of meaning (a deeper understanding of the *symbolism* of the expression) depends upon our confidence in—and use of—our intuition. Increasing our skill and confidence in decoding musical symbolism by use of our intuition necessitates the following:

- The belief that we do have intuitive abilities to "decode" much of the symbolism in music.

- The recognition that intuition, like any faculty or skill, requires exercise and development.

- The recognition that most of the cognitive skills for which we are trained or have experience do not demand the use of our intuition. Therefore, we have not been asked or encouraged by many of our cultural systems to use this faculty.

- Finally, since we are using intuition and not factual knowledge, we must always modify our responses with the *humility qualifiers:* "I think," "it might be," or "perhaps it is…"

Stories from the Human Family

"I really never had interest in 'classical' music or for that matter any other music than R&B and hip-hop. Most of the time when I got together with friends, we would make fun of anything that was not a part of what we already knew.

"When I first took the CDs home—and listened to them without anyone around, I began to realize that there were pieces of my music in these other pieces. From there I began to realize that there were also new elements and sounds in each piece that I didn't know. In time, it became an exercise for me to listen to the piece, imagine I knew what was being said, and then check it with the text.

"I very seldom had the exact meaning, especially if the song had lyrics or told a story in a language I had no clue about. Yet, I was surprised how close I would come. I'm not saying I'm as good at this as my "moms" … but I can imagine getting good at it, and that's reason enough to continue to try and use the skill.

"Maybe, in time and with lots of practice questioning and hearing music from other places, you could get real good at knowing the meaning through intuition and knowledge. I guess that's the goal— huh?" (Harvey P. Robinson, Detroit, African-American male, 24 years old)

The Power of Intuition

in·tu·i·tion (in'too-ish'un,) n.

1 a) The act or faculty of knowing or sensing without the use of rational processes; immediate cognition.

b) Knowledge gained by the use of this faculty; a perceptive insight.

2 A sense of something not evident or deducible; an impression.

Does needing to "know," having "factual" support or statistical justifications, have limitations? When we sense something to be true, is there a science in the possible interconnection of the human soul or spirit with its source of creation? Can this connection be as (or more) valid than anything that is material or tangible?

Against the backdrop of hundreds of years of education founded on material and statistical science is the generally less supported "reality" of intuition. However, becoming both keenly aware and trusting of our intuitive faculties, against the daunting task of "proving" them, has left many of us reluctant if not completely negligent in developing this marvelous ability.

The capacity for trusting and increasing our intuitive and/or spiritual powers lies first in our self-esteem and self-confidence. From there, the capacity to investigate truth, to see alternatives, and to trust that small voice whispering from within, can begin to grow.

Questions

• *Must we be school-trained in order to be "knowledgeable"?*

• *Without intuition, how do we understand someone speaking or singing in a language we do not speak? How do we understand the needs of a very young child or, perhaps, a pet?*

• *How do we know what is right or wrong, especially when the apparent "right" may be the minority opinion? How can the power of "intuition" be more fully developed and, ultimately, trusted?*

Native American Symbolism: The "World" of the Circle

"Myths by their nature need not be negative. When, however, myths that concern the construct of perceptions which diminish human potential, undermine the respect and integrity of groups of people, or restrict the implementation of cultural and social justice across centuries get implanted, it is critical that they are explored, decoded and eventually replaced in the interest of justice." In Search of Truth: A Re-examination of Western Academia in the Context of 'World,' c.2004, Center for Cultural Healing, Ann Arbor, Michigan.

Although there are many instances wherein diverse human culture groups come into contact in peace and respect for each other (which seldom make our history books), there are many as well in which the contact process is marred by a lack of understanding for the symbols and expressive features of the opposite culture group. The unfortunate nature of the European settling of the Americas and the generally negative result of the contact these individuals had with the indigenous cultures are by now mostly known. Even more devastating is the impact that the arrogance of a minority of individuals has had, through the eventual establishment of policies and institutions in government, on nearly every political, economic, and educational institution, for generations. Despite the fact that there might have been generations of individuals who would have sincerely loved a unilaterally respectful connection to Native cultures, to the sophistication of indigenous religion, to the symbolism in their honoring and respect for ancestry and their environment, and, most especially, to the enormous dignity and passion exhibited in their music and dance, there has been instead a void in Western education as well as romantic illusions that will take generations of re-education to reverse. Much of this make-up work will be in the area of learning to better understand *symbolism* and alternative perspectives to the Western mindset.

What is as relevant now as it was when native cultures first had contact is that they hold in high esteem nearly polar opposite values to those of a high percentage of the European colonizers. When one culture of governing bodies assumes supremacy over other cultures, the assumptions and interpretations of that dominant culture are exalted, documented, perpetuated, and ultimately reinforced over time and generations. Among the misinterpretations and dismissals of symbolic meaning in indigenous cultural art forms over the centuries since European colonization were the following:

- That Native Americans practiced "animism," which over time became distorted to their believing that animals had souls (equivalent to those of humans) or that they worshipped animals.

  What proved to be true: Animals, trees, rivers, and the elements of nature are, to Native Americans, representative of qualities and traits which are deemed respectable and desirable. In this sense, they possess a spirit or energy. To dance the "Eagle Dance," to name a group of your family (clan) after the wolf, the bear, or the turtle assumes that every animal or element of nature possesses a quality that is worthy of respect from humankind. For Native Americans, the relationship of humans to this Supreme Being necessitates the acquisition of spiritual traits and qualities, each of which has a parallel in the world of nature.

- That Native cultures were "primitive," unsophisticated, and unspiritual (or at least not as "spiritual" as those passing this judgment).

  What proved to be true: The degree to which Native cultures offer a valuable balance to the world of the Europeans and their steadfast perceptions of ownership, capitalism, and the equating of a person's

Pic. 3.2 and 3.2A *The pictures represent the diversity and change in symbolism in Native American cultures over time. In this case, both images reflect the respect for and qualities of the eagle, which is a powerful metaphor for responsibility to the Creator, to the world of the ancestors, and to our potential to communicate with the spirit world. When we fail to seek a deeper or flexible and changing meaning in the colors, images, and sounds of the world's art, we might disrespect the people. Even when we have a sound idea about the symbolism, we might remember that symbolism will change with each generation over time.* Photos: courtesy wikipedia.org and Joy Fera.

strength or success to material wealth has yet to find its home in the larger society. What will become clear as we examine the Native dances, the pow-wow, and a host of other symbols is that the symbolic interpretation of Native values requires a deeper use of our intuitive powers. In the majority of representations of Native wisdom in Western academia until very recently, we could see clearly the clash of the world of the *rectangle* with the world of the *circle*. That is, the perceptions of *one* world are formed based upon the symbols and values of the one interpreting.

Pic 3.3 *Grand Entry at
The University of Michigan
Native Pow-wow.* Photo: Courtesy
"Dance for Mother Earth" organizers.
Photo: Authors.

Honoring the Gift

You may have heard that it is a longstanding tradition among many Native cultures to give gifts to each other or to those whom they meet. Whether tobacco, sage, the feather of a hawk or eagle, it is not the gift, but its symbolism as a form of respect and honor to the other individual that is essential to the meeting and the gift-giving. For this reason we offer the only gift we can in a textbook: our paying of respect to these culture groups for what we have learned and will continue to learn from them:

So—we offer this gift of acknowledgement to those whose knowledge we seek:

We wish to thank our Native American brothers and sisters for contributing a wealth of cultural values and tools that bring health to us as individuals, families, and communities.

We thank you for providing us with strong *symbols* that remind us of our ancestors, of the Great Spirit, and of the many things we have to be thankful for.

Among these symbols are the circle, which reminds us of our Mother Earth, of the Sun, which gives us warmth and life, of the cycle of life that connects us to our ancestors, and of the seasons, which bring us fruits and grains and the passing of generations.

Through the cold of winter, we are reminded of the beauty and warmth of spring, just as, from the cold of your suffering, we have been given the warmth of your knowledge.

Above all, we give thanks to the Great Spirit, that through all of the hardships which have fallen upon you and your ancestors, you have remained intent upon maintaining your vision, honoring your ancestors, and treating the earth and all it sustains with respect.

Stories from the Human Family

Michael's Experience:

I was attending a world music (ethnomusicology) conference in Atlanta some years ago. The main speaker at one session was a member of the Native American community (Lakota Nation) of South Dakota. He spoke for nearly 40 minutes telling stories that seemed to blend from one to the other, with transitions as smooth as silk.

At the close of his session, he simply came to a resting point, and stopped. I, and many at this conference, which was conducted in accordance with the world of Western academia, were confused by the lack of a clear message. Where was the conclusion? What was the moral of the story? What were we to assume was the point?

Not being one to avoid an opportunity to learn the goal of the speaker's talk, I approached him and asked (more or less), "So what exactly was the essence of the story?"

He looked at me, smiled slightly, and replied, "You come from the world of the rectangle, and I come from the world of the circle."

Feeling momentarily as though I had just been called a "square," I swallowed my pride sufficiently to ask, "What should this mean?"

He replied, "You wake every morning in what-shaped bed? Look up at the ceiling—which is what shape? Walk out the what-shaped door of your room? Into rooms in what shape? You go to the ice-box which is what shape? Take out an orange juice carton— which is what shape? Get in your car and drive around blocks and buildings which are all shaped how?"

Finally I stammered, "OK, most things in my world are rectangular, but how does that relate to your story?"

He replied, "If your world is represented by images which all have a clear beginning, middle, and end, how do you suppose you think? Remember that not all things have a conclusion or point. Many things require us to grow until we have the wisdom to see their meaning, and meaning is more often multiple than singular. This is the world of the circle. My world is the circle; perhaps you will see the meaning of my stories in time."

With that, he walked away, and left me with thoughts and images that have continually been an inspiration for much of what I've come to value— not the least of which is this very unit. Atlanta, Georgia, 1994.

Within the "Circle": The Modern Pow-wow

The Native American, or "First Nation," *pow-wow* is an exciting example of the fluidity of tradition. The following is a brief introduction from a Native web-site, www.elements.nb.ca, c. 2005:

    "A Brief Look at the Evolution and the Meaning: To clearly understand the true meaning of Pow-wow in the context of its spirit, one must start at the beginning:

    It is believed by many Natives that still practice the traditional way of life, whose roots trace back to the beginning, that nature and Native peoples spoke the same language. A common belief is that when the Creator made this world, the Creator gave in nature a uniqueness and power to each tribe. Geographically, each Nation enjoyed a very respectful and harmonious relationship with Nature as a guide and provider. The relationship with the Creator was pure and its strength was at its peak, being both visible and heard through the voices of Nature.

Pow-wow time is for Aboriginal Peoples getting together to join in dancing, visiting, sleeping-over, renewing old friendships and making new ones. This is a time to renew thoughts of the old ways and to preserve a rich heritage. When early European explorers first saw these sacred dances, they thought "Pau Wau" referred to the whole dance. Actually, its Aboriginal definition refers to the medicine people and spiritual leaders. As more Nations learned the English language, they accepted the "Pow-wow" definition.[3.3]

Another account of the Pow-wow's history suggests:

"There are several different stories of how the Pow-wow was started. Some believe that the war dance societies of the Ponca and other Southern Plains tribes were the originators of the Pow-wow.

"Another belief is that when the Native Americans were forced onto reservations the government also forced them to have dances for the public to come and see. Before each dance they were led through the town in a parade, which (came to be) the beginning of the Grand Entry."[3.4]

Today's Pow-wow is a unique blend of Nations, tribal groups, and clans, each with its own symbolism in color and **regalia**.[3.5] Whatever the *Pow-wow* was, it has changed over time to become an intertribal festival or celebration of heritage and unification of indigenous peoples and a good starting place for anyone who wishes to learn more about the Native people or traditions. At the center of the music we will hear at Pow-wows are the *drum* and singers. Unlike the enormously disrespectful stereotypes of Native drumming found in cartoons or in Hollywood images or in athletic team mascot chants or dances, "the drum"—a large drum played by any number of participants who both drum and chant or sing the music for pow-wow—is a well-rehearsed, well-planned, and at times enormously complex pattern of beats, subdivided beats, accents, as well as strong (and difficult to sing) melodies or chant structures in a call-and-response form.

The Drum and the Dance

In most musical traditions around the world, music and dance are close, if not inseparable, companions. The notion that dance and music can be separated or divided into distinct departments is more the result of the Western university emphasis on specialization or division by discipline. Therefore, it is truly hard to appreciate the music of the "drum" without the movement of both the drummers/singers and the dancers with whom the complete musical and cultural experience is created. Mr. Paul Gowder writes the following on pow-wow singing and drumming:

Pic. 3.4 *The pow-wow drum is the heartbeat of the pow-wow.*

"One of the most important things in the life of a Native American is the drum. Our whole culture centers around the drum. Without the drum and the singers around it, the Native Americans could not have Pow-wows. The drum brings the heart-beat of our Earth Mother to the Pow-wow for all to feel and hear. Drumming brings everyone back into balance. Whether dancing, singing, or just listening, people around the drum can connect with Spirit.

"Being a Head Singer is a great honor. The man who receives this honor is chosen for his experience and the fact that the Singer has the right to lead all songs unless he chooses other men to lead and help carry the load. While at the drum, the singers should keep their thoughts on the songs and should keep the beat of the drum. When a Head Singer is chosen to sing for a dance, he will naturally do his best. Therefore the singers he has chosen should do their best for the Head Singer.

"Songs are started with a lead line sung by the Head Singer. This lets the drum and the dancers know what song is coming. After the lead line, the second (another person at the drum) will take up the lead line, and everyone will join in with him. At this point the dancers begin to dance. The loud accented beats during the songs, sometimes called "Honor Beats," are a time for dancers to honor the drum. In Northern singing, these beats are generally during the verses. In that he knows many songs, it is no wonder the drum should be treated with great respect." www.powwows.com, c. 2005.

The singing and beat cycles or accents in drumming will be discussed in greater depth below. But what is essential to the understanding of the drum-and-singing relationship is that each chant has deep

Pic. 3.5 *The Grand Entry at the "Dance for Mother Earth Pow-wow" on the campus of the University of Michigan, Ann Arbor, Michigan. Notice the crowd, many of which are non-natives, stand and pay respect to the dancers and "drum."* Photo: Authors.

significance to the singers and dancers, and, though frequently communicated through non-textual **vocables** that can be sung regardless of one's tribal or Nation affiliation, they are given deep meaning by all who participate—in thought and perception. Unlike speech, *vocables* have no inherent textual meaning, but when the song is announced—*honor song, grass dance,* etc.—all of the participants are required to keep the thought and focus of the dance firmly in their minds, thereby creating one of the most sophisticated examples of symbolism known to humanity.

> Of the pow-wow singing, Paul Gowder writes: *"Pow-wow singers are very important figures in the Native American culture. Without them there would be no dancing. The songs are of many varieties, from religious to social.*
>
> *"As various tribes gathered together, they would share their songs, often changing the songs so singers of different tribes could join. With these changes came the use of "vocables" to replace the words of the old songs. Thus, some songs today are sung in vocables with no words.*
>
> *"Yet, they still hold special meaning to those who know the song. Many songs are still sung in native tongue either newly composed or as revivals of old songs. These songs are reminders to the Indian people of their old ways and rich heritage."*
>
> As to the dance, in a related article on pow-wow dancing, Mr. Gowder helps us decode the myriad symbols in the pow-wow dances and music: *"To dance is to pray, to pray is to heal, to heal is to give, to give is to live, to live is to dance. These lines express my belief that the dances of American Indians are beautiful metaphors for celebrating life to the fullest. I dedicated this short poem to a friend, Reggie Brewer (Lumbee/Tuscarora), who has been a traditional dancer on the powwow circuit for the past twelve years. Reggie dances for the old people, showing them respect and honor by keeping the breath of Native ways alive. When I asked if he prays when he dances, Reggie answered, 'Yes, because sometimes the other way of praying just doesn't seem to work.'"*

"When American Indians dance, whether it is at Pow-wows or other gatherings, all senses become heightened as cultural chants, drumming, and songs fill the air. These haunting, mystical sounds transport the imagination to other times and places. The drum—its round form representing the shape of the sacred universe—emits strong, steady heartbeats that bring entrancement through repetition. This enables the dancers to put to rest the distractions of worries and cares of everyday life so that they may become one with all. Dancers from different nations in splendorous regalia dance the spirituality of their cultures into being as they pay homage to an ancestral tradition as sacred and important as rain. Agile and full of purpose, their artistic movements bring chills to the soul.

"Serious dance is prayer that can open a doorway to a connection with the total universe, a way to find that 'inner being' who recognizes and appreciates the spiritual essence of interdependence and to gratefully ask Creator for recognition of the needs of his or her people in return."

We will encounter the phenomenon of dance as prayer or worship in many other cultures (East Indian, Sufi Muslim, many African or African Diaspora cultures, etc.). What is important to consider is the role that dance plays in healing, in creating community, in demonstrating inter-connectivity, all in addition to its entertainment value. Mr. Gowder continues:

"Dancers have always been a very important part of the life of the American Indian. Most dances at Pow-wows today are social dances, which might have had different meanings in earlier days. Although dance styles and content have changed, their meaning and (especially their) importance have not. The regalia worn by the dancers, much like the styles of clothing today, evolved over time. Native culture—and Native Pow-wows—are not stagnant, but a vibrant and changing way of life."

First-time visitors to the pow-wow may be surprised by many things they see and hear, especially if that pow-wow is held, like many are today, in a large indoor arena. Perhaps lured by the romantic depictions of Native Americans dancing in the plains around the fire, or by the vision that Native Americans are clearly "Native" in appearance or personality, one quickly comes to realize the following:

Pic. 3.6 *Grand entry with the flags.* Photo: Authors.

Pic. 3.6A *Beyond the context of the pow-wow, the sheer beauty of the regalia, and the spectacle of the pow-wow's artistic and community unity – with respect for diversity.* Photo: Authors, 1999.

- Native Americans may be full-blooded, partial blooded, or in fact, "no-blooded," and of every variety and shape, hair color, or appearance. What distinguishes Native culture is that a person's "native-ness" is – to many (not all) – not as much an issue of birth or race as it is of respect and acknowledgment of the past, the living of the lifestyle, and the adherence to laws and rules which demonstrate respect for the culture.

- Pow-wows may be indoors, will likely have large sound-systems, and may have artificial lighting. In addition, dance contestants will usually be wearing numbers and often dance in competitions for money, and there may be numerous vendors selling their wares. Many things may seem in contradiction to the romantic illusion that some may bring to the pow-wow. If presumably we go to a pow-wow to upgrade our files, then it will begin with placing many of our expectations on hold in favor of the actual experiences and desires of the culture-bearers. Native Americans of all varieties are part of two worlds simultaneously, the ancient and the modern. Accepting the harmony and fusion of these worlds is critical to an accurate reading of the pow-wow and Native symbolism today.

- Pow-wows are carefully planned and organized. Native organization, though at times different from corporate structures of Western institutions, is extremely sophisticated and respectful of both experience and ancestry. Mr. Gowder writes:

  "Pow-wows are organized by committees that work for weeks before the event. At the Pow-wow, the MC runs the events. The MC works with the Arena Director to keep the Pow-wow organized and running smoothly. These two individuals along with the committee work hard to bring the people together to dance and to have fellowship together in the circle." Pow-Wows.com, c. 2005;

- There will be an immediate and confusing paradigm (construct of values) in the interrelationship of Native Americans and the United States. Native Americans will honor the United States flag, they will honor veterans of the military, but they will also speak to many issues and perceptions in "mainstream" America (in their crafts, wares, and songs) which they feel dishonor their heritage. Of these seeming contradictions, Mr. Gowder writes: *"These [the flags] are usually carried by veterans. Native Americans hold the United States flag in an honored position despite the horrible treatment received from this country. The flag has a dual meaning. First it is a way to remember all of the ancestors that fought against this country. It is also the symbol of the United States, which Native Americans are now a part. The flag here also reminds people of those people who have fought for this country."*

In the entry and honor songs, *"following the veterans are other important guests of the Pow-wow, including tribal chiefs, Princesses, elders, and Pow-wow organizers … everyone dances to the beat of the drum."* As another pow-wow attendee at The University of Michigan's "Dance for Mother Earth" Pow-wow explained: *"The symbol of the flag and our honoring of our land—America is based upon the ancestry of respect for 'home.' This is the place we live, the place we've raised our children, where we were raised, where our forefathers were raised. The warrior, in the past, was the protector of the home. Today he may be the veteran. We may not agree with much that the government has done or will do, but America is still our home and the home of our ancestors."*

If we have even a meager knowledge of the grim and difficult history of Native cultures since the beginning of colonization (late 15th century or, as one young Ojibwa student put it, *"the time that Native America discovered Columbus"*), and we then reflect upon the maturity and depth of forgiveness reflected in the above statement, we cannot help but be impressed and, hopefully, desire to listen more carefully to what our Native ancestors wish to teach.

Thinking within the "Square" or the "Circle"

Upon whatever a culture places its highest value will, over time, influence nearly all facets of that culture's lifestyle. So how, then, could cultures that has constructed a physical realm of rectangular buildings, windows, streets, and blocks become influenced by this construct in the mental and perceptual realms? That is, if in the more dominant Western cultures, physical spaces conform to rectangular shapes, is there a parallel to the way we think, process information, and define education generally?

The predominant academic conceptual model of thought —for paper-writing, speech-giving, instruction, and general life/business discourse— within the "square" or empirically-minded Western world is some variation of the following:

Begin with a thesis/hypothesis or introduction that introduces your point.

thesis

In most cases, the thesis is encouraged if not demanded to be of one perspective, a single side of a debate. Furthermore, by presenting our perspective as factual, as scientific, we create the expectation that it can be logically supported. For example, "Racism has been the result of the prolonged economic demand to produce wealth (resources) to justify and finance colonization by the empires."

Next, we support the thesis with facts and citations from others' research, attempting to solidify our argument in the "science" of already established facts or indisputable evidence.

The body of any paper, lecture, or discussion is the support material for the thesis. The more statistics and apparent facts, the more definitive the support material, the more conclusive the discussion, and the "better," by most standards, the "argument."

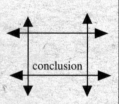

body

Example: "(Cite author/study) supports the expense of colonization, the influence of imperial competition in Europe, and the economic demand on the empires to support their global expansion, thus justifying the following….. (Citations)."

Finally, if we've done our job correctly, we bring back our thesis, which we now term the "conclusion."

Although there are many ways in which empirical or scientific methodologies can yield wonderful results, there may be as many in which this search for facts and conclusions minimizes (or even eliminates) the potential for multiple truths, for simultaneous conclusions, or for flexible discourse that does not seek goals, but rather makes the process of searching to understand -- the goal.

conclusion

This process is "circular" discourse. In the circle, we know that there may be multiple truths. We can allow for the possibility that sometimes there may be one conclusion, sometimes another, and sometimes none. Circular discourse also emphasizes the use of humility qualifiers, allowing the author to demonstrate "humble" wisdom by saying: i.e. "Although racism may have been considerably influenced by economic needs, it may also have had its roots in a prolonged history of greed, fear, religious fanaticism, and intolerance. Perhaps we can explore the multiple possibilities in this essay…. etc."

Activity

• *Pick a subject you find controversial or difficult to discuss.*

• *Can you list or discuss all the multiple truths and circumstances that might be valid?*

• *Under what circumstances might there be different or multiple "truths"?*

Pic. 3.7 *Symbolism personified:*

An Eagle feather is dropped during the Grand Entry of a pow-wow. The drum stops playing, the dancers stop moving, and pow-wow MC begins to explain: "We're going to take a break here, someone dropped an eagle feather. We want you to know that all tribes, many groups of Natives have different rules and traditions … which is good." He went on to explain that the sponsoring tribe would perform a ritual to purify the eagle feather and that "they would not penalize or punish the person who dropped the feather (as may have been done in the past or in other tribes) – just as we do not punish the eagle when he loses a feather."

Following the dance of Four Directions around the fallen feather, the feather was presented to the person who had found it, and he, in turn, immediately re-presented it to the one who had lost it. And, both the Grand Entry and the two-day pow-wow resumed. Photo: Authors.

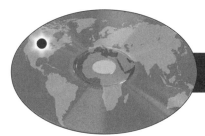 *Inside the Musician's World*

Drum Circle – Midnite Express

Note: A young "break-dancer" in one of our classes turned out to be an accomplished *Grass Dancer* now living with a Northern Michigan native community (Ojibwa). Some years later, we met him at a Pow-wow and asked him which drum group he liked. He referred us to one of the ten drum groups at the Pow-wow, saying, *"There are a lot of good drum groups these days. I like 'Midnite Express,' but really – they are all good."*

As we learned later, what might have been considered by many young folks as "un-cool" (participating in drum groups or pow-wow dancing) has seen a dramatic change in status and participation. Ever-increasing numbers of young Native, mixed, and even non-Native people are learning the ways of Native

American ancestry, particularly as expressed in the ever-changing and modulating songs and dances of the pow-wow. At any rate, we approached the *head drummer* of *Midnite Express* and asked if the group would be interested in our interviewing them or possibly contributing to the project. Then we waited, watched, and listened until, in time, we were given the nod to sit down and chat.

"Grand Entry," by Jeremy "Worm" Dearly, Jr., from the CD: **Midnite Express: Live in Cali,** c. 2005 Midnite Express Productions.

Midnite Express is a pow-wow drum and singing group from Redwood Falls, Minnesota. The group fluctuates somewhat (as do most Drum groups) in its personnel but generally maintains a close "family-like" relationship between all the members and their families, wives, and children.

The *head drummer* (the person who directs the "drum"), Opie Day-Bedeau, expressed a clear enthusiasm for helping non-native people understand that evolution in all things is natural: *"One thing I've noticed from personal experience is that just like everything else in life, music evolves … everything evolves. Maybe at one time they evolved more slowly, but evolving is human nature. At one time, when I was a little boy the way singing was then and now is quite different. I love being around the drum, I love singing, I love the feeling I get and the feeling I get—when we give this to the people.*

Pic. 3.9 *Pow-wows are filled with families and children of all ages. As Opy Day-Bedeau leads Midnite Express, you can almost see in the eyes of this little one in the arms of her mother the desire and intention that will simultaneously carry on ancient traditions and create new fusions of ideas and styles … This is the embodiment of Native culture and the powwow.* Photo: Authors.

"My dad was a singer, and that was a major influence. I wanted to be one of those people that people looked at and respected when I was little … and have my dad feel good too. There were many things he couldn't do— it made me feel good to sing for him too. It's in my blood."

When asked what he'd like non-native readers to know about his world, he replied: *"Just that it's here to stay, it's not going anywhere. Pow-wow singing is much stronger now than when I was a little boy. When I was little, I had to sit at the drum and I couldn't even use the stick until I knew the proper protocol. That's OK too, but nowadays you find a lot of young men who know the songs, and who sing and drum from an early age. That, too, is evolution. It's almost like it's a cool thing to do. I take a lot of pride in that— our culture is stronger now than it ever was."*

The Recipe of Sound

When Mr. Bedeau was asked about how the changes and the movement in the drumming and singing were orchestrated (accents in the drums, changes in volume, and entrances and directional changes of the chant), he replied: *"I think we've been doing this for so long now. The style we sing, well … a lot of people like to put Powwow singing in categories like contemporary, traditional, Northern or Southern style … the style we sing isn't really contemporary or modern, it's more a woodland style. This is how all the folks from where we come from sing. We've added our own little improvisations and hand signals. We pride ourselves on coordination and unity."*

Each member of the "drum" (usually a group of 6-12 people) will play the drum patterns together with a long padded stick and sing the high-pitched melodies (most often) in vocable (non-textual) style according to the directions of the pow-wow elders and MC. After a drum roll-call (before the Grand Entry), each *drum* will be called upon to sing for particular dances and events during the (usually) 2-day event.

The singing is generally in a "call-and-response" pattern. After beginning the drum pattern (at a tempo appropriate to the dance: Honor Songs are generally slower, Intertribal and Contest songs usually faster), the main singer will start the melody and the group will follow. When called upon to perform an "intertribal dance" or a "contest" dance (for jingle, traditional, grass, or fancy dancers at each age group from tiny tots to elderly), the group will have a particular song and drum pattern that they will have in mind for that event.

The listener should try to know the event, listen to the precision of the drumming and changes in accents or volume, altered to the communication between members and the unique style of the melody and the call and response between the group and soloist. These are the main musical elements of the drum.

In this piece, "Grand Entry," we might literally imagine that the *flag-bearers* entering into this song and the progression of dancers from hundreds of different tribes, a multitude of different-colored regalia, and thousands of years of American history are formed into a *circle*. Now, listen to the pride of ancestry, the energy and spirit of these people, and, above all, the youthful energy and passion in the song style and drumming patterns.

Crow Bellecourt, another member of Midnite Express, commented: *"We sometimes will sing songs in our ancestral languages, and if not, we sing songs for different parts of the Pow-wow or ceremonies. If an elder comes to us and asks, "Do you know what you're saying?"—we better know. If not, we'll get in trouble. That's why we practice so much and try to make sure we're solid in what we do."*

Stories from the Human Family

Sacrifice *"Just today, a student who had attended the Pow-wow over the weekend came to me and said: "Dr _____, I went to the Pow-wow over the weekend as you suggested and I was very disappointed." Teacher: "Really, what disappointed you?" Student: "I went up to one of the Indians and asked if I could interview him for the class … they treated me very cold and with no respect. All I wanted to do was show them that I wanted to respect them."*

Teacher: "This hurt, didn't it?" (Student nods.) "This is what we mean by sacrifice. You cannot expect after centuries of abuse, the exercise of 'white privilege' by those of European ancestry, and a perpetual history of people 'stealing' everything from images (sports team mascots, for example) to ideas, that you would be embraced just because that's what you wished. Your 'Higher Power' must have thought you were ready for the next stage in humility and learning: if you want equality or desire that others listen to you, you must also be willing to pay the price for their trust and their wisdom. I suspect that if you go back again next year, you will learn whom to ask, how to ask, and when and where to ask—and your experience will be much better. Are you prepared to make that sacrifice— to make the effort?" (Student nods). [Student: "European-American" female (18/19 yrs.) / Teacher "European-American" male (50 yrs.), with 25 years experience working with Native cultures.]

Songkeepers: *Music as a Way of Life*

Against the backdrop of musical contests, music "stars," and the enormous preponderance of music that is consumed in the context of entertainment, it may be hard, especially for each new young generation, to see the enormous importance of **songkeepers** in the traditions of our world's music. "Songkeepers," as the term suggests, are those individuals in any culture who have learned from their fathers or mothers, grandfathers or grandmothers, to play, sing, drum, dance, or chant music and who carry a deep and lasting respect for music to the next generations and their children or grandchildren.

In Native cultures, against the backdrop of the enormous loss in numbers of their people and restriction of their ways of life, *songkeepers* were the storytellers and history teachers who allowed generations of Native Americans, and anyone else willing to listen, to find their path back to balance. Despite the depth and duration of repression and disrespect suffered by Native cultures, forces which at times threatened personal self-esteem or community well-being, Native communities inevitably would also build and maintain tools for self-preservation and healing. The pow-wow is such a tool for Native cultures, as are the songs, stories, and melodies preserved by the storytellers and songkeepers.

Pic. 3.10 *The "Drum"— it may seem strange to some, but standard protocol for those interested in the drumming and singing at pow-wows is to come to each "drum" when they are called, and circle round the group. Even more interesting to the outsider might be the custom of tape-recording or video recording each drum song. This is actually perceived as an act of respecting the drum group rather than an act of piracy or stealing. In this sense, the innovations of a drum group are generally not to be "owned"—but to be shared.* Photo: Authors.

An example of such a songkeeper and preserver of Native traditional flute music and dancing is Kevin Locke (*Tokeya Inajin* is his Lakota name, meaning "The First to Arise"). Mr. Locke is Lakota (Sioux) and Anishinabe from the Standing Rock reservation in North Dakota. He learned all of his skills from his mother, Patricia Locke; his uncle, Abraham End-of-Horn; a mentor, Joe Rock Boy; and other elders and relatives. He has, by virtue of his performances throughout the world, become a pivotal force in the powerful revival of indigenous traditions, and especially flute traditions, which had begun to decline in the face of the technology and the rhythm of the modern world.

Mr. Locke's goals for music are that we listen deeply to the voice within us, the voice that connects all of humanity. If we are to practice listening deeply, then we must practice not only the skill of listening to the sounds and the obvious content (the surface meaning, especially if words exist) but also the skill of exploring the intent of the speaker or conveyor, the *symbolism* of the sounds. To do this, whether in conversation or music, we may wish not only to explore our mind files (which is our world, what we

Our Musical World

---

know, what we are familiar with), but also listen to the words, read the liner notes, plant the thoughts of the speaker in our mind, and then reflect upon the music as deeply as possible. At first, many of us will experience what Buddhists call "monkey mind" in attempting *deeper listening.* This is natural at first. It is simply our nerves and thoughts crying to calm themselves. Or, it is, potentially, the result of decades of living a fast-paced life, saturating our free moments with games or media, and of music which, for many, reflect these life forces with pulses and tempos that do not wish to be quieted.

Just as in conversation, it is not uncommon to listen while thinking about how we are going to respond, and thus, to more frequently misunderstand the other's intent and give the other person's words *our* meanings as opposed to their actual intent. Even more critically with music, we must attempt to gather whatever we can from the artist's world, and then quiet the "monkey" inside until we begin to see the vision of the musician, the vision of the songkeeper.

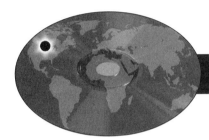

Kevin Locke (Tokeya Inajin)

Mr. Kevin Locke (Tokeya Inajin, "The First to Arise") says his goal is *"to raise awareness of the oneness we share as human beings,"* which he says is dramatically represented in many of the traditions he practices. The "Hoop Dance," for example, is a Lakota tradition which illustrates *"the roles and responsibilities that all human beings have within the hoops or circle of life."* He also says that it reflects both the virtual and symbolic Springtime, or time for renewal, which by his attitude, the songs he plays, and the dances he creates are all part of his mindset: *"All of the people have the same impulses, spirits and (deeply within) goals. Through my music and dance, I want to create a positive awareness of the oneness of humanity."*

The role of the songkeeper is therefore simultaneously essential and profound. In Mr. Locke's case, he is at once a "recorder" and disseminator of traditions which, if "lost," would greatly deprive both younger Native Americans and all humans of perspectives and visions essential to the balancing of our culture (see below: "culture balancing"). Simultaneously, however, he is advocating a vision, one that seeks through music and dance to touch the spirit—whatever lies beyond the intellect—with the reality that *"humanity is one, and the only natural fulfillment of our lives and efforts is that which leads to establishment of this awareness."* Can you hear these perspectives in his music?

"Itancanyapi" and **"Midnight Strong Heart,"** performed by Kevin Locke from the CD: <u>Midnight Strong Heart</u>, c.2003 Red Feather Music.

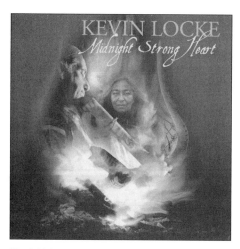

Pic. 3.12 *Patricia Locke, a powerful example of the strength of women.* Photo: Courtesy Kevin Locke JMixtlanArtists@aol.com.

This medley of two pieces, "Itancanyapi" and "Midnight Strong Heart," connects two simultaneous visions or principles to heal the divisions and harmful separations between human culture groups: *one,* the recognition of the special strengths and characteristics of women, and *the other,* the need for the "warrior" spirit in addressing the forces that subjugate human reality to forces of division.

"Itancanyapi"—*"ItaNcaNyapi, Lakota wiNyaN ki ohitka ca itaNcaNyapelo."* Translation: "They have made her their leader; because of her courage, this brave Indian woman is their leader."

This is a recent vocal composition by Clifford Tawiyaka from the Standing Buffalo Reserve, Saskatchewan. Mr. Locke writes: *"My late mother, TawaciN WaSte WiN (Patricia Locke) was ever ready to remind us that, while most of the world has been overwhelmingly patrilineal/patriarchical, here in North America the norm has always been that one's identity and birthright are inherited from the mother's side.*

"She had many stories, both historical and contemporary, of women whose superior moral courage enabled them to scale great heights of heroism. This was her favorite song, honoring this great legacy of bravery, inspiring us to strive to attain new horizons. One of my favorite quotes is, "The woman has greater moral courage than the man; she has also special gifts which enable her to govern in moments of danger and crisis. If necessary, she can become a warrior." [3.6]

"Midnight Strong Heart" – *"Ho anaguptapo mitakuyepi, kitaNla iyomakSice, Lecala inawaye wagnuni. Le TawaciN WaSte WiN eciyapi YuNkaN. OhiNni weksuyayelo. NahaN lila caNtowagnake, le olowaN hece wecicahiye. Nake nuNla wauN, nake nuNla wauN, owah'aNSuNkeca na makaSinawakiye. Ho bliheic'iyapo mitakuyepi bliheic'iyapo."* [3.7]

Translation: "Listen, my relatives. There is some sadness in my heart. I have recently lost my mom. Her Indian name was The Compassionate Woman. She is ever in my thoughts. *There is a big place for her in my heart, so this song is for her. My life is temporary, soon it will be over and I will wear the earth for a blanket. So be courageous, my relatives, be strong and courageous."* (In italics is the text of the original "Midnight Strong Heart Society" vocal composition).

Background: In the 1870s, TataNkiyotake (Sitting Bull) reorganized the CaNte T'inza Okolakiciye (Strongheart Society). Responding to the unprecedented threats from the advancing Euro-American people, he created the HaN CokaN CaNte T'inza Okolakiciye (Midnight Strongheart Society). Mr. Locke writes, *"Sitting Bull revitalized the musical repertoire with lyrics that re-emphasized the purpose of life, to renounce material comfort and well-*

Pic. 3.13 *Kevin Locke (Tokeya Inajin) on the plains of North Dakota.* Photo by Bruce Wendt.

being to serve the greater common good. I learned the song from my late uncle Joe Flying By. Today as never before, the world needs this warrior spirit to combat the rampant forces of materialism that threaten to extinguish our realization of our reality as spiritual beings."

The Recipe of Sound

"Itancanyapi" is a short chant-style song in Lakota, without drum, the rhythm of its melody being kept in the voices. Like many of the world's chants, it does not follow a set meter (a predictable and reoccurring or repetitive number of beats, which cycle over and over). Also, in most chants (see Unit V), the rhythm (flow of the music over time) is determined almost exclusively by the requirements of the lyrics, once again, in this case, a tribute to the strength and station of the woman.

"Midnight Strong Heart"—the slow and floating style of this flute piece gives ample time to ponder its meaning and, in this case, its implications to understanding "American history" in a considerably more real sense. The combination of the flute melody and the floating nature of the rhythm (flow of music over time) is what nurtures the mind into a state of reflection.

You may note that the **chordophone** (any instrument which uses a string to produce a vibration or sound) and the flute (an **areophone** or wind-instrument—any instrument which uses air or wind to produce sound) play sometimes separately and sometimes in loose unison (playing the same pitches at or nearly at the same time).

Pic 3.14 *Mike Irolla (Michigan, U.S.), the sculptor of these wood pieces, says, "Creativity is impulse, vision, communication. Children are born awake. But society and media can deaden creativity." Can we see his views in his art? Can we imagine his art from his words?* Photo: Authors.

Respecting the Circle: Culture Balancing (Healing)

"I do nothing but go about persuading you all, old and young alike, not to take thought for your persons or your properties, but chiefly to care about the greatest improvement of the soul. I tell you that virtue is not given by money, but that from virtue comes money and every other good of man, public as well as private. This is my teaching, and if this is the doctrine which corrupts the youth, I am a mischievous person." Socrates (469-399 B.C.) as quoted by Plato, The Death of Socrates.

"The means by which we live have outdistanced the end for which we live. Our scientific power has outrun our spiritual power. We have guided missiles and misguided men." Dr. Martin Luther King, Jr., Strength to Love, 1963.

There are times over the course of history when war and great upheaval, political or religious conflicts, greed, or natural disasters disturb the peace or equilibrium of a culture. As concerns the modern life-style of the last few centuries and the perpetual focus of Western cultures on technological and material advancement to a large extent over their family and community structures, it may at times feel to some of us that we are spinning out of control, out of balance. Whether in a material sense or in the decay of the strength of our families, communities, or social structures, how does one correct the imbalances that threaten to detract from our potential to enjoy the life experience?

Pic. 3.14A *The "pan" flute (Zampoña), used in Greece, Romania, and across the Inca-influenced civilizations from Mexico to the Andes, is played in this case by a young Peruvian-American in the Air Force.* Photo: Courtesy Airman 1st Class Harold Barnes III.

Culture balancing simply reiterates that all cultures have strengths and weaknesses. The simple laws of humanity imply that our individual and collective energies can only meet so many needs or be applied in so many ways. How we invest our energies will determine how we will prosper. That which we neglect will become weak or inert. When we recognize the weaknesses in our cultural systems, we can begin to exert energy toward creating alternatives and, by acquainting ourselves with other cultures and their expressions, bring balancing insight to our lives.

To *balance or heal* our cultures does not imply the giving up of positive values we may already have, nor does it imply the lessening of integrity by blindly accepting anything without choice, distinction, or logic. It is instead a process or way of thinking that assumes there are imbalances in our own personal culture, assumes value in all others, and encourages us to invest energy in finding those values that bring stability and balance to our lives. This is a natural response to, and wonderful benefit of, human exchange and the potential for interaction in the age of global communication.

In a real sense, culture balancing is *re*-education. Regardless of where someone is born or grows to maturity, every culture has enormous strengths and equally large holes in its social, political, or community lives. In the Western world, for example, much of education is predicated upon European and Euro-American belief systems, with all their good and not-so-good. In every instance, it is critical to examine the "not-so-goods." Once we understand their origin and degree of influence on us, we have the option of seeking alternatives from other cultures in the human family which may offer the *antidote* to our imbalances.

Culture balancing (healing) assumes that every culture on earth has a wealth of value and a number of problems. It assumes that technologically advanced cultures may not be sociologically balanced, that simpler communities may be in need of technology but may in turn have a sophisticated community structure or better-balanced social structures.

Culture balancing does not disallow the pain or distortions of our pasts, but accepts the diseases we inherited (e.g., racism, disparity of wealth and poverty, addictions, gender bias, and engrained separation of humans by category) as bi-products of human fear, greed, or mis-education. If we can accept the reality of humankind as being a single community with a diversity of human experiences and values, then thinking or acting as if one culture is superior to another is "simply illogical"!

Just as an artist reaches for a specific paint on his or her palette that will complete the balance in the painting, **culture balancing** is a mechanism that heals our own imbalances while sharing with others our own "wealth" (including humility and respect) by example.

Stories from the Human Family

Maybe you've had the experience of reading or reciting something, or walking by a particular park or house, and then magically one day, you notice a completely different meaning in the reading or for the first time see a different beauty in the park or house. In most cases, this is simply because at that moment in time, you were *listening (being aware)* with the depth of your *intuition (full awareness)*.

Advice from an elder:

> "To appreciate music, I would suggest you seek its knowledge. Try and hear what it has to say. If we are peaceful and it is violent, then we must remind ourselves we would not know peace if it weren't for anger. If we like lyrics, and it has none, then we must remind ourselves that talking is only one way of communicating. In the wind there are a thousand messages, but not one word. There are a whole bunch of ways of saying, "I love you," "Get off my foot," or "You are the sunshine of my life —."

> "Now I may be old, but I know how wisdom passes itself from generation to generation. You think I got these thoughts on my own? Heck no, these are the same thoughts my mama, and her mama, passed down.

> "I so wish young people today could understand the circle of life is not just a 'Lion King' song. It is how we keep our balance, how we maintain our humanity, and I got to tell you … we could stand a whole lot more of both of those." (Ester Williams, African-American female, 68 yrs.)

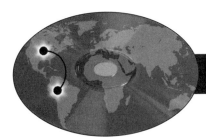

Inside the Musician's World

Ecuador Manta

Note: Many members of Quichua (Quechua) and Inca Quichua indigenous communities from the Andes Mountains of Bolivia, Peru, and Ecuador have traveled throughout Europe and the United States, playing in musical groups since the 1980s. You may have heard or seen these groups playing at summer music and art festivals. For many of the groups' members, the primary motives for leaving their homes and traveling extensively in the West are to heighten awareness of their ancient culture, to educate Western cultures about the traditional music of the Andes, and, especially, to provide for their families.

For those of us who experience this music for the first time, it is important to see the symbolism, not only in the music or of each song, but in why the musicians play it and what it represents. Since the art of playing this music has been handed down through the millennia from grandfather to father to son in order to sustain community-life and to connect to ancestral practices, it has always been essential that the songs express this connection and fortify the family and community units. This is yet another strong connection to the circle. We experienced this earlier through the music of Cesár and Inca Son, and as we visit Ecuador, we will have another opportunity to experience what must be seen as another variation of the rich traditions of Native American music.

What many indigenous communities offer to those of us who are willing to look behind the sounds and appearance is a profound appreciation for the life cycle, and in many cases, clear models of sacrifice, an essential pre-requisite for establishing close-knit communities. These are qualities that many Western cultures are currently struggling in varying degrees to manifest. The simple reason for this is that is difficult to place enormous energy in our material prosperity, career advancement, and individual concerns, while remaining perpetually balanced in our devotion and capacity to sacrifice on behalf of our families. It takes enormous wisdom to see imbalances in our cultures: it takes greater wisdom yet to have the humility to look for, and respond to, these needs.

CD 1.8

"Ecuador San Juanito / Sera," performed by Ecuador Manta from the CD: <u>**Alegrando el Alma,**</u> c.2000 Ecuador Manta.[3.10]

This medley of two pieces, "Ecuador San Juanito" and "Sera," connects the traditions of the parents and grandparents of the group members with the reality of their own world as young adults. In one piece, "Ecuador San Juanito," we hear the blending of ancient traditions and community formulas (the traditional dance rhythm of the "Wayno" or "Quenyo" and traditional Andes highland instruments) blended in a modern arrangement and recorded with modern technology and sound-processing techniques. In the other, we can hear a combination of reggae, cumbia (a Colombian dance rhythm), and both modern instrumentation and production in a poetic setting, which describes the duality of colonization as a force both destructive and innovative.

The group's director, Alfonso Burga, told us: *"Ecuador is rich in culture, in different art. People work so hard there, they make everything by hand. A lot of people are farmers who make handicrafts by hand—traditional Inca handicrafts. They work hard and play music too— nearly all the time.*

"Our ancestors, my grandfather, used to play instruments. That's how we learn. My father learned from him, I learned from my father; it's like a tradition. Our music is like a message of sadness and happiness. It's not involved with religion, or with government or the president. It's not political—it's music to make you happy or to free your soul. Our music is peaceful music. We bring our music to the United States or Europe to bring peace to them. This world is for all of us. It's not just for particular groups or countries that should lead—this is not the balance. The indigenous culture in Ecuador is like an example, a powerful example, because we have many things to fix in this country (U.S.) and everywhere. This country is not just for the rich.

"My message is that people have to wake up and see the real world. We must do for our kids what is essential for their well-being. I have my kids and I have to protect them. But I think we must change the way we live to protect them … if that is what's necessary, then that's what we must do."

The Recipe of Sound

Mr. Burga went on to say, *"I think the secret of our band is that we share everything equally. We don't give more money or other things to one more than the other. We share everything, money, pain, happiness. When someone gets sick, we get together—we share everything. Not just here, but also in Ecuador. The secret is we share.*

"We have our disagreements. We play together, there will be conflicts, but in the evening we get together, we talk, and the next day we continue as a community. This is what we have to do for each other, for our families, for our community."

So how do the sound, the combinations of notes, the rhythms, the layering of instruments, the organization of the music (form), and even the production (manner by which the recording emphasizes how and in what manner we will hear the piece)[3.8] reflect the closeness of their community?

Listen on your own and see what you can discern. You may wish to complete a sonograph of your observations while listening. Then, see if you can answer these questions: Can you hear how the instruments are layered (*texture*)? Can you hear how *tightly* or *loosely* the instruments play together (*uniform*

Pic. 3.16 *Alfonso Burga and his friends and colleagues from Ecuador Manta. Both the phenomena of exchange between cultures – and, in the case of many musicians from S. America, playing in the U.S. and Europe to support family in their home country – creates opportunities for cultural exchange and education for all.* Photo: Courtesy Ecuador Manta, Authors.

proximity to the beat)? If the instruments play tightly to the beat (pulse), does this impact our perception of their community life? How do you see the relationship between the order of the music and the order of *Quechua community life,* or to Mr. Burga's comments. And finally, in what way do the instruments support the following story/message?:

> *It will be, it will be that the wind will belong to us*
> *I will see perhaps, even though the beasts appear*
> *I do not know if it was our screams.*
> *Or if it were the few children that died for you.*
> *Oh, Oh, Oh…..*
>
> *With the sun, with the sun, with the sun of dawn.*
> *It arrived, it arrived, but which one of the snow beasts,*
> *It brings a cramming, defeated, yet a hopeful flavor,*
> *where each wants to be born here.*
> *Oh, Oh, Oh…..*
>
> *It was all a very real dream—five centuries,*
> *reached the wake up point?*
> *Fatal kiss of a world and a continent.*
> *The burden was light, peaceful, but also snake like.*
> *The shadow of yesterday gathers around my path,*
> *with its color of death, with its color of life.*
> *Oh, Oh, Oh…..*

One thing twenty-first century humans will need if they wish to reconstruct accurate and balanced files will be to build perceptions that allow for multiple truths. That is, that a single event (such as colonization) is neither completely "bad" nor "good." The settlement of European culture in South America unquestionably brought numerous grave consequences to indigenous cultures while it also brought movement, growth, and technological advancement. Alfonso's poetry (lyrics) bring the duality of truths to the forefront.

Pic. 3.16A *Two musicians from Ecuador (Native Quechua) wearing N. American Native clothing, perform a fusion of American Native music of a variety of styles, mixed professionally with synthesizers and nature sounds—to whom? Tourists from around the world in Héviz, Hungary!* Photo: Authors.

Stories from the Human Family

A Teacher's Letter

An email response from a colleague in a Southern California university read, *"Dr. Naylor, in answer to your question (What motivates your pursuit of new music and new cultural influences….?):*

"The strongest of motivations I've always had, has been my interest in justice. There was, I suppose, a point in my life when injustice did not motivate my pursuing other culture groups to the extent that I would grow to appreciate their values. But as I've grown older, I find I gain so very much by attempting, however inadequately, to understand the concerns and issues of other culture groups or individuals.

"In Native American music and culture, for example, I find an incredible power and resilience in both traditional chant and dance and in the contemporary works of young indigenous country, rock, or popular musicians. I am motivated by my desire to make 'deeds, not words, my adorning.' As such, I have logged on to various Internet sites, held conversations with many Native American friends on their music and culture, and have learned some important lessons on respecting their cultures. Among these lessons is the requirement of my simultaneously acknowledging what these culture groups have given to our world as well as the manner by which they have been so incredibly disrespected.

"I no longer purchase 'New Age' Indian artifacts unless they are made by tribal hands and the profits return to them. I no longer purchase music that claims tribal affiliation but is performed by 'gringos' (in this case: non-indigenous musicians), unless there is a respectful acknowledgment of the tribes from whom the music is borrowed, and a disclaimer that the product is anything other than the musicians' impressions of Native music. My motivation is simply justice. These seemingly small acts are the means by which I may show, however inadequately, my respect for the integrity, beauty, and depth of these culture groups, while gaining a sense of peace which stems from my own growth and increased sensitivity. A sensitivity which has in turn, taught me how to become a member of a

community, how to work in a community—and how to contribute to community-building, which was a skill I had not learned in my own world. Anyway— those are my thoughts… until next time—." ("Mixed" ethnicity colleague, 55 yrs., teaches in Southern California University; untenured faculty, name and university withheld by request)

The Talking Circle:
Listening below the Surface

Unconsciously or not, each of us has heard a tremendous variety of music and been in contact with a wide variety of cultures. In expanding our circle of contacts and our sense of *community*, that is, those with whom we live and share our identity and creative qualities, we simultaneously enlarge and potentially balance our own capabilities as well. The key to any expansion of perception, however, lies in the intensity and duration of our interaction with other human beings or culture systems. One very profound tool for increasing the intensity of the listening experience lies in the model of the Native *round house* or *talking circle*.[3.9]

We have already seen that historically Native American communities have used complex symbolism in clothing, shapes, colors, and of course, music to increase the impact and effectiveness of an event or expression. Among the most profound examples of this is the reoccurring use of the symbol of the circle to discourage rigid, finite, or self-indulgent thinking or behavior. Circular discourse, or a talking circle, is a "translated" group collaboration tool used to increase the potential of the community to solve problems, find solutions, and better understand one another. This device combines a collection of these symbols into a mechanism that fosters respectful listening and consultation in a group environment. In the end, group decision-making and a detachment from personal opinion or personal perspectives bring harmony to even the most severe problem.

Mr. Burga, when asked how their group solves problems, replied that they use the talking circle without even thinking about it. Asked how they do this, he replied: *"When possible while working in groups, do all your activities/consulting in a circle, for the circle is without hierarchy or status. There is no front or back, up or down. When conflict arises, keep in mind the symbol of the circle and its call to us to be better listeners."*

TALKING CIRCLE – (Suggested Procedures for Community Consultation)

- Arrange yourself in a circle.

- Begin consultation by first paying respect to the culture (see above). Contemplate the symbolism of the circle and our inclination to judge symbols by the literal meanings of our own cultures. (Note: This equates to "prayer" or establishing a contact with both/either your Higher Power or your ancestors).

- Select a topic that will most enhance your interaction in the group or advance the group's goals or mission. Place something symbolic of being *greater than yourselves* in the center. Frequently, a stick, as a symbol of nature, is used. However, anything from nature may be used, because these symbols represent a force greater than that of the individual human. Now observe the following:

  – That no one may speak without holding the stick; that everyone has the right to say what is on his/her mind without being judged, but only when holding the stick.

  – When someone wishes to share, he/she must first rise, go to the middle of the circle, claim the stick, and return to his/her seat before sharing;

  – That when you hold the stick, you hold a symbol of the Force or Spirit that gives life, a force greater than ourselves. Be respectful in what you say.

  – While you are listening to the person speaking, you show respect. Regardless of whether you agree, you respect the person's right to express him- or herself honestly and trust the process. Do not judge or respond quickly to what is said. The group will determine the ultimate wisdom.

  – When you are finished, place the stick (respectfully) back into the middle of the circle. At the same time, you give your thoughts and opinions to the group. You no longer own them; they belong to the group. You must let go of your opinions, or your stubbornness might dampen the spirit of the group. Now return to your seat and give your will to the group.

  – Anyone wishing to respond must wait until the previous person has sat down before rising and carrying out the ritual him- or herself.

If we are not Native, or have not spent much time befriending Native Americans (from throughout the Americas), an important part of our appreciation process will be to set aside outmoded images of tee-pees, ritual dancing, peace pipes, and headdresses, and to simply ask, "How do you (Native or First Nation people) wish us to learn of your culture?"

> In order to respect a culture with the full passion we have toward our own culture, we might ask, "How would you like to be treated?" or "What would you like me to know about you?" In this manner we return the entire process of self-determination to the people themselves, rather than repeat the same mistakes of centuries of colonization.
>
> The right of self-determination is the most essential element of respecting others. The capacity to listen to what others say in the manner they wish to convey it – is one of the most important disciplines we can learn.

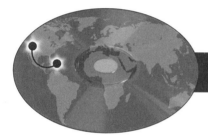

Inside the Musician's World

Lee & Stephen Tiger and Casper

Note: Perhaps the single most common mistake we are likely to make in assessing cultures for which we have little or no first-hand experience is to look for them to manifest the characteristics of our mind files. Since many of these files may be loaded with outdated information, stereotypes generated by media, or inadequate education of culture or history, we might try to give more time to our assessments. As with all cultures, Native American communities cannot be generalized into the narrow parameters of media portrayals and misinformed history lessons. In like fashion, the musicians of each generation are just as likely to fuse rock 'n' roll, reggae, or hip-hop into their musical expressions as we are.

Two examples include, first, a collaboration of brothers, Lee and Stephen Tiger, from the Miccosukee-Seminoles. This piece is an example of rock, country, and their own musical past with the stories they most wish others to hear. Many of the Tiger brothers' songs talk about the *Indian Removal Act* and the wars fought by their people for self-preservation. Lee Tiger writes, *"Originally, the Miccosukee stretched from Georgia to south Florida. However, after two major wars (1813 to 1858), soldiers pursued the Creeks, Miccosukees, and Seminoles into the Everglades."*

The second is an example of reggae/hip-hop and other genres by a young *Hopi/Diné* (the *Diné* are frequently incorrectly referred to by the Spanish name Navajo) from the Southwest, Casper Lomayesva. Casper cites his grandfather, Sankey Lomayesva, as having the biggest influence on his life and music, but then turns to cite the enormous bond that was established in 1985 between the Hopi Nation and the Island of Jamaica. *"In 1985 Freddie McGregor became the first Jamaican reggae artist ever to perform on an Indian Reservation. There was a special feeling that developed between the reggae artists that came out to the reservation and the Hopi people."*

"We'll Be Here," performed by Tiger/Tiger (Lee and Stephen Tiger), from the CD: **Space Age Indian,** c.1994 Stinger/Hopanke Music/ A Tribal Experience/Soar Corporation, www.tigertigermusic.com.[3.10]

The incredible stories of survival, in this case of the Miccosuke-Seminoles in the swamps of the Everglades, is reflected in this song. The *"Indian villages"* constructed by Lee and Stephen's ancestors were ingeniously converted to tourist attractions to generate income and to sustain their families. From crafts and art to alligator wrestling and the eventual establishment of the first "Indian Village" tourist attraction (1957), enormous hardships were overcome through the strength and bonds which connected the generations. The story also demonstrates patience and will-power as well as the power of forgiveness. In order to sustain their community, generations of the Tigers' ancestors were forced to entertain the very descendants of those who had established the systems of repression and isolation. The lyrics tell the painful story and reflect the enormous will to survive:

Verse 1: Yes our homes were devastated –We rode out the storm
Children cried and men were humbled – Now our lives are torn.

Chorus: We'll be here – We will rebuild somehow
We'll be here – We will rebuild right now

Verse 2: Now the time has come our people – Now we need our friends
Hurricane couldn't break our spirit – We're here 'til the end *Chorus -*

Verse 3: Someday when the sun is over – We'll know we were strong
No race, no gender, everybody – Helped when things went wrong *Chorus -*

Note: We wish to acknowledge with deepest sympathy, the passing of Stephen Tiger since the completion of this text. Our sincerest thoughts are with Lee and Stephen's families.

"Babylon World," performed by Casper Lomayesva, from the CD: **Honor the People,** c.2004 Third Mesa Publishing, www.3rdmesa. com

Casper writes: *"Thanks for considering me … here's what I do.*

"Being raised on indigenous lands surrounded by thieves and corporate greed has given me the need to address people of all races. As you probably already know, native lands have a history of being some of the poorest communities in the country. Suicide, alcoholism, and teenage pregnancy are just a few things I have had to endure in my years. This is the result of despair and the loss of self-esteem suffered through being controlled and dominated against our will.

"On top of this, coal and water were found under the Black Mesa in Northern Arizona, near the village I was raised in. So now we have corporate America strip mining the coal and using our pristine drinking water to slurry it to light up Los Angeles and Las Vegas ... ruining the land for our children's future use.

"I've made it my life's goal to educate the people in all directions of this unlawful act being conducted throughout our Native lands. The future of Indigenous lands must be put into the hands of our people. Through music we can reach the future generations who will someday be lawyers, judges, and maybe ... world leaders. Music has no boundaries, so this is why I do what I do! Respect."

Pic. 3.18A *Honor the people.* Copyright, Casper, 2004.

As you listen to the piece, you will easily hear how the influences of reggae, funk, and hip-hop genres which have historically been platforms for liberation and culture balancing (Unit IV) give an ideal platform for Casper's message. References to "Babylon," the Rastafarian referral to the biblical Babylon or imperial source of repression, summarizes the lyrics, which spin off the numerous means by which injustice and destruction are, according to Casper, perpetuated.

The final line summarizes the ancestral will to survive that Casper inherited from his grandfather: *"Remember you must struggle if you're going to survive. The human spirit always finds a way to stay alive."* Perhaps more important are the messages below the surface, which, according to Casper, *"are a call for action and fortitude in lieu of apathy and indifference."*

The Recipe of Sound

Certainly the main function of each of these pieces is to broadcast a message or to tell stories of struggle and survival. The question from a musical perspective is how are the instruments and production of the pieces supportive of these stories? Though different, both pieces use the *verse / chorus* formula of popular song forms that have become a formula particularly since the advent of mass media (1920s).

We can graph or chart out the form of a piece of music to see its structure. In this case, and in the case of most music produced for mass media (CD, radio, television), the verses are the vehicle for conveying the details of the message. The faster the tempo, or in the case of hip-hop if the lyrics are not sung, the more information can be provided. The chorus, on the other hand, is the location for what is called the *hook* in music. Although "hooks" can be melodic, harmonic, or part of the production or arrangement of instruments, the lyrical-melodic hook of most popular/media-formatted pieces is where we will find the essence, or the primary summary, of the story or message. Most of these *hooks* are found in the chorus and frequently are the song's titles as well. The hooks are, in the first piece:

"We'll be here / We will rebuild some how / We'll be here / We will rebuild right now"

and in the second:

"In the Babylon world every person has problems / Can't we just put aside our differences to come together and solve them?"

Cultural Healing: The Role of Education

Discussion Reflection III-C

Against a myriad of current socio-cultural problems such as racism, global warming, dysfunctional communities, health epidemics, wars or conflicts based on religious, political, or economic power struggles or greed (imbalances), and the proven ineptitude of political measures to solve the majority of our world's imbalances, emerges a rather simple question: *Who has the responsibility to begin altering (healing) the mindsets that perpetuate our world's most urgent problems?* And, *where might the re-education or "healing" of these imbalances begin?*

There is for certain one place to begin transforming the outmoded perceptions that have misinformed generations and created dysfunctional models of "value" and the purpose of life—and, more explicitly, the purpose of education itself: the very places from which each generation's parents, school teachers, doctors, or business and corporate executives or politicians are trained: the university or college.

Despite a wealth of positive, virtuous, and socially-culturally beneficial developments that have been derived from the eight centuries of the Western academy (itself predicated upon the model of the Greek academy before it), there are concerns within education that have remained largely unaddressed and that can be blamed for many of the gridlocks in our attempts to establish healthy communities today or to solve the numerous problems cited above. Among these concerns are the following:

1. Outcomes (test scores/grades/degrees) are generally more important to the student and more emphasized in all academic arenas (from primary school to higher education) than learning itself. These outcome-oriented messages (based upon the ancestry and history of the academy and its search for monolithic and mono-disciplinary "answers" and facts over processes, creative thought, and interdisciplinary learning) begin early in primary school and are reinforced throughout the academy cycle.

2. Students are inundated with concern for their material well-being and are given little training and even less encouragement to explore their emotional, mental, cultural, and even physical balance, much less their potential for happiness, spiritual health, or choice of professions based on desires to contribute to the benefit of society or to find jobs based upon self-aware perceptions of their inherent potential. Educators are increasingly concerned about the psychological/emotional health of students and the challenges ill-health imposes on learning;

3. Current systems of measuring the success of "education" by testing mandates and imposing tenure requirements on professors based upon publication and self-centered career advancement (not necessarily on "teaching") do not administer to the needs of the world in which we live. Thus students are expected to perform in a manner that does not fully account for globalization, interdisciplinarity, and full-brain learning (including emotional learning). At the same time, teachers, who realize there are alternatives to what "they know" or how they teach, are frustrated by a lack of support for allocating time and resources to broadening their own experiential base or, for changing our educational environment. [3.11]

Questions

- *Has your educational experience been effective or ineffective in teaching you emotional intelligence or cultural awareness? Why or why not?*

- *Discuss what you think would be needed to transform our educational emphasis for each of the following criteria (based on Goleman's Emotional Intelligence, 2006): self-awareness (knowing yourself, emotions, and potentials); understanding and managing your emotions; becoming self-motivated (learning and applying what you learn); and having empathy and creating or managing relationships with the widest assortment of peoples/cultures.*

Musical Terms and Concepts

Musical Note-taking—*The Sonograph*

As long as we are writing about the music event, our mind must have something to write. That is, if our pen is moving, our mind must be pushing it to speak. This exercise demands that we do not revert to passive or non-concentrated listening or remain in our comfort zone, but instead attempt to focus our energy on what the music has to say to us. Regardless of our tastes in music, concentrated listening skills have enormous benefit in our day-to-day human experience.

While listening, we might attempt to draw a **sonograph** or "sound picture" of the piece. We do this primarily to keep our focus and concentration on the music. The reason we would want to create musical notes revolves around the simple nature of how many of us use music in the context of our normal day.

Since the most predominant times that music is *heard* during the context of a normal day are while driving, dressing, working, eating, playing, or, in short, doing something other than listening deeply (focusing all of our attention exclusively on the music), it is understandable, even when we love the piece of music or sing along with it, that we may seldom ask, *Why do we like it?* The simple question *What in the music made us feel or think... whatever?* begins the process of encouraging us to listen more deeply. We are in essence asking, *What is the musical recipe or the elements in the music that led us to our thoughts?* To ask these questions and attempt to address them with our concentration is the beginning of demonstrating respect for the work and efforts of the musicians. Whenever we compliment chefs, artists, or creators of anything that we appreciate, they appreciate it more if we can specifically comment on the ingredients or nature and beauty of their work.

Unfortunately, just as with a lecture, a speech, or for that matter anything that happens over time, we may not remember much that occurred at the beginning of the listening experience by the time we reach the end. The simple nature of the human mind precludes the complete recall of events over time and will reduce the listening experience to a selected few highlights, based usually upon our preferences and biases.

Therefore, the purpose of taking musical notes is to:

- Create a map of our observations of the recipe of the piece of music.

- Help us keep our concentration on the music and not drift to unrelated thoughts.

- Help us develop our listening concentration for longer duration.

- Respect the art or artistry of the musicians by helping us understand the efforts and techniques they used in building their composition.

Although in listening to "Midnight Strong Heart" we will get more (ultimately) from a reflective or meditative approach, unless we are practiced or somewhat disciplined in this art or are comfortable with music that does not possess a strong or steady *beat* (the pulse of the music to which we tap our foot or move in regular motion), it is still, with all music, a relevant exercise to note the piece's form, structure, and elements first.

It is important to note that all sonographs will be based upon the knowledge and affinities of the note-taker. What we hear, to a large part, is based upon our preferences in, affinities for, and experiences with music. Therefore, sonographs will be the reflections of the listener and, much like snowflakes, will not— *should not* —look the same.

Pic. 3..18C *A handwritten sonograph for "Babylon World."*

In the case of this piece, we would want to use a combination of the two styles of musical note-taking we will use throughout this text:

1) A **linear** sonograph, which includes the drawing of a line on your paper and blocking of the piece by sections (that is, using vertical lines to indicate each change or new section in the music and descriptions of what we hear above or below the line).

2) The **narrative** sonograph, which is much like note-taking for a lecture or speech, but in this case is a running narrative of our thoughts and feelings about the music.

The *linear sonograph* can be effectively used for any music that has clear-cut sections. This would especially include all popular music structures that have verses, choruses, or regular changes in musical structure. To create a linear sonograph, we simply use the line as a graph of time, and then note each section or distinct change in the texture or form of the music with vertical lines as it occurs. We simply notate whatever we hear above or below the line. In the end, we will have a map of what occurred, in what order it occurred, and a relatively good indication of the *recipe* that was used in the piece of music to elicit our response.

The beginning of "writing music" starts with notating observations. With some training, anyone can move from observations of form and texture (structure and instrumental layers) to actual notation (by any system). Photo: George Argyropoulos.

For some pieces, or for some sections within a piece, the changes in the musical instruments, musical sections, or layering of musical elements (texture) occur either too quickly or too slowly. For these pieces, we will need to revert to a long-hand or *narrative sonograph* in order to maintain our concentration on the music by continuing our writing over the duration of the piece. Examples of these musical styles might be meditative pieces with erratic or no steady beats (pulses), techno/dance hall, or ritual music where changes occur only over long periods of time (leaving us without many new observations to make concerning instrumental or form changes), or certain forms of European art or "classical" music, experimental music, or what is often called *through-composed* music.

Most frequently we are called upon to combine the two styles, as would be essential for "Midnight Strong Heart." Although there are relatively clear changes in the musical events (another definition for texture), there are fairly extended periods of time during which we will have little to notate and must begin the process of contemplation in a narrative style. Once again, the primary benefit to note-taking while listening to music—even to a meditation-like piece—is that we don't lose our awareness of the music, its elements, or its recipe. Once we feel we have the discipline to maintain our focus throughout a piece of music, we can then turn it on or off at will, but we will not be locked to an exclusively passive mode (*cause and effect*) of listening.

Flute begins- bending notes	Melody goes higher/string Instrument follows flute –	Flute returns - Greater energy

Hear: slow – no real beat /random sound "string instrument"   Talking – check meaning

Narrative: possibly reminds the listener of _____ then ask why?

Speak of emotion – your own relationship to song

Possible meaning – this is where we put specific emphasis on the intuitive analysis or projection of the possible symbolism of the piece … remembering to use "humility qualifiers" such as "I think… it might be … etc.

On a 2nd listen – maybe we can carry the meaning of the piece in our mind – and try to "meditate" or close our eyes and listen with the thoughts in our mind (meditative listening)

Note: We will use the *sonograph* as a means of encouraging concentration on the music and recognition of the musical elements used to create the piece. The graphing of the form and occurrence of musical events over time encourages concentration. At times, we may suggest you attempt to draw a sonograph before reading anything about the piece. At others, we may ask you to draw a sonograph after reading the notes. Above all, don't make the sonograph into a frustrating experience. The specifics of the musical note-taking should never be used as a test of our listening capacity or in comparison to those of others. The sonograph is simply an important tool for increasing our awareness, concentration, and respect for the music (nothing more). Anything other than this is a distortion of its purpose and value.

Stories from the Human Family

Alternatives in Community

The following story was written in a student journal to express what the student thought was the difference between the manner in which many are raised in technologically competitive cultures and those of her indigenous ancestry. Although the culture groups are fictional, the message is worthy of consideration. (Used by permission on the condition of anonymity.)

Pic. 3.18D *The beauty of the concept of "unity in diversity" (understanding that "unity" does not demand "sameness" but can honor diversity) is clearly manifest at a large inter-tribal pow-wow. A single image, such as this, shows such a diverse array of regalia and color, reflecting an equally diverse heritage of Native American cultures, but still within the context of magnificent unity of purpose and ritual (see Unit VIII). What is not evident from this image, however, are the masses of families (Native and non-Native) that surround the dancers. Some may walk away after the event never to return, some will return, and some will become permanently attached to the community and be absorbed by virtue of their love and respect of the culture. This is the power of individual passion and initiative.* Photo: Joy Fera, (Kiyyah), 2005.

Pic. 3.18E *In the end, ALL forms of separation and exclusion of human beings or cultures is learned. These children (in Eastern Europe) have no problem dancing to the music of a culture as diverse and "opposite" to their own experience. And the musicians are flattered by their efforts.* Photo: Authors.

"Suppose we hypothesize a fictional culture to see how cultural traits impact musical choice. The following story might be a good portrayal of a diversity of possibilities. I do not mean this to be negative or critical, just to point out the differences as to how others might live differently, and therefore, perceive things differently.

Story: "In Zubalo culture, it is commonly believed that we should teach our children to be independent and begin pushing the children toward self-dependency at a very early age. In time (over a few generations), however, it is observed that the children begin to have increasingly less contact with their parents. They may move further away, or even grow to feel that they may no longer return to their 'homes' for any length of time once they are adults, as this would be a demonstration of failure. Many reject the music of their parents and seek to find the latest, and, frequently, most different, musical styles they can as an exercise of their independence.

"What may follow is an increasingly weakened and possibly even degenerative family structure over time. The musical chasm between parents and child may in time even become a battlefield. In general— only time is likely to bring the forces together.

"Now someone from Puchachu culture (fictitious as well) comes along. He comes from a culture wherein children are taught to be responsible, to find a trade, and to contribute equally to the well-being of the family. But amongst the Puchachus, there is no pressure at any time for the young adult to leave home if he chooses not to. This child may or may not become involved in the modern music movement. But he is likely to express respect for his parents' music, and his parents, in turn, are not likely to make the musical tastes a battlefield of wills.

"Where fusion and exchange are concerned, if the individuals of the Zubalo culture come into contact with those from the Puchachu culture, they will exchange frustrations, successes, and ideas. The result is that a change in cultural perception will be made. In short, they may learn to balance the traits of their cultures with the alternatives received by being sensitive to others. In any case, they would learn more about why or how they and their actions have been influenced by the larger cultural viewpoint.

"Anyway, does this make sense? I just felt I had to write this in a fictitious way to not offend anyone."

Unit III Activities

Activity #1: Understanding Concepts

Answer the following questions based upon your understanding of the reading:

1) What is the primary difference between reading the symbolism of a culture with intuitive understanding and nonverbal decoding versus relying solely on our perceptions of information, with the use of our mind files? What do you feel may be the primary hindrances to our development of strong intuition? How does education or our larger culture's values play a role in what we value or devalue?

2) What are some of the primary symbols found in the Pow-wow of Native American culture? What are some of the ways we see the symbolism of the circle in the Pow-wow?

3) If we are not Native, how do we come to understand the *reality* of American history from the perspective of Native culture, without being defensive or feeling useless guilt? What are the expectations (do you feel) that Native culture-bearers might have of the non-Native in showing respect for their culture?

4) What does *culture balancing* mean to you? In what ways do you see imbalances in your culture system? In what ways do you see balancing qualities or perceptual tools in Native American cultures that could fix your own culture's imbalances?

Activity #2: Listening Deeper

Now that you've had one listen to the pieces, you may wish to listen again and this time attempt to take musical notes (a *sonograph*) while listening. The purpose of the sonograph is, once again, to force ourselves to listen aggressively to the way the music is constructed and force ourselves to hear the music's recipe of sounds and instruments over time.

CD 1. 8 Artist: Ecuador Manta / 1.9 Tiger Tiger

For each of the pieces 1.8 (parts one and two) and 1.9 (part one), draw a couple of lines on your paper. As the music progresses, try to identify each new section (or repeated section) with a vertical line. See if you can label the *verses* (same melody but with different text) and *chorus* (same melody with the same text). What else can you find to distinguish each section (instrument, melody, texture)?

Make sure to also add any textual cues or a word here and there about what is being said (whatever you are able to observe while listening to the music as well). Above all, try not to worry about "what" you write. Just *write*!

CD 1.10 Artist: Casper

Due to the more intense pace in the flow of the lyrics of this piece, you may wish to put all your focus upon the story that is being told and take note of the phrases or words that "stick out." The more prolific the textual content, or the more foreign the delivery of the text, the more concentration or intuitive interpretation we will need to exert. What do you feel Casper is saying to us? What does he hope we'll come away with from listening to his message?

Note: See the Endnotes (3.10) for (sample) sonographs for 1.8 and 1.9 and lyrics for 1.10. Remember, it is not important to have the same information or thoughts. Each of us listens with the sum total of our experiences and vocabulary—*which is fine!* It is only necessary to have a "comparable number" of observations, which indicates concentration over the duration of the piece.

Activity #3: **Exercising Passion**

To demonstrate our willingness to honor any gift we receive from another culture, the proof of our gratitude lies not in our verbal acknowledgment, but the incorporation of what we've learned into our lives. One of the most profound symbols of Native lifestyles is that of the circle and, especially as concerns learning to listen more deeply, *the talking circle.*

Suggested activity:

With a group of friends, colleagues, or family, set aside one to two hours for the talking circle exercise. Then follow the steps below:

1) Arrange yourselves in a true circle.

2) Explain or read briefly the importance of the circle and usage of the talking circle as described above.

3) Explain the procedures of the talking circle, making sure to emphasize: a) no one should speak without the talking stick; b) no one should address the comments of someone else directly but, rather, apply the comments to ourselves and our own experiences; c) everyone should attempt to demonstrate attentive listening to the comments of others (including watching our body and facial language as well); d) what is said at the talking circle *stays at the talking circle;* there must be complete trust that what we say belongs to the group and will not be carried outside the circle.

Pic. 3.19 *"I hope the Great Father, who will look down upon us, will give all the tribes His blessing. That we may go forth in peace, live in peace all our days, and that He will look down upon our children as His children. That all the tribes may be His children, and as we shake hands today upon this broad plain, we may forever live in peace."* Red Cloud (Marpiya-Luta)/ Oglala Chief / late 19th century (as quoted by Lakota Native elder).

The "Blue Marble," as shot from Apollo 17 (1972), is a fitting backdrop for this group of International Women at a conference on the "equality of men and women." The balance of life, the attention to the education of children, and the reduction in tendencies toward conflict or war are substantial gains in social/cultural societies marked by equality of women and the influence of their wisdom. Collage rendering: Brandon Naylor, 2006.

Although any question or topic can be brought to the circle, some questions that frequently elicit good responses include:

– How do you feel about the overall stress and/or balance in your life today?

– What is the most important way in which someone may demonstrate respect to you?

– Under what circumstances do you feel respected or valued?

– What do you enjoy most in life, work, etc? These are things that you can offer others to balance their lives.

Or simply:

– What type of music do you dislike the most?

– How can you demonstrate respect to those who value this music?

– What part of your life or character would be enhanced by taking action to respect others?

Pic. 3.20 & 3.21 *The symbolism of the eagle – and the importance of honoring ancestry and maintaining a solid and firm interconnection between generations – is manifest in both of these images. The totem (left) is an ancient tradition that includes symbols of nation, clan, and their history. The father and daughter (above), share not only the pow-wow experience, but colors, shapes, and symbols of their ancestry. Against the backdrop of the modern world, these early childhood experiences, will keep the child respectful of her ancestry and elders – a quality she, in turn, will be able to pass on to her children.* Photos: Courtesy, istockphoto.

Activity #4: Exercising Our Own Creativity

There are so many symbols in Native culture systems that are worthy of respect. To select one in particular that you find valuable or balancing in some way to your own experiences should not be difficult. Now, how do you reflect upon that symbol in a manner that would be respectful to the culture-bearers of that group?

The key here is the depth of your listening or observations. Surface-level observations will produce graphic or surface-level art, just as deeper understanding of symbolism and a depth of perception concerning the ancestry of the symbol or event will produce a wider vocabulary from which to create your work. You may wish to contact a local Native group or reservation and set up a time to visit and interview or discuss your chosen interest. You may wish to look for Native-designed websites or Native-authored texts and deepen your perspectives of the authors' visions and understanding. Whatever you do that shows a deeper capacity to listen will take some *sacrifice* on your part.

Now as you create your own poetry, drawing, or song, or make your own fry bread, so long as you say, "This is my interpretation" or "This is based upon (such and such)," there is a very strong chance that, if the members of the culture group were present, they would feel honored by your efforts. In the final analysis, the only real criterion for creating something based upon another person's culture is that the culture-bearers would feel honored and respected by what you do. In our experience, they always will if you've taken the time to listen deeply.

Unit III: Endnotes

3.0   The Santee-Yanktonai are also listed as "Sioux." As to the origin and meaning, the Chippewa and Ottawa referred to the Iroquois as Nadowe (adder or serpent). The diminutive of this term is Nadowessiwag. The French-Canadian abbreviation of this was termed "Sioux." (Densmore, 1918, p 1). "Lakota/Dakota/Nakota" is often used to make a self-reference in the native language. English, however, lacks such a term. Hence, while "Sioux" has a negative connotation and is problematic, it is often used by North American Indians when speaking English. In most references, the words Lakota/Dakota/Nakota are used instead of "Sioux." This convention is gradually becoming the preferred usage in academic and public circles" (Koen, *"Efficacy of Music-Prayer Dynamic in Healing and Health Maintenance,"* Ohio State University, 2000).

3.1   *Symbolism,* generally defined, is the investment of words/expressions with a representative meaning. In music, symbolism of "meaning" or intent is expressed using sounds with or without words, and words which are usually metaphoric or poetic to imply meaning.

3.2   *Intuition* is generally defined as the state of being aware of or knowing something without having to discover or perceive it … something known or believed without actual evidence for it. Some call it a "gut feeling"; others, spiritual perception.

3.3   For complete listings of "pow-wows" in your area, type in "pow-wow" on any search engine and look for sites created by Native councils and communities. A very good site is: www.powwows.com.

3.4   The *Grand Entry,* as the term suggests, is the first entry of the pow-wow dancers into any arena or pow-wow setting. The pow-wow begins by the Grand Entry. This entry was originally "a parade through the town the pow-wow was in. Even today in some pow-wows, these parades are still held. During the Grand Entry, everyone is asked to stand as the flags are brought into the arena. The flags carried generally include the US flag, tribal flags, POW flag, and eagle staffs of various tribes present." www.powwows.com, c. 2005

3.5   *Regalia:* In earlier generations, each Native American nation had distinct clothing and ceremonial dress. Native regalia today is similarly latent with symbols, colors, and patterns that address the individual's Nation and clan, plus many of the events or experiences unique to the individual. For more information, you may wish to visit www.native-languages.org, c. 2005, a Native site dedicated to the preservation of Native languages.

3.6   From the writings of Abdu'l-Baha, "Abdu'l-Baha in London," p. 103.

3.7   A simplified Lakota pronunciation guide: All vowels are "long" or "open" sounding, as in the Hawaiian language. C = "ch" sound; capitalized "N" = the nasal "n" sound; capitalized "S" = "sh" sound.

3.8   Musical production – that is, how a piece is recorded and "mixed" – can be accurately compared to the darkroom or digital processing of a picture. Once we take the picture (write the piece of music or record the sounds), we have only captured the bare skeleton of the art. When we "produce" the music, we have the capacity to alter each sound, just as we might completely reconstruct the picture. In production, we can emphasize some sounds, diminish others, and, in short, completely reconstruct what the listener will hear.

3.9   The "talking circle" is a translation of a Native community principle capsulated for this text. Although some communities may actually use, or call a circular community discourse, a talking circle, this is primarily a translation of a principle for the purpose of instituting a deeper listening mechanism in a group setting, not a "universally recognized" Native institution.

3.10   Sonographs for the following: (see next page)

Equador San Juanito:

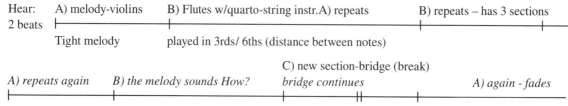

Hear:
2 beats

A) melody-violins   B) Flutes w/quarto-string instr.A) repeats   B) repeats – has 3 sections

Tight melody   played in 3rds/ 6ths (distance between notes)

A) repeats again   B) the melody sounds How?   C) new section-bridge (break)
bridge continues   *A) again - fades*

Rhythm sounds almost like a polka?

> *Narrative: If you got confused – or realized that many of the sections repeated the music – you might have begun to take notes in a narrative style (like taking notes at a lecture). This is where you can comment on the story, the emotion, relationship of what you hear to what you know, or the intuitive quality of the music and its potential symbolism. [Make sure you use "humility" qualifiers if you are guessing or are uncertain.]*

Sera: *Relaxed 2-beat (what you might clap) with accent "in between the beat" or on "off-beats"*

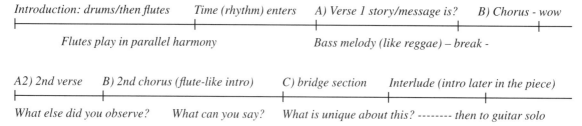

Introduction: drums/then flutes   Time (rhythm) enters   A) Verse 1 story/message is?   B) Chorus - wow

Flutes play in parallel harmony   Bass melody (like reggae) – break -

A2) 2nd verse   B) 2nd chorus (flute-like intro)   C) bridge section   Interlude (intro later in the piece)

What else did you observe?   What can you say?   What is unique about this? -------- then to guitar solo

We'll Be Here:

Intro: thunderstorm? Time: (rhythm/tempo – define: medium rock?)

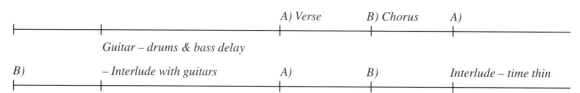

A) Verse   B) Chorus   A)

Guitar – drums & bass delay

B)   – Interlude with guitars   A)   B)   Interlude – time thin

> *Narrative: It's pretty hard to listen to a piece like this and not pay attention to both the lyrics and the guitar work. Whether or not we are interested in any piece—should have little bearing on our ability to hear its worth and value. In this case, the combination of the message—and the repetition of the chorus in short intervals—drives home the positive message: Native Americans (Seminole) will not be driven away by repression, weather, etc. The guitar lines, in this case, also show the closeness of the two brothers and their capacity to play so "tightly" (term for close synchronization of rhythmic movement) together.*

[3.11] Extracted from: *The Educator's Role in Cultural Healing and the Sacred Space of the World Music Classroom,* Léonie E. Naylor, L.L.P.C., Michael L. Naylor, Ph.D., 2007.

Note: It's not important that your sonograph matches that above. If you have musical experience, you would hopefully have a more detailed analysis . . . if not, you may have observed other things. The important focus in listening more deeply to music is that you keep your focus on the music, its sounds, and its stories and that you don't drift to your own experiences or thoughts exclusively.

Africa–America:
Tales and Visions of a Racial Legacy

UNIT

IV

Topics to Consider in Unit IV

➤ *What are some of the most "lethal" boundaries or barriers in our history and education? And – how did they develop?*

➤ *How did the perceptions of "nation" or "race" develop? And – how do they impede our collective progress?*

➤ *What are the legacies of human bias? How about "racial" biases specifically?*

➤ *How do biases develop? And – how do we overcome them?*

➤ *What are three windows by which we can understand racial history – and how it is expressed in music in the African Diaspora? (And – what is the "African Diaspora"?)*

➤ *What are the "blues," spirituals, capoeira, or calypso? And – how do musicians speak of their significance and value to us today?*

➤ *How might an accurate (unbiased) understanding of these genres in the context of American history, heal the biases and ingrained systems of institutionalized racial hierarchy in today's society?*

➤ *What are the relationships of Blues to Hip-Hop?*

➤ *What were the roles of "encoding" or signifying in the healing and reclamation of dignity in a racist culture system – such as those of the Americas?*

➤ *What are some of the similarities and differences of the PAN "African-American" or American experience (as seen through music)?*

➤ *What is "Carnival/Carnavale" and what does it mean to the people of Trinidad? What is the role or impact of the Calypsonian?*

UNIT IV

Africa–America:
Tales and Visions of a Racial Legacy

A Visit to the Land of THEM

All good people agree, and all good people say,
All nice people, like Us, are We, and everyone else is They;
But if you cross over the sea, instead of over the way,
You may end by (think of it!) looking on We, as only a sort of They!
Rudyard Kipling, 1970 [4.1]

"At the heart of the discussion of a strategy of social and economic development,
therefore, lies the issue of human rights. The shaping of such a strategy calls for
the promotion of human rights to be freed from the grip of the false dichotomies
that have so long held it hostage. Concern that each human being should enjoy
the freedom of thought and action conducive to his or her personal growth does
not justify devotion to the cult of individualism that so deeply corrupts many ar-
eas of contemporary life." The Prosperity of Humankind, 2000 [4.2]

Let's suppose the boundaries of humanity (political, national, or racial categories) are exactly the *bound-aries of human thought*. Not generally realities at all, but designations of human division, created and implemented by our ancestors. If this were so, then the designation of people by the categories of "Caucasian" or "black," "Asian" or "African," would need to be considered the *creation,* not the reality, of primitive ancestry. However ubiquitous, however entrenched in our education, our textbooks, and our media, each of these designations is still the invention without biological or scientific merit of human cultures and is not founded at all in the reality of the human condition. To develop a more accurate vision of human cultural realities, it becomes essential to simultaneously see and internalize the historical legacy of separatist thinking upon our current perceptions. This is not an easy task; it requires flexibility and fluidity of thought and contradicts the predisposition to **dualistic** (either/or) or **monolithic** (search for singular truth – viewed often as **empirical** or scientific) thinking that pervades many of our human traditions in education and communication.

As concerns music, the multiple methods by which cultures fuse, exchange, blend, and mix is essential to the perception of all music's validity and function. Yet, against a backdrop of centuries of training to see and believe in separation or of avoiding valuable and sustained contact with each other based upon these primitive paradigms, twenty-first century sojourners for truth or equity face a dilemma.

The false dichotomies in the perceptions of our history – from which the paradigms of our present were generated – are centered in the belief in and adherence to the structures of *nation* and *race*. This is … the "land of they." Understandably, before flight, telecommunications, and the World Wide Web, our collective ancestry could hardly fathom viewing history from a global perspective. But had the belief in such a ("they") *land* never existed, had race, nation, and separation of musical genres by these outmoded parameters not been our ancestry, how might we look at human cultures and music today? What vocabulary would we use to discuss our multicultural musical expressions – many of which are the result of numerous exchanges and fusions over centuries?

For now, if we can see that the evolution of our training is generally rooted in the constructs of human separation and racial/cultural division (even if we think this is still as it should be), then as this unit evolves, we will look to the development of alternative visions. Potentially, these alternatives will increase the accuracy of our perceptions, but most importantly, will help us see value in the music of cultures which have most battled these limitations and survived their smothering effects.

What perpetuates the myths of separation to the point that we become inept at seeing the forces of integration and cross-cultural exchange?

What is the mechanism (by which) "country music" is perceptually separated from "rhythm and blues?" or – European classical music seems so distant from rock 'n' roll?

Why is it a challenge (to see the "African" in the "Arabic" – and the "Arabic" in the "French"?)

Many scholarly works (in the last four decades) have pointed increasingly to the perpetual cross-influencing of cultures over the evolution of humanity, including the construction of more flexible (and thus) accurate ways to see cultures as fluid and perpetually changing phenomena.

To believe in culture or expressions (as being "pure") or even mostly distinct is a distortion of the truth … why might we remain essentially entrenched in our perceptions of "otherness"?

Pic. 4.0 *"Blind Blake" (born in 1893) was considered to be an accomplished guitarist, recorded over 80 known tracks, and performed both the blues (Delta-style) and "boogie" guitar (a style of music/rhythm known as "boogie woogie"). The guitar – based upon the Spanish guitar – and before that the Arabic "ud" – became the instrument of choice for many early blues musicians. And the music (the blues) would perpetually be fused with Caribbean, European, and multiple other musical styles as well. So – are either "Blind Blake" or his music "black?"* Photo: Author.

We can't hope to solve the problems that centuries of human wisdom have failed to solve. However, we may be able to make significant in-roads if we examine one single trait of the human condition that has played a role in every unjust, distorted, or exclusionary act of separatist thought over the course of our history: **human biases.**

The Legacy of "Culture Bias"

No one generation or century can be blamed for initiating the habit of separating human groups from each other under the guise of *otherness.* The annals of human discourse, from the Old Testament to the earliest stories of the Egyptians, Romans, Greeks, and throughout ancient China, India, and the Ottoman or Persian empires, are filled with references to other human groups as distinct *tribes, nations,* and, later, *races.* If you multiply this tendency over thousands of years, a few decades of attempting to create more fluid and accurate perceptions is not likely to make a significant dent in the entrenched vision of separatist beliefs. However, if we look at **biases** a bit more closely, we can learn to identify them in our own lives, try to understand their origin, and begin to seek information that will eradicate them. Especially those biases that may be harmful to our personal progress, the enhancement of our families and communities, and the appreciation of music outside the circle of our respect, may be worthy of examination.

Bias (noun): A perception or opinion for or against something that is unfair, partial, or based upon incomplete or inaccurate information.

We will spend little or no time on the biases that are positive or which do not have an exclusionary impact upon our perceptions. Unless a bias toward something demands an exclusion of something else, positive biases toward, say, *heavy metal, or Beethoven,* do not require adjustment. If you hear a new "metal" piece and you already enjoy the genre, you'll probably be interested in the piece. If you already love Beethoven and you hear either another piece by Beethoven or by someone influenced significantly by him, you will likely enjoy the new piece. No harm; no foul!

Pic. 4.1 *Whose vision is this anyway? Because "news" and documentary reporting may be perceived as factual and authoritative in nature, because images of other cultures or their music can be acquired entirely through movies or television programs, it becomes really difficult to know when we are getting an accurate picture and when we are getting an exclusionary or biased picture.* Photo: Courtesy of Sean Locke, 2005.

The *biases* we will address and which we encourage the reader to investigate are those deeply embedded into our perceptions, which induce us to see entire groups of humans as being other than they are or other than they see themselves. Many of these exclusionary biases are taught in our schools, are broadcast in our media, and entice us to devalue other human groups and, subsequently, their music as well.

How Do Biases Develop?

Biases of the negatively impactful variety have a few commonalities, no matter where they occur or how deeply they are imbedded in our belief systems. There are some distinct qualities and patterns to their development and to our challenges in dealing with them:

- *Few* among us will actually accept our own biases toward another culture group or music without some struggle. Initially, we may blame the bias on something we perceive to be distasteful or unpleasant. We may think that bias (and all of its synonyms: ignorance, prejudgment, prejudice) are signs of human weakness or failure, rather than being *universally human traits* often used to rationalize fear of the unknown. They may also have developed as the result of unpleasant experiences we've had. Regardless, biases usually develop over a long time, often over generations, and frequently are covertly masked by justifications.

- The most hidden biases are generally the most lethal, difficult to discover, and difficult to eliminate. Most hidden biases develop from misinformation we receive from trusted sources, i.e., family, schools, teachers (and textbooks), our larger culture, and media – particularly news and documentary media. Because many of these sources may be believed to be objective, the bias conveyed through them may go undetected well into adult life.

Pic. 4.1A *When television began in the U.S.A. to dominate the leisure time of families in the 1950s, it began also to create the images and information from which individuals would see the world around them. The time spent watching television vs. the time spent in traveling or conversing with people of diverse cultures ultimately equates to our information and files of the world around us.* Photo: Courtesy wikipedia.org.

At this point, recognition and deprogramming becomes extremely difficult.

- In all things, music included, biases usually develop from a lack of exposure to correct or valid (up-to-date) information; that is, we hear something once, not in its entirety, or from people or sources that express disrespect for the expression, culture, or idea, and we develop a sense of comfort with our justification that it is *bad, too this* or *that,* or not worthy of our time or further investigation.

How Do We Overcome Biases?

If we like country, rap, or "classical" music, our pleasure directly relates to the contacts and exposures we've had or to the correlative strategies and perceptions we've come to believe are respectable. If we dislike something (to the point that we will not seek to "respect" it), it's usually due to a lack of exposure, lack of knowledge, or an association with a single negative experience that has influenced our tastes and preferences.

In this unit, we will begin our work on overcoming biases by exploring a specific variety of bias: *racial bias*. We will try to determine how racial biases develop, are propagated, and ultimately, taught through expression of carefully worded or encoded denial. We will also look at the wealth of music that has been created out of, or in reaction to, racial bias, especially how the music itself seldom reflects the perceptual disease of separation by race. Rather, the creative nature of human cultures is attracted to and assimilates musical ideas, sounds, and inspirations without regard to distortions induced by racial perceptions.

Central to our learning to accept biases as universally existent in the human condition, and helping us to increase our motivation to recognize and ultimately do battle with their multiple dimensions and forms, is reminding ourselves that our growth and the growth of those in our care (especially children) is dependent upon our developing humility and accepting our own biases as part of the human condition. In this sense, recognition of a negative bias toward someone or something, though only one part of the equation, is a distinct sign of intelligence, not a weakness or an indication of a lack of wisdom.

Pic 4.2: *Although most of us prefer one fruit over another, few of us would say that the orange is "bad," or "too orange" if we prefer the apple. We'd simply say: "I like apples better," or "The orange is 'too acidic' for me." Therefore, we know how silly we'd sound if we implied that the "orange" had the problem. Yet, far too often, if we don't like a music (and usually have a problem with the people who make it as well), we will denounce the music as being "bad" or "too this or that," rather than recognizing that we are the ones who have the problem with the music based upon our experiences, and in some cases, our biases. We don't have to like the "fruit" or music to respect its existence and give it the chance we'd like others to give us!* Photo: Courtesy i-stockphoto.

The repair of entrenched biases requires that:

- We have courage to make a sustained effort to address or alter our biases. This is one aspect of the human condition in which the phrase "no pain, no gain" is most relevant. The more entrenched biases will require a prolonged investment of energy to "undo."

- We are motivated to do something about our biases. This is the toughest of all. What's in it for me? I'm so busy, I've got so much to do. Why should I be concerned? And the most common one: *"I just don't like that music (culture or people); everyone has their tastes."* One thing is certain: those who respect others with greatest sincerity are given the most respect by others in return. No one said we had to *like the music* or, for that matter, the people, but a casual dismissal by another group of humans of our culture or music would likely be offensive to us.

- We are willing to make adjustments in the expenditure of our energy and resources to accommodate this growth, recognizing it as an investment that will mature later. Foremost in Western societies, reversing the larger cultural emphasis on personal advancement or the assessment of one's success against material standards based on time efficacy will definitely require a reallocation of our energy toward re-education and creative exploration.

The more *educated* we see ourselves to be, or the greater our status and recognition in society, the greater might be the challenges or obstacles we may encounter in eliminating biased perceptions. The two greatest enemies of bias recognition are false pride and arrogance, for both lead to an inflated sense of self and to an unwillingness to locate the holes in our own knowledge or to fill them with the information that comes through **humility**.

Recognizing Biases Towards Music

We can start identifying our tendencies toward bias by consciously tagging the words and expressions we use to define music. We should try to recognize any word that might be disrespectful in any way to the "other" or the person who created or loves the music, as well as any terms that attempt to justify the bias and fortify the boundary. For instance, if you are someone who claims to enjoy *all kinds of music* [Reminder— to "like" or respect does not mean *tolerate* !], then probably you have already been exposed to a wider diversity of expressions, cultures, or people than many of those with whom you associate. However, this doesn't mean you are free of biases—an impossibility to be sure. It might mean, in fact, that you feel generally comfortable engaging a diversity of expressions; or it might be a strong indicator that, to you, listening to two or threes kinds of music when your friends or family listen to fewer is tantamount to enjoying *all kinds of music.*

In a literal sense, to like all kinds of music first assumes we have actually heard "all kinds of music." Secondly, it presumes that we truly like, or respect, them. Usually what is meant by "all kinds" is many kinds of music within our cultural system or in comparison to the tastes of our friends, family, or acquaintances. To others, "liking" may simply mean *"do not hate,"* or "do not have a strong negative bias." What is the effect of using a phrase such as this?

The phrase convinces us of our desire to be "open minded" and unbiased. It also shields us from the reality that, being human, we necessarily have biases. It may also insulate us from the need or desire to exert more extensive effort toward recognizing and eliminating our hidden biases.

We call phrases such as these **filtered** responses; that is, they are the result of an intricate system of *bias-disguises* that we first learn as children. Filtered responses or bias-disguises can only be stripped away when we remove most of the requirements to be politically correct or to be socially pressured by the culture that surrounds us. As we become comfortable exercising and exuding humility in our perceptions or language, we might re-work many of the comments we make. *"I try to listen to as many kinds of music as I can (or can get exposure to)"* replaces *liking all kinds of music*. In other instances, we will learn to recognize our distastes and judgments about music and later seek to understand the source of the biases' origins.

The words we use, if we examine them carefully, can give us extremely important information about ourselves, our education and experience, and, ultimately, our biases. Let's take a look at actual comments and situations gleaned from university-age students during a decade around the turn of the 21st century. The first group of comments was solicited from students as if they were in the company of their closest friends. Had we asked for their opinions of the music from the students' perspective, or had they assumed their comments would be read by their instructor, they would likely have been considerably more *filtered*.[4.3]

Stories from the Human Family

"I hate this. It sounds like a cheesy kung-fu movie. There is no beat, nothing really to listen to. I can't see why anyone would make something so harsh and so boring. This is pretty primitive stuff." (Musical example: short excerpt from a "Noh" drama/Japanese music/dance theater. Listener: 18-year-old American male, with stated preference for rock and hip-hop)

Commentary: If, upon hearing a song or seeing a dance, I say, "That's boring... cheesy... or primitive," I am using terms which, despite their original meaning, are not perceived by most of us in Western cultures as being positive. The use of such terms usually means, "I've categorized the expression quickly as being outside my tastes or *affinities;* now let me justify my bias by placing the blame on the music and move on to something I really like, something that's "good"!

An alternative way of speaking and, therefore, thinking is to say: "To *me,* the music seems a bit loud, harsh (whatever), but then I haven't had much contact with this style" or "I admit, I've never really liked it, because …" (and then state some reflection of your personal experiences). Then, either try to project how the music may be viewed by those who like it, *or simply ask the question,* "How do they (or does anyone who likes the music) relate to it?" Finally, if it is *acceptable* to speak so harshly about someone's music or culture around our friends, we may wish to re-think the quality of our friendships, for, in essence, we are solidifying our own *ignorance*[4.4] and maintaining the narrowness of the world in which we live.

The "tambourine" (in this case Brazillian) is an essential element to community music of multiple varieties.

"This is opera. I don't mind it; it's just too loud and I can't understand the story. I would prefer if they sang in English and didn't sing so loud." (Musical example: excerpt from a Verdi opera aria. Listener: 21-yr.-old American female with stated preference for R&B and gospel music)

Pic. 4.2A & B *Everywhere in the world, people's experiences and, subsequently, their tastes and values, are greatly influenced by media, commerce, and money. Whether a festival (4.2A Detroit Jazz Festival) or concert advertising (Prague, Czech. Rep.), what we see and hear around us, most often equates to what we will choose and ultimately like. To become aware of possibilities outside the scope of corporate or material influences and media-promotion takes considerable effort. The gains, however, usually match or exceed the effort invested.* Photo: Authors.

Commentary: Whenever we say "I don't mind it – but…," the "but" indicates a filtered response. We've stated how open we are, "but" then we immediately turn to the descriptors "too loud" or "too anything" to say the fault is with the music, rather than with limitations in our experience or appreciation skills. This is a classic example of how we disguise biases. We've tested especially the "too loud" aspect by playing numerous pieces at precisely the same volume: opera, heavy metal, hip-hop, country, and music of other cultures. When we don't like something, when the languages (musical and lyrical) that are used are *particularly foreign* to our ears, we hear the music as generally being "too – (something), and frequently – "too loud."

When we begin to question the music's context, that is, "What is this music used for? How did it come into existence and what purpose did it serve?" we move from passive tolerance or filtered biases to the active search for information and knowledge.

> *"That's country music. It's not my type of music. I suppose its OK for some people, but I'd never listen to it. The sound of their voices and whiney guitar – it's just not my thing."* (Musical example: 80s U.S. country piece. Listener: 22 year old, American male, with stated preference for punk and metal music)

Pic. 4.3 Photo Courtesy Jeff Jones, 2005.

Commentary: To place a musical piece in a category is not inherently negative, that is, until we have a bias for the category (see Unit V). Often, however, when we place the piece in a category, we are accepting our first impression, labeling the piece, filing it in a drawer we may seldom or never look into, and thus, feel we no longer have responsibility to investigate the piece on its own merit. Categorizing or, in this case, *stereotyping* (the more lethal variety of categorizing) reinforces our biases.

In this case, by saying, "It's not my type of music," or "I suppose it's 'OK' for some people," we are in essence patronizing (diminishing) the music and diplomatically filtering our bias. But the bias comes later, as we justify our comments by again placing the blame on the music: *"The voices and guitar are whiney."*

Finally, if every kind of music, food, or experience has to be our type, then we will remain locked in the very tiny world of our upbringing. This is deeply below the potential of our human capacity to interact with all the peoples of the world, to develop deep quality relationships, and to perpetually increase our knowledge until we reach the end of our lives.

Confronting Biases

Biases -- are a universal human dilemma, not unique to any culture group. Unfortunately, the simple desire to be "open-minded" or free of biases—especially towards perceptions of identity and expectations based upon race, nation, religious or gender stereotypes, and mis-education—is not sufficient to ridding ourselves of biases. Instead, we may wish to embark upon a consistent, life-long initiative to re-educate ourselves away from our ancestors' divisive world (based on the invention and maintenance of hierarchies and separatist beliefs) and to journey toward inclusive alternatives in our daily lives. This would include friendships and close community relationships with "other" groups that can assist us in avoiding the exclusion or marginalization of others.

If biases are perceptions or opinions that are acquired primarily from trusted sources (e.g., family, close friends, news media, education systems), then overcoming biases demands effort, courage, motivation, and a tactful approach to confrontation that seeks justice without intending to alienate or offend others.

Activity/Questions

- *Make a list of five of the strongest resentments or dislikes you have toward a culture, a group of people, race, nation, or, if you wish, a genre of music. For each, list the strength of the bias (on a scale of 1 to 10, with 10 being the strongest) and the likely source(s) of the bias.*
- *Now, in what "circular manner" (manner of multiple truths) might you better understand (and even defuse) your bias? How might you extend a less judgmental perspective to the source of the bias? What might you need to DO (e.g., allocate time or resources, or change your lifestyle)?*

"R.E.S.P.E.C.T." and the Human Condition

To be **respected** is perhaps one of a handful of universally relevant requirements in discussing the human condition. That is, every single individual on the planet, at some level, desires the dignity of being valued or *respected*, though naturally, everyone defines respect differently. For example, as concerns our right to listen to music, respect for one person may mean being able to listen to his/her music at any volume level; to another, at any time; to another, having the privacy to listen alone; to another, having the right or freedom to listen to any music, period; another, not listening at all; and to still another, having the space and ability to dance, sweat, and move to a point of achieving a state of intense religious trance. To feel that we are valued, that others see us, or that our lives have meaning, and that we are appreciated, is essential to the fulfillment of the human experience. To respect others in this manner is also the primary means by which we demonstrate our humanity or, in the worst-case scenario, by which we can disarm even the most intense forms of animosity and disrespect from others.

It is, of course, natural to gravitate toward people and expressions with whom/which we share **affinities.** However, the broader our experiences and our willingness to sample from other people, places, and things, the broader will be our *affinity-base* (experiences for which we've already perceived value and from which we can relate to new experiences reflecting some similarities). This doesn't mean we will always like the new experience or expression, but we will respectfully acknowledge it, possibly even to the satisfaction of the culture-bearers.

We *respect* others when we can either find value (appreciate) or acknowledge the essential *respect requirements or factors* on their terms. We may also see that we will be respected by these individuals in return. When others perceive that we have acknowledged an essential portion of their value, their ancestry, or their cultural expressiveness, they almost always return that respect with at least one important qualifier:

> **Depending upon the history that "our" culture group has with "theirs,"** there may need to be a proving period. Especially as we survey the holocausts that have been the outcome of the most severe and prolonged varieties of human bias, each of us may be called upon to make sacrifices on behalf of the ignorance of our ancestors.
>
> That is, depending upon where we fall across the boundaries of race, gender, religion, nationality, and all the other devices of human categorization used to perpetuate and prolong biased acts, we may need to take on a different role in the de-fusing and re-education of biases.

Two such human devastations were perpetuated by the close companions of *slavery and colonization*. These forces combined subsequently with the dominant Western-world emphasis on capitalism and cultural-centricity,[4,5] which both fanned the flame of biases and increased the depth and prolific creation of bias-filters, generating one of the most elaborate forms of bias known to humanity: that which resulted in the de-humanization and marginalization of others—based upon the creation and fortification of a myth of race, over a collective five centuries, affecting millions upon millions of individuals.

Analyzing the impact of racial biases and the filter mechanisms that disguise and obscure their presence would take much more than a single unit. However, there are some distinct cultures and their musical expressions that have been historically mis- or under-respected (or given less exposure). A closer examination of these cultures' musical expressions will give us perhaps a more accurate glimpse of racial history, as well as both the evolution of bias structures and the coping mechanisms by which individuals addressed and healed from these inhumane actions. Among such communities, we will look at the Americas' African-Diaspora cultures and their musical genres: work songs and field hollers, spirituals, the blues, reggae, calypso, capoeira, and hip-hop. Let's take a brief look into some of the ways that these genres created balance, educated, and healed, as well as communicated and reflected the biases and barriers instituted by a devastating racial/cultural myth.

Pic. 4.4 *Whatever the results of racial bias and categorization, we do not restrict ourselves to music based upon the racial myth, no matter the credence we give it. This younger Canadian musician tries to soak up the wisdom from an elder master of the blues, Freddie King.* Photo: Authors.

Understanding Racial Barriers and Biases: Music in the African Diaspora

> *"History, despite its wrenching pain, cannot be unlived, but if faced with courage, need not be lived again."* Maya Angelou

The primary focus of this section is for us to honestly and more fully understand the hidden messages, underlying currents, and tremendous educational potential latent in the African-American Disapora[4.6] through the evolution of its musical genres.

Cultures operate very much along the line of Newton's physical law: *"for every action there is an equal and opposite reaction."* That is, concerning racial biases, for every act that perpetuates a bias and re-inforces a stereotype or an unjust hierarchy within a culture, the subordinated culture will be forced to find a balance with their creativity and ingenuity with the same force and investment of that act. And so we ask ourselves, in what ways do repressed cultures find a balance, re-establish their dignity, or counter injustice?

The foundation of this text is viewing humanity through the window of the enormous creativity and depth of expression in music. Across the **African Diaspora,** music acted simultaneously as a means for assimilation (fusion), expressing the depth of despair or highest spiritual beliefs that could emote or counter and heal the impact of injustice, or as a literary tool for documenting and explaining conditions, or regaining control of the uncontrollable. Additionally, creativity born in the face of repression and spawned from a history of thousands of years of evolution in communication, harnessed the literary mechanisms of nonverbal or subtle verbosity and created layers of meaning that only those within or close to the repressed groups could accurately perceive. These educational, cultural, and ultimately musical/literary devices, born of the African-American experience, demonstrate a resilience, fortitude, and creativity that we will attempt to address through the following windows:

- **Assimilation and fusion:**[4.7] We will look at this phenomenon primarily through the *spirituals and work songs* of the North American Diaspora. We will see how the spiritual and emotional sophistication of the African cultures was creatively fused with the requirements of the dominant culture in the Americas, to spawn not only mechanisms of survival but of miraculous healing benefit to their communities. As a result, these creative expressions would later inspire or influence virtually all musical innovations globally since the close of the nineteenth century.

- **Honest communication:** The "soul" of virtually all African Diaspora music is first and foremost in the honest conveyance of feelings and thoughts. As with all challenges in life, holding pain, anger, or frustration internally, without a means for venting, is destructive. How much more so, when the injustice is completely without merit, of enormous proportions, and prolonged for centuries. We will look at this mechanism through the storytelling genres of the *blues* and the current manifestation of this principle in *hip-hop*. The blues has probably impacted nearly every popular music genre, provoking numerous exchanges across the perceived "color lines."

- **Signifying… or encoding:** When disrespect is so pervasive, dishonor so extensive, and the options for recourse so obscure, a culture will need to ceaselessly exert its energy towards the creation of counter-balancing tools which, on one hand, speak one message to the repressor, while communicating a completely different message to those within the repressed culture. This message, in essence, restores the balance and respect otherwise denied. Fortunately, for Africans brought to the Americas, the diversity of expressive modes they brought with them included numerous communication patterns built on deep networks of non-verbal or encoded mechanisms that had evolved over centuries. To look into the *signifying traditions* in African-American music, we will take a brief trip to Brazil and Trinidad to examine the genres of *capoeira* and *calypso*.

Virtually every African American musical genre prior to the development of music solely for the purpose of entertainment or commercial gain in the twentieth century was simultaneously a means of assimilation and fusion, communication and healing, and a means for the recovery of human dignity. Regardless of where on the continuum of "color" we are or consider ourselves, those of us whose larger cultural structures are the Americas, Europe, Africa, or cultures substantially influenced by these cultures, will have a direct connection to the themes and topics below. Others may need to reflect upon their own culture's system of cultural or racial hierarchy (as doubtlessly they have one), for to some degree the phenomena of action and re-action as concerns the separation and classification of human groups has imbedded itself into cultures in even the most remote parts of our planet.

Since the nature of human creativity is so far more complex and fluid than are the methodologies we use to discuss them, we can at best attempt to emphasize a couple of pertinent thoughts to facilitate the re-programming of perceptions influenced by a racially divided history:

1. **Racial harmony and an accurate understanding of history** (or sense of who "we" are) can be achieved only through an intense scrutiny of the racial disharmony and a full acknowledgement of the depth of its corrosion of our lives. The adage *"What's done is done"* is pertinent to bias structures only when they have been fully investigated, understood, and altered by methodical action. To *wish* that the issue of race would go away because we are tired of hearing about it is the greatest assault to those who daily experience racism's ramifications. To act upon its existence, then to root out every manifestation of its impact in our character, is by far a more dignified (albeit difficult) reaction.

Pic. 4.4A Photo: Courtesy of Steven Dern.

2. **No one is now—nor has ever been—white or black, red or yellow, Caucasian or Negro.** Neither do guilt, nor anger, nor resentments towards others based on race (however justified they may seem), benefit the overcoming of racial biases. It is natural to use the terms of color or race in discussion; after all, they are the product of centuries of evolution. Likewise, it is certainly important to feel our emotions, to understand that their recognition is essential to the bias-healing process, but they need not control our actions. Racial division is the means by which small groups of humans were able to gain material and psychological power over others. Since none of us were given the choice to choose our racial affiliation, identification of ourselves along these lines (again, however justifiable) gives added power to the myth, and strengthens its hold on our resources and actions. In like fashion, "blacks" dialoguing solely with "blacks, while "whites" dialogue with "whites" is the ultimate means by which the disease of racial separation strengthens its influence.

3. **If language, food, art, and music are all reflective of a culture's history and the people's values,** then the music of cultures of the African Diaspora must be reflective of the history of their collective struggles, pain, assimilation, communication, and the positive virtues born from these trials. This includes the long legacy of racial unity (races working together against injustice), which seldom if ever makes its way into our history books. The primary reason that many of us (arguably all of us) do not see the full impact of the history of race on our lives is that *history* in our educational systems is distorted by myths, half-truths, and stories passed on as "history." All of these contribute to the continuing development and maintenance of tightly woven bias-systems.

One very important means of encouragement to unravel or overcome racial biases requires simultaneously exploring the history of racial unity and interaction alongside that of injustice. Only when the races' and cultures' dialogue with each other and the intensity and duration of contact each culture has with the other matches the intensity and duration of their separation can the fullest measures of mutual respect and concern beyond myths be achieved. This generally should begin in our schools.

From: *Lies My Teacher Told Me* – by James Loewen[4.8]

- It is important that textbook authors might write history in such a way that students can feel good about themselves by feeling good about the past...but (this) imposes a burden that history cannot bear without becoming simple minded.

- While textbooks now show the horror of slavery and its impact on black America, they remain largely silent regarding the impact of slavery on white America....Without explaining its relevance to the present, extensive coverage of slavery is like extensive coverage of the Hawley-Smoot Tariff—just more facts for the hapless eleventh graders to memorize.

- No book can convey the depths of the black experience without including material from the oppressed group. Yet not one textbook (encourages) African-Americans to speak for themselves about the conditions they face(d).

- When textbooks make racism invisible in American history, they obstruct our already poor ability to see it in the present.

Assimilation and Fusion:
Perspectives on Spirituals and Gospel Music

"No culture in its totality is a commodity for export. This is why any people who, by any method, can cause another group to change its entire way of life, are building policy on a psychological unreality...culture is not a straitjacket... the restlessness of man, the creative drive of the gifted individual, the search for variety in experience, all of these assure us that man is not an automaton, nor ever has been, nor.... will ever be." Herskovits, Melville, "Cultural Relativism," 1972.[4.9]

Pic. 4.5 & 4.6 *To fully understand what we know, we must be willing to understand how we came to be. The slave ships that crossed the Atlantic and the holocaust of a past built upon the illusion of race and the supremacy one group assumed over another, however painful, helps the healing and revision of perception when properly explored. These two pictures are only a partial representation of conditions and circumstances met by early Africans in America. They also indicate the duress and pain under which spirituals, blues, and other earlier musical forms began their evolution.* Graphics: Clarkson, 1786 and Rednbacher, 1890.

Sig. 226. Sklaventransport in Afrika.

We know that **work songs** and **field hollers** were extensions of African traditions, a way of life that was carried across the ocean. In the Americas, the act of singing while laboring was clearly an indispensable part of sustaining the immense weight and injustice of slavery. Although there are more culture groups from throughout Africa involved in the slave trade than many first thought, the generality about Africans being disciplined workers who treat work almost in the spirit of "worship" (fulfillment of life's purpose), and would thus sing while working, seems to be more relevant than not.

The general perception is that these songs to relieve burdens were the means by which the **blues** would later evolve (songs to tell the truth of the moment). It is equally clear that they were initially one of the few means "allowed" by which Africans in America could express themselves openly (personal laments or early blues) or begin the process of encoding (field hollers) and thus were likely critical to all forms of African American music, including **spirituals.**

As to *spirituals,* in "Coming Home, the Black Spiritual" published by the African-American Registry (www.aaregistry.com), the authors allude to the fact that the simultaneous realities of **assimilation** (accommodation in this case of the dominant beliefs) and **fusion** (creating a blend of a culture's existing expressions with those of other cultures) is apparent:

"The Black spiritual developed by and large from white rural folk hymnody. (Blacks and Whites attended the same camp meetings and black performance style counter influenced the revival songs). Many Black spirituals resulted from the white folk music traditions and many others have melody analogues in white

American and British folk music. Black spirituals were sung not only in worship but also as work songs, and lyrics often reflect basic as well as spiritual labor." [4.11] McMickle, 2002.

Many discussions of early African-American history speak of Christianity as if it just appeared in and amongst the slaves. In truth, it was a combination of conscience, compassion, and arrogant coercion that brought Christianity by choice or force to African cultures. That is, the conscience of many European-American Christians led to dual goals to "save" the Africans and to demonstrate their humanity by increasing the African's understanding of Christianity. On the side of compassion:

"Slavery was an important issue facing Churches, as slaves were allowed to meet for Christian services. Some Christian ministers, such as J.D. Long, wrote against slavery. Rural slaves used to stay after the regular worship services, in churches or in plantations' "praise houses," for singing and dancing. But, slaveholders did not allow dancing and playing drums, as was usual in Africa." Therstrom, 1999. [4.12]

And as concerns the arrogance of coercion and the justification of slavery as "manifest destiny" justified by superficial religious connection: *"... as Europeans increasingly took over the lands and/or the resources of non-Europeans ... on behalf of "white Christian civilization," they increasingly saw themselves as the stewards of world civilization, placed on earth to elevate and guide the nonwhite masses."* Thomas, 1990. [4.13]

In many instances, this meant that slaves would be forcibly coerced to acquiesce to European cultural practices, Christianity or be punished. They also were generally not allowed to practice any of the religious or spiritual practices of their African heritage (with some variation throughout the Diaspora – see Unit VIII). But the creativity of their ancestry and human spirit would give rise to incredible solutions even in regard to forced assimilation.

As revival meetings were organized, especially in rural areas, slaves would transform the hymns and songs of their European counterparts initially into "corn ditties," "Dr. Watts," and later into *spiri-*

Pic. 4.7 *A map of the Underground Railroad, which was a means by which slaves and, later, servants, could seek their freedom at great peril. Though seldom a part of history lessons, the history of racial unity included the collaboration of "whites" and "blacks" in running and sustaining the Underground Railroad.* Image: Original source history.sandiego.edu/ copyrighted originally in 1895.

tuals. The spiritual, in essence, was not only a reflection of this assimilation of Christianity and the song and hymn forms of European-American churches but also a vibrant example of cultural fusion and exchange. The "African" community, now in America, was comprised of a huge variety of different linguistic/cultural communities (including East and South African slave populations in the Indian ocean captured by British, Spanish or French fleets and released in the Americas). Since the slaves were broken from their families, each group of slaves was immediately forced not only to assimilate the religious practices of their "enslavers" but also to creatively fuse languages and a multitude of other cultural expressions as well.

> *"Slavery in the New World, a veritable seething cauldron of cross-cultural contact, however, did serve to create a dynamic of exchange and revision among numerous previously isolated Black African cultures on a scale unprecedented in African history. Inadvertently, African slavery in the New World satisfied the preconditions for the emergence of a new African culture, a truly Pan-African culture fashioned as a colorful weave of linguistic, institutional, metaphysical, and formal threads."* Gaites, 1988.[4.14]

In most assimilations, even under the gravest of repressive systems, that which contributes to the survival or prosperity of repressed peoples is predicated in the roots of the cultures prior to the assimilation. In this case, in the majority of African religious practices, and certainly in

Pic. 4.8 *From the grave injustice of slavery continued to grow a resilience and capacity to adapt within the African (now African-American) community. Among the first manifestations of the power of music and dance to create "options" for upward mobility in spite of injustice were the successes of Black Minstrel or vaudeville performers. So universally appealing was their combination of humor, storytelling, singing, and dancing that, in no time, white performers began to paint their faces black ("blackface") and imitate their acts. Though, on one hand, this was one more stage of an equally long legacy of mis-appropriation (taking without credit) from the majority culture, it also is a clear demonstration of the cultures' perpetual exchanges despite separation. Photos: Courtesy Emmit, 1844, courtesy Hans Nathan, from Wikipedia.*

those of the Yoruba and Igbo of Nigeria, the following parallels of the existing African spiritual beliefs overlapped seamlessly with Christianity:

- The belief in an after-life. Expressed in terms of an "ancestral world" in most cases, the pervasive "Pan-African" belief in a world beyond matched closely that of Christian "heaven." Under the conditions of slavery, it became the "promised land."

- The "saints" and disciples who manifest particular qualities directly transferred to the deities of specific African topoi (traditional African themes). Similarly, themes of "fertility" (family and community), reconciliation, forgiveness, justice, and the numerous other topoi of Christian lore were creatively fused with African belief systems.

- And –singing as an essential means of worship, however different the style, would be transferred in the evolution of the spiritual and, later, African-American gospel traditions.

Although we have oversimplified one of the more incredibly creative cultural, religious, and musical developments in human history into a few paragraphs, we might also remember that these traditions' creativity did not end merely in their emergence as genres. The genres, their lyrics, and their practices were tightly linked, as is all music, with the lives of their authors. In this case, slave and later ex-slaves in servitude or in a cultural systems firmly engrained in racial separation, used music much like the "daily news" of the people—to communicate, heal, vent, and plot the inevitability of their freedom. Spirituals, therefore:

- Were a part of the "work song" tradition, elevating the spirits of the workers to the "world beyond."

- Were invested with numerous layers of meaning, including helping slaves find their way to freedom through the Underground Railroad by encoding instructions such as the famed "wade in the water" (walk in the water so that dogs could not smell your tracks), or the "chariots" (wagons or railway cars) that would denote the stations that slaves should look to for assistance.

- Would evolve to Gospel music traditions (many of which are still practiced today), would include movement, dancing, and even the fusion of trance ritual practices transplanted from Africa into the Christian milieu. The music of the religious portion of African-American life would also absorb the musical and cultural nuances of the non-religious life of the singer. In this sense, the separation of *church and state,* a seemingly distinct trait of European-American culture, had little in common with the needs and requirements of life for the African-American. Therefore, we would, until the present, see a perpetual cross-fusion of religious and "non-religious" musical traditions.

As spirituals evolved to the *gospel* traditions of the early to mid 20th century, and perhaps too, many free slaves now desired to distance themselves from many of the traditions that reminded them of slavery, the acts of assimilation and fusion—that is, the creativity of adapting cultural expressions to the dominant culture and its institutions—meant that spirituals would forever lose most of the nuances or style that had been practiced in slavery. What evolved instead, from African-American universities such as Fisk University in Nashville (Tennessee), were harmonized, composed, or arranged versions of music, generally sung in a Western "classical" (European-trained) style. Then as now, many African-American schools used the spiritual as a means of recalling or summarizing the past experiences of their ancestry, as well as in fund-raising and promotion for their schools to European or Euro-American audiences. On the other hand, most other European-American-founded schools use the Spiritual as a means of attempting to reconcile, acknowledge the past, or diversify the curriculum to, in part, recall the spirit and vibrant nature of these creative assimilations.

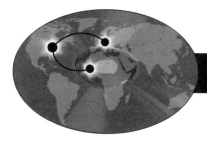

Inside the Musician's World

Augustus Hill
and the Brazeal Dennard Community Chorus

Note: Augustus Hill is a composer, conductor, and university educator. In addition to working with Brazeal Dennard, a renowned Detroit figure in spirituals, gospel, and European choral singing, he composes and conducts for a variety of ensembles. It is his vision of what can be learned through music, and in this case, spirituals that is particularly insightful. He commented to us:

Composer and chorale conductor Dr. Augustus Hill with students.

"We know there are many different kinds of spirituals: the black, white, even Appalachian white cultures, which by the way were also poor and had many of the same concerns of the black traditions. We know they evolved from the work songs, a means of getting through the day. The same songs used by the chain-gangs and prison workers.

"I think a lot of young students today don't see the connection of what those people went through so that they can be doing some of the things they are today. To many it's sort of 'Why should I be bothered with that/" But it is a rich tradition, and when the students sing the music, even here at the University, the audiences give such an enthusiastic response.

"But it's also important to tell the stories behind the music, so that it's not just all smiles or just about the music. There were enormous difficulties behind the music. For many, on an emotional level, this is a rude awakening … they have never really been exposed to the history in a personal and emotional context. If I could say a few things to students in general, I'd say:

"I think it's really important for them to get the information that is being presented. Then to really think for themselves, to understand and internalize the information— not for the grade, but for their lives. Then, to demonstrate that they heard by asking questions, being involved in their learning. That means to ask as well, 'Is this information coming from the source? Is it distorted or true?' Finally, and this is one of the main messages of the spiritual: to help each other out. To be involved in helping each other get through the class, any class, to concentrate on developing the community skills that help us feel connected and get through life. Oh yes, and to do this across the cultures.

"It's really important to stress, this music (Spirituals) is not just for or about African-Americans. Whatever traditions we come from, there is a connection to ancestry that encourages dialogue. I always say to my students: 'OK – bring something from your ancestry.' One student asked me: 'Why is most of the music we sing Christian music?' I commented: 'Well, that's what those composers wrote.' That is, both the European and the African-American were heavily influenced by their religion or wrote music based on their beliefs. But what the University is supposed to be about is expanding to meet all traditions and giving the students connection to the 'real' world they live in." Interview, March, 2006

CD 1.11

"Oh Freedom," conducted by Dr. Augustus Hill with the Brazeal Dennard Community Chorus from the CD: <u>**Spring Concert, 2003,**</u> c. 2003.

Dr. Hill commented: *"We know when the slaves came over from Africa, they were able to use their 'tonal or pitched' languages to send messages and communicate through the drums. When the slave-masters figured this out, of course, they took the drums away. Being able to send these messages in the voice, encoding the messages in the spirituals – 'crossing over into Jordan'— would tell them where the meeting was going to be, when the underground railroad would be leaving, when the plantation overseer was coming down the way – the musical tradition, and even the quilting tradition, being able to sew symbols and messages into the quilts to instruct runaways – this is all part of the tradition of communication.*

"When I think about it, the younger folks today are extremely creative in what they do today. The question is the focus: is it negative, or positive? In my mind, the focus determines the greatness of what they do. The question is to many of them, what is the financial gain? Success today is based so much more on material things, which does not necessarily connect the youth to the integrity of our ancestor's legacies, whereas before the focus then was on freedom and community. This piece, 'Oh Freedom,' was given rebirth during the Civil Rights movement. It speaks entirely about freedom – physical and spiritual.

> *Oh Freedom – Oh Freedom over me*
> *And before I'll be a slave, I'll be buried in my grave*
> *And go home to my Lord and be free*
> Later on – *No more moaning – No more moaning over me*
> *There will be singing – there will be singing over me*
> *There will be shouting – there will be shouting over me*

"The message today: if we sing, if we shout, if we live life with the understanding of the purpose beyond our physical condition, we cannot be slaves obsessed with grades, money, and things that really don't really bring enjoyment or purpose to life. For students, it really takes a while to get them out of their individualistic focus – to talk, to think, and to work together. I try to tell students, you never know which one of your classmates may be in a position to help you in the future. So the spiritual becomes a tool in 'today's' form to teach these messages."

The Recipe of Sound

If you listen carefully, you will still hear the remnant of the "lining out" style of early African-American congregational call-and-response-style singing. That would include one person calling out the lyrics or setting up the melody and the congregation following or responding to the call. The lyrical style of this piece is based upon this formula. (Note: This is one more graphic representation of how African traditions [call & response] lined up with European traditions [mass style of priest and congregational response].

Call: "Oh Freedom" or "No more moaning" or "There will be singing/shouting" etc.
Response: repeat – "Oh Freedom – Oh Freedom over me"
Known congregational repetition:
"And before I'll be a slave, I'll be buried in my grave," etc.

What is also evident is that this recording (and most recordings we can find of spirituals today) is sung, arranged, conducted, and ultimately performed within the choral tradition of Western European choruses.

Interestingly, the formula for singing spirituals in this manner was solidified during the Harlem Renaissance (1920's) and the move to "legitimize" African-American music, poetry, and art in the culture at large. "It was an evidence of a renewed race-spirit that consciously and proudly sets itself apart" (Alain Locke). But, in so doing, made the use of "black" dialect increasingly taboo, and "legitimized" the music by setting it in the more "classical" style of European harmonization and arrangement.

How Racism & Culture-Bias FEELS

Léonie's Experiences

The group of islands I come from is like much of the world today, composed of a wide diversity of cultures. However, in our case, we evolved over the last two centuries thousands of miles from other cultures, and, to a large extent, beyond the radar of colonists' intervention and attachment to our affairs for economic or political gain. As a result, the close island day-to-day life proximity of people of different "races" and cultural backgrounds helped us forge a unique "Creole whole" from the parts. Among the results:

- The culture is, for the most part, colorblind. For example, if a person commits an offense or achieves an honor, whether he/she is white, black, Chinese, Indian or any other racial mixture, he/she would be identified by name or family rather than by race, appearance, or "former" nationality (Italian-American, Indian, Black, or White);

- Family and community-life have maintained their importance to a large degree over individual accomplishment, and, most families are ethnically mixed.

I brought these preconceived ideas of identity with me to the United States. As an outsider, I was shocked to see that most of my values and beliefs did not match the perceptions in this country. I noticed that being classified as a "non-white" individual was reason enough for me to be treated differently at times. One of the examples that I have experienced rather frequently in my years, would be witnessing some of the Caucasian waiters/waitresses struggling to avoid eye contact with me as they ask my "white" husband what I wanted to eat instead of addressing me directly. At times, I have also encountered both white and non-white individuals voicing their strong disappointment in me for marrying "outside my race." While on occasions my unfamiliar accent and my "third world Island mentality" are seen as being exotic and beautiful, they are strange and primitive to others. I further noticed that mistakes, stereotypes, and misrepresentations loaded into the minds of many were often used as weapons to maintain an aura of superiority or to overemphasize typically "human" shortcomings.

In addition to being unfathomable, it was rather hurtful and confusing receiving those conflicting treatments and messages. It has been especially difficult whenever someone judged my worth or spoke of me based on their perceptions of what my culture must be like and what my accent represented, often, without having the slightest inclination that their labels or thought processes may be incorrect, corrupted, and biased.

During my twenty-five years in the United States, I have adapted to the American values that I find positive and have balanced them with the virtues of my homeland. I have been repeatedly shocked at the degree by which labeling others by race or color still manifests itself in the schools and public arenas (stores, governmental offices, businesses, etc.). These very "active" and grossly neglected "biases" that continue to cause great harm to many might have devastated my confidence, my self-worth, or, later, that of my child.

Fortunately for me, however, I was raised to know— and to "feel"—alternatives. I was instructed by my parents to let no one infringe upon my human dignity. But it must be clear: when an infringement on human justice, decency, dignity, and well-being occurs, it takes enormous energy, hurts beyond most hurts we may have known, and demands the exertion of much of our life's energy to rise above the emotional damage and to avoid its impact on creating addictions, disorders, and personal or community imbalances

Questions

- *What is your first reaction when you read the excerpt above regarding racism and other forms of prejudice many people still face today? Have you personally experienced such prejudice? If so, how did you handle it?*

- *Can you place yourself in the position of the "opposite" group in your culture's racist hierarchy? In what manner would your own development be thwarted by the disease?*

- *Can you identify a few instances wherein others have expressed their racism to you or around you? How might you effectively voice your feelings or confront racism in each instance?*

Pic. 4.9 and 4.9A *The messages in most history books is that "slaves" were, to a degree, passive objects of injustice. The integrity of African communities, the resilience of their peoples, and the transference of these qualities to the severest injustices sustained over three (plus) centuries cannot, however, be construed as anything short of magnificent in the annals of human historical accomplishments.* Photos: Detroit, Authors.

Communication from the Heart: Blues to Hip-Hop

> *"I had aimed to use all that is characteristic of the Negro from Africa to Alabama. By the time I had done all this heavy thinking and remembering, I figured it was time to get something down … so I wrote, 'I hate to see de evenin' sun go down,' and if you ever had to sleep on the cobbles down by the river in St. Louis, you'll understand that complaint. The song was off my chest, and secretly I was pleased with it, but I could scarcely wait for the public verdict."* W.C. Handy, *Father of the Blues,* c.1941 Collier.

Arguably the single most influential style of music on the evolution of today's popular music globally is that of the **blues.** Its influence can be heard in nearly every style of American music from rock 'n' roll to George Gershwin. And as global exchange through the influence of modern media would have it, the influence of *blues* and its modern-day descendant, "hip-hop," can be heard today in every corner of the world. The question we need to ask is why? What is it about the blues that has made it the backbone of nearly all country, rock, rhythm and blues, hip-hop, and jazz music in whatever form or language they may appear? The answer lies in its capacity for communicating honestly the moment's news, thoughts, or feelings.

   Neither blues nor hip-hop began, of course, in the United States. The ancient traditions of storytelling from the truth or events of the moment extend far back into the history of African cultures. The **griot** (pronounced: Gri – oh) or *Jali (djaly)* of Mali and the Western coast of Africa would tell stories about a family's heritage, what occurred that day, and improvise lyrics based upon the need of the moment (see Unit VIII). In the Americas, the tradition of storytelling, or what the beloved rhythm and blues artist B.B.

King calls "stories about the truth" became an essential companion to spirituals or gospel music. The latter was community-based music designed to bring the spirits of the community to a higher plane; the former became an essential vehicle for venting, musical competition, creating stories to cry over, laugh with, and even to turn the tables on the repressor. Unlike the overly simplistic adage that *"blues is about sadness,"* the blues were really about truth. Although truth in a racially divided society and especially for those forced to lobby for respect would frequently be sad, truth could also be anything the artist experienced: a loss of love, a finding of love, a bad day, a new child, and even—as the case frequently was—a tribute to Jesus or a venue for preaching the "good word."

As with all musical genres, the evolution of the "blues" is the result of multiple fusions of many styles and musical/cultural influences along the way. Each new manifestation (from early work and field songs, to rural blues, to Delta blues, to rhythm and blues) was influenced by the changes in culture, technology, instruments, and, in the case of the blues, the evolving dynamics of racial America over time. So in context and mode of delivery as well, the blues extended from the work songs to the porches of slave huts and shanties, to more rhythmic versions performed in clubs and speakeasies, and eventually to clubs and concert halls in Northern cities and, still later, around the world.

Pic. 4.10 *The blues evolved from ancient African traditions of storytelling and were not, as such, meant to be "written." Yet, as musicians such as W.C. Handy increasingly adapted European instrumentation and song and hymn forms to the blues and jazz, the blues would become a staple of larger ensembles.* Photo: Courtesy Wikipedia.org.

Most stages in the evolution of the blues would share a few commonalities:

- The musicians put the primary focus on the story (the truth) and used whatever instrument available in their era to accompany the story. (Early instruments, such as the Diddly-bow, resembled the one-string hunting bow instruments of West Africa or Berimbau of Brazil).

- The form (structure) of the blues evolved through a series of stages until it became solidified over time into the set formats of Delta, rhythm and blues or Chicago-style blues most commonly performed today. Resembling the call-and-response formats of work songs and early spirituals, the blues evolved into a format in which each verse had three phrases, regulated into either a 12-measure or 16-measure format (12 or 16 times 4 beats):

Phrase one: "this is what I'm thinking today"

Phrase two repeats phrase one: I said, "this is what I'm thinking today" [which also gives the "poet" time to think about the reply]

Phrase three is the consequence or reply: "Because this is what happened that made me feel this way"

In time, however, as recording technology made records available to the masses, blues artists were recorded on "race labels" (labels geared to appeal to African-American audiences) and played in "juke joints" or blues clubs, which sprang up in the South, and the blues became an important outlet for field workers, share croppers, and house servants not only during their work but also during their time off. Since social services were seldom available for blind or disabled African-Americans, playing the blues became a favorite outlet for the blind man who could not work. Parallel to the lives of the Vaudeville performers of mid to late 1800s, African-American blues musicians were eventually able to use their music as an alternative to earn respect and money as well. Of note is, as the influence of the blues grew and the music moved from private porches to the "juke joints" and clubs, associations of the blues (and later jazz) with exclusively non-spiritual environments frequently caused a split within the African-American community, one that leaves its legacy to the present day. The divide between the music of the church (soul) and the music of the heart & body (what occurs in life) meant to some that the blues would be stigmatized as the "Devil's music" by some church-goers. This historically ancient divide between sacred and secular would at times separate the African-American community, though never really the cross-exchange of the music.

As World War I, the industrial revolution, and World War II enticed thousands of African-Americans to northern industrial cities to seek a better life, "juke joints" gave way to Blues clubs, and the amplification and orchestration of the single man or women storyteller, the American griot, gave way to the evolution of **rhythm and blues.**

The majority of blues heard today is *rhythm and blues,* or what some call **"Chicago-style Blues"** (as Chicago became a major center for blues artists in the North). In truth, the over-simplistic versions of evolution (including the one above) do not do justice to the complexity and multicultural nature of the blues, which despite its origin as a voice of honesty through suffering and hardship, has become an anthem for the universal human condition of change over time:

- How the blues was performed and how it was perceived has evolved and changed over time. In the early years, many blues musicians were blind, handicapped, or incapacitated physically. These musicians would express their personal conditions and experiences. Over time the genre evolved and placed a greater emphasis on the showmanship and technical mastery of the musicians. As the rift between church and blues widened, some blues artists did not even want to be called "blues musicians" but simply "musicians" to avoid the stereotype of Blues as being non-spiritual and Blues artists as less capable. This is evidenced by the following quote from Gatemouth Brown:

> *"I'm not a blues player; I'm a musician. But all blues players, when they play, their mind is on their work, it's what they need ... not what you need. When I walk on the bandstand, I'm giving myself to all of my kids. You are too my kids – all of you. I have no color barrier and the message I have to give will hopefully help them."* [4.15]

Pic. 4.11 *"Little Freddie King" seems almost dwarfed by the immensity of the stage at the Montreal Jazz Festival. But make no mistake about it, blues in general is not "little" in stature. It is among the most influential genres or styles of music on the face of the planet – influencing nearly every American style and much of the popular music of the world since the late 1800's.* Photo: Authors.

- Despite the origins of the blues in the African-American community and the necessity not to trivialize the hardships through which the blues as a genre was born, the fact that some African-Americans mixed with Native American cultures, that all blues artists associated with and eventually often played with European-Americans or Europeans, and that blues eventually became enormously popular in Europe (evidenced by the music of the Beatles, Rolling Stones, and Eric Clapton) and later behind the iron curtain (in Russia and Poland), meant that blues had become an invaluable tool in expressing the human condition. Unfortunately, the fact that many blues (and later jazz) musicians were given more respect and appreciation abroad than in their homeland speaks to the blinding nature of racial perceptions. As to the diversity of ways by which blues (and subsequent blues-based genres such as hip-hop) continue to occupy an international status in portraying the now greatly admired human qualities of endurance, patience over hardships, and intense creativity through hardships of the African-American experience, blues artist Lowell Fulson commented:

> *"I've been to Sweden and Switzerland, Japan, Brussels, Germany, the Scandinavian countries. They know who you are and they know what you are singing about. You talk about screamin', boy. Them people study their book about that music, and them singers, entertainers, they know who they're gettin'. And they might not know the words, but the way you deliver the melody."* [4.16]

The role the blues played as an essential form of release from deep within the heart of the African-American storyteller must first be acknowledged and respected. For without this acknowledgement, again, the accomplishments and adversity of the early blues artists is, to an extent, trivialized. The Blues genre is not primarily about the chords or sound—but its history. Yet, perhaps the greatest legacy of the blues is found in the creativity of blues musicians today—and in the fact that they may be playing blues with increasing passion in Europe, Japan, a Native American reservation, and the blues artist may be Jewish, female, Polish, or Chinese. So although the experiences of blues musicians today are drawn from all races and walks of life, today's blues probably should not be compared to that of the African-American from past generations. Instead we might see blues today as an accessible vehicle for the honest communication of feelings and experiences that find validity in the commonality of the human experience.

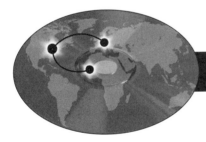

Inside the Musician's World

Robert Penn

Note: Detroit blues artist Robert Penn was animated and straightforward in telling us his experiences as a "bluesman" of nearly four decades. He commented: *"Blues was simple, in earlier days, it was the simplest way to take their ideas, circumstances, their moods or what was going on in their life… the music is simple and the message is simple. You know this music actually had its origins in Africa. The musicians were not "trained" musicians, they created straight from the heart… no theoretical mish-mash, he goes straight to it. Blues musicians knew that you'd be able to relate to the story, because even if you hadn't dealt with what they were singing, you would one day.*

"I want to emphasize that slavery was a holocaust. We as human beings have both spiritual and physical, mental or emotional needs and concerns. As humans the Gospel gave us the hope of a better life and a way out of the holocaust we were facing. That God would give us relief… "Swing low Sweet Chariot – comin' for to carry me home," whereas Blues went right at the situation and was a way of communicating human thoughts and feelings— " I don't like this," "She treated me this way and I don't like it,", or "She's so sweet / I feel so good around her." That's the Blues … not everything in our life is religious.

"Keep in mind as well, many people that liked Gospel music and condemned the Blues did not understand that to sing the Blues didn't mean you weren't spiritual, but that you were just honest about your feelings and about your "humanness." There were a whole bunch of Blues that even talked about spiritual things too. Blues is from the human spirit, and the spirit is not always happy either. I think that music comes from God – the Irish had Celtic music, every culture has its own music unique to them, a way of telling their stories and expressing their lives. Music doesn't belong to us.

"You know, I got to say, racism is a part of our life still, we've just been putting band-aids on it. We cannot turn our back on our history if we want to heal it. Just last week an event occurred to honor Black music in Detroit, but only a few black musicians were called to play. The club owners are white now, and the ideas may come from the Black man – but the resources and business still lie in the hands of others. You know, we're all getting away from some of the values of the past, the old values. Now in the Hip-Hop age, no one knows about the Blues. It's like we don't want to be reminded of our past … a type of amnesia."

CD 1.12

"Son, Sing the Blues," by Robert Penn, from the CD: <u>**Live and Mighty,**</u> c. 2004, Kimi Records.

"My uncles both played music. Uncle Bill was a cowboy, he wore a hat and the whole thing. I remember one night they'd had maybe a few drinks, and they had left the guitar in our house. I remember getting up on Saturday morning, and a voice said "look to your left." There was the guitar, and I said, "This was it." Well, I called him, and he said, "Boy, you can keep it." Well, I started playing – but everything except the Blues.

"There's a song on this CD called "Mama said, 'son … sing the blues." It's not really a low-down blues. But it's based on advice my mother gave me. You see, my mother and I were separated for years … from 7 to 14 years old, I didn't see my mother. I saw her only once until I was 24 years old. I went back to California, where I was born. You see, my mother had moved out there from Mississippi in the 1940's because they were trying to escape racism. Anyway, I used to love the Temptations and funk music; I didn't do the Blues. But my mother was pure Blues. One day I was on the phone talking to her about my band. She said, "Boy, you ought to sing the Blues, people will love it." Well, over time, that's exactly what I did. Mama had to work so hard her whole life, I think the Blues grew on me. Unfortunately, Mama died before I could get rich or buy her the home I always wanted to buy for her. But I thank her for getting me back to the Blues. Hey, ya gotta listen to the elders." R.Penn Interview, June, 2005.

Pic. 4.12A *The 1963 March on Washington D.C. of thousands of "blacks," "whites," and others is perhaps best known for Martin Luther King, Jr.'s "I Have a Dream," speech. However, it should also be known as one of many ventures in which courageous African-Americans worked with those of other races to move an immovable system towards equity. Today, thousands of "African-American" families still pay the price within their families and communities of the psychological and emotional pain of seeking human dignity and equitable respect within the system plagued by institutionalized racism.* Photo: W. Leffler, Library of Congress.

The Recipe of Sound

There are standard forms or formats for the blues. Most blues are 12 **measures** (*measures are cycles of beats – usually four beats per cycle*) or 16 measures. The standard formula for blues was based on its importance as a means for telling the "truth of the moment" (see the form above). This piece has the form unique to most standard blues songs.

Once the singing begins, there are four sections of four measures each. Over this section the story is essentially told over a steady and repetitive rhythm. The "chorus" of this piece (the section that contains the "hook," or song title) contains also a melodic line that is performed by guitar and bass in unison (playing the same notes in **octaves**).

The meter of this rhythm is what is called 12/8, or 4 beats per measure with three divisions (*sub-divisions*) per beat. This is one of the standard meters for blues, rhythm and blues, and earlier rock 'n' roll.

Passing It On –

Although we will talk about the difference between *respectful borrowing* (**appropriation** [4.16a]) and *stealing* (**misappropriation:** taking something without paying respect to the source) again in Unit X, there are so many instances where the blues has found its way into the hands of others as a perfect vehicle for the expression of *their truth*. Following are two examples: 1) a piece written by mixed Native American singer and songwriter Joe Reilly ("Pow-Wow Blues"), and 2) a piece by Jewish guitarist Shari Kane. What will become clear is that once a people dedicate themselves to the art of *truth* in storytelling and have respect for the ancestry of blues—race, gender, religion, or ethnicity have little to do with the impact of the music.

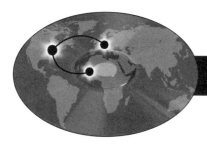

Inside the Musician's World

Joe Reilly / Shari Kane
(with Madcat Ruth)

Note: When someone from one culture learns the music of the another, how should they represent the music? How should they demonstrate the respect for the culture from whom they learned?

These are the questions we ask especially when we are borrowing or learning from a culture that has been significantly mistreated or misappropriated historically.

The following two pieces by a Native American (mixed) and Jewish (female) artist respectfully, demonstrate both the respect the musicians have for the music (blues) and culture (African-American), and the fact that when both those conditions are true, the labels we just used to define these two artists become – for the most part – *irrelevant.*

CD 1.13 – Part 1

"Pow-Wow Blues," by Joe Reilly, from the CD: **Mothers and Daughters,** c. 2001, Semper Records, www.joereilly.org.

> Joe Reilly wrote us: *"Understanding music as an expression of spirit, I write, sing, and perform in order to celebrate life and allow the spirit of God, and my ancestors to sing through me and touch listeners. I believe that music is a universal language that speaks from all that is sacred and mystical, voicing the spirit of God and creation through breath, rhythm, and melody. I have inherited music as a gift from my parents and actively nurture its development through study, practice, performance, life experience, and community building.*
>
> *"I've been inspired by folk, blues, classical, jazz, Native American, and liturgical music, I strive to create a sound that speaks to the soul of humanity and strengthens those voices inside all people that cry for justice, peace, and health.*
>
> *"As a Cherokee, Italian, and Irish American, much of my work as a musician directly reaches out to Native American and multicultural communities, social change activists, high school and college students, elders, and youth. In order to help build vibrant, inclusive communities, I also perform in venues as diverse and accessible as community centers, living rooms, coffee shops, community festivals, bars, bookstores, clubs, theatres, conferences, schools, and college campuses.*

"'Pow-Wow Love Blues' uses humor and real life experience from traveling the Pow-wow trail to highlight my romantic tendencies of falling in love with beautiful women. There are many beautiful dancers at Pow-wows, and they provide good opportunities to meet new people, enjoy food, share songs, and have fun. This song is a play on the social reality of Pow-wow culture: love, song, and, oh yes … frybread."

"I humbly offer these songs from my heart to the world like a gentle spring thunder shower, watering seeds of compassion, hope, love, understanding, healing, courage, laughter, freedom, clarity, and reconciliation in the hearts of those who choose to listen. I am grateful for all who have watered those seeds within me and who have encouraged me to take risks and share my gifts in open and honest ways." J. Reilly interview, September, 2004.

Pic. 4.14 *The injustice of "racial" vision is not only its effect on those that are its victims, but especially on those that are its perpetrators. It blinds their vision to human reality. In this case, thousands of "black Indians," the beautiful product of mixing and exchange beyond perceived limitations of the myth of race are left out of our vision and history books, primarily because they cannot be classified within the confines of a "single" race.* Photo: Bismark Indian School, Library of Congress.

"You Used to Call Me Mama," by Shari Kane, from the CD: **Madcat and Kane: Up against the Wall,** c. 2004, Hit Records.

Ms. Kane writes: *"In my experience I don't focus on the relationship between being female, or Jewish, to being a blues-woman; except that all of that falls within the realm of being 'human.' What I really feel about the blues, is that it captures human emotion, without regard to sex or race. And even though it was born out of a certain culture, it was about the people of the world, not just the people of Mississippi. However we came to be humans, we ended up with strong emotion, and a need to let that strong emotion out of us. To me, the blues is a perfect vehicle for that emotion, regardless of what the driver looks like. And so, as a person with strong emotion, I was drawn to the immediacy of the blues.*

"I was also strongly drawn to the rhythms, chord structures and the progressions of the blues. Its rhythms felt like home to me. Like breathing. And I felt a sister/brothership with the others I met in the many countries I traveled to. I remember getting on a festival stage in Poland, you know, at the end of a show when all the musicians get together for the finale, except all these guys only spoke Polish. Because the chord progressions of the blues are universal, all I had to do was look at the bass player to find the key, listen to the groove, and I was set. I remember thinking, I can't even talk to these guys, but I can play music with them.

"I also love the tradition of the blues. In so many genres there is a strong value of coming out with something 'new,' something that hasn't been done or said before. In the blues, there is a strong love for going back and getting deep into the tradition of a certain time period. I wrote 'You Used to Call Me Mama' as a tip of the hat to Magic Sam, and the Southside Chicago guitar players of the late fifties and

sixties. The lyrics were secondary; I just told a story about something that had happened to me, but the thing that I was really trying to communicate was 'Remember Magic Sam? Doesn't this groove thing in the middle just knock you out? I still remember the first time I heard it, and tried to figure out how he got all of that out of one guitar. And so on...'!" S.Kane interview, April, 2005.

Hip-Hop: Today's Voice of "Truth"

"Rap is more than music or entertainment. The words rhythmically recited, chanted, or sung over music represent a new sense of identity and belonging for young people in America—and throughout the world. Rap is the voice of a population that has been ignored by (the) mainstream ... It is a culture. The creation of young African Americans, rap reaches far beyond America's inner cities. Its booming bass and many voices resound on every continent. Rap represents the pulse – thoughts, values, and experiences – of youth worldwide." K. Maurice Jones, from Say It Loud!, 1990, Millbrook Press

"It didn't start out as black culture, either, because Hip-Hop has always been its own culture. Let me say that again, just in case you didn't catch that. Hip-Hop has always been its own culture. Not all of the fathers and godfathers of Hip-Hop were African-American. The original breakers were black and Hispanic. The first graff writer, Taki, was Greek. Speaking of graff, Seen isn't black. I could go on and on, but it would be quite long and boring, so I'll just stop here with my point that Hip Hop was composed of different races, different ethnic groups, different styles, and different cultures. Hip-Hop still is composed of all these things, as well as different age groups, different nationalities, and straight-up different people." NyceStylez

We might look at **hip-hop** as the embodiment of *fusion* or the modern-day blues or voice of *truth* heading into the 21st century. To appreciate *hip-hop,* some hip-hop artists feel that we must separate the music that is solely produced for commercial gain, or what many now call "rap" (music for "party/dance" only, or has violent or obscene lyrics solely for sensationalism and does not address a valid point, a problem, dilemma, or a significant social/cultural condition) from hip-hop as an expression or voice of a culture.

We can look at the history of hip-hop as being the latest in the ancient tradition of rhymed oration – extending from the African storytellers and griots across the ocean into the early formation of the "black" communities and the earliest orators and storytellers in their "new world."

Pic. 4.14A Hip-hop – from an ancient tradition of African storytelling to rhythm, to Caribbean rhymed recitation to a beat, to Brazilian Capoeira dance, graffiti art, the urban blues of the late 20th century—is also the pulse of racial and cultural progress and regress in much of the world. Photo: Vector Art, courtesy of Stephen Green.

As with any music that points to truths and dilemmas that many in a society would prefer to ignore (such as the continued impact and consequences of *racial categorization* and its economic, political, and human consequences), hip-hop requires of the listener, and especially the listener from another generation or culture group, the consideration of the following:

- That the genre can be a profound form of performance literature. The recitation of text in complicated rhyme schemes requires the rhythm of a percussionist, the lyric and melodic conceptualization of a singer, and the vocabulary mastery of a poet.

- Profanity, though sometimes a part of hip-hop, in the most artistic of hip-hop music is not as prevalent and when it does exist is generally not to be interpreted or understood in the same manner by those who use it as by those standing outside the culture. Though some hip-hop (Rap) will use profanity and obscenities solely for sensationalism and commercial gain, the most respected hip-hop artists historically (Run DMC, Public Enemy, TuPac Shakur, Jay-Z, etc.), are sophisticated artists with exceptional command of both language and music. Though one may not agree with the topics or manner of expression, we can listen from the perspective of compassion or a desire to understand the state of our culture.

- Because hip-hop was also born from the traditions of "Toasting" and "Ragamuffin" or Jamaican oration, the history of blues and African storytelling, and so many other influences, to consider hip-hop as anything other than a magnificent fusion of cultural elements is to shortchange its profundity; [4.16B]

And perhaps most profoundly:

"Hip-Hop is a creative and flexible tool for the articulation of consequence and responsibility by each generation of youth – and specifically youth who are experiencing the residue of injustice, disassociation or imbalances in community… wherever they may appear. The true artistic brand of Hip-Hop (left to the discernment of the listener) incorporates the voices of ancestry with the creative flexibility of each generation – crying out in one form or another … that "partial" and "equity" are oxymorons. That Hip-Hop, like nearly all styles of Blues, Rhythm and Blues, Jazz, Rock 'n' Roll or Gospel was born out of the African-American community, is a testament to the creative spirit and resilience of a people who have suffered, first, a holocaustal repression of mind and body, and who

now bear the burden of the hidden holocaust deeply within the fabric of society's institutions and status quo. That Hip-Hop, like all of its ancestors, both reflects and now belongs to any sincere artist desiring justice, balance, and a creative outlet for their voice, is equally undeniable." Anthony Morgan (a.k.a. S.K.L.F.L.), 2005.

Stories from the Human Family
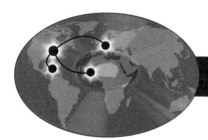

"I think racism is still alive today, mainly because of ignorance. Coming from a predominantly white school, I have seen many parents being racist and their children not being racist. This is because the youth actually had exposure to those of us from different races and the parents didn't.

"As a class we would have discussions; students would talk about their parents not wanting them to have contact with the "others"—and they began to question why. Had their only source of information about African-Americans been their parents or the way the media portrays just about everybody, they'd be racist too.

"This is a perfect example how we, as a nation, will be able to conquer racism and, yes, I believe it will be conquered. Ignorance is the fuel that feeds racism; when we eliminate ignorance, we will eliminate racism. It's just that simple." (Jameeka Williams, 18-yr.-old, African-American student)

Inside the Musician's World

S.K.L.F.L.
(Anthony Morgan)

Note (Michael N.): When a student brings an original CD to a music teacher, he/she will usually try to listen to it immediately (or forget). This practice is also the means by which instructors can keep their finger on the pulse of identity and the mindsets of those they teach. A young man, Anthony Morgan, came to us with a CD one day. We were so intrigued with his style ("flow") and lyrical ideas, that we could see he would be a great example of local talent in hip-hop.

Although anyone who desires to familiarize themselves with hip-hop may wish to look into some of the internationally known masters of the genre, still, the nature of hip-hop is to tell what is real in the world around you. Listening to any of the fusions that are in your area may provide as strong an insight into the values and insights expressed through hip-hop of today's youth. Now truly an international art-form, one that can be heard in most of the world's languages, it has evolved to become a vehicle for the voices of early 21st-century youth and, in many cases, reflects the problems and dilemmas still yet to be solved.

"Spare Change," by S.K.L.F.L. (Anthony Morgan), from the CD: **A Poet's Theme,** c. 2003, Brown Bomber Records.

Anthony (a.k.a. S.K.L.F.L.) writes: *"The song 'Spare Change' was written in August 2001 as a reflection of the schizophrenia of becoming a responsible adult in an irresponsible society. 'Spare Change' illuminates the energy of poverty, social unrest, community struggles, and the overall desire for love and human connection that seems so difficult to find at times. I was thinking about the state of the world, my nation, my community, and myself as being under nourished and mis-classified. Both the lack of melody and harmony amongst the different ethnicities, cultures, and social classes is irrational and without merit. Truly believing that the world, my world, your world, doesn't have to be or remain this/that way is why I created 'Spare Change.'*

The Recipe of Sound

There are a few distinct forces that act on the creativity of each generation of our youth's storytellers: the human desire to obtain respect for their abilities and means for sustaining life materially; the human instinct to be part of a community (whether of artists, ethnic groups, generations, or humanity generally); and in the case of most of the best artists, the attempt to change ignorance and myths to knowledge and reality.

"Spare Change" creatively uses not only the double meaning of *sparing change* – (implied: "money," / actual: change in the negative conditions in humanity), but simultaneously uses conversation, the musical conventions of modern rhythm and blues, the placement of vocal hooks, and ultimately his unique, personal *flow* (style of recitation or brand of hip-hop) to encourage thought and potential *change*.

If you are familiar with hip-hop, you will probably have little problem locking onto the lyrics and messages. If not, listen a few times to see if you pick up the ideas and messages which, in characteristic style of most hip-hop, are combined with musical layers and *samples* [4.17] that may in fact give alternative textural layers and meaning. The density of messages and textual layers or meaning in today's hip-hop requires deeper listening or, if the listener is unfamiliar with the perpetual change in language and production styles, the asking of questions.

Encoding and Signifying: Reclaiming the "Voice"

"Free of the white person's gaze, black people created their own unique vernacular structures and relished in the double play that these forms bore to white forms. Repetition and revision are fundamental to black artistic forms, from painting and sculpture to music and language use... the black tradition is "double-voiced." Henry Louis Gates, Jr., 1988, "Signifying Monkey," pp. xx-xxi

When a culture already has a long and deep history of nonverbal communication, as did most of the African cultures which contributed to African-American ethnicity, we can expect the continuance of such practices, especially when the culture is forced into subservience by another culture group. Recognizing the human universal desire to be respected or to balance disrespect, there is likely to be a strong and irrepressible drive for the repressed culture to find a means for balancing injustice. It is espe-

Pic. 4.15A *This Makonde elephant wooden carving is an example of the "trickery," double-meaning, and encoding that is essential not only to the understanding of most African art and languages but also to the creativity necessary for survival through slavery and repression by Africans in the New World. Ask yourself, what could the "carver" of this work have been saying?* Photo: Courtesy, wikipedia.org.

cially true that when war or rebellion by any physical means is not plausible, some other sort of war, or defensive measure will ensue.

The *art* of signifying, encoding, or speaking with "double meaning," basically saying one thing while appearing to others ("outsiders") to say something entirely different, is an essential means by which respect and balance was historically attained against the backdrop of enormous injustice. To accomplish this feat, the *signified* or *encoded* expression would have to be expressed without the knowledge of the majority or controlling culture group. In one sense it's very simple logic.

When misappropriation (taking something without respecting the source) and severe injustice or disrespect occur, disappointment, anger, and resistance are the natural human emotional responses. Of course, the outward expression of anger or physical resistance in the face of a lack of "justice" or judicial integrity would only lead to increased hardship or extermination. But since clearly, our African cultures in the America's survived, in addition to the deeply rooted spiritual beliefs of many, there must have been another mechanism of resistance, which perpetuated the balancing of injustice and the reclamation of respect.

By converting meaning or "re-creating" the function of an expression demanded by a repressive cultural structure, the considerably negative (lack of respect or voice in a matter) is converted into one's own concept of *self* (respect). For example, in this manner being forced to eat the entrails and leftovers of butchered animals, or the least edible plants, mustered all the creativity of the culinary artist, the mother, and the nurturer creating food that, however despicable its origins, is given altered meaning and administered with love as *soul food*. This act of converting meaning, playing within the mandates but turning them whenever and however possible to an alternative that would build, heal, or bridge the hardships and negativity of racism is an essential element of nearly every form of music that evolved from the pan-African-American communities, and too – is one of the most vivid evidences of creativity in human history.

Were it not for the creative skills to convert and alter meaning, cultures in the midst of the fires of a holocaust would be exterminated spiritually by the loss of their humanity and integrity. Instead, from the earliest of work songs, spirituals, and encoded vaudeville jokes and "coon songs," [4.18] to the poetry of the Harlem Renaissance, jazz of the 20th century, and music and literature of today, Africans throughout the Americas have used their inheritance of nonverbal and double meaning expressions to balance injustice, communicate the means for upward mobility, and psychologically, if not physically, gain the freedom that was intended for them. In this manner, the action or thing over which there was no control became a symbol of altered cultural values and *choice* to the benefit of an otherwise grossly disrespected community.

With this in mind, we have been speaking predominantly about African-American cultural processes and using music that is essentially from the United States. This is one more disservice to the reality of the human condition. Since African-Americans are not only technically but culturally any person mixed, derived, or fused culturally with African ancestry and living in the *Americas,* we are, therefore, also talking about all the islands of the Caribbean, and any African-Americans in Central America or South America. We must further now include any place where these individuals have dispersed (England, France, Spain, Holland, or Portugal) and their return and influence to the cultures and music on the continent of Africa.

Time and space cannot possibly accommodate the complexity of representation of all culture groups that are a part of or are influenced by the African Diaspora. However, since reggae, cumbia, salsa, merengue, zouk, and calypso (to name a few) are just as representational of the processes of *assimilation and fusion, communication, and encoding,* we will take two dynamic cultural/musical examples: **calypso,** from the islands of Trinidad and Tobago, and **capoeira** , from Brazil. Both *calypso* and *capoeira* are genres of music, forms of literature, and a voice for liberation that provide insightful visions into the thoughts and values of the people over time. Through slavery and repression, these genres served as the vehicle of encoding or signifying for African-Americans in both locations. Over time, however, they also became the means for conveying news, for rising against the force of politics and economics, eventually playing a major role in the movement for independence. Today, they are also pan-American symbols of resilience and the "alternative" voice performed across racial and cultural perimeters in many parts of the world.

Pic. 4.15 *Carnival in Montreal: "Pans" or steel drums are the signature instrument of Trinidad, as are the glorious costumes and regalia of Carnivale. Here a band of "pan" musicians (Trinidadian) strut their pride in their homeland and its music and culture in the far removed location of Montreal, Canada. Festivals such as this exist in nearly every major city in the world (and many smaller ones). This is the means by which most cultures share their pride and creativity—all we need do is observe.* Photo: Authors.

Pic. 4.17A *Capoeira bateria in Baltimore, MD, featuring Mestre Cobra Mansa. It's the job of the Bateria to maintain the rhythmic energy as well as interact with the capoeira practitioners. Here, three berimbaus (likely the descendant of one of the very first string instrument ever made) and one pandeiro form the bateria or rhythm section.* Photo: Courtesy Sam Fentress, c.2001.

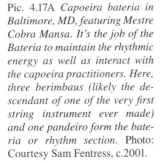

Pan "African-American"

"To neglect the interconnection of the African experience throughout the Americas is to disconnect members of the same family as being different solely because they have different names. It's bad enough that we cannot see the oneness of the human family and that we've bought into separation by race or nation to the point that our vision of the interconnectivity of all cultures historically— and especially today—is impaired. But to not see the commonalities between Capoeira and Samba of Brazil, Merengue in the Domincan Republic, Reggae in Jamaica, the Blues in the U.S., or Calypso in Trinidad—and, today, the way these genres have perpetually influenced each other—is equivalent to putting a blindfold over our search for truth and knowledge of our own selves." From *"Caught between Race and Racelessness,"* 2005, The Center for Cultural Healing.

The expressions of music, dance, language and literature that rose from the ashes of cultural arrogance and colonization should by their mere existence have sufficient cause to be elevated to the elite phenomena among culture studies in our institutions and for celebration in our art festivals and programs. The modern mind is bereft of the capacity to understand the creativity of the African in the Americas to simultaneously appease the "claimant" of their humanity and maintain a conscious connection to a spiritual world and sense of self-preservation, mentally, emotionally, and physically.

Pic. 4.15D *From Kwanzaa to the very term "African-American," the reconciliation of abused identity is made more complex by perceptions of culture and its transference through educational methods that cannot accommodate fusions of identity as an identity. Efe and Ituri ("Witness Bambuti") are both Detroit natives that passionately fuse their vision and instruments of "Africa" with their own "African-American" experience.* Photo: Courtesy "Witness Bambuti," Authors.

As we have begun to discuss, among the means by which African-Americans combated psychological repression was double meaning and encoding. A classic example of this is the genre known as *capoiera* of Brazil. A fusion of music, dance, and the combative (martial) arts, capoeira is the outgrowth of numerous African cultural groups: Malesian, Hausa, Bantu, Kkongo, Kimbundas, and Kasanjes to name a few. From the initial shipping of slaves by the Portuguese to Brazil (beginning the 1500s), each dignified community was forced to fight outwardly as well as inwardly for survival.

"As the slaves became aware that their condition was irreversible, that they were intended to be an involuntary work force forever, they began to run away. In Recife, a group of 40 slaves rebelled against their master, killed all the white employees, and burned the plantation house. They then set themselves free and decided to find a place where they could be hidden from the slave hunters. They headed to the mountains, a trip that took many months to complete. Had it not been for the help they received from the Indians, this journey would have been practically impossible to accomplish. Eventually they reached what they thought was a safe place, which … they named Palmares. In this community the first forms of Capoeira were developed." [4.19]

131

Although the documentation and historical accounts of capoeira speculate on a wide variation of events in its evolution as an art form, some common themes seem to appear:

- During slavery, capoeira was a means by which slaves practiced techniques of self-defense or skills to use in combat.
- The art form was likely developed in Brazil; no equivalent techniques have been documented in Africa prior to 1800's.
- Many slaves would practice the art with double meaning – appearing to be dancing, while in reality working to perfect the art of "kipura" (to flutter, fight, flog or flit from place to place).
- Capoeira, through the immigration of Brazilians to New York in the 1960s and 70s, is likely to have substantially influenced "break dancing" in Hip-Hop, as the movements styles are in many ways identical.

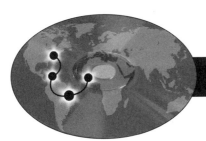

Inside the Musician's World

Preston Vismale

Note: When we attempted to locate an example of the music that is used to accompany the dance and martial arts movement of capoeira, we looked to musicians in New York, where the music and art first appeared in North America. The tempos of the music differ: very slow (the "Angolan" style) to very fast (the São Bento Regional style). Most singing is done in a "call and response" (question-and-answer) style.

The instruments used include: the *berimbau* (a one-string instrument which looks like a hunting bow with a calabash gourd attached as a amplifier), *pandeiros* (tambourines), an *agogo* (two-tone bell from West Africa), and in most cases now, the *atabaque* (a conga-like drum).

This piece, like so many of the pieces played for the evolving art today, is a fusion of "samba," jazz, and Afro-Caribbean musical styles. It is important to note, that although human beings have always been multicultural (usually much more so than their self-perceptions or self-awareness tell them), the impact of media upon an individual's options for identifying with other cultures based upon affinity has impacted most of us dramatically. In this case, a close friend of the author, Preston Vismale (his family originally from Barbados, Surinam, and Trinidad and Tobago), a professional musician and producer living in the Queens district of New York City, meets musicians regularly from around the world, including Brazilian artists, and numerous percussionists from other cultures. Their fusion of influences and musical experiences and their passion for the rhythms and cultural history of capoeira led to this piece, which like most music/cultural fusions, defies a search for "origin" and, in this case, also gives us a feel for the modern descendants of the music originally used for capoeira.

Pic. 4.16A *The berimbau of Brazil.* Photo: Courtesy Lark in the Morning, S.F.

CD 1.15

"Berimbau," by Preston Vismale, and Nego Gato from his personal recorded archives, <u>Capoeira</u>, c. 2004.

The lyrics speak of the **"berimbau,"** which, like capoeira itself, has evolved to become a "Pan-African" symbol of "Afrocentricity" and equality for the African-American, similar to the Pan-African movements of today's reggae and hip-hop. The explosion of media has expanded access to virtually all the musical genres which represent the dynamics of creative survival, and most certainly at the top of the list are those spawned throughout the African Diaspora.

Of this piece Mr. Vismale wrote us: *""In reference to the song "Berimbau"—it was actually recorded for "Deep Listening Records." The lyrics and rhythmic "bed" was composed by Nego Gato (Black Cat), a legendary capoeista and percussionist from Bahia, Brazil. The musical instrumentation and arrangement was composed by myself. The song is kind backwards in the sense that the Berimbau pattern played at the end, in an older Angolan rhythm, whereas the beginning is modern (call and response) Brazilian drum pattern, similar but not derivative of the Afro-Cuban Bata. It then goes into a jazz-samba, called "afroxe" ("African-like") before ending in the original Angolan "bow and arrow" (Berimbau) pattern.*

My interest in this music is the result of passion for music and justice. And the two, when they meet, produce something enormously special. The passion for equality and justice has fueled the creativity of the African both in the Americas and on the Continent. I don't think anyone can say one style of music is better than another. But we can say that some groups have been tested more than others. If hardship is an element in the equation of successful creativity, then you'd have to admit, African music throughout the Diaspora has the credentials for success."

Pic. 4.16B *Today's capoeira groups across much of the world (such as this group in a community college in Michigan) may have very little to do with the origins, purpose, or music and dance styles, but are born from an affinity for the art—and dynamic interconnection of music, dance, and the martial arts.* Photo: Courtesy Capoeira Club, Washtenaw Community College.

This piece represents the fusion of traditions and generational ideas that occurs in Pan–African exchange. Here, a Brazilian singer and a U.S.-born Trini (from Trinidad) meet with a conglomeration of musicians in New York from around the African Diaspora to produce a piece that begins with a "Bata-style" (Afro-Cuban) drum pattern, evolves into a jazz-samba fusion (**samba** is a musical genre of Brazil that is most associated with "Carnavale" in Brazil – see Unit VIII), and ends with a traditional style *berimbau* pattern that would be more similar to the style of music usually associated with capoeira.

Pan Have We DNA:
The Calypso and Calypsonian of Trinidad

"Where did Africans (and African-Americans) learn of "carnival?" The answer is simple: mask-making and masquerading are traditions found all over Africa as interlocking aspects of most celebrations. Masking suggests spirit-associated transformations whereby the maskers cancel or obliterate their personalities by changing into other human characters and supernatural spirits so that they are no longer themselves." "Mighty Chalkdust" (Hollis U. Liverpool, Ph.D.) [4.12]

To search for *meaning* in assessing human cultural creativity, especially across the African Diaspora, denies the highest percentage of our inclination for science, conclusion, and precision of definition. For example, the Pan-American tradition known as **"Carnival"** (or Mardi Gras in New Orleans, Louisiana) is the result of the volatile fusion of cultures in the Americas, including:

- Regions settled by one European culture, battled for, settled by, or reclaimed by other European cultures.

- The enormous diversity of African cultures combined to form what we simplistically call "African-American" populations.

- All other colonized and creolized cultures who have historically interacted with each other.[4.21]

A fascinating example of double meaning or encoding in both music and performance is that of the storyteller at *Carnival* in the islands of Trinidad and Tabago: the **calypsonian.** The islands in the western Caribbean are influenced substantially by the Spanish, French, and English, populated with Africans from the Mandinka, Fulbe, Kwakwa, Yoruba, Hausa, Igbo, and Kongo peoples, and ultimately are a part of Pan-African-American exchange with cultures in all directions.

Pic. 4.17 *"Mighty Chalkdust," a.k.a. "Chalkie," a.k.a Hollis Liverpool, Ph.D. A calypsonian (and frequent Calypso King at Carnival), Mr. Liverpool is also a professor and scholar of the history of the calypso, from which he derives his alias.* Photo: Courtesy H. Liverpool.

"Carnival" in Trinidad became a venue for fusion and transformation of all these cultures by encoding or altering meaning initially through "masking." The *calypsonian* or performer of calypso music, in turn, became the "newscaster," the humourist, the storyteller, and ultimately the source of relief for generations of Trinis (people of Trinidad) at this festival. Much like the funk or Motown performers in the 1960's in the United States, by taking on titles and persona masked by language, dress, and sound, the calypsonian could create a persona that would transcend the typical station of the musician, and, on the biggest stages of the year, at Carnival time, become more important, powerful, and influential as well.

Dr. Hollis Liverpool (a.k.a. "Chalkie") writes:

"The Calypso is in fact the music of Carnival.[4.22] Those who compose and sing the tuneful refrains are called Calypsonians. As early as the 18th century ... calypsos were bitter criticisms of the system of enslavement, and the enslaved Africans practiced a system of "ridicule and derision" which they not only in time exercised at each other (competition in all styles of African-American music is also an essential part of Calypso)–but not infrequently, at the expense of their owner or employer as well." [4.23]

Pic. 4.18 A, B, & C. *A carnival mask from the Venice Carnival, Carnival clowns in Wolfach, Germany, and a "future" carnival star in Montreal, Canada. All variations of carnival extend from the Roman Catholic traditions of celebration and usage of all foods prior to the fasting period of Lent. However, the meaning and variations in celebrating Carnival are as diverse now as the regions where carnival celebrants can be found.* Photos: (above) Venice Carnival from istockphoto, (above right) German Fashing by Eribula, and (right) Montreal's Caribbeanfest, Authors.

Although calypsonians were originally called "Chantuelles" (from the French—translated "to sing"), Dr. Liverpool writes: *"When the kalenda ('stick fights' for which the singers accompanied the competitive fighters) was outlawed by authorities, Calypsonians sang in the barrack yards of the city, turning the yards into make-shift theaters to which the middle class flocked to hear the leggos (events) of the day and the news of the hour and to see the singers engage in 'picong' (sharp, biting attacks on one another to the deafening applause of the audience)."*

Although there were multiple transformations in the meaning and importance of calypso over the years, perhaps one of the most fascinating historical elements of the role of the calypsonian in Trinidad culture is that the most famous of calypsonians and their importance and status amongst the large lower and middle classes rendered them "untouchable" to the government even before Independence. That is, the calypsonian became a means by which news, balance, and healing could be obtained in the face of racism and inequality. By creating lyrics that would play on words, that were loaded with double meaning, the calypsonian could ridicule an unjust politician, even to the point of causing him to lose the election. This unprecedented power and influence meant that the role of the musician (*calypsonian*) was not solely reactionary but instead influenced the course of Trinidad's movements for justice and equity.

For decades, calypsonians have taken on creative names (Mighty Sparrow, Mighty Chalkdust, etc.), dressed in exaggerated style, and created songs which make fun of politicians, policies, and each other, to the delight of audiences. However, the non-Trini must keep in mind the following:

- The "happy" nature and upbeat tempo of the music is a disguise (most often) for lyrics that are filled with double meaning and usually deeper significance than a casual interpretation will discern.

- The language is just as "creative" and perpetually changing as the music. As in the art of most African-Diaspora cultures, language is heavily encoded and will require that listeners use every faculty at their disposal to attempt its decoding.

- Finally, as Dr. Liverpool comments: *"Singers have cultivated their own particular styles of singing, dressing, and even dancing, so that their different personalities are exposed in a myriad of ways on the stage...."* In essence, it's unlikely that people will understand the complete communication unless they see the "live" performance, as much of the encoding is built into the visual performance as well!

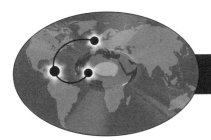

Inside the Musician's World

"Chalkie" Hollis Liverpool

Note (Michael N.): When I first met Dr. Liverpool, we were both working on our doctorates in ethnomusicology at the University of Michigan. I was fascinated not only with his view of the world of music but also his vibrant enthusiasm and virtually inexhaustible energy. As a result, we asked him to our house to give a house concert-lecture. I'm not sure that I'd ever seen (or seen since) thirty some people so enthralled with a speaker as on this night. What came across in the broadest sense was the clearest understanding that music, especially in the context of the evolution of Trinidad's calypso culture, has never been merely music but instead the vehicle through which the sum total of everything which Trinis take pride in is expressed.

CD 1.16

"Pan Have We DNA," by Chalkdust, from the CD: **Pan Have We DNA,** c. 2004, Juba Productions.

The statement of autonomy and identity, of equal respect in the world community is an essential and necessary theme in most cultures that are either smaller geographically or dominated by American/European media, politics, or economics. In this piece, the statement that political or cultural colonization (exerting one's culture over another or taking ownership of that which does not belong to you) are no longer valid justifications for the assertion of cultural supremacy. Listen carefully through the dance rhythm of the Calypso, the quick tempo, and the layers of trumpets, saxophones, and "pan" (or steeldrum) for the important message: that the steel-drum (or "pan") is not only indigenous to Trinidad culture and music but also an essential element of their cultural "DNA."

The lyrics in part are:
Out of struggle and aggression – Trinidadians made "Pan,"
To fight elite domination – Pan was Trinis' weapon,
From enslaved man throughout the years – Then Trinis swept to tears
To experiment – until they invent – this unique instrument

Chorus:
But today the U.S.A. want to say – I come from they
So they trying to fatten – the accomplishment
– so it's time we go from end
So from West to the Orient – making the statement –
Pan is we instrument

Play Mr. Panman play – Play Pan is we Visa
Play til' friends and away
– know that Pan each day from gentleman will play
Play til the USA know that Pan today – have we DNA

Pic. 4.19A *Steel drums ("pans") were original-ly large oil drums left behind after WWII that were later pounded and fashioned ingeniously into musical instruments in Trinidad. Today, they are made by skilled techni-cians and played in much of the world in everything from small combos to large pan-orchestras. You may hear pans naturally as part of calypsos but also doing versions of Beethoven and Tchaikovsky as well.* Photo: Courtesy Lark in the Morning.

Pic. 4.20 & 4.20A *The "trumpet man" (as he called himself) in this picture (above), is playing a "jazz-calypso" in the streets of San Francisco for a few coins, but especially to get some prac-tice. While in Trinidad, entire orches-tras of steel drums are setup in streets and on stages during Carnival (and for other festivals and competitions) to play everything from calypso to ren-ditions of a Beethoven symphony.* Photos: Authors and Mark Goddard.

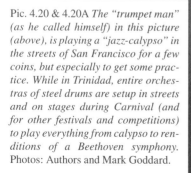

Seeing the History of Racial Unity

Undoing the legacy of human separation, racism, extreme forms of nationalism or religious intolerance will take painstaking efforts in all arenas. Such effort will begin with equity in economic opportunities and health care, since they have the most immediate impact on the physical safety and well-being of humanity. But for these and all others, we will still need to turn to "re-education," or the elimination of biases from education, including the understanding of the important history of "racial unity."

Michigan State University's American History and Race Relations Dr. Richard Thomas was among the first to explore the history of "racial unity" as an imperative for social progress. He writes, *"As a result of long years of teaching about the history of racism, I felt compelled to include the history of the 'other tradition' of American race relations, namely: the history of those who have struggled against racism and have envisioned a social order in which people not only accept each other as equal but also have a profound appreciation of each other as members of the one human family."* 1990, p. I

He further comments, *"Citizens of multiracial societies must be made aware of the relationship between racial unity and social progress. They must be exposed to the great historical cost in human misery and social conflict that racism has exacted from the entire society... where racial unity based upon social justice and nurtured by love and fellowship is lacking or absent, such multiracial societies are forced to waste precious time, energy and resources managing crisis."* ibid, pp. 4-5.

Question: with this in mind....

What are each of the musicians (CDs 1.12 through 1.16 / pick as many as you wish to explore) saying in their comments and music about the issue of recognizing the essential aspect of achieving racial unity— or the cost and impact of disunity? Finally, describe the most powerful experience of "racial unity" you have experienced and in what manner it impacted you.

CD 1.12 (Robert Penn) *"Keep in mind as well...Blues didn't mean you weren't spiritual, but that you were just honest about your feelings and about your 'humanness.' ...Blues is from the human spirit, and the spirit is not always happy either. I think that music comes from God . . . Music doesn't belong to us."*

CD 1.13A (Joe Reilly) *"Understanding music as an expression of spirit, I write, sing, and perform in order to celebrate life and allow the spirit of God and my ancestors to sing through me and touch listeners."*

CD 1.13B (Shari Kane) *"However we came to be humans, we ended up with ...a need to let that strong emotion out of us. To me, the blues is a perfect vehicle for that emotion, regardless of what the driver looks like...I was drawn to the immediacy of the blues."*

CD 1.14 (Anthony Morgan, a.k.a "Sklfl") *"The true artistic brand of Hip-Hop ... incorporates the voices of ancestry with the creative flexibility of each generation—crying out in one form or another . . . that 'partial' and 'equity' are oxymorons."*

CD 1.15 (Preston Vismale) *"I don't think anyone can say one style of music is better than another. But we can say that some groups have been tested more than others. If hardship is an element in the equation of successful creativity, then you'd have to admit, African-American music throughout the Diaspora has the credentials for success."*

CD 1.16 (Dr. Hollis "Chalkie" Liverpool) *"As early as the 18th century . . . calypsos were bitter criticisms of the system of enslavement, and the enslaved Africans practiced a system of 'ridicule and derision' which they not only in time exercised at each—but not infrequently, at the expense of their owner or employer as well."*

PIC. 4.E-1

PIC. 4.E-2

PIC. 4.E-3

How do we acquire our values?

In music as in all things, the value that we place on what should be taught and "how" something should be taught is a result of the sum total of our culture's evolution. For example, Biza Sompa's Congolese dance class (E-1) and Rev. Marvin Miller's gospel music class (E-2) at a local community college, is a rarity in the context of European or American college or university classes. In both instances, instruction is generally conveyed orally and the method of instruction parallels the values of each of the culture systems, placing greater emphasis on what the dance means or its spirit, than on its technique. Conversely, Laurice Anderson's ballet class (E-3) held in the same school, places a much larger emphasis on the values of the European/French culture's affinity for precision, technique, and unity or organized expression. Neither is superior or inferior — but certainly, the latter method is more accessible and emphasized in Western cultures and their institutions than the former two. Without exposure to a variety of cultural possibilities, many students, as well as the institutions and administrators themselves, will be prone to making the assumptions that what we do – is what should be done. This breaches academic and cultural dignity and equity.

Photo: E-1, Sarah Scherdt, E-2/3, Authors, courtesy Mr. Sompa, Mr. Miller, and Ms. Anderson and students.

PIC. 4.E-4

PIC. 4.E-6

PIC. 4.E-5

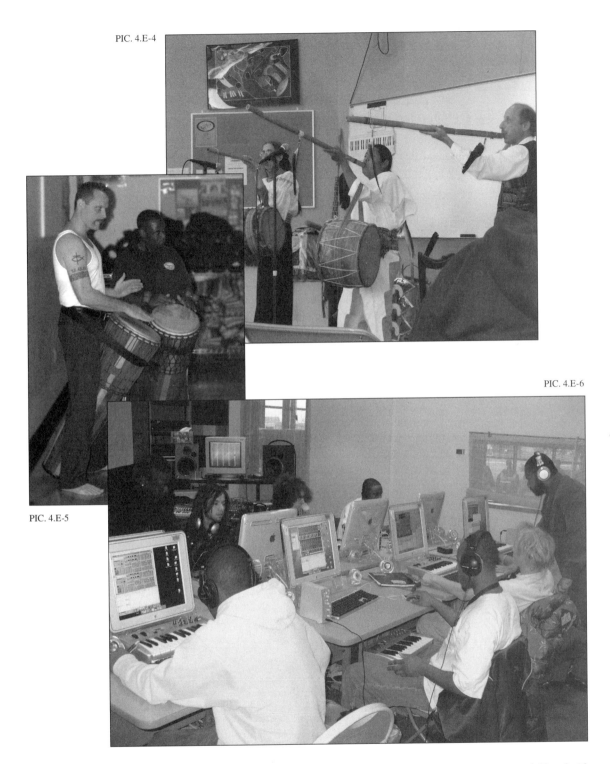

Expanding both content and methodology – but how? *The only means by which a young person can grow to adulthood with a truly healthy perspective of themselves and their culture in the context of a "world" (i.e. "equal but different" in value), is to be exposed to a variety of alternatives. Students at this community college (Washtenaw Community College/Ann Arbor, Michigan), are among the luckier to have exposure to occasional external performances from other cultures (E-4, Ecuadorian Oscar Santillian and Helen and Lazlo Slomovits), the opportunity to work with Mr. Sompa on Congolese drum techniques (E-5) and in having the opportunity to use the latest computer recording techniques (E-6) taught by two instructors Mr. Bonnie Billups (left) and Mr. John E. Lawrence (right) alongside more traditional or Western instruction. Furthermore, in the latter case (computer recording class), since both are career musicians with less academic and more experiential paths, the students are given instruction more closely tied to their own goals and designs, and less to formulas that evolved from the European University or Academy tradition. Photos: E-5 Ms. Scherdt, E-4/E-6, Authors, courtesy, Mr. Santillian, Mr. and Mrs. Slomovits, Mr. Sompa, Mr. Billups, Mr. Lawrence and their students.*

Unit IV Activities

Activity #1: Understanding Concepts

Read the following thoughts, and then respond to the questions below. Try to be honest and "non-filtered" in your responses, but also make sure that you write your responses in isolation of anyone else's influence.

1) We know that each of us has learned a sophisticated network of politically correct or filtered means of reacting to things we don't like, or of which we don't approve. In doing so, we protect our true thoughts and feelings, but we also obscure the existence of potentially harmful biases.

   A) If this is so, why do we do this?

   B) How do we learn when and where to apply filters (be more conscious of filtering) so that we can learn to recognize important biases as well?

2) We are socially sophisticated beings in many ways, and in just as many – potentially unaware. Outside in the "real world," where competition is intense and emotional sensitivity or overt honesty are frequently less emphasized, we are called upon to mask some of our natural instincts for fairness or justice towards others.

   A) Are there ways we can learn to increase our sense of fairness and equity towards others?

   B) What about when you are with a group of friends and someone articulates what is clearly a bias towards someone or their music? Is there a way to confront the bias without humiliating the person? How would you do this?

3) If we can accept the possibility that all of us are "open-minded" in some ways, and have blinders and barriers around other areas of our perceptions, we will likely see that many of the barriers are created from emotions such as fear, insecurity, or anxiety and discomfort for our safety or well-being (physical, emotional, or intellectual). Generally, we do not want others to see these emotions. Depending upon our comfort level with identifying and expressing feelings and emotions, we develop sophisticated networks of qualifying or maneuvering around them based upon learned filtering techniques or social etiquette.

   A) Did you read anything in this Unit that made you feel in any way uncomfortable or uneasy? Can you identify the passage?

   B) Can you trace what in your experience and life may have led to the feelings of discomfort with the passage? Even if you disagree with the passage, suppose for a second it is "fair" or just. What in your experience (life, education, family, etc.) might have influenced you to feel the uneasiness? (Or, how might you have been trained to believe something other than the point that was made?) Could both beliefs co-exist? (be true or partially true?)

Activity #2: Listening Deeper

When you listen to a piece of music you do not enjoy or value, try to observe your first and usually "gut-level" reaction. This is the place from where you are coming. It's your past, your culture, your family all rolled into one.

Now follow these steps in order:

1) Pick three (or more if you wish) pieces from any of the CD's for which you have the least possible affinity.

2) As you listen to each piece (or listen again, if you've already listened once to the piece), write your *completely honest responses* or comments about the music as you would if you were with your closest friends or family members – *and no one else would see your comments*. This process will help us recognize or remove the filters we use when we are around the people that mean the most to us;

3) Now, pretend the people that made the music, or the people from the culture that love that music, are in the room with you and will read what you wrote. Which of the words are remotely offensive, potentially disrespectful, or capable of being misinterpreted in a negative manner?

   Underline or highlight these words.

4) Finally, go back and look at your work. Are those *all the comments* you'd make honestly? Did you catch every word that might be offensive? (Suggestion: Pretend that someone wrote these thoughts about your music as a back-up to check the filters.) Do you know why you wrote the words that were indicators of bias? Can you trace their source to your family, friends, experiences?

Activity #3: Exercising Passion

Hopefully there were one or more of the pieces in Unit IV that you found interesting or would like to know more about. Maybe there were some musical styles that were mentioned but not covered that you have an interest in, such as reggae, merengue, samba, Delta blues, work songs, etc. If so, you might wish to try one or more of the activities below to follow up on your passion for learning.

1) Research your musical interest or culture of choice. While doing so look for sites or resources that:
   - have been created by members of the culture group.
   - offer a cross-section of historical background and information about the current practices of that musical style.

2) Make sure to ask yourself:
   - Does the source you are using paint a balanced and flexible picture about the music?
   - Is the approach to the music overtly "racially" defined (Euro-centric, or Afro-centric) or does it seem to offer a balance of perspectives?
   - Does your source "dance" around the history of racial abuse and the impact of colonization, or address it in an objective manner?

3) See if you can find a musical example of the style of music – or better yet, a performance you can attend of that musical style.
   - You may also wish to read up on the music before you listen to it.
   - Try to find commentary or actually interview someone who plays that music before or after listening (or attending the concert).

Questions you may consider asking yourself or ask of the musician or article:
   - Can you see the impact of racism and colonization on the development of the music?
   - Can you see (hear) the integration (assimilation and fusion) and unity of cultures in the music?
   - In what do you hear, see, or detect encoding or double meaning in the music or event? [Can you confirm any of your thoughts with the musicians or from sources?]

Activity #4: **Exercising Our Own Creativity**

1) Write your own blues. Keep in mind the following:

   • Blues is about the *truth*. When you sit to write your verses, make sure they are about the thing you feel most intensely at the time you write.

   • Write three lines. The first two will be more or less the same and may be in one or two phrases. The third should be a consequence or reply to the first two. Average number of syllables will vary. A general range, however, would be 10-14 syllables per line, as each phrase will go over 8-10 beats of a 16-beat pattern (four measures of four beats per measure).

2) Try to write your own "hip-hop" piece or calypso, or rhythm and blues, reggae, or simply "rhymed poetry" piece that talks about your views of race and your perceptions of the history and evolution of racial perception. Themes might include:

   • How we've come to see and talk "black and white" as if such a phenomenon of color in humanity exists, or as if racial identification is worthy of our human dignity.

   • Why we talk so little about racial history or learn so little about the evolution of racial perception in our schools. Or, if you have been taught well in your school, where and when this was, and what did you learn?

Be sure to include your vision of solutions and possibilities that would help alter the gridlock of racial and cultural stereotyping, as the best "art" usually incites thought and alternatives in addition to pointing out the conditions.

PIC. 4.21 *An elder once commented: "If you have never looked through my eyes—-if you have never seen what I've seen, then you have not experienced either the extent to which pain leads to knowledge or knowledge leads to you." This musician, having weathered pre-civil rights, the civil rights era, and nearly four decades since, must have experiences none after his time could know ... unless, of course, they asked many questions, and listened well.* Photo: Courtesy Gisele Wright, 2005.

Unit 10: Endnotes

4.1   From <u>The Collected Works of Rudyard Kipling,</u> Vol. 27, NY: Doubleday, Doran and Co., 1970, pp. 375-376.)

4.2   Published by the Baha'i International Community, Baha'i Publishing Trust, Wilmette, Illinois, U.S.A.

4.3   All the stories used in this text are actual comments used by permission of the students or interviewees. Name and demographic or anonymity is the decision of the interviewees and is indicated according to their specifications.

4.4   *Ignorance*— a lack of knowledge or education, the unawareness of something, often something important.

4.5   *Cultural centricity* will be a concept we will flesh out more in this Unit as well as in others. In general, Euro-centricity was the result of colonization, slavery, etc., on the part of the European and, later, European-American ancestors. Afro-centricity was, to a large extent, the necessary reaction to this form of arrogance, the reverse arc of the pendulum. All "culturally centric" perceptions, however perceived or seemingly justifiable, leave us void of accuracy and will continue to reinforce biases and the development of elaborate filter systems.

4.6   Though perhaps obvious, the term "America" is as accurately applied to the cultures of the Caribbean and Central and South America as it is to the United States and Canada. To see the experiences of all cultures in the Americas as simultaneously similar and distinct gives an enormous boost to the recognition and depro-gramming of biases—by means of comparison.

4.16B Mr. Vismale writes: "Hip-hop was 'originally' created in the South Bronx, New York in the early 70's by pre-dominantly Jamaican and Trinidadian kids. Derived from "toasting" and "dubbing" styles of music which were popular in the Caribbean countries—both styles inferred an ability to take a microphone and spontaneously "rap" and /or rhythm over rhythmic music. In any case, to view hip-hop without its multi-cultural and distinc-tive Caribbean creative contributions is both inaccurate and potentially disrespectful.

4.7   If we consider the experiences of the Native and African Diaspora by the intensity of repression and numbers killed, injured, or otherwise affected—and the generations of human beings of all colors who have acquired devastating biases as a result of the actions of the colonizers and their descendants over centuries, we can use no other term but *holocaust* to define this part of history. The term's strict definition is a *complete consump-tion by fire, wholesale or mass destruction, and a sacrifice that is totally consumed by fire.* Although one may argue the "totally consumed" part, were it not for the creativity, intense spirit, and spirituality of the peoples, total consumption of mind, body, and/or spirit would have been inevitable.

4.8   James Loewen wrote this book as a survey of twelve of the most used "American History" textbooks in American schools. He gives undeniable support for a preponderance of "simple-minded" perspectives that are conveyed as fact. Then he provides strong information and support for a more complete history, which would lead us to elevate the stations of "minority" cultures, or see the "founding fathers" and heroes in American History as men, many of whom made grievous errors and mistakes. In short, to re-create the manner in which we see our evolution in Western cultures gives us enormous incentive for how we think of ourselves today and, potentially, for how we will use our time and efforts in the future. See:<u>Lies My Teacher Told Me</u>, Touchstone, New York, c.1995

4.9   Melville Herskovits, "Cultural Relativism," 1972, p.71.

4.10   We will purposely avoid the usage of "black" or "white" in discussing culture whenever possible. To give any weight to color terminology in discussing culture is, in our estimation and regardless of how they may be val-ued as a symbol cultural identity by some, a support for the very biases and myths we are seeking to de-code. We will, however, use the terms in reference to quotes or passages that discuss racial dynamics in this manner.

4.11   From <u>An Encyclopedia of African American Christian Heritage</u>, by Marvin Andrew McMickle, Judson Press, c. 2002.

4.12   Cited from <u>www.negrospirituals.com</u>, as extracted from: Thernstrom, Stephan, <u>America in Black and White: One Nation Indivisible</u>, Touchstone/Simon & Schuster, 1999.

4.13   Richard Thomas, <u>Racial Unity: An Imperative of Social Progress</u>, Association of Baha'i Studies, 1990, pp. 13.

4.14   Henry Louis Gates, Jr., from <u>The Signifying Monkey</u>, Oxford University Press, 1988, pp. 4.

4.15 From "Rollin' and Tumblin': The Postwar Blues Guitarists, edited by Jas Obrecht, c.2000 Miller - Freeman Books, pp. 82.

4.16 Ibid. pp. 71.

4.16a Although "appropriation" (dictionary definition) might infer a stealing or disrespectful acquisition of an expression, idea, etc., it frequently is used to infer acquisition. We will use "mis-appropriation" to make clear a disrespectful acquisition. (see also: "Appropriation – creative or artistic forms, themes, or practices by one cultural group from another. It is in general used to describe Western appropriations of non-Western or non-white forms, and carries connotations of exploitation and dominance. The concept has come into literary and visual art criticism by analogy with the acquisition of artifacts by Western museums. *Oxford Companion to English Literature*, Oxford University Press, 2003.

4.16B Mr. Vismale writes: "Hip-hop was 'originally' created in the South Bronx, New York in the early 70's by predominantly Jamaican and Trinidadian kids. Derived from "toasting" and "dubbing" styles of music which were popular in the Caribbean countries—both styles inferred an ability to take a microphone and spontaneously "rap" and /or rhythm over rhythmic music. In any case, to view hip-hop without its multi-cultural and distinctive Caribbean creative contributions is both inaccurate and potentially disrespectful.

4.17 Sampling is an innovation brought on by the advent of digital computer technology. It is the taking of sounds or musical "samples" from one source (e.g., other recordings, instruments, or sounds) and converting them from analog vibrations into digital information. Once this is accomplished, "samples" may be layered or inserted wherever the artist feels appropriate. Although there are myriad copyright and ownership issues with sampling, artistically, sampling offers artists the options of creating multiple layers and meanings in a work. This includes the option of creating "sub-text" in hip-hop (or other genres) by quoting a source that may have meaning to only the "inner culture" of the genre.

4.18 Vaudeville and "coon songs" (frequently performed in vaudeville acts) were styles of entertainment wherein African-American performers (in the U.S.) would make jokes, sing, or dance, as a means of entertaining (frequently) "white" audiences (and earning extra money), frequently at the performers' cultural expense. Often, however, the routines and performances were heavily encoded with double meaning to poke fun at the audience, without its knowing.

4.19 A good source for information on capoeira and its history (and source of this quotation) is www.capoeiragem.com.

4.20 From The Trinidad Carnival: History, Development and Organization, by Hollis U. Liverpool, section 22.

4.21 We will address "creolization" as a specific force or slant on "creative" cultural fusion in Unit X.

4.22 "The *Carnival Season* is a holiday period during the two weeks before the traditional Christian fast of Lent. The origin of the name "Carnival" is unclear as there are several theories. The most commonly known theory states that the name comes from the Italian *carne-* or *carnovale,* from Latin *carnem* (meat) + *levare* (lighten or raise), literally 'to remove the meat' or 'stop eating meat.' It has also been claimed that it comes from the Latin words *caro* (meat) and *vale* (farewell), hence 'Farewell to meat.' Yet another theory states that it originates from the Latin *carrus navalis,* which was some kind of Greek cart carrying a statue of a god in a religious procession at the annual festivities in honour of the god Apollo. Most commonly the season began on Septuagesima, the third from the last Sunday before Ash Wednesday, but in some places it started as early as Twelfth Night, continuing until Lent. This period of celebration and partying had its origin in the need to use up all remaining meat and animal products such as eggs and butter before the fasting season. The celebration of Carnival ends on 'Mardi Gras' (French for 'Fat Tuesday,' meaning Shrove Tuesday), the day before Ash Wednesday, when the rigours of Lent's 40 days of fasting and sacrifice begin." Extracted from: *en.wikipedia.org/wiki/Carnival*

4.23 Dr. Liverpool quotes Bryan Edwards and Abrahams and Szwed, 1983, After Africa, pp. 292.

The Middle East (and Southern Asia): Religion and Music

Topics to Consider in Unit V

➤ *How can we differentiate between healthy categorization (for communication) and biased categorization (stereotyping)?*

➤ *What are possible "habits" we can develop to more fully recognize and eliminate harmful biases and stereotypes?*

➤ *What role does media and education play in our generalizations of others? What roles can they play in our "re-education"?*

➤ *What is "religion"? And – how can we better understand religion in the context of both our past and present?*

➤ *What is the role of music in religion? And – what is the impact of religion on our world's music (secular and sacred)?*

➤ *What is "counter-culture" music? And – how can we better read the evolution of counter-culture movements and their impact on us/our music?*

➤ *What is "chant" or "intonement"? And – why is chant so important to all of the world's major religions and musical genre?*

➤ *What are some of the important aspects of Hinduism, Judaism, Buddhism, Christianity, Islam and the Bahá'í Faith? And – in what way are each connected – or related both to our beliefs and cultural/ musical practices?*

➤ *What are some of the main principles or beliefs of Islam? And – how do these principles vary with many of the stereotypes current in other cultures?*

➤ *How – or in what manner do these ancient cultures offer a balancing alternative to modern Western cultures today?*

➤ *What are some classifications of instruments that serve our entire Musical World? Which Middle Eastern instruments and musical practices serve as the basis for many of the most famous Western instruments or practices (i.e. guitar, piano, or violin)?*

➤ *What is the connection between Persian poetry, music, and art?*

➤ *What can we learn from an Iraqi/Islamic rap group in Toronto, Canada?*

UNIT V

The Middle East (and Southern Asia):
Religion and Music

"In the human kingdom itself there are points of contact, properties common to all mankind; likewise, there are points of distinction which separate race from race, individual from individual. If the points of contact, which are the common properties of humanity, overcome the peculiar points of distinction, unity is assured. On the other hand, if the points of differentiation overcome the points of agreement, disunion and weakness result." `Abdu'l-Bahá, The Promulgation of Universal Peace, pp. 67-68.

"It is unwise to be too sure of one's own wisdom. It is healthy to be reminded that the strongest might weaken and the wisest might err." Mahatma Gandhi

Communication and Miscommunication of Human Experience

How do human beings communicate their thoughts about other human beings? That is, how do we take something so complex as human thought and experience and encapsulate it into neat, understandable word packages for the sake of communicating to others? How do the communication norms and standards set by the collective ancestry of the societies through which we pass determine how we think, perceive, and live? More importantly, how many of the labels that we use are based upon biased information, misconceptions, or over-generalizations, which inaccurately describe others and stunt our own growth as flexible and potentially balanced individuals?

If it were possible to be in the minds of all the people with whom we communicate, to know their history, and to read their symbolism, we'd have no problem deciding upon labels and phrases to respectfully communicate our thoughts. But given the impossibility of this, while we continually grow in our experiences, we must also learn to better scrutinize our system of labeling, categorizing, and generalizations in order to find those which lead to the very source of human conflicts and are the "arch-enemy" of appreciation ... **stereotypes.**

Summarily, to label or categorize[5.1] music, people, or cultural features is both a natural and essential element of human communication. As soon, however, as the areas of our biases are communicated to

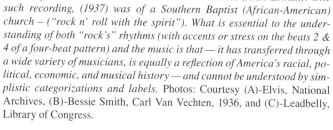

Pic. 5.1 A,B,&C *There are many types of "rock n'roll." The first document-ed use of the term was in Southern Black Churches (Alan Lomax). One such recording, (1937) was of a Southern Baptist (African-American) church – ("rock n' roll with the spirit"). What is essential to the under-standing of both "rock's" rhythms (with accents or stress on the beats 2 & 4 of a four-beat pattern) and the music is that — it has transferred through a wide variety of musicians, is equally a reflection of America's racial, po-litical, economic, and musical history — and cannot be understood by sim-plistic categorizations and labels.* Photos: Courtesy (A)-Elvis, National Archives, (B)-Bessie Smith, Carl Van Vechten, 1936, and (C)-Leadbelly, Library of Congress.

others, they will more often than not be reflected in overgeneralizations or stereotypes. The negative la-beling is based upon whether or not our words *respect* the music or people *on their terms.*

As soon as I say, "Now we are going to talk about jazz…," listeners immediately draw upon their mind files for whatever experiences they have with jazz. If our files are based on a respectful and diverse contact with the genre of "jazz," we will likely wish to interact in the discussion. If our file is virtually unloaded, or has a negative impression of jazz, based more often than not on a superficial impression or experience with it, then we may either feel no particular motivation or may have developed a bias and be unlikely to desire interaction (or do so negatively) on the subject. Whatever our opinion, the question of our being conscious of our exposure and experiences, or how we acquired our information and the validi-ty of that information, is at question. The more we are concerned with how we communicate about oth-ers, the more—much like a professional reporter—we will begin to question our sources.

More often than not, we draw our conclusions about people, music, food, and virtually all the ele-ments of human culture-systems on the basis of limited contact. This is due to the comparably short span of human life and the amount of energy that must be invested in the pursuit of careers, sustenance of fam-ilies, and the general rigor of our personal evolution through the challenges of the life-cycle.

To discern when we are respectfully categorizing for the sake of communication and when we are stereotyping or legitimizing incorrect or superficial contact with another culture or musical genre is obvi-ously not a skill to be mastered, but rather skill sets to be pursued. The following are just a partial list of the habits that can assist both the recognition and elimination of tendencies to stereotype or communicate harmful biases:

- *Questioning our perception* – As simple as this sounds, perpetual questioning of our sources of information, their accuracy, the potential that what we know may have now changed (as people and cultures in the computerized age are changing at enormous speed), or that others' needs, biases, or even greed, may be the source of our information, is not an easy skill to learn. To a great degree, placing a focus on flexibility and a willingness not to "be right" will foster humility and liberate our capacities to reach their full potential, though these skills are proportionately acquired to the development of our own sense of purpose and self-esteem.

- *Developing and trusting intuition and conscience* – Possibly, discussion of the use of intuition and conscience as a source of knowing when we are harmfully categorizing may seem both naive and unscientific. However, science and these spiritual tools may be considered essential partners in the development and maturation of respectful communication about others. To put our entire trust in research and "facts" is to put our entire trust in what we read and believe to be fact, as being fact. Given the enormous history of false categorizations and stereotyping in much of our world's historical reports, this would not be prudent.

- *Close examination of the source of information* – Where did we acquire the information we have about "music (people)"? Were the people from whom we learned about the music part of the culture? When we question not only our perception but also the source of our information, we increasingly develop our potential for objectivity or fairness in our perceptions. As we discussed earlier, people desire to be respected as *they* define respect. If we seek the voice of the cultures or the musicians themselves, and become content only when we are certain that their voices are being represented, we automatically magnify the potential that we will not be over-categorizing or stereotyping.

- *Seeing things over the continuum of time* – A deep respect or appreciation for anything is essentially derived from a deep and unbiased evaluation of its evolution over time. In music, if the listener still attributes a specific style of music to a single culture group, a single composer, or gives too much credence to labeling and categorization without consideration of the entire, complex, multi-cultural, and perpetually modulating nature of the evolution of the genre or piece over time, he or she will likely miss the true nature and validity of the piece. For example, to see jazz or country music as a specific artist, style, or radio station, outside of the context of its evolution and its role in magnifying the complex and deep history of American cultural evolution, including its touchy and essential picture of both racism and racial integration, is an injustice to the music and a distortion of its validity. To question what we know about history, beginning first with our own, and venturing slowly to the histories of others, is an essential step to learning to develop a more accurate and "just" perspective of all things.

To exercise these tools of scrutiny, let's return to a discussion of media, one of the primary sources by which we acquire both respectful labels and stereotypes. The University of Minnesota (School of Journalism & Mass Communication) posted a summary of some of the developments and historical events in the evolution of world media.[5.3] Since these developments occurred primarily in Europe or the United States, they have, therefore, influenced not only the way individuals on those two continents communicate and learn generally but also all other cultures under the influence of the media.

Media Technology Timeline Entries

Remember, as you read these "facts," you are simply getting the picture *we choose to give you*, not the *entire* picture (impossible) or even the *best* picture (unlikely). Read the information from the perspective of deepening your perception, and then reflect on the relevance of these events and how they are reported to your world.

8,000-3100 BCE: In Mesopotamia, tokens used for accounting and record-keeping

640BCE: Coins are circulated

5.2A *Sumerian language cuneiform script clay tablet, 2400-2200 BC. List of gods in order of seniority: Enlil, Ninlil, Enki, Nergal, Hendursanga, Inanna-Zabalam, Ninebgal, Inanna, Utu, Nanna. Writings from Mesopotamia (Uruk, modern Warka) are the earliest written work in the world, giving Mesopotamia the reputation of being the "Cradle of Civilization."* Photo: Courtesy wikipedia.org.

Interpretation: First, credit goes to this study for using BCE and CE to indicate *before common era* and *common era*. This recognizes the fact that the Gregorian calendar has increasingly become the calendar of international communication over time; however, it also acknowledges that, in fairness to communication globally and with other cultures and religions, it is better to denote these eras by a term accessible to all.

Secondly, although there is very little emphasis on the history of commerce, this particular discovery leads to the questioning of the evolution of value and commerce overall and, ultimately, its impact on music. From the earliest Mesopotamian, Egyptian, Roman, Persian, Greek, and Chinese civilizations, we see a perpetual increase in the role of assigning "value" to all things: land, property, and, not too far into Western evolution, intellectual and artistic works as well. What impact has this had on cultures that did not believe in ownership of land, thought, or art? What possible outcome would there be on today's music and art if there were less emphasis on its commercial value? To what extent have the principle of commerce and the assignment of value to *all things* (capitalism) affected creativity in music?

1700BCE First known alphabetic symbols, a few written by Semites in Canaan

1000BCE alphabetic writing appears in various parts of the Near East

920BCE The oldest version of the Hindu epic The Mahabharata

900BCE China's Zhou Dynasty has an organized postal service

800BCE Greeks improve Phoenician alphabet by adding vowels

600BCE First appearance of Latin / The "Near East" has coin, clocks, calendars

530BCE In Athens, a public library

500 BCE Persia develops form of "pony express"

435BCE In China, a solar calendar

Interpretation: Although the first notational systems for Western music would not become common until nearly nine centuries after the beginning of Christianity, the evolution of communication by documentation and writing as well as the establishment of writing and recording by written documentation would lead to the means by which perceptions of our world would be passed from generation to generation.

What we must learn to question, however, is that if the people of the earlier ages were prone, as in all centuries, to classification by their perceptions, and those perceptions included the designation of hierarchy based upon "nations" and "races," and those designations in turn became reinforced over centuries, how much of what we've been using to categorize our world today is accurate or fair? When you look at the generalizations we've selected above, you may get a distinct feeling that the evolution of the world's systems of language, communication, and eventually printing and media technology has truly been a multicultural endeavor. We see as much or more influence from Eastern or "near Eastern" cultures in the evolution of our systems of communication as from Western or European culture. However, once we arrive at what is labeled as the medieval period in the West, we very quickly see a narrowing of inclusions from non-European sources. Once the list begins to include such items as *the formulation of Western universities [1168CE - Oxford University is founded; 1200 - the University of Paris is granted its charter; 1222/1224CE - the University of Padua/Naples if founded],* we—in the West—very quickly begin to lose track of the other trails of evolution on our planet.

From this point on, except for the occasional entry such as "1150 Koreans start printing books from movable type" (thereby contradicting the "invention" of printing with movable type by the Europeans or Johann Gutenburg – mid-1400s), the preponderance of entries honor, exalt, or document the accomplishments of European and Western cultures, exclusive to others.

This leaves us to wonder that if the earlier evolution of communication and exchange between cultures was so critical to the evolution of our languages and communication technology, what happened to these cultures after that? Did they disappear? Do African, Chinese, Indian, Indigenous American, and Near East (Middle Eastern) cultures simply recede into the historical background, waiting for European and American innovations and culture to evolve? And, especially considering that music is an aural art, what about the cultures that practiced sophisticated transmission of their history, stories, and art orally/aurally? Since the documentation of sound communication was not possible until shortly before the twen-

tieth century, many of our world's earliest non-Western civilizations, and all civilizations that put a greater emphasis on oral transmission, are generally missing from our written and recorded vision.

Is it not possible that the memorization and oral transmission of the Indian Vedas from generation to generation (four volumes each—nearly equal to the Christian New Testament 1500-1000BCE), or that the stories and tales transmitted orally throughout the illustrious history of Africa's evolution deserve a place alongside Hippocrates'

Pic. 5.2 and 5.2A *Sanskrit and Sumerian scrolls or parchments. To what degree has our world always been "multi-cultural" and perpetually in contact? What impact would the cultures that place a greater emphasis on the technology of war and conquest – or upon the written documentation and dissemination of their history over the histories of other cultures have – on the way we communicate about and categorize our world today?* [5.4] Photos: Courtesy, wikipedia.org.

study of medicine (circa 420BCE) or Plato's establishment of the Greek Academy (386BCE)? Although these latter developments would become the basis for the European university and the values that European cultures would continually reference through the 19th century, are they a more valid representation of human accomplishment? Or, are we getting a distorted picture not only of what we know but also from whom we know it?

Categorization vs. Stereotyping: Cultural and Religious

We have already referred to the designation of humans by racial or national categorization as "myths." This does not mean that there is not enormous significance to the consideration of these categorizations in our review of history or our assessment of their impact on humanity today. Rather, by this statement we hope to greatly increase the energy that is put into seeing cultures and especially their music outside of the categories, genres, and *generalizations* that obscure their *reality*.

However, there is a far more lethal consequence of adhering to the belief in division and separation by national, racial, or even separatist religious designations, especially to the understanding of art. The desire for advancement, respect, beauty, and spiritual, aesthetic, or physical pleasure, however defined, is a natural drive or extension of the human condition. To create art, music, beautifully colored clothing, or fine buildings is essential to the enjoyment of life. This reality does not to a great degree recognize the superficiality of racial, cultural, or religious separation. Thus, the transfer of cultural, expressive, and artistic ideas between cultures historically is infinitely more dynamic and active a force than the superficial force of isolation, nor is it accurately reflected in historical documentation.

We will see this phenomenon repeatedly in all of the subsequent Units. The influence of the Romani ("gypsy") and Jewish cultures on European and Christian "art" music (and vice versa); the dynamics of inter-Asian exchange of philosophy and art between China, Korea, and Japan; and the "Pan-African" and "Pan-Latino" exchange of music between the "colonizer," the African continent, and the "New World" are all just samples of the manner by which cultural reality defies the categorization of humanity by nation or race. To see being "French" as a cultural reality, when the culture is now, and has always been, completely multicultural, confuses the human with the political. Our human artistic, spiritual, aesthetic, and emotional sensibilities do not cater to political or economic separation to a large degree. Therefore, as we will see, musical categorization by racial or national designation, more often than not, leads to stereotyping.

Does this mean that we should not consider race or nation in evaluating the history of music? Or, that race or national labels are not valid considerations in understanding the context of music? Absolutely not. Since such categorizations are the means by which human ancestry has built its institutions, taught its history, and categorized its music, we must respect the influence of these beliefs on the thinking and perceptions of the musicians and ultimately the music of the past. That the nationalism of 19th-century Europe was the predominant and essential outcome of the competitive forces of feudalism and colonization, and that it gave rise to national schools of art and music, is undeniable. However, as we will also learn, Italian or German opera, or French Ballet, was also influenced by the "folk music" of its peoples, and they included, Jewish, Gypsy, Arab, and Asian *folk* as well. So the oversimplification of labels, or the over-usage of these labels distorts our perception of the art itself. Questioning the category and reopening our investigation is a means of liberation from the ancient dogma and over-usage of stereotypes.

For us, the question is not so much *if* the music of the world is significantly more complex than categorization by musical genre or racial/national labels would imply, but rather, since it is indisputably multicultural and the result of a complex web of exchanges, are we willing to make a quest to re-evaluate — a pervasive tool of our lifestyle? To claim to be "French," "Italian-American," "African-American," or even "Christian," "Jewish," etc., is to profess an affinity for an ethnicity, a system of belief, or cultural expressions that bring us pleasure and self-esteem. However, to believe that the music, food, language, or any other element of these categories is truly separate or distinct within each designation and without extensive influences from cultures outside (potentially even from those despised or rejected by the culture) is a generalization—no, a **stereotype**—which can easily be proven inaccurate and whose promulgation will lead to a distortion of the full appreciation of any musical/cultural creativity.

Pic. 5.3 *Today, the average CD store offers opportunities to travel the world, hear the musical ancestors of our "own" music, and in general, expand our options. In markets less driven by "capital" (such as this East European store) we may find a wider selection of material, and less emphasis on categorizing by labels.* Photo: Authors.

Things to Consider

• **Many of the patterns of human categorization that separate people and music** are inaccurate to their reality and are the results of human strategies with ancient roots in bias, ignorance, and fears passed from generation to generation.

• **Undoing stereotypes and increasing our appreciation of other cultures and music** will require a patient and sustained commitment to re-educating ourselves, and we may sometimes feel alone in our efforts. [That is, many of our friends and family may not wish to move from their engrained perceptions of human categorization].

• **All culture groups which have been categorized as being "inferior" or "less than"** will have scars which will test the resolve of members of other culture groups and force them to demonstrate their sincerity in action over time. In like fashion, all culture groups, and especially those that appear privileged or elite in their culture hierarchy, will have blind spots and areas of ignorance that will test the patience and irritate the sensibilities of the historically repressed groups. Regardless of the position one occupies in one's culture system, remaining culturally blind or indifferent to imbalances, or perpetuating stereotypes, is counter-intuitive or unintelligent.

• **Musical genres are just as prone to mis-categorization** by virtue of labeling and attachment to racial, national, or religious stereotypes. When we begin to look for the inclusion (the manner by which a music incorporates influences outside its apparent genre or ethnic origin) and fusion (the unique combination of two or more influences within a specific piece), we begin to respect the music on its terms. We are not bound to perception of the work solely from the *stereotypes* or over-generalizations that may otherwise dominate our perceptions.

Music and Religion: Reconciling Belief Systems

"My religion consists of a humble admiration of the illimitable superior Spirit who reveals Himself in the slight details we are able to perceive with our frail and feeble mind... before God we are all equally wise - and equally foolish." Albert Einstein (1879-1955)

Perhaps no single phenomenon has had more impact on music than the evolution and practice of religion. Although it may seem strange to think of rock 'n' roll or hip-hop in the context of religion, not a single note, instrument, or manner of performance did not have—at some point in time—extensive ties to the evolution of our world's religions. Yet, nowhere in the annals of human history are there more generalizations and stereotypes than about this topic. More wars have been fought in the name of religion than for probably any other reason (except possibly greed). Religion has been used to justify enormous injustices and to subordinate and enslave masses of humanity; yet, despite its overwhelming importance to our understanding of history, it is arguably the single most avoided and misunderstood topic cross-culturally. To a large extent, humanity's difficulty engaging in passionate and thorough discussions of religion is not due to the principles or teachings of the religions themselves, for, as we shall see, *every* world religion advocates acceptance (love) for others; rather, it is due to the rigid or at times inflexible interpretations of the basic tenets of each religion by the religious practitioners themselves—that is, humans!

In many cases, what amounts to "dualistic thinking" [this *or* that] restricts the possibilities of *inclusiveness,* an essential ingredient in the acceptance of the validity of all religious (and non-religious) beliefs that do not advocate harm or disrespect to others. We can get a helpful picture of the sort of perceptions that have blocked religious discussion both historically and in the present by examining a few of the more predominant religious dualisms [Note: these perspectives are not made by inference that their acceptance is necessary for the reader but rather that their consideration may be essential to the appreciation of the thoughts and music that differ from one's own beliefs]:

> *Only those that accept "my religion" or "prophet" (revealer or Divine Manifestation) will be acceptable before God and/or all others will be condemned or rejected by God.*

Alternative: Perhaps the fact that each religion speaks of its teachings as "the way" or "the path," while also advocating (generally) the religions that preceded it, and most frequently, predicting other "comings" or "returns" as possible, is confusing and central to the dualism above. Essential to avoiding such a dualism which clearly cannot accommodate the respectful acknowledgement of other religions are the other core teachings of each religion:[5.5]

- That our actions (not words or expressions of belief) in this world determine our ultimate destiny in a/the "next world."

- That our acceptance (love) of others, undefined as to who those others are, is one of the central "actions" essential to acceptance of our lives by a Creator.

- That a Divine Creator (God), not man, is the essential judge. Therefore, to judge others by our perception of Faith (others believing as we do) is not only the basis for centuries of religious war and persecution, but tantamount to a rejection of the essential law of all religions: God is God and cannot be "asked" of his doings (or judgment), AND a human is a human, and it is not his/her place to judge the Faith of others.

How much of the world's music has been created in direct or indirect reference to the world's religions? How many songs and symphonies have been expressions of the composer's religious beliefs? Can we appreciate much of the world's music without respecting the musicians' religious beliefs? And, oh yes, what are the dualisms that relate to the practice of religion through music historically?

Whether we take the original Latin definition of **religion** (re- *again* / ligiare – *to connect*) as any endeavor which helps *re-connect* the human being to a purpose for life or "Higher Power" [thus implying that essentially *all music* may be "religious"] or the more pervasive definition of religion (specific belief systems based upon the teachings of a prophet or manifestation of an Unknowable Creator), there is no possibility of respecting much of the world's music without respecting the beliefs from which much of the music extends and all is connected. In short, whatever our religious beliefs, there comes a juncture where appreciating others' music requires the appreciation or respecting of their religious beliefs.

If you are reading this text, there is a strong likelihood that you have the capacity to respect other religions and listen to what they have to say or possibly to see the connections or similarities of other religions to your own beliefs. If not, if you truly believe that only your religious orientation is correct or that only if people come through the belief systems of your orientation will they be acceptable to you or your vision of the Creator, then we offer the following "Golden Rules" taken from many of the world's great religions:

Pic. 5.2C *A embodiment of both the inter-connection and conflicts between our world's great religions, the Dome of the Rock lies in the heart of Jerusalem. The Jews and Christians believe this place to be Mount Moriah, the location where Abraham almost sacrificed his son Isaac at the command of God, where Jacob saw the ladder to heaven, where the innermost chamber of the Jewish Temple stood. The rock in the center of the dome is believed by Muslims to be the spot from which Muhammad ascended through the heavens to God accompanied by the angel Gabriel.* Courtesy, wikipedia.org.

"This is the sum of all true righteousness: deal with others as thou wouldst thyself be dealt by. Do nothing to thy neighbour which thou wouldst not have him do to thee after." The Mahabharata, Hinduism

"That nature only is good when it shall not do unto another whatever is not good for its own self." Dadistan-I Dnik, 94:5, Zoroastrianism

"What is hateful to you, do not to your fellow men. That is the entire Law, all the rest is commentary." The Talmud, Shabbaat, 31a, Judaism

"Hurt not others in ways that you yourself would find hurtful." Udana-Varqa, 5;18. Buddhism

"As ye would that men should do to you, do ye also to them likewise." Luke 6:31, Christianity

"No one of you is a believer until he desires for his brother that which he desires for himself." Sunnah, Islam

"He should not wish for others that which he doth not wish for himself, nor promise that which he doth not fulfill." Gleanings from the writings of Baha'u'llah, Bahá'í Faith

Once we are aware that each of the world's religions professes the acceptance and treatment of others as "we" would like to be treated, and that none of the religions specifies that the *neighbor* must be of the same belief as ourselves or have a belief at all, then any willingness to stereotype, segregate, judge, and most certainly condemn the beliefs of others falls into full contradiction with this basic tenet. Therefore, if we can simply acknowledge that the spiritual principle of acceptance and respect of others is central to the world's major religious systems, then perhaps we can move more deeply into the core of their musical and cultural practices.[5.6]

Here too, we run into a quagmire of dualisms as to the appropriate venue for practicing one's faith through music, or for praying to (speaking to) or meditating about (listening to) the Creator or God. Throughout history, most of the world's religions have had numerous conflicts or dualistic beliefs about the place music should have in religious practice. Some of these include:

Only the recitation (chanting) of the holy texts (revealed teachings by the prophet or manifestation of God) is an acceptable form of worship and all other forms of musical practice are material and will lead to evil.

Alternative: Nearly all religions have had time periods or geographical regions wherein the practitioners of the religion believed that any musical pursuit other than the recitation of the holy verses would lead to excessive "human" or material traits. Whether the earlier centuries of Roman Catholicism or conservative Jewish or Muslim traditions, this belief countered the opposite practice of those who professed no religion or who saw music as a tool for material, sexual, or solely personal gratification, a belief which placed no restriction on its usage. We will attempt to value both perspectives, but mostly to show the impact religion and religious expression has had on music generally.

All music (creation of music for any reason) is a part of the "freedom" of expression of the individual. And no one has the right to tell anyone what he or she can or cannot say.

Pic. 5.3 *The world's temples, churches, cathedrals, and mosques – such as this Mosque of Hassan II in Casablanca, Morocco (the 2nd largest religious building in the world) – are testimony to the artistic vision and passion that may be inspired by religion.* Photo: Courtesy and copyright, Terry Abrams, 2005.

Alternative: The virtual canyon between the restriction of musical practices to the recitation of holy verses by the human voice (chant) and the enormous commercialization or what some perceive as a void in spiritual connection in commercial music will be tough to cross without a bridge. We will attempt to moderate excesses in individualism and the belief that *freedom* means we can say whatever we wish—regardless of whether it restricts the freedoms of others, or that some music may be fairly mired in sensationalism, in the business of making money, or in the advocating of promiscuity, sexuality, or even hate or violence against others, with the perspective that as mentioned it should not be the role of the individual to judge others, but to understand them. Simultaneously, to advocate using the tools and capacity of music to enlighten, inspire, heal, and create beauty and connection between humans and their purpose for living makes it difficult to accommodate any form of excess or hatred towards others.

Certainly, an individual's right or freedom of expression is a principle of creative democracy. Essential perhaps to the consideration of the *music appreciator* (respecter of music) are these questions: When does music lead to the advancement of one's spirit, the edification of one's character, and the fostering of peace or well-being between human beings—*versus*—When does it restrict not only others' freedom to advance, but potentially one's own? This is obviously a question each person must answer for him- or herself.

Since it is not the place of this text to define morality or spirituality for others, any more than to advocate one musical style over another, yet religions and religious beliefs play major roles in helping us understand and reconcile the extreme outer regions of the continuum of musical relevance:

> *"We have made it lawful for you to listen to music and singing. Take heed, however, lest listening thereto should cause you to overstep the bounds of propriety and dignity. Let your joy be the joy born of My Most Great Name, a Name that bringeth rapture to the heart, and filleth with ecstasy the minds of all who have drawn nigh unto God. We, verily, have made music as a ladder for your souls, a means whereby they may be lifted up unto the realm on high; make it not, therefore, as wings to self and passion..."* [5.7]

As to the interpretation of what is dignified, that is where individual freedom and discernment must be exercised. Unfortunately, many of the systems of commerce and media make being *human* and attempting to discern which music is creatively beneficial to the spirit and which is not, a difficult exercise. Most musicians can differentiate between the instances when spiritual magic and beauty are achieved, musical moments that bind the musicians and the audience to the music, and the times when solely anger, self-centered fears, or material pursuits that, according to religious or spiritual teachings, dull the senses or obscure perception of a Higher Power are practiced. This discernment is equally the challenge of the music appreciator.

Before continuing our discussion of religion and religious music, we should address one of the important aspects of creative music – and one that was as applicable to young people in Mozart's time as it is for youth today: the role of **countercultures** in music.

Counterculture Music

Countercultures, loosely defined, are movements or culture groups that express themselves against the grain of what is perceived as acceptable in mainstream culture. There are two main branches of *counter-culture* movements.

One: Frequently seen as expressions of a generation "gap," *counter-culture* movements may be created by student–aged groups or youth with similar affinities and a strong need to create a sense of community. These movements are most strong, graphic, and poignant in cultures where individualism, materialism, or disrespect for community or the life cycle leads parents away from intimate contact with their children. If there is animosity between parents and young people as they mature and find their own identities, the strength and degree of the "gap" and the requirement to create a sense of community elsewhere will animate the young people's attraction to "counterculture" movements.

Two: Countercultures might also develop in reaction to social, governmental, or cultural practices and especially injustices. In this sense, what is considered "normal" may actually be a distortion or abuse of human rights or logic. In such instances as killing, war, or human injustice, *counter-culture* movements may be built in reaction to provide a voice for youthful conscience.

In both cases above, the following generally also hold true:

- Counterculture movements are the strongest with youth and young adults. Their intensity varies with the degree to which the youth feel animosity and discontent with their worlds (personal or cultural).
- Counterculture movements will, as the youth and musicians age, eventually change their meaning and relationship to culture, frequently becoming *mainstream* over time.
- Each generation of counter-culture movements will need to alter the sound and strengthen the appearance and lyrical content of their music from that previously deemed "counter" in order to conflict or challenge mainstream expressions.

Can violent or negative music **cause** *violence or negative actions?*

Although this is a difficult question and one which has historically fueled animosity across generations, one general consensus amongst musicians themselves is that music and art generally act more like a mirror of one's existing state or condition than a catalyst for the creation of a state or condition. In this sense, if one is already filled with anger, hatred, or despair, then the music can further intensify what is there, possibly inciting one to act on the existing emotion. However, music, although it has amazing potential to increase emotional intensity and motivate the human spirit, cannot by itself cause a human who holds no anger or animosity to act in an angry and violent way. In short, music does not *cause* violence or negativity, but can, if listened to by people not certain of themselves, or discontent with their lives, increase the level of discontent.

When parents and elders of each generation make the music or nature of the music listened to by their youth the focus, they miss the fact that the music is really more a "letter" being sent, or mirror reflection of the emotional and mental concerns of the youth. Therefore, discussions are better directed at the feelings of the youth towards life and family generally than at the music itself. Beyond this, one should not be too quick to react, as many thoughtful and concerned messages are sent in the disguise of energetic or even aggressive music.

Pic. 5.3B *A Canadian rock band performs under the lights, with huge speaker towers, and with lyrics and stage antics designed to promote community euphoria – and challenge many of the things that young adults in urban-material Western centers challenge … not the least of which is authority itself.* Photo: istockphoto.

Role(s) and Responsibilities of Youth

Each stage or phase of the life cycle has a series of specific and non-negotiable rights and responsibilities that must be maintained (see Discussion VI-A) in order to sustain the positive welfare of the community and to provide humanity a boost of needed, positive, and creative energy. Among these, great focus must be placed on our future leaders—the youth.

However, in much of our world today, youth are forced to battle extremes in materialism, injustice, racism, inequality, dysfunctional or biased families, communities, or inequitable education; thus, their creative potential can become compromised, diverted to repairing damage or used purely for survival. Repairing this damage can occupy youth well into the adult phase of the life cycle, and deprive their communities of the needed positive, creative energy that can both heal and reform.

Suggestion: Examine the images below and consider the questions in the context of the youth in the pictures.

Pic. 5.3A1 *A mother and daughter visiting the ancient ruins of the Temple at San Gervasio (Cozumel, Mexico) which "was a site dedicated to the Mayan goddess Ixchel ("She of the Rainbows"), deity of midwifery, fertility, medicine, and weaving. Many women from the mainland… made the pilgrimage here to Ixchel´s shrine at some point in their lifetime."* www.mayasites.com.

Pic. 5.3A2 *This is a village street on an island off the coast of Honduras. The two youths spent hours engaged in creating and discussing street art.*

Questions

- *Against the backdrop of centuries of inequality between male and female, how does this picture and the description of the shrine strike you? Based solely on the picture, what do you imagine this young woman will do with her "youth cycle" years and energy? Why? (Pic. 5.3A1)*

- *Why are the youth years believed to be the period of greatest creativity and questioning? What must take place in a community to see that this energy is directed towards constructive and positive ends? What happens to youthful creative energy when adults or a culture neglects them? (Pic. 5.3A2)*

Intoning the Verses: Chant—The Melody of the Spirit

Among the methods for worship or "re-connecting" to a Higher Power (God) or passing along the teachings of all religions is the practice of **chanting** or **intonement** (putting pitches or tones to religious verses). In simplest terms, chanting slows down the text or thoughts, places them into pitched or defined frequencies, which resonate through the human voice and create the capacity through melody to attach a deeper emotional or spiritual connection of the words or thoughts to influence *the spirit, or the soul.*

Since most of us may not likely chant or listen to chanting on a regular basis, if the practice of *melodic chanting* (cantillation or intonement) were restricted to the synagogue, temple, church, or mosque, we would not need to address this in the context of music *appreciation.* However, so pervasive is the influence of chant and the melodic singing-styles of the world's religious musical systems on both the instrumental and the vocal melodies of each culture that it becomes essential to investigate *chanting* regardless of one's religious beliefs or musical tastes. Since we are entering difficult waters for some, we may wish to remember the following:

- The "boundaries" between **sacred** music (that which pertains to religious practice) and **secular** (that which is *seemingly* not religious) are seldom as pronounced as historical perspectives of either religion or music tend to indicate. In nearly all cultures, the influence of religious music on popular music and vice versa is considerable;

- Nearly *all music* has some connection to the broader definition of religion as a means of "re-connecting" humanity (or the artist) to a purpose, whether directly tied to a religion or not. In this sense, the most "non-religious" piece may, to the musician, be a question or reflection about life, its purpose and the primary means for conveying their thoughts is through lyrics tied to melody. Most melodies (arguably all) have a strong connection to religious chant.

Pic. 5.3C *Saraceni painting of Pope Gregory I, also known as Pope Gregory the Great [after whom Gregorian chant is named]. He is frequently given credit for the codification of chant and general formatting of liturgy which was passed from generation to generation orally to become the Roman Catholic mass. Later (circa 9th century), these chants (plainchants) would be documented and recorded by monks in the Roman Catholic church, through a notation system that would evolve into the musical system of notation used in documenting (notating) Western music until today.* Photo: Courtesy, wikipedia.org.

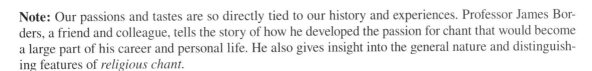

Stories from the Human Family

Note: Our passions and tastes are so directly tied to our history and experiences. Professor James Borders, a friend and colleague, tells the story of how he developed the passion for chant that would become a large part of his career and personal life. He also gives insight into the general nature and distinguishing features of *religious chant.*

> *"I grew up as a child in Chicago. I started singing in the Boys Choir when I was six years old. We had a great music teacher; her name was Sister John-Anthony. As the boys' choir got better, it would eventually blend into the larger choir, which included men and boys (the boys would sing the "soprano" or higher parts).*

> *"We learned not just the basics of music, but especially Gregorian chant. We learned how to sing on pitch, and also how to sing in the **modes** (the pitch menus derived from Greek and Arab scales). She would sometimes criticize us if we were singing G Ionian when we should be singing G mixolydian (two different modes or scales based on a common "tonic" or foundation pitch).*

"So I grew up singing Gregorian chant before Vatican II.[5.8] The popular music and even other classical music was great, but it didn't have the kind of patterns or flow of the chant. Specifically rock or jazz had standard formats (regular beat and meter structures and predictable form). Gregorian chant doesn't work by those structures. And so I guess, what stuck in my mentality was that it didn't work either tonally (pitches) or formally (form and structure). I also had a problem with the fact that the church had just thrown this chant-style music out. So chant has become a passion for me.

"In terms of what chant can mean, any chant or singing of a sacred text is different than everyday speech. It's a form of heightened speech directed either to the Creator (Deity) or to the community. A prayer is words offered to God. So to offer prayer in the same way that you would order a hamburger doesn't seem right, if you think about it that way. Another way that chant of all types represents heightened speech is a communication to the whole, sometimes communicating to a congregation or community, or the group communicating with itself. We know from yoga or meditative practices how important the breath is. So chant is not just a type of music, but a manifestation of a way of life. Gregorian chant grew up in a Monastic framework (monastery communities of monks). This must not have been lost on these people who developed it.

"Concerning the communication value of chant, this has to do with a kind of structure. Whether Buddhist, Catholic, or any chant, there is the raising of the aesthetic level. It's not just singing for the sake of singing because now I'm 'talking to God.' In the medieval context, it's something like the difference between how a monk might prepare a manuscript (with incredible care, detail, and ornamentation) and how he might write a laundry list (without concern for its appearance). So chant developed in its aesthetic dimension with increased 'flowery,' coloratura, or melisma (ornamentation of the melody).

Pic. 5.3D *Vatican City from the top of St. Peter's Basilica, also the location of both Vatican I (1869) and II (1962), the extended conferences in which major changes in Catholic policy and practice were made.* Photo: Courtesy of Paradiso.

"We know that both Jewish and Christian music were influenced by a variety of different sources and from each other. We know that Hebrew people marked the hours of the days (and nearly all religious events) with singing and chant. So there has to be a cultural connection between cultures. We also know that much of Gregorian chant comes from deep within the Mediterranean cultures. This would obviously connect to both Greek and Arabic modes. So what came down to us as 'Gregorian chant' must have been the result of a series of 'hybridizations' of all these cultures.

"The best analogy we can make is if we were building a structure in Rome during medieval times. If you built a house in a rural or deserted part of Rome, and there was a bit of column from an ancient structure, and a boulder from another time, and then bricks that the guy down the street just made. What you're doing is using what you have at hand, whatever is within the range of your vision. You still need to build a wall, and you really don't care where the ingredients come from. Gregorian chant had a very practical purpose, and that was to serve the interest of worship for the mass and prayer hours during the day. This practice had grown from practically Biblical times, so like an archeological dig, there are layers upon layers of influences and alteration over time." Interview, James Borders, Professor of Musicology, University of Michigan, May 2005.

Melodic Chanting

A *melody* is a series of pitches organized one after another. Since **pitches** are singable or of a recognizable **frequency** (a single vibration measured by vibrations per second

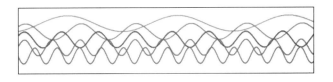

or *hertz*), any instrument that produces pitches can perform melody. The one instrument that most permeates the music of all cultures and all genres is the human voice.

Therefore, since the most intimate and closely connected instrument to the human spirit is the instrument biologically attached to the human frame—the voice—it is not illogical that religious history is permeated with musical or tonal expression of religious texts, prayers, and songs chanted by the voice. For some styles of religious chant, the voice is used to produce a *mantra* or sound that draws the human mind inward to the spirit; for others, the voice recites holy texts that are passed from generation to generation outward to an audience or congregation; and for others still, composers or trained musicians write elaborate melodies with instrumental accompaniment to praise God or exalt the listener to a heightened state of emotion. We can also generalize the following about religious chants, songs, and compositions:

- The chants and melodies of each religion greatly influence the religious chants and songs of other religions that follow. Therefore, early Christian chants (Eastern European or Russian Orthodox and "Gregorian" chants of the 9th century) were heavily influenced by Jewish and Greek chants, and Islamic chanting was heavily influenced by all these as well as Vedic and Zoroastrian chant styles.

- Chant melodies of each religion greatly impact the song or singing styles of the "folk" or popular music of each generation and region. Conversely as well, popular styles of music have impact upon the chanting or religious song styles of each generation and region.

- Chant melodies also greatly influence the instrumental compositions and melodic styles of each culture. What we learn to sing or value in the voice so too do we play. The compositions of composers from Monteverdi or Stravinsky to Muddy Waters or B.B. King ring with the musical remnants, phrasing, and sensibilities of vocalized melody based on the rhythm, meaning, and intonation of the text.

As we listen to the chants, songs, and musical compositions of the world's religions and read the commentary of the musicians or religious culture-bearers, we may also be drawn to the connection these pieces have to our own world, whatever our beliefs. We might also be intrigued by the manner in which so much of what might have appeared foreign to our experiences and beliefs is directly connected to our own cultures and music.

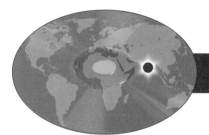

Inside the Chanter's World

Mrinalini Arkatkar
Vedic Chant

Saha Nabhavatu Saha Nau Bhunnaktu
May the Lord protect us together.
Sahaveeryam Karavaavahi
May he nourish us together
Tejasvi Naavadheetamastu
May we work together uniting our
strength for the good of humanity.[5.9]

Note: The East Indian **Vedas** are among the oldest written texts on our planet. They date back to the beginning of Indian civilization and are arguably the earliest religious works still in use today. Some believe the Vedas to have been transmitted orally for thousands of years until finally being written down between 1800 and 800 BCE. Others believe that they first came into existence with the invasion of the Aryan culture into India during that time period. Regardless of the Vedas' origin, Aryan beliefs and daily life are described through recitation of the four Vedas ("veda" meaning *knowledge*), which are a collection of poems and sacred hymns composed during what is called the *Vedic Period*.

Picture of Lord Ganesha (Ganesh)

The Vedas are divided into four groups, Rigveda, Yajurveda, Samaveda, and Atharvaveda. Each group has an original text (*mantra*) and a commentary portion (*Brahmana*). Among the Vedas, Samaveda is in verses that are to be sung and is concerned more with rituals than philosophy. Learning the chanting discipline of the Vedas was frequently begun by pupils at a very early age and required incredible discipline and respect for the teacher as well as nearly unparalleled capacity for memorization, which included learning the Sanskrit texts in varied formats (forwards, backwards, etc.) to assure complete memorization. Earlier, most of the chants (such as the one below) would use only three pitches (a base or home pitch or **drone** and two others). The reduction of pitches to a small group is universal to religious texts of longer duration. Additionally, the drone or base pitch would later become the musical formula for much Indian "classical" music and even the basis for Western music as well (although the *drone,* or *tonic,* as it is called in the West, is not sounded continually throughout the piece).

In shorter passages, meditations, and song styles, such as that in Unit IX, a wider diversity of emotion is accomplished melodically by a greater variation in the melodic **contour** (the formula of rising and falling of pitches in the melody), a greater **range** (distance between the lowest and highest pitches), and would include a wider variety of instruments for accompaniment. The *tanpura* (tambura), is commonly used to support Vedic chanting today.

CD 1.17

"Atharva Sheersha" (believed to be from the **"AtharvaVeda"**), by Mrinalini Arkatkar, from a recording made for this text, copyright, 2005.

Ms. Mrinalini Arkatkar learned her chanting and singing styles and their connections to Hindu symbolism from her **guru** (an exalted station for the teacher – see Unit IX), Dr. Patavardhan. She is very careful to give credit to her guru, and also is quick to comment that it is the chant not the chanter that should be acknowledged (thereby removing herself from credit or accolades, an important distinction between *intonement or chant* and performance). Ms. Arkatkar commented: *"This particular chant describes the moral fiber of Lord Ganesha, who is believed to be the God (a physical representation of a higher ideal … not the same as God, the Creator) of wisdom and prosperity, and is always remembered before the beginning of any event. It is written by Atharva "Muni" (Rishi) and believed to be from "Atharva-veda."*

She goes on to explain that Lord Ganesha, known as Aumkara because His body mirrors the shape of the Aum, the elephant god, is thus seen as the embodiment of the cosmos. His elephantine head symbolizes the intelligence and beatitude of the elephant, powerful yet gentle. His companion is a mouse (mooshikam), which symbolizes the nature of the intellect (small enough to find out any secret in the most remote of places), but also signifies His humility (that He keeps company with one of the earth's smaller creatures). Since he is the remover of obstacles, it is normal to invoke Him before the undertaking of any task with such incantations as *Aum Shri Ganeshaya Namah* (hail the name of Ganesha).

As you hear the drone in the background, listen also how the chant moves from the drone or center pitch to the one above or below, continually returning to the drone or center pitch. This is the simplest and most direct form of chant, which as we mentioned, lent itself to the memorization and recitation of vast textual verses over long periods of time.

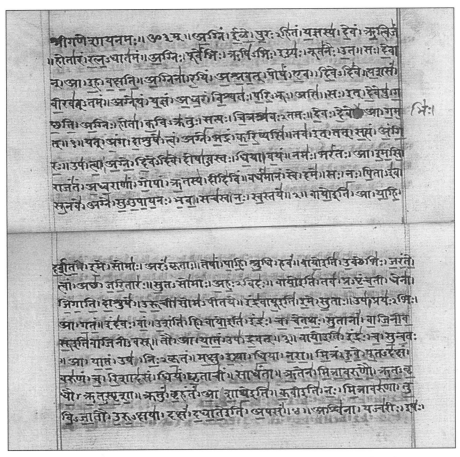

Pic. 5.4A *A Rigveda manuscript in Devanagari, early 19th century.* Photo: public domain.

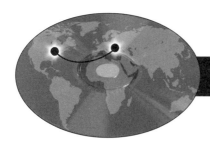 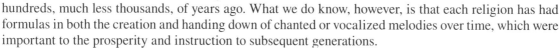

Inside the Chanter's World

Herman Slomovits

with comments by his sons – Laszlo and Sandor

CANTOR HERMAN SLOMOVITS

Remember the days of old, Consider the years of ages past;

Ask your father, he will inform you; Your elders, they will tell you. Deuteronomy

Note: We don't know exactly how the chant and musical practices of the older world's religions sounded hundreds, much less thousands, of years ago. What we do know, however, is that each religion has had formulas in both the creation and handing down of chanted or vocalized melodies over time, which were important to the prosperity and instruction to subsequent generations.

In Judaism, chanting of the holy verses, or **cantillation,** was a perpetually evolving art. In each location where Jewish communities would settle over the course of centuries, the cantor's melodies would greatly influence the musical traditions of the Jewish community, and the community's music at large would greatly influence the melodies and chant styles of the cantor. As time passed, and the melodies and music of the synagogue became increasingly influenced by instrumental music or with the song and music structures of each region, the process of adaptation and fusion in music became as natural to Jewish musicians as the desire to maintain traditions and formulas of their ancestry. Cantor Annie Rose, one of the rising number of female cantors, commented:

> *"A cantor is like a singing rabbi. The cantor 'holds the heart' of the people sometimes because of the strength of music and melody to convey things you can't just express through speech. And so if the person sang well, and he – and initially all cantors were males – really did his job, and hearts could be moved. The old expression 'from your lips to God's ears'—I usually turn around to say: 'No, I'm just you singing.' The basic role of the cantor is to interpret text through song or melody.*

> *"Whether it's a prayer, or chanting from the Torah or sacred scrolls (Jewish holy writings), the job of the cantor is to present a penetrating reality of the words through music. Whether the chants are improvised[5.10] or learned and passed down across generations is somewhat dependent upon the cantor and the needs or desires of the congregation – or whether more "Orthodox" or contemporary. In the course of a contemporary reform service, there may be twenty-five times that a cantor sings. At least ten are melodies, however short or long, that everyone knows is coming. Then another ten will be things that vary from week to week or according to the season, but are still familiar. Then the rest will vary. Even when you improvise, it is based upon particular modes or scales that you know in advance must be part of that chant or song.*

"Cantors in Europe did blend and fuse with European operatic style, and the music took on elements of 'classical' music performances of Europe. Of course, a very beautiful performance can still be very engaging and uplifting, and so this style of chanting prospered for some time. Maybe, too, that's why there were a significant number of cantors who sang opera as well. Jan Pierce or Richard Tucker clearly magnified the connection between cantorial singing and opera, as it frequently existed.

"Today, cantorial singing, and maybe this is because nearly half of the cantors these days are women, which truly would affect the role and nature of the cantor in general … the role of the cantor is more to engage the congregation spiritually. I think the feminine energy of engagement is different than that of performance, regardless of whether you're a male or female."

The example of cantor-style melody in CD 1.18 represents an older version of Ashkenazi (Eastern European-style) that reflects the intertwining of Jewish tradition with European "art" or "classical" musical performance. Cantor Herman Slomovits was born in Máramoros Sziget, Hungary, in 1910. In the late 1940's and early 1950's he sang in some of the major synagogues in Budapest, Hungary, including in the Dohány Utca Templom, the largest synagogue in Europe. He immigrated to Israel in 1957, and then to the United States in 1959, where he served as cantor in Kingston, NY, as well as in Hartford, CT, and Hallandale, FL. His two sons, Laszlo and Sandor, themselves musicians (see Unit VII), give an account of their father, his role as a cantor, and his influence on them.

"Shema – Kiddusha," (from Jewish daily prayers), by Herman Slomovits, from the CD: **Herman Slomovits, Cantor,** c. 1958.

Laszlo: *"We grew up from an early age hearing our father sing and then starting to sing with him. At first our roles were to sing 'Amen' and little things like that (laughs). Then little by little, we learned more. Our father never formally sat us down and gave us lessons; we'd just hear him sing, and then imitate. Then he might give us a few pointers like "You can try singing a third above." Then we'd say a third above what? He'd sing and then we'd do it. Most of the learning came from watching and listening. We went to the synagogue, and particularly on the Sabbath[5.11] we'd sing with him."*

Sandor: *"Father grew up in a very small village, but by the age of thirteen he was traveling around to villages near where he lived to sing. He told us that one of the first times he sang, he was so short that they put him on a box behind the altar to make him look like he was grown (laughs). He later served as Rabbi and Cantor for a small village before the war (WWII). During the war he and his family were taken away and very few came back. When he returned (November of 1944 – he was in labor camps and not the death camps), his family was gone and most of the community was gone as well."*

He used to tell us that before the war, he probably would not have been hired as a cantor as he did not come from a lineage of cantors; but after the war a lot of the cantors were gone, so the tragedy led to his opportunity to work as a cantor."

Laszlo: *"You asked how he learned to be a cantor. Just like most jazz musicians will go around to clubs, he would go around to the various synagogues and learn just by listening. Actually he did this later in life as well."*

Sandor: *"Our father knew many of the most famous cantors. Some were from Po-land or Russia; many wound up in New York or L.A. These guys all had operatic-quality voices so that they could project and fill up a large synagogue. This passage, 'Shema – Kiddusha,' is from the Daily Prayers. It was recorded in Haifa, Israel, circa 1958.*

Pic. 5.5A *Prayers for Jewish prayer services are collected in the Siddar. The hazzan or chazzan (Hebrew for 'cantor') is generally someone who specializes in both chanting the prayers of the Siddar and leading the congregation.* Photo: Courtesy Steve Nallan.

The text translates:

'Hear, O Israel, the Lord our God, the Lord is One.

One is the Eternal our God, our Father, our Sovereign, and our Savior;

and He will again in mercy proclaim in the presence of all living.'"

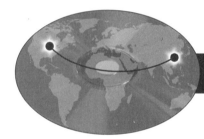

Inside the Chanter's World

Ven. Samu Sunim,
Buddhist chant

Let none through anger or ill-will wish harm upon another;
Even as a mother protects with her life her child, her only child;
So with a boundless heart,
should one cherish all living beings.
Metta Sutta

Pic. 5.6 *A bronze Buddha on Lantau Island, Hong Kong.* Photo: Stanley Yap

Note: Each religion brings numerous qualities and practices to the world, which over the course of time inspire and influence the development and evolution of all the sciences and arts within their jurisdiction. Such is the nature of all religion, as is clearly visible when one begins to investigate the history and principles of Buddhism. During roughly the same time span that Zoroastrianism had become popular in ancient Persia (500 BCE), Siddhartha Guatama (Buddha) began teaching the doctrines of detachment from this world and love for others that have animated the lives and cultural structures of much of Asia for the last two millenniums. (Note: We will deal more extensively with the influence of Buddhism on Asian music in Unit IX)

The chant you will hear is led by the Venerable Samu Sunim,[5.12] spiritual director of the Buddhist Society for Compassionate Wisdom (BSCW), which has Zen Buddhist temples in Ann Arbor, Michigan; Chicago, Illinois; Mexico City; and Toronto. Ven. Samu Sunim was born in Korea in 1941. Orphaned during the Korean War, he entered a Buddhist monastery following a period of homelessness. He completed his Zen training at Pomo-Sa monastery in Pusan, Korea, ultimately leaving his native country for New York in 1968, where he founded the BSCW. In this chant, we hear and feel the compassion and depth of devotion that religious adherents have for the ancestry of their faiths expressed, in this instance, "through the paying of homage (respect) to both the source of their beliefs and the great teachers of the past." (Interview, Joe Lukomski, 2005).

"Yebul – Homage to the Three Jewels," by the Ven. Samu Sunim, from the CD: <u>**Moon Journeying through Clouds,**</u> c. 1995 BSCW.

> The Ven. Samu Sunim writes: *"With a strike of the mok'tak (a hollow wooden instrument struck with a stick) the Buddhist chant Yebul beings … "Fragrance of Morality, fragrance of Concentration, fragrance of Wisdom … I pay homage to all Buddhas,[5.13] the Teachings, and the Spiritual Community (the three Jewels).*

> *"Yebul is chanted at morning and evening services worldwide at Buddhist temples that follow the Korean Zen tradition.[5.14] Chanting, like sitting quietly, is another form of meditation for a Buddhist. Although this particular chant is a 'prayer,' the words in most chants are not intended to be the focus but rather the sound (vibration). The restless mind should be kept still while you center your attention on the sound of your own voice. When we are strongly centered, we can be keenly aware of our emotions and feelings. Zen masters say that when you and the sound become one, you don't hear the sound; you are the sound."*

The principle above, can be applied to listening to music, any music. Practicing a focus on the music and its structure and its emotion allows us to hear rather than just listen. Try to take a few moments to sit comfortably, relax, and still your mind before playing the piece. As you listen, hear the voices rise and fall, the phrases punctuated by the mok'tak. Try to stay relaxed and focused on the sounds through the piece. As with any form of meditation, if you wander mentally, don't fight your thoughts; just return them to the music.

Pic. 5.6A *Young Buddhist monk chanting.* Photo: public domain.

When Is It Culture? … When Nation? … When Religion?

When we question whatever we read, hear, or think in the context of flexibility and exchange across the perceptual borders that we've come to use to define religious culture systems we may experience discomfort. That discomfort may occur, in light of the intimate relationship most humans have with their personal religious beliefs, is even more likely when we consider: a) the enormous contributions made to the world of music through the cross-influence and exchange *between* religions; and b) the conflicts and misinformation across or between religious cultures that have permeated history and our perception of it.

Christianity, for example, has had a profound effect on the evolution of much of the world's music. What we might call "classical" or "art" music was developed primarily in Europe and Russia, and was directly or indirectly connected to Christianity. However, European cultures evolved not despite, but as a result of, interaction with Jewish, Arab, Muslim, and Asian cultures as well. Since, as we mentioned earlier, these cultures were also the source of our universities, the common calendar, and much of what we have come to accept as "Western culture," it becomes an essential task to see the cultural and musical *realities* (a fair and respectful understanding of what actually exists without the bias of cultural preferences) if we are from a Western or Western-Christian background. For this reason, we will devote the next Unit (Unit VI) to the understanding of European music, including *folk* and *classical or art* music, the influences of the Christian church (Roman Catholic and Protestant), and the exchange of influence between Christianity and other religions. We will then spend time looking into the influences of Greek, Jewish, and Romany cultures on both folk and classical music genres of Europe (Unit VII).

By attempting to separate church and state as part of the Western (American) doctrines of democracy, we may actually have softened our scrutiny and understanding of the degree to which religion and state are inseparable. One can avoid talking about something and simultaneously be directly involved in nurturing its influence in every other manner.

Furthermore, given that so much of what we know and what we do in Western cultures is somehow connected to Western Christian culture-systems and the evolution of European values, most of which were heavily influenced by the Church, many of us may have come to accept, whether tacitly or consciously, that Western music is the *most developed* (even preferable) music. Since the most significant

Pic. 5.6A *A Bible handwritten in Latin, on display in Malmesbury Abbey, Wiltshire, England. The Bible was written in Belgium in 1407 AD, for reading aloud in a monastery.* Photo: Adrian Pingstone, 2005, and released to the public domain.

source of our perceptions is our experiences, if most around us are looking at the same phenomena and speaking the same rhetoric, we can very easily believe that this *is what is to be believed.*

In Western music education, the emphasis on European music over that of other cultures or religious systems is especially evident as we survey six of the most-used texts for the generic Music Appreciation courses taught in most colleges and universities.[5.15] Of the six, only one of the texts has 20% of its space devoted to popular or "folk", non-Western or "world," or what some still call "ethnic" music[5.16] (thereby implying

Pic. 5.7 *If we say "music," "history," or any other topic without specifying, we should now mean that of any or all cultures. Today – a "world series," "music appreciation," or "world news," event or program cannot be world – or music if it does not have the integrity of being inclusive of all (or attempting to be). Most Western universities have "music" programs or classes that include the beautiful music of orchestras such as this. What is not beautiful at all – is that they assume this to be music, thereby disrespecting much of the rest of the world – and denying their students the beauty of the music of other cultures as well.* Photo: Philharmonic Orchestra of Jalisco, courtesy Pedro Sánchez.

that European art music is "non-ethnic"- a fatal flaw to objectivity). In this sense, what many call "music appreciation" is really "Western" music appreciation, and the music of other cultures or religions is either mentioned in passing or not mentioned at all. Also, seldom mentioned is the influence or cross-influence of these other culture groups or religions in the context of the evolution of Christian or classical/art music. And for that matter, often the enormous influence of Christianity on our seemingly "non-religious" art or "classical" music is addressed only in passing.

We will continue to emphasize—what is missed by not demonstrating the integration and connection of human cultures and religions is the very perspective that human culture groups do not abide by the political separation and stereotyping passed down by our collectively biased and limited ancestral vision. When we are given accurate pictures of the alternatives of cross-cultural and religious exchange out of the ruins of overt stereotypes and mono-cultural perspectives, we increase our capacity to observe cultural phenomena of this century with our eyes open. Considering the question *"When have we not been multicultural?"* is essential to the reprogramming of stereotypical labeling with the more vibrant and accurate dynamics of perpetual cultural fusion.

Those of us living in Europe or possibly any place colonized or extensively influenced by these culture systems, will likely feel a bit of resistance to some of the considerations that follow.

Since the mindsets and values of these larger culture systems have to a large extent become our own, we may at times be forced to question, when is something "great," and when is it "great" *because* that is all we know or what we've *been trained to believe* is "greatness"? The balancing paradigm is to continue to believe in the greatness or beauty of what we know, but to place it progressively on the same scales and with the same respect to the myriad of things we do not know or have not been taught.

Obviously, being of a dominant culture group poses liabilities when living within and among institutions built upon that dominance. In like fashion, others may have, in the interest of equity and balance, begun to (i.e., in the West) reject or question *anything* that is derived from the European, Euro-Christian, or "white" culture systems. Somewhere in the middle is the mind that comprehends one's own value while seeing and extending energy towards the eradication of one's own biases and stereotypes.

To seek a balance, we'll begin by addressing what we call Middle Eastern (Mid-East/North African) and Islamic cultures so that the reader may explore more completely the perceptual tools outlined above and be able to discern healthy categorization or unhealthy stereotyping even in the midst of discussing *re-ligion.*

Overcoming Stereotypes: Melodies of the Islamic World

"O mankind, We have created you from a male and a female and have made you into nations and tribes for you to know one another... Truly, God is All-Knowing, All-Aware." Qur'an, 49:13

"But (remember that an attempt at) requiting evil may, too, become an evil: hence whoever pardons (his foe) and makes peace, his reward rests with Allah— for, verily He does not love transgressors." Qur'an 42:40

For many in the West at the start of the 21st century, one of the greatest challenges has been to acquire an unbiased understanding of the cultures that are connected to Islam. Most certainly since the Crusades of medieval times, one of the greatest challenges concerning over-labeling or generalizing to the point of stereotyping has been the reconciliation of Christian cultures with religious and culture systems which seem either foreign or in contradiction to Western beliefs. To many, the cultures labeled as *Middle East-ern* and the manner by which religion is practiced in most of the cultures of this region may seem far removed from the Western experience. As usual, though, reality and perception are at odds.[5.17] As we shall see in discussing the evolution of European cultures in Unit VI, a clearer understanding of many Islamic cultures will depend upon our ability to comprehend cultural/religious interconnectivity.

Although there is enormous diversity throughout the culture groups erroneously designated by the label **Middle Eastern** (a designation which includes parts of Southern Asia and North Africa, with extensive influences as far as Indonesia and Africa South of the Sahara as well), we will need to address both Islam and the variations by which both Islam and the music derived from the cultural traits of each region is practiced.

The subsequent section is devoted to Islam and the cultures of the Near or Middle East and Northern Africa. What we hope to demonstrate is that: 1) the Arabic and Islamic world has contributed to much of what we call Western music (thus, to be Western is to be *in part* "Middle Eastern"); 2) the manner of prayer and teachings of Islam have greatly influenced the singing styles and, through the singing, the musical styles of the "Middle East"; and 3) the poetry of Islam (Arabic/Persian) regions has influenced (though not without controversy) many song and song/dance genres that have in turn both provided and taken on influences from other regions of the world as well.

Pic. 5.8 *The "Mosque of the Prophet" (Masjid al-Nabawi) in Saudi Arabia.* Photo: Ali Mansuri.

Beyond News and Media Images

No one can justify the holocaustal conflicts that have been waged in the name of religion or that have been waged against humans because of religion over the course of human history. From the earliest conflicts in the Old Testament, through nearly 300 years of war between Christianity and Islam, to conflicts of the last 300 years, religion has been the justification for colonization, slavery, and terrorism. The aftermath of wars and conflicts in the name of religion is the source of most of our world's most lethal stereotypes and a large part of why today we have such difficulty discussing the topic in an open and unbiased manner.

We can begin to remove the residue of conflicts in human religious history when we separate the true nature of the world's religions from the greed, actions, and ultimately poor decisions made by human beings in the name of religion. In simplest terms, there is nothing (arguably) in any of the holy books of the world's religions that justifies war or the spread of religion through war. To believe that such a possibility could exist is in exact contradiction to the essence and nature of religion and the principle tenets that animate all religions, (i.e., "that we should love our neighbors as ourselves").

However, much of the media of the past century has been dominated by the sensationalism of conflict, and to this fact we owe much of our information, or perhaps misinformation. The sensationalism that is bred from misinformation engenders fear, which may be the single most profound ingredient in perpetuating and maintaining stereotypes. From the place of fear, our safety is at stake. At this point, whether historically or at present, we can justify nearly anything—how much more easily the establishment and maintenance of boundaries and stereotypes?

The separatist thinking that arises from fear-based emotions then leads to mis-education—as now our fears and emotions must be rationalized. Thus, over time, distortions that are essential to justify wars and conflicts in the forum of the masses can completely blind us to the ways in which religion has enriched humanity or influenced the development and evolution of the cultures and music in which it is practiced.[5.18] Therefore, it becomes essential to separate clearly the religion itself (and the cultural expressions and music derived from the religion) from the information and opinions that come to us from either those who incite division or conflict on the religion's or culture's behalf or on behalf of their opposition to these cultures.

Pic. 5.9 *The term "Middle East" is a generic term, not only for the countries you see on this map, but for most of North Africa and even portions of Asia. If we consider the influence of religions and cultures beyond their points of origin, the terms of "Middle East," "Western," much less terms which are completely ambiguous or denote preference (such as "first world" or "third world"), are likely to restrict our vision of cultural exchange and the true nature of human evolution.* Photo: Public domain.

Stories from the Human Family

Note: We had a wonderful interview with two local members of the Muslim community, one from Lebanon and the other from Sudan. Both were living in the United States, and both consented to the use of the interview on the grounds of anonymity (preferring not to be spokespeople for either Islam or Islamic cultures). One of the gentlemen showed me a website with numerous different versions of the Adh'an or Azan – the "Call to Prayer" that has for centuries wafted across the air throughout all regions in which Islam is a major religion. Here is the fruit of the conversation. [The Lebanese gentleman will be designated "Leban"; the Sudanese, "Sudan." Thanks to both of them for sharing their thoughts].

Leban: *"The two main misconceptions concerning Islam are the issue of women and the issue of war or fighting. These are not modern; they go way back to the European crusades. When you first meet the Westerner, the first things they talk about are terrorism or war and the treatment of women.*

"My first answer to war is that killing others is not justified unless in defense of your ability to practice your faith. He quotes the Quran: *"But (remember that an attempt at) requiting evil may, too, become an evil: hence whoever pardons (his foe) and makes peace, his reward rests with Allah—for, verily He does not love transgressors."* Qur'an 42:40

"We have clearly defined rules – we don't just take the Qur'an but also the life of Muhammad. How he lived. When he was confronted with war or conflict, how did he deal with it? This is the background upon which we can live."

Sudan: *"In the beginning, Muhammad was fooled by the tribes and he was attacked, and He prevailed over them by necessity. Later when His successors tried to spread Islam, if people did not allow them the opportunity to live their Faith or teach their beliefs, then they would wage war. Any other conflicts in Islam are usually – like families fighting. They are human and not encouraged by Islam."*

Leban: *"As to the other main stereotype, women and the role of the mother is highly respected in Islam. [He quotes: "The best among you are those who are best to their wives. (Ibn Majah #1978)] You see, one of the problems lies in Western societies' perceptions of 'freedom' and individualism. In the West the individual entity is the foundation of the society. Whether you're a man, a child, elderly. You have your right; I have mine.*

"This concept does not exist in most of the rest of the world. The most important entity is the family. How the family interacts with each other is the most important responsibility of all. As a man, you are responsible to protect the women, the children – that is your responsibility. The woman is always connected to a husband, a father, or a brother ... not to control but for protection. This is not an issue of a woman having rights to express herself or to develop, but she must be protected (as she is the care-taker or future care-taker of the children).

"You are always connected to your family; that's the smallest unit of the community. Then solid families join to become the larger unit or community. When you put the veil in the context of the family and the protection of their purity and their roles in the family, it becomes a symbol of the purity of the family. Women have a lot of 'say' in the family."

The Pillars and Practices of Islam

The Disciplines of Religion

To say that Muslims or those that practice the religion of the Prophet Muhammad are frequently misportrayed or categorized incorrectly in Western media or education is an understatement. Although there are individuals from many religions who further mis-understandings by virtue of fanaticism or selfishness, to label a religion and thousands of individuals around the world based upon an either surface-level understanding or the exaggerated portrayal through the media of the works a few individuals is a classic case of stereotyping. This form of stereotyping becomes lethal to education when it hinders our ability either to learn from these cultures or to perceive the unilateral influence they/we have had over time upon each other—religion included.

Let's begin a search for a deeper understanding of Islam with an examination of its basic "pillars" or disciplines. Each of these pillars has a direct parallel to the practices and disciplines in other religions as a means of *re-connecting* oneself with the source or purpose for life (God, Dios, Allah, etc.).

Every religion provides laws and teachings. It is believed these laws or teachings are not to confine its peoples but to liberate their spirit or potential or to keep them focused on the spiritual nature of life. This may seem to be contradictory to the concept of "freedom." But the disciplines of religion—prayer, meditation, fasting, giving to the poor, and reading of holy writings—are, for those who practice them, the means by which "freedom" (spiritual freedom or detachment from fear or material life) is believed to be achieved. As we survey the differences in the laws of each of the world's religions, we might also find direct correlations between those laws and the evolving needs of the populations and time periods each religion served.

Let's take a brief look at some of these disciplines which, though varied in their practices, are a part of all religions. In Islam, the primary principles are defined as the **five pillars**. They form the framework of a Muslim's life. Following each is some commentary provided by our Lebanese and Sudanese friends:

• The testimony of Faith - "La ilaha illa Allah, Muhammad rasoolu Allah" (There is no true God but God, and Muhammad is the Messenger (Prophet) of God).

> Leban: *"When we say five pillars –these are fundamentals that Muslims practice, what they believe. The first, is believing in God or Allah in Arabic. I believe in Christianity, this is God (with a capital G)– then in the prophets – in our case the Prophet Muhammad (may God exalt His mention and protect Him from imperfection)[5.19] There is a clear separation between what is the Creator and what is created. We say God inspired Muhammad, but that He was a true human – He was a Messenger of God."*

• Prayer – five times each day.

> Leban: *"Then we perform prayers five times each day. These are daily prayers, which are encouraged to do in congregation. You can do them individually, but a congregation is best. We also have what we call "zekr" (dhikr),[5.19a] close to meditation, but meditation to me means being in touch with the Divine. The Sufis[5.20] believe in this, zekr is much more limited and does not assume we can become one with God. On Fridays you go to the Mosque (Masjid) and there may be a sermon; this is true all over the Muslim world."*

Pic. 5.10 *The religious center of Makkah (Mecca) and place of supplication for Muslim pilgrims is the Haram Mosque (Masjid al Haram).* Photo: Ali Mansuri.

- Giving zakat or support to the poor or needy.

> Leban: *"Then we have Zakat – which is giving to the poor. This is from when Islam was also a State; it was like a tax collection. You could give to the government and they are responsible to distribute it."*

> Sudan: *"It is especially to make sure that wealth is distributed. If you are a poor man, you don't have to give Zakat. You pay based upon what you earn or have."*

- Fasting – abstinence from food, drink, or anything that is abhorrent to God, from dawn until sundown (during the month of Ramadan, which rotates according to the 28-day lunar calendar).

> Leban: *"Then there is fasting, which in the Muslim calendar is based upon the lunar cycle, so it moves around each year. We fast from before dawn until sunset. No eating, drinking, or sexual relationship. This is the month of Ramadan.*

> *"There is one thing that I want to add – there are some things that are not a "must," things which we are encouraged to do but don't have to do. But Ramadan or fasting is a must. There are other days we can fast, but Ramadan is a must."*

- Making a pilgrimage (Hajj) to Makkah (Mecca) at least once during one's lifetime, providing health and finances permit it.

Pic. 5.10-1 *The first surah in a Qur'an (Koran).* Calligraphy by Hattat Aziz Efendi.

Note: Not all religions advocate a "pilgrimage" to their holy places. A high percentage of the world's holy places are centered in a very small region of our world. Many of the world's religious practitioners would love to visit these sites. This pillar is a means of reinforcing "Faith." In one sense, any ritual which re-establishes connection with the religion's history or life of the prophet would serve, in part, the function of the pilgrimage.

Many of the contributions made by the cultures of the Arab/Persian world to music extend to the Arabic, Persian, and tribal cultures before the 7th century and the advent of Islam. Once the region became infused by Islam, a spiritual and cultural renewal followed based in no small part upon the laws and disciplines such as those of the "five pillars." This renewal included, is it does at the apex of all religions, an outpouring of artistic expression as well. However, the expression of human emotion or thought through music and art was intermittently discouraged and encouraged, based on time and location. This is why we suggest keeping multiple files open to accommodate the diversity of simultaneous "truths."

The primary element of the music of the entire region is *melody.* The human voice was the primary foundation for evolution of the intricate and highly *melissmatic* (ornamented) melodies which characterize the music of the Arab/Persian/North African regions. Imagine how the importance of melody may have been amplified when, after the advent of Islam, chanting or intonement of the holy verses of the **Qur'an** (Koran – the writings, teachings, and laws of the Prophet Muhammad) was deemed the most holy or dignified means for both worshipping the Creator and educating oneself in Islamic principles. Imagine as well how the stylizations of the non-religious-based music and instrumental music (which we will discuss later) must have both influenced and been influenced by the vocalizations of the most respected tonal music: Islamic chant.

Islamic[5.21] Chant

The role of chant and religious song (praise songs) in the pre-Islamic world prior to the 7th century (AD or CE) was based primarily upon the enormous influence of the Bedouin tribes of North Africa, the Egyptian, and Persian cultures. That melodic singing or chanting was a strong part of all the cultures of the Middle East prior to Islam is documented throughout the Bible, scrolls, and documents of ancient human history.

Musically, **chant** is melody: *the linear organization of pitches*. But it is melody that is based upon the natural rhythm and flow of the text ... and generally without a strong concern for regular meter or beat patterns. That is, the text and meaning of the text are the sole dictators of the melody. In each region, *chanting* is based upon the sound world of the chanter, therefore including all forms of melody and pitch as ordered in the "chanter's" world.

More specifically, in nearly all musical systems, melodies are based upon **scales** or **modes,** which are groups or menus of pitches that become standard to each culture over time. In Arabic music, the scales are microtonal or, to Western ears, have pitch groupings and ornaments smaller and more ornate then Western scales. Nearly all modes evolved from songs or chants of the human voice, as it is both the oldest and most accessible of all instruments, but also by itself can create only melody. Since the human voice is by far the most prolific instrument of the world's religions and also the musical cultures that evolved from or with the religions, we can safely say that the scales or modes sung by the voice became the foundation of all of the cultures' music.

From the vocal melodies of North Africa, a diverse assortment of ***maqam (maqamat)*** evolved from which eight primary modes are still used in Arabic music today. Among these, only two are similar to Western scales: *ajam* (similar to what we call *major*) and *Mahawand* (most similar to what we call *"harmonic minor"*). The other modes (*kurd, hijaz, rast, bayat, saba, and siga*), are all

Pic. 5.10A *"On the banks of the Red Sea, Moses and the children of Israel sang their triumphal song of deliverance from the hosts of Egypt; and Miriam, in celebration of the same event, exercised one of her functions as a prophetess by leading a procession of the women of the camp, chanting in chorus the burden of the song of Moses. The song of Deborah and Barak is cast in a distinctly metrical form, and was probably intended to be sung with a musical accompaniment as one of the people's songs. The simpler impromptu with which the women from the cities of Israel greeted David after the slaughter of the Philistines was apparently struck off on the spur of the moment, under the influence of the wild joy with which they welcomed their national champion... 'the darling of the sons of Israel.'" 1Samuel 18:6,7*[5.22]

much more complex and *microtonal* than the scales used in the West. *Maqamat*, like the ***dastgah*** of the Persian culture, would eventually cross-influence the evolution of Greek modes, which in turn would later be adopted by the Roman Catholic church as "church modes." Therefore, although our Western scales and their meanings have been enormously simplified over the course of European evolution, it is entirely correct to say that Western scales are the descendants of *magamat/dastgahs* in simpler form.[5.23]

To appreciate the nature of chant, we might begin with the understanding that historically, most Muslims did not consider chanting as "singing" or performance, but rather prayer with no performance context. This in part leads to the difficulty in Western understanding of Islamic chant or chant as most religions view it. The last few centuries of singing even in a religious context, along with Western music's increased compositional complexity, have created an attachment of religious song or chant to performance (as in: "I really like your song or voice"). So to many Western ears, anything that is "intoned," or chanted, is sung. And, any song is a performance of sorts. Thus, the "chanter" is a vehicle through which inspiration or melody is chanted but *not performed,* which, though it may be somewhat difficult to understand, is an essential re-conceptualization of presentation from most Western perceptions of "performance."

Although there is no single style of chanting in any religion, there are some general tendencies in all melodic recitation, in addition to those we have already discussed:

- The text and syllabic structure (accents, breaths, and emphasis of some syllables or words over others) is the basis for the chanting or melodic rendering. Thus, chanting does not generally follow a specific beat or repetitious *meter.*

- The rise and fall of melodic chanting (*melodic contour*) generally is based upon a "main" or central pitch. As the intensity of the words (meaning and intonation) rise and fall, so too will the melody. In most cases, the melody will return to the central pitch frequently during the chant and nearly always at its conclusion.

- The voice quality (*timbre* – the actual sound quality of the voice or instrument) is to a great degree predicated upon the context of the chant. As concerns the Adh'an **(Adh'an/Azan)** or *call to prayer,* only in the last century, with the advent of electronic amplification and recording technology, has the Ad'han been either pre-recorded or called out from the **musallah** (prayer hall), thus giving rise to a more relaxed *timbre* and chant *recitation* style. Prior to this, the call to prayer was sung from the *minaret* (prayer tower) of the Mosque (Muslim "church" or "temple") by the **Muazzin** (person who chants the Adh'an). Since the "call" would need to be projected over a large area, much like opera singers in Western opera theaters, an extremely focused and strong projection style of chanting was required.

Stories from the Human Family

Michael's Experience:

"It was 1977, and I was on my first musical tour to the Middle East as part of the United States initiative to build good will between the cultures (State Department tour). Although I was with a jazz group of some fifteen musicians and looked on the trip to Syria, Jordan, Egypt, and Tunisia as more of a novelty, it was not far into the trip that I realized "this would be no ordinary trip."

What became apparent after the initial observations of the diversity in climate, clothing, buildings, and food was an intense and vibrant "rhythm" in the lifestyles of the people – unique to each city and region we visited. Although I remained generally unaware of the influence of Islam, one event changed my perception dramatically.

It was around 5 a.m. and we were in a hotel in Cairo, Egypt. I awoke to pronounced chanting or a song that wafted from loudspeakers in the distance. I rose and went to the window, wondering what in the world was going on so early in the morning. As I looked out over the Cairo bazaar, there was a quiet serenity and peace that replaced the enormous activity of the day before. The

Insert; 5.11 *Sunrise in the desert – the beginning of the day – and moment of the first "call to prayer."* Photo: Public domain.

chant seemed to be a wake-up call to the region and blended perfectly with the desert sun as it peaked above the horizon, blending its rays of light with the mist that covered the streets of Cairo.

I would later come to understand that the initial call: "Allah'u'akbar" was really the English equivalent to the pronouncement that "God is the Greatest." That this was the Adh'an or call to prayer for the Muslims of the region. What I also came to feel, however, was what a great way this would be to rise from sleeping each day. The experience was powerful and did not separate itself by "religious affiliation". The chant and its meaning, however different from others, had a powerful impact on my day – perhaps even on my life. (from "The Personal Nature of Music," 1991).

In Islam, as in most religions, central to each of the pillars mentioned above is the recitation of prayers or the holy verses (of the **Qur'an/Koran**), which to some Muslims are the only legitimate form of music-like (intonement) practice. The following quote from a website put out by Alan Godlas at the University of Georgia (www.uga.edu/islam/) speaks to both the dilemma of musical legitimacy across the diversity of Islamic cultures and to the acceptance universally of Qur'anic chant and melodic recitation of prayers:

*"Music has traditionally been one of the more controversial issues in the Muslim world. While all Muslim scholars have always accepted and even encouraged chanting the call to prayer (Adh'an or Azan) and the Qur'an, the permissability of other forms of music, especially instrumental music, has been problematic. In Arabic, the word **musiqa,** which is translated as 'music,' even has a more narrow sense than does the English word 'music.' Musiqa in Arabic refers mainly to popular and instrumental music and excludes genres such as Qur'anic chanting and the Muslim call to prayer (adh'an). In spite of critiques (of musical practice), many forms of music have traditionally been present in the Muslim world and are still found throughout it today."*

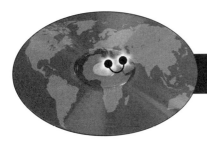

Inside the Chanter's World

Prayer Minaret of Mosque

Note: We can not include Qur'anic chant on the CD, as many Muslims would not consider it "music" at all, and some Muslims would object to its inclusion in this text (especially those who feel any association of "chanting" to music would be disrespectful). However, since melodic chanting may be the single most essential ingredient and influence on the music of the entire Islamic world, we recommend the reader take time to hear an example of the *Adh'an* (Azan), the call to prayer recited before each of the five daily prayers. We will then touch on the evolution of music in the Arab/Muslim world and perception towards music through a variety of other musical pieces.

Listening Opportunity:

Suggested Listening: (Not Available on CD)

"Adh'an (Azan)," by Hafiz Mustafa Özcan, from **www.audioQuraan.com,** a famed chanter from Turkey, c. 2005.

As the term "call to prayer" suggests, this chant is obviously a *call for people to come to pray.* In most Islamic cultures, it will be chanted or (more frequently) played in recorded form the five times each day that prayers are to be recited. In its essence, the Adh'an is a testament of faith and a preparation for prayer by transitioning the individual from the "regular" world to the world of communion with Allah—or God. A portion of the text translated to English would read:

> *Allah (God) is great (repeated four times)*
> *I bear witness there is no God but Allah (God) (repeated)*
> *I bear witness Muhammad is the Prophet of Allah (repeated)*
> *Come (rush) to prayers (repeated)*
> *Come (rush) to prosperity or [success] – (repeated)*
> *Allah (God) is great (repeated)*
> *There is no God but Allah (God)*

What becomes immediately apparent especially for those not acquainted with Islamic chant styles are the extended pauses between intoned phrases. These pauses serve numerous functions. They provide opportunity for the listener to reflect, and in the case of the Ad'han, they also provide time to perform ablutions (washing and preparing for the prayer), to find a clean, safe spot to perform the prayer, to congregate in the mosque, or to repeat the phrases after they are chanted.

The Diversity of Musical Practices

As we will also see when we discuss the diversity of Christian musical practice, the variation in branches of any given religion over time manifests a wide diversity of visions as to the proper practice of music. In Islam, both over time and across the three primary branches—Sunni, Shi'ah, and Sufi—the vision of music's proper place, beyond the chanting of the Adh'an or holy verses of the Qur'an, is quite diverse. The following quotations mark the "outer poles" of the continuum and debate concerning music amongst Muslims:

Conservative view of music and its appropriate position in Islam:

> *"If the head of the family is fond of tambourine, It is no wonder why the whole family dances!"*

> *"Whether it is through natural/physiological means or instruments, or tunes, depending on the kind or the different ways (of Islamic practice), music may be forbidden, disliked or allowed according to the variation of Islamic religious edicts. However, in any case, it is also known that Islam avoids absolutely accepting or remaining indifferent to the issue of music. It is this latter fact, i.e., a sort of position by Islam, of cautioning by not allowing music, or encouraging it without reservation. It is this position whose reason or essence we will be discussing.*

> *"It would not do justice at all to compare this position of reservation by Islam with heartsick people who are unable to appreciate the joyful effect of music which is considered by those who are fond of pleasures, as of great spiritual value.*

Pic.5.11A The Mezquita (Cordoba, Spain) was originally a mosque and converted after to a church. The interconnection and overlap of the world's religions and religious cultures is frequently overlooked due to the labeling and allegiances of prior centuries. Photo: Courtesy and copyright, Peter Williams.

Perhaps Islam does not see right to remain indifferent to music because it knows how delightful music is to our nature and how strong it is on our feelings. Our religion has an exceptionally good view in any case, in discovering the hidden dangers, which might be inherent in the sweetest and most pleasurable things. Indeed, a heavenly religion should lead to the truths, which are unattainable by man himself, as this is expected in the guiding nature of the religion." [5.24]

Note: As in so much of the history of all religions, the intensity of the debate concerning the appropriate nature of music is directly linked to music as an essential element of socialization and community entertainment. Precisely because some of the "secular" or social nature of humanity is also linked to alcohol, drugs, or promiscuity outside of marital relationships, music and its partner, dance, have precarious positions of being simultaneously the most prominent of vehicles for the connection of the spirit to its Creator and the most prolific of vehicles for the entertainment and expression of "worldly pleasures in the material world." Our Lebanese friend explained this phenomenon in Islam as follows:

"Historically there has always been a pull and push between two sources, the mystic or emotional and the traditional or conservative. The mystic (particularly Sufi or cultures with a more tolerant view of music as a means of spiritual connection) would approve of music as a source of worship or praise. The traditional Muslim culture or individual would not be as likely to encourage or listen to music – on the basis that the music might lead to an imbalance of the "human" or emotional nature over the spiritual. That's how we can look at the phases (different time periods) and cultural diversity as to how music is viewed in Islam. The praise song, which is in a Moroccan dialect, is strictly devoted to praise of God, but uses instruments which are deemed appropriate as a setting to the text in Morocco, but maybe not in Saudi Arabia or in Persia at a particular time period.

"There is a quote that music and Faith cannot co-exist; one will overtake the other. You cannot be conscious of God and at the same time being swept by music. Both passions cannot co-exist. Some feel music numbs your sense of conscience. So the wording of these songs may not be offensive at all – but the passion in the music may take me away from my true passion as a Muslim."

When Music Is Embraced by Muslims—The Sufi Path

"Many are the roads, but truth is a single path. And those who tread this way are few. They pass unrecognized, their goal unknown, while slowly and steadily they press along. Men do not know for what they were created, and most of them fail to see the path of truth." —al-Ghazzali

Although the Sufi branch of Islam has historically been the most "all embracing" of music and dance as a means of connecting to God, it was primarily as a movement of conservatism that initially led Sufis to place a strong emphasis on music and movement in an effort to pull away from the material world and increase the perpetual emotional and spiritual connection between man and God. Much like the Protestant movement in Christianity or in Hasidic Judaism, Sufism is a direct attempt to increase the emotional and spiritual experience of worship through music.

> *"Sufism is a mystical path of love, knowledge, and action, the goal of which is union with God and the completion of the human personality. Sufism involves the purification of lower personality (the ego or nafs), and the awakening of the heart as an organ of spiritual knowledge and vision. While Sufism has produced many significant spiritual, poetic, and metaphysical teachers and writers, the Persian poet Jelaluddin Rumi (d. 1273) is often regarded as exemplifying the Sufi Path of Love, while the Andalusian metaphysical scholar Ibn 'Arabi (d. 1240) is often seen as exemplifying the Sufi Path of Knowledge. At their core, however, these paths are one and the same."* [5.25]

Pic. 5.12 *The interior art and mosaic designs of the Blue Mosque in Instanbul, Turkey. The mosque is a magnificent blend of domes and arches, mosaic, and calligraphic art.* Photo: Damir Cudic.

Sufis believe that, unlike religions and philosophies that may degenerate into dogmatic intellectual or theological systems, their faith focuses on the inner reality of spiritual experience. This dichotomy between outer form and inner essence is reflected in the lines of the Persian poet Jami (1414-92):

"The rose has gone from the garden; what shall we do with the thorns?

The Shah [5.26] is not in the city; what shall we do with his court?

The fair are cages, beauty and goodness the bird;

When the bird has flown, what shall we do with the cage."

It is precisely this enormous appetite for the emotional/spiritual connection between the Creator and the created that drives the Sufi poet, musician, and even trance dancer—throughout the multiple regions in which Sufism thrives as a bridge between traditional Islam and those wishing a more intense emotional and mystical contact with the spiritual realm. Such quotes from the Qur'an as:

> *"Allah addresses the disbelievers of the Quraish as follows, "Do you marvel at this statement, and laugh and do not weep, while you amuse yourselves (proudly) in vanities? Rather, prostrate before Allah (God) and worship Him." (53:59-62)*

– are interpreted by some to imply that the use of music (outside of the context of chanting) is an amusement which dilutes spiritual practice. On the other hand, a musician colleague who practices Sufism preferred to see the issue of music and religion as follows:

> *"Those who believe God in His book believe that the Qur'an is a complete book as far as Islam is concerned and that is true regarding all the prohibition. The list of prohibitions in the Qur'an does not include music or singing. When needed, prohibitions are given clear and straightforward so as to leave no doubt in the minds of the believers. (He cites the Qur'an, 39:28).*

> *"The Qur'an teaches us that God is extremely displeased with those who prohibit anything that was not specifically prohibited in the Qur'an, (see 16:112-116). The upholding of any prohibitions not specifically mentioned in the Qur'an (e.g., prohibiting Music and singing) represent some other god besides God."* (Moroccan musician who prefers to remain unnamed)

Because of this ancient dilemma concerning the appropriate use of music, much of the archives of music in many Islamic regions are filled with poetry and *"praise songs"* which either directly give praise to God or indirectly praise God in terms that also permit the discussion of love or the "lover" without distinct reference to whether the beloved is God – or one's romantic partner.

The following are two examples of songs which praise God. The first is an example of a **madh** (praise song) from Morocco, which in its lyrics would not likely offend even the most conservative Muslim. Its musical setting and format, however, are distinctly the product of an **Andalusian** (North African/ Spanish) musical fusion to Sufism.

The second piece, also greatly influenced by the Andalusian fusion culture, represents the *veiled* version of praise songs, which have a metaphoric duality: they can represent praise to God, or they can be interpreted to mean the exaltation of the human "beloved." In both instances we have the intermingling of poetry and music, one of the ancient characteristics common to Persian and Arabic cultures in both the past and present.

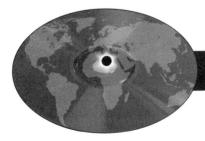

Inside the Musician's World

Orchestra Chabab al Andalouss

Note: *Madh Chanting* (poems in praise of the Prophet Muhammad, pronounced "mad-h") is most commonly done during the celebration of the birth of the prophet (*mawlid al-nabi*). In most cases, praise songs strongly express humility on the part of the human station, and exalt both God and His Manifestation or prophet (Muhammed). Praise songs generally are quite lengthy – some may extend to an hour in length. The praise song below is, in its entirety, twenty-one minutes in length. This song represents the fusion between the Arab/North African, Gypsy, and Spanish cultures – often referred to as "Andalusian" music.

"Madh" (Praise Song), by the Orchestra Chabab al Andalouss, from the CD: **Musique Arabo Andalouse Du Maroc,** c. 2004.

> Mohamed Amine Debby of the Orchestra Chabab al Andalouss from Morocco told us: *"Andalousian music is a high level of poetry talking about different issues. Some of the songs (intoned poems) are life, love, and Madh (Praise) of the Prophet; but no politics. It is a descriptive music. It has a poem for each period of the day (sunrise, sunset, night, etc.). Those chants associated with the rhythm that goes up and down and the voice that follows it make the listener travel to another world for a period of time. The key factor to enjoy listening to this music is to understand the poems and try to live them; the rest comes by itself."*

The fusion between Spanish, Gypsy, Jewish, and Christian/Catholic culture and music was ongoing from the 7th century as the "moors," or North African Muslims, invaded and later conquered Spain to spread Islam, until some seven centuries later, when Spain was reclaimed by Christianity. Still today, however, there is a strong intra-cultural exchange between the music created in Spain and that of the Arab world. This is exemplified in the Andalusian music of Morocco.

The text of this praise song in Moroccan Arabic dialect translates roughly as follows:

> *"Why should I worry for my sustenance when my Creator sustains me,*
>
> *I am the servant of my Lord,*
>
> *He has the power that makes all things easy for me,*
>
> *Though I am a weak servant,*
>
> *My Lord is strong and He is All Powerful – over all things,*
>
> *My Lord looks over me, but my vision is limited as if in the womb,*
>
> *He says: 'Be'—He is the one that creates and invigorates all things."*

Most "praise songs," whether *"madh"* or other versions such as **Qawwali** (Islamic praise songs from Pakistan), follow primarily the same formula:

- A lead singer leads the *praise song,* in some cases breaking into improvised verse or chant inspired by the moment.
- Each main verse is followed by the chorus response. This call-and-response formula is then in turn followed by the instrumental response to the vocal melody, which builds in emotion over time.

If you listen carefully when the instruments play the interlude, you will hear a considerable amount of "improvisation" both in rhythm and melody, indicating a certain amount of freedom or "allowance" to flow with the inspiration of the moment even in the role of the instrumental melodies. However, when the singers re-enter, the instruments recede to the background again.

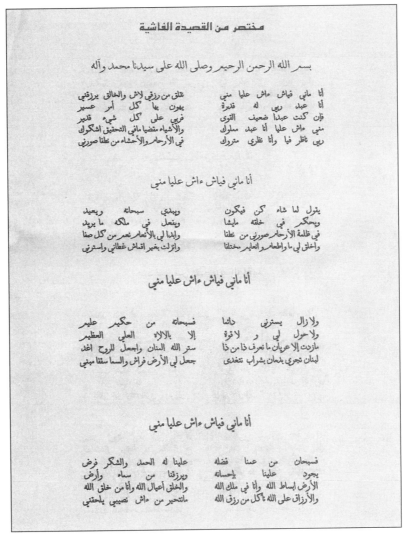

Pic. 5.13A Arabic text of the Madh.

As in nearly all instrumental and vocal collaborations of the Middle East and North Africa prior to the last few decades, the interplay of melodies or melodic dialogue between solo voices or instruments (the ensemble or orchestra) is critical to the musical texture and emotional feeling. Since little emphasis is placed on the *harmony,* or combination of pitches sounding together, there is a profound emphasis on the interplay rhythmically and melodically between all musicians. You will hear this melodic and rhythmic interplay in both this piece and the next piece from Syria.

Instrumental Music

The world's instruments can be effectively categorized into groups based upon how or in what manner the vibration (or sound) is produced. The **Hornbostel/Sachs** method of classification accommodates the world of instruments effectively in the following categories (all photos courtesy of Lark in the Morning, San Francisco, CA, USA):

Nearly all forms of music in the Middle East, other than pure chant, use instruments and particularly *chordophones* in combination with the voice. In both the *madh* above and the next song from Syria, we begin to hear the transfer of vocal melodies onto the instruments. You will also note that the instruments used are strikingly similar to those found in Western music, although the melodies sound quite different. The following are just a couple of the main musical elements and contributions of North African and

Pic. 5.14B **Aerophones:** The sound is created by the use of air. This would include all flutes, brass, harmonica, pipe organ, and even the human voice.

Pic. 5.14A **Chordophones:**[5.27] The sound is made by vibrating strings. The main groups of chordophones are **zithers,** the strings stretched across, over, or inside a resonator; **lutes,** the strings stretched across the resonator and up a neck; or **bowed,** the strings on a lute-like instrument bowed (may also be plucked).

Pic.5.14C **Membranophones:** Literally any drum or instrument which uses a *membrane* (whether an animal skin or synthetic) to produce the sound.

Photos: Courtesy of Bill Wilson and Lark in the Morning, San Francisco, CA/USA.

Pic. 5.14D **Idiophones:** Any instrument that is a solid object. This is all of the world's percussive instruments other than drums. Gongs, cymbals, even hitting a table would be in this category.

Pic. 5.14E **Electrophones:** The advent of electricity used to create vibration (mid-20th century) necessitated the creation of this category. Electricity has been used for amplification of vibration, but the generation of sound by electricity includes primarily the synthesizer. Although the electric guitar uses electricity for amplification, it is technically a *chordophone,* as the string is the means of creating vibration.

Middle Eastern cultures to Western music:

Some Middle Eastern Instruments – The three most significant instruments in Western culture are arguably the guitar (lute-like), violin (bowed), and piano (zither—strings set horizontally, played with either a plectrum or pick or with small wooden hammers). Although the origins of these instruments could possibly be traced even further into the ancient cultures of Africa, they first appear in the following instruments common to much of the Arab world. Their inclusion and development into the instruments we know today is a matter of continuous exchange between culture groups over centuries. Of the ancestors of the instruments used today, only

Pic. 5.15A *It may seem hard to imagine how intimately connected our world may be to someone else on the other side of the planet. But just as these modern Western violins are the direct descendents of the Arabic rabab, so too are we related to these other cultures by the connection of centuries of exchange.*

the ***rababa(h), rebab, or rebaba(h)*** is most often replaced by the violin; the others are still used today along with the ***dombecki, dombek, or darbukkah (tablah)***, an "hour-glass shaped" hand-drum prominent in the Syrian/Andalousian piece you will hear below. The main instruments you will hear include:

Ud/Oud – A "*lute*" (the word "lute" was derived from "ud") or guitar-like instrument with five or six strings. Although there are numerous descendants of the "ud," the most important is the guitar, believed to have been the product of exchange between Arab and Roma people in Spain over the course of Arab occupation (8th to 14th centuries) Image (P.15): Courtesy Viken Najarian, Najouds@aol.com.

Rababa(h), rebab, rebaba(h) – Originally a one-string Bedouin instrument with a sound box and played with a horsehair bow, over time this instrument evolved to three- or four-string version. As with all the instruments of the Arab world, the Rababa eventually found its way to Europe through both the Crusades and Arab occupation of Spain. It more than likely also made its appearance to a large extent through the Roma and possibly Sephardic Jewish communities.

and ***Santour (santur) and Qa'nun*** – The *santour/santûr* is a very popular court music instrument, especially in Iran but also in Turkey and Iraq. It is frequently used in classical Persian music. The name of this Middle Eastern instrument comes from the Greek *psalterion*. Just like the qanûn, its close relative (played with finger picks rather than the small hammers used to play the santour), these zithers probably arrived in Eu-

Pic. 5.15B *A vector diagram of three of the most important instruments in Arabic/N.African music: the ud, the dombecki, and the rababah.* Image: by Heidi Priesnitz.

rope first during the Moorish occupation of Spain and later through the Crusades of the Middle Ages. Today, both zithers still play important role in the music of the Balkan countries, especially with the Hungarian and Romanian Rom (Romany) communities where it is known under the name *cymbalon*. For both the santour and qa'nun, the strings must be re-tuned (movable bridges) for each piece, to match any one of the eight primary *maqamat*. On the principle of hammered stringed zither (santour), the piano was to be later built. We could say, therefore, that the santour is the grandfather of the piano.

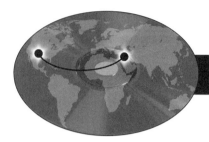

Inside the Musician's World

Zein al-Jundi

Note: When Zein al-Jundi was only five years old, she was discovered by a local Syrian TV producer, and for twelve years she became a household name on Syrian radio and TV channels as well as concert halls throughout Syria. Despite objections by her teachers and fans, in 1982 she moved to the United States and began her studies in Architecture and Urban Planning.

After eighteen years of absence from the music field, she returned to performance and recording work as well as the promotion of the art and culture of the Arab world. This CD is one of the results of her work, of which she commented: *"I formed an arts organization, World Music and Dance Productions, as an agency to promote world cultures through their music and dance. But I also teach dance and choreography and both own and manage an import business, the Arabic Bazaar in Austin, Texas."*

Photo by Ricardo Acevedo.

CD 2.1

"Aminti Billah," written by Laure Dakkash, performed by Zein Al-Jundi, from the CD: **Traditional Songs from Syria,** c. 2004.

One of the only female composers in the Arab world, Laure Dakkash was also an accomplished ud player with "one of the most beautiful voices of her era." Born into a Christian/Maronite family in what is now Lebanon (at that time "greater Syria"), she wrote and recorded some 120 songs of which *"Aminti Billah"* (composed in 1939) is one of her most famous.

As an illustration of the manner by which all cultures exchange and fuse their expressions of life, each new fusion taking on a life of its own, the lyrics of *"Aminti Billah"* are based upon an ancient classical Arabic poem (author unknown), the song's composer is the Lebanese-Christian songwriter, the singer is the Syrian-born, now U.S. citizen Zein Al-Jundi, the music is of an Andalusian character (Spanish/Arabic fusion), and the arranger/producer is the Egyptian- born, now European artist Hossam Ramzy. To simply say the music is "Middle Eastern" greatly oversimplifies the creative dynamics and heritage of this fusion.

There are many styles of songs in the Arabic world, many of which have been influenced by music created in the courts of Al-Andalus (Andalusian) Spain and Portugal at the time of Arab rule. Some of these include: *Mawwal* - (a non-metric [no steady pulse or beat] vocal improvisation on a poem, usually sung with instrumental accompaniment by ud or qunun); *Muwashshah* - (a **strophic** [repetitive melody which changes lyrics] song form originating in Al-Andalus [Spain/Portugal]. The verses are sung by a soloist alternating with a chorus in *call-and-response* fashion. This is a common format for the *Mahd* as well.); *Qadd* – (an older popular Syrian song genre whose lyrics have been replaced by new ones—usually religious to secular, secular to religious. classical to colloquial, or vice versa); or *Taqsim* – (which are instrumental improvisations [usually solo] based on one or more *maqamat,* often accompanied by percussion).

In this piece, a combination of the styles above, the author is enchanted by the beauty of a woman, a beauty so miraculous that it makes him believe in God, the woman's creator:

Refrain: Aminiti billah, Aminti billah….nour jamalek aya, aya m'nillah. Aminti billah

> *I have believed in God as your radiant beauty couldn't have been but a creation of a God.*

Verse 1: Nour jamalek, nour 'ajeeb yitfi fil qalb ellaheeb

> *Your radiant beauty is an astonishing light; it puts out the fire that burns in the heart*

Yisreb eddam' essabeeb ma khalaq na'ma siwah

> *A blessing created unlike any other; it brings out tears that pour down with no end*

Nour jamlek aya, aya m'nillah, Aminti billah
Your radiant beauty has to be a creation of God…. I believe in God

Refrain~~

Pic. 5.15C *A wall of Zithers or flat string instruments.* (Courtesy Lark in the Morning)

> Verse 2: Nour jamalek bil kamal yihyi fil qalb elamal
> *Your radiant beauty is a perfection; it resurrects hope in the heart*
>
> Wil ilah haabi el jamal wesh nikoun janbel ilah
> *And if God loved beauty enough as to create it, what chance do we stand next to God and resist such love?*
>
> Nour jamlek aya, aya m'nillah, Aminti billah
>
> *Your radiant beauty has to be a creation of God…… I believe in God*
> Refrain 2 times~~

The Recipe of Sound

The song begins with an improvisation on the ud to establish the mode (maqam) and then is followed by an improvisation and exchange between the voice and the violin—which is now a more often-used replacement for the rababa. If you listen carefully before the rhythm and song begin, you will hear the flute and violin also follow closely the voice, almost as a flock of birds flies and changes direction. This is one of the aspects of Middle Eastern music that is highly sophisticated, a form of closely integrated (community) call and response, which frequently has the dimension of improvisation followed closely by another instrument.

Pic. 5.15D *A Moroccan musician demonstrates his proficiency on the ud.* Photo: Courtesy and copyright, Terry Abrams, 2005.

The introduction (which establishes the mood) takes a full two-and-a-half minutes, which by Western standards is unheard of, until finally the rhythm enters and the lyrics begin to tell their story of "love," the single most common subject of Arabic poetry, but one which has multiple dimensions and correspondingly multiple words in the Arabic language. Listen for the following features as well:

- *Beat and meter* – Notice that the beats are not grouped into easily defined patterns of 4 as in most Western or Arabic popular dance music of today. The **Iqa'a** (plural: Iqa'at or meter) generally group beats into more complicated patterns which are designed to follow the flow and nature of the melody.

- *Melodic call and response* – One of the most common features of Arabic music throughout the ages has been call and response, both in the shorter sense [a phrase sung or performed by instruments or voice with a small or short phrase in answer] or in the sense of form [where after a melodic section of the vocalist, the instrumentalists respond with either a repeat of the melody or a response to it]. Listen also for the chorus response to the verse. This is somewhat similar to the *Muwashshah* described above.

Stories from the Human Family

Note: About five months after the terrorist tragedy in New York City of September 11, 2001, we created a series of video interviews with primarily Muslim students living in the United States to play for non-Muslim students. In one instance we were told by other Muslim students to interview an older Muslim student because he was older and *"would be able to really give us a good description of how Muslims feel."*

We interviewed him on a well-prepared and decorated stage. He said: *"I like America, and the freedom you have here."* (That was it!) The other students said, no that's not it, try again. We interviewed him in a private room with only two people. He said: *"I like America, and I miss my country, and I like the freedom here."* (That was essentially it!) The other students said, no try again. We sent a camera with a group of Arab students to their home (no non-Muslims or non-Arabic speaking people in the room) and once again, he said basically the same thing. Finally we asked him to write his thoughts, and at long last he wrote the following (which we later translated):

"When I left Jordan to come to the U.S., I was so excited. We hear so much about other countries in Jordan, especially the U.S. But even before and especially since 9/11, when I saw the way the movies and television made us look (people from Middle Eastern cultures or who practice Islam), when I saw how misrepresented my religion Islam, was, I really wanted to cry. It's true our cultures are quite different. At times we may even have opposing ideas as to how to live or what is important, but I anticipated that this was the land of the "free"— and instead, I think most Americans do not question what they see on TV or that their news or even government may be showing them the false ideas. How is this freedom?

"It takes so much energy to get up in the morning when you feel that no one really wants you here. I guess that's why many of us (Muslim or Arabic speaking) hang together. It just takes less energy." [Used by permission on condition of anonymity]

Persian Poetry and Music

The distinguished history of Persian (now Iranian) culture and its influence on the rest of the world dates back to the illustrious rise of Zoroastrianism (estimated at between 2200 and 551 BCE). Through numerous dynasties, expansion, and conquest, through the Arab-Persian wars, the Crusades, and Mongol conquests of Persia come an enormous legacy of poetry, calligraphy, and music.

One of the elements that distinguishes much of the world's music is its close relationship with poetry. Perhaps nowhere is this more graphically illustrated than in Persian music. The famous Persian-Sufi poets: Rumi, Hafez, and Jami (13th – 15th centuries) wrote poetry that is quoted, sung, chanted, and used for compositions all over the world. By connecting music to the creative poet or spiritual practices of Persian culture (and the beginning stages of Sufism, which grew from these poets and this time period), one could bask in the sounds and vibrations of music, while contemplating the most essential philosophies of human love, existence, and poetic attempts to decode the meaning of life itself.

Pic. 5.16A&B Modern Persian and Arabic artists may combine new ingredients with an eye towards seeing the ancient connection between life, spirit, and all the arts. The poem (above left) "Manifestation of God," is filled with poetic metaphor (roughly translated from Farsi): "The path is not my path, nor is the choice mine.,, For my feet are in the stirrups of the steed of time… Consciousness emerges from the magnificence of life…In that transformation the manifestation of God lies.,, What a world is the imagination! For in its light I see…although I'm earth-bound, I soar amongst the stars." The painting (above right) "Warning," (1997), concerns the agony of time passing without our serious appreciation or the fulfillment of our potentials. Mohsen Janatpour, (the artist/poet) writes: "My work does not fall under a particular school or "ism". Metaphorical elements of my art unify the diversification of my philosophical, academic, and cultural views and experiences, and expresses the world as it is reflected in my mind." All work courtesy: www.mohsensart.com

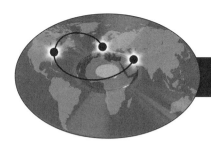

Inside the Musician's World

Mehri Vaghei and Persian Symphonic Orchestra in Iran

Note: We were not at all certain how we would accommodate the ancient connection between Persian poetry and Persian music. Despite our having had contact with Persian culture on various levels, without any direct connection to Iran, acquiring a piece of an older tradition upon which today's modern Persian songs are built seemed unlikely at best. By chance, we had a young Persian musician in one of our classes, whose own work we'll hear in the final Unit. Arash (his name) mentioned that he knew of a famous Persian singer who lived in this area. With his help we were able to contact Ms. Vaghei, who provided the recording and comments below. When we asked Ms. Vaghei about the music of her culture, we received the wonderful response below.

CD 2.2

"Celestial Lover," by Mehri Vaghei, lyrics by Moayeri, music composed by Reza Babakhanlou, arranged by Millad Omranlou, from the CD: **Music of the Persian Symphony Orchestra,** c. 2000.

> Mehri Vaghei wrote: *"Regarding your question about the connection between my music and my heritage, I can say that this piece is quite related to my culture, its emotions, and to beauty and love which are beyond any ordinary feelings. This perspective is from the heavenly parts of the human spirit, which can guide one to the secrets of existence.*
>
> *"What I would like the reader to learn about my culture and music is that we are mostly motivated by a deep love and affection. This is part of a rich tradition, which goes back to the poetry of Rumi and Hafez, which encourages the creation of art based upon the philosophy that it is intended to transcend any ordinary thoughts.*
>
> *"This piece is part of my feelings which forms my motivation for life – to be interconnected with my Higher Power – namely God. So, when I sing this piece, I express my feelings, which are deeply connected to this heritage of emotional connection to God. This type of music we call 'Persian Classical music.' In this type of music, the poetry and music are completely intertwined. There is more improvisation and the deepest possible emotion. Since improvisation allows for the emotion of the moment to be poured into the music, there are no two recordings or performances that will be the same."*

Although we can no longer call music of this nature religious in the strictest sense, it is, however, religious in the broader sense, still tied to connecting oneself with the Higher Power (God/Ghodah) or the search for the purpose in life.

> Translated lyrics (from Farsi): *"I am like your hair when I am distressed, I am the early morning wind when I am unsettled, I am the dust and I am the particles, I am the tears and I am the pain, You are the sun and you are the light, You are the love and you are the life…"*

The Recipe of Sound

Musically, the orchestrated version of a traditional or "classical" Persian song uses the symphonic orchestra (evolving from Germany during the 18th century) with traditional Arab/Persian instruments and poetic-song fusion. But since the European instruments and even the concept of the orchestra had already been in place in Persia and the Middle East, to what or whom should we give credit?

Maybe it's best not to strive to continue to label ourselves or anyone into a corner, but rather appreciate this ancient art and practice of cultural fusion in its emotional and musical beauty. In this case performed in one of the seven Persian **dastgah** (scales or modes similar to Arabic maqamat)—the dastgah that most resembles our Western minor scale. Once again, we have a complete fusion of music and poetry, ancient and modern, East and West, and specifically, the *ancient and sophisticated* art of Persian poetry—set to music.

Overcoming Religious/Cultural Separation

> *"O Children of Men! Know ye not why We created you all from the same dust? That no one should exalt himself over the other. Ponder at all times in your hearts how ye were created. Since We have created you all from one same substance, it is incumbent on you to be even as one soul, to walk with the same feet, eat with the same mouth and dwell in the same land, that from your inmost being, by your deeds and actions, the signs of oneness and the essence of detachment may be made manifest. Such is My counsel to you, O concourse of light! Heed ye this counsel that ye may obtain the fruit of holiness from the tree of wondrous glory."* "The Hidden Words of Baha'u'llah," Arabic no. 68.[5.28]

As we have discussed, much of the world's music is inextricably bound to the world's religions. The ultimate tool to respect *all* of the world's religions is in seeing them as essentially "one" religion. Although arguably all of the world's religions accept many of the religions before them and advocate the renewal of their message in the future, the human dilemma has always been how to understand the history of diverse religions as we practice our own beliefs.

The Bahá'í Faith, which began in Iran in the mid 19th century and established its International center in Haifa, Israel (prior to British occupation and Jewish/Arab divisions of the 20th century), offers distinct perspectives that might assist us to more fully respect (not merely tolerate) the perspectives of others on an equal basis, while not offending whatever it is we believe. Some of these perspectives include:

- First, as both the meditation above (from Bahá'u'lláh the Prophet of the Bahá'í faith) and the "golden rules" cited earlier might imply, humanity may be considered as one race, just as the Creator is a single Creator of all humanity. Therefore, the belief in the multiple races or nations creates a conflict with the reality of human existence.

- Secondly, the principle of "oneness" can be applied to religion. Is it possible to believe in a single God or Creator (as do arguably all religions), to espouse principles of love and justice for others (as can be found in all religious books), to believe that the manner by which we live our life determines our station or status in the next life (as do all religions), to believe that the Creator (God) is the ultimate judge of our actions and doings in this world— *and* – to simultaneously judge others who practice their religion with love, justice, and compassion as being less than ourselves? The perception of the Bahá'í faith, that all religion is one, *progressive,* and equally valid chain of guidance from a single Creator, liberates one, regardless of upbringing, to accept with equal passion not only all of the religions of the world but also the art and creativity that has emanated from religion generally. On the topic of religious inter-connectivity, Bahá'u'lláh writes:

> *"All the former and latter Books of God are adorned with His praise and extol His glory. Through Him the standard of knowledge hath been planted in the world and the ensign of the oneness of God hath been unfurled amidst all peoples. Attainment unto the divine Presence can be realized solely by attaining His presence. Through His potency everything that hath, from time immemorial, been veiled and hidden, is now revealed."* [5.29]

What about the "balance" between the material and the spiritual? How does one address this dilemma? How does religion figure into this equation? In a letter written to "the peoples of the world," the international administrative body of the Bahá'í Faith (The Universal House of Justice) outlined the conditions that face humanity, and clearly delineated the inclusion of religion (and again acceptance of the progression of religions) as part of any effective and lasting solution:

Pic. 5.17 *A view of the Shrine of the Bab (Arabic for "the Gate"). The Bab was the forerunner of Bahá'u'lláh (Arabic for "the Glory of God"). The shrine is located in Haifa, Israel.* Photo: Courtesy www.bahai.org.

"The endowments which distinguish the human race from all other forms of life are summed up in what is known as the human spirit; the mind is its essential quality. These endowments have enabled humanity to build civilizations and to prosper materially. But such accomplishments alone have never satisfied the human spirit, whose mysterious nature inclines it towards transcendence, a reaching towards an invisible realm, towards the ultimate reality, that unknowable essence of essences called God. The religions brought to mankind by a succession of spiritual luminaries have been the primary link between humanity and that ultimate reality, and have galvanized and refined mankind's capacity to achieve spiritual success together with social progress. No serious attempt to set human affairs aright, to achieve world peace, can ignore religion." "The Promise of World Peace," 1985, pp.17.

But the role of music and art in connection to religion may still remain a bit murky. Is there music which has "spiritual benefit" and possibly other music that does not? What about the conflict that religions have had with music, at times condemning its practice and at times extolling its virtues?

Just as with religion, the choice of music that one feels leads to fulfillment and balance is up to the independent investigation of the individual. No one can or should determine for another his or her beliefs. However, the son of Bahá'u'lláh (Abdu'l-Bahá) puts the dilemma concerning the possible usage of music and art in the following perspective:

" ... In this new age the Manifest light hath, in His holy Tablets, specifically proclaimed that music, sung or played, is spiritual food for soul and heart. The musician's art is among those arts worthy of the highest praise, and it moveth the hearts of all who grieve. Wherefore ... play and sing out the holy words of God with wondrous tones in the gatherings of the friends, that the listener may be freed from chains of care and sorrow, and his soul may leap for joy and humble itself in prayer to the realm of Glory." Selections from the Writings of Abdu'l-Baha, p. 112

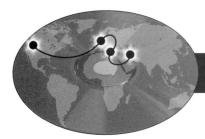

Inside the Musician's World

A Medley of Bahá'í Chants

Part I - F. Enayati (Persian/European fusions)

Part II – Lorintha Umtuch (Yakama, Native American)

Part III – Kosta Kontos (Greek)

Note: The comments above imply that music is both positive and beneficial so long as its impact and effect is one that *"frees the listener from the chains of care and sorrow."* We also might imagine, based upon the disbelief in a superior or inferior culture or musical system, that there must be a multitude of fresh and exciting ways humanity can

Shrine of the Bab.

create spiritually freeing music. Since the manifestations of music and art will reflect the particular "mission" or scope of the religion's central teachings, it is interesting to note the emerging global nature of Bahá'í artistic reflection against these core tenets of Bahá'í Faith:

- That all of the world's religions are part of a progressive chain of Guidance from the Creator, each being the fulfillment of the previous and providing the groundwork for the next. Therefore, as we have seen, each stage in the evolution of religious culture influences subsequent stages, and all are therefore equally important.

- That the world has ever been evolving to the stage of, and will fulfill, permanent unity of all its peoples. A permanent and peaceful global world commonwealth is the inevitable conclusion of centuries of strife based upon division by gender, race, religion, or nation.

- But also, that unity and equality of race, gender, religion, or diverse cultures does not imply the rejection but rather the acceptance and full appreciation of our planet's diversity and unique cultural heritages.

Based upon these principles, what would culturally diverse religious chant sound like? How would one's perception of our world's musical cultures broaden, if all of the world's previous religions and cultures were embraced and respected? The next three examples are a sampling of the variations of modern musical styles that are merged with some of the world's most ancient practices of chanting.

The first is a collaboration between Persian and European Bahá'ís living in Germany, the second is the fusion of a Bahá'í prayer with Native American ancestry (from the Yakama nation in Washington State, U.S.A.), and the third is reflective of ancient Greek-style poetry with modern Euro-American music as a setting for a Bahá'í prayer.

In the ultimate *re-ligious* setting, the longing for connection to the single Creator and the understanding of the singular nature of humankind would still accommodate the expression and unique histories of our diverse and yet singular human race.

"Hidden Words from Bahá'u'lláh," Persian no.'s 38 & 40, as intoned by F. Enayati, from the CD: **Naghmeha I,** c. 1990.

What is unique about this chant is that it follows the style of ancient Persian and Arabic chanting from pre- to post-Islam Persian melodic and poetic song styles (Mrs. Enayati is Iranian), but, because of the global cultural orientation of the Bahá'í perspectives, the piece is conciously designed to fuse diverse musical and cultural elements. In this case, the guitarist is Greek, the violinist is Persian (as is the main singer), the pianist is German, and the poem/prayer text are the following meditations (chanted in Farsi):

> O Son of Spirit – Burst thy cage asunder, and even as the phoenix of love, soar into the firmament of holiness. Renounce thyself and, filled with the Spirit of mercy, abide in the realm of Celestial Sanctity.

> O My Servant – Free thyself from the fetters of this world, and loose thy soul from the prison of self. Seize thy chance, for it will come to thee no more.

"Is There Any Remover of Difficulties," a prayer by the "Bab" (Gate) recited by Lorintha Umtuch (Yakama Nation), from the CD: **Native American Style Bahá'í Songs,** c. 2004.

Lorintha Umtuch is not a professional musician. She is the acting chief judge at the Fort McDowell Yavapai Nation's Tribal Court in Arizona. But her chanting represents the important spirit of both her heritage and faith and the role of chant historically, she says, *"to draw the heart to the Higher Above (or Great Spirit/ God)"* – a practice that is not limited to the professional singer, but is shared by any human desiring such connection.

Don Addison, an anthropologist/ethnomusicologist who teaches Native American Studies at the University of Oregon, writes about Lorintha's chant: *"Native peoples have been using music, in many forms and social settings other than the Pow-Wow. Native songs traditionally expressed gratitude to the Creator, appeals for assistance in healing ... but they could also be given from person to person as a gift of generosity.*

"Lorintha, therefore, has carried on this tradition by giving these songs to the public – a mark of true Native generosity – one that honors the Creator and the community for whom she created the CD." In drawing upon the ancestry of words and sounds having a sacred meaning beyond the obvious, Dr. Addison comments: *"... the words in the text and the expressive traditions may go back many centuries into the people's oral traditions."* Quoting Simon Ortiz (Acoma), Addison writes: *"to regard language too casually ... we forget the sacredness of it ... language is more than a functional mechanism, it is a spiritual energy that is available to all."*

This particular chant is in the NAC (Native American Church) style of chanting. The text is a Bahá'í prayer: *"Is there any remover of difficulties save God? Say: Praise be God, He is God, all are His servants and all abide by His bidding."*

CD 2.3 – Part III

"O God, Guide Me," prayer by Abdu'l-Bahá composed by Kosta Kontos, recited by Helen and Kim Kontos, from the CD: **To the Eternal I Call Thee,** c. 2005

Kosta Kontos is a professor of Audio Recording Technology at the University of Thessaloniki in Greece. Together with his wife and daughter and a group of European musicians, Mr. Kontos produced a fusion of chant dating back to the earliest styles from ancient Greece, fused with modern instrumentation, soprano saxophone, and ultimately a text which summons guidance from the Creator, one of the singly most common themes in religious chant:

Text: *"O God guide me, protect me, make of me a shining lamp..."*

Mr. Kontos commented concerning the music: *"For the most part this CD represents writings and prayers from the Bahá'í writings with a strong Greek influence."* He goes on to comment that it is the inspiration of religious focus and the connection to God that has inspired his composition and ultimately his passion for collaborating with diverse musicians or learning diverse musical styles.

This theme of interconnection between the material world and the spiritual world is the driving force for much of the world's greatest music. The greater the desire to know our purpose or feel guided in our human pursuits, the greater the emphasis by musicians and artists to hone this connection and reflect it in their art.

"Sacred" Spaces & the Classroom

Sa·cred *adj*
1. Dedicated to a deity or religious purpose.
2. Worthy of or regarded with religious veneration, worship, and respect, not to be challenged or disrespected.

Every space where education occurs is sacred. Therefore, every classroom has the potential to teach valid life skills, which include an understanding of the life cycle, the full utilization of human potential, and cultural justice (a respectful inclusion of all cultures with equal passion). We do not use the word "sacred" lightly, but we may wish to investigate the difference between spirituality, sacredness, religion, and "church," especially since Western cultures have come to conceptualize "religion" as separate from the predominant academic/scientific disciplines (i.e., the "state").

To respect the "sacred" space of the classroom as the primary venue for cultural transformation in all its forms, we may return to the original Latin definition of religion (re=again, ligiare=to connect). In the direct context, despite the evolution of "religion" as being unique to individual belief systems and/or the politics of human interpretation of religious revelation, a religious activity is any that connects the human, over the course of the life cycle, again to a purposeful fulfillment of human potential.

A science classroom that investigates the evolution of "chemistry" as a discipline, its potentials, liabilities, and possible uses for human advancement or the solving of human dilemmas, cannot help but be seen as religious. In this sense, there would be no delay in accomplishing what the majority in the health profession know or intuit: that healing by use of science cannot progress without the inclusion of human emotion, mind, culture, and spirit. If all the efforts of the global medical community have been incapable of curing some the most devastating diseases (cancer, immune disorders, etc.), then it may not be that cures are elusive, but rather that the research methodologies we are applying are not as inclusive of environment, diet, mental/emotional/spiritual health, or, culture -- as they might be.

There are, however, a few sources we know to be immediate venues for transformation of the academic exercise into a heightened "whole-person" or "sacred" space:

- All faculty/venues where cultural healing or transformation of learning and dissemination are at the core of their discipline/mission.

- All courses where "creativity" (creative thought or expression: "art") and investigation of "spirituality" (existence of a reality beyond the empirical) are essential to the curriculum.

- All courses where "inter-disciplinarity" and/or multiculturalism (even religious cultures) are at the core of the curriculum.

Questions

- *How might the world(s) of the humanities, history, music, or art figure into the transformation of the learning process at all levels? How might/must "spirituality" or the broadened context of "religion" be engaged in order to accomplish this?*

- *Is it possible to liberate ourselves to engage in religious discussion without fear that our individual beliefs will be threatened or infringed upon? How can this be done?*

- *And, finally, to what extent might we discuss spirituality or religion in order to understand the vast majority of human creative endeavors? How can we see the continuity or "brother-/sisterhood" of religions in the context of our personal beliefs?*

Extracted from: *The Educator's Role in Cultural Healing and the Sacred Space of the World Music Classroom, Léonie E. Naylor, L.L.P.C., Michael L. Naylor, Ph.D., 2007.*

Religion, Youth, and Music Today

How is the search for connection, or the religious beliefs of youth being expressed in music today?

From contemporary gospel and hip-hop to contemporary Christian music in all of its forms; from young Buddhists, Hindus, Jewish, Muslim, or Bahá'í youth, we will hear songs with digitally sampled and synthesized music that connects their creative and youthful thoughts and perceptions to the ancient river of religion and to the Bachs, Rumis and Bharata Natyam of ancient religious pasts. How does one learn to discriminate between creative art and that which is produced solely for material gain? Should we in fact discriminate? And finally, is there a place for the *counterculture* voice at the table of "re-connection?"

The final piece in this Unit is a clear indication that the modern-day tools of music and the media have as much a place in musical connection as they did at any other time in religious history.

Pic. 5.17B. *Ryman Auditorium in Nashville, Tennessee, is not only built like a church in appearance, but regularly hosts both "country" music performances of mainstream artists whose music is based frequently on Christian themes, but also contemporary Christian artists. "Contemporary religious" musical movements are a consistently progressive phenomenon – reflecting the musical vocabulary of each generation's youth in combination with their religious beliefs.* Photo: Courtesy of Ryan Kaldari, 2005.

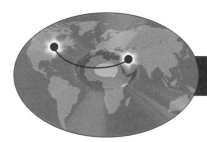

Inside the Musician's World

Euphrates

Note: The verses and poetry of Euphrates (named after the anacient river which cradles some of our planet's earliest and most profound civilizations) speak to the labeling, stereotypes, and injustices which are magnified by politics, media, and (when applicable) poor education. The group's members also spoke to the importance of hip-hop in providing a vehicle for the exploration of thought and music. They wrote:

"If we speak of our (Euphrates) culture as hip-hop, then the function of the music, in our view, is truly to expel energy off one's soul. Lyrically, I remain adamant on the fact that the process of recording itself—is therapy. The same goes for beat-making. In our philosophy, HIP-HOP stands for Highly Intellectual Planes Hovering Over Politics; nothing is a faster mover and shaker than this movement. Because it is a product of the twentieth century, it is a lot more technologically driven than other music genres, although musical instrumentation always gives hip-hop that extra control of the body and soul (i.e., the roots). Hip-Hop's influence on our lives has been more than simply musical; it is a way of life. It starts by opening your mind to understanding different conditions of living worldwide and appreciating the human plight of survival. It is the innate way to disrupt the system; by changing yourself, you can change your environment. Hip-Hop is life.

"Its purpose? To help you through the day. Its function? To change the world and bring the younger generation to the forefront of knowledge, wisdom, and understanding.

"As for our culture being of Middle Eastern descent, music is also central to our civilization. Be it Egyptian, Iraqi, Lebanese, Palestinian, Jordanian, any form of 'Arab,' music is central. A pivotal figure such as Oom Koolthoom definitely left a huge impact on our peoples, and the politicized voice of Fairouz also touched our entire peoples. Hip-Hop allowed me to achieve a pure and synthesized relationship between my Eastern beliefs and my Western upbringing. It really bridges the gap.

"Euphrates is an attempt to bring understanding to who the 'new Arab' is – as we see it and experience it. We are not camel-bearing, head-wrap-keeping, wife-beating, oil-rich tycoons. We are regular people from your neighbourhood. We are just bringing something new to the table musically and food for thought, unstereotyped. Our culture is beautiful and probably is older than the one you are sitting in right now!!"

Unfortunately, this piece, like many in the annals of human creativity, comes through the enormous sacrifice of the musician. In this case, this "Arab-North-American" hip-hop group, Euphrates, lost its founding member, Nofy Fannan, in the midst of negotiation for inclusion in this project. After hearing of this innovative group from an Irish-Catholic student in Detroit, we began communicating with Nofy, the group's leader. After numerous emails, the communication lines had gone cold, and we wondered had they lost interest?

Finally, his cousin, Yossin Alsalman emailed the following: *"So sorry we did not get back to you – but our dear brother Nofy ascended to the realm above through a tragic accident – and our pain knew nothing of this world. We would still like to be included in the project but primarily as a tribute to our dear brother. Please include whatever of our comments you wish with some tribute to Nofy. Thank you, His Cousin—Yassin."* We will keep our promise.

"Nofy Fannan: 1978-Eternity"

To you Brother, This River will keep flowing upwards while you swim to life after.

We miss you eternally, and feel you with every word, thought and action.

Love you Habibi…..we live for you, till we meet again king………..

If walls could break I would mould this hall to shake the earth and fall to birth.

If words were silent, I would rid this world of violence and hurl a sentence so quiet it would unfurl a science in verbal pious circles...to bring you back.

Son of the moon too bright to teach honest, God bless you brother, While we confess to others how you might rest above us.

Just know we hold the soul of Nofy so closely we slowly flow because you love us so deep, I wasn't so sure this planet wasn't so pure, till it swallowed my one and only cousin running from cures.

I'll watch it hover, scan, skies don't shine for another plan succumbing hand of Allah, It can't be stranded. Sanded – cover man, woman and child of a southern land.

Lift us first, your gifted worth God kissed the earth as you reached the sun and star, al hamdulilah!

"Mecca to Medina," by Euphrates, from the CD: <u>**Stereotypes Incorporated,**</u> c. Ilm Productions, 2004.

The final selection of this Unit returns us to the fact that the greatest stereotypes and injustices in human history have been in the name of the source of much of the greatest advancements in human history as well: *religion*. To learn the interconnection between religions, music, and cultures is to see the fruits of the dearest aspirations of humankind fulfilled.

As we listen to this selection (one of many from this talented group that could have been inserted here), we may wish to follow the text and contemplate the gulf between human reality and the mis-portrayal of that reality. We may also wish to reflect on the wide diversity of music and thought that have only briefly been sampled in this Unit and contemplate the interconnection of all cultures to those that have arisen from what we call the "Middle East."

Pic. 5.18A *The Hijab (or Khimar) refers to the covering of the head (and body) in modesty and reverence. Symbols such as these from all cultures or religions can be grossly misinterpreted if we do not ask questions.* Photo: Galina Barskaya.

Text: Mekka to Medina

Who said Islam was a bomb and eight wives? / Set to storm and hate lives that absolve a norm/ son of the Quraysh tribe was formed /as a Prophet to God, and our state dies Islamic/ his mind will purge sonnets;

Verses for Earth's vomit and vermin/ rhyming uncommon of sermons, honest and firm calm along it he was promised a service/ the birth of our honourable Mohammed/ 570 AD, starburst, mind heavenly baby;

Fruit of Islam, the truth in losing his mom Amina/ the emotion of the moment that he palmed Khadija for quotients born/ with stories of Moses and oceans torn/ he hoped Islam was the call for all those holding arms;

And praising sculptures/ Maybe it was enchantment or a phase in culture/ crazy but it was ranting back to him/ He wrote not of when the trees spoke/the dirt screams the rivers streams gloat;

The hurt being that our planet became/ can't it be games of a stranded innate plan to dismantle a race? / Or a canvas to paint/ Sanded he handed the hate down/ from Medina and Mecca to shift standards;

And cultivate a seed juicing cleanest of nectars/ it seems the reflection of his seeing was a fleeing from vectors/ and angles of math misunderstood concealed in a grave of the mind, at 40 he meets Gibril in a cave to find....;

Yo Ga like Meditation/ with an angel's wing touching his throat awed/ his float caught up and the sky stood silent/ his eyes' irises shook/ his mind would challenge but the sight took pilot drive; (continued)

Yassin concludes: *"I am not one to say that I am a teacher; I still feel I am a student of life. But I hope people leave our shows, or listen to our CDs and feel at one with the message we are speaking. I hope people leave our musical experience and want to come back to it, and that we deconstruct the metaphor-*

ical veil on our societies and selves as Arabs, as Muslims, as the 'other.'. We hope you will learn that we are all from the same essence and that we shouldn't believe what we see, but rather, what we see that is lived— and accept difference and embrace similarities."

The Recipe of Sound

The interconnection between the Southern Baptist/African-American style discourse, which refers to Jesus, and the lyrics of this hip-hop piece, which refers to Muhammad, paints the dynamics of "revolution," suffering, and ultimate victory that mark the lives of the Prophets or Manifestations (reflections) of God. This piece also brings together the following musical and literary components imbedded in the *texture* or layering of the music:

- The strong poetic/metaphoric traditions of Arab/Persian songs with an equally strong connection to God and, in this case, the history of Islam.

- The multidimensional (multiple layers of) meaning that can be created by "sampling" or digitally recording and setting pre-existing sounds and musical ideas into the texture of a hip-hop work. In this case, "Nature Boy," a song made famous by Nat King Cole, is set into the work, as it infers a connection to a prophet.

- And finally, a plea for justice and education in evaluating what is dear and close to the hearts of the artists. That is, the piece from an entire CD that addresses the issues of stereotyping begs listeners to simply relate their culture, their passions, and their beliefs to those of others, without the injustice that is inevitable in the act of "stereotyping," *creating an impression of human beings, human cultures, and their music upon brief and uninformed contact.*

A dombecki performer playing one of the Middle East's most flexible and beloved of instruments.

Religion and Music

The Influence of Religion on Music and Music on Religion

To undermine the value of religion on the world's creativity or to separate religion from daily life distorts the reality that life and connecting life to a Higher Power or "purpose" (however defined) are inseparable, as witnessed in much of our world's history. Musical chant, however, (the "chanting" of prayers or Holy verses) does have a unique place in both human and musical evolution. Professor Borders says about chanting: "In terms of what chant can mean, any chant or singing of a sacred text is different than everyday speech. A prayer is words offered to God. So to offer prayer in the same way that you would order a hamburger doesn't seem right."

Activity

Select a chant of your choice (suggestion: one unlike your belief or culture system). Read the quotation below, listen to the CD example, and discuss in what manner you feel that chant(s) reflects the quotation (in quality, style of recitation, emotion, or presentation):

CD 1.17 Ms. Arkatkar commented: *"This particular chant describes the moral fiber of Lord Ganesha, who is believed to be the god (a physical representation of a higher ideal . . . not the same as God, the Creator) of wisdom and prosperity, and is always remembered before the beginning of any event."*

CD 1.18 Ms. Rose comments: <I>*"Whether it's a prayer, or chanting from the Torah or sacred scrolls (Jewish holy writings), the job of the cantor is to present a penetrating reality of the words through music."*

CD 1.19 The Ven. Samu Sunim writes: <I> *Chanting, like sitting quietly, is another form of meditation for a Buddhist... the words in most chants are not intended to be the focus but rather the sound (vibration). The restless mind should be kept still while you center your attention on the sound of your own voice."*

CD 2.3 (Parts: I, II, III) From the Bahá'í writings: *"O Children of Men! Know ye not why We created you all from the same dust? That no one should exalt himself over the other. Ponder at all times in your hearts how ye were created. Since We have created you all from one same substance, it is incumbent on you to be even as one soul... and dwell in the same land."*

To further understand the impact of religion on music, you may wish to pick one (or more) of the selections below. Read the comments before listening to the music. Then discuss the relationship of the comments to the music. In what manner can you see or "hear" the person's "religious" beliefs and visions expressed in the music?

CD 2.1 In this piece, a combination of the styles above, the author is enchanted by the beauty of a woman, a beauty so miraculous that it makes him believe in God, the woman's creator: *I have believed in God as your radiant beauty couldn't have been but a creation of a God.* Verse 1: *Your radiant beauty is an astonishing light; it puts out the fire that burns in the heart."*

CD 2.2 Ms. Vaghei commented: *"What I would like the reader to learn about my culture and music is that we are mostly motivated by a deep love and affection. This is part of a rich tradition, which goes back to the poetry of Rumi and Hafez, which encourages the creation of art based upon the philosophy that it is intended to transcend any ordinary thoughts."*

CD 2.4 Yassin from the group Euphrates wrote: *"Hip-Hop's influence on our lives has been more than simply musical; it is a way of life. Hip-Hop allowed me to achieve a pure and synthesized relationship between my Eastern beliefs and my Western upbringing. Euphrates is an attempt to bring understanding to who the 'new Arab' is-- as we see it and experience it... We are just bringing something new to the table musically and food for thought, un-stereotyped!"*

Unit O Activities

Activity #1: Understanding Concepts

Based upon what you've read:

1) How can we perceive the difference between "categorizing" for the sake of communicating effectively and "stereotyping" others?

2) In what way do you see your understanding of the world's history or the manner by which you've been educated or informed about the world around you as "slanted" towards your culture? Or, is it slanted towards another's culture, and in what way?

3) What is your perception of the meaning of "religion"? Does your religion (organized religion or personal credo for life) have an equivalent to the phrase "Love your neighbor as yourself?" If yes, how do you think of this principle in terms of your "neighbors" being of other religious beliefs?

4) How do you understand the function of "chant" in the world's religions? What do you think might be the connection of "chant" to the music you most favor?

Pic. 5.19A,B&C *The art that rises from religious beliefs at each stage in the progression of the world's religions is born frequently from both the intensity of "faith" and the desire to serve that faith through the power of human creativity. Images of Andalusian Qur'an calligraphy (above left), the ceramic painting of a Mosque (Farsh-Isfahan – above right), and an actual mosque (Beirut, Lebanon – right) all bear striking similarities in their creation to the creative process used by musicians.* Images: Courtesy, wikipedia.org.

Activity #2: Listening Deeper

You may wish to listen again to the sampling of religious chants from the Hindu, Jewish, Buddhist, Islamic, and Bahá'í religions. Then contemplate the following:

1) What are the musical or aesthetic properties that are shared by all of the samples of chant included in CD examples 1.17 – 1.20 and 2.3?

2) Since we know the definition and properties of melody, what are the differences you hear in each of the melodic variations? [You might describe the differences in terms of the singing style, the contour or ornamentation of the melody, the combination of pitches (scales or modes), or the timbre or vocal quality of the person chanting.]

3) Having recognized that the term "Middle East" or even "Islam" does not give credit to the cultural diversity that is reflected in the diverse practices of either Islamic chant or the music of these regions:

   A. What are some of the main musical observations that you can make in examining the similarities and differences between each of the pieces—1.21 Andalusian/Moroccan Madh; 2.1 the Syrian/Andalousian piece performed by Zein Al-Jundi, and 2.2 the Persian poetic setting performed by Mehri Vaghei?

   B. Can you discern the relationship of the various chordophones to the vocal melodies? How would you describe this relationship?

Activity #3: Exercising Passion

Often, if we can find a fascination with one culture, and we become informed of its qualities and creative expressions, we can transfer that insight and experience over to others.

Suggestion

Find one religion or one aspect of either a religion or culture discussed in this Unit that you found fascinating. Are there people that you know from that religion or culture with whom you could discuss? If so:

   A. Ask them for a "meeting" time that is convenient for them. Prepare a list of questions to help provide yourself with more or deeper information. If you are uncertain about whether the question will offend them, simply ask them if the question [then state the question] is appropriate. Record their responses. Then ask yourself: were there any of their thoughts that you had a different perspective on than the person you interviewed? Do you think the person's perspectives represent a large percentage of their religion/culture, or do you feel the people's views may give only one perspective of the culture? Did the people seem balanced in their portrayal of their religion or culture, or were they trying to "win" you to their cause? Were you pleased or disappointed by the meeting?

The next step:

   B. Is there a favorite restaurant, cultural gathering place, or special event (concert or cultural celebration) that your source will be attending that perhaps you could attend as well? If so, ask them if it would be appropriate if you attend as well? If so, is there anything you should do to prepare yourself, or *if there is anything you could bring* (this is an act of courtesy sometimes neglected in some cultures)? Although you may not be able to "write" or record your observations of the event, make sure that you record your thoughts shortly after the event before they are distorted by time.

Alternative: If you do not have a personal source:

   Find one religion or one aspect of either a religion or culture discussed in this Unit that you found fascinating. Conduct some research on the topic by locating websites or materials produced by the culture or religious advocates. Make a list of the things you find similar to your beliefs. Make a list of the things that you find in contradiction to your beliefs and then answer the question : *How can I reconcile my beliefs with the those things I find different, to avoid stereotyping?*

Activity #4: **Exercising Our Own Creativity**

You may recall your first time on a mountain, scuba-diving or snorkeling in an ocean, the first time you saw snow or a desert. In each "first" adventure over the course of our lives, we are given dynamic and exciting new information with which we can see and appreciate our planet.

Artists often seek these life-transforming events (as they excite the deepest levels of passion and awareness) and then they attempt to convert these emotions and experiences into their art. That is, rather than simply taking a picture (unless your art is photography) that likely will find its way into a drawer or cupboard, we try to capture the excitement, the information, the form, colors, sights, or sounds of the experience into our *medium* (form of expression for which we are most passionate). Remembering that one's "art" may be as diverse as quilting, dancing, making music, or planning a trip or a dinner, we may honor another culture by incorporating the positive impressions of that culture into the expressions in our life that are dearest to us. Just try to keep the following in mind:

Pic. 5.20 and 5.21 *What do we see versus what is there? The question of perception vs. reality is a great part of the challenge of the human experience.*

In the picture (right), is anything "odd?" Perhaps that this man is playing the violin in a vertical position, that he is playing the violin at all, or is there nothing "odd" – since the violin came from the rababa(h) and would have been played in this fashion originally?

In the picture (below), what do we see? Do our eyes go immediately to the camel, since in our environment there are no camels? Do our eyes go immediately to the Mercedes Benz, since that is what we value or prefer to see? Or do we see the inevitability of evolution and, in this case, the irony of thousands of years of "transportation evolution" in a single frame? Photo: (right) Courtesy and copyright Terry Abrams, 2005; (below) Authors.

- Whatever religion or culture you choose, make sure that you ask yourself: "If someone said or created this work (whatever you make) based on my culture and represented it this way, would I feel honored?" Then make sure that you represent it as only "your impression" and not, for example, Arabic calligraphy, music, or authentic cuisine.

- Try to capture the essence or quality of whatever you find attractive. A craft is a mastering of technique and usually includes the reproduction of an existing creative piece in replica fashion. Art generally makes impressions or reflections of what we experience, but takes the liberties of re-interpretation based upon our emotional and creative sensibilities. [Again, make sure that you represent your art as interpretive and not as a literal reflection of the culture].

When possible, share your creativity with others. Art derives its primary fulfillment to the artist when it is in service to others, causes one to think, or is enlightening. In some cases, you may even wish to give your "art" away to others as a gift. This is an excellent practice, as once we create our art it is an excellent endeavor to practice detachment (letting go) of the work. This includes not being concerned with the evaluation of others, or else the beauty of creativity is compromised by our egos and our attachment to the approval of others. This is definitely not an easy concept to master, especially if we come from a culture that emphasizes "ownership" or places emphasis on the personality of the artist over the art!

Exercise

- Pick one topic, one small passage, one quote, one picture, one of the pieces of music, or one thought from the Unit above that you found inspiring.

Pic. 5.21A *Symbols in all religions are based upon values and perceptions of the time period of their construction. As each "new" religion manifests itself, the primary teachings and ultimately the symbols will change.* Photo: Authors.

- Reflect for 5-10 minutes on the quote, passage, image, sounds (you may take notes during or after your reflection): What does it mean? What does it reflect about our purpose on this earth? How do you relate to this passage?

- Now, take up your pen, jot down the first things that come to your mind as relates to your chosen instrument. How would you reflect or mirror the inspiration and impact you had from your *meditation?*

- How can you complete an artistic thought (a work of art) that will have the qualities and impact of the inspiration and thoughts you had from your reflection? Now simply do it. [Remember that your project design should be only as ambitious as the time and materials you comfortably have to commit to the project. Overzealous projects can destroy the spirit or joy of creativity—at first.]

Note: If you pick a religious passage or topic, see if you can create the emotion and spirit of the passage in your art. As artists, we reflect the spirit of our inspiration like a clean mirror. Try not to be concerned with the outcome that will dirty the mirror.

Unit 0: Endnotes

5.1 To *categorize* is to place somebody or something in a particular group and define or judge the person or thing accordingly. Though all words are labels for human thought, words that define or describe people, cultures, or their music summarily are categories. When "just" or fair, the labels are congruent or respected by those whom we are categorizing. When not, we are incorrectly *categorizing,* or *stereotyping.*

5.2 Photos: Ethel Waters, photographed by Carl Van Vechten, 1938 Aug. 28. Library of Congress; both Muddy Waters and Elvis Presley pictures are used under "fair use" previsions under United States copyright law.

5.3 The Media History Timeline (see www.hediahistory.umn.edu) is a handy source for quick information. Special scrutiny, however, should be given to nearly every entry as things rarely occur overnight, on a specific date, or year without multiple other stages and influences; European/Western cultures are given the majority of emphasis, and very little is said of the contributions of Indigenous or non-"first" world cultures.

5.4 Devimahatmya MS in Sanskrit on palm-leaf, from a monastery in Nepal, 11th century.

5.5 A strict separation between the actual writings of "holy books" of each religion and the subsequent (and frequently numerous) interpretations of the symbolism or the "sects," or divisions, of these religions based upon interpretation must be drawn. An accurate comparative understanding of religions requires both an understanding of cultural evolution and symbolism. Perceptions of meaning today of a religious teaching or concept 2000 years earlier are likely to have been distorted or altered numerous times from the context of their initial orientation or meaning.

5.6 For anyone advocating atheism or agnosticism, sticking to the belief that there is purpose for life (even if that purpose does not acknowledge a "Creator") would simply require the *recognition* that many believe the purpose of life is articulated by the "Creator" through human form (a Prophet). Although you may not agree with this, you may relate it to whatever drives your life, gives you inspiration or insights, and, ultimately, purpose.

5.7 From the "Writings of Baha'u'llah," courtesy http://reference.bahai.org.

5.8 The Second Vatican Council, or Vatican II, was an Ecumenical Council of the Roman Catholic Church opened under Pope John XXIII in 1962 and closed under Pope Paul VI in 1965. Under the pressure to liberalize Catholic worship and create better accessibility to Catholics around the world, the council allowed for mass and worship in vernacular languages and for a greater flexibility in the practice of mass, leading, in some instances, even to "folk masses" (masses sung with guitar or popular instruments) in the United States.

5.9 A mantra for meditation, from the New Bhajan Book (Hindu book of prayers and mediations).

5.10 Improvisation is the spontaneous formulation or composition of musical ideas. Although many people mistakenly think improvisation is "making up something" or creating something that is original on the spur of the moment, all forms of improvisation are based upon formulas and standards that are known in advance. Additionally, improvisation is based upon whatever the musicians have heard or experienced to that point. The *creativity* is that they formulate those formulas and existing ideas in a "new" or "fresh" manner—spontaneously.

5.11 The weekly cycle, measured by the Sabbath at the end of the week, is one of the oldest recorded divisions of time (Genesis 8:10; 29:27). *Sabbath* is the official day of rest in Judaism. The Jewish Sabbath, called Shabbat in Hebrew, begins at sundown on Friday evening and ends at sundown on Saturday evening.

5.12 Sunim is a term of respect for a monk or nun, generally meaning "teacher."

5.13 Although the reference to "Buddhas" could be construed to mean only the Buddha of the various schools of Buddhism (Theravada or Mahayana), it is also generally construed to mean all the "Manifestations of God"— that is, the Holy Prophets of "Sons of God" (reflections of an unknowable Essence) in human frame (six of which came before and thirteen of which will follow). Check out www.buddhanet.net for a comparison of schools and a general overview of Buddhism.

5.14 There are many sects or divisions of the two main schools. Zen Buddhism is one of them and relies heavily on chanting as a means of turning inward. Interview: Joe Lukomski, March 2005. "The main message which Bodhidharma (an Indian Buddhist master—remembering that Buddhism originated in India) sent to us runs like this:

"Not relying on the words and letters, Teachings are transmitted outside the Scriptures; pointing directly into one's mind, then one can see into his own nature and attains Buddhahood."

"To help people who like to do kensho (see into one's own nature), Zen masters have designed many different methods. The four main ones of them are: counting your breaths out and in, following your breaths with your mind's eye, shikantaza (just sitting in your whole awareness), and koans." (from www.zenguide.com)

5.15 We chose texts based upon a survey of known music appreciation texts (from the largest publishers of textbooks), combined with a telephone survey of regional instructors. We do not wish to embarrass or ridicule other textbooks, authors, or publishers. Note: This survey was conducted in November 2003. There may be textbooks on the market since this time that have changed their proportion of "Western" to non-Western materials (or, if non-Western focused, have included Western music in the same "ethnic"/cultural context).

5.16 To denote "non-Western" music as "ethnic music" implies that Western music is "non-ethnic." In truth, all music is ethnic, and none more or less so—Western and even "classical" or "art" music included.

5.17 We might consider that the very designation of "first world" and "third world" implies a greater-than / lesser-than status. To the extent that this perception is given ascendancy, the very cultures that hold the key to cultural balance and eradication of cultural arrogance will be held back from growth (stereotyped and disrespected), and Western cultures will be forced to continue to wallow in the imbalances of excessive materialism, disjointed communities, and imbalanced education. Moreover, one need not speak the terms to "think" them. The greatest source of biases and stereotyping is not rooted in ignorance, but in our ignorance of our ignorance.

5.18 Historically, unless in defense of life, initiators and leaders of war must create and reinforce stereotypes and mis-labeling, or create monster-like images of other humans (as enemies) in order to sustain the counter-intuitive act of taking human life. In turn, regardless of the victor, now retribution and revenge loom as distinct possibilities in the minds of the conquered, sometimes for generations or centuries.

5.19a Should be spelled "dhikr," though another common transliteration can be substituted altogether with "zekr," which gets closer to the Arabic or Persian pronunciation. Using the "d" is problematic for people that don't know Middle Eastern languages. The difference between the "dh" and the "z" versions refers not to pronunciation but to two different letters, both of which have a "z" sound—see a parallel example, Adhan and Azan. Finally, the word zekr/dhikr means "remembrance" and "mentioning," which links to an idea that is part of Islam: that people are not born sinful, but forgetful, and that through remembrance, they can become closer to God.

5.19 This is a phrase that is uttered most frequently when Muslims say the name of Muhammad to distinguish His name with respect from normal conversation.

5.20 Sufism is one of the three primary branches of Islam: Sunni, Shi'ite, and Sufi. Each of these branches uses the Qu'ran as the Holy text, but distinguish themselves in some fashion, e.g., as to who Muhammad's successor was or, in the case of Sufi-ism, how prayer or even dance may be used to heighten religious experience.

5.21 "Islam—a world religion belonging to the Semitic family; it was promulgated by the Prophet *Muhammad* in Arabia in the 7th century AD. The Arabic term *Islam,* literally "surrender," illuminates the fundamental religious idea of Islam—that the believer (called a Muslim, from the active particle of Islam) accepts 'surrender to the will of Allah (Arabic: God)'." <u>Encyclopædia Britannica</u> Article, page 1.

5.22 From an overview of Biblical music at www.bible-history.com.

5.23 We will use the term "microtonal" to describe scales or melodies based upon the scales of Middle Eastern and Indian cultures. The term "microtonal" simply refers to the fact there are infinite pitches or tones that one can produce. The scales of the world's older cultures, and melodies that were produced, initially used pitches that were closer together, had numerous associations with each scale (emotion, color, associations), and were, therefore, the focus of the music.

5.24 From: <u>A Topic of Dispute in Islam: Music</u>, by Mustafa Sabri, as published in Beyan-ul-Haq, issue 63, year: 2, vol: 3, 1910 (a journal which used to be issued by the Islamic Scholars Society). Mustafa Sabri was one of the top Ottoman scholars in the 20th century. He served as a *shaikhulislam* (Highest religious authority) in the Ottoman State. He died in 1954 in Egypt.

5.25 For more information on Sufism, you may wish to check out www.sufistudies.net or www.uga.edu, from which these quotations come. Permission was given by their founders for use in this text.

5.26 The Persian Empire and culture should be seen as distinct from those of Arabic cultures. The language *Farsi,* spoken in Iran (Persia), is as distinct language from Arabic as Hungarian is from English. The Shah was the "king," or ruler, of Iran, the last one being deposed during the revolution of 1979.

5.27 The suffix "o-phone" means "to sound" – as in what causes the instrument "to sound."

5.28 The *"Hidden Words"* written by Baha'u'llah (Prophet Founder of the Bahá'í Faith) in 1857 are a unique series of mystical and powerful meditations revealed in both Persian (Farsi) and Arabic. His son, Abdu'l-Baha, commented that *"The Hidden Words"* is "a treasury of divine mysteries" and that when one ponders its contents, "the doors of mysteries will open."

5.29 Unique to the progression of religious "Manifestations" and interpreters of religious teachings is the progression of Prophets and, later, "interpreters" of the religious teachings in the Bahá'í Faith, which has assured that the religion would not split into sects or divisions detrimental to the establishment of a "global commonwealth." Beginning with the "Bab" (the Gate) in 1844 (whose job it was to lay the foundation for the coming of the "Promised One"), extending through Bahá'u'lláh's Revelation (1863-1992), and finally through three phases of interpretation: the guidance of Abdu'l-Baha (from whose writings this selection is taken: "Writings of Abdu'l-Baha, p.112), extending through the Guardianship (Shoghi Effendi), and leading ultimately to the establishment of the Universal House of Justice, Haifa, Israel.

Pic. 5.22A, B, & C. *The silhouette, physical portrayal of Jesus, cross and church steeples are given even more symbolism by the sunset and presence of the dove (A – Prague skyline). The dualism of "good" vs. "evil," for some, is clear and graphic (all things must be one or other); to others, there may be many manifestations of potential "good" and many possibilities before "evil" (B – Kutna Hora); and to others, the multiple heritages, cultures, and time periods through which a group of people passes will find their way into their religious practices (C- Berlin Synagogue). Photos: A/B Authors, C, Courtesy of Andreas Praefcke.*

Europe:
The Influence of Ancestry and Imperialism

UNIT

VI

Topics to Consider in Unit VI

➤ *What are some of the most important influences of European cultures on our world's cultures (plus and minus)?*

➤ *What are the benefits and challenges of seeing European cultures as equally "ethnic" – or, in an equal context to the rest of the world's cultures?*

➤ *How might we (more accurately) look at the "periods" and genres of European history and "classical" music?*

➤ *What is the impact of "imperialism" on the evolution of European cultures? And – what is the impact on our culture-systems today?*

➤ *What are the challenges and benefits in seeing "history" or acknowledging ancestry on our perceptions of today's cultures?*

➤ *What are some of the major events or developments of the periods we call: Middle Ages, Renaissance, Baroque, Classical (Neoclassical), and Romantic? And – what are some of the major musical innovations, which affect our musical practices today?*

➤ *How did the European musical cultures evolve in their practice of polyphony and harmony? And – what was the influence of the Christian church on musical evolution and practice?*

➤ *What are the differences and similarities in the music of Monteverdi, Bach, Mozart, Beethoven, and Verdi? How did each composer's music reflect the values of their time? (Were there ways by which each mirrored what was to come?)*

➤ *What was the impact of the development of European musical notation on its "ethnic" music?*

➤ *What is musical texture, form or tension and release (in music)?*

➤ *How might we discuss the interconnectivity in musical evolution between (examples) early Christian Chant and Monteverdi, Bach and Stokowski, Mozart and his father, Beethoven and the Romantic period, Wagner and Nationalism, Verdi and Italian pride in opera?*

➤ *What is "programmatic music"? And – what is the impact of Romantic composition and program music on one of today's "classical" music formulas – film music?*

UNIT VI

Europe: The Influence of Ancestry and Imperialism

Revising Our Vision of Connections over Time

"Tradition may be defined as an extension of the franchise. Tradition means giving votes to the most obscure of the classes, our ancestors. It is the democracy of the dead. Tradition refuses to submit to the small and arrogant oligarchy of those who merely happen to be walking about. All democrats object to men being disqualified by the accident of birth; tradition objects to their being qualified by the accident of death.

"Democracy tells us not to neglect a good man's opinion, even if he is our groom; tradition asks us not to neglect a good man's opinion, even if he is our father."
G.K. Chesterton, "Orthodoxy,"1908, ch.4.

"What does honoring our ancestry mean, you ask? We can begin each day knowing that we are exactly where we are supposed to be.

"What's most important in life is that we don't begin tomorrow in the same place we are today, that we grow each day in some way. I'm just not sure that many young people today have a good understanding of what positive growth is. What I mean to say is, to change where we are going we must have a firm and fair knowledge of where we've been.

"I have learned, unless I honor my ancestors, I stand to do a grave injustice to myself and my children. But it's also important that I distinguish honoring— and a fair and just understanding of the past. Not everything of the past deserves honoring. This is the balance of the cycle." Wallace Martin, a wise elder, Detroit, Michigan, 1995.

Pic. 6.0 and 6.0A *This is NASA's "Blue Marble" image of Europe applied as a texture on a sphere using Art of Illusion program. The observer is centered at (50° N, 20° E), at Moon distance above the Earth. Europa was a Levantine woman in Greek mythology, from whom the name of the continent Europe was ultimately taken. The etymology of her name ("wide" or "broad" + "eye(s)" or "face") metaphorically could mean "the intelligent or open-minded" (synonymous to glaukopis).* Photo and information: Courtesy NASA, (painting - A) Gustav Mureau, 1869, and wikipedia.org.

How accurate is our understanding of history? Since much of the documentation of history has been recorded by people who did not see the multidimensional nature of human exchange across cultural boundaries, how can we be sure that what we know of history is what actually occurred? If history has frequently been reported in a slanted manner or biased by cultural centrism (a common human flaw regardless of culture), is it possible that the events we accept as fact might not actually have occurred?

Presumably we know that Christopher Columbus did not discover America (i.e., the "discovery" of America occurred possibly 30,000 years earlier and that its subsequent "discovery" may have occurred 10 to 25 other times before Columbus).[6.1] But we might wish to ask ourselves, if this very obvious fact has been only recently "discovered" (i.e., changed in most American school curriculums), while the United States still celebrates "Columbus day" rather than *"Native American Ancestry day,"* or *"Columbus the great adventurer day."* How many less obvious distortions of our[6.2] history remain still to be "discovered," especially as concerns our European ancestries? Though we have many things to celebrate, are we seeing history with clarity?

Simultaneously, Columbus's legacy still has impact on the world, just as do the legacies of the colonizers, Native Americans, slavers, and slaves alike. To see history in the context of multiple truths and with a keen eye to its impact on our daily lives is both critical and, in future-oriented societies, challenging. Certainly, despite the legacies of cultural dominance and arrogance, those who owe much of their heritage to European culture groups (the primary topic of this Unit) also have much of which to be proud. Just look at this partial list of European influences on much of our world:

- Europe has two of the strongest currencies (Euro/British pound) and the most dominant languages in international trade and communication.

- European nations, by virtue of colonization, have had an unparalleled influence on the rest of the world.

- European systems of government, commerce, and especially education (including the model of the university) are the basis for dissemination of much of the world's practices in a wide spectrum of disciplines.

- The primary religion of Europe, Christianity, has become the basis for the "common" calendar, and thus, impacts in some fashion many of the world's cultures and their rituals, holidays, and family or community events.

- European technology and the perpetual search for scientific advancement has affected nearly all aspects of how the world lives its life today. Few people are not touched by the advancements made in agriculture, science, medicine, manufacturing, or warfare technology.

And finally, as concerns music, "classical" [6.3] or "art" music from Europe (the music that evolved through either European Christianity or patronage by the ruling classes of Europe from the 7th-20th centuries) is also the foundation for much of today's film music, today's modern instruments used in popular music, and is certainly in itself, the fruit of remarkable creativity.

However, with power comes responsibility. As mentioned earlier, if we survey the preponderance of *Music Appreciation* texts and instruction programs, we see the overwhelming weight given to European classical music is grossly disproportionate to the world's other cultures and music. The same imbalance occurs in the majority of European and American university music curricula, where the musical language (music theory) and history of European music are given nearly exclusive emphasis over the world's other musical heritages. The reverse effect is nearly as disturbing. When instruction programs in "ethnic" music (ethnomusicology) are offered, they often fail to include European classical music, thus implying that classical music is somehow less "ethnic," or in any case, not placing all cultures on an equal pedagogic playing field.

Like the Columbus error, it is not really the event that is problematic, but how we view and discuss it. *How* the music of our European ancestry is taught in terms of exclusivity, disassociation from other cultures, or in failing to connect history to modern practices in an "equal but different" manner diminishes both our understanding of the relative contributions of <u>all</u> cultures to our cultural make-up, as well as the music's reality and its value and importance to us. By underemphasizing the "ethnicity" of classical music, by not showing its "multi-cultural" nature, by not underscoring the folk and popular emphasis of its musical and cultural context, or by not demonstrating with clarity the religious nature of much of its origin (without attachment to our personal religious preferences), we fail to place the music in its balanced and rightful place, or in any case to emphasize it as being *a reflection of the values and history of the European cultures that created it.* Bereft of the commonalities it has with other cultures, or with rock 'n' roll, gospel music, or salsa, both classical or art music and the cultures from which it evolved can become distorted, much as have many of the figures and events in European or American history. Such distortions actually serve to strip both music and history of its natural distinction, humanness and, ultimately, relevance to our values and lives.

Pic. 6.1 *The gravesites of Beethoven and Mozart in Austria are only a few feet from each other. This is probably also the distance of much of their music from the melodies, rhythms, and function of the music found amongst the "folk" with whom they associated throughout their lives. When we assign inferior/superiority designations to either human cultures or their art, we profoundly injure the foundations of mutual respect and potential appreciation.* Photo: Courtesy and copyright Daderot.

James Borders, from whom we heard earlier, is a professor of medieval music with strong interests in a wide variety of other musical genres. He made these observations: *"One analogy* (concerning appreciating diverse music equally) – *is that today there may be far more people into sports than music. When you*

Courtesy of the Academy of Fine Arts, Vienna, Austria.

watch Michael Jordon play basketball, Tiger Woods golf, or Muhammad Ali box, what you admire is their form. You don't have to know the sport to appreciate the way they use their bodies and skill to produce the results in each of their sports.

"I think what occurred around WWII was the development of a kind of 'middle brow' culture. I remember one of the first records I owned was 'Death and Transfiguration' (an orchestral tone poem by Richard Strauss, Germany, late 19th–early 20ᵗʰ century—see tone poems later in the unit). It had a green cover and label that said 'the world's greatest music.' But the fact that you could purchase or consume something that was believably advertised to culturally "enrich you"; that is, "if you buy this product, you will be better as a result," really loused up much of our perception of art and creativity. Especially Western concert music was viewed as something that would better you almost as a sort of religion. The religion of God, and other Gods—such as enrichment and self-improvement— especially during times when there seemed to be no God, then you end up with a formidable movement that would impact many.

These ideas probably would have been seen as ridiculous to Mozart and Beethoven. Mozart was apparently pleased when his opera tunes were being played by fiddlers or hurdy-gurdies on Viennese street corners. I think that Mozart would have a whole lot to say to musicians like Stevie Ray Vaughn (blues guitarist). They were both virtuosos in their time. In the overall scheme of things, people who do music appreciate other people who do music and it doesn't matter what that music is."

European "Classical," or "Art," Music in Perspective

To counter the tendencies to over- or under-magnify the importance or impact of European art, classical, or "ethnic" music in all of their forms, we will attempt to focus on the following themes:

- The periods and genres[6.4] of classical music should be used only as file labels for the collection of information (throughout our life). In reality, they should not be considered as definitive of the pieces, composers, or even the events of the periods themselves. Each "period," for example, began long before its assigned time and was the direct result of numerous events and exchanges with other cultures over time. Just as each work or event is far more complex than the simplistic labels or periods can imply, so are the periods in European history.

- The beliefs, perceptions, and cultural tendencies of each era will be explored as to how they contributed to European, American, or world history, as well as to what we do or practice today. For nearly every music or event, there are likely to be at least a couple of perspectives worth pursuing. For example, at times the touching beauty and profound influence of Christianity in the cultures or music will be seen or heard, while at others we may need to view the greed or cruelty of those who distorted Christianity for personal advancement. In some cases, heroes and geniuses will become people, and masterpieces will become songs. In all cases, however, we will *attempt* to see the history of the music and cultures from a globally "just" perspective.

- The pendulum swing between "classicism" (returning to Ancient Greek culture as a model for artistic/humanistic development) and "romanticism" (dramatic and highly emotional art that reflected times of enormous upheaval and change) can be a frame through which we can visualize both Europe's historical and cultural evolution. We will also see how the imperial mindset (belief and great investment in empire) evolved—through feudalism, the Crusades (holy war), colonization, slavery, nationalism, and still further to WWI and WWII—and had enormous impact on the world's economy, social systems, and music.

- We will examine the perpetual cross-influencing of folk (secular) music, especially that of "minority" European cultures such as Jewish and Romany [gypsy] (Unit VII), and sacred or art music. We will also attempt to minimize the belief that either was more or less ethnic, or that they were separate or distinct in their evolution.

- Finally, we will explore the importance of the global cultural fusions that we erroneously still categorize by nationality, (i.e.,"French," "Italian," "German," etc.) and thus, grossly neglect the multi-dimensional nature of these cultures' evolution.

Pic. 6.1A 6.1B 6.1C *We can look at painting, dance, art, architecture, or any human expressive art to understand a culture's values over its evolution. In Medieval or Gothic times, the longing for connection to God amidst the drama of Holy and feudal wars, plagues, and greater involvement in the "world" around led to the dominating influence of Christian values and the longing for heaven in many of these periods' works. Notre Dame de Paris (above), French for "Our Lady of Paris," meaning the church in Paris dedicated to Mary, the mother of Jesus, is an example of a gothic cathedral with all points ascending to the realm above. The Western (Royal) Portal at Chartres Cathedral, ca. 1145, (above right)— these architectural statues are examples of the earliest Gothic sculptures and were revolutionary in style and the model for a generation of sculptors. Meanwhile, the evolution of painting (the representation of images on a surface) during the Gothic period was practiced in four primary crafts: frescos, panel paintings, manuscript illumination, and stained glass. Frescoes such as this one by Simone Martini— 1285-1344— (below right) frequently portrayed the dark themes and high emotion characteristic of the times.* Photos: Notre Dame de Paris, southern view, at night in Spring 2001. Copyright (c) 2001 by Steven G. Johnson and donated to Wikipedia; Chartres Cathedral, photo by Eixo.

Respecting and Understanding History and Ancestry

"Nothing Comes from Nothing"

Nothing comes from nothing …
The aged man sits – head in hands
Stars above, earth below – pondering the empty lands
Drum beside him – the air grows cold
Memories of art – and rhythms of old
The wind blows east – it harbors silence
One man's passion – lost to another man's science
He rises: reminisces – imagines as he listens
The music of his heart –
still playing as the young depart

He saunters, wonders …
Will they ever know – ever perceive?
What they claim is created – evolved over centuries
It's never mine or theirs – simply white or black
To judge is neglect – denial reject –
the ancestors would remind us …
… Nothing comes from nothing!

Poem: Kaitlyn Charlebois
(By permission, student musician, May 2005)

There are many ways to look at the manner by which events or musical works connect to us over time. We might begin with the understanding that all events, all works of art, and all inventions or innovations in the world *do in fact* have some sort of impact upon the evolution of human cultures leading to us and our world. The more marked the events, such as three-hundred nearly uninterrupted years of the Crusades, the Spanish Inquisition, or the Civil Rights movement of the 1960s and '70s in the United States, the more direct and profound the impact upon our way of life. Although few can deny the impact of Martin Luther or Martin Luther King, Jr., on the course of human affairs, individuals such as these were significant figures in a chain of remarkable individuals and events over time. This is why when we read or hear that someone is the *father, mother,* or inventor of some major initiative or style of music or art we should remember that all creativity is born of the reconfiguration of prior creative initiatives. All too often, the labels and credits attached to historical events divert our attention from seeing a more accurate reflection of multiple fusions, exchange, and simultaneous "truths" not only between individuals but between cultures and across generations as well.

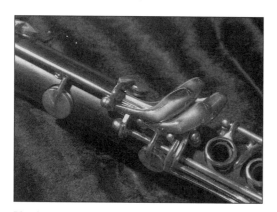

Pic. 6.1D *One online encyclopedia speaks of the evolution of the modern Western (transverse) flute: "The dimensions and key system of the modern Western concert flute and its close relatives are almost completely the work of the great flutist, composer, acoustician and silversmith, Theobald Boehm, who described his invention in his 1871 book…." In truth, however, the evolution of the recorder, multiple other flutes, and the clarinet – and all of their "inventors" – contributed to its origin as well.* Photo: Courtesy Nicole Randall.

Since the wealth of documentation of Christian art and music and/or later, of classical music (both Christian and "non"-Christian) is extensive while the act of recording or documenting one's work is one of the primary cultural aesthetics that distinguishes the European academic exercise, we will always have many resources from which to work in discussing European cultures that may not exist with other more oral cultures. But we also will need to resist, even in the smallest sense, the inference of cultural superiority to Europe's multiple cultures if we desire a balanced assessment of the processes and dynamics of European musical and cultural evolution.

Of course, we cannot do justice to the multitude of creative European musicians and composers any more than we could successfully portray the immense creativity in other parts of the world. What we can attempt is to select a few of the composers, sample their works, and attempt to paint the connection of these works and ideals to the evolution of a continent (Europe) and its subsequent impact on our world today.

You may wish to remember that for every statement you read in this or any historical summary, you are only getting a partial picture. Try not to consider this information definitive or without alternative interpretations, but rather assume we are giving one set of insights or one guide to the reconsideration of history in a more flexible mode. In this case, one which simultaneously requires:

- Seeing the evolution and influence of a single artist over his or her lifetime as a process of perpetual fusion and a reflection of the organic process of (global) human evolution. We will emphasize how artists formulated their crafts based upon ideas from other artists, over the assignment of "ownership" or credit.

- Seeing evolution and influence not only within a single genre or defined culture group *across generations,* but also in the context of the world around it. This means seeing Italy or France as a composite mixture of cultures, perpetually in contact with other cultures, despite how they may have defined themselves or documented their history. It also means seeing Italian opera of the Baroque or Romantic periods as an evolutionary process rather than as distinctive genres or periods.

Above all, we might keep the phrase, *"nothing comes from nothing"* as a mantra for the search for understanding and dialogue with others. As disconcerting as it may be, to believe that something was "initiated," "created," "begun," "founded," or "started" from any human life experience is generally inaccurate.

Periods and Labels

Remembering dates, period titles, and labels is helpful for keeping a mental framework. Below- are generalized file labels and extremely rough outlines of events that might place composers and musical achievements in a time reference.

We just need to keep a balanced perspective that each "period" began in the previous or was simultaneously occurring in the following, and that a search for a balanced understanding of the dynamics of history should take precedence over a quest for labels.

Pic. 6.2C *Contrary to many perspectives of "periods" in history, each culture reflects its "fusion" of influences and values at the time in all expressions, from music to architecture. Vienna's famed St. Stephen's Cathedral was originally started (as a parish church) in 1147. It was enlarged over centuries and became the center for many important events – from the issuing of a Crusade plea (1454) to the funeral of W.A. Mozart and performances of sacred works of Beethoven. Unique to this cathedral are the mosaic roof tiles, which were destroyed in WWII but restored later.* Photo: Authors.

Early Europe (5ᵗʰ-15ᵗʰ Centuries)

Time Frame	General Events and Empires
5th century	The "Fall" of the Roman Empire ("Dark Ages"), which led to "Middle Ages." Developments included greater emphasis on tribal or feudal confederations and overall administrative confusion within Europe.

The evolution of Christianity and two primary divisions: Eastern ("Byzantine") or Orthodox (North African, Greek, Armenian, and Slovak regions). The influence of the Holy Roman Church would evolve to "empire" status over subsequent centuries (Italy and most of Western Europe).

Musical Developments

Jewish cantillation, Greek modes, and Arabic scales became the basis for Christian chant. Diverse styles of Christian chant evolved in both Eastern and Western Europe alongside numerous (generally and documented) community music genre.

7th and 8th Centuries   Charlemagne forged an agreement with the Roman Catholic Church and aided in also forging of a "pan-European" empire of sorts. Muslims began the conquest and occupation of North Africa and Spain. A firm establishment of the Christian church as the primary "centralized" empire or governing institution. Evolution of feudalism (tribal lords evolving to feudal lordship).[6.4a]

Musical Developments

"Plainchant" (later termed *Gregorian chant* after Pope Gregory I) or the single melody (**monophonic**) chanting of liturgy (sacred texts) became formulated. In subsequent centuries, these melodies would eventually begin to be combined with others – creating **polyphony** (two or more melodies occurring at the same time).

5th–15th Centuries   ### Medieval—(Middle Ages)

Numerous transitions in power between tribal confederates, feudal lords, warrior cultures (e.g., Avars, Vikings), Aryan and Islamic cultures, and liaisons between feudal or noble kings/lords and the Holy Roman Empire occurred.

Musical Developments

The organization of chants into liturgy to mark the rite of Eucharist (Holy Communion) and later into **masses** (Ordinary and Proper) generated musical notation systems, and slowly evolved into polyphonic vocal works. Four-part harmony (the type used in choirs and choruses around the world), which is now emblematic of both Western popular and classical music, began to evolve. The affinity for strict organization (composition by notation), a strong emphasis on *harmony* (two or more different pitches occurring at the same time), and many of the "musical rules" and notation practices which would influence or govern Western music to the present day evolved during this period.

11th–13th Centuries   ### Crusades of the Middle Ages

Nine crusades occurred, which were primarily attempts on the part of European Christian and secular leadership to regain the Holy Land, expand or defend Christianity and, at other times, to convert Jews or Muslims who were believed to be in contradiction with Christianity. The first, third, fourth, and fifth crusades were the largest and were sanctioned by the Pope; all of the other crusades were undertaken primarily by rulers of France, England, Austria or other regions. A substantial percentage of the male population of Europe was lost during this time period.

Musical Developments

Much "re-exchanging" between Europe and the Middle East/North African region, including the exchange of instruments occurred during the Crusades. The Troubadours (in France, Trouvéres, or in Germany, Minnesingers) were wandering minstrels and storytellers. They developed musical plays and songs which popularized courts and became the "hits" of Europe's peasant class. So popular were their melodies that at various times they were incorporated into Roman Catholic masses. Also extremely important to all musical evolution were the enormous contributions of "folk" and religious music from Jewish and Romani groups throughout Europe (Unit VII).

Pic. 6.2A *"True history", and not a one-sided version, must account for all stories. The Crusades, which lasted nearly four centuries, included multiple dimensions of religion. Saladin, (Ruler of Egypt) countered Christian attacks, eventually recapturing Jerusalem in 1187. Equally important, however, are the numerous contacts and exchanges of ideas, inventions, and musical instruments between Christians and Muslims during this period.* Photos: Painting Saladin rex Aegypti, courtesy Wikipedia.org.

Respecting the LIFE CYCLE

Discussion
Reflection
VI-A

Respecting Ancestry and the Life Cycle

In much of the West, respect for ancestry seems to be either A) overly emphasized—as it is in the "university," where both European curricular topics and modes of dissemination of information and values based upon European ancestry receive emphasis and "respect" (over those of Native or African cultures, for example), or B) virtually non-existent—as it is in many regions where the elderly are placed in homes and their stories and wisdom are unheeded; or where being "young" or looking or feeling young is the emphasis for much of business and media, and, as a result, the young-adult portion of the life cycle is given out-of-balanced emphasis.

As we have already indicated, where cultures are in contact with their ancestry and are trained to respect and listen to their elders or to honor their departed ancestors, and, simultaneously, when the accomplishments of these elders/ancestors combine with a balanced sense of connection and an understanding of history, the relevance of "self" or importance of the individual (and especially that of "youthfulness" or youth) is kept in proper balance.

However, nurturing a healthy and well-balanced vision of wisdom and respect for ancestry yields even more benefits for the well-being of each stage of the life cycle. This condition can also exist only when adults of child-raising years reject the trend of inordinately emphasizing career advancement and self-promotion over the raising and nurturing of their children. A key component of this raising and nurturing is teaching a deeply seeded respect for elders and ancestors through their own actions. In cultures where a healthy understanding of the life cycle is present, we see the below-listed characteristics and connections between life-cycle phases:

Child/Youth: *When children and youth are the priority of adults and "elders" within a community, when they are trained to respect their teachers and elders, they will learn to listen better to the voices of wisdom and experience, to question respectfully, and not to have an imbalanced sense of self-importance.*

Young Adult: *The primary need of young adults is to take this precious time of the life cycle to find their occupation, continue their education, and prepare themselves for parenthood and the caring for the elderly. It is often best that young adults are not forced to work long hours but instead acquire education and exert energy to developing their unique abilities for later service. In addition, parents and elders in strong communities try to support the young adults, care for any children, and nurture their growth into their occupations and in preparation for parenthood.*

Adult/Parenthood: *In this phase of the life-cycle, the term "sacrifice" MUST be seen as a creative act rather than an infringement on the rights of the individual (as is so often the interpretation in cultures with a material emphasis). Such sacrifice is the means by which parents derive their fulfillment in serving their children and in caring for their elderly. Once adults'/parents' occupations are secure, this is the phase in which the life cycle is often "anchored."*

Elder: *Once the life cycle is balanced, and children are taught a healthy respect for age and experience, and adults are trained to sacrifice for the young and to care for the elderly, then the elderly are free to exercise their powers of experience and understanding of the life cycle on behalf of the entire community. If they are respected and cared for properly, their wisdom can enrich and empower each phase of the life-cycle and keep it healthy beyond their individual life-spans.*

Questions

- *In general, what do you think of the discussion above? How do you feel that your vision of the life cycle or that of your country/culture compares to the above?*

- *Do you feel you have a healthy understanding of the life cycle or your place or role in it? What about the role of your elders? If so, how? If not, why not?*

The Impact of the "Empire" Mindset

The model of social and political organization for much of the history of our world has depended to a large degree on the conceptualization, creation, and dominance of "empires." The basis for this paradigm of human governance was well established by the earliest human dynasties, including the Egyptian, Persian, and, especially, Roman empires. Much of the **imperial** strategy is anchored in the ancient mindset that one's security, prosperity, and ultimate purpose in life is determined by the degree to which one expands, conquers, and establishes (or forces) one's beliefs and manner of living over or upon others. The consequence of this is that perhaps otherwise peaceful neighbors, when confronted with the potential prospect of aggressive takeover of their worlds, must in turn, amass a militaristic defense, thus fanning the flame of the imperial cycle and creating an exaggerated focus on warfare technology. In European history, the imperial formula would impact or result in all of the following:

IMPERIAL CONSEQUENCES

- The establishment of a firm pattern of competition for "control" and ascendancy through tribal confederations, feudal lords, and eventually, "nation states" throughout Europe.

- The transfer of the imperial formula for governing to the Church (Holy Roman Empire). The perpetual integration of church and state replaced that of the Roman Empire as the governing body of much of Europe.

- The rise of former military allies of the Roman Empire to the status of feudal lords, and, later, to governing "nobles," that would further evolve to the establishment of kingdoms and nations.

- As nation states in Europe solidified out of feudalism (roughly Renaissance time frame), they pursued acquisition of other regions (Colonization), extending their empires (and fortifying the imperial mindset).

- The competitive mindset inherent in the vision of "empire" fueled human greed, leading eventually to a "colonization derby" (Renaissance/Baroque/Classical), slavery, and numerous wars in the "New World."

- Nationalism, as it evolved into its extreme form during the late 1800s and early 1900s, would lead to the ultimate clash of the national empires during World War I and World War II.

And subsequently,

- As the universities (learning institutions) of Europe evolved, the imperial mindset would find its way into the dissemination of the European "vision" of world (Cultural Imperialism), through what can best be classified as the empire of European academia. In subsequent generations, throughout Europe and European colonies, "world history," world maps, even the "World Series," would not actually mean "the world" but rather the world of those writing the books, making the maps (with Europe [Euro-America] in the center), playing baseball, or teaching and performing music.

Although there were other factors in the evolution of policy, governance, patronization, and cultural evolution, the imperial strategies that encouraged or endowed one with the right to conquer, or, conversely, the "fear" that is automatically derived from confrontation with such a mindset (i.e., that those who are "different" from us will automatically be preparing to conquer us or that they must be defeated or "colonized" for our gain and protection) were essential ingredients of a multitude of conflicts. Although imperialism is to a large extent a global phenomenon, the doctrines of Western cultures, and too, much of the magnificent art and music that would evolve from European minds were reflective of or born from this history.

Among the most influential of all the empires in the evolution of European music, and especially of what we call classical music, was that of the Holy Roman Empire. Clearly a dichotomy of spiritual reform and political conflict, the Holy Roman Empire and later the Church introduced many of the doctrines of love, peace, and spiritual discipline which unified much of an otherwise badly segmented Europe and later advocated policies such as the sanctioning of the Crusades, which led to untold destruction. In either instance, there is no denying that both the Holy Roman Empire and the Roman Catholic Church had an enormous influence on the evolution of Western culture and its art.

Let's examine some of the musical innovations from the Renaissance to modern times that grew out of Church doctrines or policies, in reaction to them, or more generally as a part of the evolution of a complex series of cultural exchanges within Europe.

The Renaissance and Harmony

To begin, the Renaissance dates (circa 1450-1600) are not literal. There are many accounts that the "re-birth," as the term implies, began much earlier, perhaps as early as the 13th century. Regardless, the *Renaissance* created a balance, sense of security, and stability out of the devastation left by the Crusades, plagues,[6.5] and centuries of imperialism in varied forms throughout Medieval times. Therefore, to some degree, the Renaissance was a period of relative prosperity and reprise from the drama of prior generations. Especially in Italy, the permanent home of the Roman Catholic Church, the arts of music, painting, and sculpture flourished (in both their religious and "humanistic," or secular, forms), returning to the values of the ancient Greek philosophers and artists.

The seeds for Opera (—a multifaceted version of storytelling with costumes, enormous set designs, dancing, and dramatic text performed in singing style) would emerge towards the end of the Renaissance. A substantial variety of *concertized* sacred music (music composed with a religious theme outside of the liturgical setting) also emerged, due in part to the emphasis upon creating "art for art's sake" or, according to the aesthetics, "reborn" from a return to Greek humanism. The subjects for many theater and later opera works were stories of Greek Gods or folklore.

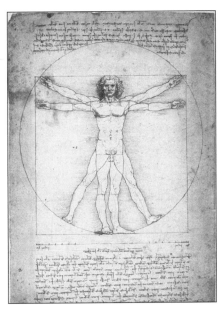

Pic. 6.3 *Leonardo da Vinci's "Vitruvian Man"— like the works of ancient Greek icons such as Aristotle, Socrates, or Plato and of the University that would evolve from this time period as a permanent institution of Western culture—blends the creativity of both the arts and sciences. However, as Western society approached the 20th century, science and technology would be given considerably more weight and emphasis than the arts* Photo: Courtesy Wikipedia.org.

Some of the **musical developments of the "Renaissance"** that would impact Western cultures until today include:

• The evolution of polyphony to the eventual establishment and emphasis of "harmony" much as we know it today (see "harmony" below).

• The creation of *concertized* formulas of composition (performances in "concert") which included the organ, instruments (of all groups), and voices in both religious and non-religious forms.

Professor Borders commented: *"At first, the church fathers (of Roman Catholicism) had a big problem with the use of instruments in church. They were associated with paganism, with pagan sacrifice, obviously with the Romans, and so it wasn't until the later Middle Ages that organs were used in church and later still other instruments. By the 16th century, however, string instruments and even some wind instruments were included. Even something like the 17th century Sonata da Chiesa (the church sonata) were pieces that were written in substitution for certain sung parts of the mass. The text could be read and the music could be substituted for the parts that would have been sung."* [6.6]

Other innovations of the time period included the "Western" orchestra, based upon formulas of "orchestra" heard in both the Middle East and Asia, being now *in evolution* to the "modern" orchestra (the standardization of instrumentation would eventually become a formula by the mid to late 18th century). Clearly, a collection of instruments and Western affinities for various groups and timbres had evolved, including specific groups of each of the instrumental groups, i.e., chordophones, aerophones, and membranophones.

And, a greater emphasis was placed on musical theater, which led to the development shortly after this period of not only what we now call opera but also religious opera (**oratorio**) and, still later, musical theater (in England) as well. If we fast-forward this development, for example, we would eventually arrive at the "musical theater" of early silent films and motion pictures and even further forward – to much of the film and music formulas of today.

Of all these musical innovations, the one that perhaps most distinguished Western music from much of the rest of the world's music (prior to recent decades) was the evolution of and emphasis on *harmony*.

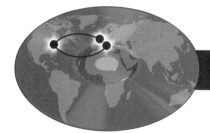

Inside the Musician's World

The Wayne State University Concert Chorale,
with Dennis Tini, Conductor

Note: Although Claudio Monteverdi lived and composed music during the later stages of the 16th century and first half of the 17th century and is therefore part of both the "Renaissance" and "Baroque" (designated) periods, his work represents the culmination of what occurred in the Italian Renaissance. Musically, polyphony (or the combining of two or more "layers" of melodies) had existed in much of European music through the Middle Ages. During the Renaissance, however, it flourished to the extent that **harmony**, or the manner in which pitches are sounded together, began to be (with considerable controversy) a primary focus of European, and especially Italian, composers.

As we will see repeatedly in examining the lives and works of classical composers, what distinguishes their lives is not only their prolific output (Monteverdi composed 18 operas, hundreds of works for church, and madrigals or popular choral works for entertainment) but also the manner by which their pursuits echoed the sentiments and values of their time and influenced subsequent generations.

In Monteverdi's case, the exaltation of the arts in the Renaissance and the rise and now post-Crusade decline of the Roman Catholic "Empire," whose erosion of control brought about a split of much of Northern Europe from Catholicism (known as the **Reformation**), gave license for composers to increase their use of harmonic tensions and compositional voicings, which served to increase the emotional depth of Western music. Despite the controversy that such new developments inevitably foster, the emphasis on how combinations of pitches would sound together spawned four-part (four voices) choral composition (subsequently referred to as: **SATB** or, *soprano, alto, tenor, bass*), an outgrowth of the Renaissance. The technique of writing for a hierarchy of high and low voices would eventually lead to the establishment of three- to four-part harmony (**chords**), and the formulation of **harmonic progressions,** or a progressive movement of chords from a home base (*tonic*) to chords that would build *tension* (increase anticipation) and then return to home (*cadence*).

Pic. 6.5 *A Portrait of Claudio Monteverdi in Venice, 1640. Painted by Bernardo Strozzi.* Photo: Public domain.

"Cantate Domine," by Claudio Monteverdi, from the CD: <u>**Glory to God,**</u> by the Wayne State Concert Chorale, Dennis Tini, Conductor, c. 1998. (recorded in 1991)

The following is a brief excerpt from a document published by The Council of Florence (CE 1438-1445) from the Bull "Cantate Domino," February 4, 1441. It states:

> *"The sacrosanct Roman Church, founded by the voice of our Lord and Savior, firmly believes, professes, and preaches one true God omnipotent, unchangeable, and eternal, Father, Son, and Holy Ghost; one in essence, three in persons … The Father alone begot the Son of His own substance; the Son alone was begotten of the Father alone; the Holy Spirit alone proceeds at the same time from the Father and Son. These three persons are one God, and not three gods, because the three have one substance, one essence, one nature, one divinity, one immensity, one eternity, where no opposition of relationship interferes."*

This piece is designed to elicit from the listener love or devotion to *God – the Father* (the Creator) for his Creation expressed through the Divine Guidance given to the *Son* (Prophet of God, in this case, Jesus Christ) and through the *Holy Spirit* (intangible spiritual influence emanating form God). What frequently occurs in all the arts is that the philosophies and perspectives of each age eventually give rise to the forms and techniques of the artist. In this case, the **trinity** of Christian belief (the *Father,* the *Son,* and the *Holy Spirit*) would become reflected in the *triad* (three-note chord or harmony) as the musical metaphor for the religious belief. By equating musical innovations with religious principles, clergy and musicians would eventually find common ground in the emphasis upon *harmony.*

Today, it may be hard to envision the openly religious statement such as the one above being made in public institutions. However, church and state—or religion and musical concerts, schools, and even politics—were still combined during the Renaissance. Although the influence of the church through the Renaissance was also used periodically to condemn those of other religions (specifically Jews and Muslims) and eventually fostered the separation of church and state in the New World (a development which would make frank and open discussion concerning religion touchy), the aspirations of the composers and many artistic religionists would inspire beautifully sensitive works of art.

As to what the performers experience in singing music of this nature, Dennis Tini, the conductor of the chorus performing this Monteverdi work, commented:

> "Conducting the chorale or the chorus and orchestra, especially after you've done all the rehearsal on the mechanics of notes or fixing the blending of voices, you come to the performance with both a concentration and a sense of obligation to release yourself from concern for those mechanics (there is nothing you can do about missed notes now) and focus on the spirit of the piece. When the focus and all variables are working together in a positive musical way, you get to some pretty intense states of music-making. It takes over everything. It's not about ego or mechanics; it becomes an expression of making the music, in this case in celebration of the Creator. It's like going into the next state of consciousness – it may be emotion or the spirituality of the piece. Whatever you want to communicate, but I get lost in it; I'm in a different sphere of consciousness."

The Recipe of Sound

When you listen to the "lilting" rhythmic feel of the beginning of this piece (in three-beat patterns), if you have ever heard the popular or folk music of the Renaissance, especially madrigals, a favorite compositional format of Monteverdi, you may see the "popular appeal" of this otherwise serious religious work. Perhaps the most important device in this piece is the manner in which the multiple layers (polyphony) of voices move in perfect rhythmic unity. The uniform and cohesive rhythm enables us to focus on the emotional nature of the pitches as they *stack up* (sound together). Pay particular attention to the musical moments where, after some independent movement, each phrase or voice comes together and forms a tonal consensus with the other voices. We call these moments a *cadence*. They are important moments in Western music and are frequently followed by a pause or break before the music begins to move again, or to build tension moving toward the next musical conclusion.

Also, like the "popular" madrigals of the time period, you will notice there are multiple sections and changes of compositional orientation in this work. A sonograph of this piece might include:

3-beat patterns (waltz-like) Cadence (resting point)   *Change of rhythm*

Balanced phrase   Repeat of phrase with extension   *Voices enter one at a time and converge*

Faster tempo   Converge to cadence   Climax of piece

Call and response between lower and higher voices   *True counterpoint – would be a device used extensively in the "Baroque" period*

Slower – somber final cadence

Pic. 6.6 St. Peter's Basilica, Vatican City, Italy. From 326 A.D. (CE.), when Constantine built over the tomb of Peter, what is believed to be the first church, to the latter part of the 19ᵗʰ century, the Catholic Church had many papal states or regions under its direct gover-nance. Only in the latter part of the 19ᵗʰ century when the "Kingdom of Italy" seized many of these properties, and in 1927 when Vatican City was given its independent status from Italy, did the dimen-sions or nature of the Roman Catholic Church change from "empire" back to influential "religion" in status. Photo: Courtesy, Vance Smith.⁶·⁶ᵃ

Stories from the Human Family

"Certainly the statement you mentioned, 'nothing comes from nothing,' I also heard from our (the author attended class with this individual) music composi-tion teacher in Miami (Florida). At first I thought, 'Man, this guy is definitely not a genius.' Of course nothing comes from nothing. But over time, after learning a bit more humility, I realized that this statement is extremely profound.

"That is, although I like to think of myself as being unique, and that my problems and accomplishments are all mine, the truth of the matter is that my most 'origi-nal' thoughts, actions, and ideas are, at best, reconfigurations of ideas and thoughts that are already in existence somewhere. From the way I learn, to the way I perceive the world, and most certainly to the music that I think jams, I am, to a much greater degree than I believe, the product of my ancestry.

"You're right about this tugging at my personal identity, but it also triggers a real sense of peace: that no matter what those around me value, I have the potential to respect myself and value my accomplishments, based on their con-nection to my ancestors or by thinking of myself as one 'cog' in a very important and ageless wheel — that of human evolution. By reducing my 'importance' (or desire to be important), I'm better able to see what I should do with my life as would respect those who have left this world and no longer have the ridiculous concerns of the material life.

"Of course I also must, as a 21st-century learning, growing organism, con-stantly change, just as the world around me is constantly changing. My ances-try can no longer be viewed as those 16ᵗʰ century English folks that got off the boat at Plymouth Rock, or the African ancestors originally taken from Ghana and dumped in Virginia. Rather, my ancestors are the sum total of the culture groups and mixed individuals who have contributed to the body of knowledge and experiences that make up my world." Interview: R. Moreno, Age: 50-ish colleague, mixed ethnicity, while working as a composer and university adjunct faculty in California, 1987.

Player organs (such as this barrel organ) and player pianos became the first means of in-home entertainment – beyond learning to play the instruments oneself.

More on Harmony

Harmony —

—the resultant sound of any two or more different pitches heard simultaneously (vertical alignment of pitches). Harmony is one of the primary musical elements for eliciting or supporting emotional diversity and depth in music.

Harmony is primarily a mechanism for deepening a sense of emotion in music. Although few non-musicians or those who have not been required to study music will likely feel inclined to decipher or decode the specific elements of harmony or to know precisely the name of the chord or the pitches that make up each harmonic unit, each listener may want to consider the important impact harmony has on how we *feel* about the music. Briefly stated:

- When the music elicits strong emotions—as during a movie—and you are made to feel something strongly without words or lyrics, then harmony is likely a major component.

- When children sing the happy songs, or you cry over the sad ones, much of what you are feeling is the result of the support *harmony* provides the story. So evocative is harmony due to the influence of pitches in combination, you would likely feel these emotions without the melody or the lyrics.

The Evolution of Notation ("writing music") is a hallmark of what we frequently call "art" or "classical" music. It is not necessarily that this music is more complex, better composed, or more sophisticated, but rather, by "notating" musical ideas, the ideas can be duplicated, disseminated, or analyzed by later generations.

Pic. 6.7A *An example of early hymn notation. Although it has a four-line "staff" (five lines are now used), it is similar to the notation still used today* Images: 6.7 and 6.7A Courtesy of Wikipedia.org.

Pic. 6.7 *Sample of Gregorian chant: Kyrie orbis factor. This shows the single melodic (monophonic) style of chant, one of the earlier notation styles.*

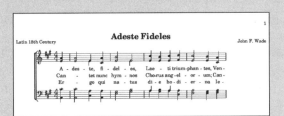

6.7B *Screenshot of score (musical notation for all singers or instruments) for "Adeste Fideles," released to public domain. In this notation example, you can see all of the "notes" aligned vertically. Since the notes are, for the most part, of equal shape and size, this is an indication that the singers move together (a similar format for most hymns) and that a large part of the focus of the piece is on the "harmony" or collective sound of the different notes.*

Pic. 6.7C *Measures 1-9 of Fuga a 3 voci by J.S. Bach, typeset in LilyPond, from www.lilypond.org. This example shows the linear or "melodic" notation of pitches, but note as well that whenever you see two or more pitches occurring at the same time vertically (directly above each other), you also have "harmony."*

One of primary qualities of European "art" or "classical" music is in its "organization." Whether that organization refers to the enormous task of keeping 65 musicians in an orchestra playing together or the organization required to maintain precise performance practice over hundreds of years, the affinity for organization is a key aesthetic to Western art and culture generally. One reflection of this, as concerns music, is the evolution of musical notation.

There is some evidence that a kind of musical notation was practiced by the Egyptians from the 3rd millennium BCE and by others in Asia in ancient times. Ancient Greece had a sophisticated form of musical notation in use from at least the 6th century BCE until approximately the 4th century CE; Knowledge of the ancient Greek notation was lost around the time of the fall of the Roman Empire. Scholar and music theorist Isidore of Seville, writing in the early 7th century, famously remarked that it was impossible to notate music. By the middle of the 9th century, however, a form of notation began to develop in monasteries in Europe for Gregorian chant, using symbols known as neumes; the earliest surviving example of the musical notation of this type is from about 850 CE.

What notation provides is the ability to document musical ideas, to see them, and to both refine them or pass them to others in order to "re-create" the musical experience. What notation also provided, however, was an intricate system to carefully plan and monitor the simultaneous sounding of pitches. Although what would be "appropriate" or preferred in each time period would change, there is no question that from the 15th century on, _harmony_ and the _notation_ of music generally would become two of the primary influences of European cultures on the world of music.

Since harmony and texture (the musical layering of voices and instruments) frequently go together, it is difficult to speak of one without the other. Often while listening to musicians, we use the phrases, *"They harmonize well," "They're in good harmony,"* or simply *"I like the harmony."* For many, the simplest definition of harmony is how things blend or sound (work) together. That's actually not too bad a definition, except that we may want to know a bit more about the *"things"* that are blending, in order to be a bit more specific.

As with melody, we frequently speak of harmony as being either **consonant** (having repose, balance, or being pleasing, probably the term to replace "good") or **dissonant** (clashing, lacking balance, frequently not pleasing or tense). These terms are completely *subjective*. What is consonant to one may be dissonant to another. However, when we speak of harmony we look to the emotions we derive from the simultaneous sounding of pitches. Finally, since the array of human emotion is vast, *harmony need not necessarily be harmonious!* If we wish to convey strong anger or anxiety, we will use combinations of pitches that are *dissonant* or potentially "displeasing."

Musical Terms and Concepts

We mentioned in the beginning of this text that appreciation is directly linked to participating in the music *as the culture would deem respectful.* Since the legacy of European classical or art music is so directly tied to the recording and teaching of notation as well as the study of music by reading, writing about, and analyzing the traditions which preceded each generation, appreciation of Western classical music requires a bit of study, or concentration on the elements of a piece.

The following are a few of the basic terms to which you may refer as you complete this Unit:

Harmony: The combined sounding of two or more different tones. May be generally consonant or dissonant. Harmony may, by itself, provide strong emotion in music. It is one of the major distinguishing components of Western music, currently being used by musical systems around the world, even those which previously were essentially melodic or rhythmic in their orientation.

Interval: The simplest combinations of pitches that can produce harmony. The *interval* is the measured distance between any two pitches, either vertically (together as harmony) or horizontally (as a melody).

Chord: The result of the simultaneous sounding of three *(triad)* or more different pitches is what we call in Western music a chord. Most chords in simple Western music (including pop, rock, etc.) are called major (somewhat "happy sounding") or *minor* (a bit melancholy). Chords move in a progression, or according to a logic that is determined by each culture, genre or style, and time period. Generally, or often, *chords* move away from a *tonic* or home pitch, eventually to a note five notes away *(dominant)*, which will pivot the music back to the home base. This movement of chords or harmony is called a *harmonic progression*.

Cadence: All of the world's music is constructed in phrases of musical thought. Most often these phrases are based on the manner in which human beings talk and sing. Therefore, even instrumental music will also have musical sentences that build and release tension in *units or phrases.* Especially in Western music phrasing, each statement (phrase) will come to a resting point or momentary point of repose. We call these cadences. Of course, the grandest of all *cadences* will usually be at the very end of the piece.

Brass instruments—such as this bugle—became first the means of military motivation and signaling. In time, they would also evolve to become many of the instruments used in today's modern bands and orchestras all over the world.

Key: Most Western classical and popular music (including rock, blues, etc.) works from pitch menus *(scales)* and *chords* based upon a *key* (the home base of which we have spoken) and, generally, an emotional character or *style of mode or scale* (as in a *major key or minor key*). The key provides a combination of a single pitch which functions as the *root* or ground tone, and the scale or pitch menu that is formulated from that tone. Keys and scales provide us a menu of pitches from which both melodies and harmonies are built.

Form: *Variations of Musical Structure or Architecture*

There are many forms in European "classical" music. Each form or structure of the music is patterned in accordance with the function and

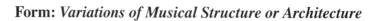

context of its creation. For example, one form that became exceedingly popular at a time when European cultures, by and large, were attempting to put order to the chaos of extensive colonization and empire building, was what was called *sonata allegro form*. This form followed the precise logic of constructing an essay or speech. Although we will see parallels to this logic in other cultures' music as well, in Western music it consisted of an *Introduction* (exposition), *development of introductory ideas* (development), *and conclusion or restatement of introductory ideas* (recapitulation) (*Sonata Allegro Form*–see below). Each form common to classical or art music in Europe would have its own logic, tied to the values of its culture and time period.

Other terms used to describe common European *musical formats (classical or folk/pop music)* include:

- **Binary / Verse-Chorus or A-B** – A musical statement is made (generally in the form of a balanced progression of melodies), followed by a second (bi) section of related, but unique content.

- **Rondo Form** – The musical form of a consistent pattern of a new melody returning to a primary and constantly main melody or theme.

- **Canon or round** – A cyclical melody that is repeated and whose harmonic structure will allow for the melody to reoccur while the first melody has not yet completed itself (e.g., "Row Your Boat).

- **Theme and variations** – A melody/rhythm or musical motive is presented upon which variations or alterations are made. An extension of this formula can be found today in movies where there is a theme or melody one associates with a character and that will appear in variations throughout the film (e.g., James Bond films).

- **Through-composed** – A term to describe music which does not have repetitious sections. It is a composition wherein repetitions are incidental to the story. Symphonic tone poems—stories told with music only, usually for symphony orchestras and some movie music—are good examples of this form.

- **Concerto, Symphony, Sonata** – Though different, each of these formats shares in common multiple movements (self-contained or fulfilling sections of music separated by breaks or pauses that allow listener and musician the opportunity to reflect on what has occurred or prepare for what will follow). Most movements are in contrasting tempos (speed) and have contrasting moods or thematic (*melodic, rhythmic, or harmonic*) vocabulary.

- **Etude** – A musical "study" of a particular technique or challenge for any instrument.

- **Song forms** – Vary over time and culture. Most tell stories by either a repetitious melody with changing lyrics or are based upon poetry, and change the melody to accommodate the lyrics. A strophic song, for example, is a song that uses the same identical melody, but simply changes the words. This is a common folk music structure. Most all song forms (including those in popular music) are determined by the text and genre of the musical style.

Texture *(Review):*

The density or layering of musical activity which, when in layers of two or more, may also define itself more specifically as listed below;

Polyphony: Two or more musical layers occurring at the same time.

Types of polyphony: Under the heading of polyphony we have a variety of sub-headings:

- **Counterpoint:** From *contra punctus (point against point)*. Two or more different melodies or the same melody occurring at different points. From the Renaissance on, counterpoint was a major part of classical music, perhaps no more so than in the Baroque period, where counterpoint took precedence over most other musical elements (see Bach below).

- **Fugue:** This is a subcategory of counterpoint. It is a melody (or group of melodies) that enter and unwind separately, each melody when it enters adding to the tension and texture of the piece. Fugues were constructed along very complicated rules and systems of governance and require the listener to listen for the exchange of focus from one melody to another, rather than being too concerned with the stacking of pitches or harmony.

Other "ophonies" (ways of sounding and organizing musical layers):

- **Heterophony:** Two or more musicians sing or play a single melody in different ways. (Ex: Unison singing in congregations, much of Asian or Middle Eastern music.)

- **Homophony:** A more specific form of polyphony wherein one dominant voice or instrument is supported by one or more simultaneously occurring parts (accompaniment). Most popular and church music fits this description.

Pic. 6.8 *Texture and harmony in Western orchestral music is achieved by the layering of multiple instruments together. Each has a defined part that is notated and must be specifically placed in time. The conductor coordinates this process.* Photo: Courtesy Stefan Junger.

Tension and Release: Past and Present

All effective events that occur over time (i.e., plays, lectures or speeches) build and release tension in an innovative manner to maintain listener interest. In movies, if the good guy just kept chasing the bad guy and never was either frustrated (missed him) or fulfilled (caught him), the build-up of tension without a release would become either irritating or boring. Progressions of harmony, along with changes in the speed of the music (tempo), **dynamics** (changes in loudness and softness), and changes in texture (the layering of musical instruments) provide for the building and release of tension. What we may find as we listen to subsequent pieces in this unit is that those of us who are accustomed to a listening diet of popular or radio-stylized music might find our attention and concentration challenged by the longer durations and the manner by which tension is built and released in the music over longer duration. These formulas, of course, extend back into our Western ancestry.

Concentration's Challenge

In a human sense, given the pervasive push in many societies to achieve, to become competitive (earlier in the life cycle), to become better professionals and career people and always more quickly, we may be less impelled to look at the relationship of our lives against those of our ancestors. As our world, and particularly our modern world, evolves more quickly, any respite from the enormously fast pace at which most of us live may help us avoid being cut off from contact with or respect for our ancestors. This may provide justification for using music of longer duration (or from any of our ancestors) as a catalyst to slow down, see things more clearly, and potentially to enjoy life more as a *journey* versus a destination.

Some believe that engagement solely in the present or in planning for the future puts us at odds not only with our elders but also with the natural cycle of life. They might advocate that we become "too important" to ourselves when we do not feel at one with our ancestry, respect our elders (by placing them above ourselves), or in general create a balance of perspectives between the importance of our lives and the equally important but different lives of those before us. Regardless, each age and generation has a tempo, a pace, and patterns of organization, which include a body of stories and preferred formats for telling them in patterns which build and release tension and emotion. In most music of earlier ages, the pace of life was slower, the space for listening or exposing oneself to music or art was generally longer, and the time taken to build or release tension corresponded to these values. In any instance, the perception of time was enormously contrasting to that of today.

Baroque: The Reformation to Bach

The factors that contributed to the **Reformation** or evolution of **Protestantism** of the 15th century, though numerous, must include the following:

Pic. 6.8A *An inspiration to the reform of Christianity (especially in Northern Europe), German monk, priest, and theologian Martin Luther may not have been solely responsible for the development of "Protestantism," but his writings greatly influenced the movement. In turn, the alteration of Christian practices in parts of Europe would increasingly permit larger and more pronounced roles for musical composers to experiment with instrumentation and form.* Public domain from Wikipedia.org.

- Unrest in the Roman Catholic Church (Avignon papacy and papal schism, 14th century) incited wars and conflicts between princes, peasants, and clergy. This included a widespread concern for perceptions of corruption in the monastic system. The Council of Constance, (1414 – 1415) reformed the Clergy and resolved the "3 popes at once" schism of the Church.

- The growth of "nations," fueled by the Renaissance explosion of "free thought" and the use of the printing press, led to greater debate and questioning about the nature of church and religion and the capacity to spread such thought.

- German princes were distracted by the threat of Islamic invasion. The protest of the masses of Northern Europe erupted in the works of Martin Luther (a university professor and Augustine monk), Huldrych Zwingli (in Switzerland), and John Calvin.

- The Church of England (under Henry VIII) separated itself from Rome in the early 16th century).

What would evolve, especially in Germany, was a change of vision about life, religion, and God. God was no longer a rational governing principle but an "arbitrary unknowable will that could not be limited." [6.7] Additionally, humanism or the reversion back to intellectual pursuits, classical traditions, and the re-emphasis of Latin and Greek scholarship were profoundly at odds with the evolving consensus that "true" religion should be a matter of inward devotion and not an outward symbol of ceremony and ritual.

What would the *Reformation* mean to composers and musicians in the northern regions of Europe? Precisely what occurs in all *counterculture* movements: a high percentage of what was deemed appropriate by prior standards would require alteration or reversal by the new standards of what, in this case, became known as "Lutheranism." Among these musical innovations were the following:

Pic. 6.8 *The "Baroque" period was, to a large degree, the product of a variety of very dramatic occurrences in Europe. Colonization, the discovery of new worlds, slavery, the Reformation (and split of the Christian church), the building of a large "middle" or "merchant class" (peasants with money), and an intensification of nationalism and competition throughout Europe were all factors in this portion of European history. As we shall see, Baroque art, architecture, and music mimicked the drama and grandiose goals of the times. The Adoration of the Magi, a 1624 oil-on-canvas painting by Peter Paul Rubens, is 447 by 336cm (15 by 11 feet) and shows enormous movement and emotion. It is currently displayed at the Koninklijk Museum voor Schone Kunsten, in Antwerp, Belgium.* Photo: Courtesy of wikipedia.org.

- *Use of pipe organs* – Despite being invented and used during Roman times (likely an evolution of centuries of *aerophones* using bellow mechanisms to force air over reeds or pipes) and used since the Middle Ages in various formats, the *pipe organ* became the ideal musical instrument to elicit the highest of emotion that would characterize *Baroque* sentiment, music, and art.

- *Orchestral evolution* – The evolution of the "orchestral-like" ensembles patterned in part from those experienced in the Middle East during the crusades and later as they evolved in the Renaissance combined with the capacity to print music, allowing for works to be written for specific instruments and disseminated with greater ease. The restrictions on the manner in which music could be performed in the church were simultaneously contested and relaxed, but in time, the use of the orchestra, the organ, and large choruses was encouraged, not only in the context of *extra-worship concretizing* (or performance) as many of the works had come to be experienced in Italy, but also as a primary means of worship throughout Northern Europe. Both the dramatic character in the style of composition *(counterpoint)* and in the texture *(layering and increased usage of massive instrumentation)* echoed the dramatic art of the time period. The impact of each of these developments can be clearly seen in the musical performances of today's artists.

- *Expansion of religious musical forms* – The evolution of a larger middle class, in part the result of the high drama of colonization and global expansion, created a need for worship music that would elicit a higher degree of participation and emotional response. **Cantatas**[6.8] and **oratorios** (smaller scale works or larger scale "religious opera" with their origins in Italy) but, specifically, **chorale hymns** (choral-style musical works for congregational singing) became the genre of choice in the Protestant church. The hymns (usually collected in volumes or books) would later become the most common of devices for religious participation in the New World as well.

Cantatas became one of the most important musical constituents of the Lutheran service. The general format of the cantata was to alternate descriptive narrative singing (**recitative**) with substantial dramatic or virtuoso aria-like singing (**arias** *are vocal works with frequently very difficult performance sections usually isolating a specific emotion or event*), choral anthem-like sections, and instrumental interludes. These devices were taken primarily from the evolution of *opera and oratorio* as well.

In Germany, a young man who grew up in a family of musicians, Johann Sebastian Bach, began to study music on his own by copying the manuscripts of numerous composers and attending performances of the greatest organists of his time. He also learned the trade of repairing and altering organs, and furthered his knowledge with "on the job training" by taking posts as an organist, later as a composer and director of music at Arstady, Mühlhausen, Weimar, and, eventually, Leipzig (all cities in Germany within roughly one hundred miles of each other).

Bach may be best known for his large number of works, which include numerous cantatas (at one point in Leipzig he ventured to write a cantata each week), vocal and instrumental works, and the propagation of the system of equalizing pitches, called **equal** *(or well)* **temperament**.[6.9] His fathering nearly two dozen children might also be considered in the context of remarkable accomplishments. Against the backdrop of the turmoil and drama of the times, perhaps the fact that Bach's innovations were accepted during his life, that he was able to support his large brood, and that he rather seldom ruffled the feathers of his patrons while being distinctly innovative in compositions for the time, are among the most impressive of all his accomplishments.

Pic. 6.8C *A manuscript of Bach's Violin Sonata No. 1 in G Minor. The Sonata (generally a work of four movements or sections) has continued to change and evolve over nearly six hundred years.* Public domain

Pic. 6.9 *Stops at the right side of the console divert the air to the various ranks, or rows, of pipes. This is a Baroque organ by Joseph Gabler, at the Basilika St. Martin, in Germany.* Photo: Courtesy Andreas Praefcke, May 2005

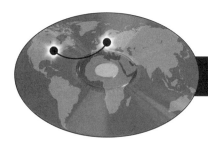

Inside the Musician's World

J.S. Bach
Leopold Stokowski, conductor,
Elaine Bovender, church organist.

*"In the architecture of my music....
I want to demonstrate to the world
the architecture of a new and
beautiful social commonwealth...
The secret of harmony? I alone know it.*

*"Each instrument in counterpoint and
as many contrapuntal parts as there are instruments.
It is the enlightened self-discipline
of the various parts...
Each voluntarily imposing on itself the limits of
its individual freedom...
for the well-being of the community. That is my
message.*

*"Not the autocracy of a single stubborn melody on the one hand.
Nor the anarchy of unchecked noise on the other.
No... a delicate balance between the two— an enlightened freedom.
The science of my art. The art of my science.
The harmony of the stars in the heavens...
the yearning for brotherhood in the heart of man.
This is the secret of my music."*

Johann Sebastian Bach (1685-1750)

Pic. 6.10 *A statue of J.S. Bach in Eisenbach, Germany.* Photo: Courtesy of Adambiswanger1.

Note: In every generation, there are those who create a great stir by offending the norms of their day. Others, by virtue of extreme circumstances or challenges in life or innate gifts, help bring together the influences of their culture in a manner never thought possible. Then there are those who possess gifts, but whose hard work within the system is the basis of their results. These are blue-collar artists, so to speak. They might conform to the needs and standards of their day, but primarily through strenuous effort they are able to create such a prolific body of works with a fresh and innovative insight that their efforts immediately become recognized, and they achieve fame within their own lifetimes.

Born in Eisenach, Germany, into a distinguished family of musicians, Bach (bok) lived and worked all his life within a one-hundred-mile radius of that town. He, and later his many children, became a stable part of the musical scene of the region, generally with neither fanfare, great fame or fortune, nor controversy.

It may seem strange to think that many of the perceptions and musical practices that we use today can be traced back to the time of Johann Sebastian Bach (17th-century Germany), or, for that matter, to the time of 19th century Italian composers Verdi or Rossini, or to an Irish country dance fiddler, or to a West African trance ritual drummer who arrived on the shores of America 350 years ago, but this is fact.

So what can we have in common with, say, Mr. Bach, when his music, his life, dress, seemingly everything, seem so distant from popular artists today, or whomever we might listen to tomorrow? Each generation is born into a world of values based solely on the standards and, yes, reactions to those values and standards of the generations before. What may seem like forever ago … say 1675 CE is, in the context of cultural evolution, really only a breath.

CD 2.6

"Christ lag in Todesbanden," from Bach's **"Cantata No. 4,"** transcribed and conducted by Leopold Stokowski, from the CD: **Leopold Stokowski: Bach-Stokowski Transcriptions,** c. by Fono Enterprises & Allegro Music, 2001.

Although this piece would initially have been performed with chorus, the love that Leopold Stokowski, one of the greatest (and most well-known) conductors, had for J.S. Bach's music is demonstrated in this *arrangement* – an instrumental version of Bach's choral work. This is one clear example of respect for ancestry. Not only was the acknowledgement and study of what had come before essential to the proper training of the classical musician in Bach's day; it remains a requirement of musicians prolific in classical/art music even today.

Stokowski, perhaps best known for his role as conductor in Disney's animated film *Fantasia,* once commented: *"It is the birthright of every man and woman to be able to hear inspired music, read great books, and live for a time*

Pic.6.11 *Leopold Stokowski.*

each year close to the earth and the beauty of nature." Although his own life resembled that of a rock star more than that of the humble homebody Bach, Stokowski constantly lobbied to bring "accessible" music to the lives and ears of the general public. At one point he commented:

"Because I believe in this, I am planning to work in Hollywood each year for three or four months, with the object of doing everything I can to help bring great music to the movies." This he did in the conducting of Disney's *Fantasia,* and would likely have done even more had he lived another five years – to the ripe old age of *one hundred* years. In this sense, maybe ninety-five years of hard work in the music profession does make Stokowski more like his idol, Bach.

Listen to the *counterpoint* (multiple moving melodies within the texture) as well as the glorious emotion (harmonic progression) that is made more or equally beautiful by the exchange of tone colors between the instruments of the modern symphonic orchestra, which in this piece transforms itself into the **ranks** (multiple banks of unique timbre [sound quality] pipes) of Bach's pipe organ. You might also wish to pick an ancestral personage that has had an impact on you and reflect on his or her contributions while listening to the aural manifestation of gratitude that Stokowski imbued in this work towards one of his *heroes.*

CD 2.7

"Fugue," from the **"Prelude and Fugue in G minor,"** by J.S. Bach, performed by Elaine Bovender, from a personal recording, c. 2005.

Note: When a student (roughly "middle age") approached us with the idea of having a recording in this text, We smiled politely and said, "Let us hear it; we can discuss it later," thinking to ourselves this would never compete for space with great professional artists. But as we got to know the student and saw how sincere her passion was for music she had learned as a church organist, and specifically the music of the

Pic. 6.12 and 6.13 *Church organist Ms. Bovender at a console organ (powered and amplified by electricity) and the "ranks" (pipe systems) of the organ in St. Paul's Cathedral, Münster, Germany.* Photos: Authors/E. Bovender (right)

"grandfather" of church organ music, Bach, we began to reconsider the focus of what to include generally. This chapter, for example, is about learning to see and appreciate connections over time. By including Elaine's music and comments, we might also see how individual passion can drive the appreciation and respect of ancestry.

Ms. Bovender wrote: *"Today, J.S. Bach is considered to be one of the greatest composers of all time. We have no real idea how Bach played his own music, but we do know on what instruments he performed: Baroque organs from the 17th and 18th century were exceptional instruments for their time, capable of colorful shading and sounds of wide dynamic and timbrel ranges. I, however, performed this on a digital keyboard, the Kurzweil K2500 XL workstation, since no organ around had sounds as good as this digital keyboard.*

"I think what I like best about Bach's music is the exquisite flow of melody in both the prelude and the weaving of these melodies in the fugue. I think it is really important not to rush the performance of this music to our modern tastes. The counterpoint of voices and tonal shading should be well defined. I hope I was able to accomplish this.

"I think as much as I love Bach's music, I am impressed by his life and faith. Bach's musical masterpieces emanate from his passion for God. After his death in 1750, they found written in the margin of his Bible, the phrase: 'Where there is devotional music, God with His grace is always present.' My personal goal in performing this work is that the listener will be able to feel the depth of Bach's passion for music and for God. Thanks for considering me in this project."

The Recipe of Sound

This is the fugue section of the Prelude and Fugue. Now we have a very clear example of the complexity of counterpoint (multiple melodies) that went into the making of the fugue. As you listen, try to let your ears move from melody to melody as each new melody enters, but also try to keep abreast of how the melodies, though different in pitch and perpetually changing, still sound *good* (balanced and harmonically "in-tune"). Despite the fact that there are at times four simultaneous melodies (often sounding as though there may be two organists), they lock together by virtue of a series of well-defined rules and intricate patterns of organization – once again, one of the main themes of European culture and its art or classical music.

Cultural Imperialism and the Academy

Cultural Imperialism: Silent Distortion

Imperialism—from its ancient Egyptian, Roman, Holy Roman, Mongol, and Islamic manifestations to its more recent extremes in nationalism or practices of colonization—has dominated much of the world's history and governmental philosophy. The primary distinction between Western and non-Western imperialism is the degree to which European colonization from the 15th to 19th centuries spread European values and perceptions around the globe. What has become part of the status quo, even to many of the colonized cultures, is that European cultural values are often viewed as the way things are, or should be. Therefore, in most professions, the models for economy, credentialing, discourse, and, thus, "success" are those perpetuated by Western cultures, and the mode of perpetuation is the Western academy.

To emphasize the implicit: Western cultural imperialism and its belief that Western values and methodologies are empirical and potentially absolute can dilute our development of the intuitive. At the same time, it veils the "other truth": namely, that people from diverse cultures and, specifically, less Westernized or technological/material societies, see the world differently but with equal validity. Let's broad-stroke the more pervasive impact of cultural imperialism:

Not only have the "loudest" and most pervasive voices in much of the world been those of Western derivation; over time, owing to the impact of colonization, those voices and values are emulated in nearly every area of human accomplishment around the globe and especially through the models of the Western academy (and its descendants: primary and secondary schools). As a result, those who otherwise would have self-evolved to employ socio-cultural solutions and value dissemination, likely more distinct and equally valuable as alternative models for cultural expression, have now, over generations, come to believe that they too must "achieve" according to the Western model. A simple example of this is that most people in the world now learn English, not because it is the "best" language (Farsi and Arabic, for example, have far larger vocabularies to intricately express human thought) but because it has now, through imperialistic dominance, become essential to global commerce and communication, further connecting language and culture to perceptions of what "should be valued."

"It would seem that the pendulum, in swinging toward the position that it is impossible to evaluate differing cultures, has overshot its mark, since it has caused us to overlook how important are the values of a given culture to the people who live under it... this is why the imposition of a foreign body of custom, backed by power, is so distressing an experience. A people may recognize ever so clearly that their own customs are best for them, yet no matter how deep their conviction of this, it is supremely difficult for them to meet the immediate argument posed by the possession of superior force." Melville Herskovits, 1972, p.8

Regrettably, the impact of cultural imperialism (superior force as the justification for cultural ascendancy) far outlasts any forms of militaristic conquest in the manner in which values are set, perpetuated, and exported. When we add the impact of media technology on the degree to which cultural voices are amplified, it becomes virtually impossible not to hear some voices more loudly than others.

Questions

In our pursuit of "truth" (a distinctly beautiful premise of academic discourse) through our Western academies (universities/colleges), we have seldom brought under scrutiny the academy itself.

- *How powerful are our Western educational institutions in transmitting cultural values?*
- *How pervasive is the influence of Western thinking in marginalizing the potential benefits offered by "other" cultures, many of whose histories transcend by thousands of years that of Europe?*
- *Do you believe that Western thinking is pervasive to the point of marginalizing the potential benefits offered by "other" cultures? Evaluate and reflect on your responses.*

Classicism[6.10] Personified

We might look at much of Western history as a sort of pendulum that swings from pole to pole. The outer poles of this pendulum of socio/cultural sentiment—and, ultimately, art—are **romanticism,** the outcome of wars, plagues, inquisitions, expansion (i.e., *"romantic"* or dramatic times with high emotion), and **classicism,** the longing for organization and order (usually a direct reversion to classical Greek culture, a time eulogized by Europeans for its art, humanist philosophies, and culture). Seeing the larger picture of ebb and flow in cultural processes in one period as they lead to the next helps us understand "cause and effect" in the context of change over time.

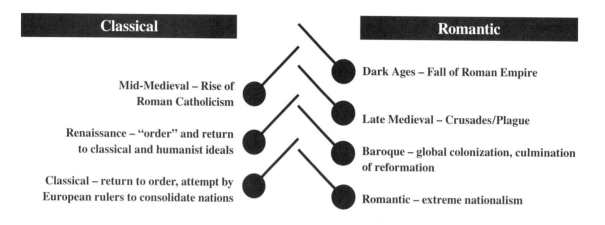

Classical	Romantic
	Dark Ages – Fall of Roman Empire
Mid-Medieval – Rise of Roman Catholicism	
	Late Medieval – Crusades/Plague
Renaissance – "order" and return to classical and humanist ideals	
	Baroque – global colonization, culmination of reformation
Classical – return to order, attempt by European rulers to consolidate nations	Romantic – extreme nationalism

Of course, this over-simplification doesn't remind us that each movement of the pendulum was initiated in the prior period or perhaps centuries earlier. That is, in the heart of the *"classical"* period lies the nearly ten-year French Revolution and a revolt against both absolute monarchy and Roman Catholic control (i.e., a stretch of prolonged revolt against classical order) that would later strongly affect the evolution to *Romanticism.* Still, we can discern important tendencies in the mindsets, cultural values, and, ultimately, art, as a result of seeing the ebb and flow of changes in order/disorder and in socio-cultural affinity.

In the period that we actually designate as "classical" (or "neo-classical"), there is a strong and undeniable surge toward establishing order politically, aesthetically and, ultimately – creatively. Even in the largely "unordered" life of the composer Wolfgang Amadeus Mozart, who is often viewed as the central figure of classicism, we hear in much of his music, the mathematical and highly synchronized movement of equally subdivided rhythms and perpetual logic.

6.14A *The Palace at Versailles: Louis Le Vau opened up the interior court to create the expansive entrance cour d'honneur, later copied all over Europe. Though actually a product of the latter stages of the "Baroque" period, the highly ornamented style of architecture is characteristic of both Rococo and Neo-classical movements (Classicism).*

Pic. 6.14B *This portrait of the Austrian classical-era composer Christoph Willibald Gluck (by Joseph Siffried Duplessis, 1775) depicts the predisposition to "perfection" and "order" of the era embodied, among other things, in the decorative lace, powdered wig, and controlled emotion in the portrait.* Image: Public domain from Wikipedia.org.

Pic. 6.14C & D *Numerous locations around the world were, by the mid 1700's, under the direct political and cultural influences of the British Empire. Modeled on the principle of prior empires, this meant, naturally, that each colonized location would have boundaries established (be subject to becoming a "country" based upon British design) and be subject to the values of British culture. This portrait of George Washington (American general and first president, by Rembrandt Peale, ca. 1795) demonstrates this influence, and the map of British territories as late as 1921 demonstrates how much of the world was under British influence—in most cases—for over two centuries.* Image: Public domain, fromWikipedia.org.

Still, a word of caution: the dangers of oversimplification can distort the lessons of the past. In this case, the lives of composers such as Mozart or Beethoven[6.11] and their role in society contrast with the backdrop of images and messages we may glean hundreds of years later. When we combine a look into the personal *human* evolution of historical figures with period context, when we attempt to see through the mist of posthumous glorification in favor of human reality, we get a much better picture not only of the individual and his or her music but also of the artist's manner of creativity and approach to life through his or her unique circumstances and challenges. Genius becomes even more dazzling in the context of human reality.

Artistry and Humanness: Mozart and Beethoven

Perhaps embedded in the events and lives of numerous artists such as Mozart, Van Gogh, Charlie Parker, Billie Holiday, Jim Morrison, or Michael Jackson are many similar lessons of life. We see in their struggle, their experiencing of hardships, as well as in issues of economics, patronization (how they were supported) or their struggles to rise above innuendo and public censoring (today – mostly experienced through media), a direct correlation between their lives and the manifestation of their art. Certainly, the archives of the world of art are filled with stories of tragedy, struggle, and pain.

Many have questioned if the *"blues – must be lived in order to be performed,"* or whether struggle and challenges help increase our efforts, our determination, and ultimately, the depth and emotion of our creative expression. The lives of Wolfgang Amadeus Mozart and the composer who would follow him in Austria, Ludwig van Beethoven, are, for different reasons, filled with pain, disenfranchisement, and struggle. The enormity of their works, by number and quality, reflects the phenomenon we see often in art: that one of the artist's primary solaces from life's difficulties is found in the expression of art itself.

Wolfgang Amadeus Mozart (1756-1791)

The following is a notice announcing one of Mozart's many early childhood performances, scheduled and promoted by a father obsessed with creating fame for himself, through and for his son:

"Mozart – the child prodigy –

The boy, who is not yet seven, will perform on the clavecin or harpsichord; he will also play a concerto for the violin, and will accompany symphonies on the clavier, the manual or keyboard being covered with a cloth, with as much faculty as if he could see the keys; he will instantly name all notes played at a distance, whether singly or in chords on the clavier, or on any other instrument, bell, glass, or clock. He will finally, both on the harpsichord and the organ, improvise as long as may be desired and in any key, thus providing that he is as thoroughly acquainted with the one instrument as with the other, great as is the difference between them."

Pic. 6.14E *Estates Theater in Prague (Czech Republic) was the site for the premier of Mozart's opera "Don Giovanni" in October 1787. The opera bridges the gap between what was is classified as "comic" or "tragic" opera. This picture was taken as the opera was being restaged in Prague with traditional costumes, instruments, and staging in July 2006. Photo: Authors.*

This was an indication of Mozart's childhood. It began not too unlike that of a circus performer. So what are the consequences of such a lifestyle? Another observer wrote of Mozart's later evolving obsessive tendencies:

"When he is in no pressing need, he is quite content and becomes indolent and inactive. Once set going he is all on fire and thinks he is going to make his fortune all at once. Nothing is allowed to stand in his way, and unfortunately it is just the cleverest people, the exceptional men of genius, who find continual obstacles in their path."

The obsessions of Mozart's father in exploiting Mozart's gifts, despite their success in propelling his musical development, would have enormous personal repercussions on the quality and balance of his life.

Labeled a child prodigy by the age of five, Wolfgang became, to his father, Leopold, a property worth exploiting. In one instance, Wolfgang's triumphs were cut short by scarlet fever. Wolfgang was in bed for nearly a month. His father wrote:

"His body's illness has meant a setback of about four weeks for although since his recovery we have taken in twenty-one ducats, this is a mere trifle, seeing that we only just manage every day on one ducat, and that daily there are additional expenses."

Wolfgang, as a young adult, would become an embodiment of the "counterculture" figure of today. He began to reflect the excesses of attention and admiration, as well as of pushing and control, exerted on him by his father. He would become prone to excess in all things, work (and especially composition), but also drinking and socializing. He also became a member and practitioner of "free masonry,"[6.12] and led a life style that frequently would extend beyond his means, even after his marriage to his wife Constanz, and later, the birth of their only child. It is the dichotomy of excess and creative ability that has led to the simultaneously self-destructive lifestyle and enormously prolific/creative output of many artists such as Mozart over the course of musical history.

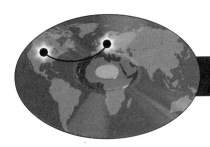

Inside the Musician's World

Wolfgang Amadeus Mozart

"I thank my God for graciously granting me the opportunity... of learning that death is the key which unlocks the door to our true happiness.

"Neither a lofty degree of intelligence nor imagination nor both together go to the making of genius. Love, love, love, that is the soul of genius.

"Music, even in situations of the greatest horror, should never be painful to the ear but should flatter and charm it, and thereby always remain music." W.A. Mozart, en.thinkexist.com.

Pic.6.15 *The so-called "Edlinger Mozart" was painted (circa 1790) by Johann Edlinger in Munich. Today it is displayed in the German Berliner Gemäldegalerie.* Photo: Public domain.

CD 2.8

"Lacrymosa," from the **"Requiem,"** by Wolfgang Amadeus Mozart, performed by the Wayne State University Concert Chorale, Dennis Tini, Conductor, from the CD: **Glory to God,** c. 1991.

At the end of a short and productive life, having struggled with the attainment of commissions and patronization to appease his "sponsors" and perpetually living beyond his means, Mozart began writing his final work, a **Requiem,** or *mass for the dead*. Despite glamorous stories that he was writing the mass for himself, that he was pressured from the grave by his father or by the meddling of one his contemporaries (Salieri), Mozart died at 35 years of age, without completing the Requiem and in general disfavor with the nobles and clergy of his time period. However, not long after his death, like many counterculture figures, both his extravagant and tragic life and his clearly beautiful creative capacity, increasingly became things of legend.

To help ourselves fathom Mozart's life and find a parallel to its impact today, we might ask: Who are the creative geniuses of our time? Will we appreciate their genius while they are living? Will they be required or encouraged to destroy human balance to gain notoriety or visibility? Is destruction and excess a pre-requisite for the intensity of creativity we can hear in music such as that of Mozart? Or do some of our societies feed the images of destructive lives and tragedy and/or build the reputations of artists beyond what anyone can accommodate in a balanced manner in an insatiable thirst for sensationalism? Does this cycle of "supporting the artist" while also making imbalanced demands on their humanity feed destruction or imbalance?

Professor Tini commented: *"The United States media and to some degree European or Western media on the whole are extremely negative and materialistic in their bent. The value of the artist and creativity of artists is undervalued. In some parts of the world the artists and their creative projects are held in higher esteem. Here everything is a commodity. Media is looking for hype and sensationalism on the artists and their lives rather than ever emphasizing the creativity of the music or projects, or the source of inspiration to the artists.*

"It's really backwards and demeaning to artists. Our culture is pigeon-holing things into glitz, shock-value, or into narrow formulas based upon what is currently selling or accessible, rather than in exploring new venues, or in emphasizing the emotional or spiritual quality that is essential to the creative, artistic experience, or frankly to the transformation of society. Remembering that in the past, in many cultures— and yes, in America as well— it was frequently artists who would initiate movements of reform or transformation. How can this be done, when nearly the entire emphasis is placed on the commercial appeal and value to a society who has begun to accept commercial formulas and sensationalism as commonplace?

"Is there a way we can transform this process? I keep looking for the positives. What can we do? I don't think our society, government, or media is supporting the emphasis on the creativity or artistry and the potential of the human spirit and human communication through the arts. I think education and performance are the places where both the example of creativity and artistry and re-education can be accomplished."

As we listen to this very emotional piece, constructed in a minor key (the harmony is built upon a minor scale) it may provide a strong backdrop for a reflection on the themes above.

Pic. 6.15A *Portrait of Beethoven by Carl Jung (ca. mid 1880's).* Public domain.

Ludwig van Beethoven (1770-1827)

"Prince, you are what you are by an accident of birth. What I am, I am through my own efforts. There have been thousands of princes and there will be thousands more; there is only one Beethoven." Beethoven, "Die Erinnerungen an Beethoven," p.212.

If Mozart's life and works reflect the duality of prolific creative output through the difficulties and even tragedies that life can bring, then the same is true of Ludwig van Beethoven's life. Although the events of his life are quite different to those of Mozart, the theme of success, innovation, and extreme confidence (if not arrogance) in his abilities coming from a painful and even tortured life – is the same. Ms. Bovender had this to say about Beethoven's life (from a student newspaper in Ann Arbor, Michigan, USA):

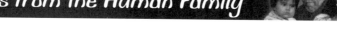

Stories from the Human Family

"My perceptions of Ludwig Van Beethoven:

"Most people today have heard the name Ludwig Van Beethoven. They have listened to or even performed his many works. Some have probably learned a little about him in a long since forgotten music appreciation class taken during their school years. His timeless musical works are still widely used by piano teachers, aspiring concert pianists, and those who simply enjoy his music. However, few know about the life of this creative musical genius and the struggles and trials that were the platform of his creative expression.

"Ludwig Van Beethoven was born in Bonn, Germany, on December 16, 1770, and died in Vienna, on March 27, 1827. He was quite famous in Vienna over the course of his life. He was often described as being eccentric, rude, temperamental, obnoxious, and a tyrant, though his musical genius was well respected. He was loved by many throughout Vienna and especially by the elite nobility.

"Beethoven suffered several physical ailments and was treated by many different physicians, whom he frequently referred to as 'bumbling doctors' or ''incompetent asses.' (The Beethoven Compendium, 164) [Note: Beethoven "began" to go deaf at the age of 28.] *In addition to his physical condition, historical information suggests that Beethoven suffered from manic bipolar depression.*

After the death of his brother, Casper, he faced many agonizing court battles in his attempt to gain custody of his nephew, Karl. He perceived his sister-in-law, Johanna, as unfit to raise his beloved nephew. Beethoven's physicians theorized that the stress produced from these grueling trials contributed to his strange and somewhat bizarre behavior. His personality characteristics were reported to be extremely contradictory. His euphoria could be quickly replaced with uncontrollable rage, intense agitation, or anxiety." E. Bovender, Student Voice, 2004.

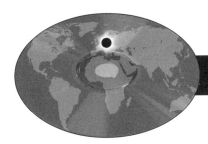

Inside the Musician's World

Ludwig van Beethoven

"For my bothers Carl and Johann Beethoven,

"Oh my fellow men, who consider me or describe me as hostile, obstinate, or misanthropic, how greatly you do me wrong. You do not know the secret reason why I appear this way.

"Since childhood I have been filled with love of humanity, and a desire to do good things. But for the last six years, I have been afflicted with an incurable complaint, made worse by incompetent doctors. From year to year my hopes for a cure have been gradually shattered. Finally, I must accept the prospect of permanent deafness.

Pic.6.16 *Painting of Beethoven by Joseph Karl Stieler (1820)*

"Though born with a passionate and sociable temperament, I was soon obliged to seclude myself and live in solitude. When I tried to ignore my infirmity, it became worse. Yet I could not bring myself to say to people: speak up, shout, for I am deaf.

"Alas! How could I possibly refer to the impairing of a sense which should be more perfectly developed in me than in others – a sense which once was perfect?

... Again I thank you, my brother Carl, in particular, for the affection you have shown me recently. I hope your life is better and more carefree than mine. Urge your children to be virtuous, for only virtue can make a person happy. Money can't. I speak from experience. Only my virtue and my art have kept me from killing myself until now...

"Well, that is all. Joyfully I go to meet death. Even if I do die, I'll be content, for death will free me from this continual suffering. Come, whenever you like, with courage I will go to meet you." Ludwig van Beethoven, "Heiligensadt," October 6th, 1802.

CD 2.9

Middle section of fourth movement, **"Symphony No. 9,"** "Choral," by Ludwig van Beethoven, conducted by Wilhelm Furtwängler with the Berlin Philharmonic Orchestra (a live recording), from the CD: **Wilhelm Furtwängler, Beethoven Symphony No. 9,** Allegro/Fono Enterprise, c. 2001.

The Symphony No. 9 in D minor, Op. 125, is the last complete symphony composed by Ludwig van Beethoven, who at this point in his life had been deaf for years. Completed in 1824, it includes part of the ode *An die Freude* ("Ode To Joy") by Friedrich Schiller, a text sung by soloists and a chorus in the last movement. His friend Anton Schindler explained: *"The master's spirits were soaring because he had finished the work for which he had the highest hopes."* It is one of the first examples of a major composer using the human voice in the context of the symphony (generally a four movement [section] work for symphony orchestra – designed essentially for music listening pleasure).

> Musicologist Bill Parker writes: *"The gala event took place on May 7, 1824. Beethoven, too deaf to conduct the work himself, sat in the middle of the orchestra attempting to follow along with the score. At the conclusion of the performance it became obvious that he had lost his place and did not realize it was over. Fräulein Unger, the alto soloist, turned him about to face the wildly cheering audience."* (From liner notes: Furtwängler, Beethoven-Symphony No. 9).

On March 24, 1827, Beethoven fell into a coma, and three days later, he passed away. On March 29, 1827, a crowd of more than 20,000 people gathered to watch Beethoven's funeral procession pass. Very much like Mozart in terms of the personal pain he suffered, but very unlike Mozart in terms of the popularity his music enjoyed during his lifetime, Ludwig Van Beethoven was personally a complex man with a rebellious nature, an unpredictable temperament, and awkward manners. He also possessed a capacity for compassion and a great love for his Creator and, more generally, for music. This love, probably more than anything else, is reflected in this work, which has been used repeatedly in plays, movies, and popular culture for decades.

Pic. 6.16A *The violin section of an orchestra performing a Beethoven symphony is just one of anywhere between 22 and 30 voices in a Beethoven score. It is the stacking and unstacking of instrumental layers that provides the depth of emotion and contrast of tension and release.* Photo: Courtesy Jean Schweitzer.

Pic. 6.16B *Although "chess" (a game of competitive logic) evolved through exchanges between India, China, ancient Persian cultures, it became popular in Europe between the 8th-10th centuries. When we attempt to decode a culture's values through its expressive arts, we must also attempt to understand the evolution of its logic over time and, whenever possible, in a multicultural context.* Photo: Courtesy John Carleton, 2005.

The Recipe of Sound

The portion we have included is only a 6.5-minute section of the final 24-minute movement (the middle of the movement) of a symphony that takes approximately one hour and a quarter to play in its entirety. Generally, **symphonies** (a specific style of work composed for the **symphony orchestra**) have four movements, each with altered formats to provide variation and tension and release throughout the entire work.

The first movement usually introduces valuable musical materials and is rather quick, energetic, or grand in proportion; the second movement is generally the slowest of movements; the third is usually based upon a lighter "dance-like" tempo, and the final, *the finale* is generally the heaviest and most pronounced of the work.

One of the traits that made Beethoven such an innovator was that he broke many of the formulas, relied heavily on insight and emotion, and (certainly no small part of the equation), in the end, could not actually hear what he had composed. Solely from the sounds in his mind, the music found its way into the world. Because of this, his work would unquestionably break, alter, and re-invent many of the conventions of that time. It is also why, as we move into the period called *Romantic* (relating to or characterized by adventure, excitement, the potential for heroic achievement), a time from which we get many of the most vivid, dramatic, and emotional works ever composed, many consider Beethoven's music the first to characterize this next stage in Europe's cultural and musical evolution.

Romanticism and Nationalism: The Culmination of Empire

The Romantic Period— (circa 1825-1900), as its name suggests, is a period of upheaval and drama. Revolutions, schools of intense nationalistic competition in politics as well as the arts, reactions to attempts to subvert, control, and repress change in classical times, were now leading Europe and later much of the world to global conflict. This period also marked the culmination of adherence to *nationhood* and the imperial doctrines and mindsets which had so longed plagued humanity.

During the Romantic period, monumental works of opera (especially in Italy and Germany), symphonies and tone poems (throughout Europe), and intimate works for piano (now the *"stereo"* or personal instrument of choice in parlors and living rooms throughout much of the world) were composed within schools characterized by *nationalist visions*. In many cases, and again modeling the ancient imperial formula of governance, each "school" vied much like athletes in the Olympics to exalt their nation's supremacy culturally and artistically over their European colleagues. Perhaps emblematic of the most terminal cases of *nationalism* of this time period were the works, and more importantly the thoughts, of Richard Wagner of Germany.

On one hand, Wagner was truly an extremely inspired and emotional musician, whose passion for music was considerable. On the other hand, he was reputed to be as arrogant and self-absorbed as nearly any musician had been. Most influential in terms of how we experience theater and movies today is his concept of *Gesamtkunstwerk* (all-together artwork). Wagner's vision of operatic performance encompassed music, theater, and the visual arts and placed great importance on "mood setting" elements, such as a darkened theater, sound effects, and seating arrangements, which focused the attention of the audience on the stage, completely immersing them in the imaginary world of the opera. These techniques are now standard in the world of theater, opera, and motion pictures as well.

Just as critical to Wagner's beliefs were his refusal to write music on any other topics than those of German lore, his promulgation of anti-Semitic sentiments (claiming that Jewish musicians were freaks of nature in appearance and action, despite the probability that he himself may have had a Jewish father, and originally a name common to Jewish people in his region and time period), and finally insisting that German art alone, could satisfy the human quest for artistic (musical) satisfaction, even serve as a replacement for religion itself.

Perhaps not to the extreme of Wagner, many European politicians, economists, educators, and artists during this period began to assert their tribal supremacy, which would once again increase the com-

Pic. 6.17 and 6.17B *From the evolution of language, music, painting, and politics as nations became truly established (and in reaction to "top-down" management by nobility in the Classical period), Nationalism, the hallmark of the Romantic period, witnessed the near exclusive emphasis on the values and ideals within each culture's supposed borders over any of their commonalities and shared evolution. In this case the "Painting of Liberty Leading the People," painted in 1830, is emblematic of both the French Revolution and the nationalist movement in France. In similar Nationalistic style, the "Church of the Savior on Blood," which was built over the spot in St. Petersburg where Tsar Alexander II of Russia had been assassinated, is constructed in a style that best evoked traditional Russian features.* Photos: Public domain.

Pic. 6.18 *A portrait of Richard Wagner (Public domain). Wagner wrote: "The Italian assimilated all those aspects of antiquity that he could imitate and reproduce, while the Frenchman, in turn, borrowed from this reproduction whatever might flatter his national sense of formal elegance; only the German recognized antiquity in all its purely human originality and as something that enjoyed a significance which, totally remote from utilitarian concerns, was uniquely suited to reproducing the purely human." KLRW IV, 17. Cf. PW IV, 155.*

"I believe in God, Mozart and Beethoven, and likewise their disciples and apostles; - I believe in the Holy Spirit and the truth of the one, indivisible Art; – I believe that this Art proceeds from God, and lives within the hearts of all illumined men; – I believe that he who once has bathed in the sublime delights of this high Art, is consecrate to Her for ever, and never can deny Her; - I believe that through Art all men are saved." Wagner, "An End in Paris," PW VII, 66-67.

petitive spirit, insecurity and, in the extreme, paranoia and ill-will that would lead to arguably the most destructive events thus far in human history. Musically, however, the emotional and dramatic events of the period spawned works that possessed wide melodic contours, contained a diversity of harmonic content, pushed the development of instrumental technology to its zenith, and gave us formulas for orchestration that would become the standard for setting stories in today's film music.

Italian Opera

Ethnic self-determination was in fact the theme that animated much of Europe's final surge to the ultimate state of nationalism during the Romantic period, before turning much of the continent in on itself. In Italy, the establishment of the Kingdom of Italy and the reduction of power of the Roman Catholic Church also fanned the flame of Italian nationalism. Opera, already considered by many Italians as an invention of Italian ingenuity, became the primary vehicle through which Italian stories and Italian sentiment for generations would be expressed.

The term **opera** comes from the Italian *opera in musica* (work in music). Although there are different labels given to "Romantic" and "modern era" opera, the most important aspects of Italian opera of this period were the simplistic stories of human drama (not too unlike exaggerated themes in soap operas from which the early TV programs [together with the soap commercials played during their airing] derived their names). Italian opera of this period placed enormous importance on exaggerated melody and the incredible expertise of the operatic performers, many of whom would receive "rock star" notoriety and status, even to the point of having entire operas composed for them.

Among the composers, Giuseppi Verdi (1813-1901) was one of the most popular and well known even within his lifetime. His flair for orchestration, for dramatic melodic composition in his arias, and for finding themes and topics which resonated with the Italian populace, made him perhaps the most popular composer in Italian history.

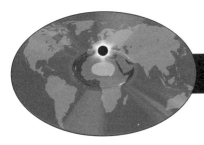

Inside the Musician's World

Note: In attempting to determine how in the world we would find a single piece to "summarize" both the Romantic Period and Italian Opera specifically, we turned to a representative from the Italian Record company "Fono Enterprises," Ms. Maria Cristina Nava, for suggestions. She wrote to us: *"I'd suggest "Va Pensiero" from Verdi's Nabucco. It is the music Italian people wanted to be the hymn for the unity of Italy and it is probably the most representative of the spirit of our Nation."*

Although the selection below is a choral anthem and does not feature a solo singer, Italian opera, and later opera in nearly all European countries and languages, became a primary form of entertainment in Europe from the 17th to the 20th centuries. In addition to the appeal of the

Pic. 6.19 *Teatro alla Scala, the famous Milan, Italy, opera house, was re-built (after a fire) and inaugurated in 1778. For many years, "La Scala" had a special relationship in the performance of Giuseppe Verdi's operas.* Photo: Courtesy O2ma.

stories, the grandiosity of the productions, and the appeal of the composer, much of the audiences' attention would be centered on the "star" appeal of the main or lead role performers. Opera houses such as "La Scala" not only were places to see the newest and latest operas or experience the classics of the past, but for the elite of the city (many of whom owned boxes in tiers to the left and right), some who would stand for the entire opera on the main floor, and still others, often the most dedicated and critical participants who would voice their approval or disapproval with whistles form the *loggione* (or gallery) located at the top of the opera house, opera provided both personal escape and a locale in which to engage in business and social or community-building relationships.

CD 2.10

"Va Pensiero," by Giuseppe Verdi from the opera: **Nabucco,** from the CD: **Nabucco,** Fono Enterprises, Italy, c. 2000.

"In the 1840s, the popularity of Verdi's music coincided with the Risorgimento, the campaign for a unified Italian nation. The wild success of Nabucco in particular put Verdi's name and music in the minds of many Italians at the time. They saw in Verdi's works a sadness, which reflected much of their own unhappiness with the status quo, and a vibrancy, which conjured romantic visions of Italian unification. Verdi's songs were especially resonant in Milan, then under Austrian occupation." [6.5] The opera, Verdi's third, is considered by many to be the one that permanently established his reputation in his homeland. *Nabucco* follows the plight of the Jews as they are assaulted and subsequently exiled from their homeland by the Babylonian King Nabucco (in English, Nebuchadnezzar). The best-known number from this opera is

Pic. 6.20 Giuseppe Verdi.

Pic. 6.21 *Much of the world's great art, such as this memorial in downtown Rome, is born out of healthy pride and patriotism. The Romantic period was a fertile ground for such art, as well as separatist sentiments with lethal consequences.* Photo: Courtesy Massimiliano, Fabrizi, 2005.

the Hebrews' Chorus, "Va pensiero, sull'ali dorate" ("Fly, though on golden wings").

Ms. Nava continues: *"In particular, the "Chorus of the Hebrew Slaves" was an immense success, and reportedly could be heard sung in the streets of Milan in 1843. Also known as Va' Pensiero from its first line, the song has been proposed from time to time as the Italian national anthem."* It begins:

Va, pensiero, sull'ali dorate; va, ti posa sui clivi, sui colli ove olezzano tepide e molli l'aure dolci del suolo natal!

Fly, thought, on wings of gold, go settle upon the slopes and the hills where the sweet airs of our native soil smell soft and mild!

Later, we hear (what is now the "Hymn of the nations"):

*The people Gloria resounds through the empyrean; it re-echoes through the highest peaks.
On this happy day the world exults with joy.
For the reign of love is nigh.
Glory! The future will remember it in song.
Glory through the skies! Glory!*

And then the final anthem, which captures the ultimate spirit of nationalism:

O Italia, o patria mia tradita, che il cielo benigno, ti sia propizio ancora, fino a quel dì che libera tu ancor risorga al sole!

O Italy, my country, o my fatherland betrayed, may merciful Heaven watch over you, until that day when, free again, you stand upright in the sun! [6.13]

Pic. 6.21A *Today, opera houses throughout much of the world (such as this one in Frankfurt, Germany) still present many of the great operas of the past. However, in order to preserve their role as a social, political, and artistic gathering point for the community, they will frequently also include performances by each generation's attractions, from musical theater, to pop stars, to Britain's "Stomp."* We should note also, the Classical Greek-style architecture. Greek influence was perpetual throughout European history.Photo: Authors.

Programmatic Music and the *Tone Poem*

One of most interesting compositional forms to receive heightened emphasis during the Romantic period was storytelling through music only: the **tone poem. Programmatic music** is essentially any music that represents non-musical (extra-musical) themes or stories through essentially – instrumental music. In one sense, programmatic music would include opera, **lieder** (art songs or poetry set to music), and any other form of music where the emotion, ideas, and even story are either set or portrayed in music.

The *tone poem,* however, is one device that developed and grew to enormous dimensions in terms of the use of all of the components of the orchestra to create mammoth tales and stories through non-literal, non-lyrical music. From the French composer Hector Berlioz's *Symphonie Fantastique* (a story about an artist with a great imagination who poisons himself with opium), told exclusively with the voicings (harmonic formulae) and full texture of the orchestra, to the tone poems of the German composer Richard Strauss, which include, among others, *Also Sprach Zarathustra,* (a complete orchestral work based on the book by Friedrich Nietzsche, perhaps best known for its use in Stanley Kubrick's 1968 film, "2001: A Space Odyssey"), tone poems explored wide variations in *orchestration* (the manner by which musical ideas are distributed amongst the orchestral instruments) to deepen the emotion and mental images one could derive from the *program.*

Today, nearly all of the musical devices developed, from Beethoven to the composers of the twentieth century (with the works of composers of the Romantic period as the centerpiece), have become the formulas of the trade for film composers of today. The wide variation of topics and subjects, from the most peaceful and soothing to the harshest and most violent, have given film composers worldwide a broad combination of sounds and compositional tools with which to work.

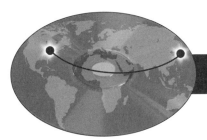

Inside the Musician's World

James Hartway composer; Kerstin Allvin, harp

An Affair of the Harp
Kerstin Allvin plays James Hartway

Note: This piece is a most striking and transparent example of programmatic music. It is based upon the work of *Matsuo Bashö,* (1644–1694) a Japanese poet of the Edo period. He is widely credited with raising the haiku[6.14] form to its highest level. "Matsuo" was the poet's family name, but he is usually referred to simply as "**Bashö**" without the surname.

Bashö was the son of a low-ranking samurai, and initially worked in the service of a local lord, Todo Yoshitada, who was only two years older than himself. They both enjoyed writing haiku. Bashö's first known work dates from 1662. By 1664 his first poems were published in Kyoto. Around this time he adopted the samurai name of Munefusa. In 1666 his master died, and Bashö opted to leave home rather than serve a new master.

Traditionally he is thought to have lived in Kyoto for at least part of the next six years. In 1672 he moved to Edo (now Tokyo). He continued to write, and by 1676 he was recognized as a master of *haikai*. He acquired a following of students, who built for him the first Bashö hut in the winter of 1680.

He lived much of his life in a series of huts, from which he could contemplate nature but to which he also welcomed many visitors. He made a number of long journeys on foot, which he recounted in diaries and which combine poems, his artistic theories, and details of his perceptions. These works were published and increased his fame as a teacher of poetry, allowing him to live on the patronage of his many students.[6.15] In capturing the essence of a thought or image, the composer, in this case Dr. Hartway, must somehow determine the instrument (or instruments) that he will use, create a series of musical devices (melodic, rhythmic, harmonic, and orchestrational), and then attempt to portray the emotion and nature of the story in sound alone. This is a difficult and challenging process, but free of the literal or more direct communication that text provides, musical poetry without text can liberate the imagination of the listener to take the suggestions of the *program* (the basis for the work) and re-conceive them in his or her own manner.

"Basho: Yellow Rose Petals," by James Hartway, based upon "haikai" by Bashö, performed by Kerstin Allvin, harp, from the CD: **An Affair of the Harp,** High Heel Records, c. 2003.

Pic. 6.23 *Lake Biwa, one of the favorite retreats of Bashö only five years before his passing, when he wrote his final haiku:*

Traveling, sick
My dreams roam
On a withered moor

The liner notes for the solo harp setting of this piece, "Yellow Rose Petals," read, *"This work is a set of eight short programmatic pieces based on the haiku of the 17th-century Japanese poet after whom they are named. In order to reflect the subtle colors of the poetry, the harp is "prepared" by wrapping strings with aluminum foil, attaching paper clips, and using brushes and coins to caress and strike the strings."*

The text or "program" is about as simple and opaque as could be imagined: [Pic. 6.22]

"Yellow rose petals... thunder... a waterfall..."

Thus, the clarity of the process of setting human thought or imagery into tone, the essential element of the tone poem, is strikingly clear. See if you can hear each of three images portrayed within the context of the piece.

Stories from the Human Family

Michael's Experience

When I enrolled in a Master's program to learn to write music for films and media, I had no idea, really, what the curriculum for learning to write "film music" would entail. To my surprise, one of the first means by which film composers learn is in the study of the past. By going back to the tone poems of composers of the 19th and 20th centuries, an enormous diversity of instrumental combinations, *timbres (tone colors)*, and orchestrational devices for eliciting emotion can be acquired.

When most of us attend films, we may get so caught up in the story that we are not aware of the tremendous impact the music makes. But the choice and nature of putting music to film is no easy process. Deciding at what point to place music, and precisely what kind of music should be used, is an extremely difficult process, easily one of the most difficult of any of the artistic decisions the director or producer might be called upon to make.

The music for a film project must support the picture and emotion but should not detract from or dilute the story. Often, music is used to enhance a scene and in some cases even make a scene that otherwise has been flawed by poor acting, timing, or technical miscues.

Perhaps, only when we see a scene without any music at all, and then see the scene again with the music added, can we fully appreciate the legacy of the great composers of the past on today's music. Film composition and the extensive work that is done to bring music to a full-length motion picture, sometime in the course of only a few weeks, is a truly amazing art. We may consider film music, as a continuance of the classical or art music repertoire tradition. Today – the programmatic music of opera of the 18th and 19th centuries, tone poems of the 19th and early 20th centuries, and art songs and concert works of the last century – have a new and respectable descendant: *film and film music.* Is this music today's "classical music"? (Reflection, 1994).

Pic 6.24 Neither people nor music can be respectfully categorized or generalized on a few contacts, as each style or genre, as well as the people who make it, is in constant flux—and is equally the product of decades, possibly centuries, of evolution. The chance of a single contact with another culture or music spawning an accurate or fully respectful perception is probably about the same as winning the lottery with a single ticket.

For example, at a quick glance: How long do you think it took Mr. Martin to sculpt these little guys from musical instruments? How do you think Mr. Martin evolved to his art? What does he want us to see, and how do we respect him by our perception? No matter how appreciative we are or desire to be, a quick or unengaged glance is not likely to produce the fullest measure of appreciation.

Mr. Martin writes: "I've been blessed as any one person could hope for. My work after 30 years has become my own life's story. As I continue on this path, I always find new ideas and am very grateful to be able to support by family as an artist." Photo: Author. Copyright: Robert Martin, Key Largo, FL, 2004.

"Classical" Music Today

"Every normal man (human) has, in some degree, creative insight (an unpopular statement) and an interest, desire and ability to express it (another unpopular statement). There are many, too many, who think they have none of it, and stop with the thought, or before the thought. There are a few who think (and encourage others to think) that they and they only have this insight, interest, etc., and that (as kind of collateral security) they and they only know how to give true expression to it. But in every human soul there is a ray of celestial beauty (Plotinus admits that) and a spark of genius (nobody admits that)." Charles Ives, "Postface," pp. 126.

Pic. 6.24A This photo from around 1913 shows Ives in his "day job": he was the director of a successful insurance agency, and composed remarkable music with little concern for how others perceived or interpreted his efforts. In many respects, the most creative art of any generation requires usually some detachment or autonomy from formulas and co-dependency on patronage or conformity to the standards of its age. Photo: Public domain. Courtesy Wikipedia.org.

In another manner, the term "classical" has come to infer "remembered" or valued over time. In this context, what will be the classical or art music of our age? What is the music that will be considered formidable, discussed, analyzed, and remembered centuries from now? Will it be music from new composers for symphony orchestra? Will it be the blues, rock 'n' roll, country, or hip-hop music of today? Do we see (hear) the difference between music that entertains and that which inspires, breaks new ground, or reflects the most vivid or emotional circumstances of our generation?

There are, in nearly every major university in Europe and United States, composition programs that may be (as one composition instructor reluctantly stressed) *"putting between one and twenty-one composers out onto the streets each year."* How will these composers make a living? Who will listen to their music? And at the pace of most of our lives, how can we work *new* music into our already very complicated life styles? When television and film are so accessible, and when symphony orchestras rarely play new compositions by new composers, from where will we gain access to new music?

Musicians, members of the music industry, and music educators ask many of these questions (or perhaps should ask them) on a daily basis. Quite naturally, there is no single answer, nor could any single response be considered unbiased. What there might be, however, are a few considerations from which to assess the artistic merit of a work regardless of whether it is a Hungarian Rhapsody (by Franz Liszt—music based upon Hungarian and Romani melodies) or Hungarian hip-hop.

- Does the piece bring anything new, valuable, or interesting to the world? Does it uplift, inspire, or cause one to think about something in a "new" or interesting manner?

- Is the music solely for entertainment or listening while doing something else, or does the music allow me to stop for a second, break my routine, and pause to contemplate some part of human existence, life, and possibly even laugh or cry?

- Is the music performed with "soul"? (The intangible quality of human sincerity, honesty, and deep emotion—in essence, *soul*.) Nearly any style of music, if played with deepest passion, can possess this quality.

- Or, regardless of genre, does the music contribute to or reinforce social or cultural excess, overt materialism, promiscuity, or characteristics that may have a negative impact on human advancement or the achievement of our potential, or does it inspire and induce thought or action that will improve the general nature of human existence (however perceived)?

We may have completely different responses to these questions, but without asking questions, the danger of becoming a "consumer" without thought about what it is we consume, is considerable. Regardless, if we give more consideration to what has come before us, we will recognize that *creative music* – however expressed, has a long and illustrious ancestry. Most of the issues we face today have been faced in the past, and nearly everything we do or have become today evolved from the past. Therefore, considering the music of the illustrious creative past (regardless of genre or culture) will help us more fully understand our world at present.

6.25 *To consider modern media to be the source of what many musicians feel to be the decay of art may be placing the blame on the wrong concern. Media is a tool, an instrument; some of the best music of our generation (and likely to be "classical" music of the future) is the music composed for films today. As discussed before, however, it is the* <u>business</u> *of media—that is, the "capitalism" of art—that is simultaneously the means by which artists generally support themselves and the basis on which creative options are restricted for artists and art appreciators alike. This continues to be one of the primary dichotomies and challenges in the creative world today.* Photo: Hollywood 1920's, Public domain.

Pic. 6.26 *It is difficult to overestimate the impact or potential for impact of today's film industry or its importance in modern life as our "opera" or musical storytelling device. Although we may question what we watch (or will spend our money for), the artistic and creative potential of film and its companion, music, is unquestionably here to stay and arguably still in its infancy. Entrance to "Universal Studios" theme park, Florida.* Photo: Authors.

Respectful Criticism

How Do We Scrutinize and Criticize—Respectfully?

A student once asked us if it was possible to not like something very much and still not offend those who do, to disagree with something to the core of your being and still find a manner of discussion that creates room for, or no disrespect to, the opposite vision.

All of us will be criticized at one time or other. In fact, if you are a creative person and committed to the fulfillment of your capacity, you'll likely be surrounded by critics. It's not unusual to be criticized for setting high goals, sharing your beliefs, taking a stand, accepting a leadership position, not compromising your principles, speaking out, or implementing change. The important thing is to understand any potential benefit the criticism might have on your growth.

Léonie's Experience

"As a counselor, whenever I come across a client who may be convinced that he/she desires to adopt a healthier way of life, but continues to practice destructive behaviors that inhibit positive growth, it is at times tempting to forget my role as an assistance provider and criticize the client. However, in order to promote positive, self-initiated growth rather than harming the client, it is imperative that I exert unconditional positive regard and remain genuine in my approach.

"If I were to tell a client that his/her views lacked substance or reasoning and could not explain in a respectful manner in what way they may wish to examine alternatives, or should I fail to time a constructive criticism to their emotional and mental capacity and benefit, I would harm the client's potential for self-initiated growth. To 'counsel' someone effectively, therefore, demands the greatest attention to maximizing the sensitivity of our words and actions in accordance with the receptivity of the client.

"Turning again to Western cultures: at issue in the very long history of debate, criticism, and critiquing of views, visions, and the arts is the creating of 'opposition' or disputing in a contestational manner. When careers are tied to the ownership and advancement of one's perspectives, competition may further fuel confrontational discourse. Finally, the history of the 'critic' is embedded in the belief in 'expertise' (the 'expert') whose opinions have (or should have) ascendancy over those of others. The critics' vision of the world or a specific idea is often believed to receive greater strength when the voices of others or competing perspectives are vehemently discredited."

Artistic Criticism

Today, we can add the fundamental quest of media—to gain viewer-/listener-ship or create "market" through sensationalizing what is in their best interest—as a huge influence on our perspectives of what "should" or should "not" be. We have become accustomed to being bombarded with the opinions of "experts" who wield the power of the critic over many aspects of creative expression.

So—*what are the alternatives?*

One option is not supporting those venues which package and market art exclusively as a commodity for financial gain, especially by disrespecting the nobility of human integrity. We might also begin to withdraw our support for any venue that masquerades critical discernment of values (essential to education and growth) under the disguise of judgmental, rude, and intrusive criticism—without responsibility to the feelings and diverse well-being of others.

Questions

- *How might we make our criticism of something we very much disagree with both constructive and respectful?*
- *Can you give an example of something or someone you strongly disagree with, and how you might approach your "criticism" in a respectful or constructive manner?*
- *How are "standards" of popularity, creativity, and human advancement in any age created? Is there a benefit to distinguishing between things that truly benefit us from those that are being placed in our path from a sensationalistic or selfish motive?*

Unit VI Activities

Activity #1: Understanding Concepts

After reading and listening to the music in Unit VI, we might have some thoughts about the degree to which we see or have a desire to see connections over time. Depending upon your perceptions, answer the following questions:

1) Are there any perceptions of culture/family as to "how things should be" (i.e., the primary "values" in how you live your life or spend your time) that you question? Can you trace how this "value" that you question may have evolved over time?

2) Regardless of your beliefs, can you see the impact of the doctrines and evolution of the Christian church of the past on any important facet of your life today? Can you cite some ways by which the Roman Catholic "Empire" of the past (i.e., its beliefs, doctrines and influence) may currently be impacting you directly? What about your music? [Note: the influence is there: "nothing comes from nothing"; our awareness of the impact of history is more the issue.]

3) If *nothing truly comes from nothing,* can you trace the music you listen to (i.e., its texture, form, harmony, or other musical devices) to musical or historical events cited in this Unit? In what way might the events distanced by centuries from you and your past have impacted your "world's" music?

Activity #2: Listening Deeper

Now that we've completed our "cliff notes" (condensed) trip through centuries of music in a few pages, play the selections CD 2.5 through 2.10 once again. This time, just us, the music, and maybe a pen to take a few notes. (Suggestion: For a frame of reference in listening, read the questions below before you listen.)

Musical Notes:

Pieces:

2.5

2.6

2.7

2.8

2.9

2.10

1) What are the changes or differences you hear in the music from piece to piece? To what (in the history or composers' lives/culture) do you attribute these changes?

2) What specifically can you say about the emotion that you feel from each piece? Can you describe the difference in the harmony (or emotion) from piece to piece?

3) Suggestion: pick a favorite selection from any of the pieces in this Unit. Why did you choose this piece? Or – What in the piece spoke to you and why? Is there any music in your world today that possesses the same traits or characteristics of the piece you selected? How would you describe any connection from this piece to what you prefer?

Activity #3: Exercising Passion

Somewhere in everything we enjoy or do with passion is a connection to some part of our history, some remote corner of our past. What we seek to understand in seeing connections over time is the path that has led to who we are or why we value (or devalue) the most critical aspects of our cultures and lifestyles. We may wish to research the connectivity of "history" to ourselves, with the understanding that appreciation of the past profoundly increases our awareness and insight today.

1) Pick a culture, specific time period, music era, genre, or musician that you'd like to find more about.

2) Gather some information (preferably from a respectful source [created by or for that culture]).

3) What interests you the most about what you've gathered?

4) Do you see any reflection of these values or traits in your world? (Ex: Some parallel reflections of the same principles or traits that are somehow reflected in what you do or value?)

5) Finally, in what manner could something you learned about this culture, era, or composer be incorporated into your life, how you spend your time, or what you do? (Or, how might you show your respect for what you've learned through an alteration in your actions or life?)

A young lady plays a recital from written notes. The formula for learning Western classical music demands strict adherence to written formulae.

Activity #4: Exercising Our Own Creativity

Programmatic art is the transference of the essence of something written, visual, or aural (from one genre) into another medium of creativity. The simplest formula in creating programmatic art includes finding an inspiration or source of topic, restricting the inspiration to a reasonable or manageable dimension, and using "our instruments," to create an impression of "the program."

Suggestion:

1) Pick an instrument for your project (writing, music, art, cooking, etc.).

2) Pick another "favorite" story, piece of music, topic, picture, photograph, etc. (not in your area of expertise). Note: Make sure it is a short, manageable "program."

3) Now ask yourself:

- What is the emotion of this source of inspiration?

- What are the qualities (especially human or nature-based) reflected in this source? [Creating natural metaphors for our perceptions gives a valuable source of symbolic tools to take us from the literal to the emotional plane.]

- What is the essence or purpose of this source?

4) Now, how can you reflect your observations in "3" above through your art?

- What form will it take? What process or steps will you take (creative art is usually made in carefully designed and frequently small steps)? Try to have fun and try *very hard* not to be too critical of yourself, the product, or the outcome. Above all, make sure you *complete* (bring to some point of closure or satisfying conclusion) whatever you begin.

Note: If we give up at the point when we need to *forge through a difficulty*, the very point where inspiration and our creative problem solving skills are waiting to be used, we will likely not fulfill or enjoy fulfillment of the creative experience. Similarly, if we are too ambitious in our undertaking, commit more time or resources than we have available, or set "goals" and outcomes, we may likely become discouraged. Best suggestion: "Keep it real."

Pic. 6.27A,B, and C *The use of musical instruments in military pursuits, such as the fife and drum units of the American Revolution (re-enactment above), date back to at least the 8th century in Turkey. However, it was the Janissary bands in Turkey from the 13th century that gave rise to European military bands (16th century) and, later, to ceremonial bands, marching bands (right), and even bands for entertainment, such as symphonic (concert) bands or Disneyworld's "Toy Soldier" bands (below). The instruments developed and used over the course of this evolutionary process remain essential to much of music today, whether performed as originally used or in synthesized form. This is what is meant by "Nothing comes from nothing."* Photos: above left, Fife & Drum, St. Louis, MO, Sean Locke; above right, drum and bugle corps, Jason Lugo; right, Disney Toy Soldier band, Authors.

Unit VI: Endnotes

6.1   See Loewen, Lies My Teacher Told Me, pp.37-74.

6.2   We will use "our" as concerns European ancestry in the same way that we will us "our" as concerns "African" ancestry or "African-American" ancestry in subsequent units. The shift in perception that we are hoping to instill in the reader is simply, regardless of what we call ourselves, if we live in a culture that has been extensively influenced now or earlier by other cultures, they are a part of our ancestry whether we look or act as "they" do or not.

6.3   We will use the term "classical" in this text without further justification. The term "art" music implies that other music is "not art," while the term "classical," though actually referring more accurately to Ancient Greek practices or to the period denoted "Classical period" (or "neo-classical," circa 1825-1900), may not be accurate, it is the most common label known by most for these Western musical genres.

6.4   The term "genre" is frequently used to refer to a category of music or art with similar form, style, or subject matter. For example, rock 'n' roll or opera. Genre may also have subgenre headings, such as Baroque opera or Italian opera.

6.4a Sister Joseph Maria, Catholic scholar from a Michigan Monastery wrote: "Pope Leo III crowned Charlemagne as emperor to unify the people and be their temporal leader and defender. this safe-guarded the church in the early centuries."

6.5   The "Black Death" or Black Plague of the 14th century killed nearly a third of the population in Europe, the Middle East, and even Asia.

6.6   Although music in the Renaissance would flourish, it was not without complications. The Council of Trent in the earlier part of the 16th century had attempted to ban the organized polyphony that would lead to the "harmonies" of today. Giovanni Pierluigi da Palestrina, one of the foremost composers of the Italian Renaissance (which was dominated by composers from Spain, France, and the Netherlands prior to Palestrina), was instrumental in forging acceptance of the chorale compositional techniques that would make up Western harmony in the future.

6.6a Sister Joseph Maria writes: "'The Holy Roman Empire' ended in 1806 with Napolean's rise to power. He refused to accept any jurisdiction of the church and thus, the alliance was broken."

6.7   From the Wikipedia discussion of Reformation history, www.wikipedia.com.

6.8   Roughly a one-hour work for orchestra, keyboard (harpsichord or organ), and both solo and chorus voices.

6.9   Prior to the Baroque period, each locality would tune its instruments slightly differently, according to its understanding of the modes or scales that had been inherited from Arab, Persian, and Greek cultures. The system of equal temperament, although it took much of the diversity from Western music, created the unified system of exactly equal distances between the pitches on the keyboard (the pitch system we use today), thus making it possible for instrumentalists to play with others anywhere in Europe.

6.10 Classicism and the more accurately defined Neo-classicism (as in "new" classicism), were periods defined by a return to classical cultural values or strong reference to values and ideals of ancient Greece. The "period" defined by these values is generally given the dates 1740-50 to 1825-30. This period absorbs "Rococo" and Neo-classical movements of the same time period.

6.11 Beethoven, like many composers, marks the transition between classicism and romanticism. Arguably, all composers will have works that do not reflect the predominant aesthetic or values of the times, or will extend themselves into genres that are "uncharacteristic," or different from those for which they are known. This is true in modern times as well: There are many "classical" musicians who play rock, country musicians who play blues, and hip-hop artists who perform in soft-drink commercials.

6.12 Freemasonry has been said to be an institutional outgrowth of the medieval guilds of stonemasons, an offshoot of the ancient Mystery schools, and the Roman Collegia, and to have many other origins. Others will claim that it dates back only to the late 17th century. Freemasonry members are joined together by shared ideals of both a moral and metaphysical nature and, in most of its branches, by a common belief in a Supreme Being. Freemasonry is an esoteric art, in that certain aspects of its internal work are not generally revealed to the public. From: en.wikipedia.org/wiki/Freemason

6.13 Extracted from Wikipedia (en.wikipedia.org/wiki/Giuseppe_Verdi).

6.14 The haiku poet (*haijin*) writes about a moment in time, a brief experience that stands out. The traditional hokku focused on nature and the place of humans in nature.

6.15 See: en.wikipedia.org/wiki/Basho for more information (Wikipedia.org).

A.

B.

C.

6.28A,B & C *The very notion of "history," as being something fixed, permanent or established is a formidable barrier in nearly all cases to an equitable understanding of human nature. First, as culture systems evolve, how we perceive or represent the past will change (A – young musicians clothed in Mozart-period clothing to advertise and sell tickets for a Mozart revival concert, Vienna). Secondly, as our needs change, how we utilize the resources, buildings, and "fruits of our ancestors' labor" will change (B – a Roman theater, then a church, now museum, center of tourism, and outdoor concert stage in Malaga, Spain). And, third, most all remnants of history have been changed, altered, added to, subtracted from, and, thus, whatever the source of their initiation, are now visions of transition as much as or more than origin.* (C – Young Czech in classical period clothing by a bicycle taxi.) Photos: Authors.

Jewish and Romani:
Stories of Creativity and Influence

Topics to Consider in Unit VII

➤ *What does the absence of an accurate portrayal of two of our world's dynamic cultures do to distort our vision of history?*

➤ *What do our Jewish and Romani (Romany/Roma/Rom) communities share in common? In what ways did they also influence each other?*

➤ *What are some of the main historical events and considerations in understanding the evolution and subsequent impact of the Jewish Diaspora on our world today?*

➤ *What is "Sephardic" or "Ashkenazi" Judaism? And – what is the impact of both these groups and the Hassidic movement on European culture and musical evolution (including that of Klezmorim)?*

➤ *What are some observations we can make about "Jewish music" from the recordings of the "Burning Bush"? And – how can we describe the difference in Sephardic and Ashkenazi music based on the recorded examples?*

➤ *What are some of the observations we can make about the influence of Jewish music and culture on today's music, musical theater, and films?*

➤ *Who may have been among the first groups to contribute (if not be solely responsible) to the development of the "guitar," the violin, and numerous other developments in European "classical"/art and "folk" music practices?*

➤ *What were the reasons that both Roma and Jewish groups likely became so proficient in musical performance?*

➤ *What are some examples of Romani music, dance, and "fusion" of cultural influences?*

➤ *What is the message of "intra-cultural" exchange and the changing dynamic of identity we can glean from the members of "Harmonium"?*

➤ *What are some of the most important dynamics in the evolution of Spain and Greece on much of our world today? And – what must we consider concerning our music today?*

➤ *What is rhythm? And – what are some of the things we can say about rhythm to distinguish the diversity of ways music flows over time?*

UNIT VII

Jewish and Romani:
Stories of Creativity and Influence

"All music is 'folk' music ... I have never heard no horse sing a song."
Louis Armstrong, New York Times, 1941

Perhaps the single-most glaring discrepancy in the documentation and instruction of European music, whether classical or otherwise, is the lack of respect and support given to the influence of a few of Europe's "minority" groups. At least as concerns the archives of scholarly documentation from which subsequent generations would operate, only scant acknowledgement is given to the creative influences of the *folk,* generally, and these groups, specifically. When, however, we do find references to the "folk" music of Europe, such references generally omit or underestimate the influence of two groups: the **Jewish** and **Romani** (Rom, Roma, or Romani). Both groups are not only formidable contributors to the evolution of Western music practices but also among the main contributors to dance, song, and instrumental repertoires of all European music genres, *folk or classical.*

For reasons and circumstances that parallel the exclusionary treatment received by African-Americans or Native Americans from the historical discussions and archives of our American/European scholars and universities, the *Jewish and Roma*[7.1] cultures have for centuries somehow managed to pass *under the radar* of most academicians, musicologists, and historians who are not, of course, Jewish or Romani. What is missed by the maintenance of centuries of prejudice and exclusion is the lesson that music, dance, and art possess the power to heal, inspire, and transcend even the most severe forms of repression. For this reason, if no other, cultures that have experienced the repression and hierarchically separatist actions of a larger culture system and contributed so much creativity to our world's music deserve an immediate seat at the table of legitimacy.

What explanation can be given for the missing voice of these communities, including their pervasive use of music, enormous creativity, and musical and technological innovations (i.e., development and transfiguration of instruments), whose influence is fundamental to what we call Western music? We'll explore this question in this unit.

Pic. 7.1A *The Dombrover Rebbe of Monsey with the Nadvorna Rebbe (Rebbes or Rabbis signified by pelz or fur coat or lining) at a ceremony to build a new facility. The Hasidic (Chassidic or Hasidism) branch of Judaism is credited to Rabbi Israel ben Eliezer (1698-1760). At a time when persecution of the Jewish people had reached a severe level, European Jews had "turned inward" to Talmud study, and many felt that "spirituality" and joy had been replaced solely by academic study. Therefore, Hasidic Judaism began to place an emphasis on the use of music and even dance as a means to "spirituality."* Photo: released to public domain, courtesy JJ211219 and Wikipedia.org.

Pic. 7.1B *A Roma family living on the edge of town in Smyrna, Turkey. Were the Roma naturally "nomadic," as many historians suggest, or were they forced into a Nomadic lifestyle because few culture groups accepted them as even remotely equal, forcing perpetual isolation and migration as a means of survival?* Photo: Courtesy Wikipedia.

Despite the fact that some members of the Jewish or Romani communities may themselves not wish to claim similarities to each other,[7.2] there are strong reasons that we can speak of these groups in nearly equal terms as concerns contributions to the evolution of European culture and music. Among these:

- Both groups were exiled or expelled from a "homeland" and spent centuries in transition, or needing to assimilate or adapt as an essentially "minority" culture.

- Both groups experienced enormous repression, ridicule, and extermination throughout Europe for *centuries,* at times being singled out for blame or persecution, often paying the ultimate penalty with loss of life, destruction of family or community for a variety of justifications (including being blamed as the cause for the "Black Death" [plague]).

- Frequently, in order to be "successful" within the societies in which they lived, both groups were required to "mask" or renounce their religions and their cultural beliefs, to take new names, to alter their associations, or to convert to either Christianity or Islam.

- Both groups had two initial paths of migration: the *northern route,* which took them through Russia and Eastern Europe to Western Europe; and the *southern route,* which extended through the Middle East, to North Africa, and into Spain. In the case of the Jewish, however, the dispersion patterns are more erratic. Often Jewish and Rom communities who were in Western Europe were disbanded or expelled to Northern or Eastern Europe, and vice versa.

- And, most important to this chapter, both groups became enormously attracted to and adept in the performing arts. In both cases, probably more than any other "ethnic groups" in Europe, the Jewish and Rom cultures used the performing arts as key elements in the sustenance, healing, and bonding essential to forge a sense of community through centuries of repression.

Because of the migratory or nomadic requirements placed on both Jewish and Romani communities, not a single "nation" and culture group in Europe can claim exclusion from strong if not predominant influences from these culture groups, especially as regards their music. Moreover, as a general principle, both groups became highly proficient at adapting to the cultures in which they found themselves. In one sense, this capacity for flexibility and adaptability created a role for both communities in interconnecting, much like "cultural honey bees," Europe's cultural and musical expressions.

Under the Radar: The Jewish Diaspora

Fragmentation of Jewish communities goes back to the conquering of the kingdom of Judea, the south-ernmost of two Jewish kingdoms (6th century BCE), after which many Jews were exiled to Babylon and others returned to Israel. Under Roman rule, Judea was first a Jewish kingdom, but increasingly came under direct Roman administration. When many in the community revolted against the Romans, a large part of the temple in Jerusalem (where currently the famed "Western Wall" now stands) was destroyed and, in time, many Jewish communities themselves were also destroyed. Others were either forced into slavery or forced to convert as loyalists to the Roman way of life.

By all definitions now a *Diaspora,* the splintered Jewish community settled in pockets throughout areas of the former Roman Empire. There are records of Jewish communities in France and Germany from the 4th century and large communities in Spain even earlier than that. During the rise of Roman Catholicism throughout the Middle Ages, Jews were frequently persecuted or systematically exterminated, especially during the Crusades of the Middle Ages.

Jewish property was frequently confiscated, and few individuals were given opportunities to prosper. At one point, because of a ban by the Catholic Church on such practices for Christians as book-keeping and money-lending (a precursor to banking), "Jews" were permitted to occupy these positions. [Note: This turn of events also contributed to age-old Jewish stereotypes, positive (thriftiness and material prosperity) and negative (overt shrewdness and pecuniary obsession)]. But without justification, Jewish property could be confiscated; Jews could be banned, exiled, or persecuted for little or no reason.

Pic. 7.2 *A Jewish cemetery (mausoleum) and former synagogue in the "Jewish Quarter" of Prague is now a place of pilgrimage of hundreds of Jewish and non-Jewish tourists who wish to remember not only the Jewish suffering of the Holocaust, but that of centuries before – and decades since.* Photo: Authors.

Pic. 7.2A1 *An equitable understanding of our world's darkest hours might not see entire nations, ethnic groups, or religions as "good" or "evil." In this sense, we should seek an equity and accountability in our own investigation of multiple truths. One example, in Germany, there is a monument in a St. Paul's Cathedral for Cardinal Clemens August Graf van Galen, who, during Nazi control, harbored, protected, and saved many Jewish refugees – and who in turn suffered for his convictions. In virtually every "holocaust" of human history, the legacy of the countless stories of cultural sacrifice or unity have yet to find their way into most of our history books.* Photo: Authors.

Pic. 7.2A *A* **Bar mitzvah**—*meaning "son of the commandment" (a rite-of-passage celebration of a boy to manhood) at the Western Wall in Jerusalem, spring of 1978.* Photo: Courtesy and copyright Leif Knutsen.

Jewish Musicians and the Importance of Music

Largely because of the enormous bias against Jewish and Romani cultures, we can read very little about their contributions in music history books. One case in point, the life and accomplishments of the 16th- and early 17th-century composer Salamone Rossi, is emblematic of the dichotomy between contributions and pervasive lack of recognition for contributing.

An article on Rossi by Raphael Mostel[7.3] begins: *"If someone told you that one of the most important, influential, and best-selling composers in Europe around 1600 was an observant Jew living in a ghetto, you'd probably think it was a joke. We are just now beginning to learn how far from a joke this Jew's story is."*

The article goes on to say that he was one of the biggest-selling composers of the time (an indication of popularity), was one of the first composers to champion the use of the violin, and was possibly the first to create a school for its use. In addition, he may have been the first to compose *the trio sonata,* one of the most popular genres to be used in a *chamber music* setting (a musical performance in a room, usually for a social event [*Fr. Chamber* – room or hall]). A direct descendant of one of the oldest Jewish families in Rome (his ancestors were brought to Rome as slaves), Rossi was able to walk the very fine line between being a practicing Jew (*he did not convert; nor did he deny his Jewish heritage—he practiced his faith both personally and through his compositions*), and a professional composer and music instructor for Christian clients.

So what happened to him? Why might non-Jews know about such efforts and contributions to Western music only if they happen to stumble upon a Jewish website, or talk to a (Jewish) musician? Perhaps Mr. Mostel's final paragraph will shed some light on this and the dynamics faced by Jewish musicians, generally, as well:

> *"What became of Rossi's grand experiment in cross-cultural collaboration? Unfortunately, after the Gonzaga[7.4] family died out, the Austrians invaded and destroyed the Jewish ghetto, murdering many of the inhabitants and scattering the rest. We have no information about what happened to Rossi. Most of the copies of his music disappeared. It was nearly 300 years before any other Jewish composer attempted something similar. It took that long for any Jewish musicians to venture out into the larger Christian society or to bring new music into Jewish society. Only with the liberalizations of the 19th century were Jews to be found once again at the center of the music world"* (i.e., part of the Western classical music field and therefore subject to documentation and inclusion in the university canon). *"But even then, most of those, like Felix Mendelssohn, Gustav Mahler, etc., found it necessary to convert to Christianity before they or their work could be accepted."*

Sephardic and Ashkenazi Music

The most commonly used divisions of Jewish culture and music are:

Sephardic – Jewish communities that evolved from the Middle East and North Africa primarily to Spain and Portugal, or those which were dispersed from Spain during the Spanish Inquisition (15th century). The term is frequently applied to include "Jews" who lived in other parts of the Middle East as well. The language is a mixture of Hebrew and Spanish (Ladino) and their songs include a mixture of North African (Arabic), Spanish/Latin, and Hebraic influences in melody, lyrics, and instrumentation.

Ashkenazi – Jewish communities extending from Russia to eastern, central, and northern parts of Europe (especially Germany and Poland). Yiddish, a blend of primarily German and Hebrew, or other blends of Slavic languages and Hebrew are the primary languages. The **Hasidic** branch of Judaism grew out of *Ashkenazim* in the 18th century. It is comparable to Islamic "Sufism" in its use of music and dance as a means for worship or drawing closer to God.

"The (Hasidic) movement was founded by Rabbi Israel ben Eliezer (1700-1760)—abbreviated as Besht. It was formed in a time of persecution of the Jewish people. Many felt that most expressions of Jewish life had become too "academic," and that they no longer had any emphasis on spirituality or joy. The Ba'al Shem Tov set out to improve the situation. The teachings of Hasidism are founded on two theoretical conceptions: religious pantheism, or the omnipresence of God, and the idea of Devekut, which refers to the belief that between the world of God and the world of humanity there is an unbroken intercourse."[7.5]

Despite the fact that there are (were) clear differences in *Sephardic and Ashkenazi* sub-cultures, especially as concerns the practice of their faith (interpretation or observation of laws and customs) and in their language and music based upon the different *fusion* of cultures, these categories, much like those of nation or period in European classical music evolution, are more important in discussing the past dynamics of Jewish culture. Over the course of the 20th century, the dispersion of the Jewish community to South Africa, Australia, New Zealand, the United States, and Canada, as well as back to Israel, make the divisions above somewhat ambiguous and perhaps more of a reference tool than a distinct reality.

As you listen to the two musical *medleys* that mark these two traditions (three samples each), consider their differences as well as their similarities. You may hear the influences of classical music or other forms of *folk* music that you've experienced before. You may recognize instruments and melodies from music of other ancestries, classical compositions, and the music of your church or culture. Why would this be? Perhaps because the capacity to adapt, create, and assimilate music as a means of strengthening the community and emoting (healing) from the hardships encountered not over decades, nor centuries, but millennia, was the source of much of Jewish music.

As concerns the exchange of musical (cultural) ideas and creations between cultures, we may never know whether the egg preceded the chicken, but one thing is certain: today we are aware that we need them both if we have any interest in creating omeletes.[7.6] That is, it is remarkable to what degree human cultures, in this case the Jewish communities, were able to assimilate the cultural traits of their host environments and conversely pass on their knowledge, creativity, and inspiration to each of these other cultures.

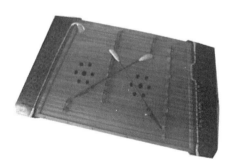

Pic. 7.2B *The cymbalum, cymbalom (most common spellings), or the tambal, tsymbaly, or santouri is a musical instrument found mainly in the Rom music of Hungary, Romania, and Ukraine. It is an outgrowth of the santour (of Persia) and the ancestor of the hammered dulcimer, harpsichord, and piano of Western Europe. It is also a symbol of the connection between the Jewish (klezmer) and Rom traditions, as it was used in both.* Photo: Courtesy Wikipedia.org.

Patronization

What Are the Causes and Effects of Marginalizing or Patronizing Others?
The lethal impact of patronization lies in the principle that we can be attempting to respect or acknowledge a person, race, religion, gender, or music and, in reality, be hurting it more devastatingly than we would with a blatant and clear form of prejudice.

To begin, let's understand patronization. Whenever we take a superior attitude towards others, marginalize or denounce something or someone as "inferior" to us, our beliefs, our culture, or our views, we are creating an "inequitable" **unreality**. Assuming that no human culture or group is inherently superior or inferior (despite human history's being written otherwise), patronizing or assuming an "air" of superiority, subtly or pronounced, is disrespectful.

In general, most of us learn early that blatant denouncing or verbally/mentally disfiguring a person, culture, or thing is an act of prejudice and injustice. However, IF we smile at, or make a superficial gesture or attempt to "allow" the object of inferiority a place in our life, but in our heart or mind it is still inferior to ourselves or our culture, belief, etc., we have now simply submerged our bias under an otherwise polite or cordial exterior, and the damage can be even greater. Not only will the object of this form of marginalization sense (but not always be certain) it is being devalued, but we may also have convinced ourselves that we are truly equitable and unbiased in our actions, thus veiling our own perceptions from this bias in our character.

Patronization may occur individually, or it may manifest itself culturally, as in the designation of a special day or month for a culture group that has been historically disrespected in lieu of a wholesale reform of culture, educational curriculum, or social and economic policies to create a truly equitable place for the other culture.

Questions

- *Have you ever been patronized? How did it feel?*
- *Can you think of someone or some culture that you have patronized? How might this be avoided?*

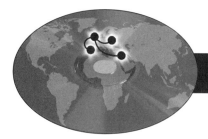

Inside the Musician's World

The Burning Bush

Note: The "Burning Bush" is a widely acclaimed Jewish musical ensemble out of Britain. Their music is the combination of research into the past and the Jewish instinct for creative fusion, which makes their music, and Jewish music historically, a vital line to the understanding of human creativity. Liner notes for this CD read in part: *"Both Ashkenazi and Sephardic musicians were happy to borrow from their non-Jewish neighbors (a universally human practice) and their music frequent-*

Merlin   Roderick   Lucie   Stuart   Robin
Shepherd   Skeaping   Skeaping   Hall   Jeffrey

ly showed clearer links with that of the surrounding Russian, Turkish or Greek environment. Among the Sephardim we find ancient romances or narrative ballads, apparently dating back to Medieval Spain, co-existing with melodies of Greek or Turkish origin."

A medley of Sephardic music in three parts. Part I: **"Quando el rey Nimrod,"** Part II: **"Arvoles lloran por lluvias,"** and Part III: **"Yendome para Marsilia,"** performed by The Burning Bush, from the CD: **Best of Yiddish, Klezmer, and Sephardic Music,** Arc Music International, c. 1996.

Part I: *Quando el rey Nimrod* (When King Nimrod): This piece is a fascinating blend of North African or Andalusian melody and drum patterns mixed with lyrics which simultaneously combine the story of the birth of Christ with that of Father Abraham. The act of creating "double meaning" remains a critical aspect of nearly all Diaspora cultures under repression. The translated text reads: *"When King Nimrod went out into the fields he looked up into the heavens among the stars and saw a holy light over the Jew-*

ish quarter—for Father Abraham was born. The wife of Terah was pregnant. Daily he asked her why her expression was so changed. She knew the good thing that she was bearing. Let us salute the Godfather and also the circumciser, that by his grace the Redeemer came to us, and took pity on all Israel; let us give praises to the truth." [7.7]

Part II: *Arvoles lloran por lluvias* (The Trees Cry for the Rain): *"A well-known text throughout the Judeo-Spanish speaking community, this love song has another even more poignant significance; the chorus was said to have been sung by the Jews of Rhodes as they were deported to Auschwitz during WWII."* The translated lyrics say: *"The trees cry for the rain and the mountains for the*

Pic. 7.3A *All things "Jewish" reflect not only the difficulties but the enormous beauty of our multicultural world and the Jewish migration through much of it. This synagogue in Budapest, Hungary, is reflection of Russian, Middle Eastern, and Andalusian influences, to name a few. Jewish food, music, theater, and religious"traditions" likewise reflect their multicultural past.* Photo: Authors.

wind; thus my eyes weep for you, my love. What will become of me? I will die in a strange land. White you are, white are your clothes, white is your body, white also are the flowers which fall from your beauty. The rain has fallen and has drenched the street and the courtyard. Go to my love and say that this water comes from my eyes."

Part III: *Yendome para Marsilia* (I went to Marseilles): Marseilles, located in the Mediterranean part of France, is, like much of Southern France, a cornucopia of cultures and influences. In this Judeo-Spanish song, the traveler comments: *"I went to Marseilles on a packet steamer; I assure you, my beloved, that I had a good time. Beautiful Marseilles, extremely beautiful … what a good life I live with the little I have. My vices are my undoing but my deeds are better than a banquet."*

The Recipe of Sound

Part I: The use of a scale that begins with a half step, an augmented second, and another half step (sometimes called a Hungarian **tetrachord** [or partial scale]) is so common in many Jewish styles of music that it is even referred to (especially by Jewish cantors or musicians) as "the Jewish scale." In fact, this mode or scale is derived from Hebrew/Arabic scales and is one of the most popular modes for the expression of sorrow or deep emotion throughout Andalusian cultures (Spain and North Africa), and much of Eastern Europe—likely also a bi-product of the migration and cross-influence with Romani culture groups. The combination of accordion, violin, and vocal melodic styling, however, reflect both Ashkenazi and Sephardic traditions, another indication that it is virtually impossible to accurately view or discuss cultures in complete separation of each other.

Part II: So pervasive is the cross-influence of classical music (European art music) on Jewish culture—and most certainly the reverse—that this piece, though possibly sounding *less "folk-like,"* reflects the dynamics of the classical style of vocal production (singing with strong support, focus in the face, and **vibrato** – waiving or vibrating in the sound) used for production in Western opera or operatic traditions.

Part III: We will find so many ways by which the Roma and Jewish cultures connect that it becomes virtually impossible at times to distinguish between them. Wherever the source of origin, one musical trait that is generally associated with perceptions of uniquely "Jewish" music is the style of clarinet melody you'll hear in this piece. With its almost humorous slurs and scoops (krekhts—"sobs"—and dreydlakh—"trills"), a mainstay of Klezmer music, we are reminded of the critical aspect of humor in sustaining ourselves through difficulties as well.

Ashkenazi Medley

Note: Jewish musician and author Yale Strom writes about the origins of **klezmer** music[7,8] by first tracing the Jewish minstrel (traveling Jewish musician) back to the Middle Ages. He cites the hardships that Jewish musicians encountered in being forbidden to play their music at times by the more rigid Jewish authorities and in part because of Jewish persecution. At times the sacred / secular wars would rage or subside; at others the war of survival would increase or ease. Through it all, however, weddings, bar/bat mitzvahs, and numerous other community events would increasingly find Jewish and/or Jewish/Roma musicians as a main part of the event.

Originally, *klezmer* (plural *klezmorim*) referred to the instruments played, then was extended to refer to the performers, and ultimately, to the genre of music. Klezmorim pieces are easily identifiable by their characteristic expressive melodies reminiscent of the human voice, complete with laughing and weeping.

CD 2.13

A medley of Ashkenazi music in three parts. Part I: **"Sirba mit Harbster Bletlekh,"** Part II: **"Una noche al borde de la mar,"** and Part III: **"Hey Zhankoye!"** by The Burning Bush, from the same CD (see above).

Part I: Liner notes for this selection indicate *"Sirba with falling leaves (the translated title) is a Rumanian Sirba (polka-like dance that increases in tempo and excitement) that may have been popular during the autumn Jewish festival of Sukkot, when God's care during the wandering in the Sinai wilderness is acknowledged and celebrated."* Listen also to klezmer-style clarinet tone and styling.

Best of Yiddish, Klezmer & Sephardic Music

THE BURNING BUSH

Part II: This is one of many "fusion" pieces that make up klezmer and Jewish music repertoire generally: a "Sephardic"-style song about a Jewish young man falling for a non-Jewish girl with dark eyes (perhaps Rom?). The song was acquired from Bulgarian repertoire, but is performed in klezmer style. Confused? Only if we're still looking for origins and distinct styles, rather than for the reality of the Jewish Diaspora, a *creole* (created) culture.

Part III: A Yiddish song. Zhankoye was a Jewish settlement in the Crimea in the 1930s. It was completely destroyed during WWII. The lyrics say:

> *"When you go to Sevastopol, not far from Simferopol, there you'll find a pretty little town. Who would need to seek other pleasure, it's the best by any measure, called Zhankoye, Zhan, Zhan, Zhan! If you ask a Jewish farmer, where's my brother, where's Abraham? He's driving a tractor like a train. The women operate machines, it's all beyond your wildest dreams in Zhankoye! Who says that Jews know only business—we have all heard that nonsense, are we not working men?"*

Jewish Music and Influences Today

From European composers Mahler, Milhaud, and Offenbach, to American composers Leonard Bernstein, Aaron Copeland, George and Ira Gershwin, and the composer many call the "father" of modern, or "atonal" music, Arnold Schoenberg, Jewish artists, performers, and composers have left an enormous

mark, not only on European music historically, but on post-19th-century music globally. As many of these artists were forced to leave their homes and come to the Americas, they brought not only a legacy of creativity and love for the performing arts, but the capacity to fuse arts from a variety of different venues and styles, perceptual skills which few other cultures had been trained to possess.

One example, musical theater, though an established practice in England, became an immediate venue for Jewish storytellers. As the Diaspora was forced into further migration during WWI and WWII, Jews in the New World made significant imprints in the evolution of all theatrical formats. From Yiddish theater in New York, to extensive involvement in the evolution of the Broadway theater industry, to eventually being instrumental in the evolution of the film industry, Jewish actors, directors, producers, and musicians/composers greatly assisted in the creation and promulgation of the American storytelling genres.

Today, you would be hard pressed to find a single film that does not have a Jewish director, producer, actor, or music composer, so extensive is the impact of this ancestry upon the collective cultural drive to tell stories or to create in these related genres. What stands out today, as a result of the tribulations of prior centu-

Pic. 7.5 *Photo of Arnold Schoenberg in Los Angeles, believed to be taken in 1948. Source of photo is the* Schoenberg Archives at USC. *Photo: Courtesy Florence Homolka.*

ries, is the pervasive Jewish capacity to remain flexible or to adapt to the changes in medium or influences of each generation. Although no one would wish the means by which these skills were honed on anyone, their evolution and their potential to affect our own perceptual skills is available for our education should we choose to avail ourselves of them.

Stories from the Human Family

The following is the concluding segment of an interview with Laszlo and Sandor Slomovits, from whom we heard in Unit V.

Question: *How does music become so ingrained and so important to a group of people who have suffered or been forced to move around so much?*

Sandor: *"It's historical, as much as anything. It's why business or banking, along with the arts, is so much associated with Jews. For a long time those were the only professions available to Jews. Those were the avenues that were open. But you also have a religion that thrived on music."*

Laszlo: *"One thing that just occurred to me is that for many Orthodox Jews, visual art is not empha-sized. And so you have one huge part of artistic ex-pression that is 'shut off.' Maybe that increases the emphasis on music."*

Sandor: *"Yes, if you look at the Hassidic Jewish practices, music is not just music, but a way of reach-ing or communicating with God. I can't help but think that if you grow up like we did, singing twice a day—well, it feels pretty natural.*

In the U.S. there is a much greater awareness now about the diversity within the Jewish communities. We saw the changes in Jewish lifestyle within our own lives. Before the war our father lived in small villages; after the war he moved to the big city, shaved his beard. Life was completely different. But when he moved to this country, then once again he had to change "who he was." Now today we're American, Jewish, men, the breadwinner, part Old World, part New. So now, if you ask me if I'm Jewish, the answer is yes! If you ask me if that is my primary identity—I don't know: is it American, a father, a musician?"

Pic. 7.5A *This Viennese street scene shows the complete cultural schizo-phrenia caused by racial or religious bias generally. A graphic memorial to the Holocaust is juxtaposed against a building (reputed to have been) designed by a Jewish architect and concert posters for a Mozart period concert in which, undoubtedly in Mozart's time as well as today, many of the orchestral members would be Jewish. One lesson: whenever we gener-alize "groups" of people based upon fears, greed, or ignorance, we great-ly devalue our own integrity.* Photo: Authors.

Question: *It seems that one of the things that is so vivid within the Jewish community— however, it may not have been chosen – is the capacity to adapt, to fuse, to change, to make something out of something else. Do you feel this to be true?*

Laszlo: *"Yes, in fact recently when Tibetan Buddhists were dislodged from their homelands, the Dalai Lama summoned a number of people from the Jewish community to help people adapt. They also learned from the Buddhists a whole new side of meditative practices. I think that this is also why there are whole groups of Jewish people that are drawn to the African-American cultures (by association of the "spirit" against all odds) and Buddhist meditation. When we moved to this country, I had never heard of Blues or Spirituals. But when I was thirteen and I heard spirituals, I recognized something in the music from my own experiences."*

Sandor: *"There is a remarkable list of musicians that have composed American popular music that are Jewish—from Irving Berlin to Bob Dylan and Paul Simon. It's a remarkable list—and then there was mainstream theater. There was the black vaudeville and then Yiddish theater. There were Yiddish radio shows and plays performed in Yiddish. It's extremely important to see the connection of Jewish culture to musical storytelling."*

Laszlo: *"People often come to us and say: "It's so great that you guys make a living playing music. I wish I could do that." I feel a hunger in them, but I don't believe it's about "making a living playing music." It's about expressing creativity in our lives. Our larger culture does not encourage creativity, which is not about being Jewish or any other ethnicity. It has to do with recognizing that creativity is a basic and vital part of being human. One of the things I feel we do in our concerts is to invite people to join us in the music making, and to encourage them when they go home to continue their creativity in whatever way is natural to them."*

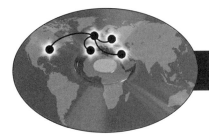

Inside the Musician's World

Sandor and Laszlo Slomovits
(Group Name: "Gemini")

Avishai Cohen,
Jazz Bassist and Composer

Note: When creating cultural musical fusions or adapting to sudden changes becomes a part of centuries of your ancestry, when flexibility becomes a part of your daily diet, and most certainly when the creative and healing potential of music, storytelling, and the collaborative performing arts become your primary mode of self-expression, then *change* is generally not something you fear. Instead, it becomes the fuel to create something new artistically. Both the music of the Slomovits brothers and that of the jazz bassist Avishai Cohen are reflections of these dynamics.

The first piece, *"The Deli Song,"* a tongue-in-cheek, klezmer-like children's song, plays on the "deli" as part of Jewish culture today, using humor and in some ways playing on the stereotypes, which generally diminishes their impact.[7.9] The second piece, *"Madrid,"* comes to us by way of Israel, Spain, Europe (generally), and the United States in the form of a jazz composition influenced by the Sephardic songs of Avishai Cohen's upbringing and his enthusiasm for rhythm, diversity in composition, and improvisation. These are some of the key elements that have also attracted numerous Jewish musicians to the field of jazz over the course of its history.

Pic. 7.8 *The resilience and determination of the human spirit is captured in this silhouette of a Jewish man praying at the Western Temple wall (Wailing Wall) in Jerusalem. Photo: Courtesy Mikhail Levit.*

"The Deli Song," performed by Sandor and Laszlo Slomovits, from the CD: <u>The Best of Gemini,</u> Gemini c. 1999.

Sandor: *"We didn't initially play for children until we were invited to play for some schools. Over a period of a couple of years we realized that we felt at home in front of those audiences. We didn't choose it; it chose us. When I started writing songs for kids, I realized I had really found my real voice.*

"'The Deli Song' is very simple in a lot of ways, and yet it has adult complexities and word play. At the same time, we've played this at every concert for the last fifteen years. If you ask someone "Is this a Jewish song?," it would never have occurred to them—and yet we've adapted it to be about Zingerman's (a famous Ann Arbor, Michigan, deli). We use Yiddish words, but that's not what they pick up on— they pick up on the spirit."

Laszlo: *"I remember sometimes people coming up to us when we used to perform cover songs (songs recorded by others) and asked us how we got into music. I'd say, "We used to be cantors"; and they'd say, "I wondered why I thought you sounded like cantors singing Bob Dylan" (laughs). Sometimes they also say, "We hear Gypsy music as well." There is definitely a connection between European Gypsy music and klezmer music as well—and, there is definitely something about being an outsider. By force or choice, when you're an outsider long enough, to some degree you have to become adaptable and flexible. Maybe that's a part of our culture."*

"Madrid," composed from the CD: <u>Avishai Cohen: At Home,</u> Razdaz Records c. 1999, gadumusic/bmi, www.avishaimusic.com

    Note: Like all of the artists in this project, Avishai Cohen and his manager, Ray, were extremely helpful in assisting us. Mr. Cohen wrote us concerning the influences that led to the creation of "Madrid:"

"I was always very excited to hear music as a kid and had many uplifting experiences from music, which made me want to be a musician. I like integrity and simplicity in music; I've always valued music of artists such as Bach and Stevie Wonder for their creative genius. I think the essence of being creative is being in touch with the inner you.

"As a man of the world and an active musician and composer, I take from life itself and the environment I'm from. This piece is a reflection of this and what I grew up on. The melody of the first part is taken from a chant that is sung on Fridays by the Sephardic Hebrew heritage. It is a Friday evening song of praising that was sung by my late grandfather, Itshak.

"I had heard it as a young child for years almost every Friday at my grandparents' house and then as a young musician wrote an arrangement for that melody which then tied into another melody of mine. I then called it "Madrid" for the Spanish connection to the piece. I thought this would best present some of my world of music. The short intro is attached to the tune as a tribute to Arabic regional music of Palestine and as a statement of peace and love between all people. I am blessed to be influenced by all music. God bless! Avishai."

The Recipe of Sound

When we contemplate the question, *"What makes creative music?,"* at the top of the list must be its uniqueness, the story or reflection of a special "fusion" of influences and, ultimately, the degree to which it leaves us with something when the listening experience is completed. Maybe for this reason, there is a large group of musicians who have come from a Jewish background that gravitated to jazz as a means of expression. When you listen to the melody of *"Madrid,"* one that is both "catchy" (repetitive and unique) and a challenge to "catch" (remember or sing after hearing), you are struck with the peaceful and relaxed quality of flute and *flugelhorn* (a softer-sounding trumpet with cylindrical bore) as it flows over the six-beat meter with flexible accents.

Majority (Influence) of "Minority" Culture

Discussion Reflection VII-B

From Euro- Musical Theater, to Yiddish Theater, to Broadway, to Hollywood

Yiddish theater consists of plays written and performed primarily by Jewish performers in Yiddish, the primary language of the European, Ashkenazi Jewish community. The range of Yiddish theatre is broad: operetta, musical comedy, and satiric or nostalgic revues; melodrama; naturalist drama; expressionist and modernist plays. At its height, its geographical scope was comparably broad: from the late 19th century until just before World War II, professional Yiddish theater could be found throughout the heavily Jewish areas of Eastern and East-Central Europe, but also in Berlin, London, Paris, and, perhaps above all, New York City.

Israil Bercovici wrote that it is through Yiddish theater that "Jewish culture entered into dialogue with the outside world," both by putting itself on display and by importing theatrical pieces from other cultures. *

Similarly, what Jewish composer John Kander calls an "interesting phenomenon that Broadway musical composers like Jerome Kern, George Gershwin and Marc Blitzstein are predominantly Jewish" comes from "the tradition established from New York's Yiddish theater." And from the first row of Ziegfeld girls in 1907 to the singing appliances in 2004's *Caroline, or Change*, the art form bears the imprint of immigrant culture—and particularly the Jewish experience.

"There would be no American musical without Jews," says Laurence Maslon, associate professor of arts at New York University. "Their influence is corollary to the influence of black musicians on jazz; there were as many Jews involved in the form" (Maslon is co-writer with Michael Kantor of the production *Broadway: The American Musical*). **

And finally, as East Coast acting troupes and, later, film entrepreneurs such as the Jewish Warner Brothers moved out to the West coast, it was not long until the formula of musical theater—dramatic music played behind the acting, formulas of tension and narrative building leading to emotional climax (song or action), and, later, a succession of technological advances from sound added to film, to fully "talking pictures," to color and advanced cinematography as we know it today—put Jewish interests and affinities for storytelling and creativity at the forefront of the most compelling innovations in motion picture evolution.

Question
- *Based on what you know or understand of the historical evolution of Jewish culture(s), why might such a passion for musical storytelling have evolved? How has this evolution impacted you or your tastes and storytelling values?*

*Bercovici, Israil, *O sut_ de ani de teatru evreiesc în România* [Translation: "One Hundred Years of Yiddish/Jewish Theater in Romania"], 2nd Romanian-language edition, Bucharest, 1998, p.103.
**From: Shapiro, Samantha, "The Arts: A Jewish Street Called Broadway," *Hadassah Magazine*, October 2004 Vol. 86 No.2. Accessed 11 February 2006).

Under the Radar (Part II): The Creativity of the "Romani"

The opening page of the Association of Gypsies / Romani International website, which assisted us in locating musicians and Roma/Rom scholars, begins with the phrase: *"Gypsy, one scattered race, like stars in the sight of God."* Then later, a poem ("The Dreamers") by Theodosia Garrison:

> *"The Gypsies passed her little gate, / She stopped her wheel to see.*
> *A brown faced pair who walked the road, / Free as the wind is free;*
> *And suddenly her tidy room / A prison seemed to be.*
> *She watched the footer (walking) Gypsies pass; / She never knew or guessed,*
> *The wistful dream that drew them close, / The longing in each ear,*
> *Some day to know a home like hers, / Wherein their hearts might rest."*

But most touching was this mission statement:

> *"The Association is a non-profit association with the intention of giving glory to God, of preserving, maintaining, promoting our Roma culture, ethnicity, pride and integrity. It is time to halt the negativism that is prevalent about us, time to dissipate the prejudice, we are loyal, intelligent, God loving people! Let us proceed in the 21st century, as one united people among all with the honest, truthful purpose of Loving God, and loving our fellow humans …"*

By varied accounts, there are between 12 and 15 million Roma in the world today. Through the changes and chances of evolution, Romani communities became highly evolved in music and dance, and created a musical legacy that is either responsible or partly responsible for the following musical developments and innovations that can be said to have affected much of our planet's music:

Pic. 7.8 *A Romani family traveling (1837 print). The perpetual need to uproot, to find a new home because of persecution and lack of acceptance contrasts with other accounts that "Rom prefer isolation or lack the desire to integrate." We might ask, should self-isolation, closely guarded community orientation, and even acts of resistance or mistrust of others occur if we continue to maintain that human beings and cultures are equal but different? What perpetuated this tendency? The simplest action is to find faults with other cultures. Especially as concerns cultures mistreated over centuries, the more difficult of paths might be to ask: What might I (my culture or my ancestors) have done to perpetuate these actions? To this extent, perhaps, Western cultures and specifically Western education are sorely in need of greater work as concerns an equal consideration of others* Photo: Public domain and courtesy Wikipedia.org.

Pic. 7.8A *From the photo series "Andalucia se escribe con c'," a Romani woman watches others against a graffiti backdrop. Regrettably, so strong has been the persecution and ill-acceptance of the Romani that only recently have (primarily young) Romani scholars, lawyers, and teachers begun to voice substantial opposition, assisted, in many cases, by others who desire to reverse the injustice of centuries.* Photo: Courtesy Alija, 2005.

- The development or assisted development of the flat-back ud—eventually to become the *vihuela* and later the "Spanish guitar," and, finally, the guitar. Theories for the design change range from the portability and capacity to play and walk that led to the convenience of creating a hollow-bodied ud with a flattened back or to acoustic (sound) qualities.

- The development or assisted-development of the violin. The "legitimization" and ultimate "invention" of the violin (from the rababa—earlier versions) to its current state is speculation. What is not speculation is that the violin appears in the music of Roma and Jewish communities as early as in any other culture group in Europe. Clearly, its use and acceptance amongst the Roma and Jewish community precedes its adoption in many other culture groups or its acceptance in church, art, or "classical" music.

- The creation of a wide body of songs and dances that may well be the most influential of all culture groups in popular or social/community settings. Even Jewish music was substantially influenced by interaction with Roma musicians. Bob Cohen writes: *"When I began to record music in Romania in the late 1980s, many of the elder Gypsy musicians I approached in Transylvania enthusiastically played Jewish tunes for me, alongside the Romanian and Transylvanian Hungarian music I was asking after. I was intrigued. Where had they learned these tunes? From playing for Jewish weddings, they answered. And so, I began to learn something of the styles and repertoire of Jewish music from the elder generation of gypsy musicians… ."*

What becomes obvious as we begin to further investigate the accomplishments of Roma culture is that this culture group, perhaps as much as or more than African-American or Native American, Jewish, or African culture groups, has been the victim of Eurocentrism and glaring omission from Western education. This version of "repression by mis-education," perhaps more than graphic persecution or blatant bias, is a more subtle, and therefore lethal, form of bias. By omitting groups wholesale from our collective history, we fortify the belief in a greater legitimacy of the majority culture. Whatever we may think or say personally, when the "less than" stigma of a culture group is reinforced by otherwise seemingly objective institutions (accomplished through minimalist or distorted inclusion), we practically *must* take on the biases, and generally without awareness.

The well-known linguist (and person of Romani descent), Ian Hancock writes:

> *"I want to be able to watch epics such as Schindler's List and learn that Gypsies were a central part of the Holocaust, too; or other films … and not hear the word 'Gypsy' except once, and then only as the name of somebody's dog."* [7.10] The Association of Romani International article goes on to say: *"(This) cynical statement reflects a notable controversy: one that concerns itself with not only the manufacturing of our current pop culture but the questioning of our historical records and the challenging of our very perception of truth, which, admittedly, is often at the mercy of blinding ethnocentrism."* [7.11]

How did such a mis-representation of some of our most vibrant culture groups go so long without a greater flood of voices confronting the injustice? Who is this culture and from where did it originate?

Originally from India, and likely an Indo-Aryan group with a linguistic mix of Punjabi and Hindi, Romani people were predominantly part of the lower class, promoted to "warrior" class to augment the Aryan warriors in meeting the Islamic conquest of the 10th and 11th centuries. They were expelled from their homeland nearly 1,000 years ago and, like the Jewish community, were forced into a lifestyle of perpetual migration and defensive posturing to sustain life and community. Some groups went South into the Middle East and North Africa; most went West across Afghanistan, Persia, Turkey, Greece, through the Balkan and Slavic states, and eventually into Western Europe. Many were made into slaves (in the Balkans—now Romania), but by the 1500s, there were documented groups of Romani in nearly every European region.[7.12]

Lifestyles of repressed or minority-status cultures are greatly determined by the doors of opportunity that are left "opened" or "unopened" for them. The creativity and enormous capacity of the human spirit then generally takes those avenues to the highest possible heights of respectability. In the case of the Romani cultures, music, dance, and the creation of elaborate social and community rituals became a regular part of community life. As these skills and predispositions evolved, they (and other skills such as blacksmithing, leatherworking, etc.) became the primary means by which exchange with non-Roma people would occur at each juncture and location of their extensive migration.

Though few nations or cultures have yet found their way to the acknowledgment of Roma contributions to their nation's musical canons, this is likely not because the influence is not there but rather because of a continuing lack of awareness, humility, or sustained prejudice toward these culture groups, perpetuated by a long history of disassociation, avoidance, and the maintenance of horrific stereotyping and mis-education.

Note: We had established contact with four diverse scholars of Romani culture in Spain, Hungary, Romania, and Minnesota (U.S.). Each seemed enamored with the project, but initially we were unable to obtain a single entry. What becomes apparent, and is discouraging in the context of the need for an accurate portrayal of Roma culture from *their voices and visions,* is the silent residue of severe and prolonged bias. Individuals of repressed and pervasively under-appreciated culture groups must/will:

Pic. 7.9 *This 19th century print of Roma musicians does not even begin to capture the plausible and important contributions of the multiplicity of Roma groups (throughout Europe and North Africa) to the evolution of both musical styles and instruments. Additionally, now with an estimated 10 million Romani descendants throughout much of the world (including the Americas, Asia, Africa, and the Pacific), it would be impossible to quantify the contributions and exchanges that have occurred between Romani and other cultures worldwide.* Photo: Courtesy Wikipedia.org and Bogdangiusca.

- Struggle more pervasively with acquiring a sense of self-esteem and self-worth. It takes so much more energy to view yourself as "worthy" when every sign around you (in society at large) points to the opposite.

- Be forced to mistrust and examine the motives and possibilities of the world around them. The natural instinct to trust, once abused and mistreated, is difficult to revive. Furthermore, techniques of proving the trust of others take considerable energy and greatly slow the rate of advancement.

- Turn on themselves as a means of venting the emotional frustrations and pain of mistreatment. The annals of conflicts within repressed communities are filled with abuse, neglect, addictions, or creation of an intricate bias system of their own.

When we see these phenomena playing out in our communities, the humanity within us should scream at perhaps the ultimate of injustices. Fortunately for us, a second attempt to reach Roma scholars, musicians, dancers, and the general worldwide Roma Diaspora (which included many non-Rom working on behalf of Romani cultures) resulted in a number of comments and submissions, which we gratefully could include.

Stories from the Human Family

Note: One submission from a non-Roma (Romani) activist was touching on numerous levels. First, it showed the pervasive and repetitive phenomenon that occupies less presence in Western scholarship than even an accurate portrayal of the repressed culture groups themselves, i.e., that there are always populations of the repressive culture groups who sacrifice on behalf of justice; second, it re-emphasized the dynamic that repressed groups' music, musicians, and creative contributions inevitably find great appeal with the masses (whenever politics leave even the smallest loophole for their emergence); but, deplorably, third, when a repressed culture group does not own the systems of "capital" and propagation (business, marketing venues), it will seldom receive a just compensation for its work and efforts in respect to its influence.

Claude Cahn was the acting executive director of the European Roma Rights Center, located in Budapest, Hungary, at the time we received his email submission. Though non-Romani himself, he has obviously been profoundly touched by the culture and has dedicated much of his life to work on its behalf. He wrote:

"In the 1970s and especially after the death of Yugoslav leader Josip Broz Titos in 1980, in the framework Yugoslavia erected to grapple with the national grievances that were a recurrent feature of its history, Romani popular culture flourished. The pre-Milosevic Yugoslav government struggled to assuage Slovene, Albanian and Croatian complaints of oppression and Serb-domination in the federal system by promoting non-Serbs and encouraging the growth of "national" and "ethnic" cultures. Romani culture—no threat to the state— was especially promoted, and Romani radio and television programs appeared on the state broadcasting network in Belgrade, Skopje, and Pristina.

"In this context, Romani popular music exploded, and the undisputed maximum king of the "Nove Romske Pesme"—the new Romani song—was Saban Bajramovic. One could call Saban the Yugoslav Romani Frank Sinatra—he is something of a crooner—but to do so would miss both his songwriting brilliance and his ambition to express something essentially Romani. But beyond a rich ear for pop melody lies an ambition to provide an honest portrayal of the Romani world; songs like "Djordjev Dan" rarely see expression via mass media such as radio and television. And when Saban sings, "Hey, another beating by the police..." to Roma in their native language, Romani audiences listening in the early 1980s must have heard a piece of their experience that they never imagined could come through the speaker of a radio. Maybe a better comparison is Woody Guthrie.

Pic. 7.9-1 *A "nomadic" lifestyle in the Romani community was the result of both persecution and, over time, the evolution of cultural preferences. It is possible that the evolution Roma culture could also lead to a pervasive disdain for "ownership," including of one's own creativity. Dragi Sestic from* <u>Mostar Sevdah Reunion</u> *wrote about Saban Bajramovic: "Over the years, his music has been constantly stolen, copied, and imitated by both famous and unknown musicians. Where others would have earned millions, he's lived as he's always lived: from day to day, making music, going wherever he wants, and not recognizing any limits at all."* Photo: Romani caravan, courtesy and copyright, Saints 4757.

"The only problem is that many non-Roma—especially Yugoslavs—cannot stomach listening to him. In the first place, he sings ballads in a language they can't understand. More importantly, his whole atmosphere is drenched in 'Gypsiness,' and anti-Romani sentiment is presently at high tide in Central and Eastern Europe. With his gold tooth and his Muslim name, he is the epitome of Romani strangeness all over the former Yugoslavia—a kind of too-familiar false Turkish

exoticism: hence the role for a cultural translator. A talented composer like Bregovic can take Bajramovic's genius for pop melody and render it suitable for non-Romani audiences.

"In late December 2000, I visited Niš, Yugoslavia, the hometown of Saban Bajramovic. Four of us—Dragan, Martin, Refika and myself—spent a snowy morning kicking around town and finally wound up in a CD shop, where Martin bought a copy of Saban Bajramovic's greatest hits, issued by a Slovene record label. A few hours after buying the CD and much excited discussion, we had worked up the nerve to go and visit Saban.

"His wife did not want to let us in. Saban was ill, and apparently quite a few Saban fans visit the Bajramovic household hoping to meet the maximum king. After some brief pleading on the doorstep and a promise not to stay long, however, she relented, and let us into the kitchen. Saban appeared in a shabby blue and green bathrobe and plastic slippers, looking distinctly less sharp than his pressed-suit-and-gold-tooth stage persona. Indeed, he looked ill, his cheeks cut with deep lines and a pair of large square wire-framed reading glasses sloping at an oblique angle across his eyebrows. Mrs. Bajramovic poured us all coffees and orange soda. A couple of children played past a door in the other room.

"'Who owned his music? Saban was evasive. Martin produced the CD he had purchased earlier that day. 'Had he ever seen it?' 'Was he receiving any royalties for it?' 'Had he been paid for it?' Saban thought he probably had signed some papers; maybe he had them somewhere. 'Could we see them?' He wasn't really sure where they were; he would have to look for them. 'Had he received any money for "Mesecina"?' Maybe, he wasn't sure. Refika explained that possibly we could help him try to secure money he might be owed if he could show us the papers. Saban looked unsure. Mrs. Bajramovic reappeared, concerned, and after another round of orange soda, we were ushered back out the door.

"He no doubt signed away all rights, we concluded, in exchange for a handful of cash that probably seemed large, but is a tiny fragment of what the underground soundtrack earns in France, where "World Music" is a cash cow." (June 2005)

Note: In another note, we gained insight into the degree of enthusiasm a vast majority of Romani people have for their culture,

Pic. 7.9A &B *Against the backdrop of an 1852 Romanian poster, which advertises an auction of 38 Roma slaves (in "fine condition") is the impact of history upon nearly 8-10 million Roma today. Many young Romani, such as these girls from Spain (1917), await any form of acceptance and acknowledgement for the significant contributions their ancestors made to nearly all European culture groups.* Photos: Public domain and courtesy Wikipedia.org.

its music, and, in particular, the enormous impact Roma musicians made on the development of the violin and its performance as exemplified by one of the greatest violin performers of all time, Niccolo Paganini. Tom Odley, media officer for the International Romani Guild. wrote:

"Dear Michael, good day to you and yours. Having regard to your request for contributions and for brief commentary concerning the influence of Romani music, I would point to the undoubted impact and influence (presumably for good?) of that renowned (Romano) virtuoso of the violin, Niccolo Paganini, of whom it was said, "He played as though inspired by the Devil himself!" Paganini's story formed the basis for the well-received film "The Magic Violin."

"Overall, I believe it rightful to claim that Paganini's music and his playing, with his mastery of the violin, will serve as a benchmark in any history of music. If music be an international language, then truly, Paganini, the most famous of all "Gypsy" violinists, spoke it as fluently as his mother-tongue, holding the world spellbound with his musical speeches. Amare Devel amensa! (Our God be with us!) O.Tom Odley, (Romanichal)"

Inside the Musician's World

Taraful Din Baia

Note: The Roma in Romania (the name "Romania" is only coincidentally similar to Roma or Romani—it was derived from connotations to the Roman Empire) are among the largest populations of Roma in Europe. However, in Romania, Romani people were slaves until the 19th century. Ute Entwistle writes: *"Even Gypsy musicians were slaves of landowners, princes, and kings or could be forcefully enlisted into army service as musicians."* Romanian Roma music is a mixture of folk songs and a musical fusion of cultures, including Romanian, Hungarian, and Russian, although songs of Greek, Spanish, Hebrew (Jewish), and any other varieties of languages and culture groups are likely to be found as well in the repertoire of the *Bidinari, or Lautari,* (small Romani bands).

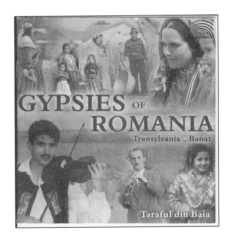

The instruments used by *Tarful Din Baia,* the group in this recording, include violin, **taragot** (the precursor to the clarinet and oboe), accordion, keyboards (today nearly all Romani bands use synthesizers or keyboards), percussion, and voice. Other instruments frequently in Romani music would include the **tambal** (cymbalum or hammer dulcimer), clarinets, trumpets, guitar or ud, and a variety of percussion, including tambourines or drums. In Moldavia, large brass bands (walking bands and the precursors to European military bands and later American military and marching bands) were an outgrowth of Rom fusion with Janissary bands from Turkey during the 14th-18th centuries.[7.13]

Taraful Din Baia plays primarily at wedding parties throughout Romania. Their music is a fusion of Romanian (Transylvanian and from Banat) and Serbian influences. If you were to trace the repertoire, instruments, songs, lyrics, and even life stories of most Romani bands, however, you would see, as with many European-born Jewish musicians as well, that looking for a "single" culture or label to attach to the musicians greatly diminishes their fusion reality. The search for origins or some mythical standard of purity trivializes the value of such cultures generally.

CD 2.16

A medley of three pieces. Part I: **"Banatana,"** Part II: **"Doina lui Cozma,"** and Part III: **"Trec Tiganii,"** by Taraful din Baia, from the CD: <u>Gypsies of Romania,</u> Arc Music International, c. 2000.

Each of the three pieces sampled below has a distinct and unique quality.

Part I: "Banatana" (Dance from Banat)

The first, an incredible dance from the Banat region of Romania, is a complex melody that requires enormous technical proficiency (*good technique in music* implies the musicians are well trained in their instrument). Listen to the *rhythmic precision* and the *togetherness* of the musicians, even as the tempo increases in speed (musicians usually say the music is *tight,* meaning well organized and synchronized with the pulse and rhythm).

Part II: "Doina lui Cozma (Cozma's doina [a song originating with the shepherds of Romania])

The second piece is a *lament,* a common song form in much of Eastern Europe and Russia. For centuries, Rom shepherds used the *taragot* (the precursor to the oboe) as a favorite instrument for passing time, and playing, in this case, what amounts to a "blues-like" piece—a song that will drain the emotion (truth) and sentiments of the moment from the musician.

Part III: "Trec Tiganii" (Gypsies are passing by)

The final piece is a song that is very familiar to most Romanians. It conveys the general story-telling qualities of Rom songs and, in this case, reveals something of the Romani lifestyle, especially the "nomadic" quality that was pervasive, especially to the musicians in each region.

Translated lyrics:

> *"In colorful wagons Gypsies are passing by*
> *A Gypsy woman with no sons counts her money*
> *Another one in a cornfield with a shell – tells the fortune of a virgin*
> *A Gypsy plays the violin with passion – Other Gypsies are dancing in a circle*
>
> *Chorus: Gypsies are passing by – They are leaving and have fun*
> *Gypsies are passing by without stopping – but they love each other*
>
> *At the end of a road they lit a fire*
> *Around the fire they started to dance*
> *The night has a magic full moon*
> *I cannot forget the love of the Gypsy woman,*
> *They live a happy life*
> *Sleeping in peace in their tents*

Pic. 7.11 and 7.11A (Left) – "Dana" Dan Daniel plays the violin and leads the band of young musicians practicing one of the oldest traditions of Romani culture: in performing for social functions. (Above) – A Rom caravan wagon and a remnant of a not-too-distant lifestyle, one virtually consistent for a period of nearly eight centuries. Photo: Courtesy and copyright, Verity Johnson.

Poetry in Motion—Romani Dance Traditions

Note: Fortunately, we also heard from a dancer and dance instructor, Simona Jovic, who was living in France at the time. She wrote:

> *"I am a Roma dance teacher and I saw your email in Romano Liloro group. Although I'm not a specialist in Roma music history, I can say that it's impossible to separate the dance from the music. To do so, you obscure the nature of the tradition. I'm fortunate to have a relatively deep knowledge of the history of Roma dances from Rajasthan and Punjab, through Egypt, Armenia, Turkey, Balkans (I'm Serbian), Central and Eastern Europe, and Spain. I've been teaching Roma dances for years now—all around Europe and am myself constantly fascinated by the diversity of dance styles and the passion with which both the music and dance are performed. They certainly show some of the mixture and diversity in Romani culture."*

Ms. Jovic wrote the following descriptions of the dances:

Kalbelya – *"This is a Romani dance from Rajahstan. It belongs to the Kalbelya casta (ethnic group), from the Thar Desert in Western India. It deals with the infamous snake charmers and magicians who entertained in the region. The dance imitates the cobra, trying to transmit the seductive mystery of its place in Indian legends. The dancer turns and moves a lot with an important emphasis on the softness of her movement. The costume basis is a black dress, from which comes the name Kalbelya, as Kalo means black."*

Ghawazee – *"This is a Romani dance from Upper Egypt. It belongs to the Rom from the Nawwar tribe, many of which were professional dancers and d musicians who showed off their talent in the streets, fairs, or weddings. A very lively and joyful dance, the movements focus mainly upon the movement of the abdomen (or belly—from which the term "belly dancing" was derived). For example, the body shakes forward, backwards. The woman who dances does so to the rhythm and rhythmic patterns of the musicians. She uses special little cymbals called Sagat. She often stops to make the public get active in the show, as participation and inclusion of all is a feature common to most Romani dances and music. The dancer usually wears a long red dress called Galabya. Today the newer costume is a shorter skirt."*

Ciftetelli/Karsilama – *"These are a couple of Romani dances from Turkey. They use two types of rhythms. There is, on the first side, the regular rhythm 8/8 (ciftetelli), which can be either fast or slow and, on the other side, the irregular rhythm 9/8 (karsilama). The Turkish dance is easy to recognize because its expression has various kinds of movements. Movements aren't really more or less sophisticated than in the oriental Egyptian dance, or in the Arabic Raq sharki. These dances are in fact related. The woman uses her body to emphasize the Karsilama accents, with a great deal of precision in her body and arm/hand movement. These body movements can vary greatly from one musical sentence to another. The use of Zills, which are the Turkish equivalent of the Egyptian Sagats (finger cymbals) is very frequent, as well as Calpara, which can be described as wooden spoons. The basic costume includes very wide trousers."*

Cocek – *"This dance comes from Southern Balkans, Macedonian, Bulgaria and the Bujanovac/ Nis Region in Serbia. It's very lively, light and gracious. It can be danced either individually by women, or together with both men and women. It remains 'Oriental' because of the five centuries of Turkish occupation. On the toes, the dancer does precise and quiet moves, with focus generally centered on the shoulders or on the ankles. The costume is a pair of wide trousers too, as well as the Opanci, Serbian traditional handmade shoes."*

The Flamenca Dance – *"This is a Romani dance from the Al Andalus (Andalusia) region of Southern Spain, which includes a fusion with Jewish and North African cultures as well. The Flamencas are where Gypsy families settled down for a very long time. They developed a very special and wide culture in which the dance (El Baile in Spanish) and the singing (El canto in Spanish), blend together and interact like a single character. Very much like the "Caracter" dance (see below), the Flamenca (Flamenco) dance can be defined as a mixing of grace and rage or extreme passion. Both men and women dance it, using the shaking of hands (las palmas) and feet (Zapateado/ Zapata=shoe in Spanish, a source of many styles of dance from Spain to Mexico). According to the type of song (el Palo), the emotions can express a very strong pain and a very deep emotion, which must have been essential to the survival of the people amidst the extreme repression that occurred after the Spanish Inquisition. This deep emotional singing is called the Canto hondo in Spanish, meaning deep chant. In addition, real joy can be also expressed. In fact, today, there is much more joy and celebration in the songs and dances."*

The "Caractere" Romani Dance – *"This is a Rom dance from Central and Eastern Europe. The countries covered by it include: Romania, Hungary, Slovakia, and Russia. In Central Europe, there are two types of Romani dances, called 'Caractere.' There are those that use the dancing songs 'Khelemaski Gil' and those that use the slow songs or 'Loki Gili,' which will be used for a very deep dance in which the dancer moves slowly for quite a long duration. The dancer uses the scarf as an accessory. Men dance as much as women, especially in Russia, where the famous kicking of the feet on the ground is found. The dances also uses high heel shoes and the shaking of hands in much the same manner as the Flamenca dance is also characteristic. The costume is a wide skirt and a scarf."*

Stories from the Human Family

Note: The following story from Peter Stan, a Rom musician brought up in Australia and now living in New York City, demonstrates a common path by which many musicians of all backgrounds come into music.

> *"I was born in a small village in the Banat in Serbia to Romanian Rom parents. My father's music, and thus my music, has always combined Romanian and Serbian Rom motifs. He always wanted to play the accordion, but his parent's couldn't afford to buy him one. Because many Rom are poor, they do not always get to play the instrument of their choice—often it is whatever is cheapest or available. By the time my father was 34 years old, he played several instruments including the nai (panflute). At 34, my father left Serbia, went to Italy, and finally made his new*

home in Melbourne, Australia, where I was born. Ever since I can remember, I heard Romani music in the home. I remember my father going to play with his accordion (he finally purchased one in Australia) for a Romani wedding where he would be away for 2-3 days. I remember being quite young and going through my father's coat pockets, which were full of money. He never had any idea of how much it was, so we would all count it together on the kitchen table.

"My father became known as one of the best accordionists playing for Romani and Balkan gigs (musical jobs) throughout Australia. And now, when I think back, I realize he was being called to perform all the time. However, he regretted that he only began playing the accordion really well at age 35 or 36. He was upset that his father didn't buy him one when he was very young. So when I was born, he made sure an accordion was in the house just for me to see it, touch it, and squeeze a note out. I thought this was really cool, so I decided to learn to play the accordion as well. After a little while, I was playing tunes by ear and everyone was encouraging me. They said I was very musical. But I never really took it seriously until I moved with my family to the United States. When I met my other relatives for the first time, I saw they were all playing music. So this encouraged me to take up the accordion more seriously. Everyone complimented me on my playing, but something was missing. They were not sure at first, and finally they realized I was not playing the mordants (melodic ornamentation) correctly. Playing the mordants in Rom music is very important. And so I began to carefully listen to the Romani violinists to see how they played the mordants, and then I tried to copy them.

"Today I play Rom, klezmer, classical, and Balkan music. What I find funny is whenever I meet someone and they find out I am Romani, they assume that I, or any Romani for that matter, am a good musician. Many of us are and, including myself, have studied music. But like any other Romani, my skill doesn't come literally from my blood. I appreciated my father's accordion playing, but if I didn't practice I wasn't going to become the musician I am today just by osmosis. Most people know very little about us. And when they think they know something, it is often a negative stereotype. Little do these people, the "gaje," know how much we have influenced the folk music in Spain, Yugoslavia, Romania, Hungary, and Russia. We Romani have given much to the various kinds of European folk musics and hope people will remember this the next time they encounter us." Peter Stan, Romani Accordionist, NYC, NY, (mrharmony03@aol.com).

Pic. 7.11D *Romani musicians Marin Florian and Bulugh Gheorghe, of Romania, make their living traveling through much of Europe playing their accordions, looking for ways to advance. When asked to play which songs they'd prefer, they smiled, mounted their accordions and played with a passion and sincere love for music. It was easy to see why Romani musicians were among the first to be called to dances and social events in much of Europe.* Photo: Courtesy Marin and Bulugh, Authors.

Jewish-Rom Connection

In attempting to get information from Rom musicians and scholars, we received a wonderful treat from a musician, documentary film director, and scholar of Jewish music, particularly klezmer music, Yale Strom. Himself an author of three books— *The Book of Klezmer* (Acapella Books), *A Wandering Feast"* (Jossey Bass), and *The Absolutely Complete Klezmer Songbook* (Transcontinental Music)— Mr. Strom's greatest legacy as an author is that he brings the sensitivity of a musician to discussions of other musicians. His books and the comments below show the respect he gives the musicians' opinions and stories. In this case, he demonstrates the connection between Jewish and Romani cultures. Yet he also speaks of the "void" or stigma that put the Rom musician even "lower" on the ladder of cultural hierarchy.

Pic. 7.12 *Romani musician Paul Babici (right) plays a tune with Yale Strom (left) as they share not only stories but the language that has transcended every form of bias, barrier, or separatist belief between religions, races, and cultures since the beginning of time: music and dance.* Photo: Courtesy Yale Strom.

"Rom Musicians Playing Klezmer"

Mr. Strom writes:

> *"The Rom and the Jews shared many similar histories during their many centuries of wandering throughout Europe. Both would (at times) be welcomed to settle in a particular country, only to be summarily expelled by the gaje/gentiles after some time and not allowed to return legally for centuries. When the Jews settled in the hinterlands of Eastern Europe (14th and 15th centuries), their relationship with the Rom was primarily an economic one. The Jews provided services for the Rom such has selling and mending clothes, shoes, household items, etc. In return, the Rom fixed and sharpened tools, sold them horses, wooden cutlery, tin bowls, and such.*

> *"These meetings between the two groups were generally cordial but not without suspicion. Unfortunately neither the Rom nor the Jews were exempt from having been influenced by the cultural prejudices and stereotypes that were rampant throughout Eastern Europe. Both groups of people held certain biases against one another, possibly until they realized that they had been treated equally as pariahs by the Nazis and their collaborators during World War II.*

> *"One specific profession, however, where the Rom and Jews shared a symbiotic relationship, and most of their members were simpatico with each other, was in the music world. Jews and Rom in Europe had been sharing the same stage since the sixteenth century. There were Jews who performed in Rom bands (and even learned to speak a Romani dialect) and Rom who played in Jewish bands (some learning to speak Yiddish). It was in the middle of the nineteenth century when the Rom musicians played a specific role in many of the **shtetl** celebrations.*

*"Specifically in Transylvania, the Carpathian Mountains, Bukovina, and Bessarabia, often the only musicians to play **klezmer** in the small villages were the Rom. The klezmorim (pl.) and Rom musicians had several things in common: they were often itinerant, they knew how to play a variety of different kinds of melodies depending on who hired them (Ukrainians, Romanians, Polish, Slovaks, etc.), generally the violinist was the leader and most revered in the band, and klezmer and Rom music shared some of the same musical principles: melismatic melodies, modal scales, and improvisation.*

"Over the many years of having conducted klezmer field research among the Jews and Rom, I met many Rom who taught me klezmer melodies (I had never heard many, or they had never been written down), as well as unique versions of some very well-known klezmer tunes.

Even among the Khasidim, one could find Rom musicians playing for the Rebbes and their followers on special occasions and holidays. The Stefaneshti Rebbe in Moldavia often was entertained by a band that had both Rom and Jews in it.

"While conducting my field research in the Carpathian village of Vilok, Ukraine, I met several Rom bands that played klezmer and Yiddish folk songs at non-Jewish dances, weddings, and other celebrations. Some of them even remembered the Yiddish lyrics and knew what they meant. But though they still played some of the Jewish repertoire, they nearly all lamented the fact that there were no Jews left to really appreciate and for whom they could play this music. One musician commented:

Pic. 7.13 *A couple of the things that draw the most unlikely of partners to the table are hardships and celebrations. In this case, Roma musicians play klezmer music at a Jewish wedding. Very little can keep culture groups apart, once they become connected by the events of the life cycle and the music that connects us to community.* Photo: Courtesy of Yale Strom.

'I had a band that had two Jews and three Rom including myself. During the 1970s through the mid-'80s, we traveled throughout the Carpathian region, even sometimes playing in Bukovina. I played the accordion, my brother the violin, my cousin the violin, and the two Jews played drums and bass. Both Jewish guys had graduated from the conservatory of music. When we played for Jewish weddings and other parties, the drummer was the leader. First, he could speak and sing in Yiddish. Secondly, the clients felt more comfortable if a Jew was leading the band, since he knew their ways. When we played for the gaje (non-Jews) like the Ukrainians or Hungarians, it was good to let them know that several of our musicians were Jewish and conservatory graduates. For them, having Jewish musicians play at their wedding meant they got the best for their money and they could be trusted more than us Rom. We played a lot, and we were all close. When the bassist and drummer immigrated to Israel I went with them to the airport in Budapest to say goodbye. We were good friends. We lost many talented musicians to Israel.' " Yale Strom, June, 2005.

Note: We received an email from Barry Fisher, a human rights lawyer (and partner at Fleishman & Fisher, L.A./CA.) who is also a musician. He has worked extensively on behalf of Romani human rights internationally, including service as the Romani claims point person on the multinational negotiations resulting in wartime claims treaties with Germany and Austria as well as claims against Swiss banks. As a Jewish musician with extensive interest in klezmer music, and a lawyer and speaker on behalf of the rights of Romani people, he learned early in his career how to combine working on legal issues and playing for weddings, engagements, and funerals. Eventually, he began to organize concerts and recordings, which addressed both music and issues of justice, thus combining his two passions. He wrote:

> *"In the 1960s I took classes from a renowned Romani scholar and traveled in Eastern Europe, where I had my initial contact with Roma communities. After much experience as a human rights lawyer, in the 1980s I began representing Romani cases both here and abroad. I successfully represented John Stevens and his wife, who were Machwaya (Serbian) Rom, in the California Supreme Court. As a result of this, sometime later in organizing 'Yiddishkayt,' a Los Angeles city-wide festival in 1998 with my group the 'Ellis Island Band,' we continued to expand the exploration of the Jewish-Rom (KlezRom) connection.*

> *"So, as one of the events for 'Yidishkayt' 2000, I suggested that we invite musicians and singers from two L.A. Romani communities and that we do a KlezRom concert exploring each other's music and playing music common to both cultures. The idea of the concert was to explore some intersections, and fusions, of the music of two marginalized peoples of Europe, the Jews and the Roma. The Jewish musicians for Central and Eastern Europe were ubiquitous in the areas where Jews were forced to live. Their repertoire and musical flavors varied with the local ethnicities, and were as modulatory and perpetually changing as the lives and conditions of the Jewish people.*

> *"Klezmorium (the plural of klezmer) played for Romani festivities and vice-versa. There were mixed groups of Romani and Jewish musicians, who, in 1880, also began migrating to America to avoid further persecution. Although klezmer music was almost forgotten following the dislocation of Jewish communities during the Holocaust, in the 1970s klezmer music, much like jazz, began to be revived, serving as a metaphor for the continual exchange of cultures in close contact with one another.*

> *"At the concert, a little more than twenty years since the beginning of a klezmer renaissance, we continued the cross-cultural dialogue with a concert of the hot music played today at Jewish and Romani weddings in Los Angeles. The concert was dedicated to Joe's father, Vanya, te avel yerto, a Rom baro and master mandolinist."* (Barry A. Fisher, Attorney/co-founder "Ellis Island Band," June 2005)

The Trans-/Intercontinental Musician: "Harmonia"

Lest we begin to think that only classical musicians, Jewish, or Roma musicians still living within the culture/country themselves have contributed to the legacies of musical exchange and creative fusions in Russia and Europe, we come to the phenomenon that is now more the norm than the exception today: *trans- or intercontinental exchange* between musicians. Virtually every piece in the compilation of recordings for this project has some form of intercontinental exchange at the core of its existence.

As one illustration, the unstable political situation of the late 19th century in much of Eastern Europe—and later the World Wars—led to massive migration of Russians and Eastern Europeans to the United States and Canada. The migration coincided with the Industrial Revolution of the United States, and large communities of Eastern Europeans congregated to many of North America's larger cities.

Following the collapse of communism in the 1990s, a new generation of Russians and Eastern European immigrants found their way to North America. Many of them were "professional musicians" whose funding by the state had now been removed. Dimitri Vietze writes on behalf of the Cleveland, Ohio-based group Harmonia:

Pic. 7.14 *So pervasive is the cross-cultural influence in the creation of our world's instruments and music. However, much of this is only visible when we spend time outside of our familiar cultural environment. From this vantage point, we begin to see our inter-connectivity— as in the music of the regions of Western Russia and Eastern Europe, brought together in a fusion of styles through "Harmonia," out of Cleveland, Ohio.* Photo: Courtesy the Itxtlan Artist's group and "Harmonium."

> *"An unexpected cultural pendulum is swinging from Eastern Europe to a city with more Slovenians than any other city in the world outside of Slovenia. In the past decade, as political and economic woes have driven Croats, Serbs, Carpatho-Rusyns, Ukrainians, and Slovaks to America, the music and culture of Eastern Europe has undergone a resurgence in the Ohio city of Cleveland."*

One of the members Harmonia explains how earlier, back "at home," people even forty kilometers away would know which village you come from by the clothes you wore or songs you sang. But this too is changing rapidly, and transcontinental exchange of music and ideas is occurring at ever-increasing rates, not only in the United States but throughout the world. Although the phenomenon of fusion and exchange is built into the fabric of the American nations or *creole* societies worldwide (see Unit X), the phenomenon of transcontinental and intercultural exchange between culture bearers in new locations and those in the "homeland" is one of most predominant and accelerated means by which our world is changing its identity. Alexander Fedoriouk, the cimbalom player and male vocalist in *Harmonia*, comments on the past:

> *"...in the Ukraine, why would Ukrainians try to play Bulgarian music, when there are hundreds of Bulgarians who can play it real well? Here (in the United States) it is different. People put things together and see what they can come up with. It's more common to collaborate, which makes it a lot easier to see the relationships between the music of one place and another."*

Pic. 7.14A *A group of young performers in Hungary perform combinations of Hungarian folk dances (modernized) and modern "techno-pop" pieces, such as this one, a fusion of global influences.* Photo: Authors.

This is the critical component not only of genuinely appreciating our ancestry but also of getting out of our culture and seeing the interconnection between cultures. For centuries, musicians and artists generally have been among the first to transcend the boundaries and barriers of politics, economics, and perceptions of "otherness." Music possesses an energy and emotion that, although not universal in its interpretation, is universal in its importance and reflection of the human condition. Walt Mahovlich, the accordionist of Harmonia, writes:

> "I'll always remember one scene clearly ... several years back we played in a coffeehouse, and it was one of the first times we drew fans from several of our cultural bases. In the same room we had Romanians, Serbs, and Croatians; grandmothers from a nearby Slovak church; and young, local artists with black leather jackets and multiple piercings. They had all heard some of our music before. But this was a moment when it all came together. From the looks of it, people were pretty much bowled-over by both the diversity of what we played and the connectedness of these regional musics."

The age-old adherence to "nationalism," not a healthy patriotism for home but instead a self-willed isolation within the "myth" of nation and general blindness to interconnectivity, still plays havoc with our perceptions of evolution and our current realities. However, when musical fusions such as Harmonium or the Rom/Jewish collaborations cited earlier occur, the exchange of ideas and particularly music becomes even more dynamic, and the anthems of our lives are passed from one region to another for others to hear. Now, freed somewhat from a superficial isolation, our commonalities reflect themselves in the spirit of music, and the diversity entices our sense of adventure to look outward—in order to learn more.

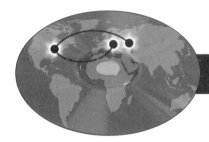

Inside the Musician's World

Harmonia

Note: When composers begin the process of creating music, they nearly always begin with an audience, a market (who will be listening?), or a specific goal. In the case of Harmonia, besides having the goal of creating music that will be fun for the musicians, having a market (anyone interested in Eastern European or Russian music), and being able to make enough money to justify the time and energy invested in the detailed business

of marketing themselves and their music (essential to musicians in any age to sustain the creative process), Alexander Fedoriouk writes:

> "We composed some of the music – but it's still within the boundaries of the 'folk.' We're trying to stay as close as possible to the traditional rootsy stuff, but still put our own personal influence on the music. It's not that different from an Indian raga, where there are 12 notes that you have to use in a certain way, and you extend it to hours, staying within the mode (the tones of the pitch menu or scale). Our pieces are short, but, similarly, we use folk standardized patterns as the basis of our compositions."

Mahovlich went on to indicate how it used to be that people thought you were "holding onto your heritage in the face of change," being stuffy and non-innovative. But he exclaimed, "Hey, I'm playing music that my grandparents played—*that's revolutionary!*" Individually, each musician still has a love of their own unique cultural heritages, but they are finding that the climate toward appreciation of others' heritage, toward better exposure of other cultures means *"there's no longer a negative stigma in the minds of these folks"* for playing the music of their homeland. And, there appears to be much less negativity for infusing their music with the influences of others' cultures and insights as well.

"Melodies from Bukovina," by Harmonia, from the CD: **Harmonia: Music of Eastern Europe,** Traditional Crossroads, c. 2003.

"Melodies from Bukovina" is named for the region in the Carpathian Mountains in Romania on the border between Romania and the Ukraine. The region has a mixed population of Ukrainians, Romanians, and a variety of other groups dispersed throughout the region. The folk music of *Bukovina* maintains the use of some of the more ancient instruments and traditions, including the small wooden shepherd's flute called *fluier* (Romanian) and *sopilka* (Ukrainian). The flute originally had six holes, but in time has been modified to have ten holes, which allow for **chromaticism** (playing essentially all of the possible notes [white and black keys] on the piano.

The Recipe of Sound

The selection opens with a free-flowing (non-metric or strict pulse) *doina* (a pastoral or relaxed style melody without a dance rhythm) and then progresses to a blistering fast dance tune known as *taraneasca* or *ruseneasca,* which is a type of "peasant" dance. While listening to this piece, we may also contemplate how vibrant the energy or synergy is between the group's members.

Maybe even as little as thirty years ago, dialogues between "ethnic" or cultural groups of this region would have seemed uncommon. Today, despite the transitions politically and economically that are occurring in the region, many musicians and artists are "discovering" the music of each other. They are now lifted from generations of mono-cultural vision, wherein other groups seemed "so different," and are now becoming much more aware of the commonalities and "dialects" of their mutual language—in this case, the music of their ancestry fused with the music of their present.

Pic. 7.15A and 7.15B *What must be considered generally universal is the natural human desire to have our "ethnicity" and histories respected. "Romanians" may not require of us to know all of the districts or regions in their country (although to know that there are many regions with diverse ethnicity and backgrounds is a great step), but they would like us to know where their country is located and demonstrate a passion for learning more.* (right) *A Romanian relief map, and the Carpathian mountains.* Both maps are public domain.

Beyond Nation: Spain

While reading previous Units and the references to "myth" of race or nation, we may have been confused or even a little irritated. If we are proud of our Italian, French, Angolan, Chinese, or American ancestry, why speak of *nationality* as myth? Clearly, there are differences between Germans and Turkish, Russians or Americans. Doesn't referring to "nationality" as a myth diminish the diversity of our human planet?

Our response: there will always be human diversity and uniquely different characteristics within the human family. This is the product of thousands of years of evolution and, as such, is part of the human condition. To be "Austrian" or "Australian" or to take pride in the accomplishments of our fellows is much like being proud of your family, your school, or your work, and is part of the joy of the human experience.

What hopefully is obvious by now, however, is that the national identities that we have adhered to, taught in our schools, and defined in the hallowed halls of politics and economics serve also as lethal tools for separatist thinking and distort a fair and accurate perception of our realities. They can create a hierarchy in human preference and serve as justifications for repression and prejudice toward others as well. The blinding forces of belief in *nationality* in this sense are destructive to any form of appreciation: cultural, musical, or simply human.

Pic. 7.16 *When we think of Spain, we might see the entire Mediterranean region, Middle East, and North Africa, for Spanish "reality" is to a very large extent the product of all these cultures.* Photo: Courtesy Wikipedia.org.

To begin to obscure any "unhealthy" vision of identity by nation, we simply need to venture out from the ancient paradigm of *nation* (as a fixed or <u>real</u> entity) and see the multiplicity of exchanges and alterations from myriad sources that go into each nation's make-up. This perpetual fusing process, ultimately, is the "stuff" from which every single nationality has acquired its perceived identity to begin with. How ironic that these identities, born of the multiplicity of intra-cultural exchanges, have now been obscured by the very titles we've invented to define the products of extended fusion and exchange. Therefore, what is required is not a change of ourselves (difficult) but simply a recognition of this distinct opportunity to adjust our perceptions to match our realities (entirely possible).

Spain – A History in Brief

Separate tribes or groups (which may have included the Basques) existed on what became known as the Iberian Peninsula. Beginning in the 9th century BCE, Celtic tribes entered the peninsula and created a unique new culture known as "Celt-Iberians" (a phenomenon that can be seen and heard in both cultures still today). The Phoenicians, Greeks, and Carthaginians each took their turn settling along the seaports of the Mediterranean, until the Romans, after two centuries of war with all the aforementioned groups, annexed it under Augustus, renaming it Hispania.

After the decay and fall of the Roman Empire, Roman Catholicism was the next major influence on the region, but there were ever-increasing populations of Jewish communities who had settled into the area as well. Christian control of the region was short lived. From the 8th to the 15th centuries, Spain and parts of the Iberian Peninsula were conquered and ruled by Muslims from North Africa (termed *Moors*). It is during this time period that the mixing of North African, Muslim, Roman Catholic, Roman/Greek/Phoenician, Jewish (Sephardic), Romani, and Celtic cultures collectively created much of what we now call Spain.

Now when we add to this cultural "concoction" the Columbus and post-Columbus-era colonization of much of the Americas, the contact with indigenous and African populations, the planting and fusing of their cultures with these other cultures, and, ultimately, the return of the "New World" Creoles to Spain in the 20th century, we have Spain's "nationality." Of course, the music reflects each and every one of these exchanges and fusions as well.

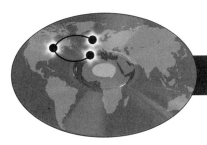

Inside the Musician's World

Galician Folk Workshop,
from the Universidad Popular de Vigo

Note: Historian Mercedes Santamaria wrote the following concerning this collection of Spanish music from the oral tradition compiled by Pedro Vaquero: *"Spanish musical folklore is very rich, varied, and unusual. Because of its location, the Iberian Peninsula is a meeting point between continents and oceans, as well as between civilizations from Africa, Northern Europe, the Far East, and even the Americas. They have all left a legacy upon Spanish popular music. Celtic, Iberian, Greek, Roman, Byzantine, Arab, Jewish, Muslim, and Christian influences are all notably a part of our traditional lyrics and melodies."*

CD 2.18

"Muñeira de Coia," by the Workshop-School for Galician folk Instruments, from the CD: **Cantes del Pueblo: Traditional Music of Spain,** Arc Music International, c. 2002.

It seems as though we should have exhausted the possible "fusions" within Spanish culture and music, but this piece and the one that follows are examples of two styles of "Spanish" music that are the resultant fusion of the multiple cultures cited earlier. Each piece is also very influential in the musical practices of other countries as well. In this case, the ***muñeira*** is a style of dance which evolved as a fusion of popular dances of the 17th and 18th centuries and a mix of Celtic traditions and practices which date well back into medieval history.

Although today we generally think of "Celtic" culture as being tied to Ireland or Great Britain, the Celts (or Gauls) inhabited and extensively influenced much of Europe prior to the Roman Empire's expansion. In recent centuries, cultures in French Brittany and the Galician region of Spain remained close *musical cousins* to the music and dances we call "Celtic" today.

This piece begins with the castanet-sounding "spoons" (which emulate the footwork of the dance) and accordion. At this point it is not hard to still "envision" Spain, or for that matter, anywhere in the Mediterranean during the 18th century. Then enters the chorus of Galician bagpipes (***gaita***) and mounted drums, reminiscent of the great pipe and drum bands of Scotland. There is no questioning the power and contrast of this music, whose dancing movements change in exact accord with the changes in rhythm and texture.

The Recipe of Sound

Besides the unique instrumentation of this piece: C-bagpipes (*gaita*- the Galician bagpipe), accordion, spoons, **charrasco** (an instrument made from a pole with a frame on the top adorned with tambourine rattles: it is played by rubbing a string along the pole with a stick), small drums and bass drums. This music has a unique form and *rhythm* (how the music flows over time) and *meter* (the way the pulses or beats and divisions of the beats are ordered).

For much of the piece, the meter is what we call "compound." In this case, it means we have two *beats* (the pulses that organize music or allow us to tap our foot, dance, or move in synchronization with the music) and three *subdivisions* (number of notes or pieces into which each beat can be divided). This particular combination of beats and subdivisions is typical of the music we call a *jig* (a common dance form in nearly all cultures touched by "Celtic" ancestry, including Appalachian dance music in the United States).

For most all of the world's music, we generally have two, three, or four beats per unit or measure and we subdivide the beats generally into two, three, or four pieces as well. *Compound meters* generally divide each beat into three pieces.

	1	2		1	2
Beats (four per "measure"):								
What you'd tap your foot to –					
	>	>		>	>
Subdivisions per Beat:	‖ ‖	‖ ‖		‖ ‖	‖ ‖

The flow of the notes (particularly of the melody) against the beat. The " >" indicates which of the three notes would coincide with the beat

The form of this piece is also interesting in the manner that it alternates sections—that are as diverse culturally as they are musically. A sonograph of the form might look as follows (the ‖: :‖ indicates the section is repeated; the numbers "8," in this case, indicate how many *measures*, or times, you will count the beats or foot taps from one to two, as in: one, 2, two, 2, three, 2, four, 2)

Melody 1	Dance w/ pipes	Melody 1	Pipes-new melody w/ drum	All the instruments
‖:   8   :‖‖:   8   :‖   8   ‖:   8   :‖:   8   :‖

No percussion (or obvious beat)	Drum/beat enters	Melody 1 returns	Full ensemble	Bridge or 2nd melody
‖   8   ‖   8   ‖   8   ‖:   8   :‖:   8   :‖

Note: if you were not told that this piece is a *jig* and has two beats per measure, you might also be correct in counting four beats per measure, which would simply reduce your measure numbers in half, as follows:

Melody 1	Dance w/ pipes	Mel. 1	Pipes-new melody w/ drum	All the instruments
‖:   4   :‖‖:   4   :‖   8   ‖:   8   :‖:   8   :‖

No percussion (or obvious beat)	Drum/beat enters	Mel. 1 returns	Full ensemble	Bridge or 2nd melody
‖   4   ‖   4   ‖   4   ‖:   4   :‖:   4   :‖

When listening to music, we may not know what exactly the composer or musicians are thinking, so we use our own ears and perceptions to break down the music to the best of our abilities.

Musical Terms and Concepts

Rhythm—The Flow of Music over Time

When asked, "What do you like about the music?" the single most common response for many music listeners is, *"I like the beat."*

Technically, the beat is not to be liked or disliked. It is merely the pulse in the majority of the world's music that is the regulator for music (especially critical to pieces that have two or more people playing at the same time). Without pulses or a beat, you must have some other form of regulation of musical events over time, such as a conductor (which is why conductors are used in symphony orchestras). What we really mean in liking the beat, is that we like the **rhythm**, *or the way the music flows over the course of time.*

The next logical questions are *"What do we like about the rhythm"* (formerly known as beat)? and *"What can we decipher about the music's flow that distinguishes it?* Here are some terms and concepts that might help us understand with better clarity *the flow of music over time.*

Beat – is the pulse in music. This is the measuring stick that divides up time in a predictable fashion so that musicians can play together or anticipate musical events. We naturally will tap our foot to the beat with most music where the pulse or beat is predominant and critical to the flow. Not all music has beats, nor are all beats regulated. In these instances other conventions are used to keep multiple musicians together.

Meter – Beats may be organized or grouped into measures. We generally group beats or pulses into patterns by which they may be organized and counted so that we can anticipate musical sections or form. In the vast majority of modern popular music, the *meter* will contain *four beats per cycle or measure.* The majority of the world's music organizes beats in patterns of two, three, or four beats per cycle. Some of the world's music, however, is much more complicated. For example, in some Bulgarian (Eastern European dances), Indian (tala), and certainly much of Africa's earlier traditions, the meter might be in much larger beat cycles or have multiple simultaneous cycles (*polymeter*).

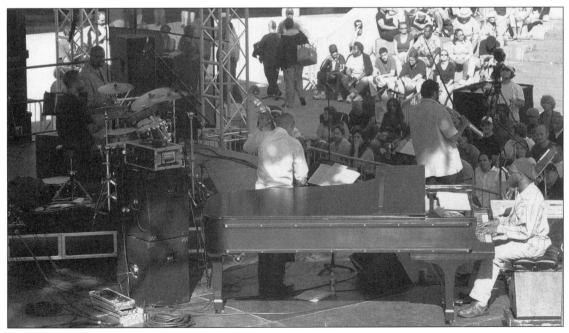

Pic. 7.17A2 *It is the texture or layering of instruments and how they flow over time that gives us the "beat" or rhythm of a piece. The rhythm of this piece (performed by Sean Jones Quintet) is essentially established and maintained by the* **rhythm section:** *piano, bass, and drums – over which the soprano sax or trumpet "cruises." Sean (left) observes the progress of the rhythm section.* Photo: Authors.

Subdivisions – We can "sub"-divide the beat into divisions (most often) of two, three, or four, creating a sense of movement in the melodies or accompaniment of the music *against the flow of the beat.* The more subdivisions, the more the excitement or movement in the music. In some cases (as in much of the music of the African Diaspora), subdivisions do not fit into equal divisions of the beat. Some forms of *swing* or mathematically unequal divisions of the beat must be "felt" to some degree and cannot be notated accurately in Western music notation.

Tempo – is the rate or pace of the beats over time. When hearing music, we can't always be certain which of the pulses or subdivisions is *actually the beat* (the one the musicians are *thinking*). However, once we determine the pulse—whatever we think it is—we can then determine both the *tempo* and cycles of beats, or *measures.*

Building and releasing tension (*including changing tempo or rhythmic focus*) – are ways to alter the flow of music over time. Among the most significant of these are changing the pace of the beat or tempo, adding or subtracting layers of instruments (texture), or altering the accents or emphasis (the strongest emphasis of the rhythms). We use the first of these extensively in classical music written for symphony orchestra (or other large ensembles) by having a conductor who can provide greater liberty to stray from regular beat structures in his or her conducting pattern.

In nearly all of the world's music, adding or subtracting layers is an essential mechanism for increasing or decreasing tension (emotion, energy, excitement). Common "beats" (layers of rhythms) in the world's ritual, popular, and dance music are made by *placing special emphasis* on various beats or subdivisions of the beat. This is the manner by which it can be said we *put the rock in rock 'n' roll, the "reg" in reggae, or the "funk" in the funk.* The following (mostly in Italian) are also common musical terms for altering the flow of the beats:

Changing the tempo:

Ritardando / rallentando — slows the *tempo* gradually.

Accelerando — gradually speeds up the tempo.

Hold or fermata – a technique for coming to a long pause or hold in the music.

Pic. 7.17B *All of life is rhythmic. Here in the streets of Broadway (New York City) there is not only the rhythm of the soundtracks of the musical plays piped through speakes but also the rhythm of the lights, the cars, the pace of life, and the strides and heartbeats of Broadway's patrons.* Photo: Authors.

Changing the flow or accents in the music:

Staccato / Legato —how the notes are performed (played short or sustained long).

Rhythm and Blues and Rock (all varieties) – placing strong accents on the 2nd and 4th beat of a four-beat pattern.

Syncopation – placing accents or stress in between the beats (especially important in most modern music and essential to nearly all music of Africa and the African Diaspora).

Polyrhythm – two or more different rhythms being sounded simultaneously.

Polymeter *or Polycycle* – two or more meters or cycles being sounded simultaneously.

Flamenco—
The Anthem of Spanish Fusion

To a degree, all of the factors of the last three units—the history and dynamics of Middle Eastern and European cultures and music, the ebb and flow of politics and religion in Europe, and, most certainly, the history of Jewish and especially Romani cultures—and their culmination in the music known as *flamenco*. *Flamenco* is an outgrowth of some of the most turbulent times in human history: *the Reconquista* (five centuries of attempts to reclaim Spain and Portugal from the Muslim conquerors) and, ultimately, the *Spanish Inquisition* (period of ethnic "cleansing" after the reclaiming of Spain by Christian rulers).

Pic. 7.18 *Photograph of flamenco dancer Belen Maya by © Gilles Larrain.* Photo: Courtesy of dancer Belen Maya by © Gilles Larrain, taken at Gilles Larrain Studio, 2001.

One summary of the cultural evolution which would lead to Flamenco's diverse and dramatic character reads: *"Granada, the last Muslim stronghold, fell in 1492 when the armies of the Catholic King Ferdinand II of Aragon and Queen Isabella of Castile reconquered this city after about 800 years of mainly Moorish rule. The Treaty of Granada was created to have a formal base for upholding religious tolerance, and this paved the way for the Moors to surrender peacefully. For a few years there was a tense calm in and around Granada; however, the Inquisition did not like the religious tolerance toward Muslims and Jews. Therefore, the Inquisition used religious arguments to convince Ferdinand and Isabella to break the treaty and force the Moors, Jews, and Gitanos (Spanish for Gypsy) to become*

Pic. 7.19 *The elaborate "honeycomb" mocárabe vaulting in the Salon of Alhambra. "Alhambra" (al-hamra or "the Red Castle") was an mosque, palace, and fortress complex of the "Moorish" monarchs of Granada, Spain, for the region known as "Al-Andalus." Today, both the Alhambra, and the entire region are a reminder of an incredibly complex and diverse history. And it is precisely the cultural diversity of the Romani, Jewish, Christian, and Muslim exchanges that have led to the influence of "Spanish" music through much of the world.* Photo: Courtesy Petrusbarbygere.

Christians or leave Spain for good. In 1499, about 50,000 Moors were coerced into taking part in a mass baptism. During the uprising that followed, people who refused the choices of baptism or deportation to Africa were systematically eliminated." [7.14]

What followed the repression and coercion was a mass exodus of Moors (many to North Africa), of the Jewish communities (large communities to Poland and other parts of Europe), and samplings of all the groups (with many of the Roma) to the villages, mountain regions, and the rural country of Andalusia (southernmost part of Spain). It was largely the commonality of exile that facilitated the fusion of the musical cultures of the Moors, Sephardic Jews, and Roma to form the basis of flamenco music.

Flamenco is, among other things, a culture, dance, and way of life. It is characterized by a North African (Arabic) singing style, expressing deep emotion, which (initially) was about people's hard lives in Andalusia. This music and dance genre contains also different *compas* (rhythm styles); rhythmic hand clapping that uses a *hocketing*, or alternating, technique (wherein one group or person claps on the beats and others clap *off the beats*); and dramatic circular-*zapateado* dance movements (*heel tap-style* dance movements that mirror the fast subdivisions of the rhythms with expressive hand and arm movements). Many of the songs in *flamenco* still reflect the spirit of desperation, struggle, hope, and pride of the people during this time.[7.15]

To a very large extent, flamenco is similar to the blues of American culture in its spontaneity of storytelling of the *truth of the moment,* extensive use of improvisation between the guitar and vocalist, and its influence on popular music and dance (in this case, from the tango, to salsa, to nearly all forms of Arabic popular music over the last three to four centuries). But what distinguishes flamenco and endears it to anyone who has the opportunity of experiencing it is the spontaneous communication that occurs between the singer, guitarist, dancer, and all those who become a part of the experience.

Stories from the Human Family

The Authors' Experiences

We decided to take a trip to Barcelona (Costa Bravo or eastern coast of Spain) with our son, Brandon. By chance, a musician friend of ours told us about a club that served dinner and featured Romani *flamenco* performers from Andalusia (the southern coast of Spain). Although we had heard of flamenco, we were unprepared for the connection this music made to our experiences in all African-American blues or jazz genres.

Pic. 7.20 *The authors' son (Brandon—at nine years of age) participating in his first flamenco experience under the spontaneous tutelage of Andalusian Roma dancers and musicians in Barcelona.* Photo: Authors.

The interaction between the musicians (yelling, talking, and especially laughing) and the connection or close bond between the audience and performers (yelling requests, clapping with the musicians, and even laughing or dialoguing about a missed note, a joke that was made, or a facial or hand gesture by a dancer) made the music, and the night, a magical experience of connection among all involved.

What has remained with us to this day (as being generally true) is the degree to which spontaneity and improvisatory expressions become essential, especially to groups that undergo the greatest forms of cultural repression and disrespect. What also occurs to us is how willing most of these groups seem to be to let the outsider in, so long as one is willing to go through a small "proving period." This period (which varies in duration) is a duration in which the outsider's desire to learn and respect the culture is tested by those within. In our case, after smiling, laughing, and participating with the music through the night, we were called upon to dance with the performers. We were so impressed with our son's capacity to plug himself into this new cultural experience, with the immediate acceptance of the musicians and dancers toward him, that we almost forgot: *we could (and would) be next!*

The Guitar—
Ancestors and Descendants

The primary musician, and usually the "guide" for the flamenco experience, is the guitarist. The flamenco guitar (and the very similar classical guitar) is a descendant of the *ud* (oud). The first guitars (as we know them today) are thought to have originated in Spain by the 15th century, the same time that the Roma began to express themselves through this fascinating fusion of cultures using the guitar as their main mode of expression.

During the so-called golden age of flamenco, between 1869 and 1910, flamenco music developed rapidly in music cafés called *cafés cantantes.* Flamenco dancers also became one of the major attractions for those frequenting the cafés. Similarly, guitar players supporting the dancers increasingly gained a reputation, and so flamenco guitar as an art form by itself was "born." In time, composers throughout Europe began to compose for the guitar based on the melodic, rhythmic, and compositional elements of flamenco.

The artist (guitarist) featured below, Lee Dyament, wrote to us: *"The guitar holds the distinction of being one of a few instruments that is as much a part of popular culture as the concert stage. There are disagreements among scholars as to the origins of the instrument. Theories point to a lineage of the Greek kithara, Arabic oud, short-necked lutes of Central Asia, and the long-necked Medieval European lute. The Renaissance guitar began with four paired strings, and, during the 15th century, the Spanish vihuela expanded to five pairs, then a sixth single string. The transition from five to six strings was a gradual process during the late 18th through the late 19th century."* (Interview, July, 2005)

Pic. 7.20A *This may not seem to be the ideal location to practice something as complicated as "Asturias" (Leyenda) by Albeniz (listen to CD2.19), but that is precisely what this young classical guitarist was playing while also collecting donations and attempting to sell CD's.* Photo: Prague, Czech Republic, Authors.

Although today the modifications of the guitar, and the variations in guitar styles, might look more like a musical roll-call of the United Nations, there is no question that the Spanish colonizers of the "New World" not only brought flamenco and related music/dance genres but also the guitar, which, because of its mobility and flexibility, became the perfect instrument for everything from accompanying story songs of cowboys and rock stars, to soloist work on the concert stage.

(Primarily for guitarists) Dyament continues: *"The family tree (of guitar evolution) split in the 1920s, when the C.F. Martin Company produced the first steel-string guitar, called the Dreadnought. The classic guitar shape was structurally altered, creating a larger body, narrower shoulder, and re-*

designed bracing to accept the heavier-gauge steel strings. The added volume and distinctive tone of the steel strings made this guitar a favorite among folk, country, and blues musicians. The L-5 arched-top guitar designed by Gibson, whose top was similar in design to the violin, became a favorite among jazz musicians.

"Over the centuries the guitar design evolved due to demands for more volume and an expanded tonal range. The arch top became amplified in the 1940s, and then in 1952 the Gibson Les Paul became the first commercially viable solid-body electric guitar. In the 1980s pickups were designed for the classic guitar. Concert artists adopted the technology and currently use it both for solo concerts and concerto appearances with orchestra where the added volume is needed. In the late 1980s the technological advance of MIDI (Musical Instrument Digital Interface) allowed the guitar not only to sound like any other instrument but also to create new sounds as well." Today, owing to its mobility and innovations in design and technology, the guitar has been embraced as arguably the most used and popular instrument world-wide.

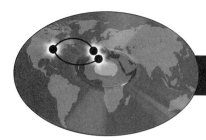

Inside the Musician's World

Lee Dyament

Note: When we first met Mr. Dyament, he was assisting us with facility problems at Detroit's Wayne State University. In time, the dialogue moved to the guitar near his desk and, within minutes, we had the experience that we had just been ushered into a new world. Passion, as a rule, must be discovered within each person, then nurtured and its character brought out, much like we would polish a rough stone into a shiny gem.

In Mr. Dyament's case, his passion was the guitar—not just how to play the instrument (al-

Pic. 7.21 *Lee Dyament (R) in recording session with Audio technician Steve Shelton (L).*

though he clearly loves performance), but also its history, how it is made, and virtually any aspect of its evolution. His performance below of the Albeniz *Suite Española (the section played is Asturias or Leyenda)* epitomizes the codependency of Spanish flamenco and the guitar's first emergence as a musical force in "classical" music.

CD 2.19

"Asturias (Leyenda)," from the <u>Suite Española, Op. 47,</u>[7.16] by Isaac Albeniz, from a live recording CD c. 2005.

Mr. Dyament writes: *"Asturias (Leyenda) is the fifth movement of the Suite Es-panola, Op.47 composed by Isaac Albeniz (1860-1909). The first Spanish composer to write in a truly nationalistic style, Albeniz infused folk melodies, flamenco rhythms, and the spirit of the regions of Spain into his works. Although Albeniz composed over 400 piano works, he never specifically wrote for the gui-*

tar. Yet, his intimate knowledge of folkloric music (flamenco) is convincingly conveyed in his pieces. Because of this, several of the pieces contained in the Suite Espanola, Op.47 (Granada, Sevilla, Pavane-capricho, Cataluna, Cuba, and Asturias) are best known as guitar transcriptions."

The Recipe of Sound

"Leyenda" is one of the composer Albeniz's most famous pieces. The piece evokes the Moorish character of Andalusia, with its Flamenco-like melodies (use of *Phrygian* mode) and harmonies (*harmonic minor chord progressions*). Composed in traditional ABA form (first section, second section, first section repeated), the outer sections are rhythmic and dance-like, with an introspective, slow middle section. The version recorded by Mr. Dyament is based on a transcription by *Andres Segovia,* who is considered perhaps the most well-known guitar virtuoso of all time. With Segovia's performance of this piece in the early 1920s, its place as a standard in the guitar repertoire became confirmed.

7.21A *The mandolin, the ud, the ukulele, and, especially, the guitar glean their enormous popularity from their portability and flexibility across diverse genres.* Photo: Courtesy Lark in the Morning, San Francisco, CA (www.larkinthemorning.com).

Greece—The "Cradle" of Western Civilization?

There is little possibility that the history and influence of Greece on the cultures and music of Europe can be overestimated. In Unit VI, we mentioned that "classical" references are actually a perpetually reoccurring referral throughout much of Europe to ancient Greek culture and values that extended from the 15th century through the 19th-century (neo-classical)) movements. But in truth, the influence of Greek culture from the Mycenaean period (1600-1100 BCE) and especially what most call "ancient Greece" (776-323 BCE, the period that produced *Homer, Sophocles, Euripides, Alexander the Great. Plato, and Aristotle*), extending even through the Roman rule of Greece and the eventual creation of a "Greek-dominated" Eastern Roman Empire (eventually known as the *Byzantine Empire* [330-1453CE], whose capital was *Constantinople,* or the modern- day *Istanbul, Turkey*) also included periods of intense warfare and numerous contacts with Egyptian, Persian, Roman, and the Ottoman cultures (to name a few).

A central component of the legacy of Greek culture was the manner by which the Greeks placed emphasis on the development of systems of documentation (writing) and education that not only preserved their ancient history, but later became the models for the establishment of education, democracy, and, eventually, the university itself. It is not so much that Greece represents a "pure" culture, for by now we certainly know such a phenomenon does not exist, but rather that Greece produced numerous formulae for learning and the dissemination of knowledge that would serve as models for many of the developments in Western thought. These systems, in turn, through colonization, further warfare, and the eventual rise of Western economics and politics, dominate many of our world's institutions today.

However, since Greece is also a fusion of cultures and influences, we can now begin to look for the means by which other cultures' visions and expressions were translated through Greek vision. We might also note, that potentially the last vestige of hope for those who might still predicate their vision of the world on the basis of nationality (Greece) was equally a culture that appears to have evolved predicated upon a thirst to learn and acquire knowledge from other sources and cultures as well.

Pic. 7.22 *The best known "Acropolis" ("high city") in the world is arguably that of Athens. Rising 150 meters above sea level, it was also known as Cecropia, in honor of the legendary serpent-man and first Athenian king. Most of the buildings, including the Parthenoń, were constructed between the 6th and 4th centuries BCE. Today, the influence of Greek architecture, the Greek columns, and much of Greek administrative procedures or cultural ideas can be seen around the world.* Photo: Courtesy and copyright Sandra vom Stein.

A few such examples include: the Greek *kitara or lyre*, which may well have been the descendant of the African *kora*; the *Greek modes or scales* (upon which Western scales are based), which were largely a fusion of Arabic and Persian modes; and "classical" and folk music from the Middle Ages to present-day Greek music, which are largely the result of exchanges with every possible culture from the Romani to Roman Catholic. One thing is certain, however: music and dance have always been a major part of the Greek culture's heritage and a centerpiece of Greek community life. Today, they also provide solace and a connection to home (intra-cultural fusion) for large groups of Greeks living in many parts of the world.

Stories from the Human Family

"As long as I can remember, there was always music around me. Maybe because we lived far from our homeland, my parents made sure that the Greek elements were present—through music, newspapers, going to Greek churches, participating in the local community's events, etc. But what was always present was the Greek music (and most of the time, dancing).

"I guess that must have been the reason that I started to learn piano. I started off with classical music. I still focused and tried to play the new songs from the radio, but I also played the older Greek folk songs and modern Greek songs, which really made everyone around happy.

"Even though people might think of **syrtaki**[7.17] *as the only dance and music—usually accompanied by breaking dishes and bellydancing—there is a lot more to the music than that. There are a lot of forms, transitions, influences up to this day. Even though a lot of people have accused Greek music of being too influenced*

from outside, they forget that there are always Greek elements at the base. Besides, what makes Greek music is not that everything comes from Greece, but that you are playing it with or for Greeks, or while thinking about Greece ... then it becomes Greek." Yanni Dionisopoulos, 24-yr.-old university student, living in Detroit, Michigan.

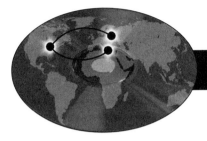

Inside the Musician's World

Kypros Markou and Sinfonietta Cracovia

Note: *Kypros Markou* is the Director of Orchestra and the chair of the string program at Wayne State University, Detroit, Michigan (U.S.A.). He also is (was at the time) Music Director of the Westmoreland Symphony Orchestra, in Greensburg, Pennsylvania, and the Dearborn Symphony Orchestra, in Dearborn, Michigan. He had his early training at the National Conservatory of Greece in his native city, Nicosia, Cyprus, where he learned his passion not only for the music but also for teaching music and the cultural connections collectively. He loves Cyprus and his Greek heritage, but he also sees the enormous impact Greece has made on what many call "classical" music and what Greek culture has contributed to his career as a conductor of orchestras as well. He comments:

"The classical spirit of Greece had a certain simplicity, an elegance; it was the world of the ideal... much of this comes from the Pericles era, signified by the Parthenon. [The first temples of the Acropolis were built during the Mycenaean times, but were destroyed by wars. They were rebuilt in the 5th century BC by Pericles – the period known as "classical" Greece]. Then the period when Christianity came along – there's a bit of a contradiction here; the Hellenistic/Christian civilization, somehow we managed to combine it – even though they were pretty distinct cultures. Then Byzantium, which was not really Greek, but if you talk to a Greek, they'll say that was part of our history. Then there is modern Greece.

"In Cyprus, I had a teacher who liked to say that the Greek people who were cut off from the main body in Athens, like in Cyprus, might be more able to preserve

Pic. 7.23A & B *We do not need to look far to see the influence of Greek culture. In nearly every large city in the world (such as these two in Vienna (above) and Budapest (right), we will find buildings of commerce, politics, and art are still built in classical Greek style.* Photos: Authors.

the traditional Greek culture than on the mainland. If you come to a Greek community in Australia, as in where my sister visited and said to them, "You people are more like Greece was in the 1950s." People who leave their homeland become even more fanatic about the preservation of the old culture. They need their roots – but the culture meanwhile, continues to change.

"At any rate, we forget that our music today is the result of the last 3000 years, as the aesthetic can be traced back to the Classical tragedy. When Glück was writing his operas, I can see the connection. Then in modern music, it is passed on again. Someone like Stravinsky got so much influence from Rimsky-Korsakov, from "Scheherazade" (orchestral "story"— or programmatic music to the ballet "The Firebird"); there are so many harmonies in Stravinsky that are only one step from Rimsky-Korsakov.

"What I was also saying before, one of the aesthetics of Plato is that he talks about the world of ideas that have a reflection here in this world. When you hear Mozart's music, he describes to me the world in its ideal form – through the ages there are still those who share that vision. When I go to Schubert, Schumann, or later Wagner— then you get into the emotional world … the way we feel here— now. The music may be timeless, but those composers deal with very specific emotions.

So like we see, the pendulum goes back and forth. So you can have the same aesthetics in the 16th century and again later in the 20th century. The language may be different (vocabulary changes), but the aesthetics or visions are the same." [Can you hear this in the music? Can you find a connection to your own musical world?] Interview: Kyrpos Markou, June 2005.

"Kleftikos," from **"Five Greek Dances"** for String Orchestra, by Nikos Skalkottas (1904-1949), Publisher, Universal Edition, Wien. *Recording copyright: Apollo Classics, performed by the Sinfonietta Cracovia (from Kraków, Poland).*

The composer, Nikos Skalkottas, was at the forefront of the Greek nationalist movement with his use of Greek and Cretan folk music. On the heels of European "nationalism," which reached its apex prior to the World Wars (again the outcome of the severe nationalism which had "begun" some 300 years earlier), Skalkottas was well versed in the "atonal" and avant-garde works of his contemporaries and even studied with Arnold Schoenberg for a brief period. This created an interesting fusion of some of the oldest traditions in Western music (Greek folk dances) with some of the most challenging and subjective music ever composed. Musicologist Mary Wischusen writes in the liner notes, *"He composed 36 Greek Dances for orchestra between 1934 and 1936, re-orchestrating them in 1948, the year before he died."* She goes on to say about the music itself, *"These charming dances, five of which are recorded here, capture the spirit of the original folk tunes. However, Skalkottas has transformed the traditional melody in diverse and inventive ways."*

"Kleftikos" is rhythmically as much an up-tempo dance piece as one would expect to find at any Greek celebration. Yet, Skalkottas takes numerous side trips (*transitions or movements away from thematic material*), straying at times into different tonal centers (also referred to as "modulations"). Then, there is a bit of *dissonance,* which is a device that was used particularly by European composers through the years and events during and after the two World Wars. Most of these techniques are more common in concert "art" music than in "folk" traditions. However, perhaps even in this fascinating fusion you can hear the influences of the Rom, Jewish, or classical works of previous eras, the influences that may have crossed the paths of the composer during his musical life.

When History Is Distorted

How/Why Has Romani (European…World) History Been Distorted?

When history is distorted, the integrity of all cultures is compromised. For example, the manner in which Romani people have been grossly overlooked for their enormous contributions in virtually all areas of culture (especially in Europe) is by itself among the most glaring injustices in human history. However, far worse is the reality that they have been victims of the most inhumane treatment for over 700 years, with only a trickle of non-Romani voices raised on their behalf. As a result, we must begin to grapple with the manner in which this history has been suppressed, altered, and manipulated and, without hesitation, investigate cultural arrogance and injustice with increased rigor. Fortunately, scholars such as Dr. Ian Hancock provide some of the facts for bringing the plight and contributions of Romani cultures to light.

From: *The Patrin Web Journal* with permission, by *Ian Hancock*. *Posted originally 1 March 1997*
"The Roma, or 'Gypsies,' entered southeastern Europe in the last quarter of the 13th Century, caught up in the Ottoman expansion westward. Originating in India as a composite, non-Aryan military population assembled to resist the Muslim incursions led by the Ghaznavids, they left through the Hindu Kush during the first quarter of the 11th century, moving through Persia, Armenia and the Byzantine Empire towards the West (Hancock, 1995:17-28).

"'By the thirteenth century, [Roma] began to be enslaved for a variety of economic, military, social and possibly racial reasons' (1991:61). The condition of slavery so defined, however, emerged later, out of the increasingly stringent measures taken by the landowners, the court and the monasteries to prevent their Romani labor force from leaving the principalities, as they were beginning to do in response to the ever more burdensome demands upon their skills, and from the shift of their 'limited fiscal dependency upon the Romanian princes' to an 'unlimited personal dependency on the big landlords of the country, the monasteries and the boyars'(Gheorghe, 1983:23).

"While the enslavement of Roma in the Balkans is the most extensively documented, Gypsies have also been enslaved at different times in other parts of the world. In Renaissance England, King Edward VI passed a law stating that Gypsies be 'branded with a V on their breast, and then enslaved for two years,' and if they escaped and were recaptured, they were then branded with an S and made slaves for life. During the same period in Spain, according to a decree issued in 1538, Gypsies were enslaved for perpetuity to individuals as a punishment for escaping. Spain had already begun shipping Gypsies to the Americas in the 15th century; three were transported by Columbus to the Caribbean on his third voyage in 1498.

"Spain's later *solucion americans* involved the shipping of Gypsy slaves to its colony in 18th century Louisiana. An Afro-Gypsy community today lives in St. Martin's Parish, and reportedly there is another one in central Cuba, both descended from intermarriage between the two enslaved peoples. In the 16th century, Portugal shipped Gypsies as an unwilling labor force to its colonies in Maranhão (now Brazil), Angola and even India, the Romas' country of origin, which they had left five centuries earlier. They were made Slaves of the Crown in 18th century Russia during the reign of Catherine the Great, while in Scotland during the same period they were employed "in a state of slavery" in the coal mines. England and Scotland had shipped Roma to Virginia and the Caribbean as slaves during the 17th and 18th centuries; John Moreton, in his *West India Customs and Manners* (1793), describes seeing 'many Gypsies (in Jamaica) subject from the age of eleven to thirty to the prostitution and lust of overseers, book-keepers, negroes, &c. (and) taken into keeping by gentlemen who paid exorbitant hire for their use.'" *Extracted 09/07/07 from http://www.geocities.com/~Patrin/slavery, Special thanks to Dr. Hancock.*

Questions

- *What do you think causes such gross neglect of historical truth? What is the impact on successive generations of the "majority" culture? What is the impact on the "minority" or misrepresented group (Romani)?*

- *What might you do as an individual to alter historical misrepresentation?*

Unit VII Activities

Activity #1: Understanding Concepts

There is a combination of extremely disturbing and uplifting information in this chapter as concerns, especially, the lives, conditions, and acknowledgement or acceptance of Jewish and Romani cultures.

1) Make a list of the things/events you found most disturbing concerning the experiences of both the Jewish and Romani cultures (you might supplement your thoughts with Internet research if you wish).

2) From the reading, make a list of the things/events you found most inspirational about each of the two culture groups and explain their impact on you.

3) Since blame or condemnation has never benefited either our understanding of the negative aspects of history or the manner by which we heal from their wounds, how can you understand (not justify) the fears or perceptions upon which European culture groups may have acted to cause the repression of these groups?

4) Other approaches: What do you think might be the cause of the continued disproportionate teaching of European values over the consideration of Jewish and Romani cultures?

5) A knowledge of ancient Greek culture and its influence on the evolution of modern Europe and American cultures is essential to some degree in order to see what we do—and why we do it. Other than what has been cited in the book, can you find other events, philosophies, and cultural expressions of ancient Greece that are manifest in modern Western culture?

Activity #2: Listening Deeper

There are a few tools we can use to focus our listening more directly upon the music itself while attempting to de-emphasize our natural tendency to see things through our prior experiences or musical preferences:

• Music – may be appreciated by *understanding or identifying with the expertise of the performers,* their vocal or instrumental prowess, the sound quality (*timbre*) of their voice or instrument, the difficulty of the music, or, simply, through an appreciation of the time and passion the artists have invested in their art.

• Music – may be appreciated by *analyzing the manner or style of its flow in time.* That is, the nature of the melody, harmony, as it *rhythmically* flows through time (*all terms that were introduced in this or prior Units*). To do this, we must know something about the way music is organized, the components or pieces of the music. What did the composer do that was unique or special? What are the components or pieces of the musical puzzle, which elicited our reaction (good or bad)?

• Music – may be listened to from the perspective of its inherent ability to assist us in training our minds to process information, to focus, or to develop listening discipline, stamina, and emotional sensitivity. For this reason alone, if we apply our analytical skills to concentrating on the musical components or elements, our listening concentration can not help but improve.

1) Pick one (or two) of the pieces in this Unit.

2) Listen three times to the single piece without external distractions and while doing nothing other than listening (and writing). Concentrate each time on a different perspective, as follows:

First Time: Make notes to yourself about the composition or *performance* and the expertise of the performers in playing their instruments or singing. What was unique, special, or, in your estimation, particularly innovative or special in their performance?

Second Time: Make a sonograph of the music as it moves over time. Try to write in perspectives of what you hear only and avoid, as much as possible, judging or critiquing the music based on your experiences and preferences. Your associations and experiences aren't going anywhere. They'll be with you until you take your last breath. But we may wish to learn to relate to the music on *its terms and not ours.* Make sure to indicate what you hear in the melody, the texture, the rhythm, and the form of the music.

Third Time: By now, you will have really broken down much of the recipe of the music. Listen again from the perspective of the emotional, mental, or physiological properties of the music. What characteristics are most prevalent in the music? In what way is your knowledge or understanding about the people or culture broadened from listening to this piece?

Activity #3: Exercising Passion

It would be difficult for a somewhat objective mind not to see the positive characteristics in the artistic and cultural legacies of our Jewish and Romani cultures, created despite extreme tribulations. But how did these experiences fuel creativity?

Pick an artist (music, painting, theater, etc.) that you admire. Research that person's life and the relationship of their experiences to their art.

1) What were the most difficult trials endured by your artist?

2) How did they react to these difficulties?

3) What impact did the difficulties have on their artistic expression? OR, in what manner was their artistry reflective of their difficulties?

4) Examine your own life: What are the things you've accomplished in your own life of which you are most proud? What impact did the difficulties and challenges that you endured have upon your accomplishments?

5) Finally, what is the relationship of *test or difficulties* generally to the most innovative, creative, or moving human art?

Activity #4: Exercising Our Own Creativity

In Unit VI, we discussed programmatic music and how music can be based upon experiences, stories, or images. In Unit VII, we reiterated the fact that much of the world's best music is born from the tribulations as well as the honest reflections or healing properties that severe trials induce.

Suggestion: You may use the images of nature provided (below and page 302), or you may describe in two sentences or so the most difficult challenges you've endured in life (this is your program). Try as best you can, using your artistic passion, to model the emotion and form of your experience or the image you select in your art, as follows:

Pic. 7.24 A-D Art from visual images:

Each of the images in nature has a contour that suggests movement over time, texture, emotion, or other qualities that relate to our human existence. Pick the image of your choice; analyze its properties and contour; and try, in your medium or with your instrument, to model what you perceive from the image. Do not worry about your expression making sense... it will as long as you complete your idea without concern for the outcome. Note: In most all instances, the world's music reflects its natural visual and sound environment. Photos: Courtesy of David Earl.

Art from Experience

Music of Jewish, Romani, African-American, and a host of other culture groups over the course of history has been composed from the deepest recesses of the human spirit in overcoming or expressing the travesties of repression or suffering. After you reflect on your most difficult moments:

1) Try to put these moments down in writing.

2) Use symbols or references to nature (*tornados, the ocean, a rain storm*) in order to capture the essence of emotion, and then transfer the event to a metaphor (*like or as*) which will spawn a deeper emotion in your art.

> Example: *I remember when I was a child, I fell and broke my arm;*

> Feeling: *Falling and injuring yourself as a child is a violation of innocence – our parents could not protect us – and we realized that pain is a part of life — this is like —* Nature metaphor: *The trees and blossoms of summer suddenly frozen by an early winter storm.*

3) Now, using your medium or instrument, see whether you can reflect the emotion (why you perceived your event as difficult) and the metaphor (reflection in the natural word) within your medium. Be sure to observe the pattern or contour of the event, its form, and its texture. For most visual genres, these will be requirements for conversion to your art. For Art from images, see photo caption, page 301.

Pic. 7.24 *"Romani" musicians playing two of the most characteristic instruments of both Jewish popular and Romani music: the clarinet and the violin. So intermingled are the histories of these two groups with those cultures through which they have passed that attempting to discriminate could be a grave injustice to both the cultural realities and, certainly, their music.* Photo: Copyright Demonoid.

Unit VII: Endnotes

7.1   The terms Roma, Rom, or Romani (Romany) will be used from this point on to refer to "gypsy" culture. The term "gypsy" is the word used in English from the belief that the Rom or Romani had evolved or come from Egypt. It, much as similar words used by other European groups in a negative context, is generally distasteful to many people of Rom descent. Therefore, as in all forms of "appreciation," it is essential that the right of self-determination come from the groups themselves.

7.2   A common phenomenon among groups that have experienced repression is a refusal to extend respect to other repressed groups. That is, as humans, if we have been severely disrespected, until the imbalances have been acknowledged, we may less often desire to extend respect to others. In addition, many repressed culture groups are forced to insulate or isolate themselves within their own communities for protection, physically and psychologically. This insular approach tends to further isolate the group from the mainstream and, frequently, from each other.

7.3   From "Meet Europe's Hottest Composer, c. 1600: A Devout Ghetto Dweller Mamed Rossi," from <u>Arts and Letters</u>, 2002/02.11 (<u>www.forward.com/issues/2002/02.11.29</u>).

7.4   Despite the fact that Jews could regularly be persecuted or hanged for acts such as teenagers teasing their Christian neighbors (which occurred during Rossi's time), the *Gonzaga* family ruled Mantua, Italy, in a manner that was more just and less prone to persecution than most places in Italy at the time.

7.6   As mentioned earlier, the search for origins and definition has defined the vast majority of Western research. Much of this orientation, however valuable, has made us blind to perhaps the more vivid and dynamic nature of human fusions and the processes and dynamics of *creolization* (human creativity). See Unit IX.

7.7   All descriptions and translations are from liner notes by Lucie Skeaping and Robin Jeffrey.

7.8   See Mr. Strom's publications later in the Unit. They include <u>The Book of Klezmer</u> (Acapella Books), <u>A Wandering Feast</u> (Jossey Bass), and <u>The Absolutely Complete Klezmer Songbook</u> (Transcontinental Music).

Pic. 7.25 *It's not certain who is having more fun or enjoying the performance more – the listeners or the performers themselves. Regardless, this group, "Tuna de Derecho de Valencia," is not only performing on behalf of their entire city (representatives of a traditional regional community music and dance ensemble) but also enjoying the holiday in Eastern Europe as well.* Photo: Authors.

7.9   Is there a parallel between the circumstances and events in African-American and Jewish history and the number and diversity of comedians that come from these communities? The role humor plays in the arts creates a critical balance with "blues-like" (personal storytelling) genres for the venting of truth and emotion.

7.10   Hancock, Ian. Pariah Syndrome. Karoma Publishers, Inc. Michigan, 1988; pg. 68.

7.11   The term *Niger* (Latin for "black") became a pervasively standardized term used by Europeans to discuss people of African descent, regardless of the depth or darkness of their pigmentation. However, some sources denote the term being used long before the 15th century (possibly as early as the 11th century) to describe the "Romani" peoples out of India.

7.12   From "Origins of the Romani People," by linguist Ian Hancock, as quoted in: http://www.geocities.com/Paris/5121/.

7.13   Romani musicians were frequently employed to play in the military bands of the Ottoman Empire. Their music, in turn, influenced Western musicians such as Mozart, Beethoven, and even Wagner. The combination of brass instruments, cymbals, and the enormously dramatic quality of the Janissary bands would be the impetus for Western military bands, concert bands, marching bands, and all music that would later use these instruments as a central part of their instrumentation.

7.14   Extracted from the article on Flamenco history from wikipedia.com.

7.15   Extracted and summarized from wikipedia.com (http://en.wikipedia.org/wiki/Flamenco.).

7.16   These numbers "Opus 47," etc., are notations of classification used to distinguish and codify a composer's work by sequence, order, or genre.

7.17   *Syrtaki* is a dance and music style that really began with the creation of the music for Zorba the Greek (1964). A blend of slow and fast dances (*Hasapiko*) with a name taken from *syrtos* (a name for a group of traditional dances), the music has immediate appeal, as it starts slowly, increases speed over time, and encourages participation by all involved.

Africa and Latin America:
Rites, Rituals, and Community Life

Topics to Consider in Unit VIII

➤ *What must be present in a "healthy" community? And – what role does music, dance, and creativity play?*

➤ *What are some of the primary discrepancies between Western value systems and those of African cultures? And – what is the impact of media, cultural colonization, and education in perpetuating discrepancies of "value"?*

➤ *What are "rites" or rituals? And – how important are they to the sustenance of healthy community life?*

➤ *What are some of the most glaring omissions about African cultures and their value in Western education? And – in what ways might Western cultures learn from African cultures to the benefit of altering their most predominant cultural imbalances?*

➤ *What/who is the "griot" or "djaly" – and what is the influence of this practice on modern Western music?*

➤ *How might we reflect on the comments of Mr. Sompa in the context of appreciating ancestry? What is the impact of a solid appreciation of the life cycle and ancestry upon the solidarity of community life? And – what role does drumming and dancing play in this regard?*

➤ *How can the evolution of "highlife" music be explained in the context of colonization and de-colonization?*

➤ *What can be understood by "pan-latino" exchange? What are some of the most striking similarities and differences in the music and cultural lives of the people of Cuba, Puerto Rico, the Dominican Republic, Mexico, Colombia, and Brazil?*

➤ *In what manner are the songs, dances, and musical expressions of Pan-Latino cultures critical to their community life? What are some of the unique ways Roman Catholicism, West African rituals, and Spanish musical genres combined in the evolution of Rumba, Salsa, Merengue, Mariachi, or Cumbia?*

➤ *What are some alternatives to the separation of religion and music, dance and music, and community ritual and deeply interactive (not consumed) music — that are expressed in African and Latino cultures, which might enhance community life elsewhere?*

UNIT VIII

Africa and Latin America: Rites, Rituals, and Community Life

"One generation plants the trees; another gets the shade." Chinese proverb

"We were born to unite with our fellow men, and to join in community with the human race." Cicero

"This is the duty of our generation as we enter the twenty-first century— solidarity with the weak, the persecuted, the lonely, the sick, and those in despair. It is expressed by the desire to give a noble and humanizing meaning to a community in which all members will define themselves not by their own identity but by that of others." Elie Wiesel, Holocaust survivor and winner of the Nobel Peace Prize, 1986.

*"How does one keep from 'growing old inside'? Surely only in community.
The only way to make friends with time is to stay friends with people…. Taking
community seriously not only gives us the companionship we need, it also
relieves us of the notion that we are indispensable."*
Robert McAfee Brown

At the apex of the commonalities in the human experience is the "cycle of life" and the simple and undeniable fact that human beings are essentially designed to mark or support each other through the cycle in communities. The extended family unit (*community*) is an institution structured to guard children, care for the elderly, and sustain the unit members over the course of their experience in the life cycle.

The effects of dysfunctional community within the family or extended family on the lives of the individual are readily apparent in societies or pockets of society where little emphasis is placed upon the community dynamics. In such instances, individuals and individual "freedoms" are given priority over the well-being of the community, and family and community life begins to decay. At this juncture, the individual is forced to fend alone for balance and cohesion within his or her journey through the cycle of life, bereft of the benefits of a strong support-system.

A healthy community structure provides:

A) The assurance that, in one manner or another, the physical necessities of food, water, shelter, and safety will be shared. This sense of personal security liberates the human spirit and its potential to engage willingly in the lives, successes, and trials of one's fellow community members, which in turn reaffirms a repetitive and healthy understanding of the *life cycle.*

B) The reinforcement of "belonging," regardless of the trials and difficulties encountered. Whether in rural Africa, South America, China, or Russia, whether in the midst of the hardships of the absolutely gravest tribulations in human history, strong communities endure, comfort and fortify their members during the trials through which they pass. Weak community structures generally crumble, or are divided or breached by sustained difficulties, so that the individuals experience considerable fear and resentment, or resort to "self-preservation" as the motivation for their actions.

We can also see the impact of community-*lessness* on youth in extensively material- or technology-oriented culture systems. It is a simple law of energy or cultural economics. In some cultures imbalanced by their orientation towards capital, personal wealth, and individual accomplishment, communities lose cohesion by the shear impact of decreased energy investment on behalf of the community. However, human nature (instinct) still requires safety, security, and belonging as well as both the need to care and be cared for. In such instances, the roles of counterculture, social or religious communities, communities based on interests or hobbies, will often serve as replacements for the extended family or village community.

Communities of this nature might include music groups, drug or gang groups, sport or hobby groups, recovery groups, and any host of other *communities*, some of which can have enormous positive effects in their replacement value on the individual's recovery of community life; others simply provide a temporary belonging, but with potentially destructive long-term consequences.

We've mentioned before the law of cultural economics: if we accept the potential that all human cultures are equal, but different, in the way they manifest their capacity, creativity, and intelligence, then the manner by which each culture group or society *is* sophisticated will likely be determined by where they invest their energies and capacities. In simplest terms, if you invest your capacity in playing basketball, or knitting, then you will likely be successful in those endeavors. At the same time, if you spend the majority of your energy engaged in making money or promoting your career, the likelihood that you will be an exceptional knitter begins to diminish.

Although this is a simplistic example of *cultural economics,* when we consider many of the communities of Africa, South America, and the Caribbean, to which we will devote this Unit, we generally find cultures whose investment in the area of human capital is more profound than in material capital. That is, the economics of community life have generally received greater emphasis (historically) than those of material life. In some cases where struggles, war, disease or starvation have occurred (more frequently documented in Western media than are the cultures' sophisticated communities), we may find thousands of years of community focus have been circumvented by

Pic. 8.1 *The Masai (now primarily of Kenya) were known to be "warriors" in much of Western literature. Externally, they are perhaps best known for the warrior "jumping" dance, in which young Masai morani (youth) leap into the air from a standing position in order to demonstrate their strength and agility. Not included in Western literature is the fact that the Masai have an enormously strong sense of community and recognize that, whether to accomplish the task of herding cattle, finding water, or sustaining life in the face of droughts or other natural trials, they must work together—a phenomenon which likely results, in part, from the fact that the women have a very strong voice in community affairs. Photo: Courtesy Wikipedia.org.*

Pic. 8.2A / 8.2B *The pursuit of profit over loss and the assignment of value to nearly all aspects of human culture (including thought) is one primary aspect of capitalism. Strong communities can be involved in the affairs of capital, but investment in the life cycle and human concerns generally takes precedence over concerns for material profit or loss.* Photo (below): Courtesy Wikipedia.org. *The second photograph is one of a farming community in Burkina Faso.* Public domain.

colonization and material-based values. Western colonizers encouraged placing **capital** (the assignment of value) to natural resources, land, and even human life (as property, or capital). Transplanted to African cultures, we should not be surprised to find an extraordinarily negative (or perhaps "un-African") impact on both human creativity and their community life as a result of this sudden shift of values.

> Hernando de Soto writes: *"In the west, by contrast, every parcel of land, every building, every piece of equipment, or store of inventories is represented in a property document that is the visible sign of a vast hidden process that connects all these assets to the rest of the economy ... assets can lead to an invisible parallel life along side their material existence ... by this process the West injects life into assets and makes them generate capital.*
>
> *"'Third world' and former communist nations do not have this representational process. As a result, most of them are undercapitalized ... without representations."* [8.1]

Despite relatively small pockets of African community dysfunction (regions riddled with inter-tribal wars and greed, a topic which we will address later), what has ultimately occurred is not a lack of sophisticated development in African nations, but rather a stark *difference* in the manner by which they are developed or sophisticated. Perceived against the values of Western culture (capital/ownership and technological or scientific advancement), many African culture groups whose standards of advancement were centered in the cycle of life and the prosperity of community life have found a hard road to gain respect from Western societies. Against the initial forceful nature of colonization (*"he with the largest gun wins"*), the pervasiveness of Western media (*perpetual broadcasting of Western values to the world*), and, today, Western economics and a now-global hunger for technology (*which generally demands that all cultures compete against the standards of materialism and technology established by Western powers*), much of Africa and the cultures termed "third world" still place considerable emphasis on the extended family or village community.[8.2] Against the "louder" voices of Western education and media Western cultures are almost certain to over-emphasize their material and technological values through the tools of their own design, while devaluing arguably their greatest need (and the primary export of many African cultures)— the "technology" of community-development.

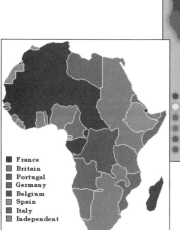

Pic. 8.2C & D *Against the reality of thousands of years of human evolution in Africa, African nations (see map 8.2C) and virtually thousands of "divisions" within these "nations" (divided primarily by natural boundaries), are the last few hundred years of post-colonial African history (see 8.2D). It is primarily that the latter history and boundaries do not conform to the ancient ancestry of the former (including the mismatch of many colonial institutions, such as capitalism or politics that do not recognize the life cycle), that most of the conflict currently being experienced in this rich continent now exists.* Images: 8.2C courtesy of Mark Dingemanse, and 8.2D the CIA Factbook.

Although we've previously made mention sometimes in seemingly critical connotations of the Western affinity for material advancement, individualism, and technology, most certainly, there are numerous benefits to technological and material advancement. However, in order to see many of the world's cultures and their community-derived creative expressions with some objectivity, and in order to attempt to perceive accurately the difference between a healthy (balanced) community or excessive emphasis on materialism and individualism, we may benefit from an exterior look to African and Pan-Latino community life. Such a benefit, cannot be acquired, however, without a somewhat direct approach to addressing:

a) the discrepancies between Western and non-Western values;

b) a thorough look at the impact of *cultural colonization (cultural imperialism)*; and

c) the imbalanced impact of Western media and education in perpetuating Western values. Thus, a respectful understanding of African cultures for most people in the West will require a shift in perspectives of "value."

Let's explore some of the means by which community structures in Africa, the African Diaspora, and Latin America evolved and are sustained, and examine the roles that music and dance have played in creating healthy communities over generations. We'll begin by taking a brief look at *ritual* — and its role in fortifying community over the life cycle.

Rituals – *Community Rites of Passage*

> *"Ritual is one of the constants of human activity, in any human society, central to the understanding and negotiation of the life cycle. Though the forms may change from time to time, there is remarkable similarity...from one culture to another. English society during and after the Reformation may have moved from Catholic to Protestant versions of Christianity, but ritual practice continued to serve many of the same ends despite variations in its forms of expression."* Cressy, David, *Ritual Religion and the Life Cycle in Tudor and Stuart England,* NY: Oxford Univ. Press, 1997, pp.656.

A **ritual,** by definition, is a *series of symbolic actions or events, usually held in repetitive formats (once per life, per year, etc).* Of course, rituals exist in all areas of daily life—from daily brushing our teeth to our final ritual—the funeral. But particularly in the West, the understanding of ritual, its study, and even its practices, have declined because of the prevalent perception that rituals are performed by tribes or "other" cultures, or again, because of the ever-increasing trends in migration away from extended family (which requires maintenance of regular rituals wherein most in the community are in close proximity) to nuclear family models or individualism.

Here is a simple demonstration of this trend: When 126 students were asked to what degree they felt *rituals* played an important role in their lives, 60% of the sample (U.S.A., ages 18-25 years old) responded that they do not see many/any of the events in which they participate as being rituals, or do not see ritual as essential to building strong community lives.[8.3] Additionally, when asked to define community, the majority defined community as either their nuclear family or their peers, or the larger village, town, or city groups, indicating that extended family or larger community structures that encompassed their family had been replaced or altered substantially.

The role played by community rituals is profound in terms of the solidification of community and the reconciliation of individual security and group harmony within the cycle of life, as follows:

- The attachment and respect for ancestry, elders, or those who are deceased is directly proportionate to the degree to which their values, and ways of life, are acknowledged or celebrated.[8.4] When *community rituals* do not acknowledge past generations in some manner, each subsequent generation's vision of self-importance becomes enlarged. Subsequently, the interconnectivity over the course of generations and the emphasis on the commonality of the human experience in a community context diminishes.

- With community reinforcement of the roles of elders, parents, youth, and children through ritual, each member at each stage of the life cycle is given a "place" and is subsequently trained to acknowledge both former and future stages. Generally in healthy communities, as one gets older, one is granted an ever-increasing portion of respect and decision-making within the community and more important roles in its rituals. Community *rite of passage rituals* reinforce the life process and distinguish the stages, assuring each individual respect and dignity through the full course of life. When rituals are diminished in frequency or fail in efficacy to instill respect for each stage in the full course of the life cycle, various phases of the cycle of life (such as youth, young adulthood, or mid-life—the time of fullest development of economic potential) may become disproportionate in their importance.

Pic. 8.3 *Graduation ceremonies, which extend back to the late Medieval/early Renaissance time period, because of their pomp and circumstance, may not be viewed by many who participate in them as "ritual," but by all definitions they are one of the more important and oldest community rituals in Western cultures. To some it may be viewed as an individual rite of passage. The function of the ritual, however, and its greatest value, is bringing the community (extended family) together in celebration of the individual's accomplishments.* Photo: Jeppe Barnwell.

- Finally, emphasizing community ritual in all of the significant stages of the **life cycle**—*birth, coming of age, marriage, and death*— reduces fear of change or discomfort with the inevitability of the passage of life and time. Such rituals also provide a significant venue for celebration, individual acknowledgement, grieving, and the "re-gathering" of community (extended family). If the frequency or participation in community rituals declines, possibly to the celebration of "once in a lifetime" rituals only (generally marriage or funerals) or the intimacy of the rituals is diminished in favor of group interactions of limited duration or

Pic. 8.4A *A wedding group preparing for the photos at Thornbury Castle, Thornbury, near Bristol, England.* Photo: Taken by Adrian Pingstone in September 2004 and released to the public domain.

Pic. 8.4B *Japanese funeral arrange-ment, Tokyo. The white decoration on the green mountains in the back is all flowers.* Photo: Courtesy of Chris 73, administrator for Wikipedia.org.

intensity of contact, community life will also decline in quality. (*Example:* A community which previously had numerous songs or dances that they created or performed at large community events replaces these with a DJ, or replaces the preparation of food as a group with a caterer. The acts of collaborative participation thus become diminished, as does the depth and duration of contact between community members).

Hopefully, we might accept the premise that community rituals are essential to the function and overall health of the community. Addressing, however, the manner of their celebration or specifically under-standing the role of music and dance in the rituals gets a bit trickier. If overly packaged (most preparation being done outside the community), condensed in time, or requiring little or no interaction on the part of community celebrants, the event will have less impact as a binding force on community members.

If, however, music, dancing, singing, cooking together, decorating together, or gathering for extend-ed pre- or post-ritual events are planned and held as a community, or the event incorporates numerous in-ter-active events appropriate to all stages of the life-cycle, the ritual will have a more intimate and lasting effect upon community participants.

Generally, the extent to which the community experiences the binding energy of *ritual* upon the closeness or desirability to reconvene is directly proportionate to the degree of interaction and engage-ment within the ritual. For this reason, as a generalization, in many African countries, especially prior to colonization and the influx of Western values, most communities maintained numerous rituals and com-munity events marked by considerable use of music and dance.

Along these lines, we simply cannot speak of dance without music, or music without dance, nor could we imagine most community rituals without either. It is assumed, therefore, that music and dance have been an integral part of African community rituals for as long as many of these cultures have exist-ed and that, by their nature, these rituals are among the primary means of facilitating the highest level of group or community interaction.

"Rites of Passage" Rituals

The term "rites of passage" is believed to have been first used by the Belgian anthropologist Arnold van Gennep (1873-1957) to refer to the basic life changes marked over the passage of life by ritual. Specifically in rituals that honor the individual in a community setting, each change is marked by a transitional peri-od that serves a variety of purposes, including:

- Removing the individual from his or her former status.
- Readmitting the individual into society in the newly acquired status.
- Bringing the family and community together to adjust to and honor the change of status.

As we attempt to appreciate the rituals of others, among the most important considerations we will need to make is that each "rite" is likely to be shrouded in generations of symbolism. To honor or seek understanding of others' symbolism is to honor their ancestry. This can be challenging, depending on our own experiences and depth of knowledge in reading symbolism, respecting cultural diversity, and understanding the life-cycle.

Because not all of what we see or hear will speak with the aesthetics or values of our own experiences, it is critical to remember the universals mentioned thus far, i.e., that most rituals contribute to our understanding life generally, assist us to fully experience emotions collectively, and ease us in our passage through the life-cycle by creating social bonds that give us comfort and a sense of stability. In this sense, we can know that however "foreign" an experience may seem to us, somewhere in our own culture there is (or was) a parallel activity.

The idea of rituals being "primitive" or "tribal" is as irrelevant and outdated as the generally held view of primitiveness itself. First, most related communities *are,* in essence, tribes. Therefore, all such community rituals are *tribal* rituals and vice versa. Secondly, few rituals in the world today practice physical abuse or contain harmful practices that may be seen as detrimental to the individuals involved. Instead, rituals are generally an anchor connecting us through deepened human experience to the crucial stages of the passing of our lives.

Finally, the vast majority of effective and influential rituals throughout our world, utilize music, dance, and variations of theatrical expressions as the means by which they deepen, enhance, and create a profound emotional attachment within the community to the event.

Pic. 8.4C & D *The symbolism and practices in most of our rituals today are as multicultural as our communities. A wedding at the famous "Guildhall" in Windsor (site of numerous royal functions and the 2005 Wedding of Prince Charles to Camilla). The white bridal gown is an extension of the dress worn and solidified as tradition (now through much of the world) by Queen Victoria in 1840 for her own wedding. Meanwhile, the important history of marking the burial of our dead with monuments, crypts, and mausoleums is magnified by this grave located at the cemetery in Sedlec (Czech Republic) outside Kutná Hora. This burial site by the "All Saints Church" became "superstiously" famous among nobles to the point that thousands more were buried than the grave could accommodate. As a result – space was needed and the bones and skulls of prior tenants were used to create sculptures of religious symbolism by, according to legend, a blind Cistercian monk (see pic. p. 20).* Photos: Brandon Naylor.

Pic. 8.5, 8.5A & B *The "Big House" (football stadium for the University of Michigan) accommodates over 107,000 people on any given Saturday for a football game – and a "rally" drummer in a small German village during the 2006 World Cup match between Germany and Italy, watched on televisions of all sizes by billions of people worldwide. Although these may be "games," they are among the most magnificent rituals in our world and are equally descendants of the ancient Roman and Greek games. Such "competitions" have served as community rituals for centuries and are also frequently enhanced by drums and rhythms, which motivate participants and spectators alike. Large sporting events today also provide ample opportunity for vendors and artists alike. This stage is built next to the cathedral in Köln (Cologne) and was the site of nearly non-stop music during the 2006 World Cup in Germany. The Cathedral, meanwhile, is the greatest Gothic cathedral in Germany and has been Cologne's most famous landmark and site of hundreds of performances and life cycle rituals over centuries. Once the tallest building in the world, Cologne Cathedral still boasts the world's largest church façade. It is also built over the site of a 4th century Roman temple.* Photos: (8. 5) Keks Mattson and Authors.

Stories from the Human Family

Student response to the question: "Are your rituals as important, significant, primitive, or sophisticated… as those of other culture groups?"

"I had never really thought of ritual as being important. I always thought of ritual in the context of Native American ceremonies or something. I suppose if you look at ritual, we have some of the most momentous, primitive, and "ritualistic" rituals on the planet. I've attended American football games since I was a little boy. If you think about this ritual – you can't help but think someone would really be amazed.

You come to the stadium and everyone is wearing the same 'tribal colors.' They all hand the entry pass to the 'gatekeeper.' Now they file up to their specific locations (based on economic status) and await the beginning of the events.

"Much like gladiator ceremonies of ancient times, a group of people come out with instruments and matching costumes playing the village song (that everyone knows). Everybody stands and sings 'Hail to the conquering heroes,' etc. Now the warriors enter the stadium dressed in their warrior costumes and paints. Heck, if you follow this through the tribal elders (referees), the ritual receptions (hot dogs at half time), and the clash of the titans (the actual game), you have one of the most magnificent rituals playing out right before our eyes." (Robert James, 24-yr.-old student and former H.S. football player, 2004)

The following are quotations from **The Circle of Life.. Rituals from the Human Family Album, 1991,** Cohen Publishers, which are helpful in framing a few of the most predominant rites (rituals) of passage:

"For most of humanity's history, **marriage** was more an alliance between families than a bonding of two individuals in love. In traditional societies, parents or professional matchmakers usually selected mates in a way that reinforced kinship lines or improved the social or economic status of the families involved. In time…the revolutionary belief in romantic love took hold… (but whether about) love, sex, life-long commitment, procreation…never has one institution tried to encompass so much." (p. 111)

"Five hundred years before the birth of Christ, Saracen **brides** in what is now Syria held sprigs of orange blossoms to ensure fruitful marriages. In ancient Rome and Greece, brides carried stems of wheat and wreaths of holly. By the nineteenth century, Victorian brides were surrounded by garlands of flowers, ring bearers and flower girls, symbols that are now used around the world." (Ibid. p. 116)

"When **death** separates us from a loved one, we experience a gamut of emotions: denial, anger, grief, and, finally, acceptance. To help us make this transition…and to squarely face our own mortality…societies throughout the world have created an enormously diverse set of rituals. These rites honor the deceased and consecrate their passage to the next world. They also serve the survivors in important ways. 'The living mourners and the deceased constitute a special group, situated between the world of the living and the world of the dead,' writes Arnold van Gennep. 'In this liminal state, we come to comprehend our own inevitable demise and, more importantly, the value of our lives.'" (Ibid. p. 193)

Developing Meaningful Community Ritual(s)

Developing Meaningful Community Rituals

To develop or to sustain strong and deeply nurturing community life, there must be a combination of meaningful, enjoyable, and rites or rituals that bring the community together regularly, enhance the relationships of the community members, create a sense of comfort and well-being with the life-cycle and the changes in life itself, and, in most cases, create a strong connection between the community members and the Creator or a higher sense of purpose (religion).

But even when ritual events are created (and they can be created within a single generation), two of the above conditions must be emphasized if the role of ritual in strengthening the bonds of human/community interaction is to be maximized:

1) Rituals within a community must have some semblance of frequency. Members of the community must be able to maintain some connection with each other at frequent or regular intervals to sustain communication.

2) Rituals must contain activities that facilitate the deepest possible level of human interaction.

In the first instance, any ritual (midday lunch, sit-down dinner, late evening sing-a-long) that occurs regularly will encourage community members to reserve time for it in their busy schedules. However, when the frequency decreases (when weekly dinners become monthly, annual, or biannual, for example), the closeness of the community bond will dissipate.

But it is the second instance, the depth of human interaction, wherein most communities—especially in this age of cable television, videos, video-games, and sporting events—have seen a marked decrease in focus. When our community rituals include singing, telling stories or jokes, making "homemade movies," cooking together, having talent shows, dancing together, or enjoying any other activity wherein community members share their creative abilities, work together, experience and resolve conflicts, and interact "eye to eye," the opportunities for dialogue or sharing emotional connections increase. In contrast, passive activities, even when the whole community is present, are far less likely to elicit a deep connection among community members.

Questions

- *How would you evaluate the frequency of rituals in your community (extended family)?*
- *How would you evaluate the depth of personal interaction in your rituals?*
- *If you feel they could be improved, what specific events or ideas do you have to increase the depth of community interaction?*

Africa – *Respecting Ancestry / Protecting the Community*

To assist in the process of countering the inadequate and grossly negligent communication about communities on the African continent in much of the West, we will focus on a small sampling of African music and dance traditions. Specifically, we will address how they benefit or help sustain community life. We might assume that the longer a culture group has been in existence, the longer and more varied will be that culture's rituals, rites, and music.

Furthermore, since written documentation of the history of ancient African civilizations was not a part of the value systems of many African groups, much of what we

Pic. 8.6 Africa has more than 50 "countries," the majority of which have political boundaries formulated during or after colonization by Europeans. The "real" Africa, however, is a host of communities—pre-dating by centuries the presence of and colonization by any of the European culture groups. . Photo: Public domain, map of 1890.

have available to us concerning African history is either from oral traditions or colored by the biases of the "outsider" Westerner. For these reasons, as we have done thus far with other cultures, we must go to the culture-bearers to acquire their voice and perspectives.

The Griot—The Ancestry of Storytelling

Storytelling may actually be no more important in the diverse regions of Africa than it is elsewhere in the world. But whereas some cultures may have a few hundred or a couple of thousand years of stories, many African communities have many thousands of years of stories and strong oral traditions through which these stories have been passed.

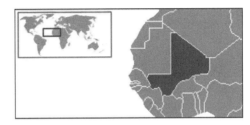

Pic. 8.7 *Location map for Mali.* Photo: Originally created for English Wikipedia by Vardion.

You may have already noticed that a high percentage of the artists and composers from whom we've already heard came into music through early contacts with music in their families. Many of them had parents and others—grandparents, for example—who were musicians and from whom they could learn both the techniques and passion for music. This is certainly true amongst the musicians, storytellers, and dance masters in most African communities. One of the most distinguished traditions is that of the *griot* (pronounced "gree – oh") or *jali (jeliyah, djaly),* a professional storyteller of western and northwestern Africa.

The *griot* is a West African poet and musician, and a repository of oral tradition. The griots' job is to spin tales and stories of their countries' leaders in a manner that is both pleasing and innovative. In other cases, families employ griots for special community events to enhance their importance or impact. The griots' original home was the territory of the *Mande* peoples in Mali, Gambia, Guinea, and Senegal, where their craft and musical storytelling is still alive today. (Note: the "griot" is also called *jeli (djely)* in northern Mande areas and *jali (djaly)* in southern Mande domains).

The Malinké term *jeliya (djelys)* means "transmission by blood." This translation in no small way defines the manner in which griots are honored in receiving their craft by virtue of the hereditary passing down of the skills and stories. *Jeliya* comes from the root word jeli (blood), which is also the title given to griots in areas corresponding to the former Mali Empire.

"In the Epic of Sundiata, King Naré Maghann Konaté offered his son, Sundiata, a griot, Balla Fasséké, to advise him in his reign. Balla Fasséké is thus considered the first griot and the founder of the Kouyaté line of griots that exists to this day. Each family of griots accompanied a family of warrior-kings, which they called diatigui. In traditional culture, no griot can be without diatigui, and no diatigui can be without a griot; the two are inseparable, and worthless without the other." [8.5]

Pic. 8.7A *Mady Kouyaté, a descendant of the ancient griot (djaly) tradition, plays his kora and sings a song for passersby.* Photo: Authors.

At its height, in the middle of the fourteenth century, the Empire of Mali extended from central Africa (today's Chad and Niger) to West Africa (today's Mali and Senegal). The Empire was founded by Sundiata Keita, whose exploits remain celebrated in Mali today.

What is spellbinding about this tradition is the pride and reverence its practitioners have for their ancestry, an essential prerequisite in the development of close communities. Despite colonization, modernization, and even some disrespect for their craft within their own cultures, the griots have thrived. The passing of family names, traditions, and rituals across generations, such as that of the griot, is *not* a sign of primitiveness, but rather, in the context of building communities, highly sophisticated and desirable.[8.6] Most griots become accomplished musicians, lyricists, and improvisers. Even more important for those of us in the United States and Europe, the tradition of the griot is likely the specific root from which all forms of the blues and hip-hop have sprung.

Therefore, the impact and role of the griots' stories (or similar storytelling genres) must be considered enormously important to the world of music. Another issue of importance relates to one of the instruments most commonly used by the griot, the **kora** (see below). The kora and its ancestors may well be the precursors of the harp, lyre, and possibly even the *ud* and guitar. The instrument (technically a "harp-lute") has two rows of multiple strings strung parallel to each other, but does not use a *fretboard*. Instead it is played by plucking the strings with both hands in complex picking patterns, somewhat like the *mbira or kalimba*.

Inside the Musician's World

Mady Kouyaté

Michael's Experience:

Note A young man walked in to the college one afternoon with the strangest instrument case I'd seen. With confidence and pride he asked where the auditorium was located. I began to suspect he was a special individual simply by the demeanor with which he carried himself. He had arrived to contribute to an international showcase of student talent at the college. As his time came to have his "soundcheck," he took the beautifully ornate *kora* gently from its case, went through a series of carefully calculated tuning procedures to prepare it and then proceeded to play some of the most complex and involved music from a single instrument I had heard.

I later learned he was Mady Kouyate (as he tells it): *"I was born in Senegal to Djely Mamadou and Korotoumou Kouyate. These were the best teachers along with my uncle Djimo Kouyate and my brother Soriba Kouyate. But later, I wanted a better understanding of my Manding roots (culture and language of the Bambara, Mandinka, and Maninka peoples). I returned to Mali and was fortunate to acquire an apprenticeship with Toumany Diabate and at the same time attended the L'Institute Naionale des Arts."*

Mady began playing professionally and touring several African countries with Toumany's symphony band. In 2000, Mady made his first international tour to the United States with the Ballet Afrique Noire. He now lives in the United States, and says simply: *"I wish to share the wisdom of my fathers with people here."*

CD 3.1

"Kumbuna," by Mady Kouyate, from the CD: <u>**Kelemagni,**</u> c. 2004.

Note(cont.): When we asked Mady if he'd be interested in sharing his music and thoughts in this project, he calmly replied, *"Let's meet and we can talk."* When we were together, we realized what dignity and pride Mady had, not only for his tradition, but for how it would be represented and whether it would bring dignity to his craft and his ancestry. When asked which selection he'd like us to use, he paused, took a breath, and then said: *"I think Kumbuna—this is really a tribute to my father, and if only one piece will be heard, then I think it should be the one which honors the source of my gift."*

Members of his family go way back to Sundiata Keita, the King of the Manding empire. The *djelys or griots* were the musicians and *praise singers* who acted as advisors to the king, helping him to make wise and fair choices. But the griot ultimately was also responsible for helping each family and community maintain a deep respect for its ancestry as well. It would seem that Mady, through his mastery of kora playing and the dignity of his attitude toward his father, grandfather, and the ancestry of the tradition, would be making the Kouyaté family proud.

Pic. 8.9 *The multiple-string kora has been the primary instrument used by griots or djelys for centuries.* Photo: Courtesy of www.kora-music.com.

The Recipe of Sound

While listening to this piece and contemplating the history of the griot, take time to reflect on the most critical element of continuity in the cycle of life: *respect for that which has come before us.* In this piece, besides musical patterns that could just as well be played by a virtuoso ud or guitarist, multiple melodies are being played simultaneously, not unlike the counterpoint texture of the Baroque period. Additionally, a perpetual *drone* or home-base pitch, which we will discuss further in Unit IX (as relates to Indian *raags*), is also maintained throughout as an important musical device to facilitate the thought process of the storyteller.

In some cases, the griot's songs would contain text, in others, the text is implied by the piece's title or the introduction made by the performer in a poetic context. When the piece is solely instrumental, we are left to the devices of *program music,* instrumental portrayal of thought, similar to Dr. Hartway's harp piece in Unit VI.

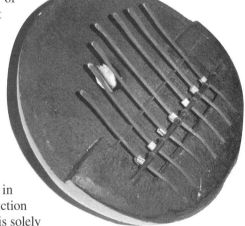

Pic. 8.8A *The Mbira or Kalimba (thumb piano) is a common instrument in much of Africa to accompany storytelling.*

Now, in contemplating the meaning of this piece, how might we relate it to the subject of "community" or ritual as the basis for solidification of community?

When people's perception of community encompasses hundreds of years and numerous generations and their personal identity is tied to the honoring of those upon whose lives they now build their identity, we have the essential groundwork of solid community life. This respect for ancestry is *one of the essential components of community,* which, in the griot's case, is based upon the ritual of learning the trade, craft, and art from elders as well.

Growing Up with Music –
Congolese Drums, Dance, and Community

One of the veils that impedes Western acknowledgment of African values in general and particularly that of their strong community life, is the result of political/economic instability in much of the continent. The *Republique du Congo* (Republic of the Congo, not to be confused with the *Democratic Republic of the Congo,* or former Zaire), is undergoing numerous transitions as a result of **decolonization** (attempting to recover from the negative aspects of colonization) and the attempt to re-establish community principles at the level of government. While contending with the economic and cultural values of Europe (specifically France) from the 19th and 20th centuries and the impact these cultural clashes had on the ancient and established traditions of the region, the Congo is now more deeply in need of their ancient use of drums, dance, and song than ever before.

Pic. 8.10 Map of the Republic of the Congo. Courtesy Wikipedia.org.

Against the forces of technology, materialism, and images of success in terms of Western perceptions, such countries throughout Africa now struggle to find their own voices and reconcile their past histories (including colonization and the ancient traditions). In contrast to the whirlwind changes many African cultures face in establishing balanced political and economic policy from these divergent forces is the stability that is created by centuries of drum and dance rituals, most of which are anchored by an extremely strong and natural understanding of the life cycle.

Stories from the Human Family

Authors' note: For years, we've known and admired Jean-Claude (Biza) Sompa as a colleague, a musician, and a dancer, but especially in his role as a father. We were excited that he consented to be a part of this project. So many of his comments became the basis for our selection of both topics and music for this Unit sampling of African cultural values through music. We include parts of our discussions as follows:

> "*For me, music is like everyday life. From the time I was a baby, music was there, everywhere. I grew up in a family that most of the people liked to dance and play music. A few of them were musicians, including my father and my uncle. They played drums, and my father played a string instrument a little bit like a kora, but it has a variety of strings.*
>
> "*I didn't grow up in the village, I grew up in Brazzaville (capital city), but cultures in both the city and village will use music. Whether it's at night, after working hard all day, people come home— and there may only be one person in the village or the neighborhood who would make everybody come down, and he'd play the music to help everyone forget about the hard work during the day.*
>
> "*So I grew up constantly around music. My mother used to tell me: 'Every time you hear the music, dance—do something with it.' Maybe at 8 or 9, I began to pay more attention to the music, but the encouragement from my mother made me feel that I could always do something with the music. At that time I wasn't thinking about being a musician or dancer; it was just something I loved to be around.*

Pic. 8.10A & B *Throughout Africa, a few principles can be generalized with acute accuracy: 1)many/most Africans are encouraged to dance and sing from a very early age; 2) all music and dance "traditions" will change with each generation both in context and presentation; and, 3) each generation of youth will be instrumental in the modulations of the expressions.* Photo: Authors.

"You know at home when somebody wanted to do a performance, it wasn't the same as here with a poster or flier everywhere. There, most people didn't have the money or equipment to make posters and things, so you would rent a truck, and one person would sit on top of the truck and others would hold his legs, and in the back of the truck were all the musicians playing – and the person on top would dance. It would attract people and they would follow the truck all the way to the theater where they would perform. People would then pay a bit and get into the theater.

"At that time, I was with some of my friends and we were planning on playing on a soccer team, and we heard the drum and followed it all the way to the theater. I remember we had collected some money, and we were hoping to buy a soccer ball and some jerseys—you know, kids dreaming even if we didn't have enough money. But instead we took our money and we bought tickets to see the group. They had a young guy that looked to be about my age, maybe a bit older, but not that old. I said, 'Wow! He's the youngest one in the group – and he can do this, maybe I can do it too.' After that, we went back home and now the soccer team became a dance company." Interview: June 2005

In cultures where an abundance (at times, a sufficiency) of material goods is a consideration; in many cases where politicians hold control of the fragile material resources, or where jobs or venues for self-betterment such as colleges or universities are absent, creativity is given a boost. When the toy store is not an option, toys must be made. When grocery stores seldom have already prepared food or possibly the staples required for dinner, you must find a way to gather and prepare the food yourself. When musical instruments, manufactured recordings, or other musical supplies may be non-existent, individuals must learn to make, create, copy, and with few resources and by their own initiative, solve the problems at hand. This is where the strength of the community again plays its hand. Although things are constantly changing in all cultures as we speak, when individuals act on behalf of the community, not themselves, their place within the community will also be protected and enhanced. Mr. Sompa commented:

"We started taking the big tomato cans and made them into drums. We took the patterns we had heard—you know, also from my family and my cousins. The cans, whatever we had around us, became the tools. You know you can make wonderful things that sound great—instruments are all around us. It was not too long, that I saw one of the musicians in the street. He invited me, and basically even though I went over there as a naive boy, that's pretty much how my career started. I realized if I could use what I had in some way to better myself and help my family, then I had an obligation to do so.

"It wasn't long and I got a chance to be part of the national dance company (Ballet Nationale). We did modern Congolese dancing, not ballet as you may think. We went to Germany and to Russia. I remember being excited about the way people who didn't even know this kind of music … received us. I began to think, 'Maybe it's time for me to go somewhere else and share what I know.' At the age of 19, I went to Paris, and then later to the United States. But I have to tell you, oh yes, maybe I wanted success for myself at times, I'm human, but mostly what I was searching for was a way to help my family. How I owe my parents, my uncles, my brothers and sisters so much for what they gave me … and now I have my own family, and everything in the world that I can do to help my children appreciate their lives and develop their abilities and a strong respect for community as well, I must do. Then, I'll take extra work so that I can help my family back at home as well."

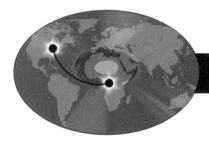

Inside the Musician's World

Jean-Claude Biza Sompa

Concerning music and community rituals, Mr. Sompa writes:

"Yes, music is something for everyday life— it brings the community together. A lot of time, people would sing for different reasons. The healer person would use music, because they believed some of the spirit of the music would go into them— and they would use music for healing.

"Then there is the marriage ceremony. Or maybe, if you were going to have twins, in African cultures, because we don't use fertility drugs, if you are going to have twins, that's a very big deal. This doesn't happen often, so people put on a big ceremony to honor the couple who is going to have two kids at the same time.

Jean-Claude Biza Sompa teaches students Congolese drum patterns.

"Then, of course there is funeral music, which is different for different funerals. You know in most African cultures, we have a strong understanding of the cycle of life, and we don't believe that someone should die earlier than reaching the end of the cycle. We start here (draws a half circle) and then we come through here, and then we leave … that's how it's supposed to happen. But a lot of us, we may not make it all the way

through the circle—and the community handles each situation differently. My grandmother lived to be 105 years old, and she died like a little baby—the complete cycle. When that happens, yes, there is a mixed feeling. There may be crying, but because they are grateful she completed the whole cycle. When a young person dies, people cry, but its really crying from grief. That ceremony is different.

"When my grandmother died, she had never been in the hospital: she called my mother's name, and that was it. Of course, we're sad, but we celebrated her life with singing, dancing – she made it all the way through the cycle. Maybe most of us won't ever reach that point.

"When she passed, we blocked the entire street from one side to the other— no car could pass. We had two or three different groups of performers; there were legendary guys that came: Mundanda—he's a very famous kalimba player (a finger piano, like the mbira), everybody was shocked to see these guys there … but that's how special the cycle of life is: everybody celebrated that day. That's how we approach the music; it's for healing, for every part of the cycle, even after the person dies.

"We believe that after the person dies, their spirit stays around with us for a while. Then we know there will be a day when we do another ceremony, and at that point the spirit will go to its home. In fact, in a couple of weeks, we will be returning home so that we can have the second celebration for my grandmother. There will be a big party, maybe even bigger than when she passed, more music, more danc-

ing. We let her go then; she's gone, and we can release her spirit in our minds and hearts. That's how music is incorporated into everyday life— and shows you how important we hold these rituals in the life cycle."

Question: How do you instill these community values in your children growing up in Europe or America?

"I grew up in a different time and a different culture. We have a lot of problems, as you know, in Africa, but they are much different than the problems here. As a father, raising my children in this country, it is a challenge. People generally educate their children much different here than we do. There are a lot of things they allow their children to do that we never would—and other things they don't allow their children that we do. Of course, you can't say that everybody in any country does the same thing, but the majority of people in my culture treat everyone in their neighborhood as family (according to their place in the life cycle).

Pic. 8.10E *Where the cycle of life is balanced, adults sacrifice for their children, spend time, model skills – and youth copy their examples and are taught to respect them. The patience of the elder and respect of the youth will produce magnificent results – down the line.* Photo: Authors.

Everybody was a father, an uncle, mother, brother, or cousin. When we were growing up, we never called our elders by their name. Blood or not, when I look at someone the same age as my father, he's my father. The same age as my mother— she's my mother. I would say 'Tata' (father) and his name. My brother's friend— I would say 'Yaya' (big brother) and his name … so I can't just go and say: ' Hey Michael' to an elder. They would just look at me and say: 'What did you say?'

"This is all about respect. Even today, when my mother is with her friends, I call my mother ('Mama') and the others 'Mama Yengo'—that's my mother's friend. I always use mother first. Here, it's really a challenge; it doesn't matter what you do in the house, when they go to school, they're in another world. You challenge them in the house, and their friends challenge them at school. It's hard on the children too, but what we are trying to teach our children is that life is a series of steps.

You can't jump the steps; you can't be 10 years and be acting like you're 15. If you move faster than the life cycle, or treat people older the same as you would your friends, you are breaking the cycle. I teach my kids, if you disrespect someone my age, you are directly disrespecting me. It's the job of the parents to show the respect to the children and to model the life cycle for them. If you don't respect them, they will return whatever you give them.

"Anything in life, whatever you put into it determines what you get back. If you plant the plant and put lots of energy into it, you reap the harvest. This is an African philosophy: If you work hard, you get good results; if you don't, you won't. This is the same for our communities."

Dancing and Drumming and the Family / Community-

"What I try to do is tell people if they have children—that the children are welcome in the class (Congolese drum and dance class). Not many people teach what we teach. If I can expose them to this culture while they are 5, 6, 7, or 8, the chances are they will have fun and feel comfortable dancing. Believe it or not, they teach the older students better. They see them, and maybe they feel like I dance or play the drums too complicated or difficult, but they look at the children and they say: 'If they can do it, maybe I can too –' The kids try without any reservation. This is why the whole village must live and work and dance and play together. I don't make my kids dance; I want them to come because they want to come. That's how I learned from my parents. The same goes with school; and, whatever they choose, I will support them."

Pic. 8.10F *African drums – are they merely instruments? Are they artwork? Are they remnants of history? Are they a means of communicating, telling stories, and remembering ancestors? Are they for music, dance, or theater? Or are they all of these?* Photo: Authors.

Mr. Sompa teaches Congolese dance at both the local community college and university. He works the same principles of community and extended family into his dance class. There is a hierarchy based upon age, experience, and the life cycle. Students who respect this, according to Mr. Sompa, will progress even more quickly in the dance. At one point we are viewing a rehearsal of some of the ex-students, who are now part of his dance company, *Bichini Bia Congo.* The students are enormously concentrated and energetic. I ask: "Have the people back home seen your students dance? How do they think of it?" *"Oh they think it's great. They can't believe that Americans can dance Congolese dance this well."* [8.7]

"Sava Maiyaka," by Jean-Claude Biza Sompa and Bichini Bia Congo, from the DVD **Bichini Bia Congo,** c. 2004.

> *"I choreograph my dances with examples from everyday life. Sava Maiyaka (the making of kassav). This is the staple food back at home, and it takes a bit of work. You have to get the roots from the ground; then you might soak the maiyaka for four days until the starch starts to come out. So the dance imitates the sounds and actions of collecting the maiyaka. They come with the basket, and they prepare it and put it in a big pot, and they cook it. Then the result is good, and they can have fun now that it's prepared. You know, I want to teach that you can work extremely hard, but you don't use as much energy if you are happy about your work. It makes the work easy. This is how the slaves in this country were able to survive.*
>
> *"Much of this was also the ability to take the sounds and the rhythm of the work itself and incorporate it into the music. This is what we've been doing with our songs and dances for centuries. The chopping of a different plant can actually make a melody. I believe that a lot of the music—since it would not be written— was tied to the sounds of the work they did. As a musician, you listen and you use your hands to produce the sounds, melodies, and rhythms in the drums. This is why we say they are 'talking.' You play and share with other people. This is the idea of this piece. They are making fun with the work. The drums, dance, and life are all combined as they always have been—and always will be. We work together as groups...we play as groups. My grandmother says: 'I have to eat with others, or I don't have an appetite. If I eat with others, the family, the community, the food tastes better.'"*

Highlife – *A Fusion of Functions and Cultures*

As we move from the older to the more modern music of today's Africa, we will begin to see that, despite the respect for ancestry and the musical traditions of the past, in many cultures touched by colonization (which were the majority), music became precisely what the cultures themselves had become— a fusion of diverse influences. Added to this, we must address the paradox between maintaining ancestral traditions and creating new fusions, which nearly all cultures with ancient traditions experience as a result of the communication boom of the 20th century.

What may seem confusing to many outside Africa is that most African cultures have very effectively adapted the musical innovations of the Americas or Europe to their own ancient musical traditions. Although not always without an internal struggle, they have frequently found ways to merge their ancient community practices and rituals, with modern technology and innovations.

There are a number of reasons that creating musical or generational fusions has not proven as

Pic. "South African born and globally revered, reggae artist Lucky Dube was one of the country's beloved artists. His music touched millions around the world." Prior to his tragic death in October, 2007 at the hands of a car-jacker, Mr. Dube embodied the creative spirit of modern African musicians, fusing Zulu, English, Caribbean, and a host of other influences to a strong social and political awareness. Photo and information courtesy: www.luckydubemusic.com

difficult nor been objected to by many African communities and, specifically, musicians. For one, whether in the South African fusion of Zulu song and dance styles with American gospel, Angolan traditional music fused with the samba of Brazil, or the myriad of popular styles of "Afro-pop" or "Afro-beat" music fused with everything from American Country music (Juju) to hip-hop fused both with existing forms of traditional or already fused popular music, creativity and adaptation are essential to healthy community life. Another reason, however, is the natural human-exchange process of *affinity transfer.*

Every American music genre, and now most of those in Europe, already possesses many of the African aesthetics of sound and organization, instruments, and other expressive features. These are deeply embedded in the Pan-African fusions and have been part of the cultural/musical fabric of the "new world" cultures since early slavery days. From this vantage point, it is relatively easy for any generation of musical innovators in Africa to see themselves mirrored in the traditions of the blues, R&B, country, funk, rock 'n' roll, salsa, rumba, hip-hop, and the multitude of other fusions in the Americas and now Europe.

This isn't to say there are not generational objections or even stiff opposition to some musical movements. But as a rule, healthy communities are much more likely to accept the flux or change in traditions across generations as the natural course of life. Of course, this occurs as well when the youthful explorers in the young adult phase of the life cycle (the phase that dominates change and creativity within the community) demonstrate a knowledge, affinity, and respect for the music of their elders. To be sure, youth will explore, experiment, and diverge from their parents in search of their place and occupation in life.

But in strong communities, the following also occurs: (see also page 217)

- **Parents** are directly and intensely involved in the daily lives (and music) of their youth. One of the main benefits of parenting in a healthy community environment is seeing your children grow to respect the generations before them. This, of course, is done by example. The amount of time and effort the parents spend nurturing (respecting) the children is generally reciprocated by the children. Strong communities know this and will generally guard space and time for family and community needs.

- **The youthful years** do not have a designation for their completion (18 yrs. or 21 yrs.), but are rather based upon the individual's maturity or responsibilities. Youth may live with parents into their 30's or even 40's, if the pace at which they progress through the cycle evolves more slowly or their services are needed to take care of elders, children, etc.

- And finally, **most community events** are structured to allow for the diversity of expressions across generations. There may be more strict ritual dances and music that observe age-old customs, directly alongside DJs and modern dancing of *soukous or reggae.*

Once the balance of generational respect is in place, the adaptation of the music of the past to changes brought on by the present can occur without disrupting the natural balance of community. But what about the rituals and events which served as the cement for community life? How will the community celebrations that mark the life cycle be altered when traditional drumming and dance events now use electric guitars and brass instruments? And most especially, what was the effect of the imposition of the European political, economic, and cultural *will* upon the musical traditions of ancient African music and dance genres?

As we cited from the onset, the diversity of African cultures and musical systems is mind-boggling. Those of us living in the Americas and Europe cannot possibly imagine having ten completely different linguistic systems in a country the size of France or even Switzerland. But when you add a two- to four-hundred year period of *colonization*[8.8] by a foreign culture *on your soil* and, more recently, the boom in global cultural exchange through technology, the dynamics of community life (and how much more so political and economic life), become ever more complicated to decode. To illustrate some of the impact of colonization, as well as some of the current concerns of post-colonization Africa, let's take a look at one particular style of music from Ghana and East Nigeria, called **highlife.**

Highlife

Highlife is a style of community dance music performed mostly in Ghana and Eastern Nigeria. It has been one of the 20th century's most popular fusions of African traditional music and Western music *on the continent* of Africa. Originally, early highlife followed the patterns of early jazz in America, incorporating the military band instruments of British ceremony and military bands[8.9] into the rhythmic, dance, and ritual music of the native (Ghanaian or Nigerian) cultures. By the late '40s and '50s, highlife had also incorporated the music of the American big band (for which it shared a direct affinity) and Afro-Cuban *mambo* and *rumba* music.

By 1970, highlife had further incorporated other African-descendant music: calypso, rhythm and blues, and even American Motown and funk music into the already unique fusion of earlier highlife. Over the course of time, it ruled dance floors and became the favored music at community gatherings, parties, and receptions across much of West Africa. One of the first highlife musicians, trumpeter and bandleader E.T. Mensah (born in 1919 in Accra, Ghana), formed his first band in 1930s and went on to be crowned the King of Highlife.[8.10]

With the rise of Congolese music in the 1960s, highlife's popularity began to wane. But what would not diminish was the increased velocity amongst young African musicians in striving to incorporate and re-create fusions of *exterior and interior* musical styles. What would also not decrease was the enormous popularity of these fusions at nearly all community and social functions. In one sense, the fusion process embodied in highlife was the reconciliation of one the most absurd phenomena in human history: *the settling and claiming of ownership of someone else's home*, as embodied in *colonization* (in all its forms). Highlife was more than a musical style; it became an emblem for the simultaneous reclaiming and adaptation of the African musical voice from, and with, the exterior world. Now, with brass, drums, and electric guitars, highlife would embody the fusion processes as had been done in every other scenario of cultures in contact. Despite this, however, the functionality of highlife would adhere to centuries of traditions in which music and dance remain at the apex of community "rituals."

Now, challenged by perpetual exposure to European and American music videos, movies, and other media that paint a clear delineation between the "material have's and have not's," African communities are daily challenged to maintain a balance between the two "worlds," while African youth struggle to find contentment within their own borders against the images they see of "success" as defined in Western media. Therefore, the challenge of young Africans today remains to honor their ancient past against a backdrop of information that does not reflect their heritage or, to a large extent, their community values.

Pic. 8.11 *Perhaps the most challenging aspect of being a 21ˢᵗ-century citizen is maintaining simultaneous files on ancient, transitional, and "current" for every culture group. "African music" of whatever variation encompasses the traditional as played in the current, Afro-pop, Afro-beat, Juju, Highlife, and a host of "formerly" modern variations—and today, nearly every brand of fusion – not only from within the continent – but continually with the African Diaspora. Accommodating all of these possibilities defies any predisposition to exclusivity or cultural "purity" in any form.* Photo: Courtesy Peter Viisma.

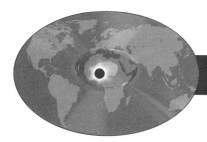

Oliver de Coque

Note: When a young Nigerian student heard we were looking for some highlife music to represent the earlier stages of African fusion, he told us, *"My sister works with Oliver De Coque—he's a real well-known artist."* We told him, if he thought Mr. De Coque would be interested, to invite him to participate. Within weeks, we received the following information, the CD selection used below, and some personal comments from Mr. De Coque.

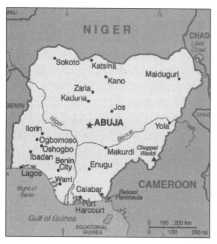

Pic. 8.13 *Nigeria is one of the largest countries in West Africa and was only officially a colony of Britain between 1914 and 1960. The Yoruba were a major influence in their transfer to the "new world," particularly Cuba and Brazil. But Nigeria also is home to the Hausa-Fulani (Muslim majority in the North), the Igbo (the largest ethnic group in the southeast), Nupe, Tiv, Kanuri, Efik, Ibibio/Annang, and Ijaw (the country's fourth-largest ethnic group). Map courtesy Wikipedia.org.*

The bio Mr. De Coque sent read: *"Chief Sunday Oliver Akanite (a.k.a. Chief Oliver de Coque) was born in Umudiani village in Ezinifite, Anambra State of Nigeria. His father, the late Chief Julius Akanite, was an accomplished local musician and his mother, Lolo Uchejigbo Akanite, was a practioner of natural medicine.*

"A singer, composer, and guitarist, Oliver came into prominence in the 1980s. But his music is the product of the vibrant guitar highlife that emerged in the Eastern part of Nigeria immediately after the civil war in 1970. As a showman, a major part of the Highlife stage performances, Oliver would dress in a suit with a bowler hat and walking stick and dance or involve the audience in nearly every piece. In 1979, Oliver released 'I Salute Africa,' which was a praise track (praise song) on the album. Later, he would shed some of the popular traditions and introduce elements of traditional highlife rooted in the Ekpili' rhythms of the Igbo people."

"Bjrj Ka Mbjrj (Life and Let Live)," by Oliver De Coque, from the CD: **Live and Let Live,** c. 2004.

When asked about his music, Mr. De Coque commented: *"Composing music comes natural to me, but that is because it is the result of my culture, my community, and the people I know or events of my life. What can be more natural than to say what you've lived?"*

When asked about what he'd like to say to youth today, he replied: *"Youth are becoming less eager to learn from their elders, to work hard in their chosen profession. Musicians that spend their time in nightclubs or miming other people's music can't find the song in their own souls. Also, drugs and alcohol do not enhance performance as some think. You cannot be creative or compose music if you yourself are not "composed." Personally, I really like music that is fresh or original in some way. We all learn from each other, but if you emulate others blindly, you cannot discover your own hidden abilities or style, nor will you remain as fully respectful of your ancestry, which might, if I can say so, be our greatest potential 'export' to the West."*

The Recipe of Sound

After the introduction, which might be seen as a drum call to the musicians and dancers of earlier drum and dance music of Igbo or Yoruba traditions (now transferred to instruments), the piece settles into enormously intricate rhythms of multiple layers. Multiple layers of rhythmically diverse patterns such as these (and virtually any music for which we generally say the "beat is good") are the result of varying degrees of complexity in the texture. In this piece, there are numerous layers (at some points 10-12 layers) before the voices enter. Each layer has a relatively simple pattern, but together they weave a thick fabric of interlocking rhythms, in this case, in a meter of six pulses per measure or beat pattern.

Just to give you a feel for the intricate nature of this piece rhythmically, let's look at a breakdown of its layers (texture). We should note that we are only getting a small five-minute sample of this piece. In its entirety, it would be nearly twenty minutes long, with numerous variations in its textural layers. The song's duration indicates the important function it serves in sustaining dance and story for a prolonged community activity.

Guitar:	usually two guitars, with contrasting melodic lines that play at both regular and irregular intervals, primarily to keep the energetic flow of the music. At times, between vocal choruses, the lead guitar will break out with a solo line.
Organ:	used in the introduction and sparingly in later parts of the piece.
Timeline:	the grandfather of the *clavé* rhythms we will hear in the section on Latin American music and the precursor to the back-beats (accents) on beats two and four of rhythm and blues or rock 'n' roll. Against a six-beat meter, this timeline is:

```
        1     2     3     4     5     6
Beats:  |     |     |     |     |     |
              >
Timeline: |  |  |  | rest  |     |     |
```

Kalimba:	the **kalimba** or fusion instrument of the **balophone** (the first ancestor of the xylophone or marimba) and **mbira** (the "thumb" or finger piano), together with the guitars, provides a constantly running pattern (much like sound of running water in a rain forest) that maintains the constant feeling of energy in the music.
Bells/Agogo/Shakers:	a variety of instruments are added or subtracted from the texture to increase or decrease tension throughout the piece. The changes are subtle, but when you listen for them, you might also hear some of them "cue" what will occur next or alter the *feel (actual rhythm)* of the piece.
Drums:	both hand drums (traditional drums of ancient ancestry) and the snare and bass drums or drum set, used in most popular music throughout the world, are present. The roles of each of the drums vary. If you listen, you will hear perpetual or constant rhythms at times in the hand drums; at other times, they will break or provide accents at the end of a section. The snare drum, in contrast, frequently plays only the sixth beat of alternating measures.

Bass: and finally there is the bass, which alternates rhythms throughout, but whose primary rhythm would be:

	1	2	3	4	5	6
Beats:	|	|	|	|	|	|
		>				
Bass:	|	|	rest	rest	| |	rest

A musician doing an accurate transcription of this piece (in Western notation) would have a challenge, as the rhythms of the diverse layers do not lock up precisely with the beat. Many of the layers are **syncopated;** that is, they use accents or stress on notes slightly before or after the beats.

To all of the above are added the layers of vocal storytelling and choral harmonization. The vocal melodies seem to ride the rhythms, enter and recede possibly to those accustomed to radio-play music, also without a clear-cut predictability. This is the beauty of the earlier fusions in African music: they maintained the original complexity of the ancestral musical practices, while including the instruments and regularity of popular styles of the Western world.

Process – *Not* Goal

Not far from Mr. De Coque, and right next to Mr. Sompa, is the homeland of Mr. Mulopo Mulomede, the Democratic Republic of the Congo (formerly known as Zaire). What was striking in the conversation with Mr. Mulomede was something we had also heard in conversation with other musicians from many regions of Africa: that spirituality, prayer, music, dance – or in other words, religion and life are synonymous, and intimately connected, activities. Mr. Mulomede writes:

"Prayer, dance, song, praise, and worship are all interrelated in my homeland. If someone can't dance physically, his/her mind does go to different directions with the rhythm. These prayers and music are like an invocation to God to help their family, their communities, and humankind (we have many prayers for humanity as well). But mostly now, the prayers are for the people from my homeland who need it right now. Most of these pieces are also linked to our ancestors. These pieces are a reminder for me when I listen, to reinforce my belief and to testify my weakness to the Creator— so that He can help me."

In the case of the establishment of rituals which mark the life cycle and bond the community to its common existence, the separation of religion from family or extended family activities, or the music and dance from either, or the division of any of these experiences from the humility and wisdom that is derived from ancestral respect and cohesion across generations is (or was previously), to many Africans, nearly unfathomable. Mr. Mulomede writes:

Pic. 8.14 *A view of the vast and diverse continent of Africa from the space shuttle.* Photo: Public domain, courtesy of NASA.

"As I said before, the stories we tell and the use of music to carry the message across time to our elders and ancestors has a big place in the continuation of the family. In African cultures, there is always music as a part of most ceremonies and events. When there is a speech, you can hear someone in the back starting to sing a song that has the meaning of the speech given and then everyone pitches in to give the song its harmony. People in Africa can't live without music. It is their therapy and a major part of life ... and it was encouraged at schools.

"I remember in elementary school, we used to go to the blackboard to make up a song that is not already known as a part of the music lesson. We did not have piano, guitar, singing lessons, etc., but were able to learn by ear and compose melodies, harmonies, and songs with new words and so on. This type of composition is done when one lets his or her mind guide him (/her). The melodies come and go every day. Everything in life has a rhythm, and it starts with our heartbeat. The music carries the message to somebody more quickly than a message given by itself.

"Music brings people to a certain state of mind depending on what type of music is played or heard. Some music has an impact on one's spirit, and I sometimes wonder: 'Why I can listen to a piece of music and keep on hearing that piece of music several hours and days later?' The music has a certain power—which impacts the mind or soul of the musician. It can be used to construct or deconstruct ... . That's human choice." Interview: March 2005.

Struggles in Africa –
Balancing the Equation

Since respect (appreciation) of other cultures is directly linked to experience, and since much of Western experience of Africa pales greatly in comparison to its knowledge of itself, understanding the poverty, inter-tribal wars, epidemics, and health concerns most prolifically broadcast by Western media about Africa, generally, is critical to the acquisition of knowledge and respect for its people. We asked Mr. Mulomede how we should understand much of the information which dominates Western media about Africa, which affects both the progress of achieving internal balance and external perceptions and, ultimately, Western motivation to respect and learn from African cultures. He wrote:

Pic. 8.15 *A map of the Democratic Republic of the Congo (former Zaire).* Courtesy: Public domain, CIA factbook.

"As to the poverty, war, the images most see about Africa—we need to make some small statement on the conflict of cultures (colonization) and influence of capitalism on the social structure and "human greed" factor. That is, we cannot allow Western students to remain with the image that the poverty, war, etc., was completely 'self-induced' or a sign of the 'primitiveness' of the culture—when our cultures are contrarily very sophisticated.

"So regarding poverty, war, and the like ... it is all human greed and a lack of understanding about the place or intent of material wealth. For sure, colonization did induce a new structure into the way most Africans lived in the past. So Africa did not reach its destination of its own accord. When the Western powers that colonized Africa left the countries, Africans were left with half of each.

"What I mean is that Africans did not achieve what they started as Africans and did not complete what was brought by the 'superpowers' that colonized them. The African leaders became so confused about the leadership of countries and have been bounc-

ing between following the old way of ruling and the new way of ruling that was brought in by Westerners.

"When I look closely to this whole thing, I find that the West brought good things and bad things and Africans have the choice to select good things from both cultures (Western and African) to make Africans effective leaders of their own affairs. As for war, it is a conflict between old and new ideas or good and bad ideas. There is no example to follow. Africa wants to be like the West but can't get rid of some of the things of the past that make it unique— many wonderful characteristics— and some not good."

"What is certain, however, is that the sense of community in which the strongest exploit the weak ones, or those who have the means dominate those who do not— a mirror of war, colonization, and thousands of years of negative human history is ineffective. We feel guilt if we do not do many things with respect for how our ancestors did them. We feel inadequate if we do not do things as the media and Western world operates and places value upon us.

"The world evolves, and people from different corners of the world meet and share. This sharing brings new understanding, and to move forward means to learn from others and use what fits in at the appropriate time. There are some countries in Africa that did not go through the colonization process but are still struggling. There are also some colonized countries in Africa that were colonized but are doing fairly well to some extent. There is a big struggle between capitalism and the community life that was practiced in the past. But what Africans have—maybe better than much of the world—and now must learn to apply, not only to their problems but to help the Western world as well, is that we know people cannot survive on their own as individuals. They can only prosper if everyone in the community does at least something to contribute to the common goal. In this manner, many things can be achieved. But there is always the need for a leading body to have a vision. Africa is struggling to get a just or fair vision. If you listen to the majority of music coming out of Africa today, these are the themes you will hear."

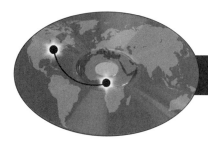

Inside the Musician's World

Mulopo Mulomede

"Hello, my name is Mulopo Mulomede, originally from the Democratic Republic of Congo (former Zaire). You asked about my perceptions of creativity – and music: I think everyone is born with a sense of creativity. Some use it to its potential and others say that they can't do it, due to encountering difficulties, feelings that things are not moving quickly enough, or discouragement from other people. Being

creative is being open to whatever comes in one's mind. I remember growing up in Africa where advice, stories, wisdom were sent down to children in the oral form. I remember going to sleep with my mother's voice singing the songs that sometimes made my mind wander to get the songs' meaning.

"Now, I look back and see that most songs taught to us as children, had wisdom in them. These songs were teaching moral behaviors, courage, sense of joy and happiness, sense of being alive. They connected us firmly to our elders.

"In the Congo, there is a lot of suffering right now with war, starvation, and disease, but the human spirit has always been kept up by the variety of music. It is the soul of life itself, no matter what happens. People sing to lessen the suffering and heal themselves and have hope for the future. The so-called "griots" or storytellers are doing an amazing thing to spread any message to the community by the use of musical instruments and their voices. The modern music in Congo has now become the art/media used for criticism among musicians, singing about love between men and women, daily issues, education, etc.... At the same time, music is used extensively in churches. If you have a church without music, you won't get people."

"Mvidi Mukulu," by Mulopo Mulomede, from the CD: <u>**My Hope,**</u> c. 2004.

Mr. Mulomede writes: "I think it's important to remember... *creativity is a part of every human being. Those who succeed are those that try to accept the shortcomings and disappointments. I listened to a variety of music growing up, and that itself gave me the courage to try. I also read about the biography of most musicians and found out that they had an attitude to enjoy making music. I am not a professional musician ... .I have a regular job, and music is my passion. But I treat music with the seriousness and passion of my faith and my family ... as I know it can provide a stability of spirit to me and to others. I hope you enjoy my piece."*

Pic. 8.16A1 & A2 *That the vision of "unity" is not only a human desire, but also a human requirement can be seen in sculptures such as these (above from Nigeria / below Townshend International School – Czech Republic) everywhere in the world. To dismiss "unity" (with respect to human diversity) as naïve or utopic would be to dismiss centuries of stories, songs, and the work of thousands of mature individuals worldwide.* Photos: Authors.

This unity prayer,[8.11] sung in Tshiluba, begins:

"Eyi Mvidi Mukulu Wanyi! Eyi Mvidi Mukulu Wanyi!
Sangisha Mioyo ya basadidi bebe
Kaba kamwee ne ubaleja dijinga diebe
Kijinga diebe dinene bua balame mikenji yebe
Ne balonda meyi eba bambuluisha"

Which translated means: *"O My God, unite the hearts of Thy servants and reveal to them Thy great purpose. May they follow Thy commandments and abide by Thy laws. Help them, O God, in their endeavors and grant them strength to serve Thee. O God, leave them not to themselves, but guide their steps by the light of Thy knowledge, and cheer their hearts by Thy love. Verily, Thou art Their Helper and their Lord."*

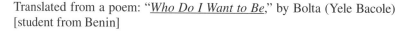

Translated from a poem: "*Who Do I Want to Be*," by Bolta (Yele Bacole) [student from Benin]

I was born centuries ago … but I did not have the vision of conquest
Therefore, I stayed hidden … and I'm asking why?
Who do I want to be?
> *My people were sent away … wounded for centuries, I remained*
> *Absent from your vision … asking –*
> *Who do I want to be?*
My "saviors" destroyed my soil … the soil
Of my heart, they planted greed … and I asked –
Who do I want to be?
Now in freedom … I feel the full burden of the slave
To material existence … searching for stability … I ask again –
Who do I want to be?
> *Under feigned democracy … I start to flourish*
> *But in what do I flourish … I ask –*
> *Who do I want to be?*
Look now I have a pretty tri-colored flag, Green –
For hope in a better future, Red –
For the courage of my ancestors, Yellow –
A sign of my wealth … and still I ask –
Who do I want to be?
> *You may judge me now, naked, black, and diseased,*
> *But I know I'm clothed*
> *But I know I'm not black*
> *But I know the only disease that can kill me – is self-hatred, I ask again –*
> *Who do I want to be now?*
Can you see me? I don't require everything you value … Just learn of me as I've learned
of you … Perhaps I know now – Benin, I am
> *Who do you want me to be?* (edited for space by permission)

Today's Africa

So quickly is the process of cultural and musical exchange occurring within nearly all regions of Africa, that by the time each one of us reads this, the popular artists from the tip of South Africa to the northern-most tip of Eritrea will have created more fascinating fusions and blends of music, each more complex, more encompassing of the music in other parts of the world, and more creative in their unique blend of elements. Currently, on a radio station devoted to African music, you might hear South African reggae

Pic. 8.16A *The world-famous Harlem Globetrotters (not originally from Harlem, but Chicago) are not merely an American icon of perseverance against racism and the manifestation of resilience and special talent; they also manifest a host of qualities which are reflected in African communities: closeness, trickery, choreographed "dance" (basketball moves), and a strong orientation towards establishing and entertaining community.* Photo: Courtesy the Harlem Globetrotters, www.harlemglobetrotters.com.

artist *Lucky Dube,* or the famous *Ladysmith Black Mambazo,* next to Benin superstar *Angelique Kidjo,* next to Ethiopian star *Aster Aweke,* next to African musicians living in Paris, Amsterdam, London, or the United States.

What you may also hear, however, especially from the artists living still on the continent, is the eternal concern to remain attached to their ancestral music and culture. This may occur in the use of ancient instruments; it may be the quotation of an ancient proverb, the use of their non-European language, references to their parents, their uncles, or the musician elders of their communities. But somewhere in the artists who are truly respected beyond a passing glance or social application of a single hit will be this perpetual connection to the past.

Many Africans who have lived away are returning to their homelands and attempting to convey the message:

"We must maintain the sophistication of our community life. Outside, much of the world is in dire need of what we have. Without our communities, without our rituals, music and dance, without maintaining the respect we have for our ancestors, we truly will have nothing." (Biza Sompa, July 2005). A metaphor for the struggle of spirit but the slowly increasing voice, in those who have reconciled their "African-ness" with the voices of the Western world is this selection from the 1994 Inaugural Speech of Nelson Mandela:

"Our deepest fear is not that we are inadequate –
Our deepest fear is that we are powerful beyond measure,
It is our Light, not our darkness, that frightens us.
We ask ourselves, who am I to be brilliant, gorgeous and fabulous?

Actually, who are you not to be?
You are a child of God.

Your playing small doesn't serve the world.
There's nothing enlightened about shrinking
So that other people won't feel insecure around you.

We are born to make manifest the Glory of God that is within us,
It's not just in some of us; it's in everyone.

And as we let our own light shine,
We unconsciously give other people permission to do the same,
As we are liberated from our fears,
Our presence automatically liberates others.
Let our Light Shine – (from Nelson Mandela's 1994 Inaugural Speech)

What We "Hear" vs What Is...

Ethiopia: What Lies Behind Media Images
(Léonie's Experience)

"In 1985, I remember well the images that accompanied the 'We Are the World' musical project for relief of famine in Ethiopia. Against the backdrop of perpetual images of starving children and, then later, the news that Ethiopia had been (unbeknownst to much of the Western world) submerged in a 30-year war with their neighbors in Eritrea, it seemed by all accounts that Ethiopians and Eritreans were deserving of 'pity' or, perhaps, the 'third world' labels that would become perpetually attributed to them over the years that followed.

"I had seen such labeling toward some of my friends' cultures and was, therefore, not prone to believing much of it. Fortunately for me, only two years later, I became very close friends with a family by the name of Tekie (take-ee-yea) from Eritrea and later, Ethiopia. A very strong mother and father sent all nine of their children one by one to countries around the globe, that they might be safe and have secure futures. Two sisters went to Germany; three brothers and sisters to Toronto, Canada; and the remainder to our area.

"Not only did I have the opportunity to learn much about this incredible family, the strength of community-life in Ethiopia and Eritrea, and the incredible music, dance, clothing, and food of the cultures; but I also learned how important their history was as a bedrock of Western civilization itself:

- *Ethiopia/Eritrea (D'mt) were among the oldest nations in the world (human remains dating back 5.9 million years), dating back to the eighth century BCE and the Aksumite Kingdom (1st century CE).*

- *Ethiopia/Eritrea were among the first countries to accept Christianity (in the 4th century) and have maintained a comparatively open policy towards many religions historically.*

- *Ethiopia/Eritrea figure prominently in the histories of Judaism, Christianity, and Islam, and are mentioned in all of the Holy books of these religions. They are also the 'homeland' of the Rastafarian movement of Jamaica (a religious movement for 'black liberation' and the basis for many reggae artists from the 1960s until today).*

- *Ethiopia/Eritrea have over eighty indigenous languages, among the most important of which are Amharic, Tigrinya, Somali, Wolaita, Sidama, Afar, Hadiya, and Gamo. However, many Ethiopians and Eritreans also speak English and, as a result of Italian occupation during WWII, Italian.*

- *Speaking of occupation, Ethiopia was among the only regions in Africa to successfully resist European colonization by the Italians in the late 19th century.*

"We could continue the list of accomplishments and fascinating aspects of these cultures, which have streamed from our brothers and sisters in Ethiopia and Eritrea since ancient times, in art, architecture, science, and all aspects of culture. However, I have learned repeatedly over the years (and perhaps nowhere more than in my contacts with Ethiopian and Eritrean friends) that what we hear about others is seldom their reality. The closeness of families and communities in Ethiopia and Eritrea, despite the portrayal of the media, once experienced, opens the door to respect what they have contributed to the evolution of our world community."

Questions

- *What was your vision of Ethiopia prior to the above discussion? Had you heard of Eritrea or the war? Why do you think our vision of these cultures might be so distinct from their "reality?"*

- *How do politics, media, mis-education, or cultural superficiality influence our perceptions of others? How might it influence their perceptions of themselves (or our perception of ourselves)?*

Fluidity in Latin America Communities

"...all cultures provide men with façades to protect their egos. However, that which serves as a façade in his own culture may be stripped away by exposure to another culture and the learner may suddenly find himself standing psychologically naked. Therefore, the main prerequisites to second culture learning are receptivity, plus normal intelligence and a good measure of inner security." Kleinjans (1972, p.18)

At times, it is very difficult to find a balance between fully acknowledging the negativities in colonization, and slavery, and the effect of its arrogant and selfish origins on cultures today (not properly acknowledging this history offends the descendents of such indignities), while at the same time acknowledging the thrilling results of the unimaginable mixing and creativity these events spawned.

One area of the world offering multiple examples of the fusion process that occurred as the result of this rocky history is the Caribbean and South American African/Spanish Diaspora. For reasons that have something to do with the Spanish style of colonization (i.e., versus the French or British), the enormity of fusions already experienced in Spanish cultures and, ultimately, the manner by which Spanish descendents mixed with indigenous and African cultures throughout, what we call **Latin America** is a vast blending of cultures that are emblematic of the cross-cultural exchange process in our musical world.

What we call *"Pan-Latino"* cultures are all the cultures in Latin America (South and Central America,

Pic. 8.18 *General map of the enormous area we call "Latin America."* Courtesy Public domain, CIA factbook.

Mexico, and the Caribbean Islands) where, for over five hundred years, the *"Spanish"* (see previous Unit VII—Spain's history of fusion) both clashed and blended with indigenous, multiple African, and other European cultures. The following events occurred with only slight variation in degree, intensity, or time period in each and every "Latino"[8.12] culture:

- All Latino cultures had some form of indigenous ancestry in place prior to the late 1490s and early 1500s. In some cases, this ancestry may only have been in place for a few hundred years (as on some Caribbean islands); in others, such as in Mexico or parts of South America, indigenous populations may have predated colonization by as much as or more than 1500 years.

- All Latino cultures were colonized by Spain (or Portugal) between the years 1492CE and 1510CE.

- All Latino cultures experienced a significant decline in their indigenous populations, primarily as a result of a lack of immunity to European diseases, but in some cases due to slavery or extermination. In a few cases, indigenous cultures welcomed the Europeans as guests and a semi-symbiotic relationship developed.

- All Latino cultures (including Mexico) had some degree of infusion of (primarily) West African cultures into their mixing process within the first 20-100 years. The majority of Africans were from the Ghana/Nigeria regions (many were Yoruba).

- All Latino cultures eventually gained independence from the Spanish (or in some cases Spanish/French, Spanish/English, or Spanish/United States) colonizers. Most achieved this status in the 19th century, but a few (Ex: Puerto Rico) remain as territories of other countries (Ex: United States).

- All Latino cultures' music, food, dance, and religious expressiveness result from numerous fusions that were the product of the above dynamics *and* from the continued mixing with other Latino cultures which are essentially the product of nearly identical histories.

A subsidiary of the belief that we are all one human family is the very striking reality that, for example, in Latino cultures wherever they exist, there is a significant historical bond supported by mutual exchange and fusion between cultures. At some points, the differences in cultural dynamics (Ex: Cuba and Mexico) were more significant (see below), but over the course of the last century and most certainly the last few decades, *pan-Latino* cultures have exchanged identity through music, television, movies, religious rites, and virtually every form of human expressiveness, and have created a significant bond—not only with each other, but in all cultures (i.e., North America/U.S.A.) where Latinos reside. As with cultures we've discussed in prior units, citizens in Afro-Latino cultures, which comprise the majority of Latin America, were forced for centuries to survive and sustain themselves through life's trials by the creation and maintenance of strong community life. By virtue of the paradox of similar histories, "they" have now exchanged many of the cultural fruits of their histories with each other while still maintaining cultural distinction as well.

The following is brief encapsulation of just a few of the Latino cultures we will represent in this Unit. You will see both diversity and striking similarities in the dynamics of their evolution and ultimate creativity in their music. Once we feel we have an understanding of older traditions in Latino music, we will demonstrate how pan-Latino sentiment on the wings of 21st century media is catapulting the already enormous affinity for community-based fusion music into overdrive.

> *"Nice project. Well, you can say this … Latin music and rhythm and blues have had a profound effect on my life. The African-Asian-Indigenous rhythms, along with Cuban influences found in Latin music, have given me a strong sense of human esteem."* Edward James Olmos (Letter received, April 5, 2004)

CUBA

Original Inhabitants

Taino (Taiwo), Siboney, Guanajatabey (thousands died on reservations). Some mixing early: Mestizos ("guajiros" – to Cubanos). No known date of initial settlement.

Colonized

1492 – Columbus. Spain ruled until 1892 and the Spanish American War. Received independence in 1902.

African Population

Imported from Florida and the Bahamas. Emancipation occurred: 1886. Most slaves were coerced or recruited into Roman Catholicism and created a fusion of Catholic (and mostly) Yoruba religious practices with a strong worship (or respect) of Saints (**Santeria**).

Other Significant Events

It is believed that the Natives showed the Spaniards how to grow most crops (e.g., tobacco) and the Spanish brought with them sugar cane (although the origin of sugar cane is disputed to have been African). Style of colonization and even treatment of African population was "comparatively" loose compared to that in the United States. Africans were able to create *cabildos* (sacred clubs) which fostered the maintenance of a higher percentage of their African religious and musical practices (see music). Castro and the beginning of Socialist/Communist Cuba in 1953 altered the political/economic flow of evolution from other Latino states considerably.

Musically

Spain brought **Zapateo** (foot or tap/heel dances), Fandango and Flamenco (song/dances), and *cancions* (songs), Roman Catholic masses, and later (1700s through 1800s) a continued influx of European "popular music," including: *contredans* (country dances), waltzes, minuets, gavottes, mazurkas, and polkas [all are pan-European dances, each of which had become the "craze" at various points in time].

Africa (primarily Ghana and Nigeria) introduced *bata and yuka* drums and dance (evolved into *rumbas* [dance and music] and evolution of *conga* drums). Also, brought and maintained numerous dances and songs based primarily on Yoruba practices. Dances included introduction of *clavé* rhythms (the time line or specific rhythm that holds nearly all Latino music together. It is also the backbone for the creation of backbeats, such as accents on beats 2 and 4 in rhythm and blues, funk, and rock 'n' roll) and multiple drum layers (critical to most Latino music).

      Note: It is believed that the *guiro* (a gourd /scraper instrument) and *maracas* (gourd shakers with handles) were introduced by native culture. Also, even Chinese and East Indian influenced the music and culture (latter part of 19th and mid-20th century). One example is the "Chinese cornet" (*corneto chino*) that is played by carnival groups in Cuba.

Pic. 8.19A, B, & C *The sights and sounds of the diverse nature-scapes (ocean, desert, and rainforest), cultural and community practices, religions, and aesthetics all contribute to the cultural/musical fusions that go into the creation of Latino identities and communities. Note: The "deafening sound" of the rainforests during a rain and the complex rhythms and energy of a rumba bear striking similarities. Just as we generalize the numerous similarities that exist between Latin American cultures resulting from similar fusions, colonization, and culture-evolution processes, we can marvel at the diversity of sights, landscapes, and cultural variations, including: a Havana, Cuba, street,* Photo by: Hajor, June 2002; *A pond in Costa Rica (left)* Photo: Courtesy of Wikipedia.org; *and this view of Havana, (below)* Photo: Courtesy Arthur Kwiatkowski.

Created Music/Dance Fusions (A Partial List)

Son Cubano – a mixture of Spanish *cancion* and African rhythms accompanied by guitar and percussion.

Danzón – a mixture of *contradans* and already existing *Spanish/African* fusions.

Bolero – a different style of *son Cubano* with a steady slow rhythm (usually about love and relationships).

Rumba (rhumba) – a variety of dance styles that merged African dances and rhythms with Flamenco, Spanish songs, and, later, American jazz. All of these (and *Trio Sons* – urbanized "sons" fused with jazz from the U.S./Cuban fusions of the 1920s-1950s) would eventually merge to create: *Salsa* (see Puerto Rico as well), a fusion of *conjunto son, mambo, conga, and rumba.*

DOMINICAN REPUBLIC (Originally, Hispaniola)

Original Inhabitants

Tainos (Taiwo), a branch of Arawak (see Puerto Rico). In 1492 (Columbus's first visit), the Taino thought the *Guamikena* (or covered ones – because they wore so much clothing) were a special people. They honored them as guests and there was little conflict or killing until eventually (as in other colonized locations) disease took the life of most or all of the culture.

Colonized

1492 – The French occupied the west side of the island (Haiti); The island had a history of numerous leadership changes: Spain to France to Spain (to 1821), to Haiti (independent French colony to 1844), to Spain to the United States occupation (1916). The first democratic election occurred in 1924.

African Population

First slaves were brought to the island in the early 16th century. Contributing groups—likely similar in origin to those in Cuba and Puerto Rico. A substantial African (Yoruba/Fon-Ewe [Benin]) influence has also been made on the population, some of it through the evolution of Haiti's culture (which shares the island).

Other Significant Events

The Dominican Republic was believed to be the first country to open its doors to European Jewish exiles from Europe during WWII. There is a substantial Jewish population still there today. The single island contains both the Dominican Republic and Haiti, and represents simultaneously the most confusing and fascinating mixtures of cultures and politics on a single island, possibly in the world.

Musically

Spain – similar to Cuba.

Africa – similar to Cuba, but stronger representation from Benin and French/African cultures through Haitian influence.

Created Fusion (A Partial List)

Many similar to Cuba, and *Bachata* – a song form from the lower middle class, which spoke on the important topics and themes of the day (blues-like genre).

Suavé – an honoring of the "saints" ceremony of almost direct African lineage, with strong similarities to *Haitian Voodoo.*

Merengue – far and away the most important contribution to Latino music, merengue (in its various stages and forms) represents (like *salsa*) the embodiment of Latino cultural fusions. The music (named after the whipped egg whites and sugar culinary delight) is a blending of European *contradans* (country dances), the *polka,* the *bachata,* and other Dominican genres, fused with '40s through '60s music from jazz to rock. Merengue was also the platform for speaking out against injustice or for reform, frequently using the "encoding techniques" of calypso or blues. Today, merengue rhythms and basic textures can be heard mixed with everything from hip-hop to reggae.[8.12A]

Stories from the Human Family

Note: Wesley Reynoso was born in the Dominican Republic. His father was a pastor and his large family deeply religious. He grew up listening to vocal music and watching his brothers and friends play instruments. In time, Wesley began to play guitar, and later piano, completely on his own. In his mid-twenties, after playing shows with salsa greats such as the late *Celia Cruz* (the *Queen* of Salsa), he moved to Spanish Harlem in New York, where he met musicians from every part of Latin America and the United States as well. He developed his skills as a jazz pianist, but still prides himself on his ability to play most Latino musical styles. He comments:

"For me music is the most important thing. I was born and brought up listening to music. Everything has music—the car, the train ... I found music everywhere. When I was five, my brother played the guitar. He played all the time and taught me a bit. The sound of the guitar was special.

"My mother sang all the time. She told me when I was a little boy – 'I was singing for you.' And then she'd stop and I was crying and said, 'No, don't stop, sing again.' I loved how she sang; my father sang, brothers, everybody sang. My father was a pastor in the church. In fact, every Sunday morning my father and mother would sing a duet. Everybody expected this.

"No, my sisters sang too—they would also sing a duet. We have nine children in our family. My father and mother taught us everything based on their involvement in the church. That's how we got a strong foundation in both religion and music.

Pic. 8.19D *Not only is singing and dancing important in nearly all Latino cultures, but so too is their enormous devotion both to religion (predominantly Catholicism) and the religious symbols or icons of their religion. Nearly everywhere one walks, one can see reflections of Christian saints, the Virgin Mary (as in this exterior shrine), or some other symbol of their religious beliefs.* Photo: Authors.

"In most Latin communities, actually everywhere in Latin America, music is the heart and soul of the pueblos (villages). A country without music? Oh – that's impossible to even imagine. For many of us, music is our identity.

"For example, in the Dominican Republic, merengue, bachata (more of a slow dance), or merengue typico (rural meringue) is music from the people of the country. Everyone knows it. And when we leave home, people really love the music even more. It helps them connect in their minds to our island culture, to our past.

"I think when you look at the music and people of Cuba, Puerto Rico, Venezuela— really the people and the cultures are very similar. Yes, we have our differences, we all have the fusion of Spanish and African; when I look at Cumbia, Merengue, Son Cubano, Salsa…they are really like cousins. And in our culture, cousins are really just a part of your family. When you say family, you don't just mean brothers and sisters; everyone even remotely related is family. In fact, if you hang out at my house long enough, you will be called 'brother,' 'uncle,' maybe even 'father/papa' from the people of different ages. The music is the same. We may have more of a passion for the music that originated from our home, but when we hear cumbia, or salsa, we see ourselves and most of what we value in this music too.

"A lot of people in my country want to come to the United States. But when you get here, you find that money is too important. Then you find the things you take for granted in your homeland— your family, the way of life, the fact that you are like family everywhere you go at home—these you don't find here.

"In my country, people are really very community-minded and friendly. Everybody greets each other; they make an effort to get to know each other. The musicians too— you may compete with each other, but it's always in a friendly sort of way. I don't know— here, you don't know your neighbor; you don't know who to say 'hi' to. For example, my mother was here last week. She said, 'Oh my God, I don't know anybody here—and nobody seems to want to know me.' You know, everybody says in the Dominican Republic, 'Hey primo, que pasa?' That's like, 'Hey cousin, what's happening?' To everybody we say that.

"Even in our Merengue, we talk about things like this. One famous song is 'Tango Primo' (I have a primo [good friend]). Another song, Buscando Visa (I have to find a visa for my dreams— is how it goes), talks about getting a visa to come to America, and then finding out the dream was really a dream. Our songs really

place a strong focus on the things we like most about life. Then, when many of us leave the island and we hear those songs—and now we don't have those things—we love the songs and our island even more. This means our communities get even stronger both here and back at home. We don't want to lose that sense of family, and our music always speaks to this.

"I think that the Spanish cancion, the song, and all of the dance music of Spain and Africa has to be credited with the formation of Merengue. You hear all those things in the music, and you hear our values in the words. That's what music is in Latin America: it says who we are, what we want, and sets these thoughts to music that lifts your heart. What (more) do you want from music? (laughs)" Wesley Reynoso, Dominican musician, Interview: April 2005.

Tambora drum used in Merengue.

PUERTO RICO

Original Inhabitants

Tainos (Taiwo), Arawak Natives (no known date of origin). Believed to have been mostly killed (influences similar to Cuba).

Colonized

1493 / settled 1508

17th/18th century – Fortified as a Spanish trade port.

1897 – Drafted charter for autonomy (both Cuba and Puerto Rico).

1898 – Spanish-American War – became a colony of the U.S. Experienced multiple changes until …

1946 – Appointment of first Puerto Rican governor. Remains a U.S. commonwealth today.

African Population

No clear record – estimates are early 16th century. Contributing groups likely similar origin as Cuba.

1868 – "El Grito de Lares" was an uprising to abolish slavery and to gain autonomy;

Greater control by European colonizers and by Roman Catholic Church and a smaller island than Cuba, influenced less preservation (or intensity) of the African cultural elements.

Other Significant Events

Since 1930 there have been multiple waves of Puerto Rican migrations to New York City (and back again). There is a very strong similarity between Puerto Rican and Cuban history prior to Castro and the influx of Socialism/Communism into Cuba. From this point on, Puerto Rico becomes exceedingly more fluid in exchanging with U.S. and other Latino cultures (including Cubans in the U.S.).

Musically

Spain – same as Cuba. The influence of the Iberian Peninsula (and Moorish/Roma/Jewish/Spanish fusion is evident in nearly all the music). The guitar gave birth to a smaller "mandolin"-style lute, called the *cuatro* (a similar instrument is used in most of Latin America).

Pic. 8.18B *A percussion line in Puerto Rico mixes a creative blend of timbres, including congas, bongos, timbales, maracas, and guiros.* Photo: i-stockphoto.

Africa (primarily Ghana and Nigeria) – same as Cuba. *Santeria* or African-based worship of Catholic saints (with parallel to Orisha, or Yoruba, "Saints"), also spawned *improvisation y controversia* (improvisational dialogue of music and lyrics). This would become an important part of salsa in later years (the coro section of a salsa piece is virtually a dialogue between a soloist who improvises his lyrics and melody [based upon the theme of the song and the moment of the performance], alternating with the chorus response [the hook or theme of the song]).

Created Fusion (A Partial List)

Many similar to Cuba, Bomba – is a *Rumba*-style dance that fosters competition between the dancers and drummers. *Competitive*–musical sparring between the musicians (and/or dancers)—likely evolved from West African genre, but became even more prevalent as an outlet of emotion under repression (Examples: "the dozens," "capoiera").

Danza – much like the Cuban *habanera* – the first place where we see *guiro* and *maracas* used.

Salsa – *el barrio* of New York (the Puerto Rican/Cuban area of New York—now primarily Spanish Harlem) was the migration point for Puerto Ricans and Cubans into the United States (Miami or southern Florida was another "hotbed" of fusion). The fusion of jazz, rhythm and blues, and further extensions of these fusions (e.g., Latin jazz) were the basis for the creation of *salsa,* a "sauce" of musical genres.

Note: This process of Puerto Rican/Cuban and now pan-Latino fusion of island music with their expatriot communities living in the United States is perpetual and nearly simultaneous. Today *Reggaeton* or Latino hip-hop are examples of music that fuse reggae, R&B, nearly any and every form of pan-Latino, Caribbean, and American music together almost as quickly as they appear, regardless of location of "origin."

Inside the Musician's World

Trío los Favoritos

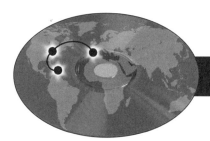

Note: When a student came back from a trip to one of our favorite islands (Puerto Rico), he said he had heard a trio and that they should be on the CD for this project *"because of how much they enjoy playing their music."* For anyone who has not been to Puerto Rico, this may seem like a fairly bland criteria for inclusion, but the passion and the example of the *Son* or *Bolero Puerto Ricaño,* a classic example of the Latino *bolero* or ballad, make a great entry point to Latino music and the values of the cultures as they appear in the music. Most of these songs are like a cultural newspaper of their generation (actually true of most music). But what many of these older *sons/boleros* speak to is family, community, and the values of sustained relationships.

When we contacted the group *Trío los Favoritos,* we received both immediate response and precisely the enthusiasm the student had conveyed. To love something so much that it is fresh and exciting every day must be a joy for these three (actually four) individuals: William Delgado, José, Héctor, and Jaime.

CD 3.5

"No Quiero Nada Mas," by Trío los Favoritos, from the CD: <u>**Trío los Favoritos,**</u> c. 2004.

> Mr. Reynoso commented: *"This is beautiful music. He says he loves God. He's looking for a nice woman who has values, integrity, and principles. He says she will love me for who I am, not for what I have.*
>
> *"This music is like a Bolero or romantic song. It has a steady rhythm to dance to, but especially the lyrics speak to older values and to the simplicity of life, or in this case, true love. That is, a dedication of two people to each other, not just romance like you see in the nouvellas (Spanish language soap operas – which are extremely popular throughout Latin America), or about physical or sexual attraction, but the kind of love that really holds up until the people get old. That is how most of us see our parents and grandparents— how they got old together— and when you see something like that, hear it in your songs and dances, you begin to think about it, desire it, and compose it into your own songs.*
>
> *"You know, even though I'm young, I like the old music better than a lot of the young music, as far as the stories and values. There are so many ways music can touch you. The rhythms drives your heart and energy to your body, the melody and harmony touch your soul, and the story, that is what goes to your mind and makes you think of all the things life should be or could be."*

This piece uses a *cuatro* (small *mandolin-style* lute), a guitar, and an acoustic bass guitar (*gitarrón*), as well as hand percussion—*bongos*. The three-part harmonization of the chorus is a typical style of the boleros and songs of earlier generations, and it has transferred into the *coros* (chorus sections) of modern salsa as well. The harmonized melodies of the cuatro and guitar (synchronized melodic movement) are also enjoyable.

Salsa—The *Sauce* of Life

What **salsa** (the musical sauce) means to Latinos worldwide, and thousands of musicians or people fascinated by Latino culture and its music, food, and family orientation, is hard to put into words. At its root is the culmination of everything we've spoken about in the evolution of Spanish *flamenco*; plus, everything listed in the music of Cuba, Puerto Rico, and much of Latin America; the very essence of *jazz,*and the importance of the New York, Miami, and Los Angeles musical communities; and finally the visions and intense hard work of a few individuals who served as ambassadors for the cultures and music when stereotypes and prejudice initially threatened the lives and spirits of many Latinos living in the *barrios* of America's large urban areas.

From the first portrayals of Latino music on the "I Love Lucy" show with Desi Arnez; to the salsa orchestras of Ray Barretto, Tito Puente, the Fania All-stars, Eddie and Charlie Palmieri, or Willie Colon; to the vocal stylizations and bubbly character of Celia Cruz; to the fusions of R & B, rock 'n' roll, and Latino music of Carlos Santana, Latino music has built into its musical DNA, the code for creative fusion. It is, therefore, a metaphor for human existence and life. That the music is such a critical part of Latino communities everywhere is evidenced in these emails sent to the families or media concerning Tito Puente or Celia Cruz shortly after their passing:

"To Whom It May Concern:

Many of us (in the military) who have our roots in NY are cognizant of the loss you have suffered. However, speaking for myself, "Tito" was more than a musician. He was a positive role model/mentor as well. I say this because he proved that if one man could get out of the 'barrios' of N.Y. through hard work, we all had a chance. Listening to Tito's music relaxed me through college and law school, as well as through other trying moments in my life. Additionally, his music opened the eyes of others who thought that 'Latin music' was a trivial art form. Lastly, Tito will not only be missed for his music, but for what his music accomplished. He was one of the better unofficial ambassadors of good will this nation ever produced. Thank you for your time." Sincerely, M.J. Lewis

"This morning I woke up and received the news that Tito had passed away. My heart felt sadness, and it was just last night that while watching Carlos Santana play 'Oye Como Va' (written by Tito Puente) to a sell-out crowd on his Fox TV special that I thought of Tito and his wonderful music how it has influenced many young musicians. I first heard of Tito when a 'drumming-friend' of mine grabbed me and dragged me to where he was playing a concert. Being a drummer myself, I was awestruck by his genius, his music, but most of all his friendliness. After his show, I met him, and we talked drums. He said, 'It doesn't matter what style you play...Latin, rock, whatever. When you play it though...feel it... live it....' His smile, his warmth, his enthusiasm caught hold of me, and I've been in love with his music and did hear him when he spoke. Tito... we'll miss you!!! I'm feeling it right now!!! Tomorrow night I'll play a song for you!" Fred Axberg, drummer in Minneapolis

"No matter how far away from Havana her career or political differences took her, Celia was still one of us. She was a national symbol of pride in how far we could go when we combined our hard work with a hearty laugh and a good dance. As famous as Cuban cigars, the warmth of our people, and the beauty of our beaches, Celia was the voice of Cuba. And by making the world jam, she became our greatest cultural export." From: *Celia Was Cuba,* by Jeordan Legon, CNN, Saturday, November 22, 2003.

Salsa's roots can be traced back to the continent of Africa. In West Africa, it was commonplace to find people playing instruments that resembled the *bata* drums or *conga* drums of Cuba and Puerto Rico or

Pic. 8.25 *A Harlem residential brownstone in Spanish Harlem, mid-December 2004. Out of the daily communications in close quarters of Latinos from a variety of cultures, salsa and the New York-based recording company Fania Records was created. The company introduced many of first-generation salsa singers and musicians to the world. Founded by Dominican flutist and band-leader Johnny Pacheco and impresario Jerry Masucci, Fania began its illustrious influence with Willie Colón and Héctor Lavoe's El Malo in 1967. This was followed by a series of updated son montuno and plena tunes that are "credited" to have contributed greatly to salsa by 1973.* Photo: Released to public domain by Moncrief. [8.13]

the *pandereta* (tambourine/tambur) in a manner common to that of salsa. Salsa's most direct antecedent is Cuban *son montuno,* which itself is a combination of African and European influences. Puerto Rican plena, Trinidadian calypso, Jamaican reggae, American rock, Dominican merengue, and Colombian cumbia were also major sources of musical inspiration during the 1970s in the Latino melting pot of New York City. So salsa (very much like the sauce) is a complete mixture of musical/cultural elements. In the last four to five decades of the 20th century, modulating influences of *mambo, rumba, chachachá,* and *charanga* altered the elements of *son montuno,* giving birth to salsa, which currently enjoys a global appeal.

Today's modern salsa, however, is said to have begun in the streets of New York in the late 1960s. At this time, Latin pop was not as much a force in American music as were doo-wop, R&B, and rock and roll. The influence of Latino immigrants, in particular Cubans, Puerto Ricans, and Dominicans in New York, and both the strong sense of creative flexibility and fusion (embedded in the cultures through their history) and the need to "re-create" a sense of community in the new environment ushered in the creation of today's salsa and the force that is now as globally influential as it is *pan-Latino.*

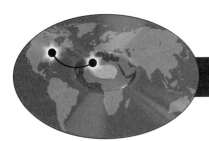

Salsa

Note: When we began to look for a single example of Salsa, we wondered how we would embody the global nature of its fusions in a single piece. One thought was to get a selection from the all-Japanese Salsa group *Orchestra de la Luz,* since their affinity for Salsa exemplifies the effect that salsa has had on the world community. Another example, *Salsa Tumbao,* recorded by Arc Music International, landed in our laps (so to speak). This recording features musicians from Chile, the Dominican Republic, Mexico, and Europe—not a single

Salsa (a "Pan-Latino" music and dance genre) incorporates a fusion of Spanish-style "feet" dancing, Afro-Cuban-style rumba, African percussion, New York-style jazz and blues horn sections, and, today, nearly every other style of music found in the Americas—hence, a "sauce" of dance and music styles. Photo: Courtesy Joe Brandt.

Puerto Ricano or Cubano among them. Yet, you will hear the passion and multiple rhythmic layers that are essential to the *sauce of rhythms and dances* that we call salsa.

"Candela y Tumbao," by Arc studio band (featuring Gastón de Avila, vocals), from the CD: **Salsa Tumbao,** Arc Music International c. 2002.

Mr. Reynoso commented: *"The clavé (rhythm of the clavé) is grouped 2 – 3 rather than 3 to 2 (referring to the organization of rhythmic accents in the timeline or clavé rhythms, –* the basic rhythm which all other rhythms lock to). *You can hear this rhythm right at the beginning of the piece. Then, bit by bit, the layers of texture are added.*

"They sing: 'Listen we are going to enjoy the bass melody' then, basically 'enjoy the music.' Of course this music is designed to bring people together. I think this is the most famous Latino music, because like its name, 'sauce,' it takes a little bit from everyone. But when you hear it, you don't hear 'Cuban' or 'Mexican' or 'New York barrio'; you hear everyone.

Pic. 8.26A *Conga drums, the heart and soul of pan-Latino community and dance music.* Photo: Courtesy, Larkinthemorning.com.

"They also sing: 'We are going to dance and enjoy the 'son' [a specific son cubano].' I have a friend, who doesn't mean disrespect, but to show you how important our music is to us— you know the 'trinity' ['in the name of the Father, the Son, and the Holy Ghost']—he says, 'in the name of the Rumba, the Clavés and the Chachacha.' (laughs) But it's true, when you get to the Mambo (the exciting part of the music after the Coro – where the instruments 'take off' [circa 2:23 in the piece]), you can't help feel the passion as deeply for the music almost as you do for our Creator.

"You really don't need to translate this whole thing; you focus on the musical energy and respect the musicianship and diversity of sweat, pain, cultural history, and the basics of Latino fusion over centuries That's the essence of this piece." Additionally, it is the conga (coon-ga) drums which characterize a vast majority of today's pan-Latino music.

The Recipe of Sound

It is the layering of instruments—pulling them in, taking them out—that creates the tension and release and, ultimately, the excitement of salsa. The sonograph for this piece might indicate these exchanges of instruments as follows:

Introduction:
| Clavé rhythm 2-3 pattern) | Piano (montuno style) ||: Brass Melody #1 | Brass Melody #2   :||
                                  Percussion/Vibraphone [8.14]
                                                              Interlude: like the intro.

|| Sung – "Coro" (chorus) | Brass Melody #2 || Coro | Brass Melody #2 || Clavé |

| Congas(perc.) || Brass Mel. #1 | Brass Mel. #2 ||: Coro #2 | Vocal solo   :||
                                                                   improvised on topic of song

Mambo – a rise in energy and rhythmic complexity
||: Piano | Brass Melody #3 (altered #2) : || Vibraphone solo ||: Perc. | Brass Mel.#3   :||

| Percussion solo (conga drums – pronounced koon-ga)
                              Fade to the end

Mexican Hospitality

Pic. 8.26 & 8.27 *This mural (carved rock and mosaic) in Monterrey, Mexico, represents "the daily triumph of civilization and culture over the dark forces of stagnation and apathy." Generally, there is nothing stagnant about human evolution and the perpetual exchange of "culture" or mixing of ideas since the earliest civilizations. To understand "Mexican" culture, however, requires also the recognition that 60-70% of Mexican communities are "Mestizo"—or, a mixture of Spanish (European) and indigenous cultures.* Photo: Mural – Jorge Gonzaléz Camerena, by Nathaniel C. Sheetz, and a street festival in Mexico City, by abalcazar.

MEXICO

Original Inhabitants

There is a 3,000-year history of Mesoamerican civilizations, including Aztec, Olmecs, Toltecs, and Mayans. The Aztecs probably reached the height of their civilization around the 10th or 11th centuries. Their influence, and the influence of Native Americans throughout much of Southwestern North America, is intimately woven into the fabric of Mexican cultures, more so than most in the Caribbean Latino fusions above. *Mestizos* (mixed Amerindian and Spanish) make up roughly 60-70% of the Mexican population. The integration and mixing of the Native and Spanish cultures is an important characteristic of nearly all Latino cultures in Central and South America as well.

Colonized

Spanish arrived early 16th century. They defeated the *Mexica* (primarily Aztecs) in 1521 and began a three-hundred-year reign in what became known as "new Spain."

1810 – Catholic Priest (Miquel Costilla) declared independence from Spain. War lasted until 1821 Independence.

Mid 1800s – Mexican government issued "land grants" to United States immigrants (many of whom were European immigrants from Slovak, Polish, or other central/Eastern European nations).

1836 – Texas won independence / 1840s Mexican-American war: United States "acquired" California, Nevada, Utah, Arizona, New Mexico, and Colorado.

African Population

There is less of a population of African descent in Mexico than nearly anywhere in Latin America. However, along the coastal regions (east coast), populations of African slaves and escaped slaves contributed to some of the musical and cultural forms. In the north, many escaped slaves from the United States found their way to Mexico. In many cases, Africans and indigenous cultures fully integrated without conflict.

Other Significant Events

"Mexico" at one point included the vast majority of the western United States. The Spanish/Mestizo culture was present even before the massive migration of Mexicans to the United States in the mid-to-late 20th century.

Musically

Spain – similar to Cuba. But the various regions reflect the dynamics of fusion differently. *Mexican Son, Zapateado* (tap-like/heel dances) – were among the most popular (see fusion below);

Africa / Indigenous – little was written about these cultures, and there is little comparison to the dynamics of the island cultures. There are indications in the *son nordeño,* and later fusion styles of Aztec/Mayan music (use of flute, drums, and other percussion instruments) to indicate fusion.

Pic. 8.18D *A Mestizo (dressed in Aztec regalia) plays the flute, conch shell, and drum, while a young Mexican man dances without inhibitions. It becomes for the most part pointless to see "who is Native and who isn't" when in Mexico and much of the southwestern part of the United States. The mixing of Spanish and Native cultures over centuries has nearly obliterated the lines of ethnic origin and separation.* Photo: Authors.

Created Fusions (A Partial List)

In addition to the above (*Mestizo*) fusions:

Mariachi – the emblem of Mexican music to outside cultures, was a fusion of *son* (song in Spanish), *Nordeno*–mixing of Bohemian miners' music (primarily 19th-century polkas and waltzes), and the use of accordion, violins, and even trumpets. *Mariachi* both influenced the creation of, and has been influenced by (a common process of cross-influencing of musical genres in all cultures), *Mexican Ranchera, Tex-Mex, Tejano,* and *Banda* (Mexican "big band" music of the 1990's). Although Mariachi music was once a more distinct fusion from most of Latin American music, the broad popularity of Mexican *novellas* (soap operas), movies, and the incorporation of other Latino or Mexican-American music into Mexican son and Mariachi-style music have created an ever-narrowing gap between Mexican Latinos and other Latin Americans.

Stories from the Human Family

On a recent trip to *Mexicali* (Baha California), the northwesternmost province of Mexico, we sat down to have lunch and were taken as tourists by groups of strolling musicians who asked what we wanted to hear. Soloists, trios, and quartets all paraded through the streets to play their music for tourist dollars. To one group, we responded, *'What do you like to play the most?'* Taken somewhat aback by this request, when they had just played *"La Cucaracha"* (the famous "cockroach" song) three times in the same venue, they paused.

One of the musicians, clearly the elder of the group, said, *"If you really want to hear what we would like, you must be prepared to listen for a while longer."* We said, "No problem," and they began to play. The song was a form of music, *Nordeño,* which incorporated the accordion, the guitar, the bass, and drums, in this case in the singing of an older *ranchera-style* (Western country music fusion) waltz (in a 3-beat meter).

Pic. 8.21 *A group of some of the most dignified and hardworking musicians the author has ever met, who, though desiring to remain nameless, represented the depth of passion for music and storytelling not uncommon in Mexican culture.* Photo: Authors.

Michael's Experience:

At first, I could see they were tired; it was already nearly eight p.m. They may have been playing since early in the afternoon. But as the multi-verse song progressed, and they began to smile, to close their eyes as they harmonized in three parts (everyone but the drummer), you could increasingly see that they had transported themselves to another world: the world of musical storytelling.

I have played music, composed music, heard music all my life, but never have I been in a position where I was playing music in such a locale where I could very well be disrespected (playing for tourists, some of whom may not look at them as artists and passionate musicians, but as a novelty) and yet still played music with such passion from the depths of my soul.

After their song, we chatted about music, about Mexico, and their families, and about how they got into music (as well as our Spanish would hold out—thank you, Léonie [my wife], for bailing me out!) I asked them if they would like to be included in our book; they said yes, but no names. So I include this story, the picture, and a recommendation: if you ever get to Mexicali, and you see these guys, *listen hard*. They definitely have a lot to teach us! Author, July 2004.

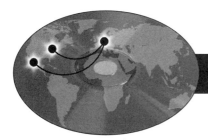 Inside the Musician's World

Mariachi Sol

Note: The following notes are included in this ARC CD by *Mariachi Sol* (Mexican folkloric group), recorded in Hamburg, Germany: *"Mariachi – is the name of traditional Mexican street music. While in earlier times only the violin (vihuela) and the gitarrón (large acoustic bass guitar) were used (and occasionally a harp), today many more instruments are involved in Mariachi music. The trumpet was incorporated at the end of the 1950s, and later (occasionally) a small flute (flautín) was used.*

"Mariachi music can be romantic but also lively. It is well suited for public festivals and weddings. Guerrero music is real 'farmer's' music. It represents the dances of the farmers and of the cowboys (Ganaderos).

The various pieces in the medley below include a traditional *Mariachi piece ("La Negra"), a Huapango ("El Pastor,"* a lively dance of Spanish origin from the Gulf coast that mixes two-beat [duple] and three-beat [triple] meters), and a *Son Guerrerense ("El Arrancazacate,"* a "farmer's" song that uses the harp).

A Medley of Mexican music, including: **"La Negra (The Black Woman)," "El Pastor (The Pastor),"** and **"El Arrancazacate,"** by Mariachi Sol, from the CD: **Mexico Lindo,** Arc Music International, c. 1999.

La Negra – ("The Dark/Black Woman")

Mr. Reynoso comments: *"This is a typico (standard) Mariachi-style piece."* He translates: *"'go ahead, say yes to anybody … but only love me.'* In Spanish, to love has different meanings. You can care for someone and still not give your heart. But the type of love that most songs talk about is the type where you devote your heart, and this really means your life, to the other person.*

Pic. 8.23 *A street musician in Northern Mexico with a large repertoire of songs (asking for requests – and over a fifteen-minute period, knew them all) takes his music very seriously.* Photo: Authors.

"He says: 'Where is my 'black' woman; I want her here with me.' You know, to the majority of Latinos, 'black' has no real negative connotation. What is great about Mariachi is that, unlike much of the rest of Latin America, each of its themes and even its sounds have a bit different fusion. Those of us from the islands relate a bit different to some forms of Mexican music, because it doesn't have quite as much of the African rhythms as most of the rest of our music."* Note: In modern Mexican music, the influence and fusion of other Latino cultures is greatly influencing today's young musicians.

El Pastor – ("The Pastor")

Mr. Reynoso translates: *"She says, 'The pastor is like a shepherd and with his flute draws in the lamb to his flock.' This is great metaphor for how many people see the priest or pastor—or even religion generally in Latin America. The concept generally is, you cannot have a community if you don't have a leader or someone to guide. When the African cultures and indigenous cultures came and mixed with the Spanish Catholic religion, the saints, and the disciples of Christ ... became the 'saints' or 'orishas' of West African religion, and I'm sure the same parallel to the Natives."*

The yodeling style of singing is both a tradition in some Mexican music (largely an influx of central European song and dance forms, including Alpine yodeling and Polish [Europe-wide] polka). The long-held notes are a standard means for building tension, increasing excitement, and then, usually, releasing the note and tension to a chorus of responses and yells from the audience.

There are (on average) about three "holidays" or mini-festivals every month in all or parts of Mexico. Many of them are religion-based, including some which honor *saints (Ex: Día de los Santos Reyes, Fiesta of Saint Peter and Saint Paul), Catholic celebrations (Navidad—Christmas, Semana Santa—the week of Easter), and "pagan" or Native/Catholic fusions (El Dia de los Muertos – Day of the Dead, or Carnaval),* plus birthdays, coming of age, and virtually any other reason for the extended families to come together.

El Arrancazacate

Mr. Reynoso further commented: *"You know, a few years back, you would not hear much of this kind of music in my community. This is more music from Uruguay, Paraguay....It has the music of the 'Indios' (native cultures) mixed with Spanish. The harp—who knows how it got there* (brought over from Spain to Mexico and South America during colonization) *– is a favorite instrument of some of these people. But because the music is good, I mean really exciting to listen to, you can hear some of their techniques, at times even the instrument transferred onto other Latin American music."*

The Recipe of Sound

Piece I: "La Negra"– This is a classic example of Mariachi *classico* (classical style) with the introduction that slowly winds to the 3-beat waltz rhythm. But the rhythm itself shifts as the accents of the guitars (which take on the role of percussion) also shift. The formula of harmony is close voicing (close prox-

Pic. 8.24 *Perhaps like Mexican food, Mexican music and musicians have strong appeal throughout the world. It is not unusual, in a common city accessible to tourists, to have 20-100 musicians or numerous groups strolling or playing in restaurants or clubs at any given time.* Photo: Authors.

imity of notes) in a moving triadic (simple chord harmony). The basic formula for Mariachi is to play a small section of music, follow this with a repetitive section by the chorus, then back to either the violins or the trumpets in alternating fashion. Because it is highly participatory (audience and group interact with calls and yells), Mariachi is one of the main highlights at important life cycle events or community celebrations (see "El Pastor" list of festivals).

Piece II: "El Pastor"– A similar 3-beat meter (a favorite meter in much of Mexican music). This piece uses the voice in an imitative fashion to mimic the flute used by the shepherd. The main feature of this song after the flute imitation and repetitive melody is the sustained "chorus" or second section and the "yodel"-style technique, which in vocal terms switches from the "chest" or main voice to the **falsetto** or false/head-resonated voice.

Piece III: "El Arrancazacate"– This piece, besides being fast and exciting, and uses the harp, which is believed to have come from the Indigenous cultures and not from European (though some feel it may have come from African *kora-like* instruments). The piece uses two simultaneously different accent patterns in the 6/8 or *compound meter.* Against a running pattern of 6 notes per measure, you have both groups of two (three per measure) and groups of three (two per measure) being accented at the same time. This, together with the fast tempo, makes an otherwise simple piece very energetic and compelling (formerly: the "good" beat).

South American Fusion

In earlier Units we explored some of the fusions of indigenous cultures and their music in Ecuador, Bolivia, or Peru. But this is also only the tip of the musical iceberg in the South American culture/music exchange:

- Argentina – sports the fusions of European popular music with Spanish music (and less African contact) – perhaps best embodied in the *tango.*
- Uruguay and Paraguay – both have various blends of Spanish and indigenous cultures, with Uruguay having been more influenced by European and Brazilian music and Paraguay more by indigenous cultures (Guarani and Bolivian Quechua), with a special affinity for and use of the harp.
- Chile, Peru, Bolivia, and Ecuador all share the mixtures of Quechua and Spanish culture with varying influences from African cultures.
- Venezuela, Columbia, the Guyanas, Surinam, and Brazil are all dramatic fusions of indigenous, Spanish, and various African cultures, with Brazil replacing "Spanish" with "Portuguese."

Although there is still enormous diversity in the geography, the cultural history, and the politics of each of these cultures, they share many common experiences, including their fusion processes having begun at the same time, having followed many of the same dynamics, and are now equally affected by the global phenomenon of cultural sharing— which has been given wings by modern media. Although any of these musical cultures would have brought enormous energy to this project, Brazil, known for its *samba, bossa nova,* and *carnival*, and Colombia, known especially for its *cumbia,* are the two we'll touch upon.

Samba—The Music of, and for, Community

Anyone who has experienced the huge ritual of *carnaval* (carnival) Brazilian style has also experienced one of the largest "community" celebrations in the world. Such a fortunate individual may also have been exposed to a music that is designed by communities —for— community participation. In its essence, the evolution of the role of *samba* (and, for that matter, many aspects of Brazilian culture) resemble the fusion processes of Cuban, Puerto Rican, or Colombian musical genres and culture. What is different is that the Spanish culture was not the colonizer; and although many of the African inhabitants did come from Yoruba and Quimbundu areas of West Africa (now Nigeria, Benin, and Angola), the country that would become the primary African colonizer and exchange partner was Portugal, which also colonized the African territory of Angola. As a result, the triangle of influences has enormous similarities to those of other Latino cultures, but shifts its points of origin to encompass Portugal, Angola, and Brazil.

Samba probably got its name from the Angolan/Portuguese term *semba (mesemba)*. Originating as a fusion of Portuguese music (Spanish/Moor/Portuguese) and African dance and songs, it found a higher degree of preservation of its African "roots" than did the music of many colonized countries. By the 1960s, samba had become directly tied with *samba schools (escola de samba),* or large neighborhoods or communities that prepared costumes, floats, and their own music for carnaval. Samba gained an enormous insurgence of energy from the dictator Getúlio Vargas, who declared samba Brazil's national music.

Like every genre that takes precedence in a culture, samba has undergone multiple variations, and its use has been reflected over the course of generations. The essence of samba makes it one of the largest and most participatory *"community musical genres"* in the world.

As each samba school prepares its themes, costumes, and parade ideas for the subsequent year's carnaval, the musicians in the school begin to write the lyrics, design a melody, and ultimately, arrange the music to the school's (community's) theme. Frequently, the message is something that is at the core of the public's sentiment. It may be political, anti-political, social, or simply samba, music, carnaval, or Brazil. At the center of the music, besides and infectious and layered rhythm – is the melody. It will be sung by everyone in the school and if "catchy" enough, will also be voted as the "samba of the year." Minimally, it may catch on in the public at large as the school parades its colors, floats, and enormous pride through the streets of Brazil's cities and villages during carnaval.

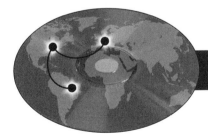

Inside the Musician's World

Arc Studio Musicians

Pic. 8.28 *Similar to this group of musicians playing "Canadian Jazz-Samba" in Montreal, a different fusion of samba and bossa nova has become enormously popular among jazz musicians in North America and Europe.* Photo: Authors.

"Brisa Marina," by Arc Studio Ensemble from the CD: <u>**Samba Bossa do Brazil,**</u> Arc Music International c. 1999.

Both the *Samba* and *Bossa Nova* (a slower personal or political commentary style of music – emblematic to the Blues) found their way to the United States in the late 1950's and early 1960's primarily through the compositional efforts of João Gilberto and Antonio Carlos Jobim, now considered the *fathers* of Bossa Nova and Brazilian jazz. Out of the context of its original affiliation with the community festival of *carnaval,* the vibrant rhythmic layering – like that of rumba and eventually salsa – and the complex and well-developed melodies, plus Brazilian affinity for improvisation, eventually found an immediate audience in the jazz community.

Pieces such as the piece *"Marine Breeze" (Brisa Marina)* named after the feel and smells of one of the largest and most popular stretches of beach that connect Brazil's two largest cities – Sao Paulo and Rio de Janeiro (and homes of the two most magnificent *carnaval* celebrations) represent the perpetual fusions that go on between all of the regions of the Americas, their European colonizers, and their African roots.

> **Note:** An article, *"The Man Who Invented Bossa Nova,"* by Daniella Thompson, appeared under the title "Plain João" in the May 1998 issue of Brazil magazine that can also be found on the website: www.joaogilberto.org/daniella.htm. She writes: *"Bossa nova, that most personal and international of Brazilian musical forms, has been blessed with numerous gifted composers. By far the greatest was Antônio Carlos (Tom) Jobim. Alone or in partnership with poet Vinícius de Moraes, fellow composer Newton Mendonça, and other illustrious collaborators, Jobim created some of the most famous and enduring bossa nova standards, such as "Garota de Ipanema," "Desafinado," and "Corcovado."*
>
> *"Tom Jobim and Vinícius de Moraes, the seminal bossa nova songwriting team, met in 1956, but the songs they turned out at the time were not particularly innovative. For two years, Jobim/de Moraes tunes sounded like traditional samba-canção (samba-song, a slower and more lyrical version of samba). Nobody got particularly excited over them. Then a certain young singer and guitarist (João Gilberto) came out of nowhere to give these songs a new vocal interpretation and a new beat. The year was 1958, and the new beat was soon known throughout the world as bossa nova."*

The Recipe of Sound

Although this piece is a *jazz-samba,* and not that played by samba-schools or of an older lineage, the basic *shuffle rhythm* of the bass and bass drum (caixa – or large tom) are present, as are the layered rhythms of the triangle and *tamborim* (small tambourine) which create the backbone of the *samba* rhythm.

In this piece, the flute plays actually a melody that resembles those found in the highlands of the distant Western part of Brazil or neighboring Bolivia. Meanwhile, the improvisational

Pic. 8.34 *Samba schools, their percussionists, dancers, float builders, costume designers, and all of their families, make carnaval (Brazilian style), not only arguably the largest community ritual on the planet, but one which sustains the "community" for the duration of much of the year in preparation.*
Photo: Courtesy Nadine Lind

section, resembles the feel of the *samba melody,* as it extends itself beyond the traditional popular melody length of eight to twelve measures and include multiple sections or choruses.

In *samba* – designed for carnaval, the melodies will go on for an extended duration, and will have multiple sections. Additionally, they will generally not be harmonized, as the primary purpose of the music is to create musical and community solidarity — *everyone singing along with the melody in unison.* The rhythm layering of a samba school piece will generally include anywhere from five to ten percussion layers, one of which is the *cuica,* a fascinating drum that is not played by striking the head, but by rubbing a bamboo stick attached to the head, resulting in an almost human sound.

COLOMBIA

Original Inhabitants

Native culture dates back to approximately 1450BCE.

The "cacicazgos" (the Cacique), with a pyramidal structure of power, and, especially, the Muisca or Chibcha people populated much of Colombia, which at one time included parts of Venezuela and Ecuador, and were the second-most populated indigenous groups after the Incas.

Colonized

1500 – Spanish conquest and settlement began.

1525 – First settlement on Atlantic (Gulf of Mexico) coast was established.

16th century – Spanish brought African slaves from other islands to work plantations.

1819 – Achieved independent status as a republic (one of the first to do so, setting off a chain of independent movements through Central and South America, which preceded nearly all movements for independence in the Caribbean.

African Population

The first settlement was in the early 16th century and was likely a fusion of West African culture groups, including re-population of groups from the Caribbean.

Other Significant Events

Civil wars and drug trade have paralyzed much of Colombia's economy and politics since the 1940s. However, although the politics and economy have suffered innumerable transitions, Colombian culture itself has proven to be very receptive to exchange with other cultures, as evidenced by the diversity of music which now permeates the airwaves.

Musically

Spain – similar to Cuba and other regions in origin.

Africa – similar to Cuba/Dominican Republic in origin.

Stirred Together You Get (A Partial List)…

Colombia's proximity to Venezuela, Ecuador, Central America, and the Caribbean (e.g., Trinidad, Cuba, and Jamaica) has made it a hub of cultural mixing for an extended period of time. Slavery was abolished in the early 19th century, but the culture freely mixed both before the abolishment and even more so afterwards.

Cumbia – The national dance of Colombia, like *merengue* in the Dominican Republic, has a series of stages in its evolution that include a strong fusion of African dance and percussion, the *Santeria*-style fusion of religious celebration through music, and the incorporation of big band influences of the 1940s in the United States, which brought the use of saxophones, trumpets, and trombones to Latino music. The *cumbia* has also both contributed to, and itself taken on, numerous influences from salsa and most Latino popular styles.

Colombian Cumbia

It may by now be apparent that since the earliest records of human history, some of the greatest or most inspirational music and art masterpieces have been born from the most significant, emotional, and diverse circumstances of human existence. When all three – enormous difficulties, extreme emotion, and the greatest possible diversity of "race," culture, and musical genres—are present, attractive and vibrant fusions are fostered. This is, in some ways, the cultural parallel to the impact of a diverse gene pool on strengthening genetic inheritance.

Pic. 8.29 *Young women dancing Colombia's national dance—the Cumbia—with Hungarian-born percussionist Istvan Dely.* Photo: Courtesy/copyright Istvan Dely, 2005.

In Colombia, as a result of the same Spanish conquest, the repetitive phenomenon of indigenous presence, the recurring theme of African slavery, and the cyclical updates in cultural infusion brought on by cultures in contact, conflicts, exterior intervention, and perpetual interaction with other culture groups, cumbia was born. Now the national music and dance of Colombia, cumbia has become a metaphor for human cultural exchange and fusion.

One take on cumbia reads: *"Cumbia is the net intersection of three cultures that settled in Colombia at different times: indigenous peoples, Spanish/Moorish, and African slaves. Some claim that cumbia began as a courtship dance among the slave population. It has now spread to the "world music" community and is highly popular in the Latin music scene.*[8.15]

In attempting to distinguish the audience and practitioners of the music/dance form, the article continues: *"Cumbia is very popular in all of South America (except Brazil), and there are lots of different flavors of it. It can be compared to country music and dance orchestras … It is also the music that bus drivers all over South America play to keep awake. In fact, it is mostly popular with the lower social classes and often scorned by the upper classes. In Argentina, this social divide is exemplified by the cumbia villera phenomenon. Villa miserias refer to the shanty towns where the most marginalized members of society live, and cumbia villera is their music."*[8.16]

In one sense, the origins and context of cumbia bring us full circle to the topics of initial discussion. Africa and Latin America sustain human communities that practice regular use of ritual connected to the motion of the life cycle. Both regularly use music and dance as a means of actively building a synergy of human interaction. Wherever in the world members of these communities may later move and meet again, they are likely to continue to perpetuate regular and frequent self-sustaining and community-building social rituals, aided greatly by their music and dance traditions.

Stories from the Human Family

Note: Hungarian-born Istvan Dely moved to Colombia in 1977 because of his passion for Afro-Caribbean/South American percussion. Having learned to play *congas* in Cuba, he was among the first to introduce Latin percussion to his native Hungary and Central Europe. Because he already had a passion for jazz and Afro-Caribbean music, the transplantation of his roots to Colombia seemed to have been born from a natural affinity. He married an Afro-Colombian singer-songwriter and created his family musical group, *Millero Congo,* in Cartegena, Colombia. He wrote:

"I really like this quote: 'Music is not merely an artifact designed to entertain and to please: it constitutes an essential part of the existence and the well-being of both the individual and the community (Richard Carlin).'

"As with speech, another of God's gifts that distinguishes man from all other forms of life, music is an innate potential which requires cultural training. Not all of us can or need become professionals, virtuosos, geniuses, but we, each and all, can and need to learn to give (produce) and not only receive (consume) music. In an age when our 'civilization' in the West has lost nearly all sense and experience of community, of belonging, and of solidarity, it is all the more important to regain the practice of communal music and dance, which of all the art forms are the most socially binding, rallying, and community-forging, which frees us from our 'separateness.'

"Here's another of my favorites: 'Music is a social game, in which every member of the community has a place of his own; and this is the purpose of the game: to find our place in society (Ray Lema).'

"To me, music is a language. Its close relationship to—and common origin with—speech is evident to anyone who has ever observed a baby. Even before he/she can utter the first word, he/she hums and sings. To many researchers, music as a form of communication appeared in man long before words acquired meaning. To Russian composer M. Mussorgsky, 'Music is not an end in itself but a means to speak with the people.' Hence the responsibility of the musician is great.

"Master drummer from Mali, Yaya Diallo, teaches that 'throughout a musical apprenticeship, you need to be conscious that you are emitting sounds and that these sounds have an impact upon people. You can see it when you play music and people cry in response to some sounds and dance in response to others. If such reactions are so evident to our eyes, how much more does music affect our health and minds! When you are playing music, you need to be conscious of how you are affecting people. I have met many musicians in North America who only want to make a hit record, regardless of the value of the music on deeper levels. They are not aware of the subtle effects of music on human well-being, but musicians should be aware of their role. They can build or destroy. They can produce tears, fatigue, excitement, or calm in people. Playing music to benefit the people was the fundamental value of our musical culture.'

Pic. 8.29A *A brass band from St. Peter's School in York, U.K., performs in Prague's St. Nicholas Church. The possibility to provide young people with the opportunity to experience new cultures or to work with other youth as a "musical community" drives instructors of music dance, such as their director Chris Blood. What is also, however, indefinable is the power that music, multiple vibrations organized to create strong emotion and communicate our common human experience, has on the human soul.* Photo: Authors.

"I like this too: 'Music is spiritual food for the soul (Abdu'l-Bahá).' Because music is food for the soul, to me all music of enduring quality, of whatever type, age, or people, though transmitted through material channels—that is, the vibrations of the air that we call sound— is an expression of the spiritual dimension in man. The human voice and the musical sounds produced on instruments arise from intentions in the invisible human interior and penetrate to the invisible interior of listeners, as well as to the surrounding invisible realm of spirits and ancestors. 'Music thus can be a potent force for maintaining or restoring human harmony with the cosmos (Yaya Diallo).' Hope that helps!" Istvan Dely, Hungary/ Colombia, June 2005.

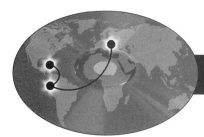

Inside the Musician's World

Istvan Dely and family group
Millero Congo, with Leonor, David, and Shangó

Note: One of the more fascinating stories of cultural migration in this text came from Istvan Dely's musical/cultural journey: *"Having been born and raised in landlocked Hungary, also locked up at the time behind the Iron Curtain of the Communist Bloc, I felt an irresistible call to the tropical South and to the African peoples and their music, especially drumming, ever since I was a child.*

"I was sent on a scholarship to Cuba in 1966 to write up my Master's Degree thesis on contemporary Latin American literature. I threw myself body and soul into the thriving Afro- Cuban religious music, learned my drumming trade, and ended up as an initiated tatan'ganga (Congo priest). After three years, I brought back to Hungary the first- ever conga drums and other Latin percussion. I taught my brother László, and together we became a legend of sorts, playing, recording, and touring with many of the major progressive Hungarian rock and jazz groups of the seventies."

CD 3.9

"Cumbia Cienagüera," by Istvan Dely & Millero Congo, from the CD: **Millero Congo,** Insignia Records c. 1996.

Mr. Dely wrote:*"Once you get infected with the fever of the Black Caribbean, you never get rid of it; you can never get enough of it. So in 1977, at the peak of my career as percussionist and translator of North and South American literature, I escaped back and settled for good in Cartagena, Colombia. With my Afro-Colombian wife, singer-songwriter Leonor, and our all-round musician sons*

*David and Shangó, we embarked upon a joint venture of passionate and success-
ful 'cultural ecology,' attempting to 'rescue' (in a sense) and develop the African
and Native American heritage in the music of Colombia and the Caribbean
among city youth. I also had the opportunity to travel widely with the same mission, ever learning and teaching drumming, in West Africa (Ivory Coast, Ghana,
Gambia, Guinea Bissau) and the Circum-Caribbean (Haiti, Honduras, the
Dominican Republic, Guadeloupe, Martinique, French Guyana, Suriname,
Guyana, Brazil, and the U.S.A.). The fruits of all this four-decade-long spiritual
and musical journey can be glimpsed on our recent albums Amame and Talisman."*
Note: Both are produced and published by multi-Grammy Award-winning pro-
ducer K.C. Porter under his Insignia Records label.

The Recipe of Sound

Cumbia Cienagüera

Listen carefully to the layers of rhythm that make up the cumbia. You will also hear the aesthetics of
African culture and music, as well as the affinity that cumbia shares with many of the other styles of music in this Unit. Normally, we might not include the names and listings of the musicians, but as might be
the case on over 70% of community-based Latino recordings, you will find brothers, sisters, or other family members involved in creating music collectively. In this case the Delys—mother, father, and children—
have made music not only a passion, but a source of their collective community. [Musicians include:
Leonor Dely, lead vocals; Istvan Dely, congolese drums, llamador, vocals; David Dely gaita flute, vocals;
Shangó Dely, gaita flute, alegre drum, djembé, bongós, shékere, vocals; Freddy Bolaño, tambora, cowbell;
Einar Escaf, drums, vocals; José Luis Tovío, percussion, vocals; Lina Babilonia, maracas, vocals].

Mr. Dely wrote: *"This piece is a classic of Colombian folklore by composer Luis
Enrique Martinez, clothed in new attire. It is acoustic fusion at its best: Afro-
Colombian cumbia, Afro-Cuban ruku-ruku, and Anglo funky rock merged together. It also represents the tri-ethnic makeup of Colombia and much of Central
and South America: African drums, Native American indigenous flutes and maracas, European drum set and the language of the song (Spanish)."*

Dance and Music—*Unit Postscript*

*"You cannot have waltzes/polkas, by separating the music and dance. You can-
not have dance without the music, you cannot have music without the dance."*
Interview: David Andre, Seychelles, 1994

*"You can't just play good mu-
sic, and the people all just
stand there and look at you.
You get the people to move. If*

Pic. 8.30A *As may be expected, in much of the world
today, DJs spin the popular hits of today's generation's community events. In addition to being the
means by which the music reaches young and old at
community events, clubs, and parties, the turntables
are also an "instrument" unto themselves—and the
means by which "beats" (recorded tracks) and dance
merge, and young adults forge a sense of community.*
Photo: i-stockphoto, 2006.

Sokwe (my group) comes here... even for free... people will hit glass bottles... I'll get everyone on the floor to play percussion. I get everyone on the floor and dance... you know Sega Tomba (a type of dance)...? I get two ladies and make them do it. It's funny, yes, but at the same time, it gets them to break the rhythm of just sitting back and watching.

"Once the music builds up... if there is no participation—the music will build up inside them, there must be an outlet. If you are an entertainer, you know. Once you see their feet tapping and their hands clapping, you reach for them and get them involved. Remember now that... they are becoming creole. Can you imagine a type of music... that does not make you want to move? ... and if you are moving, isn't that the beginnings of dance...and if it's a mixture...who's music or dance is it?" Interview: Kevin Valentine, Seychelles, 1994

What is dance?
How do dance and music relate?
Can music and dance be separated?

The human body is essentially rhythmic in all its functions (the heart, breathing, brain waves, circulation systems, etc.) and is, therefore, subject to excitability whenever it's around rhythm and vibration. The combination of music and dance is, in most cultures, the foundation of all rituals and *rites of*

Pic. 8.38 Courtesy Jamie Duplass.

passage ceremonies. Since, in the West, we frequently talk about music and dance separately, when it comes to a large portion of the world's music, the separation of these two phenomena severely distorts the nature and functions of their essentially integrated nature. We'll explore the dynamics of dance briefly and then consider the cohesive and inseparable natures of music and dance collectively.

First, concerning what they have in common, John Blacking explores the notion that ideas and feelings can be expressed collectively through dance or music before they can be articulated in speech. He writes:

"Dance (and music) are nonverbal modes of discourse, whose logic and forms can be precisely expressed and understood, but not always clearly articulated in words.... we should recognize that there are coherent, structured languages of dance, and that the transfer of decision making from verbal to nonverbal discourse constitutes the core of the dance experience." Blacking, 1977, p. 64.

Anya Peterson-Royce is an anthropologist who has studied the relationship of dance to culture. She believes some flexibility can be acquired by examining the differences in the ways others articulate value and affinity of their dance and music traditions (meaning, listen from within the culture). She writes: *"What we, as anthropologists, must consider are people's perceptions and explanations of the features that make up their particular universe."* (1977, p. 9). In short, anthropologists and culture-learners alike should attempt whenever humanly possible not to impose external definition on others' cultural values or expressions.

Many cultures have a word which has a parallel meaning to the English word *dance,* as well as a variety of terms which address particular types, styles, or, more importantly, usages for the expression. Examples of this include the Sanskrit *nrtta* (pure dance) and *nrtya* (pantomimic dance). Similarly, the perception

Pic. 8.27B *From community dance rituals ancient and extended in time, to formally choreographed ballet with drilled and impeccable precision, to modern dances such as this group in Heviz, Hungary, dance and music together may be one of the most powerful and all-encompassing expressions of human passion and senses.* Photo: Authors.

of dance as an experience extending well beyond movement is equally important. In the above examples, both *nrtta* and *nrtya* are considered integrated musical, dance, and theatrical experiences (Peterson-Royce, 1977, p. 13).

Understanding how the music and dance experiences express the needs and values of the people who define it as their *tradition* assists the process of recognizing the genres' collective importance as factors in community ritual events. Because dance, music, movement, ritual, non-verbal communication, and the "other" spheres of human activity are all so closely related, speaking of the world's expressive rituals requires an analysis of the integrated disciplines. To emphasize the multi-faceted nature of dance and its importance to life cycle rituals, we could attempt to encapsulate just a sampling of the descriptions found in scholarly literature relating to dance.

Dance has been defined as "culturally interpretive" [Merriam, 1974, p. 15]; "ritual inducing" or "ritual enhancing" [Spencer, 1985, p. 17]; "inner (spiritual) experience(s)" [Spencer, 1985, p. 1]; "patterned...or rhythmic expression"(s) which both "define human behavior" and "defy human categorization" [Royce, 1977, p. 3], and which are crucial vehicles for the understanding of both the passage of life... and how we mark these rituals in the establishment of traditions (Royce, 1977, p. 13). Kealinohomoku writes: [8.17]

> *"Dance is "an entire configuration, rather than just a performance... the implicit as well as explicit aspects of the dance and its reason for being; the entire conception of the dance within the larger culture, both on a diachronic basis through time and on a synchronic basis of the several parts occurring at the same time."*

> *"I was just reading a North American book, which discussed the fact that so much of music and dance are discussed separately. For instance, the ballet and opera were discussed as if they had nothing in common. It's a challenge to discuss the music and dance together... but shouldn't they be?"* Interview: Jean-Claude Mahoune, 1994.

In practice, *all* dances and music reflect the values and functions or purposes of the culture. To observe the movement, the position of the dancers, whether they dance touching or separate, whether the men are with the women, or whether the young are with the old—all are indicators of the culture's views and values. For instance, the dances of the *country dance* (square dance) and the *kwadril* of St. Lucia, are evident throughout Europe—and subsequently all the locations colonized by Europe, and reflect through movement the values of both the time and place of their origin. J. Guilbault writes:

> *"The posture of the St. Lucian kwadril dancers differs strikingly from the normal posture of the other St. Lucian dances...In most dances, the face and the body are very relaxed and the hips move slightly from side to side. In contrast, the kwadril dancers assume a very serious expression, hold their torsos rigid, and to not move their hips."* Guilbault, 1984, p. 168.

As we evaluate the nature and importance in marking the passage of life through rituals rooted to music and dance, we might consider:

- **The face** — Facial expressions frequently indicate emotion and tension in the ritual.

- **The shape or style of movement** — Do people dance in circles? Close or wide circles? Do they dance in patterns?

- **Who** (in the community) **will dance...** and how?

- **What are some different ways** that culture-groups **look** at music and dance?

- **How do different cultures-groups use music** (and/or dance) to mark the passage of life through rituals?

- **What is particularly unique,** refreshing, or interesting about each culture group's use of music and dance?

- **In what way does each example diffe**r from what we know or value from our culture? In what way(s) might they be similar?

Dance, Music, and Ritual

The Intermarriage of Dance and Music

There are very few instances wherein we will find strong community life without dance and music at community gatherings. Whether to mark the birth of a child, bring families together in marriage, or simply celebrate a birthday, anniversary, or public holiday, dance and music create an undeniable energy or synergy among community members.

The "historyworld" website (History of Dance) begins its synopsis of dance as follows:
"It is unlikely that any human society (at any rate until the invention of Puritanism) has denied itself the excitement and pleasure of dancing. Like cave painting, the first purpose of dance is probably ritual - appeasing a nature spirit or accompanying a rite of passage. But losing oneself in rhythmic movement with other people is an easy form of intoxication. Pleasure can never have been far away.
    "Rhythm, indispensable in dancing, is also a basic element of music. It is natural to beat out the rhythm of the dance with sticks. It is natural to accompany the movement of the dance with rhythmic chanting. Dance and music begin as partners in the service of ritual."
www.historyworld.net/wrldhis (History of Dance, 7/2007, p.1)

Although there are cultures that may study or speak of dance and music separately, historically, the two have been nearly always intertwined—as important in rituals, worship, and spiritual events as in social and community gatherings, and, along with food, essential to the planning and success of most large community events.

Questions
- *What are your experiences with dance and movement?*
- *In what manner does dance increase or enhance the depth of interaction at community events?*
- *What styles of dance or movement are most advantageous to community interactions or building healthy relationships? Are there some that are not? Why/why not?*

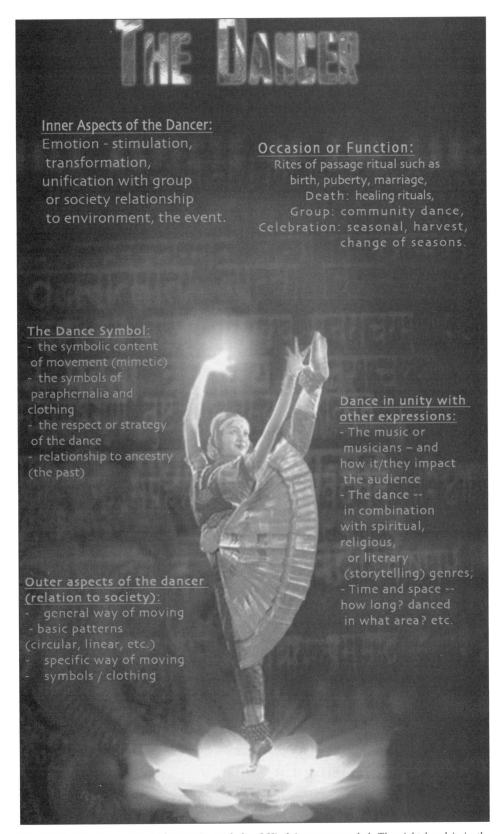

THE DANCER

Inner Aspects of the Dancer:
Emotion - stimulation,
transformation,
unification with group
or society relationship
to environment, the event.

Occasion or Function:
Rites of passage ritual such as
birth, puberty, marriage,
Death: healing rituals,
Group: community dance,
Celebration: seasonal, harvest,
change of seasons.

The Dance Symbol:
- the symbolic content
of movement (mimetic)
- the symbols of
paraphernalia and
clothing
- the respect or strategy
of the dance
- relationship to ancestry
(the past)

**Dance in unity with
other expressions:**
- The music or
musicians – and
how it/they impact
the audience
- The dance --
in combination
with spiritual,
religious,
or literary
(storytelling) genres;
- Time and space --
how long? danced
in what area? etc.

**Outer aspects of the dancer
(relation to society):**
- general way of moving
- basic patterns
(circular, linear, etc.)
- specific way of moving
- symbols / clothing

Pic. 8.31 *In this dance image, the mystic symbols of Hinduism are revealed. The right hand is in the Bhramara (bumblebee) Hasta. The bumblebee is regarded as auspicious. The left hand's fingers are in Alapadma Hasta, the rotating lotus of spiritual light. The eyes are directed toward the Supreme Lord. The left leg is lifted, symbolizing the swift ascent of the consciousness in one step from Earth to Heaven.*

Image: By permission, en.wikipedia.org/wiki/Indian, courtesy org@medha.org, adaptation with background and text, Brandon Naylor, 2005.

Unit VIII Activities

Activity #1: Understanding Concepts

Ultimately, retention and use of any knowledge or new ideas and information is based upon our perception of its relevance to our lives or our motivation to apply what we've learned (repeat its influence). Answer the following questions based on your perception of the reading discussion:

1) What are the essential qualities or elements of establishing and maintaining a strong community?

2) The life cycle (inevitably) does not complete itself for all in the same manner:

   a. How do strong communities help us reconcile the difficulties and challenges of life?

   b. What might the components of a strong community celebration of any one of the various stages of the life cycle include?

3) Effective community "rituals" must contain what … in your opinion?

4) Although all communities (regardless of strength or dysfunction) have community rituals of some variety:

   a. What are some of the ways strong music and dance participation enhances community life?

   b. Does your "community" (extended family, village, or town) have strong music/dance participation at its rituals?

   c. If so, in what way? If not, how could these rituals be enhanced or changed to strengthen their impact on the community?

Activity #2: Listening Deeper

Hearing the ingredients of a specific music's "fusion" is identical to tasting a culinary dish and decoding the recipe. By listening to a piece of music from the knowledge that *it is a fusion,* we can, in time, take delight in knowing *what sort of fusion it is!* This, of course, requires exposure to the ingredients of musical ancestry and a sensitivity (and desire) for hearing both the musical elements and decoding the musical *texture.*

1) Listen to CD examples 3.1, 3.2, and 3.8. These are the "older" ancestors of the more modern pieces in the Unit.

2) Make a list of the musical qualities of each piece's ingredients. For each, what can you say about the:
Melody:
Rhythm:
Instrumentation or texture:
Harmony:
Form or structure:
Purpose or function (for the community):

3) Now pick any two pieces from CD 3.3-3.7. Make a list of the musical elements you hear that connect to—or are influenced by—the ancestral music (it may only be one or a few of the elements: melody, texture, etc.).

4) Of all the music in the Unit, which would you play at a community event to solidify or connect members of the community? How, why, or in what manner?

Activity #3: Exercising Passion

In general, whenever we attempt researching, studying, or simply participating at any level with another culture group, there are a few questions to ask ourselves, which will enhance the experience:

• How do we know that what we read is a respectful analysis of the culture group?

• How do we know if it is a *voice* from *within* the culture?

• What should we choose to retain or demonstrate to others about another culture?

Some general thoughts: We always have choices about what we choose to include about other cultures.

When possible, choose the communications about others that will open doors to understanding and appreciation, even if (and this is also true of all cultures) we stumble onto things about the "other" that may truly seem unjust or "primitive" to us. That is, until we're willing to take the time to investigate the history and evolution of that "negative" expression (which will take time), we should remain focused on those cultural traits which might enhance our own lives (and, by action, more greatly honor the host culture).

We know, of course, that "Africa" is a huge, diverse continent and that Latin America is equally broad and diverse. We also know, for the most part, that the majority of us in the West have serious deficiencies in our knowledge of and respect for Africa, and, possibly to a lesser degree, for Latino cultures and their contributions to our world.

1) Select a country or community group (S.Africa/Zulu, Nigeria/Yoruba or Igbo, Bolivia-Peru/Quechua, Afro-Cuba, etc.), preferably one about which you could talk to someone from your work, school, community, or religious groups, etc.

2) Conduct Internet research on the culture. Look for sites posted by culture-bearers. Make lists of cultural strengths and cultural challenges.

3) If possible, interview someone from the culture. Ask about his or her perceptions of the cultural strengths. If you feel "close enough," you might pick one of the "challenges" and ask what, in his or her opinion, contributed to this "culture challenge/weakness" (how it evolved/from which circumstances)?

4) Make a list of the specific strengths and weaknesses of your own culture. What are the similarities of your two lists? In what way does the African/Latino culture offer a sophisticated balance to your culture's weaknesses?

Activity #4: Exercising Our *Own* Creativity

The most critical components of "community rituals" are the care, passion, and creativity that community members invest in their interaction. When elders and children are given priority, when the stages of the cycle of life are properly acknowledged, and when communal interaction in the cooking, preparation, and activities incorporate the widest and deepest interaction of the community members, the solidarity of the community will be enhanced.

Enhancing Ritual

1) Pick or *create* an event for your current community: it can be your family, your extended family, your friends/housemates, or members of a community group to which you belong.

2) In what way can you use your talents or "instruments" *together* with other members of your group to enhance, enliven, or deepen the effect of the ritual event you have chosen (or create)?

3) Since one of the primary components of community ritual is participation, in what way will others at the event be able to "participate" in a fun, meaningful, or otherwise uplifting and memorable manner?

4) If your talents or skills, or those in your community, do not include the use of music or dance, you may wish to think of a way by which music and dance can be incorporated to deepen the impact of your "ritual" event.

- Might this ritual be repeated (maintained over time)?

- In what manner might you increase the opportunity for further creativity and meaningful interaction at this ritual in the future?

- Above all, does your ritual help bind the members of the community to common human experiences we share in traveling through the life cycle?

Note: If possible, document your event with pictures, video, or in writing to refer to in subsequent years.

Pic 8.32 *On a stage in front of 400 high school students, "Grupo Folklorica" (above), a Mexican and indigenous dance group from Dallas, Texas, brings a group of students on stage to try a dance with them. Director Eduardo Jesus points out, "For many of these students this will be the first contact with the diversity of Mexican dance—and therefore culture. We are a fusion of Spanish and indigenous cultures over centuries. If any of these students find a portion of the magnificence we see in our culture, we will have done our job." In truth, young Hispanic students left proud of their heritage, and the vast majority of others learned a new and deeper respect for Mexican and indigenous culture that would in many ways be balancing to their own. As a 15-year-old student remarked while leaving, "I can't believe how into it they are—I wish our school did something like that!"* Photo: Authors.

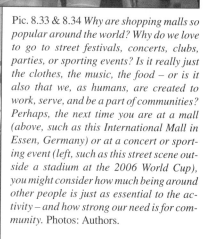

Pic. 8.33 & 8.34 *Why are shopping malls so popular around the world? Why do we love to go to street festivals, concerts, clubs, parties, or sporting events? Is it really just the clothes, the music, the food – or is it also that we, as humans, are created to work, serve, and be a part of communities? Perhaps, the next time you are at a mall (above, such as this International Mall in Essen, Germany) or at a concert or sporting event (left, such as this street scene outside a stadium at the 2006 World Cup), you might consider how much being around other people is just as essential to the activity – and how strong our need is for community.* Photos: Authors.

Unit VIII: Endnotes

8.1   De Soto, <u>The Mystery of Capital</u>, c. 2000, p.6

8.2   The term "*Third World*" was used to distinguish nations that aligned with neither the West nor the East during the Cold War. Many were members of the Non-Aligned Movement. Today, however, the term is used to denote nations with the smallest UN Human Development Index (HDI) in the world, independent of their political status. These countries are also known as developing countries, or least developed countries, all terms that reinforce stereotypes and "material wealth" as the standards by which we perceive either sophistication or development.

8.3   The survey (2003) was conducted, by the author, of college-aged students (18-25 yrs. old, Midwest United States). Questions ranged from the students' perceptions of ritual, to the importance of ritual in sustaining strong community life, to the students' own participation in family or extended-family community rituals. 32% of those surveyed (126 samples) indicated acknowledgement of ritual as important to community life, but only 8% indicated experiencing regular community rituals as an essential part of their lives, and only 12% indicated a strong desire to increase community rituals and their impact to "enhance" their lives. This was only an informal study and does not take culture or "race" into account.

8.4   As we have also seen, most rituals will change somewhat in their practice generationally. But the recognition of their importance, if maintained, will sustain community acknowledgement of the past as well as balance in the present, a critical function to the diminishing of personal ego or self-importance in the interest of community.

8.5   You may wish to visit http://en.wikipedia.org/wiki/Griot (source of this quotation) or informational websites such as *Keepers of History*, www.rps.psu.edu/0205/keepers.html, for more information.

8.6   Because most *griots* traditionally are attached or employed by the rich or politically powerful, if these figures are corrupt or unpopular figures, the general public may look upon *griots* with disfavor.

8.7   The Mbuti, and various groups of Bantu to which Biza belongs, are called *Pygmies* by Western historians and anthropologists (rather than, for example, *Bantu*, which means "the people"). Because terms such as *pygmy* have become so negatively loaded over time and are not chosen by the people themselves, they should immediately and permanently be replaced by terms preferred by the culture group.

8.8   To say that France administratively colonized Senegal or Guinea simply implies that their numbers were not sufficient to dominate the culture, only the military and administrative power structures. This is a substantially different "style" of colonization than that experienced in the Americas.

8.9   The fusion process in the earlier stages—and arguably the source of the tongue-in-cheek name – Highlife comes from Ghanaian and Nigerian references to British parties and events where, frequently, local natives, eventually trained on British military band instruments, would serenade the party-goers with the pomp and circumstance of British marches, waltzes, and country dance music. No doubt this was a humorous spectacle to most of the local residents.

8.10   Mensah's career is said to have reached a peak when he performed with the great Louis Armstrong in Ghana. This is one more illustration of the perpetual exchange and affinity transfer processes that have pre-dated modern examples of cultural fusion.

8.11   This prayer, according to Mr. Mulomede, *"is used through much of world as to reflect human purpose and incite action over words."*

8.12   We will use the term "Latino" to refer to all people from *Latin America* or Spanish (and Portuguese) influenced countries within Central, South, and Caribbean American and Mexico. We include, naturally, as well, anyone from or with ancestry from these regions who may be living elsewhere in North America, Europe, Africa, etc. Although some people reject the broader terms, our purpose is to show, at least in music, that the predominant influence today is cross-influence and exchange based upon numerous common affinities. Ultimately, however, we should ask the individuals what they wish to be called, whether by name of country, Latino, or even the broader term, *Hispanic* (virtually anyone of Spanish descent).

8.12A   Mr. Vismale writes concerning Merengue (see pages 131-132): "I think it must be pointed out that the present day Merengue came about in part, because the ethnic and racial biases of former president Rafael Trujillo. In his despotic tenure, he sought to eradicate most vestiges of African and Native American sensibilities, in all aspects of Dominican culture including music. His goal was to equate the Dominican Republic cultures with that of Europe. As an example, he gave refuge to Germans and other Europeans fleeing Europe during WWII. The polka influences of Dominican Merengue music can be directly attributed to the German music teachers he state-sanctioned to teach the "new" music to his constituents.

8.13   Contributions to the dates and information include articles on *salsa, Fania All-stars, Spanish Harlem, and Puerto Rican and Cuban cultures and music,* were confirmed by discussions with the musicians in the Unit.

8.14   A type of horizontal "xylophone" or marimba, with metal bars and electronically rotating vibrator tubes. Not, however, in this case used with the electronic mechanized vibrato/vibration.

8.15   Extracts from the wikipedia.com article on *cumbia.*

8.16   Ibid, p.1

8.17   All research on dance cited is from "Interdisciplinarity of Music and Dance," Michael L. Naylor, 1996, University of Michigan, Ann Arbor, MI.

Pic. 8.42 *When we contemplate just how strong the human instinct is to "belong" to something, to be a part of community, we can easily see why some of the most magnificent musical spectacles are dependent upon large groups of people practicing long hours, moving, creating matching or coordinated costuming, and rituals of magnificent proportions. Is it the event alone – or the camaraderie and bonds that are established in preparation, performance, and through difficulties and in triumph – that make performance groups (such as this drum and bugle corps) so attractive?* Photo: Courtesy, Jason Lugo.

Asia:
Seeking Balance (and Healing) Through Music

UNIT

IX

Topics to Consider in Unit IX

➤ *What can be understood by "balance"? And – what role can music play in balancing the various areas of the human condition?*

➤ *What are some general areas in which music can be used to "heal"?*

➤ *In what manners can music and storytelling be combined to balance or heal both human and cultural imbalances? And – what are some ways in which Indian, Chinese, Korean, Japanese, and Indonesian cultures apply the ancient art of "balancing" through musical storytelling?*

➤ *In what manner does music and dance overlap in the Hindu history and religious practices? And – what can be understood by the "raag," "rasa," the "drone," or the symbolism of Hindu stories in the context of balancing?*

➤ *What is the role or status of the teacher in Indian culture?*

➤ *In what manner can the influence of "spirit" over reality be seen in Chinese art forms (of all variety)?*

➤ *How might we understand the diversity and complexity of Chinese evolution in the context of "Chinese music" or today's China?*

➤ *What are some of the important aspects of creating balance through the art of storytelling in Chinese "opera," Korean Pansori, Japanese Noh or Kabuki, and Indonesian Gamelan?*

➤ *How is sound and space different in the older genres of China, Korea, and Japan from that of Western music – or the modern music of these cultures?*

➤ *What are important considerations in understanding Korean and Japanese culture — and much of their modern music over the last century? And – what was the impact of the last centuries wars on "balance" in these cultures?*

➤ *In what manner do young Chinese, Japanese, or Indonesian musicians carry forward their ancestry and the art of balance while combining the voices and sounds of their generation? And – how might we understand this principle as relates to a natural understanding of the "cycle of life"?*

UNIT IX

Asia:
Seeking Balance (and Healing)
Through Music

"Thus have I heard. Once the Blessed One was staying at Savatthi, in Jeta's Grove, Anathapindika's monastery. There he addressed the monks thus: 'Monks.' –

'Venerable sir,' they replied. The Blessed One said this:

"'Monks, suppose a cloth were clean and bright, and a dyer dipped it in some dye or other, whether blue or yellow or red or pink, it would take the dye well and be pure in colour. And why is that? Because the cloth was clean. So too, monks, when the mind is undefiled, a happy destination [in a future existence] may be expected.'

"He abides, having suffused with a mind of compassion...of sympathetic joy...of equanimity one direction ... and so above, below, around and everywhere, and to all as to himself; he abides suffusing the entire universe with equanimity, with a mind grown great, lofty, boundless and free from enmity and ill will. He understands what exists, what is low, what is excellent, and what escape there is from this [whole] field of perception." Buddhism, Excerpts Vatthupama Sutta, The Simile of the Cloth 1-14

When we think of the enormous geographic region known as "Asia," and its vast cultural diversity, the task of encapsulating Asian history and music into a single unit is imposing. Even conceptualizing "Chinese" or "Indian" culture or history as separate entities is attempting to understand large, culturally and geographically diverse regions with thousands of years of history interrelated to numerous other cultures. As with the similarly large continent of Africa, unless we are fortunate to have a professional or personal connection with someone from a region of Asia that will extend our contact indefinitely, we are left to seek a means of learning about cultures or their expressions (music) that might provide us an incentive (motivation) to continue contact over time. Although multicultural exchange, symbolism, religion, change or exchange over time, community, and virtually any topic discussed thus far could be the "frame" for a discussion of Asian cultures, we have chosen the topic of *healing*, or creating balance in all areas of human experience: physical, emotional, mentally, spiritual, and cultural.

At the height of today's media explosion and what some feel is an imposing surplus of information at times leading to a depersonalization of the human experience, breakdowns in family and community life, and desensitization to the beauty of the human experience, we may find ourselves seeking a better sense of **balance** in our lives. The *balance* required might include that of the *physical* (muscles, circulation, nervous system, etc.); *emotional* (a sense of stability or the conversion of sadness, anxiety, or anger to calmness or serenity); *mental* (calming what some Buddhists refer to as "monkey mind"—the overly active mind) in order to retain important information, displace the unimportant, (and know the difference between the two); *spiritual* (a combination of all elements with a heightened connection to a Higher Value or Power), and finally, *social, cultural or communal* balance (the activities, relationships, family, and community interactions that greatly affect our perceptions of balance in the prior three categories).

We can see this yearning for balance in virtually all of the world's art, but especially in that Asian music, art, or storytelling over the past three to four millennia. Why is it we see so pervasively the images of nature and the emphasis on being harmonious (in balance) with nature in the music and dance of nearly all Asian cultures? Why is creating an internal balance within oneself so emphasized in the ancient stories of Asian cultures? Despite the impact of modern media and technology, are the ancient principles still practiced or present? If not, why not? If so, how? These are all questions worthy of consideration.

Finding, creating, and maintaining a sense of balance in life between one's history and one's present, and between oneself and the world around one, is an essential feature of the majority of Asian philosophies and historical practices (see below). It is, therefore, just as critical to the appreciation of the culture's music.

Pic. 9.1 *A replica of an ancient statue of Gautama Buddha, found in Sarnath, near Varanasi. In general, statues of Buddha are used to remind practitioners to practice "right living."* Photo: Public Domain, courtesy DhJ.

Important Influences in Asian Music and Art

- The long history of Hinduism and Buddhism in much of Asia.

- The focus of these religions on creating a sense of balance with oneself, with nature, and with the world around us.

- The long and ancient history of storytelling as a means of passing the philosophies of these ancient religions (and teachings) through the generations.

- The emphasis on music and dance as an *encouraged*, if not primary, means by which stories have been passed through the centuries.

Before we begin exploring the music of Asia specifically, it is first important that we consider the manner in which music affects us physically, emotionally, mentally, and culturally. Because music is the ordering of vibrations, how these vibrations affect us, and how music is used to balance each of the areas of human experience and perception, is an important discussion by itself. A high percentage (if not all) of the music we choose to listen to is consciously or unconsciously selected according to its potential to bring us "balance" or fulfillment.

After a short discussion of music's "healing" power, we may better understand how the music of India, China, Korea, Japan, and Indonesia's cultures have for centuries focused on creating harmony and balance in the human experience. It is precisely in their stories and how they form and manipulate vibration that we will get a glimpse of the healing (balancing) power in music.

Understanding the "Healing" (Balancing) Powers of Music

"Do not be proud of wealth, kindred and youth;
Time takes away all these in a moment.
Leaving aside this entire (world) which is of the nature of an illusion,
and knowing the state of brahman,[9.1] enter into it."
[Extracted from Bhajans to Lord Ganesha]

A majority of music we choose to listen to, we do so in order to create a *balance* or sense of equilibrium, at some level, with our current state, based upon learned preferences and aesthetics. Whether the CDs we choose to play while driving our cars, cleaning our houses, for our parties or special functions, or the concerts we attend, regardless of genre, style, or culture, music is more often than not a means of establishing human equilibrium. In what manner does music interact with our human senses and perceptions to calm the mind, increase energy, diminish anger or frustration, or incite us to dance or to move, possibly even to the point exhaustion or euphoria?

Music is the conscious ordering (or perception) of sounds (vibrations) as experienced, perceived, and understood by individuals and cultures according to their values. Because all sound is vibration, when we hear these vibrations in the context of life, they become a part of our memory, as do smells, sensations, and experiences. In time, we begin to construct a network of sound preferences through our associations and experiences.

Although these networks of preferences and bodies of sounds will change as influenced by our experiences and cultural exposures, the pattern of contact with sound and music and the ultimate process of selection or rejection is universally applicable within the human experience. Equally universal to an individual's selection or rejection of sound, organized and perceived as "music," are the following:

- All humans use music, in part, to enhance or induce human emotion. And all humans experience the same range of human emotions, although each culture determines the proper expression for both type and desired method of expressing the intensity of each emotion.

- All humans participate in various musical experiences from levels of extreme passivity to extreme physical/emotional/spiritual engagement. Generally, the greater the engagement in the musical experience, the deeper or more memorable the impact.

- Most musical expressions are created by converting some aspects of the human experience into ordered vibrations, according to the learned values and experiences of the musician. Each musical experience will impact one or more of the areas of human perception (physical, mental, emotional, spiritual, and cultural). Assuming the listener "likes" or chooses the experience, it can be assumed that the musical ordering (how the vibrations have been composed) will affect "balance" or "healing" in the widest sense for the listener. The range or combinations of human perception and the extent or intensity of balance derived from the musical experience is both universal (to human physiology) and culturally specific (to time, cultural aesthetic, and place).

Music has a direct impact on us from a very early age. Before we are aware of life itself, we can sense vibrations or, in essence, hear music. We begin to learn patterns of sounds and to create associations. It's not at all uncommon for parents to sing or play a song for a fetus prior to birth and later to notice a distinct change in

Pic. 9.1A *Lord Shiva, part of the "Trimurti" (or Holy Trinity) of Hinduism, is a perfect example of balance with the attributes of being: the Creator, Preserver, Destroyer, hiding sins and providing blessings. This statue of Shiva meditating (in Bangalore, S. India) also demonstrates the principle of symmetry found in nearly all Hindu art.* Photo: Courtesy Deepak Gupta.

the newborn child's conscious reaction to that song. Is this coincidence? Probably not. The child has intense contact with vibration and patterns of sound; the brain, though still developing, is likely to recall and retain associations to the music as it will increasingly throughout life. Therefore, familiarity breeds recognition, and recognition is the basis for our selection and use of music later in life, as in: *"I've heard that before…. It reminds me of…."*

The right hemisphere of the brain has to do with feelings, imagery, dreams, and the unconscious. It is highly susceptible to the influences of vibration, especially as patterned and layered in music. Therefore, since the earliest times, in all cultures, and as a basis for most rites of the life-cycle, the ordering of vibration in music has a significant impact physiologically, as well as emotionally, intellectually, spiritually, and culturally on the life experience:

> *"Since ancient times, music has been recognized as having therapeutic value. The Bible recounts that young David was summoned to play the harp for the tormented King Saul: "Whenever the spirit from God came upon Saul, David would take his harp and play. Then relief would come to Saul; he would feel better, and the evil spirit would leave him" (I Samuel 16:23). Among the ancient Greeks, the god Apollo was most associated with the cultivated arts of music and medicine."*
> "Music Therapists Chime in with Data on Medical Results," JAMA, Feb. 9, 2000, v283 i6, p.731.

Scientists, educators, and musicians have attempted to explain and quantify the musical experience and its potential impact on all facets of the human experience. Much of the work has been done recently by **music therapists,** practitioners of a distinct profession that has evolved considerably over the last few decades of the 20th century. Beyond entertainment, passive enjoyment, or the social/casual functions music frequently appears to occupy in its social function, a good majority of the time, music possesses a special capacity to impact and truly balance or "heal" all facets of the human condition. The stories that follow might help us decode the mystery of music and the manner in which it helps us balance the human experience. As you read these stories, you might ask whether you agree with the experiences or observations, and if so, how or why? Or, if you think the experiences of these individuals overestimate the power of ordered vibration (a.k.a. music), then why or in what manner?

Stories from the Human Family

> *"After being diagnosed with breast cancer last year, Kathy Winter searched for ways to help ease her fears, boost her spirits and get her through treatment. 'I was facing weeks of chemotherapy and was dreading the whole experience,' she says. 'I was anxious and wanted something to support me.'*

> *"She discovered the therapeutic power of music. Winter scheduled sessions with a music therapist to coincide with her treatments at the Ireland Cancer Center in Cleveland. Her therapist brought along an electronic keyboard, sang soothing songs and played classical compositions chosen by Winter.*

> *"'There was less discomfort,' Winter says. 'When you're anxious, your whole body is tense and you feel more pain. I don't know how I would have gone through that without the music therapy. It was a long, dark tunnel, and the music therapy helped bring some light to it.'*

> *"Winter is among a growing number of people who are tapping into the healing powers of music. Health care professionals recognize its value too, embracing a new modality-music therapy for an array of medicinal purposes, from helping to ease anxiety to helping stroke victims in physical rehabilitation.*

"Music therapy has been shown to be valuable in pain reduction, coping with stress, easing depression, decreasing memory loss and stimulating the immune system, according to the American Music Therapy Association. It is used in conjunction with conventional medicine, functioning largely as a psychological aid." From the "Feature Article:" www.discoveryhealth.com, Sept. 2005.

*   *   *

"Certainly physical healing is important. A body that experiences pain has little room for the enjoyment of life. And some bodies, like premature babies, will have no life if they cannot gain weight, grow, and become strong enough to continue.

"My husband and I personally watched our son, born only 1lb., 8oz. due to medical complications, grow to a healthy weight (and eventually into a wonderful young adult), with no small influence of the musical tape recording we prepared for him while he was still in the incubator. Thankfully, my insistence on spending nearly every waking moment at his side was likely the most critical of influences; still there were numerous hours where our child had to be left to the sights and sounds of the sterile hospital environment.

"This tape played gentle and soothing music round the clock at his little incubator until he was released, some three months later at the 'enormous weight' of three pounds. So, his little life still in limbo, we continued the process through the next few turbulent years, until he achieved full health.

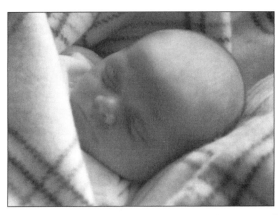

"But perhaps even more astounding than the role music played in his survival from the low birth weight was, if you could have seen his eyes at the age of 7 or 8, when he heard one of the pieces that was on the initial tape used in the hospital. I'm not sure I would have believed how important sound, and in particular the ordering of sounds and pitches—what we call music—can be, if I hadn't seen its impact on my own son years later." Léonie Naylor, "Reflections," Personal Essays, 1992.

Pic. 9.2 *The human listening experience and the sensing of vibration begins long before the baby enters the world. In the mother's womb, vibrations are felt with incredible intensity in the water of the womb—so too while the baby is sleeping.* Photo: Courtesy Robert Broadie, taken: January 1, 2005.

The observations above are supported by a 1986 study by Jayne Standley, Ph.D., published in the Journal of Music Therapy, in which she found that premature babies who were exposed to music were calmer and used oxygen more efficiently. The babies also gained weight faster and required shorter periods of hospitalization than the other babies studied.

Here are some other areas in which recent research has found musical therapy effective:

- ***Helping control patients' breathing and heart rate***—Several studies have shown that music and rhythm work in sync with people's circulatory and respiratory systems. A University of Iowa study of patients needing ventilation assistance found a single music therapy session was effective in decreasing anxiety and promoting relaxation, as indicated by decreases in heart and respiratory rates.

- ***Helping premature infants recover faster***—At Florida State University's Center for Music Research, researchers found that exposing premature infants to lullaby singing and multimodal stimulation helped reduce the number of days to discharge and helped increase weight gain.

- ***Helping ease pain and discomfort for children during hospital stays, and aiding breathing for young asthma patients***—At Beth Israel Medical Center in New York City, music is used to help ease the anxiety of the hospital experience by relaxing children when staff draw blood, insert IV needles, and perform spinal taps or other painful procedures. A pediatric music therapy program also is being used for asthma treatments. By learning to play music or recorders, the patients find that their ability to breathe is enhanced.

- *Managing pain*—Music has been shown both to help relieve pain or the perception of pain by distraction, altering mood, and promoting relaxation. In one study at Yale University, patients undergoing urologic procedures with spinal anesthesia who listened to music with headsets had decrease needs for sedatives and analgesics.

- *Improving mood and easing depression*—A study based at Michigan State University showed elderly people who take keyboard lessons significantly improved anxiety, depression, and loneliness, which are three factors critical in coping with stress, stimulating the immune system, and improving health, according to Frederick Tims, Ph.D., who was the principal investigator. In the same study, he found these lessons also significantly increased existing levels of the human growth hormone, which has been linked to improving a wide range of health concerns, including osteoporosis, energy levels, wrinkling, sexual function, muscle mass, and simple aches and pains.

Our perceptions of music are distributed over many centers in the brain and can change with experience or in differing contexts of listening or playing. Consequently, there is really no single center in the brain for performing, recalling, associating, emoting to, or comprehending music. Instead, many areas of the brain interact and cross paths in order to accommodate the multiple effects of music on human physiology and each area of human perception.

Once we become sensitive to vibration (which begins before we even enter the world), we begin to learn patterns of interaction and participation with music based on our cultural experiences, which, in turn, evolve into preferences. In some cultural settings, music is primarily used as a background to activity. In others, music can be the core activity, by itself bringing the participant to the most intense stages of fulfillment or complete use of all the centers of the brain affecting emotion, physical sensation, and satisfaction. Here is a partial list of musical experiences and an approximation of their potential effect on the different faculties of human perception and physiology:

Musical Experience	Faculties Affected	Degree of Involvement
Background – (in stores, elevators, doctors' offices)	Physical, mental (calming)	Passive – Used to assist in slowing nervous impulses and decrease anxiety or movement.
Background –	Physical (motivational), stimulates problem-solving (mental)	Passive to moderate – Might include singing along or tapping a foot to the music. Each would increase engagement.
Community ritual –	Physical, mental, emotional (spiritual/cultural)	Moderate to active – The stronger the community, the more widespread the participation from an early age, and the greater the impact or later associations that will be made with the event. In the case of holidays and family/religious events, if very special, a mere few tones of a specific piece can set off emotions and memories.
Performing music –	Physical, mental, emotional (Spiritual/Cultural)	Moderate to extremely active – When one actually plays or dances to music, the impact of personal engagement generally increases response in all areas. When we play the music ourselves, we access numerous parts of the brain in creating and sensing the vibration. At times, musicians, dancers, and even deep listeners report being overcome or transported from the temporal world to a timeless world beyond normal conscious recognition and concern.

Although the above list represents only a few of the circumstances in which music is created and processed, the impact of music is derived from the level of engagement, depth of associations, and parts of the brain or number of human perceptual tools that are affected. Deeper still, and much more difficult to quantify, are the reactions to music that some refer to as "spiritual experiences."

In the case of the biblical description of David's musical aptitude, the passion of and euphoria experienced by many of the musicians we see on a stage, the complete absorption of the trance dancer, or the deep meditative state of the religious chanter, the overall impact of the musical experience can be enormously profound, encompassing all dimensions of perception, including the deepest cultural beliefs and expectations.

Musicians and the deepest of music appreciators frequently refer to their most intense experiences with music as their having been "lost in the music" or of having had a "spiritual" experience. Although the spiritual plane of human experience is generally accepted in most cultures, it does pose a problem for science, as it is virtually impossible to prove or encapsulate.[9.1A] What may be assumed for now is that the "spiritual plane" likely involves most, if not all, of the areas of the human perceptual experience and is frequently generated by an intense connection of the musical experience to one's religious or spiritual beliefs about the importance of life itself. Individuals who come from cultures that tie music directly to religion, to mental/emotional/spiritual balancing, and even to states

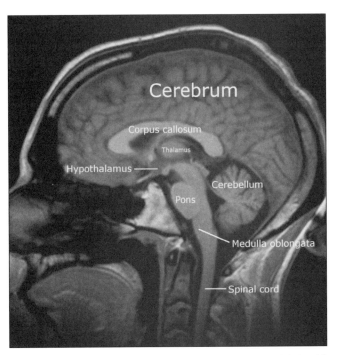

Pic. 9.3 *Although each section of the human brain is responsible for different functions of the human body and human perception, the multiple dimensions of musical vibration can simultaneously impact the listener— physically, mentally, and emotionally. As a result, many scientists believe much of the brain is used in a comprehensive musical experience.* Photo: Public domain.

of ecstasy (as in *trance* states) generally claim no need for proof that intense participation with music can move one to a state that transcends both human consciousness and human limitations. Regardless of the seeming resistance of the "spiritual" plane to empirical verification, *all* professional musicians can relate to at least a few moments when, while creating music, they lost all contact with time, space, or physical consciousness.

One example of how participation with music elicits deeply absorbing responses across the range of human capacities lies in the nature of rhythm in music. Beyond the impact of vibration (sound) itself on the nervous system, the flow of music over time, generally includes beats or pulses in music. These allow the listeners/participators to lock not only their body movement to the music but also their breathing, their heart rate, and even their brain activity. Mickey Hart, longtime drummer of the Grateful Dead rock group and world percussionist, views vibration and rhythm as universal essentials to the well-being of both the individual and human cultures. In Hart's view, rhythm and health are synonymous. He writes: *"The body is a rhythm machine, and when the coordination stops, disease steps in."*

Music therapy is actually an ancient practice. For millennia, spiritual healers have used musical sounds and vibration to chase diseases from the body. In ancient Egypt, physician-priests sang their medical scriptures in specific, curative tones. The Greek mathematician Pythagoras proposed that music might in some patients restore proper balance among the four humors and their associated temperaments.

In the United States, music is increasingly seen as a modulator of mood, or as a diversion, but not yet as a treatment. In this sense, it is more suited to an auditorium than a rehab center. Never are the words "Listen to a jazz piece or reggae piece and call me in the morning" or "Listen as needed" scrawled on a doctor's prescription pad.

Pic. 9.4 *Music inspires stories, stories inspire art, art is inspired by music – and the perpetual motion of the arts crossing boundaries to inspire yet another story is an infinitely older tradition than is the separation of the arts. Deborah Hoover's watercolors of musicians show movement, depict the color of music, and tell the stories of the musicians and dancers. While honoring musicians, such as in this work, "Blue Door Jazz," she also brings to life the interconnection between the arts in her own form of storytelling.* Photo: Authors, courtesy and copyright, Deborah Hoover, 2005.

> *"Music has been used for entertainment for so long, people forget it's a powerful medicine," said Hart. "I go to old age homes (nursing homes) in the community. They gather around in their wheelchairs or whatever and I give them drums (and tell them) ... it's impossible to make a mistake, (this) gives them self-esteem. Some of them can hardly comb their hair, but if they make a sound on their own they've done something powerful, they've made an original creation from absolutely nothing. It's true creation and it's a heartwarming thing. They usually start before I'm even ready."*

The "Healing" Power in Musical Storytelling

What the elders share in all cultures around the world are the greatest of stories and the longest traditions of participation with music. It is in fact when the two converge—music and storytelling—that we can glean from this interaction the most fascinating understanding of every culture's values and perspectives on life itself. To a large degree, this is also where we can gain a perspective on what *balance* and equilibrium mean to each culture as well.

To the heavy metal guitarist, the stories might reflect the strength of counterculture, the discontentment with mainstream society, and the aggression and energy that can purify the musician and listener alike of their own aggression or even anger. To the opera buff, the jazz aficionado, or any other active listener, the stories (whether in language and music or in music alone) will also be the mouthpiece of particular values, aspirations, and experiences. And "their" music will elicit passion, evoke emotion, and bring fulfillment—some of the requirements of daily life.

Beyond the importance of storytelling in connecting individuals to their musical passion is the impact stories have more generally in grounding individuals to their ancestry and in teaching "culture," values, and the very meaning of life itself. Although many of these stories will find their way into the music and dance of each subsequent generation, storytelling, generally, is a powerful force in the human experience.

> *"In China it's very important for us to respect and honor our parents. My parents saved all the money to send me here to school. Sometimes I feel a lot of pressure, it's true. Maybe that's a problem we have in China... but also... our families are very connected. What I really miss here—is being part of a family. It seems like people here are too busy. They never talk to me; I feel very lonely much of the time. I'm glad there are other Chinese students, but I'd really like to have American friends as well.*

"I sometimes ask myself as well, 'How can students not bow to their instructors, give their seats on buses to elders, or treat their guests (anyone not from the culture) with special respect?" It's interesting to me that you asked where I learned these things—from stories my mother and grandmother told me. Many they sang to me in lullabies. I think most everything we learn is from stories. They start telling the stories when we're babies—and don't stop until we begin to tell the stories to our babies." Mei Li [Li, Mei], Taiwanese student, four years in the United States, 2005.

Although using music as a therapeutic tool in healing is a relatively recent focus of study in the West, in most of the world, the transformative powers of music have been conveyed through musical storytelling genres for centuries. How do we know this? How do we know what was important to Bach, or to the Malian griot? It is through the choices of sounds and lyrics, and the ordering of thoughts and sounds in their musical stories. Their values are recorded in songs and symphonies for all ears to hear. Storytelling through music is arguably the most beloved means of conveying human experience. From the simplest of lullabies to the most complex of musical theater, musical storytelling takes numerous forms and dimensions. And, in most of these stories, we will find the striving for understanding and balance in the human experience.

"Out of India"— History and Music

Across the Generations

India has at least a five-thousand-year documented history. It is currently home to more than one billion people, and one of the most prolific storytelling traditions in human history. At present, *"Bollywood,"* the film industry in Bombay, India, turns out more films than any single culture on the planet – and nearly as

Pic. 9.4B *This Hindu temple (Krishna Temple in Mathura, India) not only shows the dynamic contrast of geometry common in temple architecture, but (if you read the sign to the right), a predominant spirit of sharing and "lack of ownership" that pervades Hindu communities generally.* Photo: Courtesy Dhirad.

many as all of the cultures combined. Additionally, we might mention that nearly every film made in India since the industry's conception in the mid-1940s, has been essentially **musical theater** (theatrical stories told with musical breaks [arias] used to emphasize the most critical moments of the story).

An Indian student (Krunal Patel) wrote in a paper concerning his musical preferences: *"We love our films, what can I say? There is an intense desire on the part of most Indians when the work-day is finished to escape the harsh reality of life. You may use your television or video games, but in India we use our musical stories. I don't know why. I'm an engineer. But this is how we keep our balance."* Used by permission, April 2004.

Since we can be certain nothing comes from nothing (nothing exists independent of something that had preceding it), how in the world did such an appetite for the telling of stories – especially through music and dance—become transplanted in the Indian psyche? Is there a correlation between the ancient art forms of the Vedas or Hinduism and the modern storytelling of a Bollywood film?

Malini Srirama is a classically trained Indian dancer and director of her own dance troupe in the United States. She writes: *"In India both music and dance were used as a form of worship in the temples, and thus both have a religious basis. Throughout their development in the last four millennia, both Hinduism and myth[9.2] have exercised a tremendous impact on them.*

"In Hinduism, gods not only are creators and destroyers, but they are also supreme artists. Siva-Nataraja, the god of dance, represents both creation and de-

Pic. 9.5 *Bharata Natyam is the manifestation of the South Indian idea of the celebration of the eternal universe through celebration of the beauty of the material body in musical dance storytelling. In Hindu mythology, the whole universe is the dance of the Supreme Dancer, Nataraja, a name for Lord Shiva, the Hindu ascetic yogi and divine purveyor of destruction of evil.*

The Natya Shastra (a treatise on Indian dance and music from between 200 BCE and 200 CE) reads, "... I have seen the Kaisiki style during the dance of the blue-throated lord (Shiva). It consists of elaborate gestures (Mridu Angaharas, movements of limbs), sentiments (Rasas), emotional states (Bhavas). Actions (Kriyas) are its soul. The costume should be charmingly beautiful and the erotic sentiment (Sringara) is its foundation." (Nat. Shast, I.44) In short, nearly all of the ingredients for musical theater were prescribed in this treatise written nearly 2,000 years ago. Photo: Courtesy Medha, org@medha.org, 2005 and Nataraja.

Pic. 9.6 *Malini Srirama embodies the love and detachment many Indian dancers and musicians have for their art. By not taking ownership of their skills and crafts, but deferring the credit either to God or to their teacher (guru), they are able to remain more devoted to the purity of the art and free from the potential problems brought about by success or notoriety. Frequently, Ms. Srirama would come to our class to speak without any desire to discuss payment; this, after decades of training and practice as a performer and instructor.* Photo: Courtesy M.Srirama, 2004.

struction. *He symbolizes the eternal cycle of birth and death. Goddess Parvathi, the consort of Shiva (Siva), is the precursor of Laasya, or feminine grace. The god Krishna plays eternal melodies on his flute and was a good dancer. Saraswathi, the goddess of knowledge, played the Indian flute of Veena."*

Ms. Srirama continues: *"You must understand that Indians, like the deities themselves, have never been without the arts. Their traditional arts have always been dedicated to their deities. In the traditional arts, the aesthetic and philosophical views did not compete or conflict with each other. These existed in unison. It became an instrument of fulfillment.*

"According to the Hindu mythology, the world was begun when Lord Siva danced. Ever since, the gods of India have always danced in competition to celebrate victories or for their own amusement. In the Hindu pantheon, even the equivalents of the heavenly beings are known as apsaras and gandharvas, or, to translate in one way, the dancing and singing deities."

Along with religion, storytelling with the use of mythology also played an important role in the development of music and dance in India. Like other ancient religions, Hinduism abounds in myth. The appeal of these myths easily found its way into music and dance, emphasized by the myths themselves. Ms. Srirama writes: *"In several aspects, Hindu mythology could be compared to Greek mythology with its array of gods and goddesses. The myths explained the message of the symbols of Hinduism, and its morals were conveyed to the audience through the enactment or singing of mythological stories. It is always toward the deities that an Indian artist will address the dance or music, but his or her audience, foreign and far afield, may still draw from it a common humanity of love and beauty."*

Stories from the Human Family

Michael's Experience: You may find in the following "story" numerous ideas that can help balance mind, emotion, and even cultural perception. In all cases, you will see the enormous importance placed on storytelling. A very courteous and knowledgeable woman from India, who has now been in the United States over ten years, volunteered to come to my class to talk about Indian culture and music. After the class, I asked her how she learned about her culture's music. She said from her "guru," or teacher, in the United States (since she came to the U.S.). I asked her if there would be any way that I might meet her "guru." The meeting with *Mrinalini Arkatkar* (from whom we heard in Unit V) was arranged and the following discussion resulted:

"For Indian culture, we don't have a single particular book to follow. There are many things that are not written. So, generally changes that occur in our culture, we are ready to accept and make a part of us. In the Bhagvad Gita (a collection of stories where God expounded to the warrior Arjuna the teachings and values), there are not many specific things that say this is what a man or woman should do. So the combination of Indian history (multiple influences from Aryan, Persian, Arab, Chinese, and, later, British/European cultures) and the flexibility of our religion makes Indian culture (despite many people's perceptions), a very <u>flexible</u> culture system.

"That's why for generations we've learned to adapt. Most people of my generation have learned to keep our feet in both worlds (ancient and modern). That's also why you can find so many different philosophies and practices in India. Each different group may follow a different Guru who places an emphasis on a different part of life or religious practice. Even each caste— you know we had four castes [Brahmins—priestly class, Kshatriyas—warriors/defenders, Vaishyas—craftsmen/women and merchants, and Shudras—the peasant or servant class]—*was not originally based on hierarchy or station and certainly not race, but primarily on occupation and therefore would practice religion or adhere to certain philosophies different from the other classes. Only over time did the system begin to be exclusionary and based on color, or the belief that you could not move from one class to another. You know there have also been so many conquests and exchanges in Indian culture. We divide our country culturally into two regions, the Carnatic (Karnatic) and Hindustani* (Carnatic [Karnatic]—in the South, Hindustani—in the North), *primarily because of how the culture evolved."*

Pic. 9.7 *Characters from the Ramayana – Lord Ram, Laxman, Sita, and Hanuman (crouching). The Ramayana (Sanskrit: march [ayana] of Rama) is part of the Hindu smriti. This epic of 24,000 verses tells of a Raghuvamsa prince, Rama of Ayodhya, whose wife Sita is abducted by the rakshasa, or demon, Ravana. The Ramayana had an important influence on later Sanskrit poetry, but like its epic cousin, the Mahabharata, the Ramayana is not just a grand epic. It contains the teachings of the ancient Hindu sages and presents them through allegory in narrative and devotional discourse. Many feel this epic poem is fundamental to the cultural consciousness of India.* Image: Public domain, courtesy wikipedia.org.

Note: The history of India is as fluid and diverse as may exist anywhere. Although the history extends back to 7000 BCE, much of what India was to become began its cultural evolution during the Indo-Aryan migration, circa 1000 BCE (time period for the composition of the Vedas, and later, the Bhagavad Gita [Upanishad], which contains the text for the epic poem Mahabharata). This period not only ushered in Hinduism but also established musical-dance theater as an essential means of worship. The stories of the epic dramas and life of Krishna became the basis upon which Buddhism would later be established (circa 537 BCE) as well.

When asked about the misunderstandings she felt most people had about Hinduism, Ms. Arkatkar was quick to reply:

"There are a lot of misunderstandings about the 'gods' [9.3] *in Hinduism. Lord Ganesha, as an example, is the deity of knowledge and wisdom—that's the symbolism of the 'elephant head.' He is also humble to all creatures (symbolized by his holding a mouse) and has a large belly, which symbolizes his taking all of our sins inside. Each of us may gravitate to one deity more than another. My husband is fond of Lord Vishnu, who symbolizes prosperity. Everything is symbolic and not literal. The same is with our music. We use the music to balance ourselves, to get peace of mind. A lot of people don't know about this."*

Note: Numerous dynasties, and the influence of the Greeks, Persians, Turks, and Arabs over the centuries meant that India would not only be ruled by numerous diverse cultures and rulers but also (as Ms. Arkatkar continues),*"when people invade, they don't just bring their politics, but also their culture, their music, even their food."*

"Even in our Carnatic culture, in the Southern part of India, which had less influence from other cultures, we still have a variety of different influences. It's true Carnatic dance and music has less of an outside influence, but today, there is so much cross-influence between music and dance styles that even these terms mean much less."

Indian Diaspora

"In the older centuries, I don't think many people voluntarily wanted to leave India—and nearly everyone wanted to be a part of India. It has such diverse climates, resources, mountains, ocean on three sides – I think there are many consequences of being conquered and colonized so much. Many were also taken as slaves or laborers to Africa or the Americas. For one, Indian people became adaptable and flexible in their abilities. But after the British colonization, when we got our independence back (1947), it was total chaos in India. Many intelligent people couldn't get jobs or had no opportunity of advancement. This is when massive numbers of Indians left India for Africa, South America, the Caribbean, parts of Europe, and the United States. This is also when the split between Pakistan and India occurred." It is also the beginning of generations of Indians establishing themselves as citizens in most parts of the world, further contributing to global exchange and the flow of new stories and musical influences between India and these other cultures.

The Role of the Teacher

For centuries, a generally accepted hierarchy in India has placed teachers at or only slightly below the level of God in importance.[9.3A]

God
Teachers
Parents & Elders

In this sense, it was (is) believed that teachers have an extremely high station and are, in essence, the means by which one comes closer to God or, ultimately, would achieve *Nirvana*, or oneness with the Supreme Being. Among the teachers is a very special "teacher" known as a **Guru.** Ms. Arkatkar explained the role of *Guru* (and *Pundit* – the "Guru's Guru")[9.36] and the means through which both the stories and musical/dance skills for conveying them are learned, as follows: *"People go to different institutions (or, in music and dance, "schools" of thought), and they would learn from a master teacher. In the old days, you would go and live with the teacher. You would demonstrate your respect for the teacher, and then if you earned the right—the teacher would teach you what they knew. Otherwise, you would absorb what you could from being around the Guru. At any rate, each school or guru would have a specific orientation to music and dance. In the old days, the styles were very separate and unique, but today many of the styles and schools are blending together more.*

> *"One of the main things we, as teachers, have a responsibility to teach our students is that when they perform they must have a close dialogue with their audience. This we call entertainment. It's not like you may think of entertainment in a passive sense – it is the fulfillment of emotion. In classical music, we close our eyes, and we get into the vibrations of the music. There is a healing or more deeply emotional potential in this form of (meditative) listening. The Raag (Rag) touches your heart. Unless the help of God comes into your heart, you cannot touch the audience. You must go to the level of the audience.*
>
> *"My guru always used to say: 'Unless you are selfless in your approach, you can't put your knowledge out in the world.' He used to say: 'When you go out there to sit on the stage to perform, first thank God, not just for giving you an opportunity to perform, but for giving you the opportunity to learn.' God gave you the opportunity through your Guru to learn. Any performance is a mirror image of you. It reflects what you are—whatever in the universe you've learned from your Guru, you deliver it to your audience."*

What occurs in the dynamics of such a level of respect given to the teacher by the student, regardless of the faults or inadequacies of the teacher, is a synergy, which—by virtue of the humility of the student—will likely produce the following:

- The student will remain more receptive to any wisdom that may come from the teacher and find wisdom when and where other students may not be looking.

- Students will reaffirm the roles of the life cycle and may, in turn, attain the station of "teacher" or guru at some stage in their own lives. This would occur, however, only by virtue of their ability, discipline, practice of humility, and service to their teacher.

- Students will learn the qualities of service and forgiveness, or extending a "sin-covering" eye to their teacher or elder, which will serve them throughout their lives and relationships.

- And today, students will counter the forces of individualism and disrespect for age and experience that might otherwise threaten to disrupt their natural understanding of the life cycle and result in an imbalance or "disease" in the perception of ancestry and aging.

Although "freedom of speech" has its benefits, according to Indian belief systems, when such freedom permits evaluating or criticizing your teachers or elders, the basic status of the life cycle and our respective

Pic. 9.8A Swami Vivekananda was one of the first Gurus to travel from India to the West. He addressed the World Parliament of Religions, (Chicago, Illinois) in 1893. It is the life-long commitment of the "Guru" to expand his or her knowledge and share it with others solely for the purpose of "enlightenment." Photo: Public domain.

places in that cycle are compromised. By modeling a deep respect for cultural/musical ancestry and a serious and humble approach to its mastery, the student is led by example to acquire these same qualities. This will garner them respect in their later years and serve as a foundation upon which they can, in turn, teach their children or students, later in the life cycle.

Respecting the Teacher

Respect: Who Benefits? The Teacher or Student?
Léonie's Experience

"I was still in primary school, when I returned home after a class one day, angry about a comment a teacher had made. 'So and so really needs to do such and such,' I blurted within the hearing range of my parents. Within seconds, both my parents had pulled me onto the porch, sat me down, and with nearly the same exact words simultaneously said, in effect:

> 'We don't ever want to hear you speak of your teachers in such a manner. There is nothing you can learn or benefit from, if you begin to disrespect the very person from whom you must learn. As soon as you take this attitude, you are not only disrespecting them, but you are disrespecting us—your elders and parents, and, most importantly, disrespecting yourself— for you will never learn what they have to give you if you carry animosity in your heart. And, in addition (they concluded), you may pass this on to your little brothers, sisters, or classmates.'

"Initially, I was completely surprised by my parents' response. The action of the teacher was, clearly in my estimation, incorrect. They had made a mistake; of this, I was certain. Why should I not be justified in my criticism? But, as their words penetrated my heart, it became very clear that little learning (if any) could occur, so long as I made disagreeing with my teachers, resenting their ways, or contesting their perceptions my focus.

"My parents went on to explain that I did not have to agree with or even absorb everything a teacher says—they are human, will make mistakes, have views that are not mine, or give information or ideas that are even incorrect. But, by respecting every teacher, I will generate the best relationships with them, encourage them to give their best, and, in turn, I will have the best mindset from which to learn as much as possible.

"I suppose—against the backdrop of some cultures' perspectives of 'freedom of speech,' of creating informality and openness in the classroom to the degree of calling teachers by their first name and arguing a teacher's comments in class, or back-biting the teacher to others when we do not like their perspectives or mannerisms—my parents' perspectives might seem 'old-fashioned.' But as I see the result of handing a student an instructor evaluation form every semester to 'critique' the instructor, witness the extreme informality in some classrooms, see the degree to which learning and education are often taken so lightly by an increasing population of students,or witness how teachers are treated with contempt, I now, ever so clearly, see my parents' wisdom: *It is our (the student's) receptivity and openness that closes when we become occupied with criticizing or resenting an instructor.* And, if another person respects me or my opportunity for growth, but has a problem with the teacher as well and has not yet been instructed to respect their teacher, I would fan the flame of their resentments and learning dysfunction by contributing to the criticism."

Questions

- *How have you been trained to think of your teachers?*
- *Do you agree or disagree with Ms. Naylor's perspectives? Why or why not?*
- *Do you see the potential benefit in attempting to respect your teachers regardless of their actions?*
- *What roles must teachers also play in fostering such respect?*

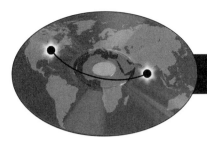

Inside the Musician's World

Mrinalini Arkatkar

Ms. Arkatkar commented: *"Both Bharata Natyam and Carnatic dance styles would have been done in the temples to tell the stories of Lord Vishnu or Krishna. Each dance would begin with the process of honoring the Gods, and would be done not as a performance to please people but to please the gods (deities).*[9.4] *Later, after the invasion of the Muslims (which began in the 8th century and intensified through the eleventh century) more of*

Pic. # 9.9 / Mrinalini Arkatkar with her husband Aniruddha, daughter Mrinmai, and son Anooj.

the 'human' or emotional elements of human love—still about Lord Krishna, but the romantic stories would find their way into music and dance, to entertain people. They were not just about His station as a God, but also had the dual metaphor of His human exploits. Kathak dance styles in particular are more modern than Bharata Natyam. Much of the Kathak style comes from the fusion with other styles and stories that resulted from Mughal (Muslim) occupation.

"Keep in mind, though, we like to simplify things with labels. There have always been hundreds of regions in India that have their own folk dance and music styles as well. This complicates the picture even more, as we have to assume that some of these influences found their way into the more classical music and dance and vice versa. It's a traditional classic dance form of northern India. Kathak uses the body as a medium of communication. This dance can be traced to the period between 1300 and 1400 CE.

"The dance was originated in remote temples of northern India. Kathak means 'story telling.' Traditionally, these stories were about the Hindu

Pic. 9.9A *Mrinalini's daughter Mrinmai demonstrating a Kathak position. She has learned nearly all of what she knows about India, Indian (Kathak) dance and music, and the culture generally in the United States. Her passion for her "other" culture, that of her ancestry, can only be learned by respecting her parents and teachers. This respect must be carefully nurtured, however, and does not come naturally in material-based or individualized societies. Photo: Courtesy Aniruddha and Mrinalini Arkatkar, 2005.*

Gods and Goddesses. But the Mughal invasion of north India had a serious impact on dance. The dance was taken from the temples to the Mughal court to entertain the kings and queens. Today's kathak style is a beautiful blend of both traditions: the expressive and devotional style from temples and the rhythmic and entertaining style from the courts."

CD 3.10

"Song by Saint Eknath," by Mrinalini Arkatkar, tabla by Shyam Kane, from the CD: **For Saint Eknath**, c. 2005.

Ms. Arkatkar comments: *"This is written by Saint Eknath. The song describes both the power of the Lord Krishna and his human nature within. It tells the story about young Krishna. Lord Krishna was believed to be surrounded by 'Gopis' (his friends), and was always mischievous to them. Somewhere in the middle of the song, you will notice that there are several cycles of rhythm, where you hear just the percussion instrument the tabla. The dancer requested me to have a space in the performance where she would act as a Gopi and her daughter will act as Lord Krishna, and they will put up a small display of Lord Krishna playing several childhood games with the Gopi. During that time, the harmonium player just keeps playing the same cycle of notes over and over again and lets the tabla player play different 'kayadas' (variety of sequences of rhythmic notes) to support the typical actions of the dancers.*

"This is my own music composition, and it is also sung by me. The story in the song is about Lord Krishna's childhood. The composition is based on raag (rag) Kalavati and the rhythmic cycle is of 16 beats, known as Tintaal. The percussionist Shyam Kani has improvised the rhythmic beats to support the dance actions."

The Recipe of Sound

Ms. Arkatkar explains: *"The Kathak piece has been composed in raag "Kalavati." In this rag, the 2nd note ("rishabha") and the 4th note ("madhyam") are not used. The seventh note ("nishad") is in the flat version. The mood of this raag is very happy and romantic and was appropriate for the lyrics, where the Gopis are enjoying discussing the Lord Krishna's nature and power."*

This piece uses the *harmonium* (a small accordion in a box-like frame with a keyboard), *tablas* (the familiar term for two, small finger or hand drums), and the

Pic. 9.10 *Mrinalini and husband Aniruddha (to her left) playing harmonium with the ensemble: (L. to R.) tablas, chorus, Mrinalini, Aniruddha, and a second harmonium.* Photo: Courtesy M. Arkatkar, 2005.

tambura (tanpura) (which a large lute-like instrument similar to the sitar that is used to produce the drone in Indian music.) *"My husband (Aniruddha) used to play violin and started playing harmonium only after coming to the U.S.A., learning on his own. I needed someone to accompany me during my concerts, and I could not think of anyone better than him to support me for the performances."*

"That is why for last 15 years, he has accompanied me on keyboard and harmonium for all my concerts. By profession he is a software engineer, but at heart he is a musician. Together we always enjoy discussing and listening to music and, of course, performing our concerts. This helps us to be in touch with our ancient traditions. We believe that we are blessed with music, which brings more joy and happiness to our entire family. Our daughter is now very much into music and dance as well—primarily as a means of deepening her cultural knowledge and attachment to India's musical past."

Indian Instrumental Music

Since the 1960s when Ravi Shankar began to work with George Harrison of the Beatles, the **sitar, tablas, and tambura** *(tanpura)*, as well as other instruments of the Northern (Hindustani) region of India, have become more widely known to musicians in the West. There are a number of potential reasons for this growth in fascination with Indian instruments and music:

- The *sitar* (see Pic.9.10A) – an instrument with 6-7 strings that also has 12 sympathetic strings that vibrate and resonate as the instrument is played. A complex instrument that can be tuned differently to accommodate each raag, the sitar is the premier solo instrument of Indian instrumental music.

- The **raags** *(rags)* – as mentioned, are very complicated tonal systems with multiple non-musical dimensions. The raags use tones (microtones) that are often smaller than those in Western music. They are also bound by numerous rules that determine which notes should be emphasized. Most raags have distinct pitch organization in both upward and downward motion, making raags generally much more complicated than Western scales or modes.[9.5]

- The meters (**tala**) – that are used as the rhythmic structure for the raags can have as few as three beats or as many as one hundred beats per cycle or measure. Rhythms played by the tabla (two single-headed drums—see Pic. 9.10B) or mridangam (one double-headed drum) are usually learned to be sung with vocal syllables (theka or bols) before the instrumentalists will begin playing their drums.

- The *drone* – usually produced by the four-string tambura (tanpura), which plays primarily root notes and notes five pitches (a fifth) higher. The tambura sustains these pitches throughout the piece, adding only rhythmic intensity as the rhythms and tempos increase. This is called a drone, as it is the core or central point of focus for meditative listening.

Pic. 9.10A, B, & C – The sitar (A-top), tablas (B-above middle), and the harmonium and tambura (C-above), together with the violin and flute (not pictured), are among the core instruments used in Indian music today. Although earlier there had been a considerably more pronounced distinction between Hindustani (North Indian) and Carnatic (South Indian) cultures, today younger musicians are more likely to utilize instruments and sounds with infinitely less concern for geographical distinctions. Photos: Courtesy Lark in the Morning, and wikipedia.org, 2005.

Since rags played with the configuration of sitar, tablas, and tambura are based on both instruments and musical formulas inherited from Arabic, Persian, and Eastern European cultures, this music also shares an aesthetic connection with those regions. Perhaps the most fascinating dynamic of the instrumental music of Northern India is the formula for building and releasing tension, which in many ways defines the most prevalent pattern of building tension in large musical works.

The beginning of the raag is called an *alap* in Hindustani music and an *alapana* in Carnatic music. The general function of the *alap* is to slowly introduce the *raag* and to encourage the listener and musicians alike to resonate, or bring themselves from the outside world into the world of the raag.

Once the rag is established, the ornamental accompaniment around the raag becomes increasingly pronounced in its rhythm (i.e., introduces the *tala* or meter), gradually speeding up. This section is called the *jor*. Frequently within the *jor* are set melodies and patterns, which conform to the rules of the raag. After the jor climaxes, everything stops and the audience frequently applauds. Finally, the percussionist begins to play, interacting with the soloist, and eventually reaching the spontaneous and competitive *jhala* section, which is highly improvisational and very much like the sections in an improvisational jazz piece. Perhaps for this reason as well, the majority of fusions between Indian "classical" music (as this music is sometimes called) and Western music occur with Western musicians schooled in blues, rock, or jazz improvisation.

In summary, in many (not all) Hindustani pieces, the building of the raag—from its free-flowing introduction (alap), to its melodic and rhythmic introduction (jor), and finally to the rhythmic and melodic improvisations which build to the climax of the piece (jhala) – serves the natural function of perpetually increasing tension. Perhaps even more profound than the complexity of the melody and rhythm as they build and release tension are the roles and mindsets expected of both the performer and the *active listener* in fulfilling the musical experience.

Rasa and the "Rasika"

Ms. Arkatkar commented: *"You know part of the music is what we call rasa. It is the musical soul or fulfillment of the music. Yes, it is like the triangle, but when I perform, I extend my heart to the audience."* What is this triangle she speaks of? What does "extend your heart to the audience" mean? And what, if you ever watch the audience during a classical music concert, are they doing with their fingers, and their eyes closed? What about watching the musicians fly around on the instruments?

Stories from the Human Family

Michael's Experience:

"I've always had trouble figuring out how to teach Western musicians to overcome performance anxiety—that is, being more than 'passionately nervous' when performing. One stretch of my life, in Germany, I was able to work for a short time with an Indian classical musician in a jazz group.

"First, he would sit down on the floor, usually do a small prayer before each rehearsal or concert (sometimes with an image of Shiva before him), and then would close his eyes and might not open them or look at the other musicians until the end of the performance or rehearsal. But more importantly, no matter how many people we'd perform for, nor the situation or venue, he seemed never to be nervous. I finally had to ask him: 'How do you stay so calm?' His reply, 'Rasa!'

"Many years later, I asked other Indian musicians what "rasa" was—and, to my delight, I learned (at least on some small level) one of the most profound techniques for overcoming performance anxiety, which I try to apply not only in my own life, but in teaching others as well:

– by detaching ourselves from the performance, allowing ourselves to become channels for the inspiration and beauty of the creation, and never allowing ourselves to take ownership of the result, we are free to do the best we as channels of inspiration are capable."

The basic concept of *rasa* ("sap/juice or essence") is realizing the depth of emotion or the "soul" of the piece through an understanding of its spiritual connection and remembering that music's healing potential and ultimate beauty do not lie with the performers' abilities and preparation alone but with the acknowledgement that musical fulfillment has a circular structure. Performers and audience alike have roles in the fulfillment of the experience.

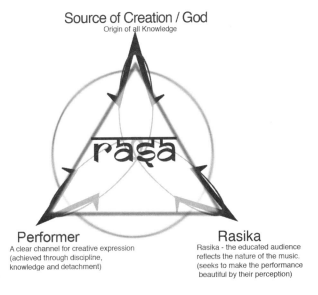

The concept of Indian *rasa* begins with the realization that all creativity (and music) already exists. In this sense, we cannot actually *"create"* anything new. The Creator has all knowledge. Therefore, our ideas and any potential musical piece (now or in the future) preexists our recognition of it. Once the performer perfects his technique, is humble before his teacher, and learns everything that he has the capacity to learn, he must then "detach" himself from the performance (or renounce ownership of the performance).

Ms. Artkatkar referred to this as *"selfless—giving of beauty or a gift to the audience."* This is a distinctly "egoless" approach to performance. It not only clears performers' minds to do their best for reasons that cannot get entwined with ego or selfishness but also reinforces the fact that, if the performers do their best in this regard, they are immune from *judgment* or criticism, the most common basis for performance anxiety.

Finally, we arrive at the audience, the listener, or the "appreciator." The *rasika* is the educated listener whose job it is to prepare him- or herself for the performance (i.e., learn about the opera, blues, or Congolese drum patterns), then learn the proper mechanism for interacting with the music. To a large extent, participating or listening in the deepest manner according to the music's tradition, requires having knowledge of musical discipline and then overlooking the flaws or inadequacies of the performance by *making the music beautiful by our perception*. This is a distinctly different perspective from the role of the music critic, to be sure.

Although this may only scratch the surface of what rasa implies, imagine the effect of such a change in perception on our appreciation of music generally. What effect would such an attitude have on the perception of the music or movie critic? Or upon us when we take on the role of critic? We could no longer go to concerts or movies expecting something to be entertaining, or "good." Instead, we would be forced to say to ourselves, "I don't have control over how the musicians play the music, but I do have control over how I *listen* to it," and therefore, we should work to make the music beautiful (fulfilling) by virtue of our knowledge and perception of it!

From the musician's perspective (as well as that of anyone who performs in other ways, such as taking exams, beginning a new job, or any other time-based performance), to give all you can to preparation and to release yourself from the outcome liberates you from fear of failure or concerns that might inhibit you from giving your best attention to the experience. *Rasa* in this sense, is a metaphor for doing our best as human beings and appreciating the best in others.

Pic. 9.11 *Indian curries (now common throughout the Diaspora) are the result of thousands of years of culinary "fusion." Curries are generally the result of many different spices: cloves, turmeric, cumin, hot pepper, curry leaves, cinnamon – all coming together in a single pot. Although comparisons of culinary arts to music or art may seem vague, in India, the colors (timbre), aroma (rhythm), and fusion of influences is precisely the manner by which the music of India came into being.* Photo: Courtesy wikipedia.org, 2005.

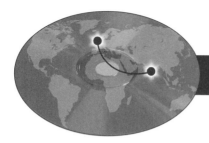

Inside the Musician's World

Baluji Shrivastav

Note: Although born blind, Baluji Shrivastav has never used this fact for anything but self-betterment. Considered a "master" of the sitar and Hindustani classical music, he exhibits great strength to command complex rhythms and enthrall audiences with his improvisational skills.

After acquiring a B.A. and M.A. in performance studies in India, Mr. Shrivastav went on to Europe (U.K.), where he has been living, performing, and teaching. The notes that accompanied this recording commented: *"Most recently Baluji's talents have taken him into other forms of music including jazz where, in addition to his own band, Jazz Orient, he is a regular member of the 'Grand Union Orchestra,' a multi-instrument ensemble."*

CD 3.11

"**Raga Shuddha Sarang,**" by Baluji Shrivastav, from the CD: **Classical Indian Sitar and Surbahar Ragas,** Arc Music International, c. 1999.

This is an afternoon raag; the time for performance or reciting of the music would be around noon. The mood of this rag is a *"happy swinging one, expressing the bracing feeling of coolness in the weather with the sun occasionally breaking through."*

Now how do we respond as listeners? It's the job of the *rasikas,* while listening, to keep the emotion and images above planted in their thoughts, to concentrate on the music (performed by sitar and tablas), and to create the imagery and emotion described above. This is the manner of *perceiving beauty* required for this particular piece. Suggestion: First read "The Recipe of Sound" (below), to become more knowledgeable, create an image in your mind based on the above description, and then attempt to hold onto that image (or return to it) as you listen to the music. Remember to create a balance between comfort and tension in the mind and body to increase receptivity to the music, yet avoid falling asleep.

The Recipe of Sound

Rhythmically, this piece is a *Drut Gat* (fast composition) in a 16-beat meter (called *Teental* [Tintal]). The patterns of the meter are generally 4 beats + 4 beats + 4 beats + 4 beats. However, because the overall meter is 16 beats before it begins to recycle again, the instrumentalists may divide the 16-beat pattern into diverse combinations of beats up to sixteen. The tempo of this piece increases from medium to fast, and the improvisation takes the form of questions and answers (call and response) between the sitar and tabla. The piece concludes with a jhala section, which includes improvisation. (Note: This is only a four-minute selection from a ten-minute composition. Most instrumental rags would likely extend longer than ten minutes).

The Ancient and the Modern

The challenge facing many of the cultures we have discussed thus far—and all to be discussed in this unit—is how to reconcile the ancient traditions of the past with the modern innovations and developments in today's world. In modern India, the musical soundscape and media are dominated by the melodies and rhythms that come from Bollywood, or the Indian film industry centered in Bombay. You might have discerned after reading the above passages that storytelling and musical perception of emotion and associations in music are also very important in Indian culture. But how do the ancient and the modern reconcile these values in today's India?

Pic. 9.12A *A stone figurine goddess playing the veena (multi-stringed lute) is one of many representations of spirituality and music being closely connected in Indian culture and religion. Vibration, sound, and their combinations in music have ancient roots in the Hindu religion and religious practices.* Photo: Copyright Hi-Design Graphics.

Mrinalini Arkatkar comments on the paradox of finding a balance between respect for the past and acknowledgment of the present: *"In this country (U.S.A.), to promote our music and our culture is very hard. Many young Indian students come to me, and the first thing they want to learn are Bollywood songs (songs from recent movie-musicals).*

"Today, I select a song from a Bollywood film, and then I teach the rag through the song they are familiar with. There are many ways to teach; you cannot teach people things that are inaccessible to them. That's what my Guru also meant by going to their level. Presenting music that can enlighten according to the capacity of the audience. I'm getting good response, and that's important. If people are afraid of the concept of 'classical music' (older traditions of Indian music and dance), then you must help them overcome their fears by giving them something that they can build on.

"Even when I teach the rags (I know they may not remember much of what I teach musically), but I relate how I learned from my Guru and how he learned from his – so that they can learn the respect and understanding of the history or culture and the respect for education that I was able to learn from.

"Today, what the producers are doing is using ancient rags and traditions. They are keeping many of the

Pic. 9.12B *A student (Usman Chohan), cell-phone and all, at a sitar workshop in Islamabad, Pakistan.* Photo: Courtesy Uchohan.

musical traditions alive, but they are creating fusions with the world around them. They are blending the influences—in the same tradition that Indian classical music used to blend traditions. Naturally, today, they are blending songs that are easy to sing, to dance to, to participate with. This is what makes them popular.

"Of course, another impact is there are so many difficulties — unemployment, and difficulties in life in general. This is an outlet, a chance to get into another world. They take this passion for storytelling and they use it as a means for creating a balance in their lives. This is very important to Indian culture today."

China—Spirit Greater than Reality?

Chinese Opera to the Music of Today

If you have ever visited a "Chinatown" in many large Western cities, watched the Olympic Chinese gymnasts perform, been to an exquisite Chinese buffet, viewed a wonderful Chinese painting, piece of furniture, or vase, then you may have marveled at the colors, the manner of discipline, commitment, sense of community, and passion that appear in much of what we call "Chinese." Although many of these qualities and traits do seem to exist and will be addressed in part below, what does not exist is a singular or uniform "Chinese" culture per se.

The history of China is marked and codified by civilizations or dynasties which ruled much or all of China beginning with the first (recorded) Xia civilization (2200 BCE–1750 BCE). Each of these dynasties had unique yet diverse characteristics. We will also see a history of exchange through conflict and war, as well as through trade and cultural exchange that makes Chinese identity difficult to encapsulate.

As a frame of reference, the following is a brief overview of Chinese dynasties and some of the events that occurred during these time periods, which contributed to the "multicultural fusions" we now generally refer to as *Chinese*. As before, we try to use the dates, events, and developments of their history to set up a flexible file of context into which we can place the music, art, architecture, and especially the history of interaction and impact of each culture on us today (thereby recognizing "their" history as important to "our" history).

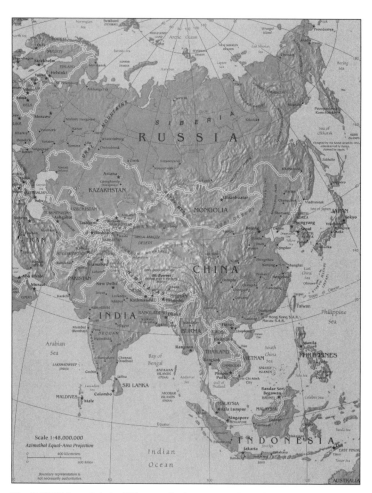

Pic. 9.12C Map of Asia: *When we look at a map from the perspective of cultures, we look at it to see which "bordering countries" contributed to the fusion and exchange process. Culturally, to look at a map from the perspective of boundaries and divisions is counterintuitive and counterproductive. India and China (and later we will address Korea, Japan, and Indonesia), despite having unique cultural aspects and expressions, have evolved, as have all cultures, through enormous efforts to adapt, defend, and both exchange and integrate with numerous other cultures over a very long period.* Image: Courtesy (www.cia.gov/cia/publications/factbook).

Chinese Dynasties and Civilization
Notable Events and Developments

Note: *There is a wide variation of dates for the earlier dynasties. The dates used here are the consensus of the different estimates. We include comments by a Chinese graduate student of history, which gives the "street perspective" (as learned by young Chinese students) of the "dates and information" we gathered. We'll hear more from that student, XiangDong, Che, later.*

Shang (1766-1040 BCE)

- *First dynasty to leave records in writing (the basis for the system in use today).*
- *Sophisticated bronze art, governmental structure, and military, which expanded the borders from Mongolia to the Pacific Ocean.*

Chou (1040-256 BCE)

- *Semi-nomadic, the Chou (from the West) overthrew the Shang Dynasty.*
- *Developed a feudal social system. Chou rulers taxed subjects, but used money to build irrigation systems and walls of protection around feudal cities.*
- *May have been the first, or among the first, to extract iron from rocks (iron ore).*
- *Persian Empire invaded and occupied portions of Western China (550-330 BCE).*

Ch'in [Qin](221-206 BCE)

- *Confucius initiated a campaign for a "just" government from warring clans.*
- *Ironically, one of the shortest dynasties, is also likely the one with which Western cultures first had contact (and the one from which the name "China" was derived).*
- *Weights and measures and Chinese writing system were unified.*
- *Began creation of the Great Wall of China and first documented use of the "silk road."*

XiangDong writes: *"The first Emperor of Ch'in has been considered as a hero recently by some people, because he brought the whole country together. But he and his son were really brutal to their people, which directly caused the collapse of their empire."*

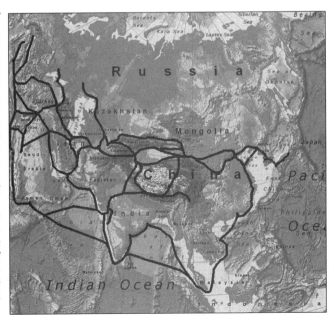

Pic. 9.13 *The "Silk Road" was actually thousands of miles of roads that stretched from China through northern Tibet, parts of southern Asia, and the northern Arabian peninsula to the Mediterranean Sea, southeastern Russia, Eastern Europe, and, in time, as far east as Korea and Japan. Few people traveled the whole length of the Silk Road but instead created a chain of outposts linking the trade routes. Not only were the routes critical for trade from East to West, but they became a means for the transference of important cultural ideals, such as Buddhism (which is believed to have come from Northern India into China through this route during the Han dynasty), the exchange of Western and Eastern technology and inventions, and, most certainly, musical instruments, musical ideas, and arts generally. Marco Polo used this route to explore China during the Yuan (Mongol) dynasty. The Silk Road became less viable as sea routes, established by such explorers as Portugal's Vasco da Gama, became a quicker and more practical means of trade and travel.* Map courtesy of "free worldmaps" and Roylee, public domain, 2005.

Han (206 BCE-220 CE)

- *Considered the "Golden Age" of Chinese History by many.*

- *"Chinese" to a "Chinese" person means "a man of Han."*

- *China officially became a "Confucian" state.*

- *Although comparisons are made between the Han dynasty and the Roman Empire (as China spread to include Vietnam, Central Asia, Mongolia, and Korea), it is actually divided into subperiods.*

- *Paper is said to have been "invented" during this time period.*

Three Kingdoms (220-589 CE)(Wei, Wu, and Su)

- *This period marked the breakup of the Han dynasty, wherein all three regions were ruled by emperors.*

- *This historical period has been greatly romanticized in the cultures of China, Japan, Korea, and throughout Southeast Asia. It became the topic of numerous operas, folk stories, novels, and, in more recent times, films, television serials, and video games. The best known of these is un-doubtedly The Romance of the Three Kingdoms.*

Sui (589-618 CE) / Tang (618-907 CE) / Song (960-1279 CE)

- *Collectively these three periods marked the end of the age of warlords and the reunification and flourishing of Chinese art and culture, primarily under Confucianism.*

- *The Great wall was expanded and reinforced.*

- *Increased contact with India, the Middle East, the expansion of Buddhism, block printing, and standardized coinage and economic system marked these periods.*

- *The Turks seized much of what is now Western China from the 10th century through Ottoman rule to the 16th century.*

- *Wars with Korea, and military figures eventually taking over parts of China, weakened the state.*

Xiang Dong commented: "From my understanding, the Tang Dynasty is the most prosperous period in China's history. China became the greatest power in Asia during Tang. In the late Tang Dynasty, people suffered a lot from wars and poverty. But during most parts of the Tang Dynasty, people could live relatively peaceful lives. The population increased, and a lot of great artists and poets living in Tang produced priceless masterpieces of art. It is rightfully ranked as the classical period of Chinese art and literature, as it set the high standard to which later poets, painters, and sculptors aspired.

"As to the Song dynasty, some researchers consider Song as the beginning of the fall of Chinese culture, because the philosophy adopted by the Song Emperors and administration had been considered a poison to people's creative thinking and freedom of speech."

Yuan [Mongol] (1279-1368 CE)

- *Timüjin (better known as Genghis Khan)united the fractured Mongolian tribes, first against Northern China, later middle China, and finally, through his lineage, parts of Persia, Russia, Poland, and Hungary, stopping only shortly before moving on to Vienna.*

- *The Mongols were considered "foreigners" by most Chinese and remained so through much of the Yuan dynasty. Kublai Khan eventually established stronger relations with other foreign cultures; most notable was his relationship with Marco Polo.*

Xiang Dong writes: "That's right. Yuan is also one of the shortest dynasties in China's history. The main reason was that the majority of the Chinese people were "Han" and never considered Yuan Emperor as their own Emperor. Rebellions could be seen in lots of places in China throughout the history of Yuan."

Pic. 9.14 *The Great Wall of China, first built during the Ch'in dynasty (221 BCE – 206 BCE), was designed to keep foreign invaders from the north out of China. The wall was expanded through numerous other dynasties, but China, by virtue of its geographic proximity to India, Persia, Arabia, Russia, Mongolia, and, later, Japan, Korea, and Southeast Asia as well as European lands, became a major partner for "trade" and cultural exchange with and between all of these cultures. Moral of the story: "Walls," physical or in the labeling of human cultures, cannot prevent human interaction, exchange, or fusion.* Photo: Courtesy Hao Wei, China.

Subsequent dynasties:

Ming 1368-1644 CE

- *A Buddhist monk led a peasant army to victory over the Mongols, which led to enormous exploration and Chinese expansion into the Indian Ocean). XiangDong wrote: "Ming is the Dynasty when Chinese Han culture was badly depressed due to the Ming Empire's restrictive laws and policing policies to oppress different voices, and possibly, any rebellion."*

Qing (Manchu) 1644-1911 CE

- *Effectively the last Chinese dynasty and one which frequently used repression and coercion to subjugate the Han Chinese prior to the establishment of the Republic of China (1911), and later, the People's Republic of China (1949) after WWII. XiangDong commented: "Qing is the dynasty when China really fell in many respects and became further behind other cultures in some respects."*

The fascinating, dramatic, and enormously multicultural history of China only partially cited above would, over time, repeatedly be the topic and inspiration for Chinese art, pottery, and most certainly one of the most dramatic forms of musical storytelling … what we in the West refer to as *Chinese Opera*. In Chinese music in general, and specifically its musical theater, we get the sense of striving to achieve balance that was an important theme in the stories and creative aesthetics of Chinese culture over the course of its evolution. Much of this was the result of Confucian and Buddhist philosophies and the emphasis on creative and philosophical balance in living and expression, which worked to counter or balance the disjointing impact of the militaristic regimes and the history of battles and conflicts. The storytelling of balancing life we will find throughout one of the most richly diverse traditions in Chinese music, "Chinese Opera."

Chinese "Opera"—Dynamic Stories of a Complex History

When we speak of "Chinese" opera, it's very much like speaking of European opera, i.e., there is French, Italian, or German opera. Then, there is French, Italian, or German opera from the Renaissance, Baroque, Classical, or Romantic "periods." In similar fashion, Chinese opera has existed as a nearly inde-

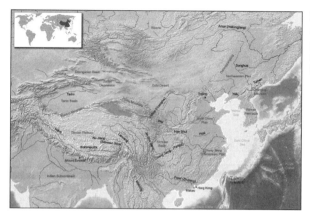

Pic. 9.15 *Each corner or region of China represents a substantially different fusion of cultures. Therefore, each region's "opera" will reflect the dialect, stories, politics, and sensibilities of that region's history.* Map: Public domain, CIA factbook, 2004.

pendent art form in every region of China from the 8th century to the present. Just as "folk" music and dances reflected each region's cultural dynamics, so too did the mixture of folk music and tales, tempered always by the dynasty or group who possessed "God's mandate" for each region over history.

To acquaint ourselves with the diversity of this art form, let's briefly scan some of Chinese opera's notable formats:

- The earliest form of opera (musical voiced or sung dramatic stories with musical accompaniment, dance or movement, and full costumes/staging) was from the Tang dynasty and Emperor Xuanzong (712-755 CE). He founded the "Pear Garden," likely the world's first "opera troupe," and China's first as well. The troupe performed mostly for the emperor's personal pleasure. To this day, operatic professionals are still often referred to as "Disciples of the Pear Garden."

- Song dynasty—"Nanxi," from Hangzhou, the capital of the dynasty in the 12th century. This early form included rhymed verse (sung or spoken). It was composed by "writing societies" and did not identify "composers," but rather functioned as an anonymous creative community. Other features included no divisions within the work (such as "acts"); an "orchestra" of aerophones and chordophones; and an offstage chorus, which accompanied the soloist. Note: Effectively Chinese "opera" in all senses of the word, preceded European opera by nearly 400 years.

- In the Yuan dynasty (1279-1368), the Mongol emperor Kublai Khan patronized opera from the Northern region of China (particularly for "high society"), which became known as *Zaju* (variety plays). The main character sang a lyric verse using a single rhyme scheme for each of the four acts. During this time, four specialized roles became the "tradition." These roles included:

Pic. 9.15A *Characters such as the Monkey King (one sub-character of the "Chou" tradition) have a special place in the hearts of all who are interested in Chinese opera. Played by an exceptionally talented Wu Sheng actor, the Monkey King holds every minute of the audience's attention with the quick, agile movements of his lithe body and his blinking eyes. He is traditionally supposed to have accompanied a Buddhist monk who went on a long journey across the mountains from China to India to collect the Buddhist scriptures and bring them back to China. The Monkey King also possesses special supernatural powers to combat evil spirits encountered along the way.* Photo: istock, 2005.

> **"Dan"** (main female),
> **"Sheng"** (a young male),
> **"Jing"** (a painted-face male), and
> **"Chou"** (the comic or clown)

- During the same time, in Southern regions, a folk opera, "Chuanqi" (marvelous tales), flourished in the Zhejiang and Jiangsu regions. The operas of the "folk" reflected the tension between loyalty to the throne (at this point occupied by Mongol leaders perceived as "foreign") and Confucian or Buddhist beliefs. Some credit the stories and plays of this genre for eventually inciting the masses to "revolt." [9.6]

- The 16th century was the home of what some consider to be China's most eloquent operatic form, "Kunqu." From the Kunshan (near Suzhou), Kunqu, was characterized by soft singing and minimal orchestral accompaniment: typically the clapper (a wooden clapper which issued the beats and accents to cue the performers or sometimes a drum) and a bamboo flute. Kunqu rose to the status of "National Opera" in the 17th and 18th centuries. Because of the simplicity of the music, the operas themselves became more ornate in story line and vocal style.

An estimated 300-plus different forms of Chinese Opera (or musical storytelling) are known to have been created to reflect the diverse "histories" in China's evolution. The best known of styles is *Beijing*, or *Peking, opera,* which assumed its present form in the mid-19th century but was extremely popular in the Qing Dynasty (1644-1911).[9.7]

In Beijing Opera, traditional Chinese string and percussion instruments provide the accompaniment to the acting. The acting is based on allusion, i.e., gestures, footwork, and other body movements that express such actions as riding a horse, rowing a boat, or opening a door. Spoken dialogue is divided into recitative and Beijing colloquial speech, the former used by serious characters and the latter by young females and clowns. Character roles are strictly defined and augmented by elaborate make-up designs and color symbolizing the character of the actor. One interpretation of these colors and their qualities reads: [9.8]

Pic. 9.16 *This is a photo of the Chinese opera stage in the Summer Palace near Beijing, where the Chinese royal family, more specifically the Empress Dowager Cixi, watched the shows. As with much of Asian architecture and art, the detail in decorative art, mosaic, and painting reflects the emphasis on patience, discipline, and service.* Photo: Courtesy Richard Chambers, AAA Yangtze Sampler tour, May 2004.

Red: *courage, loyalty, and straightforwardness;*
Black: *integrity;* **Blue:** *cruelty;*
White: *wickedness;* **Purple:** *wisdom.*

Today, Beijing, or Peking, opera is known to include more than 1,000 works. The vast majority of these are taken from historical novels about political and military struggles. Despite the political overtones, there are, in every Chinese theatrical work, a couple of important characteristics typical of Chinese art in most genres.

- Chinese art generally places an emphasis on *spirit* over *reality.* Even in today's Chinese films, the characters may frequently perform tasks completely "unrealistic" to the Western viewer, such as dancing on the tops of bamboo stalks, or perhaps flying through the air. But actions such as these are projections of the spirit, and are not intended to reflect everyday reality. To further this characteristic, "nature metaphors" are employed in nearly all forms of Chinese art wherein, much as in Native American culture, nature provides a spirit or quality to the actors and the story.

Pic. 9.16A This is an example of Chinese painting from the 13th century. The work, by Ma Lin, shows the "spirit" (the venerable master is much larger than the servant) and the "space" (much of the canvas is suggestive or empty). The ancient principle of striving for balance (yin and yang) is among the most essential philosophies in Chinese culture. The striving to reflect both spirit and balance is present in nearly all Chinese art, even in the present day.[9.9]

- Chinese art and music gives considerable emphasis to space or silence in balance to activity or sound. As each generation has become increasingly more mechanized and faster-paced, art will naturally reflect these changes. Yet, in much of Chinese painting, you may see large areas where there is "no paint." Similarly, Chinese music uses silence, or lack of sound, as a form of "music" to set up and balance the impact of another type of music—sound itself.

- The role of one's service to the community, to the group, and to the larger configuration of human grouping generally receives greater emphasis than the significance of the individual. This dynamic, despite its apparent distortions by some of the dynasties and regimes over China's long history, is, in its purest form, an embodiment of selflessness and commitment to a community ideal. It is not uncommon, for example, for an entire generation of one family to work and save money so that one single family member can come to the West to study and be successful in a university program. This person, in turn, will likely use all of his or her energy to do the absolute best he or she can to be successful—not for the self, but to honor the community.

Let's see how the above principles are reflected in the two musical examples below.

Stories from the Human Family

Michael's Experience: When I first met Che, Xien (Sean),[9.10] he was a computer-engineering student enrolled in my course "just for interest." A bit older than most university students, he was very passionate about music. When I discovered that he was from China (People's Republic), I tried to learn more about his background and interests. What followed was an important learning experience for us both. He gave me samples of the music he most often listens to, which included primarily Chinese popular music. Like most Chinese young adults, he said he seldom listens to Chinese "traditional" music. However, he was interested in learning more about it. I told him I was trying to get musical material and commentary for this text directly from China. We had already obtained the rights to a recording by international artist Wei Li (listen below), and we were hoping to get more information. His first response:

> *"Thanks so much for treating me as your friend. I am very honored and I will be very glad to help. I found contact information on Wei Kang, Li, who is a famous singer in the Peking Opera, but probably not the one on the CD. I got the info where she works, so I will call them, and, if this doesn't work, I could send a letter to their addresses. This will probably take some time. About the selections, in my humble opinion:*
>
> - *"Peking Opera definitely is one of the good choices. There are so many people who love Peking Opera in China. Not only elder people but also foreigners love Peking Opera for its beautiful costumes, face make-up, amazing "dancing" and "fighting," as well as the music. One disadvantage: Peking Opera usually is easier to be appreciated on visual media than on audio media, especially for people from other cultures.*
>
> - *"As for modern fusion music by younger Chinese people, we have too many choices. Before the last 10 years, these kinds of modern fusions were mostly from Hong Kong and Taiwan. But in recent years, many great songs are from mainland China. I really don't want to pick one now because I guess there are too many and I am sure after a while I will feel regret on whatever I picked. Best Regards, Sean."* November, 2004.

After numerous attempts to contact both Master Li and her superiors by letter and phone, Xien was able to locate not the Wei Li on the recording below (now living in London, U.K.), but the Wei Kang, Li who, at the time, was still an illustrious member of the Peking Opera.

> Xien wrote: *"About the selection of the music piece. Wei Kang,Li mentioned that since Peking Opera is such a complicated and deep art form, it would be impossible to select one piece to represent the beauty of it. She mentioned Peking Opera*

could have different types of music in one act, different background music types and different ways of singing. I actually made a suggestion to her: She could select three pieces of Peking Opera so it would be easier to make the choice.

[As the discussion of time continued, it became even more apparent that selecting a two- to four-minute selection representing twelve centuries of evolution would be impossible.]

Xien continued: *"She said that the melody may be classified into two groups: 'xipi' and 'erhong'—and that each of these can be performed in different ways: guiding pattern, original pattern, slow pattern, quick pattern, or desultory (random and unpredictable) pattern. These are the main patterns.' She said that Peking Opera is too big for her to choose a piece or two to present. At any rate, you could tell she knew so much. It was a pleasure to talk with her. I later found interesting articles on Master Li. She is called "the queen or best" for Qing Yi (the Dan—or female role) in China.*

Pic. 9.17 *These actors are waiting for their turn to go on stage. The character on the right is in a Mandarin official costume. The colorful characters in the middle are typical scholars. The burgundy characters at the back are wuxias (known to practice martial arts chivalry). The picture was taken on Sept 8, 2004, in the San Francisco Bay Area, CA, USA. The photographer believes the costumes are based on the Ming Dynasty's garment styles.* Photo: Courtesy Kowloonese and wikipedia.org.

In the end, the lines of communication with the Chinese government went silent, and we had to content ourselves with what we could find in the "Western world." At one point, Sean had written: *"Master Li is an old-style person who has been through times when the USA was an enemy to China. This is why she is very careful, which is typical of her generation. At one point she asked me if this would help the youth learn to value Chinese stories and their history. I said I was sure it would."*

"He who speaks without modesty will find it difficult to make his words good.

"He with whom neither slander – that gradually soaks into the mind, nor statements – that startle like a wound in the flesh, may be considered successful and be called intelligent indeed.

"I am not one who was born in the possession of knowledge; I am one who is fond of antiquity, and earnest in seeking it there.

"If a man takes no thought about what is distant, he will find sorrow near at hand.

"If a man withdraws his mind from the love of beauty, and applies it as sincerely to the love of the virtuous; if, in serving his parents, he can exert his utmost strength; if, in serving his prince, he can devote his life; if in his intercourse with his friends, his words are sincere—although men say that he has not learned, I will certainly say that he has."

Confucius, from *The Confucian Analects*

Pic. 9.17 *An engraving of Confucius.* Drawing: Public Domain.

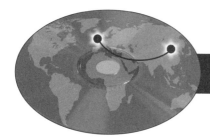

Inside the Musician's World

Wei Li
and the Far Eastern Music Ensemble

Note: Since Chinese opera may be the first of the world's operatic genres, its diversity over centuries and regions is virtually impossible to represent. However, in the sample we acquired, from Wei Li and the "Far Eastern Music Ensemble" in London (U.K.), we at least get a sample of the intensity of the singing style, the accompaniment, and the lyrical content, as well as the instruments used. As to our artist, Ms. Wei Li received her formal training beginning at the age of six in the Guangdong Music College and eventually learned many of the techniques required to sing Chinese opera.

Upon moving to the West, she also began to study Western opera. She now distinguishes herself by being able to proficiently sing in either style. In this sample, she is accompanied by some of the most familiar musical instruments in traditional Chinese music, including:

Pic. 9.18A

Pic. 9.18A The Yang Qin (yang chin)—a Chinese dulcimer probably derived from the Persian santour.

Pic. 9.18B The Erhu (air – [h]oo)—a bowed lute- or violin-like instrument played in a vertical position.

Pic. 9.18C The Pipa (peep-ah)—is a lute cousin of the ud. In this photo played by now Quebec Canadian artist Liu Fang, formerly of the Yunnan province of China. Courtesy liufangmusic.net

Pic. 9.18D Other instruments frequently used in Chinese opera include: GuZheng (or Zheng [chen])—the most famous of Asian zithers and parent of the Japanese koto and Korean kayageum, the dizi—a small, high-pitched flute; and gongs, clappers, and cymbals of various dimensions and sound qualities.

[Photos: Other than pipa, courtesy Lark in the Morning].

Pic. 9.18B

Pic. 9.18C

Pic. 9.18D

CD 3.12

"Die Lian Hua," by Wei Li, from the CD: **<u>Classical Chinese Folksongs and Opera,</u>** Arc Music International, c. 1997.

> Che, Xien wrote: *"Wei Kang, Li is a female Peking Opera artist, and as I mentioned in the previous email, she is very famous and she actually did perform a Peking Opera called 'Die Lian Hua.' She indicated, 'Wei Li's version of 'Die Lian Hua' is likely based on the Peking Opera version.'*
>
> *"By the way, 'Die Lian Hua' in Chinese opera usually refers to the story of former Chinese leader Mao, Zhe Dong and his first wife, Yang, Kai Hui. Mao wrote a poem to express the feeling of sadness after he lost his wife. So, basically, this is a contemporary Chinese opera piece in a traditional Chinese opera form. There are many versions of 'Die Lian Hua'— to name a few, the Peking Opera version and the Suzhou Opera version. I am also sure there are lots of other versions created in local Chinese opera forms, considering this is a story about a political leader who used to be almost like a 'God' for many Chinese people."*

As discussed earlier, the stories of the world's cultures are prime sources for getting a vision of the perceptions of *balance* of each culture. In Chinese history, not only is the importance of balance emphasized, but in the face of wars, conflicts, and strife, musical theater took on a prestigious role in emphasizing the characteristics of balance, in grieving losses, and in expressing the desires of the spirit. This selection does all of these. The lyrics, translated, are:

Pic. 9.18E *Hand-painted New Year's poetry, Lijiang, Yunnan, China.* Photo: Courtesy, Peter Morgan.

*I lost my wife Yang and you lost your husband Liu
Liu and Yang have become great souls
– flying to the top of heaven
When they asked the moon-guard,
Wu Gang, what he had to offer—
Wu Gang presented them
– with sweet-scented osmanthus wine.*

*The lonely Chang Er spread her sleeves
– and danced in memory of past heroes,
But upon suddenly hearing that monsters
– had been defeated in the world,
She wept and cried joyfully with overflowing tears.*

The Recipe of Sound

The beginning of the piece begins like an "overture" (or musical initiation) into the story. As the voice enters, time is suspended and the ornamentation of the voice calls attention to the theme of the story. The vocal style is a blend between Chinese operatic performance style and Western practices, as are the careers and interests of artists such as Wei Li living in the West.

We say that Chinese music (and much earlier music throughout Eastern Asia) is **pentatonic;** that is, it is based upon a five-note (penta) scale. Mostly this is true, although as modern Western and Chinese practices begin to intersect, the seven-note (diatonic) scale also finds its way into Chinese music as well. This is especially true of popular music of the last few decades.

Listen to the changes in tempo, melodic style, and texture. These changes are designed much like "art songs" in Western classical music to create an emotional setting that balances the text. At the close of the selection, much as in the performance of an Italian opera aria, the virtuosity of the soloist is emphasized. This generally means that, as listeners, our attention will alternate between absorption in the story and a focus upon the artist's expertise.

Chinese Music Today

Throughout the world, including in those cultures that have ancient traditions, perceiving change over time (the transferal of the ancient to the modern) is among the greatest requirements of any modern-day rasika, or music appreciator. But change over generations seldom completely dismisses its ancestry. So, if we listen carefully to the stories and storytelling methods of young Chinese, Japanese, Koreans, or people of virtually any culture, we will be able to maintain a connection to aesthetics and values of their pasts.

As you listen to the piece below by a young Chinese artist now living in the United States (or if you come upon music from popular musicians such as Cui Juan, The Twelve Girls Band, or any number of Chinese popular musicians from Hong Kong, Taiwan, Mainland China or living, as both our examples illustrate, somewhere else in the world), you will hear the same dynamics of fusion that have, on some level, animated every piece we've heard thus far. What we may want to look for in the music of the young composer of today is how the stories, values, and qualities of the past find their way into the modern-day expressions through the ancient art of *creative fusion*.

In any case, we also look at how the perception of "otherness" continues to be outmoded in the sound worlds of creative youth globally. The artist below, Xiao Dong, writes of her love for Western (American) cultures as follows:

> *"America is multi-cultured country; it helps with learning to appreciate and value all types of culture. It's the only way that people from the entire world can live together.*
>
> *And American music is this way as well. I love the variety of music you can find here. America has fertile soil for growing new ideas.*
>
> *"In some ways, American attitudes encourage you to do what you really want to do. For example, I wanted to parachute; when I told my Chinese friends, most of them said I'm crazy, it's dangerous, etc., and most of my American friends said 'Go for it.' China is an old country, so we saw yesterday, and we think about tomorrow. American is like a young kid, fearless. They don't see a past. They're always talking about tomorrow; they say, 'Who knows what can be done?'"*

Xiao, however, also writes about the balancing characteristics, particularly in family and community—and how individuals are expected to honor the life cycle of their Chinese upbringing:

> *"Most Chinese people have very strong family values. I would say more than 50% of our elders are staying with their children until they die. I feel it's hard for old*

people living in America—as in most parts of the country, you need to drive to be able get somewhere, even the grocery stores, I often wonder how they get around when they are too old to drive, since there is not much public transportation.

"And as for children here, I do feel they have a little bit too much freedom. It's great that Americans respect children as 'individual people,' but I think it's like a little tree growing. Sometimes you have to correct its growth to make it grow straight. Sometimes I see teenage mothers. I feel it's a pity they go into that adult life before they could even understand what the life of an adult is all about. They never complete the cycle of childhood and may not even know what they have missed. We have social problems in China as well. In the final sense, I think this is what balance means. You learn what you don't know from someone who has what you need to know. Somewhere among all the world's cultures is the balance."

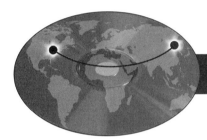

Inside the Musician's World

Xiao Dong Wei

Xiao Dong writes: *"I was born in Heilongjiang Province (Northeastern China, near the Russian border) in 1968, in a small town that produces coal. My dad was working at the worker's union as a leader of the entertainment department; he was quite famous at our town. He plays several Chinese instruments, erhu (Chinese two-string violin), dizi (Chinese flute, made of bamboo), yangqin (an instrument played with bamboo sticks) and sheng (Chinese flute-reed aerophone). I started learning erhu from him at age of five. He was going to teach my older sister as he thought I was too young for it (I have two older sisters and one younger sister—no brothers).*

At that time in China, people still thought the boys would carry on the family name. But I have a interesting story about my birth: at the time I was born, China was in its 'cultural revolution.' There were two major parties fighting with each other. My father was the leader of his team, the so-called 'San Shi' team, and he was the general of the team;

Pic. 9.19A *So complete is the intermingling of our world's diasporas and cultures that we will seldom find a location where we cannot find members of "other" cultures. Especially, in China, parents will save their whole lives so that their children can have the best education, and focus primarily if not exclusively on their studies for the betterment of not just themselves, but their families as well.* Photo: Chinese students in Vienna, Authors.

they called him 'General Wei.' They were going to beat him, when my mom gave birth to me. We called him home. He was supposed to report back the next day, but he never did and quit the team after that. So he was very grateful for my birth in two ways. He still tells me the story up to this day that when he saw me the first time he said, 'This girl is our family lucky sign.'

"Later, to show you how parents and families will sacrifice so much for their children, when I was at the age of ten, my dad decided to take me to see the world a little bit, to help me find my future. He took me to Beijing, Shanghai, Shenyang, etc., the big cities, and to meet some of the famous musicians in the nation. He also wanted the musician's opinion about my musical talent. Apparently everyone who met me was impressed. This gave my dad enough confidence to take me to Beijing to take the exam the next year for the music school affiliated with 'The Central Conservatory of Music.' I passed the exam, one of only two erhu students the school accepted for the whole nation that year. I played as a professional for years, including playing in the motion picture orchestra in Beijing until 1998. That's when I came to the United States." Interview: May 2005.

CD 3.13

"Sorrow of Separation," by Xiao Dong Wei, from the CD: **Sorrow of Separation,** c. 2005. xdwei@aol.com

Xiao Dong writes: *"My goal: I would love to continue to bring Chinese music to American people and learn more about American music. I want to make music that has both elements in it. To me, this is my balance and my destiny. I think I can also take what I have learned in America back to China when the chance comes one day.*

"This song is structured on poems from the Song Dynasty from nearly a thousand years ago. I've always loved this style of poetry. You can hear the ancient values of nature's balance. Many feel our highest cultural expressions came from the Tang and Song dynasties. Music pieces from the Song era, though, were freer in form and allowed for the expression of more emotion." Note: The perceived power of music, from the earliest of times, is made clear, in this case, by metaphors to nature. Listen for the principles cited earlier in both the translated lyrics and musical setting by Xiao Dong.

Pic. 9.19A *Separation or isolation are values neither cherished nor generally practiced by communities throughout the Chinese Diaspora. In New York's "Chinatown," for instance, hundreds of shops, restaurants, and doctors' offices create a community of resources that in turn attract others, trade with family members in China, and create an environment that allows New York's Chinese community to feel at home, while giving thousands of others contact with Chinese values—from thousands of miles away.* Photo: Authors.

"Sorrow of Separation"

How deep the autumn is,
The rain at night, filled with sorrow,
One can't sleep on the lonely blanket in isolation,
The pillow is moistened by the tears of sadness.

Music comforts me gently,
It comforts forever my affectionate heart,
The sorrow of separation is much like the grass,
It gets stronger the farther one goes.

Confucianism, Daoism (Taoism), Buddhism... and "the way"

Discussion Reflection IX-B

The Evolution and Influence of Chinese Philosophies

There are no means by which we can measure which of the primary spiritual/religious philosophies or religions influenced the evolution of "China" by degree, in as much as a) each state or region in China is diverse in its cultural makeup and evolution and b) each of the spiritual schools influenced each other substantially over more than two millennia.

However, if we examine rudimentary introductory dates and make a thumbnail sketch of essential beliefs or elements of each, we most certainly see a direct lineage to the practices and values in much of the region today, especially as concerns Chinese visual and performance art.

Confucius (551-479BCE) co-mingled teachings and instruction that crossed politics, religion, education, and culture. "Confucius' social philosophy largely revolves around the concept of ren, 'compassion' or 'loving others.'...This meant being sure to avoid artful speech or an ingratiating manner that would create a false impression and lead to self-aggrandizement (Lunyu 1.3)... Learning self-restraint involves studying and mastering li, the ritual forms and rules of propriety through which one expresses respect for superiors and enacts his role in society in such a way that he himself is worthy of respect and admiration."*

Daoism (Taoism) (evolved over time from 400BCE [Zhuang, philosopher] through the Han period [200BCE to 200CE]) represented both a formidable alternative to Confucianism ["Theoretical Daoism focused on the insolubility of this ru-mo Confucian-Mohist debate"] and, in practice, a helpmate: "We know the myriad natural kinds—all have both that which is acceptable and that which is unacceptable. So they said, 'If you select then you cannot be comprehensive, if you teach you cannot convey all of it. Dao way/guide does not leave anything out,'" or "the key lesson: open-minded receptivity to all the different voices of dao." *

Buddhism (5th century BCE): "Meantime, Buddhism came armed with a paradox that would delight thinkers of a Daoist turn of mind—the fabled paradox of desire. Rebirth was caused by desire and Nirvana could be achieved only by the cessation of desire. That meant that in order to achieve Nirvana, one had to cease to want to achieve it." (http://plato.stanford.edu/entries/taoism, ibid.) Although there are many life-guiding spiritual principles in the various practices of Buddhism, the "eightfold path" is included in all: "And this, monks, is the noble truth of the way of practice leading to the cessation of suffering—precisely this Noble Eightfold Path right view, right resolve, right speech, right action, right livelihood, right effort, right mindfulness, right concentration" Samyutta Nikaya LVI.11.

*Excerpted or paraphrased from: http://plato.stanford.edu/entries/confucius,2002/2006.

Questions

- *How do you interpret each of the "samples" of Chinese philosophies/religions above?*

- *Based upon what you've read in the Unit about Chinese cultural evolution and its music (or what else you may have experienced from media, education, etc.), what connections do you see between any of these belief systems and Chinese cultural values today?*

Korea and Japan—Cultures of Contrast

There are multiple challenges in discussing cultures that have both ancient traditions extending over thousands of years as well as abrupt and violent changes in the course of the evolution of their modern identities. To discuss the ancient and modern (when they may appear to have so little in common) we must remain flexible and willing to see multiple possibilities simultaneously. To single out a dynamic, trait, or experience as the standard by which we assess others will nearly always distort the potential for a balanced perspective, just as it will compromise the rights of the culture to self-determination and our acceptance of its *multiple* identities.

In both Korea and Japan, we have cultures that evolved over centuries, and have cultural histories, which, though greatly influenced by their evolution from Chinese cultures in earlier centuries, evolved over time to become unique and special in their own right. Much like China, both cultures have long histories, and must be understood in the context of time since each has extensive interactions with the cultures around them, including each other.

Both Korea and Japan, share a rather remarkable dichotomy and challenge. Marked by extensive wars in the 20th century and moderate to considerable modernization in the 19th century, each culture was forced into abrupt and irreversible culture cycles of Westernization or cultural fusions that did not follow a "self-chosen" (or natural) course. Similar to many of the culture groups in Africa, periods of sudden contact and conflict with other cultures—in this case, the events of WWII and the Korean War abruptly altered their evolution. Although the events and roles each culture experienced or played differs, the result for each was a sudden and extensive focus on modernization and Westernization (modeled after European and American culture systems), which had simultaneously positive and negative repercussions:

(+)

• Each culture had access to a multiplicity of alternative influences: from Western religions, to industrialization, to political or economic models.

Pic. 9.28A *Taiko drumming was historically used in festivals or street music (matsuri bayashi) – but today, modern ensembles combine choreography, acrobatics, and the use of a wide variety of drums patterned after the taiko and odaiko to create fabulous theatrical displays. This modernization of older traditions is far more the norm than the exception in today's musical world.* Photo: Courtesy, Michael Langhals.

• Each culture began a process of fusion that would increase the rate and depth of exchange with the Western world: from inter-marriages between Western soldiers and Korean/Japanese natives, to exchanges of language, students, trade, technology, and, ultimately, culture.

(-)

• Each culture to a large extent was *forced* to make these changes. Many feel that the loss of honor or of self-determination resulting from the wars (important characteristics in both cultures historically) gave rise to an overt and pervasive focus on industrialization, technological advancement, and materialism—to the extent that much of their history and earlier characteristics were abruptly altered if not ignored altogether.

(-/+)

• Progressively, each generation is being required to reconcile its ancient past with its recent history. Although many youth today are, to varying degrees, (-) lacking either a passion for or knowledge of their past, (+) ever-increasing numbers of youth (especially many now studying in Europe and America) are beginning to find their way back to the study and acknowledgement of their history and their ancient cultural traditions as a healing and balancing force to sudden Westernization.

With these factors in mind, a student of either culture must be willing to maintain simultaneous consideration for the ancient past and the modern present. We might also recognize that to understand what it is "to be" Korean or Japanese may require a larger sampling of expressions from varied culture-bearers, since each may be at different stages in the reconciliation process. In our sampling below, we will attempt to represent at least one sample of the "ancient" before reflecting upon the modern.

Korean Pansori—A Study of Time and Order

On Korean music:

"To bring emotions into harmony;
To add distinction to conduct;
To glorify heaven and earth;
... and bring about perfect balance

"... we must discriminate
sounds in order to know
the airs; the airs in order
to know the music, and
the music in order to know
the government. Having at-
tained to this, we are fully pro-
vided with the methods
of good order."

Li Chi (Book of Rites)

Although Korean legends date their history back to 2333 BCE (Go-Joseon legends), we can more accurately date the initial phase in Korean evolution to 1122 BCE (Gija Joseon), when a Chinese exile Jizi (Gija) led followers to the peninsula and merged with existing populations that date back to more than 70,000 years. Much of Korean history is marked by the wars with the dynasties of Western China's *commanderies*, extending through to the *"Three Kingdoms"* era of Chinese history. In roughly the sixth century, the state of Balhae was founded and expanded its boundaries from the Korean Peninsula north to Manchuria. In the centuries leading to the establishment of Balhae, Confucian scholarship, Chinese script, and numerous other influences from China (and especially the Southern *Han* culture) became the basis for what would later evolve into Korean culture.

Korea would enjoy a relative calm period of self-contained cultural development that would lead to the evolution of much of its unique language and art through the *Goryeo* period until the invasion of the *Monguls* in 1231. From this period forth, a cultural tennis match of sorts that included invasions, annexation, and the perpetual reformatting of boundaries between China, Korea, and Japan would continue until the 19th and 20th centuries. The competitive struggle for power increased its impact on Korea's cultural evolution further when, after the American Civil War, the United States (1871), Japan (1894), and Russia (1904) each successively controlled or altered Korean policy by force or coercion. Finally in 1910, Japan annexed Korea, at times even banning the practice of anything "Korean," a condition which existed until the WWII Japanese surrender in August, 1945. At this point, Korea was divided, a condition that was intended to be a temporary sharing of rehabilitation by the United States and Europe (South Korea) and the Soviet Union (North Korea). However, suspicion, and a division of political ideology, evolved into the "Cold War," eventually escalating to the Korean War (1950) and the permanent division of what had been, by much of the rest of the world's standards, a relatively non-aggressive culture.

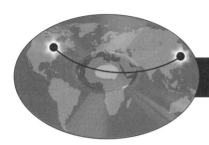

Inside the Musician's World

Min-su Kim
from the Chung Woong Korean Traditional Music Ensemble, Snag-Ryong Lee, director

Telling the stories of pain, heroism, good over evil, and, of course, the human drama of survival, love, and passion (for country, nature, or life itself) are cornerstones of Korean musical genres. However beautiful the music of Korean symphonic orchestras, opera, Christian songs, or popular music that use the modern influences of Japanese or Western recording technology, what stand out as most representative of Korean culture are its Court music (Hyangak), the folk songs accompanied by the gayageum (12-string zither similar to the Japanese koto), and the vocal art forms and, in particular, **Pansori.**

Pansori is a vocal and percussion genre performed by a single vocalist (*sorikkun,*) who performs all of the roles of the story, and a drummer (*gosu,*) who accompanies on the drum but also provides vocal cues and words of encouragement, (*or chuimsae*). What is absolutely remarkable about pansori is that it possesses all of the traits of nearly all of the world's musical theater: *narrative passages*, where the singer fills in the gaps of the story; *songs (arias)*, where the singer focuses musically on a single emotion or event in the story and emphasizes the strong emotions with more musically pronounced melody; and *interludes*, where the drummer may play and the actor may make a transition through movements, gestures, or facial expressions leading to the next part of the story.

But in pansori, quite amazingly, a single vocalist is called upon to give voice to all of the characters, a multitude of emotion, and to carry this story, oftentimes for hours in an open public setting ("pan'—a place where people gather). In this setting, vendors may sell food, people may drift in and out, and the vocalist must stay in character and continue to amaze the audience with some of the most contrasting styles of vocal production (manner of singing), timbres (sound qualities), and expressive diversity known to musical theater.

Pic. 9.21 This Korean Internet advertisement is for Juri Kim, an amazing young Pansori artist in Korea who, without a break, sang two Pansori works lasting 9 hours and 20 minutes at the Haenam Culture and Art Center on March 14, 2003. Perhaps most amazingly, she was only nine years old at the time. Courtesy: café.daum.net/juri and jurikim.com.

"Shimch'ong'ga," by Min-Su Kim & the Chung Woong Ensemble, from the CD: <u>**Traditional Music of Korea,**</u> Arc Music International c. 1999.

> *"Korean music and culture derives from the country's climate and landscape; it is intimately related to the country's religion and philosophy; it echoes the people's constitution and character. Traditional Korean music is divided into <u>chong-ak,</u> which is the intellectual, solemn, calm, dignified, and contemplative music, and <u>minsok-ak</u> which is emotional, unrestrained, direct, and exuberant.*

> *"A leisurely tempo is a general characteristic of Korean music. The slow pace is related to an emphasis on breathing: the tempo is set to a cycle of exhaling and inhaling. Korean music conveys a gentle, warm timbre. The subtle tone colors can be attributed to the fact that Korean instruments are made of natural materials. Wind instruments tend to be made solely of wood and even stringed instruments have strings made of silk instead of wire. The tempo distribution of traditional Korean music is also one which follows a natural progression ... usually beginning with a slow tempo that accelerates as the piece progresses."* (Professor Sang-Ryong Lee, Director of the Chung Woong Traditional Music Ensemble)

"Shimch'ong'ga" is a famous traditional Korean piece. It is a lament in which the blind *Shim* goes to bury his wife, who died after having given birth to a daughter.

The Recipe of Sound

When we listen to a vocal marvel of this nature, we ultimately will pay less attention to the technical aspects of the music, i.e., the notes, beats, or texture since these elements have less significance than the diversity and depth of vocal *timbres* (voice qualities) produced by the pansori singer. Vocalists frequently refer to singing by virtue of the place of resonance: a *chest voice* (has a deep throaty quality) versus a *head voice* (which is focused in the mask or front of the face).

As we listen to this piece, we see that not only the *range* of the melody is extremely large (distance from bottom to top pitch, or tone, of the melody), but so too is the range of timbres and production styles. Any vocalist who has ever sung continually for 30 to 60 minutes will tell you it can really put a strain on the voice. Imagine how much more difficult this style of singing is! Now, imagine singing this way from four to nine hours straight.

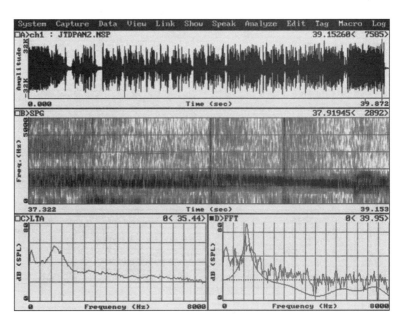

Pic. 9.22 *This is a graph indicating the diversity of range (frequency), volume, and variation in vibration of a Pansori singer. To produce such a range of sounds is extremely difficult in itself, but to maintain such a production over hours is nearly unimaginable.* Image: Public domain.

Telling Stories of Others:
Seeking a Balance in Presentation

We've mentioned the process of learning from other cultures in the context of "healing" cultural imbalances. The wisdom derived from nearly every in-depth excursion into another culture will inevitably offer insights and perspectives that can balance our own, if for no other reason than to provide us a means of comparison or alternatives to what we know.

As concerns Korean pansori discussed above, we can be fascinated with not only the discipline, endurance, and vocal flexibility in the performance of pansori but also the novel manner in which stories of history and humanity are told over time and space. We will find a parallel to the magnificence of pansori as a storytelling musical theater genre in Japanese *Noh* and *Kabuki* theater, as well as in the epic dramas of Indonesian *Gamelan*. Although there are now many sources written by Japanese or Indonesian performers and historians of these theatrical spectacles, among the first "Westerners" to explore the genres in depth over a lifetime are University of Michigan professors Dr. William Malm ("student" of Japanese music and culture) and Dr. Judith Becker ("student" of Indonesian music and culture).

As valuable as may be the information we might learn about *Noh, Kabuki, and Gamelan* musical theater and musical genres (shared below), we may learn something even more valuable about the nature of cultural exploration itself. To begin with, our investigation into the worlds of "others" is a process that generally occurs in stages that might be summarized as follows:

- **First,** we generally fall into contact with cultures outside of our experience (and "fall" is usually the manner in which contact initially occurs). Afterwards, we must choose to sustain a prolonged and continual progression of subsequent contacts and explorations or not. Frequently only sustained and prolonged contact can help us over our external perceptions and human tendencies to generalize, in favor of a deeper and more respectful understanding of another's culture.

Pic. 9.23 *Next to an upscale boating dock and mall in Fuengirola, Spain (outside of Malaga), a Chinese-imported "yacht" attracts enormous attention against the backdrop of otherwise modern boats. When the owner was asked how he became interested in Chinese boats (and, we later found out, art as well), he replied: "I had visited and lived in China for a while. I find the sails and style of the boat so beautiful. Well, I just kept going back." And now, these experiences are a large part of his life.* Photo: Authors.

Pic. 9.24 In "Chinatown" in Los Angeles, California, a small child is surrounded by gardens, architecture, and art of her parents' ancestry. But only 100 feet away are the streets that will lead her to her schools and to most of the experiences that will shape her life, and they do not reflect the cultural "oasis" of her parents' homeland. She will need to spend her entire life struggling to find and understand her multicultural "identity." She will become a mixture of values and experiences that will not be definable by any single standard or culture. Among her greatest challenges will be learning to effectively exercise her right to determine (and, if necessary, enforce) the standards by which she will be respected and valued. Photo: Authors.

- **Second,** cultural growth, the elimination of biases, and the wisdom to know when and how to report our findings and observations will move through stages. We may move from being fascinated observers of the "foreign" experience (for many of us reported in theses or dissertations related to the academic environment), progressively through stages of acquiring greater information, until at some point we recognize that our greatest strength (and comfort) is derived in adopting the role of facilitator or magnifier of the voices of each culture to our world. Of course, we will also make many mistakes along the way in direct proportion to our own awareness and sensitivity.

- **Finally,** through experience, age, and maturity comes the insight that whatever we've gleaned from other cultures should be attributed to, and paid back, to these cultures: intellectually, personally, financially, or through other means. The history of the "outsider" reporting of "other cultures" (especially in the West) is strewn with the debris of arrogance and assumption, and ultimately, with "ownership" and the propagation of these perspectives as fact. To present what we know as only what we know and to harness all of our resources in respecting the right of each culture to determine its own portrayal cannot help but increase actual knowledge, while modeling processes over goals and humility over a search for conclusions and definition. Frank Wu wrote about his experiences as an "Asian-American" struggling with self-perception against the tyranny of media portrayal as follows:

> *"I alternate between being conspicuous and vanishing, being stared at or looked through. Although the conditions may seem contradictory, they have in common the loss of control. In most instances, I am who others perceive me to be rather than how I perceive myself to be. Considered by the strong sense of individualism inherent to American society, the inability to define one's self is the greatest loss of liberty possible."* Frank Wu: *Yellow*, 2002, p. 8.

The voice of the "outsider" explorer (what each of us is to every culture but our own) has, nonetheless, value. We offer these two examples of individuals who, by their own admission, stumbled into the worlds of other cultures, but who over time persevered in their quest for knowledge and insight, eventually emerging with perspectives that would serve as "bridges" between cultures for others. Most importantly, it would appear in both careers, through numerous mistakes, miscommunications, misunderstandings, and continued efforts to return and re-examine their perspectives, they have earned the respect of the cultures they studied and described. This must be considered the ultimate test of our "knowledge" and humility: that each culture determines how it wishes to be portrayed, that we respect its wishes, and that in the end, we earn its respect for our efforts and sincerity in representing the members of the culture according to *their* values.

Japanese Storytelling—Contrasts in Time and Space

Pic. 9.24A *An illustrated scroll of the famous story "Tale of Genji" (Murasaki Shikibu, 11th century), the source of multiple dramas.* Photo: Public domain, courtesy Tokugawa Museum, Japan.

Michael's Experience: A favorite former professor at the University of Michigan and a long-time scholar of Japanese music, William P. Malm continually impressed students and scholars with his passion for music generally, and specifically for the culture and music of Japan. I remember seeing a transformation occur and his eyes light up as he talked not only about Japanese music, but about the Japanese people themselves. What I gathered from interacting with Dr. Malm in classes, participating in a Japanese music ensemble (Matsuri Bayashi or Shinto festival music), and working on visual exhibits of Japanese instruments for the Stearns Musical Instrument collection was that Japan offered enormous contrasts in its variety of perceptions concerning "time" and "space."

Much like those of China, the older traditions of Japanese music offered strikingly alternative visions into the unique possibilities of considering silence to be music, and tension and release in musical performance to be composed of subtle, nearly imperceptible changes in the ordering of musical sounds. Against the backdrop of Japan's technology, animation, and development of modern musical genres (including everything from heavy metal to salsa to blues and jazz), the opportunities to experience musically diverse perceptions of time (the manner by which the music flows over time) and space (the ordering of sounds acoustically or texturally) can be exciting. We'll explore just a few of the possibilities below.

Stories from the Human Family

We begin our conversation with Professor Malm, who talked first about music education in a general sense.

"So much of education is based upon short-term memory. When I teach, I try not to focus on terms and information, but anything that makes the student project their thoughts and understanding. You never can ask questions as being "true" or "false" because then the student is not encouraged to think or consider all the things in between.

"I had a motto when I was teaching: 'Music is not an international language – it consists of a whole series of equally valuable and distinguishable elements.' *The point being, we cannot assume understanding without effort. You have to have an arsenal of tools and stories to motivate students.*

"Where did I get this arsenal? Naturally, from my life's experiences. I was originally a composition student and my original interest was musical analysis. Then I came across music of other cultures and initially Indonesian gamelan, and my tools didn't work. I had a Master's degree and had invested so much in education, and now I could only analyze 10% of the world's music … that from Western Europe or part of America.

"So I began exploring other parts of the world in 1949. I was part of a performance project where I became sort of a one-man <u>"gamelan"</u> [Indonesian tuned-gong orchestra—see later in this Unit], playing for dancers and learning a variety of musical forms. I later became aware of <u>nagauta</u> [ensemble for Kabuki theater—see below] and Japanese music, and eventually became attracted to the <u>shamisen.</u> During the Korean War, I was in Washington D.C. and spent a lot of my time at the Library of Congress. As my interest in Japan grew, I remember taking a train to New York City and going to a particular bookstore that had lots of books on Japanese music. I came back with a footlocker full and read them all.

"When I left the army, I performed with some famous dance groups in New York City. At that time I also got a package from Japan sent by my brother. I opened it up and there was a shamisen. I knew what it was, but I didn't know how to play it. Then there was also musical notation, but I couldn't read it. So any musician will be frustrated by this, and I immediately looked for a place to get lessons. I also realized that I should get a Ph.D., and so I ended up going to UCLA.

"If you were looking for research funding at that time, there were a few foundations, but they only gave money for sociology. There was no funding for musicology at all. So I wrote a grant to the Ford Foundation: "Music as an acculturational phenomenon in an urban area of Japan." But when I got the grant, in essence it gave me a chance to physically touch, hear, and sense Japanese culture and music. You can't just look or read about a culture; you actually have to get in and play with it. So I got there and I took lessons in shamisen and in singing, flute, and all these instruments."

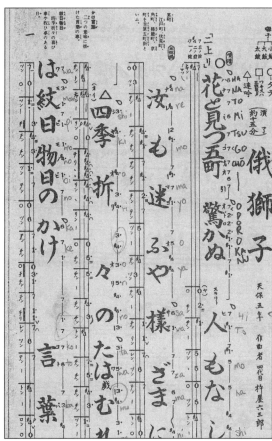

Pic. 9.24B *Notation of Japanese traditional music is both vertically organized and includes musical notation for both instruments and voice, as well as the text for the singer. This text also has the English phonetics written in to help someone outside the culture learn to sing the passage.*

Question: What impressed you most about Japanese culture? Its aesthetics (perceptions of beauty or value)? How did you get immersed in it? [Professor Malm hands me the new edition of one of his books on Japanese music, saying: *"Read this, it will explain a lot."* I read:]

"My wife and I were having dinner with Mr. Yamaguchi, January 9, 1952. Late in the meal he mentioned that Meredith Weatherby wanted to know if I was interested in writing a book on Japanese music. The fact that I was a 28-year-old graduate student who had only been in Japan four months, and that I had never published a thing, did not appear to be a problem. Rather the challenge would be that, with all the books on flower arranging, the tea ceremony, judo, sumo, and theater, there was nothing on Japanese music. Thus I turned in my first manuscript in 1957." Professor Malm followed this up: *"I was in Japan two years, 1955-1957. I was supposed to be writing a thesis, and, instead, I wrote this book and, later, my thesis off the book (he laughs).*

Pic. 9.25 *Born in Korea, moved by his family to Shanghai (1949), Paul Namkung later moved to Hong Kong, where his parents were bent on their children becoming United States citizens. After further moves to Tokyo (after the War), in 1957 Paul moved to California, where he eventually became a social worker, a profession he maintained for thirty-four years. Paul mentions that his family had written documentation of the first-born males that traced back to 16th-century China. He said: "I was supposed to be the one that followed a traditional path—but look at me now … I'm making drums and instruments."*

Paul's instruments are based upon both Native American drums and "boxes," which he describes as follows: "I started to make these wooden box-drums before I knew there was a history. Two years I developed the drums, and then I met a Peruvian drummer who said the drum was similar to one in his country. As it turned out, slaves in Cuba, the Caribbean, and, eventually, South America played a wooden box or upon a table because the drums were not allowed. When the master or someone would come around, it would again be a box or table. Otherwise, it was a great drum. The best part of that is you can enslave someone, but you can never kill their spirit." Music and art are among the clearest means for visualizing human adaptability and resiliency. Paul's own path shows this resilient spirit and innovative curiosity extended over time and space. Perhaps, too, his life shows the futility of assessing either human beings or their creative expressions from within the misleading boundaries of categorizations such as those of race or nationality. Photo: Author, copyright: Paul Namkung, worlddrums@yahoo.com, 2005.

Coming to Know "Noh" (or Kabuki)

In discussing **Noh** drama and its more modern descendant, **Kabuki** theater, two distinct yet related genres of Japanese musical storytelling, Professor Malm referred me to the following passages from one of his primary books on Japanese music: *Six Hidden Views of Japanese Music*. The first refers to the basic elements of *Noh* drama: *"…it is sufficient to say that Noh music consists of the chanting of actors (the shite, u'aki) and a unison chorus (ji). Such chanting may or may not be accompanied by members of the instrumental ensemble collectively known as the Hayashi, which consists of a flute (nokan) and the three drums (taiko and the o and ko tsuzumi hand drums)."* What is equally important, however, is that the Noh form relies on "hidden" or covert clues, which *"help the listener sense the forward progression of the composition."*

In another source, *Noh, Principles and Perspectives* (1983), the author and *taiko* (traditional drum) master Konio Komparu writes: *"Noh is the classical stage art of Japan, developed from a variety of sacred rituals and festival entertainment arts and brought to a state of refinement during the Muromachi period (1336-1568). The form of Noh that we know today has a history of six centuries"* (pp. xvi).

Mr. Komparu goes on to summarize the primary elements of Noh theater as follows:

Vocal music	*Utai* (a form of chant)
Instrumental music	*Hayashi* (an orchestra composed of a flute and three drums)
Acting techniques	*Kata* (dance poses or actions)
Dance elements	*Mai* (dances accompanied by utai and hayashi)
Fine arts and crafts	Masks, robes, and instruments
Architecture	Noh stage – an independent structure
Time	The distortion and slowing of time
Space	The unified space of stage plus audience (they are essentially one)

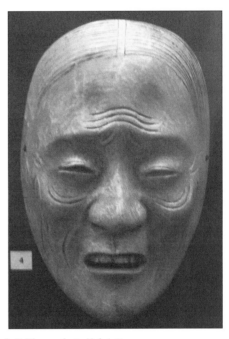

As to Kabuki theater, the more active, sensationalistic, and faster-paced theater form from which the *Nagauta* ensemble was formed (by augmenting the Noh ensemble with an equal ratio of shamisen performers to singers and the use of the bamboo flute, or *shinohue*), a popular website from Japan summarizes: *"Kabuki is a traditional Japanese form of theater with its origins in the Edo period. Kabuki, in contrast to the older surviving Japanese art forms such as Noh, was the popular culture of the townspeople and not of the higher social classes.*

"Kabuki plays are about historical events, moral conflicts in love relationships and the like. The actors use an old-fashioned language, which is difficult to understand even for some

Pic. 9.26 A & B *The masks in Noh (nÿ-men or omote) all express particular characteristics and have names. Generally, only the main player (Shite) takes the mask. The Noh masks are used to portray a female or nonhuman (divine, demonic, or animal) character. There are also Noh masks to represent youngsters or old men. On the other hand, the Noh actor who takes no mask plays the role of an adult man in his twenties, thirties, or forties. The best Noh masks have the ability to change emotions according to how the light strikes the mask. An inanimate mask can have the appearance of being happy, sad, angry, or a variety of other emotions simply by changing how the light strikes the contours of the mask. Photo: Courtesy Rama and wikipedia.org.*

Japanese people. The kabuki stage (kabuki no butai) is a rotating stage and is further equipped with several gadgets like trapdoors through which the actors can appear and disappear. Another specialty of the kabuki stage is a footbridge (hanamichi) that leads through the audience.

"In the early years, both men and women acted in Kabuki plays. Later, during the Edo period, the Tokugawa shogunate forbade the acting by women, a restriction that survives to the present day. Several male kabuki actors are, therefore, specialized in playing female roles (onnagata). During kabuki plays, fanatic fans in the audience shout the names of their favorite actors at the right moments during short pauses." (www.japan-guide.com)

Comparing Japanese musical theater to Western music, Professor Malm writes that there are *"several insights into performance practices from a Japanese perspective. Perhaps the most important principle has been the concept of relativity in relation to composition. It should be evident that one cannot view a traditional Japanese composition with the same 'absolutism' with which one usually regards a Western classical piece. In the West, considerable time and effort have been spent in recent decades searching for authentic renditions of Western classical or art musical works, despite the fact that there are continually newer renditions of the works for guitar, etc."*

"In Nagauta, we know that composition tends to be a communal activity. We also know that most performers are members of special guilds that assert their identity by the way they perform a given standard piece. Different combinations of musicians may result in a discernibly different performance ... although the same musicians performing the same piece are diligent in their accuracy and correctness." In conversation, he added: *"You must also consider transparency as an essential ingredient of Noh. In Mozart, then later Brahms, and finally Wagner, density and perpetual sound becomes essential to the Western perspective of music. But in Japanese music, the transparency of sound and its relationship to silence is essential."*

An initial contact with either Noh or Kabuki may be fascinating for many of the same reasons we find in Western opera or musical theater (costumes, staging, storylines, etc.), and, too, a famous phrase (from Zeami) quoted by Mr. Komparu: *"Never forget the beginner's mind,"* infers that Japanese musical theater is meant to be accessible. However, the most striking and notable difference, and one that may require more effort and quieter concentration to appreciate, especially in the more ancient manifestations of traditional Japanese musical theater, is the transparency of sound over "time" and "space."

Mr. Komparu writes: *"To best experience Noh, one should respond emotionally rather than observe intellectually ... The chorus chants in unison in a way*

that seems to reach into one's soul. This contrasts with the sharp vibrations of the drums and the eerie calls of the drummers. The melody of the flute seems to represent the state of mind of the character, and the character's heart reveals itself through a mask... and through beautifully choreographed movements." ("Noh..." ibid, p. xxii)

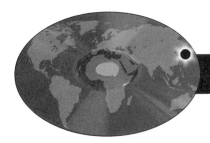

Inside the Musician's World

Kabuki (excerpt)

Beyond the magic of the enormously disciplined actors of Noh and Kabuki theater and their movements which often bring time to a crawl; beyond the incredible nature by which flutes, drums, singers, and actors lock their internal time mechanisms to a flow over time often without regularly paced beats or conductors; and beyond the ancient stories, costumes, architecture, and instruments, which merge together to create both Noh and Kabuki theater is the transparency of the art and alternative perspectives of silence and sound to those of our modern world.

For many in the exceedingly fast-paced age of technology, to hear a portion of either Noh or Kabuki without at least a brief introduction to the alternative perspectives of time and sound is not likely to yield a positive reaction. However, when we consider that the aesthetic of silence being essential to balance sound is not unique to Japanese music, but permeates Chinese, Korean, and probably many of the musical styles of non-Asian cultures as well, and if we consider these perspectives as antidotes to the ever-increasing impatience and time-constrained lifestyles in our technologically advancing age, the time spent in searching for at least a partial appreciation of Japanese musical drama and its aesthetics acquires newfound validity.

Pic. 9.27 *Painting of Kabuki actor Shunsho Katsukawa (1726-1792).*

Professor Malm writes: *"A hidden aspect of time in Japanese music is the concept of <u>ma</u>—the space between events. This concept is well known in most Japanese arts. In music it provides a rhythmic elasticity in which silence is as powerful as sound. Awareness of the art of 'ma' is one of the rewards of enlightened listening."* Six Hidden Views, p. 43.

At times during the conversation, Professor Malm's emotional attachment to his experiences with Japanese music and with Noh and Nagauta (Kabuki) performance became so filled with passion that his voice dropped to an intense whisper, and transcription of the interview became virtually impossible. Only the memory of the experience and his intense love for Japanese culture and music could be preserved. He commented:

"I personally never really played much Noh music, but in experiencing it you cannot possibly get an understanding from the musical notation itself. In Japan, each "guild" (performance group) has a unique style and manner of interpretation. You expect shamisens to play together, but the drums, voice, and actors are locked to a time structure that reflects the spirit of relativity. This flexibility is possible because the accents (and flow) of Japanese melodic lines are perceived more in the context of entire phrases, independent of bar lines (measured beats or bars)." Interview, June 2005.

Raijo, bridge from <u>**Shakkyo,**</u> a recording compiled by William Malm for: <u>**Six Hidden Views of Japanese Music,**</u> 1981.

As Professor Malm played this short narrative passage from a Kabuki performance "Shakkyo" ("The Stone Bridge"), adapted from the original Noh drama, he commented: *"There's no conductor, no beat. This is **raijo*** (or a "coming-out" introduction which serves as a narrative bridge between sections of the performance)." In fact, this piece uses the Nagauta ensemble of the more modern Kabuki theater, including the shamisen. It is also a bridge between Noh and Kabuki, as it has the aesthetics concerning time and space that are common to Noh as well. How does a modern listener (even if from Japan), bombarded with sound in everyday life and whose music is equally measured across regular beats or pulses relate to something so contrasting in its flow over time and space?

> Mr. Kamparu writes: *"One more requirement for a good experience of Noh is that one let oneself go when watching the play. Noh plays take place in a dimension of fantasy that transcends time and space, so one cannot become absorbed in a Noh play if one is attempting to make what is happening conform to logic and common sense. By extinguishing momentarily the bright flame of realistic consciousness and darkening the mind, one will enable the deeper consciousness to surface. This is very close to a state of sleep, but the state of being half awake and half asleep, this feeling of being halfway between dreaming and reality, is the territory of time and space where the nonrealistic consciousness of Noh dwells."* ("Noh…," ibid, p. xxiv)

Pic. 9.28 *This is the outside view of Kabukiza (kabuki theater) in Ginza-Tokyo, Japan. The aesthetics and, in fact, "theater" itself extend not only to the actors, musicians, or stage performance, but to the theater, the setting for the audience, and even to the outside of the theater and the approach to the experience itself. Everything is a stage in the transition from the external world to the transcendental world of Japanese storytelling.* Photo: Public domain, courtesy wikipedia.org.

The Recipe of Sound

Initially, hearing the calls of the drummers (which help anticipate the drum strike and provide a means for regulating the flow of sound and movement) and the guttural-style singing of the actor (as he narrates the events leading to the "lion dance"), many listeners may be struck with the absolute contrast to virtually all forms of Western or popular music.

But as we pay attention to the contrasting manner in which time and space are manipulated, we begin to see the creativity and "dimension of fantasy" spoken of above. A sonograph of the musical sections and the contrasts in time and space might read:

Voice/calls by drummers Slow increase in tempo Shamisen and voice play same melody, but not exactly together	Time and beat are established beat speeds—but is regular	Time abruptly halts shrill flute enters (almost playing abstractly with drum pulses)
:35	:42	1:16

Drum pulses very quietly— with ever increasing space between (listener anticipation is at absolute height)	Loud drum beat—calls and flute re-enter—calls increase in frequency – tempo becomes frantic and…	Abruptly halts again— One final increase in tempo and density to the final beat
2:08	2:35	3:05

As I watched Professor Malm listen to this piece, I saw that he was achieving everything Mr. Kamparu had written concerning the requirements of the listener. As the music increased in excitement, however subtle or pronounced the change, Professor Malm's voice and eyes also changed, but especially as the drums came to a halt, and the spaces between sounds grew, he would hold his breath, extend his hands, and wait for each beat, saying: *"Listen—do you hear the silence… the space?"* and then (long pause) … *"clack"* (the drum) … fulfillment!

Japan Today!

Japanese culture has produced a plethora of creative innovations in technology, music, animation, cinema, and art since WWII. On the heels of one of the most shocking and devastating human tragedies in our world's history (WWII and the atomic bombing of Hiroshima and Nagasaki), an otherwise very proud culture, whose government at times, historically, had been ruthless in its own desire to "build empire," had lost its allies, two of its cities, and a sizable percentage of its physical property and economic base. All of this equaled a substantial loss of honor. It may well have been this loss of honor, combined with the physical need to rebuild and the creativity, discipline, and community orientation of the Japanese people that fanned the flames of modernization and technological advancement to Japan's current status.

Foremost in the lives of the children and youth to be born over the post-war generations was an ever-increasing dichotomy between finding solace and pride in their ancient Japanese heritage, while balancing a nearly fanatical push to re-establish a Japanese economy and identity through material advancement and modernization. Musically, over the last thirty years of the 20th century, young Japanese musicians began to model their music after the likes of the Beatles, Bob Dylan, the Rolling Stones, or James Brown. In the widest variety of musical genres from Yo-Yo Ma's classical-fusion cello performances to Orchestra de la Luz (Japanese salsa), from Blue Hearts (metal), M-Flo (R&B) to Toshiko Akiyoshi (jazz), Japa-

Pic. 9.29 *Toshiko Akiyoshi is one of the finest jazz pianists and innovators in large ensemble jazz. Over the years, she has demonstrated an incredible knowledge and love for jazz that is generally appreciated by nearly all who are experienced in the genre. The keys for people who desire to pursue a music "outside" of their culture of birth are respect for the music, a dedication to mastering its technique, and a humility that encourages those whose language we are learning to respect our efforts.* Photo: Courtesy of Robert Bartley, (and Toshiko Akiyoshi) c.2005.

nese musicians have shown a remarkable capacity to devote discipline and tenacity to the learning and perfection of many things beyond their shores, thus transforming the external language into their own internal fusion or artistic vision.[9.11]

Even more recently, however, as historians, storytellers, and parents began to re-discover parts of their ancestry and history that may have been veiled by the abrupt and consuming forces of material and technological advancement, more of the stories and aesthetics of Japan's rich cultural past have begun to surface. Certainly in modern Japan, as in Western cultures, creating space and time for teaching respect for something as slow-paced as Noh or even Kabuki would be nearly impossible in the large metropolitan areas, or among most youth, but in the small island regions or rural settings, some were able to maintain a deeper connection to Japan's past as a balance to the modern lifestyle which now finds its voice in every aspect of media.

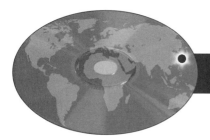

Inside the Musician's World

Painu Kajipito Marchan

Note: We were excited when we received notice that Painu Kajipito Marchan would be willing to lend his music to this project, as we had heard he was one of the younger musicians to combine older traditions of Japanese storytelling with a mix of traditional instruments (i.e., shamisen) and modern concert formulas. More importantly, as we later found out, he also put enormous focus in his lyrics and songs on connecting youth to nature, older values, and their ancestry, much of which had been obscured by modernization both before and after WWII. He wrote to us:

"I come from Iriomote Island in Okinawa prefecture, on the southernmost tip of Japan. Lately I've been holding my Sanshin (shamisen) concerts in Osaka, the second capital city of Japan ... this is the basis of my musical activity. The starting point of my music is songs and dances, which have been handed down from the very distant past in Iriomote Island, because I was brought up with such songs and dances.

"I suppose, to a large extent, my music is all connected with nature and the history of our past—in our cultural songs. Much of my music is created by the concept called "Kajipito" (this is an Okinawan dialect word. The literal translation in English would be "a person who lives with the wind").

"Takaramono (Treasure)/Sabani wo Koide," by Painu Kajipito Marchan, from the CDs: **<u>Takamono</u>** and **<u>Iriomote,</u>** Painukaji c. 2001/2004.

"The first song means 'treasure' and refers to the treasure that is found in honoring my homeland and my ancestors. This is how I find my own honor as well.
The second portion deals with the concept of 'Kajipito,' which basically says that if a person has feelings at all, they must try to live in a balanced manner with nature.

"I think people are gradually forgetting to create something and to live with their feelings. The wind is invisible. However, if the wind did not blow, clouds never drifted in the sky; if it never rained, flowers were never in bloom—then both nature and the hearts of men would perish. I think there is such "invisible wind" in our society, those are our feelings—the passion of the human heart.

"Human beings change the earth for our own convenience and live with many materials for their comfort. However, have we forgotten the most important thing? Shouldn't we stop pursuing material things for convenience and physical comfort alone? When human beings are connected by nature to the wind – then they will also remain connected to each other by feeling and emotion."

Text summary: *"Sabani wo Koide" (Island Iriomote/Okinawa)*
What is important in life?
How do you live or behave?
How people live with nature ... the feelings of the people of Okinawa
The important thing is to live with nature ... in peace.

Modeling Cultural Motion: Indonesia

In the final Units, we will be discussing the importance of the dynamic of cultural "fusion" and exchange as relates to the music of the Americas. However, located in the *Malay Archipelago* (the world's largest) between Indochina and Australia, dividing the Indian and Pacific Oceans, lies the Republic of Indonesia, arguably one of the most creatively diverse fusion-cultures in the world. Indonesia's history since the 7th century reads more like a world travelogue than any "typical" or fixed progression of evolution. Briefly:

- The population of the islands is composed of many different ethnic groups, all within the very large ethnic grouping classified as Malayo-Polynesian. From the 7th to 14th centuries, the islands of Sumatra and Java became kingdoms under the influence of Hinduism and Buddhism.

- Arab traders from India later brought Islam, which became the dominant religion in most parts of the island as the Hindu and Buddhist kingdoms collapsed.

- The Europeans arrived in the early 16th century. In the 17th century, the Dutch emerged as the most powerful of the Europeans, ousting the Spanish and Portuguese, whose influence on the language and culture had already been made (the island of Timor remained under Portuguese rule).

- The "East Indies," as they were called externally, were a major contributor to the world spice market through the *Dutch East India Company (VOC)*. After the Napoleonic Wars, they were "awarded" to the United Kingdom of the Netherlands (1815).

- During the Nazi invasion of the Netherlands, Japan captured Java; and, after the war, Sukarno (who would become Indonesia's first president) was released from prison and lobbied successfully to attain Independence on August 17, 1945.

- Afterwards, the influence of the Dutch, the socialist bloc (and Soviet Union), Western cultures, conflicts with Malaysia, and substantial interactions with China, Japan, and other regions of the Pacific Southwest (including Australia and the Philippines) combined with a perpetual influx of people from India, all over Asia and the Muslim world (including Africa) to complete the cultural "melange" referred to as "Indonesia."

Generally, once we are aware of which culture groups contribute to a given cultural mix (and obviously no culture is exempt from this process), we can also visualize their contributions to unique fusions of food, dress, art, and music/dance. An embodiment of the history of mixing and cultural fusion in the Republic of Indonesia is the remarkable music and frequent venue for elaborate storytelling known as *gamelan*.

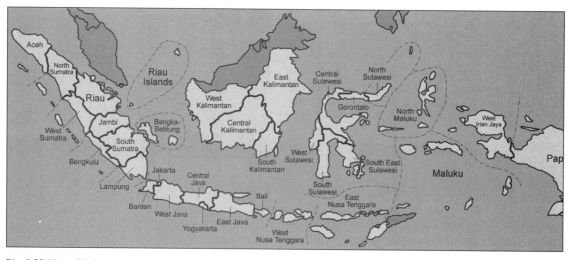

Pic. 9.32 *Map of Indonesia*. Courtesy CIA factbook.

Gamelan – "Outside In"

How should we summarize or understand a Javanese[9.12] musical ensemble of gongs and metal xylophones, frequently used to set stories from Hindu origins with substantial influences from Burma, Thailand, Laos, Cambodia, and Malaysia, to name a few, set in a culture of primarily Islamic orientation with a subsequent mix of population arguably as diverse as anywhere in the world? Objectively, we cannot! Subjectively, we try to examine the context of the genre's performance and the expressed values of the performers, generally in contrast to *what we know.*

Pic. 32.A *A traditional gamelan (as beautiful to look at as to hear) will have numerous metalophones, xylophones, gongs, and drums – whose origins can be traced across much of Asia. Most interesting is that music is perceived, and performed, in cycles (colotomy) marked at each new cycle by the "gong ageng."* Photo: Courtesy the Indonesian Embassy in Canberra and Peter Firus.

University of Michigan professor and long-time student of Indonesian culture and *gamelan,* Judith Becker begins one of her articles ("Traditional Music in Modern Java: Gamelan in a Changing Society," 1980, University of Hawaii Press) as follows:

> *"Gamelan music can be defined by the internal features of instrumentation, musical structure, and form. In addition, specifically musical aspects of gamelan are related to and interact with the cultural environment of the gamelan, including the history of gongmaking, the political and intellectual history of Java, and the uses of gamelan music in Java." (p. 1)*

She then goes on to describe the stories, impact, and depth of associations the Javanese bring to gamelan as both an artform and ritual genre as follows: *"The gamelan participates in a wide variety of activities in Java, some of which could be classified as artistic, while others more properly belong to ritual. Rarely is gamelan music heard in a concert situation with no other activity occurring simultaneously. More commonly, gamelan music enhances a ritual or accompanies a drama.*

> *Music, dance, poetry, and drama are often not separable except on an analytic level."* She later reiterates a quality we've experienced earlier: that musicians or "artists" in Indonesia, including those in the gamelan, do not separate themselves into a special category. *"The arts are not considered vehicles for personal expression ... on the contrary, it is the performer who is the vehicle through which the traditions are continually renewed and vitalized." (p. 6)*

So how might discoveries, such as those made by Dr. Becker, be understood by those of us whose cultures place so much value on ownership and individual identity? Here is a small excerpt of her story:

Stories from the Human Family

"When I first went to college, there really wasn't such a thing as 'ethnomusicology'—no one was really studying world music, at least not in an academic environment. My husband got a job teaching English in Burma; we lived in the North Eastern section in a very remote provincial town.

"I was a pianist at that point, and there was no piano for four hundred miles. We ended up staying there for three years, and you can imagine how little piano playing was done in those three years. There was such incredible music going on around me—and I couldn't make heads nor tails of it. I couldn't figure it out; it made absolutely no sense to me.

"Do you know the Burmese s'ain wain?[9.13] This is one of the most vibrant ensembles you can possibly imagine. Everything in the music is fast and moving. It is a percussive ensemble related in some ways to the gamelan, but the music is really nothing like the gamelan.

"Initially I found the music very offensive. It had the very strident oboe (double reed instrument—Hne) found in much of the Far East [China and Korea—used most often in court or processional music], and the harp (saun'gau), which at least didn't jar on my aesthetic sensibilities. So I was able to study the harp. That's how I began to learn how the music worked, how it was put together. In time, well along the line, I began to learn that the harp repertoire and the s'ain wain repertoire were the same. It was the timbre or tone quality to which I reacted. In time, the s'ain wain has become one of my favorite musical experiences.

Pic. 9.33 (below) *Professor Becker looks on with approval as her students in the University of Michigan Gamelan Ensemble begin learning gamelan pieces. Courses such of these, if taught from the perspective that we can only "sample" and engage the music, not ever perfect or own it (as Dr. Becker instructs), are helpful means to engage a culture's music and, in turn, respect the culture by our actions (sacrifice of time) as well.* Photo: Courtesy, Judith Becker and The University of Michigan, School of Music.

"After three years of Burmese music, I was getting farther and farther away from Chopin. In fact, my whole career has been a series of accidents, not planned moves. We came back to the United States, which is when I first discovered this thing called 'ethnomusicology,' as Bill Malm was here.9.14 I was able to get a Master's degree but not a Ph.D. So as much as I had loved Western music, I felt that I could no longer invest energy in studying Western music to get my doctorate. So, with the help of my husband, I managed to get a doctorate established in Southeast Asian studies. It wasn't really a 'music' degree."

Transition in Focus

"Initially, I had assumed I'd get back to Burma and write my dissertation on Burmese music, but Burma closed down in 1962 to all foreigners. When my husband, Pete, who now had a Ph.D. in linguistics, received a job teaching in East Java, I thought, 'Oh all right, I'll make that the topic of my dissertation.' We stayed there two-and-one-half years. And this stay resulted in my initial work on gamelan. I didn't set a goal and move toward it. I just remained receptive and things just sort of happened, and I just went along with it.

"The first thing that caught my attention about gamelan music was this

Pic. 9.33 A1 *These young Balinese dancers are performing the Legong Keraton, created in the 18th-century and based on the 13th-century legend of the King of Lasem.* Photo: Courtesy, G. Larson.

repetition. How they go over and over and over the same patterns and material, something that in the West might be considered "bad" or unsophisticated. But I thought, these are bright, intelligent people; this has to be meaningful. The challenge was: why is this music important to these intelligent, sensitive people? That's what guided me in this direction.

"In time, I discovered all of these parallels – that the music structure is, in essence, reflective of a whole notion of how the culture perceives the world. Their calendars are cyclical, their philosophical systems and general manner of looking at the world are all cyclical. Things that I found in the music to be odd were profoundly meaningful. All this took me, oh … twenty years to sort out.

"There are many other observations I was able to learn from as well—for instance, in Indonesia, getting angry is a much bigger deal there than it is here. Anger is an indication of a lack of control or a lack of balance. Indonesians generally find anger very frightening. Whereas, here (in the United States), people use anger as a manipulative device. You may get angry to get someone to do what you want. If someone gets angry in Indonesia, there's a kind of 'uhh…..' (shock), as that sort of reaction is a clear indication of a lack of balance. Actually, we would agree. The same thing goes for being depressed. This also indicates a lack of balance.

"In the latter case, there is a general perception (in Indonesia) that being alone is very dangerous. You must be extremely powerful to sustain being alone. That's why going off and meditating in the forest is a big, big deal. When you're alone, you are vulnerable. Indonesians want to be close together. Human interaction and community are extremely important.

"For instance, supposing you're on a bus alone—you come to the first stop and one person enters the bus (with all the seats vacant). That person will likely come

Pic. 9.33A *A performance in Peliatan, Bali of Gamelan Jegog.* Photo: Courtesy Samuel Wantman, 1989.

and sit next to you, even though all the other seats are vacant. That would never occur in most Western cultures; we are always trying to maintain that space. Indonesians generally prefer to eliminate that space or distance.

"Gamelan reflects this community dynamic and closeness to a very high degree. There are no solo instruments. Everyone is equally important; you can't play this music by yourself. This was, for me, such a relief to see and experience: to lose one's sense of self in the activity of the group, whether you are a performer or listener (listeners lose themselves too). In playing in a gamelan, it is very easy to lose yourself in it. You can't mess it up or distort its purpose.

"You play gamelan because it improves you or is good for you. The structure of the gamelan is set up so that you can have any degree of experience and you can still contribute. If an ensemble has just a small number of competent (experienced) players, they can carry a number of inexperienced participants. Indonesians generally don't subscribe to the notion of innate musical talent to the degree that we do. The general idea is that everybody is musical. If you're a human being, you're musical." Dr. Judith Becker, 2006.

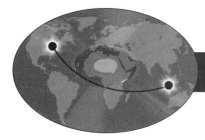

Inside the Musician's World

Dr. Judith Becker
and the University of Michigan Gamelan

Professor Becker commented: "When I first started teaching gamelan, I had to listen to the LPs and study the music in order to try to figure out what to teach. At that point, I'd never been to Java or

Bali. I did the best I could; finally we got a Javanese teacher.

"The first thing he requested was, 'Play me something.' So we played the little piece I had taught everyone from figuring out the LP. We stopped; there was a long silence. Then he said: 'Well … there's Yoga style, and there's Cirebon style, and there's Surakarta style … (and then he paused), and then there's Ann Arbor style.' (She laughs.) He was very sweet, and that was the beginning of my education. Despite the fact that I've been involved in gamelan studies for years, I'm still a beginner.

"For the last three years now, we've had Javanese performers come here. And I have to say, American students respond very well, better to teachers from these cultures than to myself. There is a wonderful quality in many Americans that they desire to 'please' the people from these other cultures. I think that's a sweet quality about American students.

"We frequently bring over young artists, as the older masters have so much, maybe too much, knowledge, and our students wouldn't be able to respond to much of it. The young musicians or dancers are closer in age to our students. The connection is made more deeply, and the material is more easily translated to their younger aesthetics and inexperience. Our students are both respectful and fond of our Javanese artists. They learn many things: about rehearsals, how to learn the piece, what's important in the piece—and in very different ways (both the music and means or methodology of learning reflect the Indonesian aesthetic). If I try to convey it, it's nothing like a Javanese teacher.

"One of things that also help our performances is that we always have a lot of Indonesians that attend. My impression is that psychologically, if there is someone in the audience sitting next to you who is from that culture (and you are not), there is a synergy and sense of humility and focus that is fostered (in both performers and audience). Without this, you can be cool and superior, (or possibly be inclined to take greater "ownership" of what you are doing). It really enhances the audience experience as well. The 'other' is not so 'other' when you also have the model of the reactionary or culture-bearer participant in the audience."

CD 3.17

"Excerpt ("Early Krishna"), from the Mahabharata," a Javanese Gamelan Dance Drama performed by the University of Michigan Gamelan, Susan Walton, Director, with Wasi Bantolo and Pak Parmardi, a live recording, (performed March 27, 2005).

Professor Becker describes this collaboration between university students (some Indonesian, some not) and guests from Indonesia as follows: *"This is a contemporary gamelan work—a more modern tradition of gamelan. Most of the pieces are not 'traditional' (of an earlier tradition). There are a few, but most are a modern presentation or more recent tradition. They use traditional instruments; it's gamelan-like, but with much more dynamic contrast, and faster (in that sense*

Pic. 9.34A *So abundant, colorful, and interdisciplinary are the storytelling genres of Indonesia. Many are extensions of Hindu story genres such as Wyang Kulit (spirit or shadow theater or play).* Photo: Courtesy Daniel Tang.

more like Bali). So it's what young people who play gamelan today like to do. This is the world of music today. They are very much in the twenty-first century. They are not an archaic culture by any means.

"The primary guests in this performance are Wasi Bantolo and his teacher Pak (which means 'father') Pamardi. Mr. Bantolo plays Krishna, and Pak Parmardi plays Durna, the two main characters in this presentation of the epic drama (Note: The Mahabharata is one of two epic stories from India that have been adopted in Indonesia). The presentation of these stories has taken numerous forms in all cultures touched or impacted by Indian culture."

Moving Ahead in Time

As we move into the final Units, we will address more specifically how we can "read" cultural fusions in the context of both their past ancestry and their unique mixture of influences. Both views are ultimately essential to respect any cultural expression. Without the context of any culture's *multiple histories* (or the complexity of their multi-faceted realities), we lose the perspective of universal humanness and respect for the life cycle, that in essence, ties "us" and our experiences to "them" (others). Without focusing in part or entirely on the nature or manner by which a culture blends its unique past with the decidedly multicultural present, we miss important clues as to the unique manner in which each culture is migrating and reassigning its values and creative energies. We also miss opportunities to update our files according to the visions and perspectives of each culture.

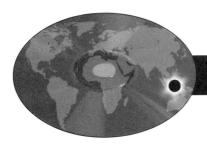

Inside the Musician's World

Sipakatau Ensemble

The word "Sipakatau" is derived from the Makassar (South Sulawesi) language which means "togethernes." The meaning of the word Sipakatau has also become the motto of this band (from "togetherness music is born"). The band was formed by Ethnomusicology students of The Institute of Art in Surakarta, Central Java, Indonesia in 2003. The members of the band are diverse in ethnicity—from Chinese, Javanese and Makassarase heritages. In making music, the Sipakatau Ensemble includes diverse instrumentation frequently in combination with dance composers/dancers or musical instruments from other cultures, such as the West African drum, "Djembe," East Java's drum, "Dog-Dog," and a variety of sizes of "Klunthung Sapi" or Indonesian cowbell, or non-per-

Pic. 9.34B Sipakatau ensemble, (Photo by Sipakatau ensemble, 2006.).

cussive instruments, such as the Kecapi Makassar (Kecapi- the general term for the boat lute in Central and South Sulawesi), classical guitar, Indian harmonium, Javanese gamelan, Irish tin whistle, recorders, and many other kinds of Suling or bamboo flutes from Indonesia.

After we contacted the group, Bagus Utomo forwarded this note to us, which we then translated. *"Of course our environment and our understanding of culture is important in establishing our approach to creativity. We were burnt-out with the development of popular music lately. We see the commercial music industry as very restrictive on imagination and creativity. We wanted to play music within the limitations of what we have, which includes a minimum of instruments and the use of bottles, pans, or whatever we have around us. In this sense, we hoped to break down the limitations of time and space, much as you might find in our ancestral music like gamelan.*

"In Indonesia, many teenagers prefer popular music and popular culture. Sometimes they get so caught up in what is popular that they forget their own cultural creativity and the beauty of their ancestry. This is primarily the result of a lack in education and especially instruction in traditional culture that was passed to them from their ancestors."

CD 3.18

"Tongkuilangji," by Sipakatau, from the DVD: <u>**New Experiments in Percussion**</u> c. 2004.

The music piece, "Tongkuilangji," from the Sipakatau DVD was actually an end result of collaboration with dance composers and dancers. *"Our diversity is our strength. For example, we have adopted drum patterns and rhythms from Makas-*

sar, Bali, and Java—and the sum total of the sounds each of us heard on the different islands while growing up. Our name (Sipakatau) can also mean: "new experiments in percussion," which depends on this diversity. We also hope to keep the live music component of our performance even in our recordings. Isn't the interaction of the musicians just as important as the sounds they make?

"I guess our hope is that with our music, we can open up new possibilities not only here for our youth but maybe elsewhere as well... especially with percussionists and people who love rhythm. We have a long history of percussion, and we hope to continue to make music whenever and wherever we are—without letting ourselves get bound by limitations."

Summary: Music and the Power of Balance

Pic. 9.34C *Musicians from the Yunnan province of Nakhi (Naxi), creating vibrations in many directions, modes, and emotional states.* Photo: Courtesy, Peter Morgan.

Note: When we began this Unit, our initial intention was to focus solely on the multiple styles of storytelling and the wonderfully rich sounds, instruments, and metaphoric connections of life to nature that pervade nearly all forms of storytelling from Pakistan to Japan. What instead emerged to become the emphasis was a perspective on the ancient art of "finding balance" in life: physically, emotionally, mentally, and, somewhat to our surprise, culturally. We also were reinforced in our premise that the natural human instinct to find balance very frequently finds its home in our creating and listening to music. When we look at time as flexible (our human lifespan inclusive) and space as only the limitation of our perceptions (nation, race, and human divisions inclusive), the opportunities to change, alter, and re-evaluate how we live and how we look at our lives increase beyond the scope of much current human perception and practice. Similarly, the potential influence of music and artistic creativity expands as well.

What is it about music that is so attractive to the emotional, mental, physical, and spiritual dimensions of the human experience? We asked a friend, Benjamin D. Koen, Ph.D., a professor of Medical and Cognitive Ethnomusicology at Florida State University, to give us some of his insights. He wrote:

"OK, here are a few thoughts on music, healing, and balancing. Perhaps you knew that everything is in vibration? From the subatomic particles that make up the pages of this book, to our bodies, to all levels of the natural world throughout the universe, to all the sounds and music that permeate our lives—virtually everything can be understood in terms of vibration. Even our thoughts can be seen as projections of vibrating energy. At one level, music is made up of all sorts of different sounds, and sounds are nothing more than vibrations of energy in the air—but look how powerful the sounds of music can be. Music can change us in a moment's time, make us feel stronger or weaker, more alert or confused, connected to or distant from other people, elicit all kinds of emotions, and even spiritually uplift or depress.

"Have you ever had the frustrating experience of having a song or piece of music that you can't stand stick in your head? Does the music seem to dominate your experience in those moments? Why should this happen? Why should a tune stub-

Pic. 9.35 Robert Bartley from West Bloomfield, Michigan, is a fourth-grade teacher, photographer, musician, artist, and creative mind of significance. He says: "There's an old song called 'trick bag'—and a trick bag is all the diverse things that we can do, by switching up styles and ideas. I like to have lots of things—whether fractals, photography, or mixing old Kandinsky paintings with jazz photography that I make myself. The idea is to have as many things in your trick bag to meet the emotion and mood that you have at any given moment. I'm never tired of art, I have so many directions to go—so many techniques to discover, perfect and then re-combine." Photo: Courtesy/copyright Robert Bartley, July 2005.

bornly and solidly plant itself in your mind and refuse to leave when you clearly don't want it there? Conversely, have you ever consciously decided to use music, either by listening to it or playing it yourself to change your emotions or state of mind? Why does music have such a power? In part, the answer has been expressed in the analogy that music is like food that we consume—which really gives a different angle to the term 'music consumer'! Music has often been called spiritual food, food for the soul, or even soul-food. But arguably unlike food that we eat with our mouth and digest in our stomachs, we consume the sound and meaning of music with all aspects of our beings—we feel and absorb the physical vibrations with our bodies, the meanings of music penetrate our minds, hearts, and emotions, and even reach that spiritual aspect of our being, which seems capable of transforming everything. Also, we digest music immediately! How often have you scanned through the radio dial for music (food) that you would like to listen to (consume), and in a matter of one or two seconds you can tell whether or not you should stay on that station or move on—the sound (taste) of the music is immediately apparent to your ears (tastebuds).

"I sometimes like to think of music as being a kind of energy or power that is connected to five broad areas or domains of human life—the physical, psychological, social, emotional, and spiritual. We probably all have had experiences of sound or music being a powerful force in these areas of our lives. But have you thought of music being a vibrating energy that can create balance or imbalance in these areas—balance being critical for health and healing, and imbalance leading to illness and disease? In medicine, when the body is in a balanced state, it is called homeostasis. In Integrative, Complementary, and Alternative Medicine (ICAM), the term 'balance' is preferred since it can speak to all areas, including the mind, emotions, relationships, and the spiritual aspect, in addition to the body. Interestingly, sound and music are intimately connected to all of these areas. What is more important is that these areas are often integrated in our experiences of life. For example, in exercise, sports, dancing, worship, studying, and practically all human activity, it is difficult if not impossible to say that something is only physical, psychological, social, emotional, or spiritual—it almost always has some mix of these aspects in varying degrees.

"A classic example of the physical power of sound and music is the image of the opera singer's voice being so strong that it can shatter a glass!—a wonderful example of the power of sound creating an imbalance in the molecules or the physical stuff that makes up the glass, so much so that it is destroyed. Just imagine what sound can do to the molecules of our bodies. Does this have anything to do

with why we like or dislike certain music, voices, or other sounds? Can negative sounds and music harm or destroy the cells of our bodies, and can positive sounds and music repair or reconstruct damaged cells? On the balancing side of things, music has been used by musicians and healers the world over, throughout history to create health in all of the five aspects of a human being. In such cases, music is most often linked to or expressive of spirituality or religious belief. Additionally, when music is used for healing, it often functions as prayer and is interwoven with multiple practices and behaviors, intentions and expectations about healing and life.

"What experiences have you had where music creates balance or imbalance, strengthens or weakens relationships, gives you energy or drains you, or evokes positive or negative emotions? If music can influence us in such important ways, how might we bring more of the positive energies of music into our lives, into the lives of children and older people, in education, in communities, and any area of life?

"Most often, a sound or music that we find beautiful, peaceful, energizing, or healing, as well as music that we find to be negative relates both to the physical sound itself and the meaning that we associate with it. Such meaning is informed by cultural influences that might be unique to an individual, family, community, region, country, or even humanity as a whole. Today, a great deal of music is linked to videos, movies, television, and other media with powerful images, all of which add to the meaning we associate with music and the experience we have with it. In addition, the lyrics of songs and words that are associated with different kinds of music convey powerful meanings.

"We can think of all the different levels of meaning in music as its messages. So, an important question immediately comes to mind—what messages do you want in

Pic. 9.36A & B The lotus flower is a powerful symbol in many Asian stories. As a symbol of balance, its unfolding petals suggest the expansion of the soul. The growth of its pure beauty from the mud of its origin is reflective of spiritual promise. Photos: (above left) Courtesy of Robert H. Mohlenbrock @ USDA-NRCS PLANTS Database / USDA NRCS. 1995. (left) Courtesy of the Bahá'i (Lotus) Temple in India, and the International Bahá'i Community, www.bahai.org.

your life? What messages do you want for your family and friends, and for all the people of the world? When you think of your favorite song or video, music that you love, music that you dislike, or music that you'd like to know better, what are all of the messages that it sends out to its listeners and viewers? Are the messages constructive or destructive? Do they create health or disease, balance or imbalance?

"For instance, the overwhelming majority of music videos promote the inequality of women and men. Typically, this is done by explicitly or implicitly portraying women as sex objects and men as their controllers, which demeans both women and men. Relatively few music videos actually emphasize the inherent nobility of people, honor human virtue, or represent healthy relationships and equality between men and women.

"The representation of women in such music and videos is not limited to the image of a sex object, however. The typical image shows women with a kind of ignorant "happiness" with their status, a lack of intelligence, and submissiveness to the desires of men. Returning to the music/food analogy, consider the dramatic effect of a steady diet of sexist music and video on the health of individuals, relationships, family, and community. Now, before taking the stance that 'music is art' and therefore 'anything goes,' I'll ask you to consider another point of view. If we agree that music has power, which means that music has the ability to effect a change or influence something (thoughts, behaviors, beliefs, emotions, the body), then isn't there a moral and ethical underpinning that must be respected and observed? In other words, isn't making or listening to music a moral and ethical activity? Importantly, this point has nothing to do with censorship or controlling what people can or cannot listen to. Rather, it has everything to do with understanding and respecting the power of music and the effects it has in our world.

"Many cultures are aware of this power of music and have many rules or laws that govern how certain songs, instruments, rituals, or ceremonies can be used. However, in the global pop music and video world, the opposite is true—a chaotic and frenetic free-for-all dominates, where a shallow concept of liberty suggests that since music is art, the artists are 'free' to express whatever they desire, irrespective of the effect. Again, I am not suggesting censorship or stifling creativity—but that people must be better educated about the effects of music, which like food, can either bring balance or imbalance to a person, create health or disease.

"The point here is to think more deeply about music's power. Consider how we treat other forms of power where we make laws about how that power can be executed. The same holds for most professions, for example, physicians, teachers, counselors, pharmacists, and many others. While people might abuse these powers, the point remains that people have recognized the role of these powers in society and have created a framework of rules to guide and govern their use. In the case of music, which includes language and many other ways of representing meaning, how can the freedom and creativity of artists be preserved, while its power and influence are recognized and expressed in a dignified context?

"Finally, since music consists of physical vibrations, as well as vibrations that exist at inaudible levels, like the frequencies of our thoughts, beliefs, hopes, aspirations, and all the messages that go along with these elements of music, it seems that music could be a powerful vehicle to create balance at the individual and societal levels. To get a sense of how you can play a more active role in using mu-

Pic. 9.36C *This Balinese temple Tamaloth overlooks the ocean at sunset. A plaque near the temple reads: "The purpose of prayer is connection, the purpose of connection is fulfillment, the essence of fulfillment is perfect balance."* Photo: Mlenny.

sic's energy in powerful and positive ways, take a few days to simply observe your environment and all the people, sounds, and music in it. Take note of how music and sound are used in highly specific positive and negative ways, both directly and indirectly, and then share your experiences with others. Then repeat the exercise with a heightened sense of awareness, listening to all the sounds and music of life, from your own breath, to the wind and rain, to the sounds on the street, and anywhere your ears can perceive the vibrations in the air."

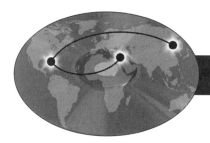 *Inside the Musician's World*

Benjamín Koen—"Reliance"

Artist and professor Koen writes: *"This piece was created through the process of prayer, meditation, composition, and improvisation. It arises from a sacred text that calls people to live as the spiritual beings that we are, reflective of all the virtues of God, and that when we do this, it will bring the long-promised kingdom of God on earth. The fourth valley comes from a passage in "The Seven Valleys,"* [9.15]

which, to me, represents a stage of development where the individual is in a process attaining the highest degree of spirituality.

This piece is also based on the concept of oneness—that there is only one indivisible divine source, unknowable essence, or God, and that creation is also one. Hence, the so-called physical world has the potential to be expressive of all the attributes of its spiritual source."

"The Fourth Valley," by Benjamin Koen, from the CD: **Reliance,** c. 1997.

"An aspect of the oneness of humanity is diversity, which is expressed throughout the music and relates to spiritual themes and creating balance and peace in the world. For instance, the first sounds are rainsticks from Brazil and Chile, and wooden chimes from Guinea, all of which convey the feeling of water and were inspired by the spiritual and purifying water of life, a concept found throughout all cultures and religions. The next sounds are three Chinese metal prayer bowls, which are used in Buddhist and Taoist temples throughout China. I was given these bowls by their maker and encouraged to use them in my music. The Chinese xiao (end-blown bamboo flute) then enters and is immediately followed by Tibetan cymbals.

Pic. 9.38 *A mime in southern Spain takes a deep breath, moves his body into position on top of a narrow pedestal, and closes his eyes. He then remains in this position—a human statue embodying perfect balance for nearly thirty minutes while crowds gather in fascination and admiration at this feat of endurance and balance.* Photo: Authors.

"Ma" and Mindfulness

Creating and Appreciating "Ma"

Probably one of the most vivid paradoxes in the evolution of humanity is the ancient principle of "ma" (space or atmosphere) as an ingredient in creating mindfulness through space in storytelling and performance aesthetics in Japan, pitted against a history of conflict, today's pace of life, and modern perceptions of both time and "honor."

This principle of "ma" is set in contrast to much of Japan's socio-cultural evolution over the last 1800 years. From Japan's earliest conflicts with neighboring Korea and China, to the post-shogunate Boshin Sens ("War of the Year of the Dragon," 1868-69), to WWII, to the establishment of "the Three Non-Nuclear Principles" (1967), and, eventually, to the extrication of Japanese energies nationally from the creation of nuclear or non-nuclear arms or, essentially, from "war" itself, Japan abruptly fluctuated from a significant military empire to a country that would now be forced to re-evaluate nationally its perception of "honor."

For roughly three generations, urban-living Japanese have given increasing energy to exalting themselves and their communities to honor through the portals of Western values: materialism, manufacturing technology, and, later, high-tech. As an added sub-plot, against the ancient codes of chivalry and honor in feudal periods that were marked by perpetual battles and skirmishes between Shogun, Samurai, courts, and clans (Yamato through Sengoku, 250-1603CE), we also see the perpetual influence of Buddhism and, later, Zen Buddhism (Soto, Rinzai, and Obaku schools), which emerged in Japan at approximately the same time as the evolution of "Noh" drama as a prominent storytelling genre (circa 12th century).

"Ma" as a principle ingredient in Japanese storytelling is likely to have developed from the teachings of Zen Buddhism (i.e., "Four Noble Truths") and the disciplines that became essential to the practice of the "Eightfold path"—centered on finding inner peace and balance and attainment of the fourth "jhana," which includes purity of equanimity and mindfulness. A monk of the Theravadin tradition, Bhikkhu Bodhi, addresses mindfulness as follows:

> "The mind is deliberately kept at the level of bare attention, a detached observation of what is happening within us and around us in the present moment. In the practice of right mindfulness the mind is trained to remain in the present, open, quiet, and alert, contemplating the present event. All judgments and interpretations have to be suspended, or if they occur, just registered and dropped." Bhikkhu Bodhi. The Noble Eightfold Path: The Way to the End of Suffering. Retrieved 4 July, 2006.

Young Japanese actress, photographer, singer, and songwriter Toko Shiiki is an example of a trend amongst youth to revert to some of the pre-"Boshin Sens" traditions as a means of creating and understanding balance. She wrote, "Ma, the relationship between participants and the space in an event or in the universe, is well known in most Japanese arts. In music it provides a rhythmic elasticity in which silence is as powerful as sound. Awareness of the art of "ma" is one of the rewards of enlightened listening. A moment of silence allows us to share spirituality with each other. Because of silence, we appreciate the vibration of the sounds, the power of the story, and the spirituality in space." by permission, from an Email received Nov. 2006.

Questions

- How do you understand the concept of "ma" in general? What about as relates to performance?
- In what manner might understanding "ma" and achieving "right-mindedness" serve as a balance to today's life-pace and conceptualization of "time"?

Unit IX Activities

Activity #1: Understanding Concepts

Finding balance physically, emotionally, mentally, and spiritually in the context of human existence extends deeply into the history of nearly all Asian cultures' art.

1) Concerning music, can you summarize how or in what manner music can impact us? (Note: you may wish to return to both the beginning and ending [Dr. Koen's] segments of the Unit for insights)

   a. Physically:

   b. Emotionally:

   c. Mentally:

   d. Spiritually (you may also try and define what you mean by this):

2) About You

   a. Which of the above aspects of human balance do you think is addressed best by the majority of your musical choices? How does your music accomplish this?

   b. In which of the areas do you wish you had greater balance? What music (from Unit IX) might you listen to more often, in order to increase your balance in that area?

3) The history of music in India, China, Korea, Japan, and Indonesia is strongly connected to the principles of achieving balance in nature—culturally, socially, and in the context of community interaction as well. From the reading (and music), what examples can you cite of the influence of musical storytelling in encouraging balance in nature, culture, and community?

Activity #2: Listening Deeper

Since we know we have probably experienced the only smallest sample of music from most cultures, we try to guard against putting the information we collect from a "few" or isolated experiences in our permanent files as being *representative* of these cultures. (Note: especially since each generation molds the music and perspectives to the values of its time—and there have been so many generations in each of these cultures). Still, we attempt to look for connections to and distinctions from "our" world of experiences.

Taiko and Odaiko drums were used in street festivals in the past. Today, they serve a similar function – although in completely altered contexts.

Listen to the CD examples below. You may also wish to re-read "Inside the Musician's World" for insights. Make a list of the similarities and differences within each country's representations of storytelling with those of your musical world. You may wish to contrast their form, texture, rhythm, melody or harmony, and instruments as well as the musical context and meaning or value of the music to the music makers:

1) India: CD #'s 3.10 and 3.11

   a. Similarities:

   b. Differences:

2) China – Korea – Japan – Indonesia: CD #'s 3.12, 3.14, 3.15, 3.17

   a. Similarities:

   b. Differences:

3) Finally, although distinctions between the "older" and modern stories of China, Japan, and Indonesia may be obvious (flow of rhythm over time, modern instrumentation, etc.), what similarities in subject or theme (story), emotion, or time and aesthetics do you hear in the following "older" and "newer" traditions?

   a. China: CD#'s 3.12 and 3.13

   b. Japan: CD#'s 3.15 and 3.16

   c. Indonesia: CD#'s 3.17 and 3.18

Activity #3: Exercising Passion

If creating a "balance" or, in essence, healing an imbalance is a large part of how most of us consciously or unconsciously use music in our daily lives, then learning to be "conscious" of both the imbalances and the possible alternatives is critical to our advancement.

1) In the stories and insights from India, China, Korea, Japan, or Indonesia, what perspectives did you find most fascinating and potentially balancing to the way you live life?

List:

2) You may wish to expand the duration of time (duration of impact) and diversity of experience (depth/diversity of contact) by picking the culture(s) that interest you the most (whose perspectives offered keys to balancing your own) and seek deeper and more prolonged contact in any of the following ways:

   a. Interviews: Try to find at least two (2) representatives from the culture you choose, representing a span of time (generations: an elder and a youth, etc). Ask questions concerning the area of your interests. Examples: how fast was the pace of life for you growing up? What difference do you see then versus now (in your country)? How would you compare lifestyles in your home and here/where you live now?

   b. Films or videos: Find one film (or more) made by filmmakers in the country for the people of that country. What differences in story, filmmaking style, music, effects, etc., do you see? How and in what manner do they vary from your own? Why do you think this is?

   c. Pick a particular musical genre you found interesting in Unit IX. Look for other recordings as well as interviews (comments) made by the culture-bearers or musicians. What do you find most refreshing or insightful (ultimately, balancing) about the music or insights?

Pic. 9.39 *Logically, gongs and cymbals most likely existed when humans first began creating objects from metal. But in much of Asia, the art of creating these instruments not just for percussive sound but for melody and creating balance is the finest of arts.* Photo: Courtesy Lark in the Morning.

Activity #4: Exercising Our Own Creativity

The beauty of art is that it becomes "freshest" when our experiences are refreshed or re-infused with the insights and perspectives that ignite our passions and imagination. If you found one or more of the stories, musical selections, or insights in this Unit fascinating, then to further your exposure to its influence you may wish to do the following:

1) Reread and/or listen to the culture's perspectives/music you found most interesting. Make a list of the insights that strike you as the most fascinating.

2) Research further: surf the Internet, listen to other music, go to the library to research the culture's perspectives related to your passions/art, or visit temples, concerts, restaurants, etc. Add to your list especially as concerns our "instrument" from these contacts.

3) Now, see if you can convert your list of insights, perspectives, emotions, and information into a creative artwork that reflects similar dimensions, aesthetics, and values. Note: You may wish to share this work with someone of the culture for a reaction—but if you do, do not expect that the person will see your insights or connections as you did. Much of the work of translating the beauty of blance from others' cultures into our own is personal. Our perspectives may not, at first, be perceivable by others.

Note: In the ultimate exchange, if our world is transformed in some manner by another's, we may wish to present our work to those that inspired us – as a gift. After all, whatever sacrifice we may make will seldom outweigh the life-enhancing benefit of our newly "enlarged" world.

Pic. 9.40A & B *When we separate the disciplines and expressive features of human existence to the point of losing a vision of their interconnectiveness, when "specialization" becomes emphasized beyond the scope of holism, and when acting and moving for the purpose of sustaining material life overtakes the essence of life itself (the depth of spiritual and community connections), we may soon lose our contact with ourselves and the balance that is the art of living. Photos: A – Beach drumming (Seychelles Islands) – and B – Outdoor concert (who has got the proper "reaction" to the music?): fusions of movement, color, sound, form, and social interaction* – Authors.

Unit IX: Endnotes

9.1   In Vedic Sanskrit: *brahma* (nominative singular), *brahman* (stem) (neuter gender) means "growth," "development," "swelling"; and then "pious utterance," "worship," perhaps via the idea of saying during prayers and ceremonies that God or the gods are great. It also can be a reference to God Him-/Her-/Itself.

9.1A Dr. Ben Koen writes: "It is at this crossroads where Ethnomusicology and the growing fields of Medical and Cognitive Ethnomusicology make a significant contribution to a holistic approach to health and healing, often employing scientific methods while also being keenly aware of and concerned with the spiritual dimension of human experience that is usually central to music's power to heal across world cultures."

9.2   A *myth* is a narrative with usually a lesson or deep explanatory or symbolic meaning to the culture. Most myths have ancient origins and are passed orally by storytellers. Myths are especially pronounced in cultures having a strong respect for the wisdom of their elders or ancient traditions.

9.3   A distinction should be made between *gods* and *God (Brahma)*. The individual *gods* in Hinduism function very similarly to the saints of Christianity. They have unique qualities and remind the practitioner to strive to attain these qualities and thus are different beings from *God*, the Creator of all that is.

9.3A Ms. Arkatkar wrote: "Some people do believe that teachers come even 'before God'—as the means by which you attain perfection. You can include this if you want."

9.3B Pandit is a title awarded to scholars of a particular discipline for their achievements

9.4   An important consideration in learning to achieve balance as a performer is the acquisition of some level of personal detachment from one's performance. By placing focusing upon the honoring of "something" greater than oneself, the performer is able to become somewhat less self-absorbed with his or her own role or performance, as well as with the reaction of the audience to the performance.

9.5   In some ways (pitch orders), the Western parallel to the *rag* is the *melodic minor* scale, which also has one ascending group of notes and alters two of the notes as it descends. Because this scale is more complex than the other modes or scales in Western music, it is hardly ever used in today's compositions.

9.6   Opera in China, though it predates by centuries the appearance of opera in Europe, still reflects many of the same dynamics it would acquire in the West. These include:

- Singers were forced to develop styles of singing that could project for large distances and be heard in large rooms or areas. In the West, the style of singing included deep diaphragm support and very wide vibrato. In China, the sound was equally projected and supported, but very narrow and focused in the face or mask of the singer.

- Two styles of singing or storytelling generally included: providing narration and moving the story along (in Western opera, *recitative*) and then moments where the focus would be on a particular event or emotion (in Western opera, *the aria*).

- Orchestras consisting of string and winds. In China, a greater emphasis on idiophones (gongs, bells, and blocks).

- Costuming and staging, usually quite elaborate, and naturally suited to the period and theme of the story. Both styles of opera used ingenious techniques in lighting and set design, given the fact that electricity was not used or available for much of the evolution of the art forms.

9.7   Basic overview was informed from <u>Chinese Opera: A Brief History</u> by Tomas A. Wilson (Department of History, Hamilton College), and Wikipedia.com: *Chinese opera*.

9.8   Although colors, shapes, movement styles, and gestures are significant in virtually all Asian art forms, the association with these colors has modulated over time. Today, for example, in modern Chinese films, red may sometimes be associated with anger or injustice. Nevertheless, it's important to be aware of the importance of color in interpreting *symbolism* in storytelling. This can provide a completely new layer to the story text.

9.9   The concept of *yin and yang* originates in ancient Chinese philosophy and metaphysics, which describes two primal opposing but complementary forces found in all things in the universe. Yin, the darker element, is passive, dark, feminine, and corresponds to the night; yang, the brighter element, is active, light, masculine, and corresponds to the day. The pair probably goes back to ancient agrarian religion; yin and yang are complementary opposites rather than absolutes. Most forces in nature can be broken down into their respective yin and yang states.

9.10   In many cultures, such as in China, the family name is both spoken and written first, before the surname, as in: Smith, John. This is, in one sense, another indicator that family or ancestry (community) is more highly emphasized than personal (individual) identity.

9.11   We might emphasize that the phenomenon of being forced to change one's internal vision or identity by external influences has numerous parallels in human history (e.g., "imperial" strategies, colonization, and enslavement). The conforming of one's voice (the subjugated group) to the controlling group, however, should never be seen culturally as a unilateral transformation, but instead a mutual transformation with no qualitative attachment. In this sense, what Japan became—whatever the political, economic, or cultural motivation, or however subjugated their prior cultural practices—is not "Western" but still *Japanese*. Just another "snapshot," or version of the culture, on the time-line of evolution.

9.12   With over 18,000 (counted) islands spanning more than 2 million miles (the largest islands Sumatra, Kalimantan, Sulawesi, and Java to the smallest islands, many owned privately), Indonesia is one of the most diversely populated culture-groups in the world.

9.13   The Burmese classical/theatrical orchestra is called the *s'ain* 'ensemble'. Its instruments can be divided into two kinds, depending upon whether they have fixed or variable notes. The fixed notes include the *ci: wain* (gong circle), *Maun: s'ain* (gong chime), and *patala* (xylophone). The moveable-note instruments are the *hne* (oboe), *saun:gau* (harp), *pa wain* (drum circle), and the various string instruments.

9.14   Now emeritus faculty, William Malm (from whom we heard earlier) was one of the first "ethnomusicologists" in the United States. He spent decades studying Japanese music, teaching, and writing books about Japanese musical genres.

9.15   The *"Seven Valleys"* is among the multiple writings of Bahá'u'lláh. Some contain laws and prescriptions for the evolution of a world commonwealth; others are prescriptions for the spiritual development of each human, while others (such as the *"Seven Valleys"*) are more mystical and address the journey, in deep metaphors, that each soul must traverse on route to becoming one with the Creator.

Creolization:
Creating Community Beyond Race and Nation

UNIT

X

Topics to Consider in Unit X

➤ *What do we mean by "humanity's" coming of age – and what must take place for this to occur?*

➤ *What is "creolization" and how is it a metaphor for the human condition?*

➤ *How did the origins of "racial" distinction both distort our perception of creolization (and cultural/human reality) and facilitate the exchange between cultures – leading to much of what we value today? And – how do we maintain simultaneous truths (or develop flexible perception) as we evolve to "equity"?*

➤ *What are some of the alternatives to perception based on race – offered by the Seychelles Island's cultural evolution and "kreolité"?*

➤ *In what way can jazz be seen as both a reflection of the disease of racism and an embodiment of American creolization?*

➤ *What do each stage in jazz evolution: ragtime, traditional jazz, big band, be-bop, or modern jazz reflect of both creolization and racism?*

➤ *What are critical musical elements of any "jazz" genre?*

➤ *What do musicians such as Charlie Gabriel, Michael Zaporsky, Dennis Tini, Chris Collins, or Ben Koen say about different manner in which jazz is a fusion of influences and cultures?*

➤ *How can we understand creolization as a dynamic in Celtic-based cultures (or for that matter European cultures as well)? And – what does such an understanding do to liberate us from culture biases and hierarchy or cultural centrism?*

➤ *What might we expect to find in the music of modern day Arab, Persian, Gospel, or other modern fusions? Is there any culture exempt from the process of extensive creolization?*

➤ *What does a Hungarian born – Afro-Cuban-conga playing musician, living in Columbia, playing the music of Bach with a Slovak orchestra say about human creativity and the ancient art of "creolization"?*

➤ *How might we understand the different phases of creative community in the group creative process? What role must individuals first have? How do we honor the creativity of the individual in the context of community building?*

UNIT X

Creolization: Creating Community Beyond Race and Nation

"Culture is an historical process: man is at once the creator of culture and creation of culture. Like language and religion or law and art, science, technology and the economy are primarily cultural phenomena created by societies in the course of their history, shaping their ongoing development." "The Multi-cultural Planet," UNESCO International expert group, 1993, p. 189.

"World order can be founded only on an unshakable consciousness of the oneness of mankind, a spiritual truth which all the human sciences confirm. Anthropology, physiology, psychology recognize only one human species, albeit infinitely varied in the secondary aspects of life. Recognition of this truth requires abandonment of prejudice – of every kind – race, class, color, creed, nation, sex, degree of material civilization, everything which enables people to consider themselves superior to others." "The Promise of World Peace," The Universal House of Justice, Haifa, Israel, pp. 28/29.

By now, we might see all humanity as a perpetually evolving single community, one that despite diverse traits or having experienced a diversity of events—has yet to learn how to reconcile its vision of itself to a more mature and realistic perception of its reality. We know today, that to truly "come of age" (mature) would minimally include:

- The understanding of the **universal human experience** as reflecting itself through symbols of diverse but equally universal proportion.

- The recognition of **bias structures** as a severe impediment to the perception of reality and justice.

- The understanding of **religious continuity** and the importance of such a recognition in undoing stereotypes and separatist visions (stereotypes that have been at the root of the worst conflicts in human history).

- A deeper recognition of the importance of seeing the **impact of history** (positive or negative) – as important to a clearer perception of our own goals and perceptions of life's purposes.

Pic. 10.0 *A group of students holding a talking circle (roundhouse). They are discussing the creative abilities and passions they wish to contribute to their "community" in creating their own performance piece. The development of a collaborative artistic or creative vision should not be viewed as limited to artists, but is in reality an essential feature of community building and, more generally, the acquisition of an equitable vision of ourselves in the context of our world.* Photo: Courtesy Washtenaw Community College students, Authors.

- A recognition that we can and must **balance the inequities** and imbalances of our cultures—especially those that marginalize other culture groups in even the slightest fashion.

- That our **communities** have now evolved to include members from the farthest corners of the earth. The challenge of creating strong communities demands the development of meaningful rites and rituals which mark the life cycle and solidify community life.

- The understanding that **balancing (healing)** in all areas of human existence can be fostered through a better understanding of the other members of the human family, their assets and needs, and, ultimately, through a greater emphasis on the arts, spiritual disciplines, and storytelling.

— and of course — *that all of these areas of understanding and growth can be enhanced with a deeper understanding of the world's creative expressions, arts, and music* — **through the development our own creative capacities as well.**

We might also have noticed that the absolute greatest distance and most fortified barriers between cultures or "races" are powerless to thwart the exchange of musical ideas or cultural information. Even in instances when dissension, hatred, or conflict exist between groups, the singular reality of our human condition and general appreciation of human creativity will prevail over the contingent perception of human division. Where music is concerned, affinities for the diverse combinations of vibrations and the manner by which they fulfill or reflect human experience will penetrate the opaque boundaries of politics and human bias based upon cultural differences.

We might also consider that nearly everything in our human institutions of learning, commerce, and culture is tainted by divisive perceptions and must be scrutinized and understood in that context if any hope of accuracy or a sweeping re-inventory of human history and, subsequently, our human reality is to be envisioned. This is the dichotomy of the "coming of age" of humanity: i.e., we are called upon to recognize with equal intensity the divisive reality of our past history and the mind- and spirit-expanding ramifications of an ever-emerging global reality.

"Racism (nationalism, etc.) is an expression of power. Therefore, it is ever-present in public and private institutions (schools, businesses, government bodies, etc.). In practical terms, institutional racism treats in an inferior manner or marginalizes 'ethnic groups.' Institutional racism results in imbalanced representations of people from 'minorities' in public life, in higher education, and in positions of responsibility at all levels of society. Those who advocate abolishment of affirmative action, saying… that getting a job or getting into a university should be based on merit and not on an individual's cultural background… fail to recognize that methods of merit assessment are geared toward a majoritarian conception of desirable traits, which do not take important cultural differences into account. To combat institutional racism, anti-racism training at all levels is necessary, and those who are vulnerable to racism must be given a say in how institutions can be improved so as to increase the participation of 'minorities' in the actual running of our institutions." From "Information on Racism in Ireland," Internet: Institutional Racism in Ireland, 2004, http://www.tcd.ie/Education/Teachers

It is difficult to see the manner in which cross-cultural fusion and the creative dimensions of human exchange have been perpetually advancing over our perceptual boundaries of racial or cultural division. This is in part because perceptions and the methodology of human social structures (much like sound) move slowly, while human exchange (much like light) moves incredibly fast. Therefore, we may find ourselves using labels of ethnic designation, or we may categorize and discuss cultures with dysfunctional perceptual tools that we've inherited. However, we may also find ourselves longing consciously or unconsciously to be free of the burdens of such labels as "white/black," "classical/folk," or even "French/Italian," especially when they carry with them implications of greater or lesser value. In essence, the creativity of our world's cultures has vastly outgrown many of our perceptions of history and our methodologies of discourse to grasp both intellectually and emotionally our own collective essence.

As concerns a search for alternative perspectives, we may find ourselves attracted, once again, to the world's diasporas or cultures that most represent the graphic clashing and mingling of diverse cultural influences. For example, each island, country, or continent in the Americas has had a three-hundred-year head-start in the intense processes of global exchange and ***creolization*** (creative dynamic of cross-cultural fusion and exchange – see below) as they have escalated over the course of this last century.

As concerns American[10.1] music, each expression or genre that we call "American" (pan-American) has undergone numerous fusions and cross-cultural exchanges. However, there may be a substantial void between the true nature of any American musical expression or genre and the manner in which many are trained to perceive it. Especially cultures having a history burdened by extensive intrusions into human dignity through slavery and the institutionalization of racial division are unable, proportionate to the abuse, to see their own cultures' integration accurately alongside their divisive history. Is it possible to overcome perceptions of separate cultures and music to see sufficiently the patterns of integration, while maintaining (or developing) and understanding of one's divisive history and its impact upon our lives?

*   *   *

Pic. 10.1 A (Paris) & B (USA) *The clichés "When we were children, we didn't see race," or "Everything I ever needed I learned in kindergarten" have particular validity as we contemplate the simple reality of human existence against the enormously complex process of deprogramming deeply entrenched biases. These children on a fieldtrip in downtown Paris and in a playground in the Midwestern U. S.A. are now completely devoid of the capacity to see race, and would remain so were it not for the education and experience they will soon acquire to see simple differences as "distinct" races or cultures.* Photos: Authors.

Pic. 10.1C *Brazilian youth play percussion, which spans virtually 500 years and hundreds exchanges or modifications between cultures over time.* Photo: Courtesy Karina Taglieber.

The patterns and dynamics of American ethnic exchange through music demonstrate the general phenomenon of the "law of balance." At some point in a society where there is clearly an "empowered majority" and a (perceived) "less than powerful minority," the natural desire for justice, balance, and human dignity will begin a course of evolution until it prevails. Among other things, the language, art, and music of the repressed culture will take on an even stronger significance, will be energized by those very acts of repression, and will alter, grow, or "re-create" itself at a rate in direct proportion to the established hierarchy and racial/cultural disproportion. In the case of African-American music, both the spirit and culture of the African people, as well as the creativity with which they combined their African heritage with that of their European counterparts, would perpetually and creatively mix, combine, and intertwine into expressions, which nearly single-handedly uplifted entire communities from the abusive disrespect of human hierarchy.

From the early fifteenth century to the present, an ever-evolving fusion of cultural exchanges between diverse culture groups would become a part of the musical DNA of the Americas. In this context, the most enduring expressions in the evolution of spirituals and gospel music, samba, rumba, calypso and reggae, in jazz, blues, and rhythm and blues, acquired their expressive qualities, not in spite of repression but because of it and not in lieu of European influences, but by the creative fusion of all cultural components over time.

We might wish to consider the following questions:

- If we know cultural fusions are the natural results of human cultures in contact and are fueled by a natural human instinct toward establishing a dignified or just environment, why might we, as a collective, resist seeing fusion, culturally or musically, across the lines of racial or national designation?

Pic. 10.2 *In Detroit, a mommy (right) rallies the troops to sing: "We Are Family" Karaoke-style. The bond of motherhood, family, and community have historically merged with creative expression to balance inequities and preserve human integrity. {P.S.: They "wowed" the audience as well.}* Photo: Courtesy, Detroit Jazz Festival, Ford, (and this family), Authors.

- If one of the primary purposes of intellectual inquiry and education is to discover "truth," why might our educational institutions still grant ascendancy and superior status to some cultures, both in content and methodology, over others? (In other words, when does "de-colonization" or a move to balance inequity between cultures find equality in the means and manner by which we educate subsequent generations?)

- If creative and enduring human expressions have always been fueled by the mingling of diverse and creative influences across cultural boundaries, why might each culture group continue to feel compelled to either "own" its history and experiences or isolate them from "others" or from the creative fusions that have perpetually occurred between groups?

- And, if "American" music in all its forms is the direct result of hundreds, if not thousands, of fusions of expressive features across cultures, races, or perceptual boundaries, many directly between the dominant European and subjugated African or Indigenous cultures in the Americas, how do we sufficiently and simultaneously acknowledge the impact of subjugation and celebrate the reality of fusion?

Music in the United States—"Take Two"

In all cultures, fusion and exchange are the inevitable result of human interaction. Regardless of our primary culture system(s) (i.e., that/those in which we were raised or acquired most of our experiential files), we naturally view our world and our respective uniqueness and interconnectivity with others in light of those core cultural experiences. In much of the Americas, as in any culture born from the simultaneous forces of severe inequality and intense multicultural fusion, individuals' recognition of the degree to which they and their expressive values represent both the impact of division *and* the results of a culturally *creative* fusion is easily distorted.

Although we've addressed many of the **challenges to the development of a flexible perception** earlier, we might briefly summarize them as follows:

- The pervasive Western emphasis on seeking a singular (monolithic) truth or solution to an issue or problem.

- A prolonged history of divisive and imperialistic actions between cultures. This has in turn influenced perceptions of history and the difficulty to detect the influence of these perceptions in assessing human value.

- Extended imperialism, the pervasive emphasis of capitalism, materialism, and the competitive thrust to exalt oneself over others based upon accomplishments and material gain that can veil or deaden one's instincts for justice and balance.

How do individuals vary in their desire (motivation) to acquire both new information from outside their immediate cultural experiences and the resolve to act upon the information? We can mark the outer poles in a continuum of "action" as follows: becoming agents for sustained re-education and growth in the manifestation of equity or justice in their personal character/lives, or remaining fixed in the perpetuation of isolation, dualism, and mis-categorization. Where people fall on this continuum will generally relate directly to the *motivation* with which they perceive their accomplishments and ultimately their value in life as being linked or not linked to the pursuit of "re"-education and/or justice.

Generally, however, we must understand that there is a blindness in the institutions and structures of most Western cultures to the entrenched connection of social status to capitalism. A verbal or political commitment to the principles of "freedom" or "equality" is not synonymous with their presence. A general unawareness of the extent to which lifestyle and community life is being eroded by the perpetuation of capital as the "God" of advancement has proven to paralyze any attempt to generate sustained and lasting change not only in undoing divisive thinking ("black/white," "African/European," etc.) but also in the creation of equity throughout the institutions of nearly all culturally and racially diverse societies based on solid human interaction and not exclusively capital. When the welfare of one's family, community, and planet takes precedence over individual concerns and material capital, equity and justice will receive

Pic. 10.2A & B *The actualization of true "justice" in a world riddled with inequities ultimately demands sacrifice in direct proportion to one's privileges. Generally, a pattern of applauding the great accomplishments of individuals such as Billie Holiday (left/top) and John Coltrane (below/left and right), or to speak of equity and justice is easier than making sacrifices (giving of one's status or comfort for the benefit of others). "If you hear the song, but not the artist — did you hear the story?"* Photos: Authors.

higher priority than one's professional and personal choices or material well-being. Similarly, when one's own family or community includes integration with people of other cultures and (supposed) races, then one will have still further motivation for engaging in the processes demanded by equitable and perpetual – re-education.

Individuals who may be conscious of the fusion process connecting their culture's history with that of others and who understand through life experience many of the dynamics of racism and cultural division may still not feel motivated to expend their energies beyond a narrow vision of mono-cultural community and thus insulate themselves from those of other culture groups. It is, therefore, the lack of activity and cross-cultural interaction and dialogue, and not awareness alone, that hinders reform and repair of both personal and cultural biases. A solid example of this is institutionalized racism, or the manner in which racist views can predominate in an entire corporation, educational system, etc., while simultaneously the individuals within this system claim (and truly desire) to be fair-minded and just. Conversely, individuals who are generally unaware of the fusion process or even of the history of division but who *humbly* integrate themselves regularly and in a sustained manner with members of both/all the culture groups will obtain, proportionate to their efforts, the wisdom, knowledge, and respect of these groups.

Pic. 10.3 *A 1912 Frank Bond map illustrating the Louisiana Purchase. Much of our history education is predicated upon the inclusion of "facts" and information that treat such phenomena as labor disputes, racism, and economic or political injustice as having been (past tense) rather than still being (present tense). James Loewen writes: "With such omissions, textbook authors can construe labor history as something that happened long ago, like slavery, and that, like slavery, was corrected long ago."* Lies My Teacher Told Me, *pp. 201, Map: Courtesy of wikipedia.org.*

Toward a "Just" Perception

Music and the perception of its value are greatly affected by an individual's experiences, especially in any society stratified along unequal racial, cultural, or religious lines.

Some of the influences affecting the acquisition of the necessary perceptual tools include:

- **The race or culture of birth:** To what race(s) or culture group(s) is the individual born?

- **Time:** At what stage(s) in the *de-racification/decolonization*, etc., of the culture is the individual raised?

- **Location:** In what location(s) (white/black suburban, black/white inner-city, etc.) is the person raised? Or, in that location, what is the nature or status of biases or cultural hierarchies?

- **Motivators:** What motivations (religious, professional, personal, communal) does the individual have to re-educate him- or herself?

The first two (race and time) are accidents of birth. Location, to a large degree, will be determined by conditions of family history as affected by race and time. Motivators, however, despite being influenced by the three previous conditions, are largely alterable, especially in adulthood.

Moving Toward "Equity"

The process of re-inventing perceptions, re-viewing history, and, to a large extent, re-defining the very purpose for which we live and by which we communicate, by necessity, goes through numerous stages. Motivated by the "accidents" of time, location, and birth into a racist cultural system, African-American academicians in the United States, past and present (L. Hughes, DuBois, H.L. Gates, Jr.), as well as musicologists (L. Jones, S. Floyd, P. Maultsby), were among the first to sound the "wake-up call" to begin the reversal of the processes of Euro-centrism (European-centered thinking or values). Over time, and in isolated locations, this movement would help swing the pendulum of cultural energy and respect in the *other* direction, to reverse the pendulum's nearly exclusive attachment to European values, to a vision of America at least partly inclusive of the perspective of African- or African-American "ness." Now, alongside the otherwise meager attempts to legislate equity in the political realm of the U.S., there was an

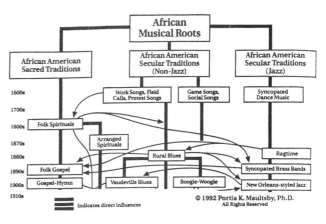

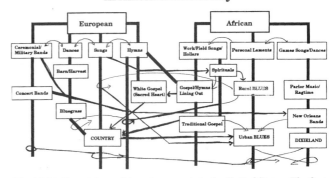

Pic. 10.3A *Two visions of American music in the United States. The first was an essential effort to move American academicians from the inertia of Euro-centrism and to an awareness of the essential and equally valid dynamics of African-American contributions to music. Based on Dr. Maultsby's graph, the second is a version by the author which (though not intended to be accurate or diminish Dr. Maultsby's work) demonstrates the type of vision that would be required to see "United States" music in its more accurate manifestation: creole reality.* Courtesy, Dr. Portia Maultsby, copyright, 1992, and author, 1997.

attempt to bring equity to fruition through the establishment of books, courses, and media images that would present, in part, an "Afro-centric" vision of cultural evolution and begin the process of questioning not only what we teach but also how we teach it.

An excellent illustration of this reversed polarity is the innovative and informative timeline of African-American musical genres created by Portia Maultsby (University of Indiana) in 1992, a pictorial of the *Evolution of African American Music"* The graph indicates the processes of exchange and evolution over time within the African-American culture.

Dr. Maultsby's graph served the purpose of assisting to break the inertia that predominates in Western-based academic circles (in this case, in Musicology) from their exclusive attachment to European ideological perceptions. By helping to generate awareness and pride in the tremendous variety and valuable contributions of African-American artists' musical expressions, efforts such as this would put in motion a balancing dynamic (especially in large institutions predicated upon European values, such as the university) to create real (not partial) equity. Still, today, however, the lack of pervasive and intensive dialogue between communities and groups divided by their histories dissipates enormous amounts of energy and potential from within Diaspora nations.

Stories from the Human Family

Personal Commentary (M. Naylor)

A variety of factors about American ethnicity are implied in the two graphs on the previous page. For one, both Dr. Maultsby and I are "Americans." Most of our American colleagues, however, would—by birth—designate her as African-American, and me as European-American. Although we both grew up and were educated—in time—during the American civil rights movement of 1960s and 1970s, we lived in predominantly distinct and separate communities. Similarly, while we – location/value – may both be ethnomusicologists, teaching in universities or colleges and while we may share many family concerns or musical affinities, because of the nature of America's racial history, our racial affiliation affects our status in society, dominates much of our professional and private lives, and permanently influences our perspectives in analyzing "American" music. Subsequently, we are both forced to address the issue of "re-educating" or attempting to diversify American education—time again (based on when, in the span of an evolving world, we come to live our cycle)—in our own ways. To a large extent, at present, given the world's racial history, the positions we occupy in voicing our concerns about America's racial polarity cannot, except to a limited extent, cross-over into each other's realm of experience.

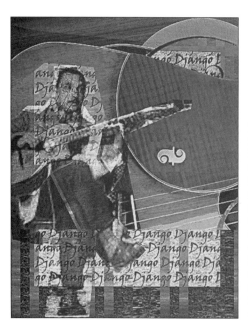

As a result of this, in the first example (see above), Dr. Maultsby's (because Maultsby is perceived as "black" and must live in this identity) must (generally) assume the role as advocate of African-American culture, pushing the pendulum of academic awareness in musical circles from its outer pole of Euro-centrism. Her work thrusts into our

Pic. 10.4 This collage of Django Reinhart by Robert Bartley demonstrates the power of the collage medium and its musical synonym—jazz. Django Reinhart was a "gypsy" (Roma) who settled with his parents near the Choisy Gate of old Paris. Because he was born to the "minority" status that greeted Romani people, his life from the earliest age included both a contention with racism and a passion for music of all varieties. After suffering the tragedy of being burned in a fire that consumed all his worldly possessions, Reinhart was forced to play guitar with only a couple of fingers on his left hand (fretboard hand) and amazed all by developing this technique to a level that catapulted him to the top of the European jazz world. Mr. Bartley's collage captures the essence of the confusion, fusion, and diffusion in Reinhart's life and music, a significant metaphor for the culturally schizophrenic nature of living in a racially divided society and coping with the indignities—through musical expression. Courtesy and copyright: Robert Bartley, 2005.

consciousness African-American contributions in a racially divided society, breaking the inertia of centuries of entrenched disregard for the enormous creativity and contributions of Africans in America. As an outwardly "white male," however, I cannot speak on behalf of the African-American *experience,* nor can I fully understand the impact of being perceived as "black," whatever my level of sensitivity.

As a result, the second example mirrors my experiences and what I can by race, time, location, and motivation accomplish. My family is racially "creole" (*creatively* black, white, and mixed), and my wife comes from a *creole* culture that is largely devoid of the racial stigmatization of the Americas. These factors, therefore, grant me the "authority" to address a vision of the creolization process (see below). Yet, I must also aspire to (though never fully achieve) an ever-growing sense of "cultural justice" and an unfiltered understanding of racism's effect on the lives of me, my family, and those throughout the world who have suffered as a result of its influence.

Finally (back to music), because African-American musical genres from blues to hip-hop are formidable contributors to all innovations in American music (including American "classical" music), any attempt to accurately perceive and appreciate American music must first embrace a deeper and perpetually growing understanding of American history that recognizes the impact of racism, ***and*** an ever-increasing understanding of **creolization,** i.e., the creative fusing, mixing, and exchange of cultural information beyond the confines of race.

*   *   *

> *"The hope of a secure and livable world lies with disciplined nonconformists who are dedicated to justice, peace, and brotherhood. The good neighbor looks beyond the external accidents and discerns those inner qualities that make all men human and, therefore, brothers."* Strength of Love, Dr. Martin Luther King, Jr., Harper & Row, NY, 1963.

Perpetually motivated by the pressing need to generate a respectful and fully equal environment for all of the world's inhabitants, a core of "non-conformists" who value justice and equity is called upon to press for balance against the larger forces of materialism, capitalism, inequity in privileges, and a pervasive decline in the quality of life in Western cultures. It is becoming clear that a *creative mindset* in all of its forms (especially one including the arts and music) is essential to reversing the polarizing influences of selfishness, self-centeredness, and racism (as well as other forms of "ism") that at present appear to be holding hostage the quality of community life, respect for the life cycle, understanding of "religion" in its inclusive nature, and sense of responsibility to our global interdependence. Against this backdrop, we must now search for alternatives.

One such alternative is offered to us by linguists such as Givón and Hancock concerning *human creativity, or creolization,* relevant to the manner in which mixed cultures create languages. As the Latin root of creole, *"crear" (to create)* implies, recognizing humans to be *creole* (of creative or created ethnicity) frees the mind from ethnic prioritization in favor of a more accurate dynamic, that being that every human being is part of the ancient *tradition* of change, of both extensive and multiple creative fusions over time, and is, therefore, essentially *creole.*

The perception of humanity from the *creole mindset* represents a vision unfamiliar to racially polarized cultures and is arguably the most accurate descriptor for American cultural and musical evolution. Hopefully, through the more fascinating examples of racial *kreolité (creolization in the Seychelles Islands)* and one of the most vibrant examples of musical creolization in the United States, *"jazz,"* we can gain a more accurate vision of the process of human exchange, fusion, and creative mixing that has, over centuries, become the basis for one of the more accurate classifications of the human condition.

Creolization—Acceptance of the Human Condition

> *"I am 'Creole' (created blend of cultures) and I accept this. Because you are Creole too, but you don't yet understand or accept it … you are confused with your times. Yes, that's it … you fight with the process of the fusions, multicultural, global, and advanced communication your own hands have created. The myths of race created by our collective ancestors, and the belief in "nationality," which*

contradicts human reality and the nature of evolution, are devoid of capacity to help us live in harmony with our surroundings. We must turn elsewhere. Be more creative in our thinking. Be willing to see the "creativity in culture." Quoted from Léonie E. (Isaac) Naylor, *"The Creativity in Culture: Music and Culture of the Seychelles Islands,"* Naylor, Univeristy of Michigan Press, 1997.

"No culture… is a closed system of rigid molds to which the behavior of all members of a society must conform… they vary too, in the degree to which they desire change, as whole cultures vary. This is just another way in which we see that culture is flexible and holds many possibilities of choice within its framework, and that to recognize the values held by a given people in no wise implies that these values are a constant factor in the lives of succeeding generations of the same group." *"Cultural Relativism: perspectives in cultural pluralism,"* M.J. Herskovits, 1972, pp. 15-16

Pic. 10.5 *A beautiful array of culinary art in a small village on the coast of Normandy (France). In a very real sense, a vision of humanity must allow for the recognition of distinction and even preference (we can see the pastries, the tortes, and the pies—and may prefer one over the other), but without the emotional attachment to preference based on ideas of superior/inferior, or a bias that denies the inherent equality of any of the parts or ignores their collective beauty.* Photo: Authors.

One of the primary requirements of citizenry as our planet comes of age is the acceptance of new and different perspectives of the human experience. At its center, if there is to be any aspiration to cultural equity, lies acceptance of individuals (and culture groups) based on their unique personalities and personally expressed requirements for respect and a diminished emphasis on categorization based upon nationality, culture, generation (old/new), religion, or race. To speed up the process, we might envision each of us as sharing the common identity – more dynamically than any other – of being "creole."

*   *   *

The study of *creolization* first found validity in the area of linguistics (Hancock, Givón, Mühlhäuser, Romaine). In this context, creolization was defined as: two or more linguistic systems coming together to form another linguistic system. The creolization process takes elements of the original two languages while altering their tone, grammar, and application over time, and simultaneously creating new expressions and applications. This also describes precisely the means by which creolization occurs in all facets of culture. Ian Hancock writes:

"Creole studies embrace a wide range of disciplines: history, ethnography, geography, sociology, etc.; the phenomenon of creolization has come to be recognized as so widespread that it may scarcely be regarded as the 'zanfan deho' of linguistics any longer. Creolization presupposes contact, and that is a human universal." Hancock, *Readings in Creole Studies*, 1979, p. vii.

What is at stake for much of the world, and especially for the creole cultures of the African Diaspora, is to find a balance of perspectives that accounts for their "reality." The violent swings of the pendulum in Diaspora culture from Eurocentrism to Afrocentrism have left some creole cultures with scars as well as a limited precrception of either the fusion process or the wealth and rich nature of their cultures. Haitian scholars Bernabé, Chamoiseau, and Confiant wrote:

"Negritude replaced the illusion of Europe by an African illusion. Initially motivated by the wish of embedding us into the actuality of our being, Negritude soon manifested itself in many kinds of exteriority: the exteriority of aspirations (to mother Africa, mythical Africa) and the exteriority of self assertion (we are Africans). It was a necessary dialectical moment, an indispensable development. But it remains a great challenge to step out of it in order to finally build a new yet temporary synthesis on the open path of history.... our history..... interior vision is a result of self-acceptance. Bernabé, Chamoiseau, Confiant, *Éloge de la Créolité*, 1990, pp. 889-890.

Therefore, as we examine creolization in music, we will see a variety of phenomena. In each, however, attempting to appreciate the music of distinctly creole cultures requires a flexibility that may be foreign to cultures still rooted to a search for origins/purity, or division. Consider the following:

- *Many of the innovative and creative qualities of creole music (especially that of the African Diaspora) are derived not in spite of, but because of, multi-racial/cultural contacts.*

- *Creole culture groups assimilate the very repression, conflict, racism, and struggle for survival into cultural and musical expressions, which accounts for a large part of the diversity and rate or speed of creolization (i.e. rate of fusion and change).*

- *Musical genres, religions, symbolism, and all the musical elements, including rhythm, texture, melody, harmony, and form, as well as the instruments themselves, were exchanged from culture to culture to such a degree that lines or degrees of contribution cannot be quantified.*

- *Having experienced ongoing contact with changing culture groups both within their nation/island (a main ingredient of the "creole" mindset) and with those in other cultures reflecting similar racial/cultural dimensions, affinity transfer between cultures is perpetual and extensive.* [Ex: Jamaican "rap" or "toasting" mixed with reggae) pre-existed and incited the "creation" of rap (hip-hop), and the reverse: U.S. R&B and Motown greatly affected the development of reggae and ragamuffin (i.e., background singers, use of horns, etc.)]

The Seychelles Islands and "Kreolité"

Although *creolization* (and its synonyms) may be arguably the most relevant manner by which to perceive the evolution and identity of our world's diverse cultures, nonetheless, few cultures recognize that being *creole* is the most accurate representation of their *race or identity*. As each generation's affinities and cultural expressions (language, music, etc.) move farther from their supposed racial/cultural sources of origin, awareness of the contradiction between self-definition (based on ancient paradigms of separation) and the multicultural reality that has resulted from centuries of cross-cultural fusion— must either be nurtured, or perpetual confusion and continued conflict is inevitable. In other words, as sociopolitical and educational institutions, commerce, technological advances, tourism, and international business or trade actively enhance these cultural exchanges between culture groups, we will need to become increasingly aware of new modes of discourse and cultural/social description. To view the world as a "cultural pharmacy" of sorts, enables us to envision that somewhere, there might be a culture that has developed the antidote for our cultural diseases.

Pic. 10.6 *This is the late Jacob-Marie, otherwise known in Seychelles as "Ton-Pa." He was perhaps one of the final keepers of the oldest musical traditions in the culture, specifically the local hunting-bow genre known simply as "music of the bombe." This form of chanting stories improvised from the moment to the repetitive playing of the bow is identical to the African ancestry of the blues.* Photo: Courtesy Seychelles National Archives.

A Perceptual Alternative: Creolization

— is the process of perpetual human fusion and exchange, or of becoming constantly RE-created. It is a metaphor for this "newer" vision of a connected and perpetually changing humanity.

Especially in cultures where there is considerable ethnic diversity (today—anywhere in the world), but especially in the United States, the Caribbean, much of South America, and in most island cultures such as the **Seychelles Islands** (pronounced: *say-shells*, located in the Indian Ocean), multiple active exchanges between vastly diverse cultures, render notions of a "pure" or distinct ethnicity or race, as generally irrelevant. However, only when one accepts their "kreolité" (state of being "creole") does one benefit from the full power and freedom from racial distinction and separatist history.

Pic. 10.7 *It's not that a fully functional creole culture does not see color or the diversity of individual complexion, "race," or cultural identity; rather, that "color" or human categorization is generally viewed in a healthy non-racist (non-hierarchical) manner. As a result of this, most creole families are intensely mixed, diverse, and generally very loyal to each other. The picture (above)– shows a complete amalgamation of racial and cultural backgrounds. Léonie Isaac-Naylor writes: "The family in Seychelles is almost sacred and of utmost importance to the Seychellois national identity, including that of the government itself. Since most families are mixed or have ancestry and family members from around the world, it is not the skin color or national identity but the family unit and sense of community regardless of a perception of racial/national identity that matters. This perception of community – in diversity – transfers to the larger national or creole identity as well."* Photos, graphics: B. Naylor.

*   *   *

If we could create a "culture" from which we could gain a perception of *kreolité* (the state of being creole) as an antidote to the disease of cultural separatism and racially motivated hierarchies, we might end up with a wish-list of events and scenarios that would in many aspects parallel the history of the *Seychelles Islands,* located near the middle of the Indian Ocean.

- An island culture, a remote in location, a close proximity of the peoples (small islands), and the fact that all must buy their fish and rice at the same market or work together in finding resources for all from outside their islands led to the development of a single "fusion" language and cultural mentality that borrowed equally from all the contributors—and became recognized as being "creole."

- Composed of diverse cultures, slavery was short-lived, and control or economic need for the territory was minimal, causing evolution of nearly equal status of members of the populace over time.

- With increasing globalization, populations of Indian, Chinese, Indonesian, Arab, and others would migrate into the culture; although some might, for a time, remain unto themselves, most populations mingled and mixed with intense frequency.

- And finally (as concerns the music), only one radio station and one theater would shape the people's affinities for music and exchange of information – up until this last decade. This radio station played African, European, American, Indian, country, R&B, folk, reggae, and the widest variety of music of the culture (across generations) so that successive generations might develop a flexible and diverse affinity for music.

Pic. 10.8 *Location of the Seychelles Islands, Indian Ocean.* Courtesy: CIA factbook.

The above is only a partial history of the Seychelles Islands, a group of islands located four degrees below the equator and roughly 2,000 miles from any land mass in the Indian Ocean. So remote are the Seychelles that they for the most part escaped many of the dynamics of slavery and codependence on racial identification that shaped most other cultures. From the first discovery of the islands in 1744 (by France), to their independence from any political affiliation (British, 1976), the people of the Seychelles (initially 60% African, 30% European, and 10% "other") experienced their diversity in the most intimate of settings.[10.2]

Around the time of WWII and the independence of India (1947), numerous people from India, China, and Singapore, as well as from the American and later Russian military joined the mixing process. Not until well into the 20th century did the eyes of European cultures or the rest of the world turn to the Seychelles, and then, primarily as a venue for trade or tourism. This new influx of non-Seychellois, coupled with the recent influx of media and technology, now feed both the speed and dimension of the culture's already existent *creolization.*

Stories from the Human Family

Michael's Experience: *First Contact with the Seychelles Islands*
"Had I never met my wife (then, Léonie Isaac) from the Seychelles while I was living in Germany, I might never have known of the island group (97 islands). Furthermore, I might never have been exposed to an alternative view of a 'multi-dimensional/colored' culture from a non-racist perspective. One experience illustrates the importance of being exposed to alternative cultures and learning flexibility in understanding the nature of human exchange. Both occurred during a trip to the Seychelles Islands, located in the Indian Ocean, that I made in 1989. Both helped to broaden my initial thinking (i.e., from categorizing music as being either European/African or black/white) and provide my first awareness of kreolité *or creolization (the state of being creole).*

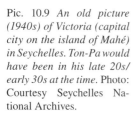

Pic. 10.9 *An old picture (1940s) of Victoria (capital city on the island of Mahé) in Seychelles. Ton-Pa would have been in his late 20s/ early 30s at the time.* Photo: Courtesy Seychelles National Archives.

"I attended a musical performance by one of the more well-known Seychellois musicians, Patrick Victor. I had been seeking "traditional" Seychelles music, music that would be distinct (from the music of my own culture), unique to the region, that used "traditional"(old) instruments, and clearly reflected the earliest African or European heritage from which the Seychelles culture was initially forged. Because such research was, at the time, primarily the "stuff" of Ph.D. dissertations in music, I'd be able to write my piece, get my degree, and continue the building of my career (hopefully, now as an 'expert' on the region). I had no idea that my contact with the wise and deeply just perspectives of the Seychellois would lead to new perspectives that would help heal my own divisive mind-set and provide insights that would thereafter guide my personal and professional life.

"I was to film one of Mr. Victor's performances for my study. It was a fast-paced show of primarily original music by Mr. Victor and six other Seychellois musicians, as well as some traditional music mixed with modern instrumentation, technology, and showmanship, which seemed jarringly Western and—to my tastes at the time—'commercial.' The audience was made up of a large group of Italian tourists, a privileged group of Seychellois elite, and a sprinkling of 'others' to which

Pic. 10.10 *Color everywhere! This painting of the main market in Victoria (Mahé, Seychelles) is as colorful as the market—and Seychelles culture— themselves. But far more important than the color is the "composite," the acceptance that this is how it is—and should be. What "goes together" or does not is a matter of individual perception and preference, and has nothing to do with the colors themselves.* Painting: Loié Barbotin, copyright, 2001.

I belonged. Like me, the tourists made video recordings and took numerous photos, perhaps hoping to capture a piece of "native" culture to exhibit upon their return home.

"Viewed as a reflection of Seychellois values and their modulating kreolité, however, the performance was not what I saw (disparagingly) as a commercialized version of Seychelles traditional music. Rather, my superimposition of outsider values in a quasi-quest for the 'traditional' blocked me from realizing that the 'traditional' in Seychellois culture was, in fact, the transitional. The separate origins had long since been obscured—but, unlike what I had learned in my own culture—most Seychellois did not see this method of categorization as valid in the least" (see Mr. Victor's comments below).[10.3]

Heeding the Creole Voice

Although we will examine specific dynamics of creolization in musical fusions such as jazz and gospel music of the United States later in this Unit, let's listen first to the insights and perspectives of artists, educators, and musicians from the Seychelles. We will hear how the creolization process across generations, racial or cultural/country boundaries, genres, and between other creole cultures is reflected in their comments and music. We may wish to examine how these perspectives differ from or are similar to our own and whether we can hear any of these perspectives in the music of Jean-Marc Volcy, the representative of Seychelles music we have chosen.

Pic. 10.11 and 10.11A *Modern performances of older Seychelles musical traditions (above L to R) Mutia, Kamtolé, and (Right) an older fusion ("Sega," being performed by a band), like most of the world's older traditions, are not at all now as they once were. However, at creole festivals, each generation re-invents its recollection, based upon the sounds, sights, and stories of their experience. This group of young dancers "re-connects" and, in essence, "re-invents" an older tradition of the Sega in public performance.* Photos: Courtesy National Arts Council of Seychelles.

Stories from the Human Family

Patrick Victor, musician, educator, and innovator, Seychelles - 1997

"I believe in this: I'm part of humanity so you're part of me. I'm part of you. If you can do wrong, I can do wrong! It's humanity. When I see something good happens to you, it happens to me. That's the way I see things.

"Anyway, I remember saying to the band: 'OK guys, let's go back to our roots.' But our roots were changing. I tried to organize these things... and I started hating myself. Why should I try to organize these things? On one hand, I said, let it be. But on the other, I realized it was not just organizing, but encouraging people to love their culture, themselves, their kreolité. At one time, people went to the brush and got the mutia drum. Later they brushed off the dust, but they had forgotten how to make the drums. I'm sure, now, I make the drums a different way. Isn't this life?

"We had lost valuable time criticizing, being jealous or scared of one another, working our muscles and emotions in that direction, leaving little strength to reach out to where the real source of the music was. Music is one with the people. Creativity is from the real source. It's there; we have to reach out. Every one of

Pic. 10.11B *An evening street festival is filled with traditional food, crafts, music, and dance. Located by ocean resorts, it invites tourists and Seychellois of every generation to mingle and learn from each other. This is a mechanism for achieving balance among generations and cultures.* Photo: Authors.

Pic. 10.12A & B *Does media impact the creolization process? Oh, if we only knew how much! (right) The only theater in Victoria for years played a perpetually rotating array of European, American, and Indian films which fueled the active creole minds of young and old. (below) In Malaga, musicians are interviewed and broadcast on a local TV station, which in turn is viewed by thousands of tourists, not only from throughout the Hispanic Diaspora but also from a host of other nations on summer vacation in Spain. Against this backdrop of modulating images, how does one remain immune to the creolization process?* Photos: Courtesy Seychelles National Archives and Authors.

us who has been privileged to have a beautiful tune come from his or her mouth had its source from somewhere else. It's not for him- or herself.

"Now when I look back at that time, I think I was running or competing against myself. Sometimes you see guys running against each other. But this is not perfection. For me, being more in tune with the finer things within every day, every minute, is more important. For a while, when we were touring France and we had done so many things, I realized that many among us, deep down, would rather not live this way— constantly pursuing things that relate to our own egos and not to our purpose on this earth.

"I recall a line from a song: 'In my mind there will be firecrackers — Dan Legliz (in the church),' well—it is for us. I don't know if it's the same for you—the bells begin ringing (sings one bell) then another starts (sings higher), then bells, high notes, lots of notes, bells everywhere. You can imagine this sort of thing going in your psyche. This is kreolité. This became the inspiration for my acceptance of myself and my culture, an attempt to resolve the contradiction from without, but one that lived as well within." Interview: August 1997.

Léon Radegonde, painter/art educator, Seychelles - 1994

"Of course, I'm a Creole! I'm a painter... but I'm also a Creole....Although I may not be certain how I evolved to this point, I clearly belong to a definite culture. I am part of a world that is really like a big family. It's like starting from a family of four, then you go out and establish new contacts, the family enlarges. When you live on a small island, the way of living is very different from people living on continents. Eventually, you develop your own way of seeing things. And many of these islands are made up of people who come from various parts of the world.

They have been put together, and they have to forge their own ways of life, away from the mainland. Obviously, they bring the influences from their country of origin, which are referred to in Kreole as "métisage" (metisaz). That's when people of different races mix together and create a 'whole from the parts.' If I am not mistaken, the term originally meant to be a mixture of East Indian and European, but its meaning is now broader. I think, in many ways, this is a broader vision of our planet, don't you think?

"Let's not forget that there are many cultures that share quite similar experiences (to those here in Seychelles). But although there may be a larger distance between some of us, everyone changes. This is Kreolité." Interview: June 1994.

Marcel Rosalie, National Heritage/Archives, Seychelles - 1994

"This is the process... (referring to rapid cultural exchange as the norm) whether accepted or rejected... It's all a process of evolution, in that something new was created, which is why I like the word 'creole.' The word itself is a creolization from the Latin 'cre,' which means to create or generate, to move. So I find creolization to be a certain dynamic of change and creation in culture." Interview: June 1994.

Jerry Souris, musician/music instructor, Seychelles - 1997

"There had been a lot of communication between Mauritians and Seychellois. Whites and mixed-race Mauritians called themselves Creoles. In Seychelles, nearly everyone thinks of themselves as Creoles. That's an important difference. There are some Indians—and the names aren't important—that are business merchants. They've managed to isolate or stay to themselves for 100 years or so. They kept to themselves for a long time. But now the youth of these families, perhaps the third generation or more, consider themselves Creoles, marry other Seychellois. You can try to stay alone for a while... then something will compel you to change.

"A saying in Seychelles goes: 'Si ou en etranze ou vin Sesel, ou konmans fer lakot en pti fiy Seselwa ou etranze pou fini ou pou vin Seselwa.' The translation is: 'If you're a foreigner and you come to Seychelles and start courting a Seychelloise, your 'foreign-ness' will slowly take a back seat as your Seychellois-like behavior develops.' This is true." Interview: July 1997.

Creolization of Tambur - Mutia -- now as performance.

Pic. 10.13 *We cannot halt, retard, or hinder creolization (creative cultural fusion). We can only refuse to embrace or accept it as the natural result of evolution or the human condition. So vivid is the active creole mind of many of the Seychelles people (Seychellois[e]), that it extends to their awareness and acceptance of their kreolité as well. This older picture, collected from the Seychelles archives, has had a comment placed on it reflecting a conscious awareness of creolization in the context of performance.* Photo: Courtesy Seychelles National Archives.

David André, musician and educator, Seychelles - 1999

"I personally believe that we can teach the rest of the world many things. Like I say, I have traveled a little bit. What we have here, in fact, is something that we've inherited, in the sense that everyone here in Seychelles can belong to any society in the world. If you dump me in India, I'll be fine; put me in the North Pole, I'll be fine; put me in the heart of Africa, I'll be all right. Most every Seychellois has the ability to adapt very, very well to any kind of situation, and this is very positive and to our advantage. Maybe this will help us to be a model to some of the rest of the world.

"As teachers, we must be open. We are the ones who must create that environment, that climate. If we just stay here and think that no one can touch us, or this is what we do and if you don't do it our way, then you're out of it... then this is a very bad attitude. This is one thing that we hope we will not lose. It gives me pleasure when you tell me that many people have told you that they are comfortable with me. I feel good anywhere... This is what I want people to learn from and appreciate. Hopefully, this will shine as an example to others." Interview: June 1999.

Jean-Claude Mahoune, anthropologist/archivist, Seychelles - 1994

"You asked for comments. I have to admit that Kamtole and Contredanse are somewhat complicated for the novice (non-dancer), and my research was never concentrated on the dances considered to be of 'European origin.' However, today I am starting to rethink and reassess my research notes and am coming to the conclusion that, though Kamtole was of European origin, it was played, danced, and re-created by Creole-Africans and has become, therefore, as creole as jazz, blues, and other musical genres of your (American) culture." Interview: July 1994.

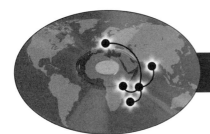

Inside the Musician's World

Jean-Marc Volcy

Note: Because of globalization and the importation/exportation of culture through media, nearly all non-Western cultures receive information from European and American media at a rate equaling or often surpassing the frequency with which they hear or see themselves. In small island communities such as the Seychelles, young artists are challenged increasingly to maintain a balance of respect between their history with its practice of the age-old art of creolization and cultural fusion and the other "tradition" of their ancestry. Jimmy Savi, formerly from the Lenstiti Kreol (Creole Institute of Seychelles) wrote of the artist, Jean-Marc Volcy, featured here:

"It seems that early on in the '70s and '80s we didn't think about Sega or our own music. At that time we were more concerned with the music that was coming from Europe, especially with international television coming to Seychelles. Everybody was trying to copy the European styles of music, and sometime later, the Caribbean style like the zouk. But since roughly 1990, it seems that the young Seychellois are starting to go back to our own music, you know, trying to develop our own music. They started to do research back into our own music and lyrics, and started to rearrange it in modern style. That's why Jean-Marc Volcy won the prize for the Radio France International 'Decouverte.' He looked back at the music...and pushed it up in time."

Mr. Volcy himself wrote to us the following:

"Well...the kind of life the Seychellois is living is becoming more and more like the European life. We have the influence from Europe in everything. You know we are a small island. We didn't use to have television—that's only very recent. We have inherited much of our culture and a tendency to take on new influences. I think this is the case. Everything that is developed new... we feel like we have to get that... have that... I think this is the problem. I think we get influenced by all these things and not always in good ways.

"Musically, we need to learn to listen to music with our heart. We should let it flow through our soul and speak to us. I believe that music that incorporates our past is the most powerful music, especially compared to commercial music, which only has a brief life. Music that extends into our past can live forever as it is the way the nation thinks, feels … . It's a creole fusion.

"We must continue to exchange ideas from culture to culture to learn other points of view. I've always had a vision of music and art being placed next to politics as the means of promoting morality, peace, and the exchange of ideas for the betterment of humanity. But we should also share with others how we got here. The balance is essential. Thanks so much for the opportunity to participate in such a meaningful project."

CD 4.1

"Kil Pake/Selo," by Jean-Marc Volcy, from the CD: **Bel Koud Kannon,** c. 2002.

Mr. Volcy commented: *"I believe creativity is fundamental to expressing one's true self and the enjoyment of life generally. I use my music primarily to educate people—both in a sense of morality and in not forgetting our cultural identity and our ancestry. Of course it can also be used just to make people happy and to dance.*

"You know you must move to create vibration. Movement can tell you much about a person's thoughts or behavior—sounds that can make people move are powerful tools. I don't just mean to dance, but also motivate (move) us to consider other points of view, to use abilities in a manner that can bring some happiness to this troubled world."

A summary of the stories and lyrics would include *(Translation and communication assistance courtesy of Francis Higby, Director of Planning and Development, National Arts Council of Seychelles, and Leonie E. Naylor, co-Author Executive Director, The Center for Cultural Healing):*

Kil Pake – "Clear the Floor!"

Chorus: *Clear the floor, guests, clear the floor!*

Clear the floor, I ask you, clear the floor! Clear the floor, give the newlyweds space to enjoy their waltz. Clear the floor, guests, clear the floor! Filozenn & Polizenn are going to dance.

Verses: *The wedding of Filozenn and Polizenn was a beautiful wedding in a **lasal ver** [temporary structure made of bamboo, thatched with coconut leaves]— which you need to **sot kap** [struggle over difficult terrain] to get there. I climbed, I slipped, but I got there.*

*I went around and greeted the guests. Miss Edna was giving me the eye (checking me out). I returned the gesture by blowing her a kiss **[mon anvoy beko]** I shouted 'It's time to clear the floor!'* (Chorus)

I held Miss Edna so tight. I was the guest of honor and looking for luck.

I was giving her the glad eye and she to me: Soon there'll be another wedding.

*Aunty Philo was dancing the sega. Her big rear end **[pake lenz** – a pile of linen]** took all the space.*

*The bride's mother came really vexed. She said 'Move your big rear **[pake lenz]***

I'll have space to waltz'. (Chorus)

Selo

("Sail-ho," a cry signaling the arrival of a boat from the outer islands plying cargoes between, for example, Durban and Karachi. Historically, about 70% of Seychelles' cinnamon and copra was exported to Karachi).

Selo the big ship's in port
(3 times)

*Let's go **savoy savoye** [porter, carry, hump, load heavy stuff] (twice) La, la, la …*

Carry sacks of guano, carry sacks of coconuts, carry sacks of cinnamon, carry sacks of copra

Pic. 10.17 *Jean-Marc Volcy, eyes closed, deeply involved in telling a story from the past, reminds young people that a fully balanced creole culture must continually create new fusions with an ever-constant and respectful eye on its past. Photo: courtesy J.M. Volcy.*

Pic. 10.17A *A blend of accordion, conga drums, djembe (West African drum), and electronic bass and guitar add to the mixture of European country dances and African rhythms to create the "creole" blend. Mr. Valentine, the leader and drummer, shrugs: "This is what it means to be creole. Not only do you do what everyone in the world does, but you accept it as natural—and look forward to the next thing you can learn."* Photo: Authors.

Come on my brother, come on my sister, carry Uncle

*In **goni** sacks, in **goni** sacks [goni: rough hessian, a type of Indian hemp fiber]
Na, na, na …*

Don't just sit Bolo[1]-Zelida, The boat is here Bolo

Don't just sit Bolo old pal, Oh le, le, le … na, na ,na

*Selo Revenan - has come, **Selo Nordver** - has come, **Selo Aoa** - has come. Let's
go **savoy savoye**, Let's go **savoy savoye**. La, la, la … la, la, la*

The Recipe of Sound

Although the lyrics and stories of both *Kil Pake and Selo* are the essential focus of both pieces, the unmistakable triplet subdivision of each of the rhythmic textures (three notes being played per beat) is critical to the overall rhythm. Blending the strict and equal subdivision of the European Kotis (or Kotis Anglisan) with the Mutia, which has a loose (swing-like) three-subdivision-per-beat rhythm, these Sega-esque rhythms are not "classic" Sega (an earlier tradition). Rather, like most pieces composed today, they blend rhythms and textures from diverse contacts, including everything from Soukous (West African popular music from the Congo) to hip-hop. *Note to musicians: Pay special attention to the snare drum accents, as they provide the timeline (much like a clavé rhythm in salsa).*

Ethnicity (Identity) Today

Re-evaluating "Ethnicity" Beyond Outmoded Identities

(Léonie's Experience)

"There is, of course, nothing wrong with being loyal to our country, ethnicity, or heritage. If we wish to claim an 'ethnic' identity and to honor that identity through our allegiance or by extending our time and resources to events or rituals that celebrate a shared perception of identity, this can only be seen as part of the beauty of human diversity. What becomes problematic, however, is when we become so attached to this identity that we are inflexible to the reality of human change and exchange… and yes, ethnicity.

"In most island or diaspora cultures around the world, there is an extensive history of multicultural exchange and fusion. In food, ideas of governance, language, perceptions of value, time, beauty, and even the purpose of life or religion, 'ethnicity' is a perpetually moving target. Therefore, perceptions of identity at some point either convert to human reality (become 'creole') or are frustrated by attempts to lock the myths of 'national identity' or 'race' to an otherwise moving process: life and the evolution of our planet.

"Generally (and I've personally seen this repeatedly over the course of my life), someone may arrive on the islands from France, India, or Kenya, but over the course of their life, they *must* interact in the 'fusion' culture, speak the fusion language, be subject to the same concerns (*Is the sea rough? Did the rice shipment come in?, etc.*); and, if not within that person's lifetime, in the lives of their children (the 2nd generation), they convert completely (almost inevitably) to an acceptance of 'creole' (creative cultural fusion) identity. That is, their allegiance to an identity other than that of being 'creole,' or a creative fusion of multiple cultures, becomes redundant if not futile.

"What I think is essential to recognize is that there can be tremendous comfort and joy in accepting cultural fusion *as an identity*! That is, despite centuries of adherence to being, for example, 'British' (when all of England has been in perpetual contact and exchange with much of Europe and all of its colonies) or any other cultural title, the accumulation of centuries of exchange through travel, war, art, or religion has virtually assured us that *every ethnicity today is just another variation of 'creole.'* This further suggests that we all have a common identity— 'variations of fusion… of kreolité.'"

Questions

- *What makes the superficial adherence to "ethnicity" by nationality or race more sustainable in large countries or continents?*

- *How does isolating ourselves with those who share similar affinities for identity increase or decrease our awareness of creolization (cultural fusion)?*

- *Why do you suppose it is less likely in smaller island cultures to profess being anything but "creole" or to not accept cultural fusion as one's identity?*
Photo: Roatan, Honduras, Authors.

Jazz: An Embodiment of the American Creole

"As long as there is democracy, there will be people wanting to play jazz because nothing else will ever so perfectly capture the democratic process in sound. Jazz means working things out musically with other people. You have to listen to other musicians and play with them, even if you don't agree with what they're playing. It teaches you the very opposite of racism." Wynton Marsalis, http://photomatt.net/jazzquotes

"Put it this way: Jazz is a good barometer of freedom… In its beginnings, the United States of America spawned certain ideals of freedom and independence through which, eventually, jazz was evolved, and the music is so free that many people say it is the only unhampered, unhindered expression of complete freedom yet produced in this country—It is becoming increasingly difficult to decide where jazz starts or where it stops, where Tin Pan Alley begins and jazz ends, or even where the borderline lies between classical music and jazz. I feel there is no boundary line. I don't believe in categories of any kind, and when you speak of problems between blacks and whites in the U.S.A. you are referring to categories again." "Duke" Ellington, http://photomatt.net/jazzquotes

Pic. 10.17B & C *Jazz may have seemed to originate in the United States. but having been the product of centuries of European and African evolution prior to the "formation" of the U.S., it was only a matter of time before it would find its way to Germany and Holland (B - the "Doohackedoodles") and Prague (C). Jazz in all of its varieties can be heard in much of the world today.* Photos: Authors.

Beyond the borders and barriers of economics, social status, and human perception lie the unmistakable human realities we all share. Through music, these realities find one of their noblest expressions of our diverse, yet related experiences. In the Americas in particular, a diversity of cultures and the distortions of colonization and slavery drove the creolization processes, and the fire that was ignited in the minds and souls of a core of its population fueled a cyclical reinvention of American musical genres. Each of these genres became a re-fusion of the sounds that filtered into the environment from a myriad of possible sources, and each became a chapter in American cultural history through which subsequent generations would obtain a perspective of an often tumultuous but highly creative past.

In the United States, *field hollers* (work songs) fused with European song forms and the ancient traditions of the West African *jalli/griot*, and the blues were born. Spirituals combined Christian European hymns with ritual songs and dances of West Africa to create *Gospel* music. In subsequent generations, each style would morph again, taking on new influences from the social, political, and economic fabric of the era, although the musicians and the genres themselves would continue to be categorized and stereotyped by labels still tainted by their divisive history.

In the context of time, gospel music of the 1940s would fuse with swing rhythms, gospel of the 1960s gave rise to Motown and funk, and in turn reinfused those influences back into the music of the black church. Simultaneously, both church and secular music of the "white"/European-American cultures, many of which had previously depended upon racist policies to prosper economically, would pervasively re-infuse their own church music, dances, and songs (from Appalachia to Western ranches) with the fresh expressions of African-American creole culture, perpetually creating their own creole music. In this context, elements of Irish and British country dance music would fuse with swing, blues, and gospel to create *creolizations* later to be dubbed country music, Western swing, or bluegrass. Nothing in American music could avoid the enormously vital process of creolization.

Emblematic of this fusion process is the genre of music known as *jazz*. Called by some the "classical music" of America (classical in the context of "classic," or a reflection of), jazz is a metaphor for the creolization process of the United States. As we trace the evolution of jazz in the United States, we will be holding a mirror to the face of America's cultural and racial evolution. Jazz models the processes of creolization in the United States. We will learn about some of the major innovations central to American popular music, and, thus, to the popular music of much of the world.

American Jazz reflects:

1) The chronology of "fusions" representing the culture's history — each stage begins as the "modern" present.

2) The dynamics and politics of racial perception and exchange in each generation.

3) The degree of exchange with acknowledgement (appropriation) or without acknowledgement (misappropriation) between the races (and especially of the 'majority' to the 'minority' culture group);

4) The fusion of musical/cultural elements with other musical genres both inside and outside the culture.

John Birks "Dizzy" Gillespie, one of the founders of "be-bop" (a fast-paced jazz form with extended improvisations) and arguably the "father" of "world-beat," or world-fusion jazz. Photo: Courtesy Library of Congress, Prints & Photographs Division, Carl Van Vechten Collection, [reproduction number, e.g., LC-USZ62-54231], photo taken in 1955.

Pic. 10.18A (left) & B (below) *To believe that creolization affects only the modern fusions and expressions of each generation overlooks its ancient roots—and its presence even in manifestations of our ancient histories. This medieval cathedral (Saint Séverin – Paris), built in the 13th century (left), houses artifacts of every subsequent century, including the most modern of 20th-century stained-glass art (below). Creolization always includes a juxtaposition of past and present.* Photos: Authors.

An Evolving Creole Art

Although "jazz" began its evolution thousands of years ago in the evolution of African and European expressions, it surfaced with the house servants' access to pianos in the mid-to-late 1800s. Musicians of "jazz" history, translated the already-altered dance rhythms of their African and Caribbean pasts into *"ragging,"* later to *"ragtime,"* and still later to the most modern jazz on radio stations or recordings today. However, each genre of jazz has shared common elements:

- *Improvisation,* or spontaneously interpreted or composed music. Each stage will have melodic, structural, and rhythmic *conventions* (formulas that give the genre its character) over which musicians spontaneously fuse the sum total of their technique and musical awareness (called *"licks"*) and reconfigure ("make-up") their knowledge music in the moment.

- A *"groove"* or rhythmic texture laden with accents generally not on the beat (syncopation) and created by a textured layering of diverse instruments, each having a specialized role. Each genre of jazz serves both the community according to the time period and cultural group of its creation.

- *Group communication and spontaneous interaction among musicians.* Except for the individual's improvisation, spontaneous communication and interaction between group members is by far the next most dynamic element of jazz and one that can also be found in blues and *jam bands* (bands based upon a spontaneous format, from Chicago blues to the Grateful Dead), to *rock and gospel bands/ensembles* (from Eric Clapton or Jeff Beck to the hottest gospel choirs of today). Here the improvisatory feature of jazz manifests itself in a "musical community," the intricate connection of the musicians to each other. More generally, jazz is based upon a negotiated format of:

  - *introduction / a "head" or song form (melody, chords/harmony, and rhythmic structure [or "groove"]).*

  - *an ordering of solos (who will solo and for how long).*

  - *a reiteration of the "head" or song form and finally a conclusion.*

Each musician simultaneously assumes a distinct role, while interacting perpetually in a spontaneous fashion with the other musicians. At its best, the communication in a jazz ensemble provides the ultimate in spontaneous (honest/of-the-moment) human musical interaction. This dynamic is found in other inter-active group music from Indian rag, to Arabic classical music, to African drum ensembles, and to most African-based music strongly rooted in *spontaneous group interaction*.

Additionally, as mentioned above, jazz in all of its forms reflects the interrelationships (positive and negative) of American racial dynamics. Among these, some clear patterns emerge:

• Every style of jazz is a fusion of European instruments (many of which evolved from Africa or the Middle East in prior centuries), harmony, structure, and form creatively fused with the rhythmic, context, style of ex-pression, and improvisational design of the African and *creole* in America. However, due to the heightened emphasis on spontaneity and improvisation in African cultures, fueled in American communities by the re-pression of liberties and the general absence of human respect in American culture, nearly all "new" jazz styles can be said to have originated within the African-American community.

• New jazz "genres," or stages in the evolution of jazz, emerged every ten to twenty years, and until very re-cently were ostensibly born in the African-American community and then either appropriated by or shared with European-American musicians and culture. In many cases, white and black jazz musicians ignored the racial separation of their times, and instead created friendships that stepped over the "color lines." And, just as frequently, the racial privilege of "white" America placed white musicians, media, and business owners in positions of power. From this position, they often *mis*-appropriated or, in essence, *stole* African-Ameri-can creativity.[10.4] In turn, this fueled the need for the "black" community to reclaim the art form, to express its individuality and community pride in music by *re-creating* yet another expression (genre) and returning the music to its community.

Pic. 10.19A & B *Appropriately, this mural paint-ed in Victoria, Seychelles (left), and of New Or-leans Mardi Gras – in Detroit, MI (below), com-bines the visual "artistic," cultural, and musical processing of "creative fusion and exchange" generally – and their connection to "jazz culture" specifically. The conscious creole mind under-stands the dynamics of cultural fusion as the es-sential dynamic, not only of the creole-artform jazz but of the creation of art itself.* Photo: 10.19A Courtesy, The National Arts Council of Sey-chelles, 10.19B, Authors.

Early Jazz—and the Legacy of "New Orleans"

Most jazz scholars begin their discussion of jazz origins with the creation of a musical style originally termed "ragging" (as in a manner of performance) and later "ragtime." Ortiz Walton, on the significance and context of ragtime, writes:

> *"In addition to being the first black instrumental music in America, Ragtime was also the first program music on a popular level in America. The banjo-Ragtime rhythms of minstrel "coon" songs were employed in this respect as accompaniment to such dances as the buck-and-wing and cakewalk. Later, Ragtime served to provide aural meaning to silent and later Western movies accentuating the mood."* Walton, *Music: Black, White, and Blue,* 1972, pp 40-41.

What emerged in the creation of ragtime were patterns of formulae that captured American musical creolization. First was the manner in which *ragging,*[10.5] initially on banjos, later on pianos, and still later through a style of instrumentation that would become known as "Dixie" or "traditional jazz," synthesized the rhythms and dance/melodic patterns of Caribbean and African-American spirituals and minstrel songs. Second was the manner in which technology would increase the means by which this music quickly became popular throughout the United States – almost as a balance to the social conditions of the late 1890s, when the nation was still healing from the wounds of the Civil War, racial and economic turmoil, and an erratic transition to industrialization.

Decades prior to this period of intense change, sheet music played on home-parlor pianos was the primary means of bringing music into the home. Later, the "pianola" (or player piano) which had been invented in 1825, by 1897, had been revamped to accommodate piano rolls which did not require any performance skills. Sales of "ragtime" piano rolls soared and both the music and medium became the "rage" of social events in much of the United States.

However, in the "business of ragtime," or the manner of propagation and distribution of the music, we see the racial dynamic of misappropriation. Scott Joplin, considered the most significant composer of rags, composed the "Maple Leaf Rag," which after 1899 became the largest selling sheet music and piano roll of the times. Its popularity perpetuated the creation of numerous dances and other rags. But Joplin's own publisher (John Stark) deserted him after his "Maple Leaf" success and took both the music and the piano rolls to white publishers. Piano rolls were soon manufactured without Joplin's "rags," without Joplin's presence, and without compensation of credit or money for his efforts in creating nearly 500 compositions. Though his music was played for celebrations, played, sung, and danced to in homes and nightclubs, and talked about on the streets, Scott Joplin died in a condition of insanity and poverty, much if not entirely due to the dynamics of racism.

Pic. 10.20 *Scott Joplin, considered to be one of America's most innovative composers, also composed two ragtime operas (Guest of Honor and Treemonisha). Were these also attempts to gain respect for his art in the larger culture? Tragically, Mr. Joplin spent the last year of his life in the Manhattan State (mental) Hospital. Upon his death, it was written, "For one day, Scott Joplin was a famous man even in Harlem. That was the day of his long and impressive funeral."*[10.6] Photo: Public domain.

A pre-requisite for any semi-accurate perception of creolization demands flexibility and the maintenance of simultaneous "truths." As such, the impact and irony of racism demands the acknowledgment unfiltered because of its unpleasantness, of the fact that no matter how hard African-Americans strived, musicians played, or African-American composers created, and no matter how embraced they and their efforts may be by the larger community or society as a whole, they would not be justly respected or honored for their efforts (a condition still visible as we write). Walton writes, *"In each black music era from early slavery to the present, the music has first been keenly listened to by whites and then imitated (usually by technology) and fed to the white culture, making (white culture) all the richer and Afro-American artists all the poorer."*[10.7] Walton, *Music: Black, White, and Blue,* p. 15.

New Orleans and "Traditional Jazz"

In the early 1800s, France "purchased" a large area of America from Spain; Napoleon later sold it back to the United States in what was called the Louisiana Purchase. This purchase nearly doubled the size of the United States. It also served to magnify the tensions between Spain and the United States that would evolve into war. Louisiana's port city, New Orleans, lies at the mouth of the Mississippi River, the United States' largest waterway. However, long before this purchase, New Orleans was already unique, owing to its diverse cultural mixture. Initially colonized by the Spanish, it had become a haven for escaped slaves, Native Americans, and later the Arcadian French who had migrated there after their expulsion from Canada.

"Whites" (from various European and especially French cultures), "blacks" from both the United States (mostly runaway slaves) and the Caribbean (including large populations of Haitians in 1809), and Native Americans (fleeing wars and the misappropriation of their homelands) created a cultural, racial, and musical dynamic of sustained fusion. What also resulted was the eventual mixing of all cultures and races both physically and culturally into a "created" culture that became known as Louisiana *Creole*. Within this mix, "black Natives" and "mixed race Creoles" also blended elements of African rituals, Haitian and Caribbean festivals and religious practices, and French festival music and dance. The backdrop was set for one of the most dynamic creolization processes in North America.

Additionally, when Civil War bands from both the North and South left their instruments deep in Southern regions at the end of the Civil War, the practice of ragging found its way onto these band instruments in the heart of New Orleans. At the turn of the 20th century, this creolization process brought about the musical fusion we now call *Traditional Jazz*, which would also become New Orleans' preferred music.

Traditional jazz, sometimes called "Dixieland," (*not* a term preferred by Creole or Black musicians who perform the music, since it was derived from reference to the Mason-Dixon line, or the line which separated freedom from Southern slavery), over a two-decade period quickly became the emblem of life in the *Big Easy* (New Orleans). Within a few years, this style of *jazzing* the songs made its way up the Mississippi River (late 1910s to early 1920s), finding homes along the waterway and finally making it to Chicago along the Illinois River.

Through the dynamics of this intense creolization process in New Orleans, traditional jazz continued to evolve, achieving its greatest creativity through the musicianship and charismatic talents of performers such as Jelly Roll Morton (pianist), Joe "King" Oliver (bandleader and cornetist), and Louis Armstrong (trumpet/vocalist). The success of these three great musicians was not the norm in the early years of traditional jazz. Much of the music from the early 20th century that we now call traditional jazz (and heard in the early recordings and later radio), was popularized by white musicians. Especially up the Mississippi, in St. Louis, Davenport (Iowa), and eventually in Chicago (with the creation of *Chicago-style "Dixieland"*). the Creole/African origins of jazz would be, in essence, colonized by white media and commerce. Simultaneously, white and black musicians themselves frequently intermingled, and the result of this intense creolization was music that found enormous appeal throughout the United States.

Perhaps as important as the music in the legacy of traditional jazz is its contribution of two important innovations to today's popular music *globally:*

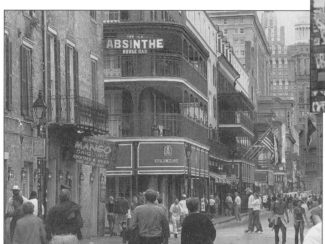

Pic. 10.21 A & B *Canal Street, New Orleans, 1920s, from a period postcard (Top). The photo apparently predates the Pearly Thomas 400 streetcars that replaced the smaller trolleys seen in the photo. The photo might have been taken in the 1910s, with more autos added by a postcard company artist. Bourbon Street (looking toward Canal Street – bottom) was the home of jazz music once it extended from the funerals and community rituals of its birth.*

- The invention and utilization of the "drum set," or "contraption," as it was originally called. The drum set is a compilation of marching band percussion: bass drum, snare drum, and cymbals. The "trap set" (later drum set) evolved from African/Creole funeral celebrations (after the burial), and allowed one musician to play all three percussion instruments.

- The creation of the "rhythm section." Each instrument in the rhythm section—i.e., drums, bass, and chordal (piano or guitar)—performs a role unique to the instrument. Collectively, the texture of the rhythm section provides the "rhythms" (also called frequently "the beat" or groove) of each musical piece. The earliest rhythm sections consisted of tuba (the bass instrument), "contraption" (the early drum set), and banjo (the chordal instrument).

Initially using a two-beat (1,2, 1,2, 1,2) style of rhythm section "swing," and later a four- beat style (1,2,3,4—with accents on 2 and 4), *early jazz* also used a type of free-style counterpoint between the "marching band instruments"—cornet or trumpet, trombone, and clarinet. Each of these instruments had a specific role: the trumpet played the melody, the trombone answered the melody, and the clarinet floated above each, flying between the melodic lines of the other two instruments. As the process of creolization progressed, traditional jazz, would also absorb and influence the melodies of Tin Pan Alley (New York's music publication district), as well as nearly any other musical resource with which its musicians came into contact. Thus, the creolization and fusion in jazz and the freedom it gave to the creative musician were united in the genre throughout its evolution.

Pic. 10.22 *Musicians such as Louis Armstrong, with his charismatic personality, large smile, and great sense of humor, needed to be geniuses of both improvisation and racial relations. Mr. Armstrong, Duke Ellington, and a handful of other "black" musicians were able to prosper despite enormous difficulties in a musical business constructed by and for "white" culture.* Photo: Public domain, courtesy Montaigne andWikipedia.org.

Pic. 10.21C *The modern-day drum set (or "contraption") with (L to R) a ride cymbal, toms, bass drum, snare drum, and hi-hat, is arguably the most important instrument in popular or dance music around the world. Even electronic sequences, which use exclusively synthesizers and digital/electronic equipment, depend on the layering of rhythms created by this instrument.*

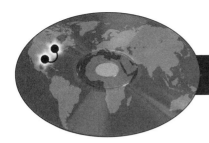

Inside the Musician's World

Charlie Gabriel

Note: Born in New Orleans in 1932, Charlie Gabriel comes from three generations of musicians whose lives span the entire history of the music we call jazz. When his family moved to Detroit in the early 1940s, they kept alive the respect for the tradition, its ancestry, and (above all) its spirit. Charlie's enthusiasm and love for both New Orleans and the history of jazz are still strong:

"In 1946, I was playing professionally ever since I was a kid – there were so many bands around New Orleans. What it is ... well, I'm gonna go back into my family. My great grandfather, Narcisse Gabriel, was a bass player. He came from Santa Domingo back in 1856. He came to New Orleans ... And my grandfather, Martin Joseph Gabriel, from New Orleans, was an accordion player and later on became a cornetist and founded the 'National Orchestra.' Then my dad was born in New Orleans in 1898—he became a drummer; you see, my grandfather had a jazz band. Well, the jazz band played with all the famous folks—Sidney Bechet ... my dad told me all about this as I was growing up. [The 'Gabriel Brothers Band' endured even after relocating to Detroit] To be honest, I didn't pay much attention to all this, until in 1969, I went to Paris with Aretha Franklin, and then I found out about the legacy of my family.

"Then I found out that back in 1917 all the jazz was just in that one part of New Orleans, when WW I was goin' on. Well, let me back up a bit. Before the music was called 'ragtime,' it was really called 'raggedy' music, because it was for slaves and common folk. Later on, the tempo changed, and it was called 'ragtime.' It was still the same music, just with a faster time (tempo). Scott Joplin used to play music, the piano at a music store for the owner; they'd sell his compositions for $.05 a copy. Well, you know what I'm talkin' about...so the cat that bought Joplin's music made millions.

"Anyway, I as a young musician thought that everyone played this type of music. I later found out that when they closed down 'Storyville' (the jazz district of New Orleans), the musicians got on the riverboats, and it moved up North. Ya see, the music is a spirit; it is colorless. They used to say it was 'dirty' music, it was from the slaves, the poor black folk. Well, let's see about that. We got the African drums, the European horns, it's a mixture and marriage of all the folks and cultures. You don't have to be a musician; somewhere your ancestry is in this music. New Orleans was like a melting pot. We had the Germans, we had the French, we had the Spanish, we had the Africans, Indians, and Caribbean. That's why New Orleans jazz was, and is, so infectious. It's America's music. We're all in this music.

"I think New Orleans music comes from the spiritual side of all the races, all the people. It's in the beat, it's in the music—and it's in our hearts."

"High Society" (Armand Piron/Clarence Williams, 1929) and **"That's a Plenty"** (Traditional Jazz, Lew Pollack/RayGilbert, 1914), Charlie Gabriel, from the CD: **Gabriel Traditional Jazz Band ... and Friends** (featuring Marcus Belgrave), c. 1993.

"High Society"—Ragtime style

> Mr. Gabriel commented: *"Now this piece here is "High Society." The solo was written (first created) by Alphonce Picou. He played in a band with my father. My father learned the solo. This is the solo that I learned from my dad. Now this is how it's done. Now I've handed it down to Taslimah Bey. That lady plays ragtime, here in Detroit.*
>
> *"When I got to France, a guy told me—and that's why I've now learned so much about my father and grandfather—the guy told me about my family and this solo. That's why I say— we really have to respect our ancestry and see this music as a spirit."*

Now, of course, the younger musicians playing with Charlie—and Charlie's own growth as a musician—will mean that creolization will continue. As Charlie progresses in his solo, he "swings" in and out of the traditional solo style. The drums, in turn, move to a swing (4-beat swing feel), more an element of the 30s and 40s, and the piece builds to its end—the melody being present only as background. In this case, what appears to be a simple "solo" is really a complex web of ancestry, history, and a tribute to Charlie's family and the spirit of New Orleans.

"That's a Plenty"—Traditional Jazz style

> *"When it (traditional jazz) moved up the river, it continued to take on a new life. I think if you have a soul, you have to feel the music. It's a godly gift from the Creator. It touches you if you're a human being. Once it moves into you, it doesn't stop. You're going to sing it from a different perspective—your own perspective.*

Pic. 10.24 *New Orleans-born and "traditional" jazz–raised Charlie Gabriel stands next to a mantel that holds pictures of his creole mother, father, and descendants. In this family of musicians, like many musicians in America's evolving creole culture, the affinity for multiple disciplines of music was passed from generation to generation, in Charlie's case, with great pride and respect for that ancestry.* Photo: author by permission, C. Gabriel, 2005.

The spirit of who we are, what we have in our head, comes out of our instruments. Who could imagine all the things that Dizzy Gillespie would play? And it moves on up to the kids of today. There are so many things yet to learn— it's unimaginable. That's why we have to keep our heads and our hearts open.

"Someone once asked Duke: 'Hey, isn't all this guitar playing terrible? Isn't it bad music!' Duke said, 'It may be distasteful to you at a given time, but it's never bad.' And I said, one time when I was in Singapore, we did a recording there with Elder Young and Red Holt, they asked us what we're going to play without music (notation). Well, I told them: 'We're gonna have a musical conversation that will keep us from having complications.'" (He laughs.)

The Recipe of Sound

"High Society"–From the beginning drum roll, we can hear the influence of the "march" and fusion of the marching band and funeral processional from which traditional jazz was born. But both the piano style and the clarinet phrasing is, well… "raggedy" (syncopated with accents placed between the beats). Later, the solo played by Charlie (clarinet) is a "learned- by-rote," complex melody (passed through generations) that outlines or paraphrases the original melody, played in the background by the piano. This melody, though more rigid than complete improvisation, was, as mentioned by Charlie, a labor of love… a musical tribute to the ancestry of his family. Oh yes, a respect for which he had to go to France to reacquire a deeper sense of appreciation.

"That's a Plenty" begins with a drum roll; then the form is: A) traditional melody with cadence [repeats], B) bridge—that elevates the emotion and raises the pitch [progression of harmony moves from tonic] (repeat again); then the return of the march-like beginning acts as a bridge to the improvised solos.

Solos: Improvised solos (in all genres) are a combination of pre-learned "licks" (pre-learned patterns on the instrument) and the spontaneous arrangement of these patterns or musical ideas. Musicians such as Charlie (clarinet) and Marcus Belgrave (trumpet) have learned a large number of ideas and are, therefore, free to go as their emotions and mind dictate. We as listeners are equally "free" to ride their solos like a roller coaster until, after a brief segment where they dialogue (trade or exchange solos), they finally come back to the "roll-off," or march-like melody, to complete the piece.

As heard by the audience response, most "jazz," even that used for dancing, must first be seen as an art of communication. If it's good, if the spirit is truly moving and the dialogue effective, the listener will be moved as well.

Jazz—From Mainstream to Backroom

The late John Birks "Dizzy" Gillespie, an innovator and ambassador for the art of jazz was once asked, "How should one teach jazz?" He reportedly said, *"I always try to teach by example and not force my ideas on a young musician. One of the reasons we're here is to be a part of this process of exchange."* As with all forms of American *creole music,* from R&B or rock to country or hip-hop, jazz has a multitude of variations, but what each shares is the capacity to express the deepest emotion of the musician—and serve as both a tie to the past and as an expression of the time in which he or she lives.

Each time we talk of one phase of the perpetually changing process of creolization in cultures as dynamically charged as those in the Americas, we hold an image or sound of an expression (tradition) that will have since moved on to new forms of expression. In each phase, the hearts of each generation would have new things to speak of, and jazz accommodated these changes.

In much of the United States between the late teens and the late 1940s, jazz became the rage. This period spanned the early industrial movement during WWI, when a migratory surge of workers from the rural South pushed into the industrial centers of the Midwest and Northeast to find work. Later, the Depression, Prohibition, WWII, and an explosion of technology that included massive expansion in the

Pic.10.25 *It may be important to remember the manner in which creolization constantly influenced the fusion of cultures and the movement of innovations between the "races." The King & Carter Jazzing Orchestra is a classic example of just such creolization: a Texas "traditional jazz band" using "orchestral" instruments. In time, these instruments, particularly the double bass (string bass), would become standard in jazz music.* Photo: Public domain, courtesy of Robert Runyon, 1921.

Pic. 10.26 *An image scanned from an original 1918 promotional postcard— the "Original Dixieland Band," as they were playing at Reisenweber's Cafe in New York City. White musicians became the most recorded and, later, most prolifically broadcast ensembles of the 1920s. Paul Whiteman's orchestra of the 20s/30s assumed the name "The King of Jazz." Regrettably, such titles ("original" and "king") ignored the "primary" origins of jazz within the African-American community and continued the perpetuation of misappropriation that would continue for decades.* Photo: Public domain, courtesy wikipedia.org.

use of electricity, the development of recording technology, and the eventual creation and mass marketing of radio (and not much later) television, would leave their mark on the evolution of jazz.

As traditional jazz became popular throughout the Northern cities, only a handful of the New Orleans musicians would be involved in the more highly visible or recorded groups. The "unequal" nature of racism in contrast to the "natural" human instinct to prosper or advance equally incited an increase also of African-Americans who chose to use their talents and skills in entertainment outside of their immediate communities.

Many African-American males also served as "Pullman porters" on the railroad. As race-records ("black" music recorded by "white" record companies) became more commonplace, these porters would also sell and distribute the recordings, which, in combination with a broader acceptance of recording industry technology and the affordability of Edison's "phonographs," made "jazz" a preferred music in much of the United States.

In a relatively short time-span, large pools of creative musicians accumulated in places such as the south side of Chicago, and in parts of Detroit, Philadelphia, and, especially, Harlem, New York. Fueled by Prohibition (1920-1933) and the establishment of "speakeasies" (underground jazz clubs that served alcohol) as well as by radio programming in many urban centers, intensive creolization continued, leading to what would later be called *big band jazz* (or jazz orchestras), but still further to the development of rhythm and blues and a host of other creole developments in gospel, blues, and even rock 'n' roll.

At this phase in jazz creolization, the horn section of the traditional band (trumpet, clarinet, and trombone) multiplied to three or four times its original dimension (3-4 trumpets, 3-4 clarinets, and 3 trombones). Not much later, saxophones, invented by the Belgian-born Parisian Adolphe Sax, would become common. These larger bands began to surface first at *rent parties*[10.8] and larger community gatherings of African-Americans, particularly in Harlem. The first "big band" on record was that of Fletcher

Henderson of Harlem (1922). In a very short time, their number and popularity grew, due in no small part to the Depression and WWII. Fueled by the speed and ease with which music reached the public by "radio" and the evolution of "mass media," big band "superstars" were made. Soon *big bands, ballrooms, and ballroom-style swing dancing* could be heard over much of the United States.

Be-Bop to Modern Jazz

When jazz left the ballrooms and "airways" of radio and moved to the smoke-filled clubs and private collections of jazz *aficionados,* it receded from mainstream America. Some view jazz as a swinging pendulum, passed between the "black" and "white" communities. However, the failure of "white-jazz" musicians and institutions to acknowledge African-American contributions can be seen as the creative impetus for new innovations within the "black" community. Perhaps in part because African-Americans wanted or needed to retain ownership or reclaim their voice, racism (and its effects politically, economically, and socially) was also at the core of creolization.

In another picture of creolization, both white and black musicians such as Benny Goodman (Jewish/NY band leader), Louis Armstrong, Fletcher Henderson (who arranged for Goodman), and a host of musicians throughout jazz history ignored color-barriers—or, better said, persevered through them. Either way, *jazz was a reflection of a dynamic creole-America* that is also, in its musical essence, a mixing of the races and cultures in near equal proportions.

As the big-band era of the 1930s and 1940s progressed, only a handful of African-American *jazz orchestras* managed to continually support their musicians through performance and recording, most notably "Duke" Ellington and "Count" Basie. "Black" jazz musicians and a handful of "white" musicians who rejected the commercialization of jazz or who were simply striving for innovation began to migrate to the smaller jazz clubs to perform their newest musical creolizations.

Jazz musicians such as Charlie "Bird" Parker and John Burkes "Dizzy" Gillespie began to play melodies that were no

Pic. 10.27 (above) *Edward Kennedy "Duke" Ellington, the grandson of a South Carolinian slave, son of a White House butler, was born in Washington, D.C. Ellington catapulted past many of the protocols of racist hierarchy by virtue of an articulate, well-dressed, and exceedingly debonair demeanor. Within ten years of forming his first band, he was hired to play at Harlem's swank "Cotton Club" (a club primarily designed for white folks to experience "black" jazz). Few of Ellington's generation were able to achieve his "cross-over" popularity with the "white" audiences who would subsidize his band, while maintaining the artistic and creative integrity in his music that would appeal to the "black" community. Considered by many to be one of the most innovative American composers, Ellington created in his music a perpetually changing blend of sounds, orchestral layerings, and musical storylines. In each piece, we hear the American creole experience through the power of a blending of European ("classical") compositional organization and the spontaneity and spirit of African-American culture.* Photo: Public domain.

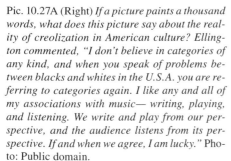

Pic. 10.27A (Right) *If a picture paints a thousand words, what does this picture say about the reality of creolization in American culture? Ellington commented, "I don't believe in categories of any kind, and when you speak of problems between blacks and whites in the U.S.A. you are referring to categories again. I like any and all of my associations with music— writing, playing, and listening. We write and play from our perspective, and the audience listens from its perspective. If and when we agree, I am lucky."* Photo: Public domain.

longer singable and that returned jazz to its primarily improvisational art form of communication between musicians or between audience and musicians. In this context, the jazz melodies of what became known as "be-bop" were intricate and complex with fast-driving tempos and often long and extended improvisational solos. It would not be until the late 1970s that jazz would occasionally find a place in the popular mainstream. Although musicians such as Herbie Hancock, Freddie Hubbard, and Chick Corea would later combine jazz elements with modern influences from R&B, funk, or soul music to bring jazz closer to a popular context, jazz would, for better or worse, never again enjoy the popularity it had during the "traditional jazz" and "big band" eras.

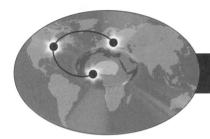

Inside the Musician's World

Michael Zaporski

Note: Michael began playing piano early in his life. He became interested in jazz in his teens. In his late teens, he was mentored by Sam Sanders, an elder jazz musician in the African-American community who made it clear to Michael that playing jazz was not about race, but did require a respect for ancestry (including racial history) as well as honesty in one's musical expression. Michael learned from many of the jazz masters in the Detroit area and spent time in parts of Europe and Africa. His compositions and interests came to reflect both a global vision of jazz and a perspective of "justice" that takes into account the impact that the sacrifices of the African-American jazz community have had on his own career. His comments illuminate the importance of understanding the ancestry of one's art, of respecting the wisdom that has come before you, and of recognizing the general dynamic of *creolization* that has shaped his own life and career:

> *"When I was a teenager, my father was a church organist. I learned to play piano… all the classic jazz. I just fell in love with it. I listened to a lot of things, from Bach to jazz artists. I quit sports and went into music. About this time, I heard Sam Sanders play, and I wanted to be able to play with those guys. Luckily, God gifted me to be able to play. When I was 18, I started to work with the cats in Detroit. They were all very supportive. If you were blowing it, they'd let you know. But most of the learning was on the scene, and most of the cats you played with were way better than you. That makes a difference.*

> *"I started playing cocktail jobs, in restaurants, worked with vocalists, and playing arrangements that were from show, to classical, to jazz. Charles Boles, (a local Detroit legend) said, 'You have to listen to the masters to get it.'*

> *"I hate to speak of black and white; I deplore the racial division. But in Africa, age increases your social status and respect. In villages, the older wise-man sits in the middle of the circle. Sam Sanders took me on a tour to Africa. I remember Sam used to say, 'You aren't really mature until you are older.' It's a heavy respect for the life cycle. This is very similar to how jazz is learned— it's an oral history—and one that must be based upon respect for your elders.*

"In education circles, if it's not written, it may be perceived as less legitimate. But the oral history is the basis of learning jazz and much of African tradition as well. There are a lot of excellent jazz musicians who could probably write out their solos, but the point of jazz is not to play it the same way twice. I believe that having that much of a gift for creativity is special. There's a correlation between the respect or lack of respect musical styles receive in the university based upon how close they are to the tradition of perfecting something that has been written down.

"In jazz, you respected the ancestry. Like any art form, culture, language, you're always learning based upon what comes before you. People say improvisation is spontaneous creativity— but it's really creative re-ordering. I mean you have to know the sounds and patterns to play them. The past leads to the future. You're re-ordering the sounds.

"Art Tatum (pianist from the 1920s through early 1950s) was so advanced harmonically, but much of what he did led to the McCoy Tyner's or Herbie Hancock's (contemporary pianists from the 1960s to the beginning of 21st century). If you did not stay connected to the music of the past, your own work would not grow.

"I respect the sacrifice of our American 'griots' or storytellers, which is a lot of what our blues and jazz musicians are ... musical storytellers. Much of what we have in our culture is blocked by the perceptions of race. And there is still so much institutionalized racism.

Pic. 10.28A *Jazz musicians and teacher Vincent York and "Jazzistry" play and teach the ancestry of jazz – as a creative reminder of the importance of learning about our ancestry.* Photo: Courtesy V. York, Authors.

Even people who don't think they are affected are definitely affected because if you live here, your mind has to be divided.

"What I have to do as a white artist is recognize that this history exists. Then I must make my actions and my music demonstrate—not in words, but action— that I am trying to respect and grasp the depth of the sacrifice our African-American ancestors—especially those musicians from the past—made on my, and all of our behalves.

"Clearly, jazz is the embodiment of the world of fusion. But for now, much of this world vision has been forged upon the sacrifices of primarily black musicians ... and this must be respected if you are to play or appreciate jazz." (Interview: April 2005)

CD 4.3

"12 Steps," by Michael Zaporski, from the CD: <u>**Insight,**</u> c. Daddy Z., 2003.

Mr. Zaporski commented: *"Jazz is constantly morphing. If you take the piece the "12 Steps," I'm using 20th-century music from a classical context, with all my other experiences, especially the blues. Like all the old cats used to say, 'It's all based upon the blues.' There are blues overtones in all American music. The '12 Steps' is based upon the 12-bar blues (a repetitive twelve-measure structure). Much of it also takes elements that I learned from Sam (Sanders). The whole idea about hooking African musical culture to 'America's classical music'— which is what I consider jazz to be— is to create a fusion of the present connected to the past.*

"We flat the 3rd, 5th, and 7th of our scale—and we call that blues. But that's because that's the best adaptation we have on our European instruments of how our African-American ancestry carried their tonal scales into our evolution. At any rate, I try to synthesize the sum total of my experiences. I'll use the example of Bartok; I take certain structures of what I know and adapt them to my experiences, just as Bartok did with the music of the 'gypsy' cultures in many of his compositions.

"Do you have to feel the blues to play it? Of course! You have to know the history, and it must be understood, not only in your head, but in your heart. It's not the notes; it's not a formula that can be learned like you study algebra. Anyway, that's where I'm at today. And one of my greatest mentors, Sam Sanders, told me repeatedly, 'Anything is possible.' Maybe that's the best definition of jazz or creolization: anything is possible!"

Other "Visions" of Creolization

Once we see humanity beyond the narrow perspectives of race, nation, gender, religion, or other categories that obscure or block integration, fusion, and exchange (or their perception), then we become liberated to see and value the dynamics of creolization, cultural fusion, and exchange. Perhaps only then do we acquire the perceptual tools to fully appreciate "jazz" and the creativity in many other musical styles throughout the world.

Some of the music we will explore below share the formulae innate to jazz (i.e., those of creating a structure over which improvisation and spontaneous creativity are laid). Other styles are more structured and composed (i.e., their improvisations are negotiated and solidified for precise repetition). All, however, share the dynamics of creating a *fusion* of the cultural and musical worlds of the musicians. In this sense, the music reflects the natural law of human existence—that we view and assimilate elements of our environment, then merge them with the unique expressions of our experiences. The active creole, or creative, mind, and especially that of the artist, is therefore not limited by restrictions of race, time, or space, but rather freely explores the interconnections that exist between all things.

Stories from the Human Family

"I've been in the states (U.S.A.) two years now. I'm from Eritrea (a small country north of Ethiopia in North Africa). I'm so grateful to have the opportunity to study in the U.S.A. American students really don't know how many opportunities they have. I would never have been able to study as I do now if I were still in Er-

itrea. So I make sure I take advantage of every course, every opportunity. I don't understand why many American students are so careless with their opportunities. And, also — I really don't like the racial division — both whites and blacks, as they call each other, are so quick to judge each other. But not based upon a full understanding— before they even get to know each other.

"Unfortunately, there is a way you're supposed to act when you're 'black' and another way when you're 'white.' Each person is

Pic. 10.28B *The Hager Fikir Theatre in Addis Ababa (capital city of Ethiopia) is not only one of the oldest "indigenous" theaters in one of the oldest civilizations in Africa, but the natural home for the blending of ancient storytelling traditions with traditions as diverse as Shakespeare and modern jazz.* Photo: Courtesy, Steffen Wurzel.

therefore bound not by who they potentially can become, but by some ridiculous belief in what a "white or black" person is supposed to be. I'm "black," and I'm going to be an architect. My friends are from every part of the world, and I have not been raised with the limitations most people in the U.S. feel compelled to live by. Although so many people think that we are primitive in Africa–the news broadcasts and the absence of our history in their schools and on the news except for the famines and wars is a clear indication of what they think of Africa.

Pic. 10.29 *Greek-born artist Georges Behrakis works on a painting in the artist district of Montmarte, Paris. He told us that his dad had left Greece and gone to the United States—and that later he came to Paris to study art. He has now been there for more than forty years. He emphasized: "No culture owns art. Art is the product of the human mind and spirit. No culture has a monopoly on that." Perhaps that is why every art form is both subject to change and unbound by a nationality.* Photo: Authors.

But in the context of a healthy global vision … who is primitive? The one that still lives by imaginary categories and who ignores a high percentage of the world, who does not have a global vision; or the one that sees not only history more accurately, but the world as a single country—and therefore sees all the opportunities and options our planet offers?" Alexander Tekie, Eritrea (born) / Ethiopia (lived), now in Washington, D.C., 2001.

The question is not *whether* a culture has undergone an extensive process of creolization or cultural fusion and exchange over time, but *in what manner* and to what degree it *recognizes* or values the inevitable human phenomenon. In present-day societies, the mere presence of movie theaters, televisions, airports, and computers with Internet access makes it virtually impossible for any culture to exclude itself from either global contact or exchange. The more important issue, however, is the degree to which a culture is conscious of the extent to which their values and identity have been altered over time. In this sense, it is entirely possible for a culture group to be unaware of its singular cultural identity, unwilling to expand beyond ideas of a fixed ancestry, or ignorant of the manner in which their own "traditions" are changing. Creolization waits for no closed mind, or closed perception, to its existence!

In most parts of the world, what many call *folkloric* music (older stages in a country's creolization process) is performed on stages and in festivals honoring the culture's ancestry. The young adults of each generation who learn these traditions wear new interpretations of traditional costumes, dance altered versions of dances, and perform to music played by instruments and through sound systems, on stages and in settings never envisioned by the ancestors they honor. Some connected to these celebrations feel that the loss of ancestry would be a tragedy and that it should be preserved at all cost. Others may embrace the changes and feel that the nature of life itself is change. In most cases, there is little likelihood that many of us are able to recognize the degree to which even the most ancient of our traditions and practices have morphed and changed over time. It is a challenge to nearly all of our ancestors' perception of the world, to re-envision history through the lens of creolization. But without this alteration in our perception, is it history we are viewing?

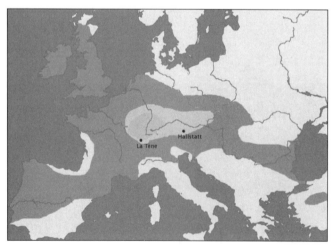
Map displaying Celtic presence 800-400BCE.

Celtic Connections

The influence of the Celts and the subsequent Indo-European languages spawned by Celtic-derived cultures dates back further than 500 BCE and reaches from the furthest point of western Spain to the westernmost part of China. The influence and culture of the Celts (Keltos), originally from Central Europe, varied according to the political or religious values of each people and time period. From the 17th century on, "Celtic" culture and history were centered in what some historians call "the seven Celtic nations": Ireland, Wales, Scotland, Cornwall, the Isle of Man, Brittany, and Galicia. This region stretches from the British Isles through western France to northwestern Spain.

Thus, Celtic influence is variously evident in French, Anglo-Saxon, and Germanic communities. In turn, *nearly all the cultures* colonized by Western Europe or settled by Western Europeans are extensively influenced by these Celtic-based cultures. In terms of music and dance, Celtic-derived creolizations, from the country dances or contredanse of the British and French to the jigs and reels of the Irish and Scottish, are contributors to a high percentage of today's music.

Naturally, each style of music and dance as practiced in Europe has changed in both function and expression. However, the creolization process of these musical and dance forms in Canada and the United States remains vivid. The music of Appalachia, bluegrass music, Western swing, country or square dances, and later fusions—polkas, waltzes, and other popular music and dance styles—all evolved from the European continent and its "pan-Celtic" fusions.

In recent decades, European dance and song forms have easily crossed the ocean into the Americas by transport or airwaves. Celtic-derived music, particularly the jigs and reels with improvisatory roots (formulas which encourage metamorphosis through continued 're-creativity'), fused with African and African-American music to emerge as zydeco and country-western swing, or "Riverdance" and clogging-style dances, from the "gumboot" dancing of South Africa, to "step-dancing" performed in many sororities and fraternities throughout the United States. In fact, the similarity of such musical-dance elements as "foot tapping/ dancing" in clogging and tap dancing; the improvisational melodies in country dances, bluegrass, jazz, and blues; and the similarities of community and social contexts in which these music and dance genres appear, cause one to delight in how diverse and far-reaching the creolization process can extend.

Pic. 10.29A *Steven Duffy, of Scottish background in his pipers' garb, takes a break in a Windsor pub after having played a wedding in Windsor's famed "Guild Hall." Although the history among the British, Scottish, and Irish has been rocky at best, after centuries of exchange, cross-influencing, and intermarriage, the reality is generally quite different than the perception.* Photo: Authors.

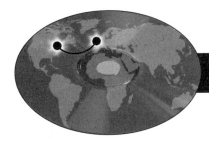

Inside the Musician's World

Mackinaw,
Music from Quebec

Note: Creolization in Ireland began with the migratory settlement of the Celts (700-500 BCE); then followed the occupation of the Vikings, and much later the Normans (from Normandy). After nearly 400 years of military campaigns by England, Ireland's many cultures were "united" as a political addendum to the British Empire in the 16th century.

Although a part of the United Kingdom politically, the Irish (and particularly its Catholic majority) suffered

numerous forms of discrimination at the hands of the largely Protestant British government. In the mid-1800s a combination of repressive politics and the potato blight caused by poor agricultural technique led to nearly a half-million deaths and the migration of millions of Irish to the Americas.

In the Americas, many Irish again experienced discrimination at the hands of the British-derived majority. In the United States, large Irish populations moved into the mountain regions of the U.S. (Appalachian, Blue Ridge) and to Quebec, Canada. In the latter, the Irish would find greater acceptance in the French regions, the French-Canadian population having also experienced discrimination both during and since the establishment of British rule in 1760.

In addition to the connections of Quebec's culture to the Irish/Celtic past cited above, a substantial part of France was home to the earliest Celtic settlements in western and northern France (Normandy). As we have seen in prior units, fueled by repression and "minority-hood" (the state of being considered less valid in a culture's hierarchy), cultures generally place greater importance upon their musical/dance identity. In such instances, the creolization process (creative exchange and fusion) also is given a boost through spontaneous creativity (improvisation).

CD 4.4

Pic. 10.30A *Everywhere in the African Diaspora, we can find music that blends Celtic, European, and African-American (Pan-African-American) influences. The music of zydeco in general, and of Buckwheat Zydeco (pictured here), is a complete blend of musical innovations from around the planet — with a good dose of individual creativity thrown in for good measure.* Photo: Courtesy, "Horsepunchkid."

"Reel des éboulements (Rockfall Reel)," by Mackinac, from the CD: <u>**Folk Music from Quebec,**</u> Arc Music International, c. 2000.

The group "Mackinaw" takes its name from a local Native American word used to describe the checkered jacket worn by the Canadian lumberjacks. The group members write about their Quebec origins: *"Since Mackinaw's foundation in 1974, hundreds of folklorists and lovers of popular art have fashioned this company and propelled it beyond its initial status of a dance troupe."* As "Mackinaw" performs its multiple variations of Canadian music not only for its own people but also for others at "international festivals," they continue to craft changes in their "traditional" music. Having toured France, Switzerland, Hungary, South Korea, Spain, (the former) Yugoslavia, Tunisia, Belgium, Italy, and widely throughout the United States and Canada, they have learned that each trip brings a "new" idea, an altered movement, or a change in props or costuming.

In all cases, the musicians exchange qualities and components with musicians and dancers throughout regions influenced by Celtic cultures or the Francophone regions colonized by France. It is common to hear similarities in such diverse cultures as northeastern Canada; both the French and British Islands of the Caribbean; Irish, Scottish and French-influenced regions of Europe (Belgium, Switzerland, and France); and virtually every other region colonized or settled by French or British Isle (Celtic-derived) cultures.

The Recipe of Sound

The music's "cut-time" meter, shuffle rhythm (a four-beat structure that emphasizes only the first and third beats that essentially becomes a two-beat structure with four sub-divisions per beat) is immediately reminiscent of the "quadrilles" and contredanse (country dances) heard in nearly all Celtic/French-influenced regions. Somewhere between a binary form (two repeating sections moving from the tonic to dominant and back to the tonic) and a rondo (a repeating section alternating with new melodic sections), this piece features a contrast between the stabile, repetitive form of the music and the varied "improvisational" influences of the rhythm section (the bass, drums and piano). A sonograph of the piece might read:

A Main Melody	B 2nd Melody
Intro ‖: 2-beat (polka)- 8 measures w/alternate endings :‖	‖: Similar rhythm, stronger accents, beats: 2 & 4 :‖

A	C 3rd Melody
‖: Repeat Main Melody :‖	‖: Begins 2-beat—moves to walking (4-beat) jazz bass pattern :‖

A Repeat Main melody	B Repeat 2nd Melody
‖: Note increase of rhythm activity :‖	‖: Utilizes walking bass and stronger accents on 2 & 4 throughout :‖

A Repeat Main Melody	C Repeat 3rd melody (one time only to end)
‖: Increase in rhythmic improvisation :‖	‖: Special improvisation in piano to ending ‖

Creolization is clearly evident in the relationship of the rhythm section musicians to the melody. In the strongly accented shuffle rhythms (with accents on the blues/rhythm-and-blues-influenced back beats on beats two and four), the walking bass, and the instrumentally improvised communication between rhythm section members, the parallel affinities between Celtic-fusion music (which has these qualities) and that of many American or African Diaspora fusions (including zydeco, rhythm-and-blues, and jazz) can be heard.

Our World Today

There are many reasons why we might attach ourselves to our pasts even though they are based upon nationally, racially, or culturally-divided traditions or perceptions. Much of our personal history is woven into the myths, stories, and instructions of our parents and grandparents. Engaging in a predisposition towards nation or race, or the focusing on any of the stages in a culture's creolization, are not negative if balanced by both a regard for the value of others' cultural/human evolution, and the larger picture of creolization or human exchange globally. However, specific expressions or cultural manifestations in technology (instruments), stories (songs, lyrics, poetry, and expressions in language), and musical formulae are the tools by which our humanity has been passed from culture to culture with ever-increasing speed and intensity over successive generations.

To conclude this look into "Our Musical World," as our flexibility and understanding of creolization (as well as all processes of interconnectivity) increases, we will no longer focus solely on the manner in which people and expressions are separate from "our world," but instead the manner in which they reflect inclusion and inter-connection to it. The following are some of the ways to examine creative fusion in musical genres:

Musical Creolization Principles and Dynamics

Does the music demonstrate clear-cut connections across generations through—

➤ The transference of older instruments or sounds of instruments (frequently experienced today through the use of digital sampling and synthesis)?

➤ The incorporation of melodies, rhythms, or form and structure of genres from the past to the present?

Does the music demonstrate clear-cut connections across cultures through—

➤ The incorporation of instruments or musical elements, especially the flow of the music over time (rhythm)?

➤ The transference of practice and connection to events which marke the cycle of life or to the natural processes of building and maintaining human communities (concerts/events)?

Does the music defy common stereotypes, biases, and perceived boundaries of separation, especially between—

➤ "Races"? Musical genres that are frequently perceived as being connected to "white," "Asian," "black," etc. – are seldom, if ever, relevant in this context.

➤ National identities? Again, the political foundation of "nation states" bears little resemblance to the evolution of human cultures, and the nature of creolization seldom is influenced substantially by these political/economic entities or creations.

Pic. 10.31 A & B *In the midst of perpetual fusion, tourists move from culture to culture much like honey bees between flowers. Each visit, each film, each piece of music, or, in this case, a boat ride down the Seine through Paris (above) places individuals from around the world in direct contact with another culture's creolization process. Our perceptions of "who" or "what" a culture is are based on the numerous layers of information we take in. Here, (right), the original 'Statue of Liberty' is superimposed upon the headquarters of multinational corporations of modern-day France. Nevertheless, tourists generally will take with them the images and perceptions of their own design. What we seek, we will find—but will this be either the reality or the nature of the culture as it perceives itself?* Photos: Authors.

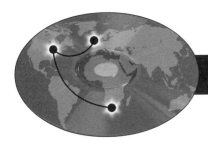 *Inside the Musician's World*

Chris Collins

"Nearly five years ago, while I was on a jazz concert tour in Scotland, a good friend from Glasgow took me to Dublin, Ireland, to hear the music of my cultural heritage. As a jazz musician, I immediately felt comfortable walking into the pub that served as the performance venue for this unfamiliar folk music. As we waded our way through the pool of Guinness-drinking patrons, I began to hear bits of exhilarating music poking through the din of conversation in the pub. The closer we got to the collected tables that formed the make-shift bandstand at the back of the pub, the quieter the crowd. Once we had squeezed our way into the back room, I found families, young and old, focused on three fiddlers, two flautists, a button accordion player, and a bohdran player playing music that, although it occasionally provoked complimentary hoots and foot stomping, consistently encouraged reverence and sheer joy from all gathered around.

"After my initial awe of the scene, my musical mind began to focus on the unique dance rhythms, interactive thematic improvisations, endless repertoire, and performance practice. Despite the dance roots and folk appeal of this music, it displayed a stunning level of thematic complexity, improvisation, and interaction. Although much of this music was foreign to my ears, the idea of a music of the people built on an underlying foundation of complex elements and technical demands was a paradigm familiar to me as an American jazz artist, including the following key foundational practices:

1. *stylistic/thematic improvisation;*

2. *a history of aural dissemination;*

3. *strong influence and connection to dance and movement;*

4. *regional stylistic variations;*

5. *dissemination of repertoire and performance practice from master to student at sessions in common venues (pubs, clubs, etc.) as opposed to concert-hall performances;*

6. *intensive interaction between performers determines melodic variations, style, and repertoire of each performance;*

7. *embracement by all socioeconomic levels with both genres artistically rendering history, folklore, and life experiences of the performers and composers;*

8. *performer's aesthetic.*

"This exposure to the live folk music of Ireland was the first step in a new direction in my life. As an Irish-American musician, I have found the intensive study of this music's history, repertoire, and methods of dissemination a key to understanding my cultural heritage and an aid to defining my individualism as a jazz

musician and composer.

"Over the past four years, the musical and conceptual elements of the research began to naturally seep into my jazz woodwind playing and compositional style. Throughout its history, jazz music has embraced many world music influences. I have been committed to creating a true fusion that demonstrates respect for the history, depth, and artists from both cultures. This work was not about simply putting a backbeat behind a jig or over a traditional Irish reel.

"Over the course of this project, the participating American jazz and Irish folk musicians experienced a heightened awareness of each other's culture, history, and musical vocabulary. Generally, common points of reference instill confidence in participants and listeners while the artistic fusion of two musical cultures and vocabularies inspires fresh thinking and new creative goals. Research and artistic initiatives of this type inevitably facilitate new lines of communication, reveal music/artistic/cultural commonalities, and create fresh collaborative artistic goals between artists of different cultures."

"Muirruhgachs, Mermaids, and Mami Wata," by Chris Collins, from the CD: **Chris Collins and Jazz from the Shamrock Shore,** c. Harriett Jazz Records, 2005.

Mr. Collins commented, *"The CD presented my compositions for penny whistle, harp, fiddle, Irish flute, drums, piano, bass, clarinet, and saxophone. During my global travels as a performing jazz musician, I have developed numerous long-term personal and artistic relationships. I have found the cross-cultural artistic and academic collaborations that result from these relationships to be*

Pic. 10.32A *An Irish band at Penn State University demonstrates the vibrant creole nature of Irish/Celtic cultures, the influence of generations of "repression" of the creative intensity of the culture, and the flexibility of individuals brought up in such cultures to adapt (creolize) to new influences.* Photo: Courtesy, "Deeptrivia."

a guiding force in my artistic evolution and the key to my cultural awareness and sensitivity.

"'Muirruhgachs, Mermaids, and Mami Wata' features Susan Bailey on fiddle, Gary Schunk on piano, Kersten Allvin on harp, Jeff Halsey on bass, and David Taylor on drums and percussion, along with myself on clarinet, penny whistles, tenor sax, and flute.

"Nearly every culture in the world has a legend describing a creature which is half-man and half-fish. In Ireland, these are known as Muirruhgachs and Murrows. The females are described as quite beautiful while the males are a bit goofy with large noses, bright red hair, and a passion for brandy. This composition uses low-D whistle, fiddle, clarinet, jazz improvisation, and African percussive and rhythmic elements to impressionistically capture a joyous reunion of the Muirruhgachs of Ireland, the Mermaids of America, and the Mami Wata of Africa. In 2002, my 'Jazz from the Shamrock Shore' band toured throughout South Africa presenting concerts and educational workshops. Each concert concluded with a performance of 'Muirruhgachs, Mermaids, and Mami Wata.'"

The Recipe of Sound

Mr. Collins writes: *"Musically, the composition draws on Irish melodic themes/ instruments, jazz harmonies, and African polyrhythms. The unique balance of cultural elements allowed South African percussionists, whistle players, and fiddle players to join us for an inspiring concert closer. The joint rehearsal and resulting performance demonstrated knowledge of each other's folk music and respect for our similarities and differences."*

This piece begins with many of the elements standard to jazz repertoire: an ostinato or repetitive pattern in the rhythm section to introduce the "groove" or rhythmic flow, a "head" or melody (in this case, Irish melody on penny whistle), a bridge or second melody that elevates the tension from the first melody, and then the third section– compositionally complex and which features perpetual interplay between the clarinet, violin, piano, and rhythm section. It includes the exchange of melody, multiple breaks and transitions in time and rhythm, and other elements, which suggest a fusion of modern 20th-century "classical" (art) music formulas with jazz. This fusion of "classical" and jazz is also a facet of creolization not to be taken lightly.

From Scott Joplin's rag opera "Tremonisha" and Duke Ellington's "Concerto for Cootie" to numerous compositions of the present, the creole nature of American jazz has continually re-fused its elements with those of European and African cultural origins.

Pic. 10.32B *It may seem natural to see such a complete "hodge-podge" of instruments on a single stage—and it should! For centuries, our collective ancestors have been passing traditions, ideas, and the products of their creativity to the farthest corners of the Earth. What may be "new," and the bi-product of recent technologies, is our perception of this ancient tradition.* Photo: Authors.

The JAZZ Experience

Michael's Experience with Jazz Improvisation

Have you ever "free-styled" (spontaneously made up) a poem, speech, or rap? Spontaneously doodled or drawn an image (where you did not anticipate the outcome)? Invented a culinary dish, or made up a story "on the spot"? If you have, then you are familiar with the art of improvisation (or spontaneous composition). The art of improvisation is marvelous in fostering trust in one's creativity. It is the centerpiece of jazz music. But there is a series of steps every single jazz musician follows on the path to spontaneous creativity:

- **First** – Every jazz musician must learn a vocabulary of expressive traits and techniques on their instrument: scales, patterns of notes, an assortment of keys; learn to change or alter their tone quality according to the style of the music; learn how to keep an internal and regular beat and to play over this beat with a variety of rhythms; and learn to listen carefully to what is being played by others. (In the jazz world, pre-learned patterns on an instrument are called "licks.")

- **Second** – Each jazz musician will (to varying degrees) learn a variety of "standards" or musical pieces from the evolution of jazz ancestry. As in all areas of music (and this is probably true in all areas of art in general), the degree to which a musician will obtain respect for the ancestry of the genre or draw from the widest possible range of musicians in their field will determine the degree to which they are given respect by those knowledgeable about the genre.

  "Once you... buy into this idea of a youth-driven culture, you've bought into one of the greatest fallacies ever perpetrated on a group of younger people: that you have to be removed from older people in order to express your youth. They (elders) bring a wisdom and an understanding to you, and you bring an exuberance to them." From: "Wynton Marsalis Speaks Out," February 27, 2004, Franz A. Matzner, http://www.allaboutjazz.com

- **Third** – Each jazz musician will need to create a sense of community with other musicians. In most cases, it is even more important that the musicians work together well, are interested in each other's lives, and are concerned for each other's development, than that they are exceptional musicians. After some rehearsal or discussion, or just based on experience wherein a plan for the form (flow) of the piece is made, they are ready for the "jazz" experience.

- **Finally** – With the first three prerequisites in place, the jazz experience may now begin. If the musicians have prepared themselves personally and professionally, they may now play through the composition—and "create spontaneously" (improvise) based on the emotion and synergy of the group, the outpouring of energy, and the connectivity between musicians and audience. This—IS jazz.

Activity: Group Work

- *Pick a topic of interest to everyone in the group. (If you wish, discuss some of the important features or concerns of the topic in the group).*

- *Next, establish a steady beat/pulse (moderately slow to begin) over which each person in the group will "spontaneously create" (improvise) a poem, a "rap," a story-dance, a mime piece, or a rhythmic or theatrical story, etc. (Those creating the beat may also "improvise" changes in the rhythm to support the rap, story, etc.).*

- *Finally, return to the original beat after each as you go from one member of the group to another, each creating their work spontaneously.*

- *Try not to acknowledge "mistakes"—as there are no mistakes when we improvise, only a stream of creative energy (try not to break the stream until you feel you've completed what you have to say). Above all...have fun.*

Stories from the Human Family

Note: One of the most deceptive myths among appreciators of "classical" or "art" music and those of secular or "folk" music is the distinct possibility that these *separate worlds* rarely if ever exist in complete autonomy. Since the beginning of recorded history, the everyday world and the world explored by the "best" (most innovative and creative) composers, musicians, and artists, or those that seek to connect us with the Creator and those that reflect our everyday existence, have been intermingled and mutually influential. Many of our world's folk artists and bearers of oral traditions have written songs and pieces inspired by their perception of the "Creator" or based on either the influence of "classical" composers or the "schooled" and lauded artists of their own generations. Similarly, not a single piece of classical or sacred art is bereft of the influence of the street musicians, artists, and creative improvisers of their day. Human creativity seldom is exclusive and is far less pious, political, or separatist than generally believed by many who have critiqued or categorized it over time.

From this perspective, it is very possible for one to revel in the beauty of a Beethoven symphony and yet still feel equally the depth of a blues piece or a Ghanaian drum pattern. The prerequisite, then, is never to place a greater-than or lesser-than value on either the music or the culture from which it comes.

We met Professor Tini in Unit VI as a chorale conductor. Now we have the opportunity to hear from him again, this time as a jazz artist and educator. The critical element is to see the possibility of connecting music across not only cultures but also the formidable boundaries reinforced by the systems used in the education of music itself. In elevating or demoting one music as being more "classic" or worthy of study, other musical genres could become less "worthy." To bridge the worlds of music and find equal value requires a strong sense of justice and self-worth as well as a certain amount of tenacity in dealing with institutional practices. Professor Tini tells his story:

"I started music at an early age. My father was a professional musician. He influenced all of us—my brother Ray who plays bass, my cousin Larry who played woodwinds, and myself. We started at five years old. He was an accordionist who had made it nationally. We all started on accordion; then I switched to piano. We had music around us all the time. He did radio broadcasts in New York as he was both a classical accordionist as well as popular. We always had band musicians around us. Even at family parties, the uncles and everybody would all play, and then we were the "B" band, the sons and cousins who would play afterwards. In time, we would go out to play.

"In public school I became heavily involved in the classical end of music. In junior high school, they would let me write arrangements, and then in high school I would begin to conduct. It was also in high school that I would do the jazz thing as well, working three nights a week playing in restaurants or clubs.

"Keeping the two cultures open was important. During the daytime I would do classical music and studies, and then at night I would play jazz. There was a time when there was a lot of resistance to doing jazz in the university environment. At one point, I even left the university because it seemed that jazz would not

Pic. 10.32C *St. Charles Bridge in Prague (Czech Republic) models the ancient reality of "classical (trained) art" and "folk art" mingling and cross-influencing each other—now over centuries.* Photo: Authors.

be respected. That was in the late 1960s. After doing some film work and playing regularly as a jazz pianist, I eventually returned to the university. Keeping them both going is essential to me. It's much like the yin and yang process. It keeps me balanced. It feels perfectly natural to me."

Concerning music education, Professor Tini commented: "In this country (U. S.A.) we're a bit behind other parts of the world in teaching or nurturing creativity through music. I think we're pretty rigid still. Although I see the curriculum, I think that there is not enough fluidity and interdisciplinarity yet. We nurture techniques and skills, but we do not necessarily teach risk-taking, creativity, and the flexibility that the students will need to make music later. If the student has the passion, they may follow this path on their own, but if not, they will not get it from the curriculum.

"Today, we tend to teach technicians, many of whom may have a passion for the music, but the creativity and spirit of the composers that created these works, or the degree to which the spirit of those creative moments of the past are generated in the works of the musicians of today, are somewhat stunted by the manner of education. I think a lot of our people have to find it outside of the classroom. The boxes are somewhat in error. Music may be like a sphere, but we're frequently attempting to put it into square holes."

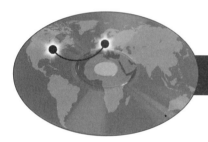

Inside the Musician's World

Dennis Tini and Quartet

"Conducting the chorale or the chorus and orchestra, especially after you've done all the rehearsal on the mechanics of notes or fixing the blending of voices, I find that because of a concentration and focus and all variables are working together in a positive musical way, I get to some pretty intense states of music making. It takes over everything. It's not about ego or mechanics; it becomes an expression of making the music. It's like going into the next state of consciousness—it may be emotion or the spirituality of the piece— whatever you want to communicate, but I get lost in it. I'm in a different sphere of consciousness.

Dennis Tini (right) on piano.

"In the jazz area, it comes in a different way. It comes frequently when you're working with good musicians and you can go beyond the normal or mechanical. Even on bad nights, we have good moments—those moments when the musicians get to the same plane. There are different mechanics in jazz and classical music. There is more of a spontaneous reaction process that is essential to jazz. In classical music, the reaction to the moment is less spontaneous and is based upon organization, rehearsal, and collective unity, whereas in jazz there is a collective unity, but it is based upon the moment and the conversation musically between the musicians."

"Les Yeux de la Jeunesse (The Eyes of Youth)," by Dennis Tini, from the CD: **The Eyes of Youth,** c. Nicole Tini Music 2004.

"I wrote the piece when I was living in Switzerland. The little kids, nieces, and nephews were sitting by the fireplace. One night I was just looking at their eyes sparkling by the fire, and I just sat down at the piano, and the melody just came out. Inspired by those little kids and their purity, it just flowed out as a complete entity. Later that night, I woke up and went back to the piano, and the lyrics just poured out as well. I hadn't written a lot of lyrics—but they just poured out as well.

"This was in the French part of Switzerland, and since I had been hearing so much French, the title, "Les Yeux de la Jeunese." At any rate, I had initially thought of it as a male voice, but when I gave it to my wife, who is an accomplished jazz singer and instructor of vocal jazz, she did a beautiful job with it as well. This piece was just one of those inspirational moments that seemed to have a destiny of its own."

Fusion Example: Gospel Music Today

In the United States, as spirituals became more closely connected to the Christian-African community, and as African-Americans moved north (especially during the Industrial Revolution of the 1920s and '30s), the devotional music of the now-urban African-American community changed to reflect the new environment. Just as traditional jazz and delta blues made their way north into urban centers, and singing and handclapping became more extensively augmented with urban technology and instruments, especially the organ, spirituals gave way to what has since been classified simply as *"gospel music."*

As with other musical genres, there is no shortage of documented evidence to show the cross-assimilation of gospel music across the racial and cultural divides. As African-American gospel music evolved, more pervasively than ever, the assimilation of European hymnody and church rituals influenced the evolution of the "black" church's music. Just as pervasive in European-American churches in the South, however, was the fusion and "borrowing" of African-American spirituals and gospel music in the evolution

Pic. 10.34 *Whether in the United States, South America, or, in this case, Cuba, musicians on street corners through much of the week would find themselves in church or at mass on the weekends or special occasions. In many cases, the instruments and song forms from the street would immediately appear in church, or the music from the church would end up on the street. Sometimes, as in Catholic exchanges, the influences might be more subtle, but still present.* Photo: Courtesy of "Faut," 1961, Montreal.

Pic. 10.35 *Mahalia Jackson (October 26, 1911–January 13, 1972) was widely regarded as one of the best in the history of gospel music. She grew up in the "Black Pearl" section of the Carrollton neighborhood of uptown New Orleans, Louisiana, and began singing in a Baptist church. She moved to Chicago, Illinois, in 1927, where she sang with The Johnson Brothers, one of the earliest professional gospel groups. Jackson's fame in the late 1950s and early 1960s continued to rise when she recorded with Percy Faith and performed at both the 1958 Newport Jazz Festival and the inauguration of John F. Kennedy. She also sang at the funeral of her friend, Martin Luther King, Jr. Jackson died in 1972 in Chicago and was buried in Providence Memorial Park, Metairie, Louisiana. She was posthumously inducted into the Gospel Music Association's Gospel Music Hall of Fame in 1978.*

of "white" church music, its revivals, and its own brand of gospel music. What can never be over-emphasized, however, is the role "gospel" music has played in the solidarity of the "black" community, especially in the face of racism.

In Northern urban centers such as New York, Philadelphia, Detroit, and Chicago, the African-American church proliferated in neighborhoods, just as blues joints and social clubs were used for the after-hours release from arduous work schedules. But just as important, young musicians streamed out of the churches into social settings and, later, into recording studios. The evolution, therefore, of gospel music parallels, and has been influenced by many of America's musical genres.

Thomas A. Dorsey, James Cleveland, and Mahalia Jackson are among those who made gospel music not just music, but a way of life. In Detroit, for example, as the automobile industry began to thrive, African-Americans gravitated into the city for employment and a chance for a better material life. The newly formed churches and revival centers became breeding grounds for some of America's most loved and influential artists and musical styles. Now, the integration of religion and daily life, so essential to African-American survival from the depths of slavery, was given new life in the North. Out of the church in Detroit alone evolved the music of Barry Gordy and "Motown," including artists such as Diana Ross, the Temptations, the Four Tops, Stevie Wonder, the Jacksons, and later, nearly every artist from early Motown to Aretha Franklin and the Winan family.

Generally, the African-American church and the music and cultural life extending from the church gave hope to the people growing up in a repressive system. It also gave a wealth of vibrant music to the world. Since most African cultures did not separate religion and the affairs of daily life, to hear the songs and sounds of work, love, and life in the streets and then later in the churches, or the reverse — that the sounds of the church would influence the songs of the "streets" – should not be surprising. This is yet another variation of creolization.

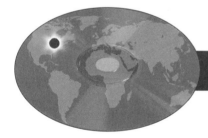

Inside the Musician's World

Carl B. Phillips
and the PAB Singers

Note: Any number of gospel groups in a large city such as Detroit, Michigan, could have contributed a diversity of expressive music that demonstrates the fu-

sion of gospel music's past with the present. We sent out a call to numerous churches locally, and within moments received responses. Among them, this song and comments from Mr. Carl Phillips. Mr. Phillips wrote, *"During the Civil Rights movements of the '60s and the early '70s, the black church was a dominant force in driving for racial equality for the African-American community. The pulpit gave a weekly platform for the black preachers to compare the bondage of the Israelites to the bondage of the black community in the United States. From these weekly platforms, such black leaders as Rev. Martin Luther King Jr., Rev. Jessie Jackson, and even Malcolm X, rose to national prominence as they empowered the black community through their riveting sermons and speeches.*

"Today's black church takes a different role by encouraging the 'bringing down of walls' so that all races can worship together and respect each other's cultures. For example, religious leaders such as Bishop T.D. Jakes advocate crossing racial barriers; the role of the black church is less militant in its attempt to bring healing from racism. The days of the Civil Rights movements also incorporated early gospel singers such as Mahalia Jackson, Sam Cooke, and Aretha Franklin to sing messages of hope and freedom for the blacks that were enduring racial inequalities. Such songs as Mahalia's 'How I Got Over,' Aretha's 'Precious Lord,' and Sam Cooke's 'A Change Is Gonna Come' reminded those in the struggle of God's promise to deliver them.

"Over time, gospel music has changed and fused continually with the needs and sounds of each age. In the late '60s, a youth choir from California, in an effort to raise funds for their church organization, made a recording of the church hymn "Oh Happy Day" (from the musical Godspell). The choir's recording, under the leadership of Edwin Hawkins, continues to be popular to this day. Such gospel artists as Kirk Franklin, Yolanda Adams, Donnie McClurkin, Hezekiah Walker, and J Moss now have their music played on secular and gospel radio. Gospel artists now have gold and platinum albums representing sales from 500,000 to 1,000,00. Gospel music has always reflected the music of the day, from the blues keyboards of the father of gospel music, Thomas Dorsey, to the sampling of secular music by the father of hip- hop gospel music, Kirk Franklin. The method of delivery has changed; however, the message and context of gospel music remains the same."

"Let Them See Jesus," by Carl Phillips and the PAB Singers, Detroit, Michigan, from the CD: <u>**Let Them See Jesus,**</u> c. 2005.

The potential for creolization in any culture's history is based upon adaptation, fusion, and, in some cases, physical, spiritual, and cultural survival. In the case of the African-American experience, survival and healing is facilitated by creativity in all areas, not the least of which is in its music. A traditional formula for the African-American gospel choir includes the dialogue between a preacher, soloist or musical minister, and, in a live setting, the choir and the congregation. This song "Let Them See Jesus" follows this call-and-response format. As gospel music has evolved, each singer, choir, or church musician will generally include new sounds, modern instruments, new slants on religious praise and worship into the lyrics, and the creolization process is given perpetual and on-going input.

This piece, from its initial "bass-line" (bass melody) on synthesizer and its drum pattern, would just as likely be the basis for an R&B or hip-hop/house piece as a gospel work. But as soon as the unmistakable quality of the choir and the full voices (singing at full projection) enters, we are introduced to one of the most important features in gospel music, past or present: *full commitment to the music, the emotion, and the message.*

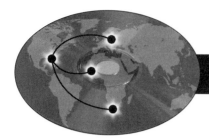

Inside the Musician's World

Ben Koen

Ben Koen and family. Dr. Koen writes: "My family is composed of a diverse background. Mom is from Seneca Indian and Welsh descent; Dad is Spanish, born in Greece, raised Jewish; Saba is from Iran and grew up in India; and our children came from all of this."

Note: Assimilation in the music of the Americas has never been solely bi-lateral (between two cultures). Today, we recognize the influences in gospel music from parts of Africa and the Caribbean, as well as from other forms of global creolization. But the key ingredients remain: the focus on achieving a closeness or oneness with a "Higher Power," the unburdening of sorrow or pain, and, in singing freely from the heart, the release and balancing of emotions, mind, and spirit while creating an intimate sense of community with others. Although these are traits and characteristics common to much of the world's religious music, they are essential to gospel music. In all its forms throughout the African Diaspora, gospel music is one of the most prolific and influential musical genres of an inspirational nature in modern history.

In this piece, we have a fusion of jazz and gospel music. Historically, these are two styles of music whose mixing was not necessarily embraced by the church. As mentioned in Unit IV, mixing what were perceived to be the world of the spirit (gospel music) and world of the devil (blues and jazz) was often condemned by church leaders. But since both genres, like the many other genres of music in the United States, are reflective of the American creolization process, they became integrated and remain essential to the understanding of American cultural and racial evolution. In this sense, although the setting in clubs or bars for blues or jazz may be in opposition to religious teachings, jazz or blues music and inspirational music, sharing as they do the healing messages and musical creolization of spiritually minded individuals, are never disjoint. Ben Koen makes a strong case for the nature of healing racism and its relationship to both jazz and gospel music:

"More than anything else, jazz and gospel music is spiritual music, the spirit is one, and its musical expressions are infinite. Jazz and gospel both grew out of the vast diversity that is America and at their core are expressive of the concept of 'unity in diversity.' The well known American motto and yet to be fully realized promise of 'E Pluribus Unum,' which literally means 'out of many, one,' is an essential goal to not only heal racism—but social injustice in all its forms. A full unity thrives on diversity and dies with sameness, which means that for something to be whole and healthy it must have diversity at all levels. When the opposite notion of 'unity in sameness' takes the upper hand, any system will start to die, whether it is a human organ system, social system, or ecosystem. Jazz and gospel music also grew out of a culture where the dominant view was one that humanity was composed of different races, which were not expressive of unity, but of a hierarchy within the human species. That view was based on a scientific fallacy and a misunderstanding of religious truth.

"In his now-published doctoral dissertation, historian Bruce Dain eloquently makes three profound points with just nine words in his shocking and powerful ti-

Pic. 10.35C *Centuries of rooftops and church or cathedral towers graphically reflect the merging of sacred and secular in architecture across generations and cultures.* Photo: Authors.

tle, <u>A Hideous Monster of the Mind: American Race Theory, 1787-1859.</u> All three points are key: first, that 'race' is a 'theory,' not an absolute reality or truth; second, that this 'theory' is a 'hideous monster'; and third, that this 'hideous monster' is in and of 'the mind.'

"In a similar characterization, psychiatrist James Woodal makes a strong case that 'racism is a disease,' a disease of the mind, with myriad symptoms, that continues to afflict all of society. Now, consider that humans overwhelmingly have organized themselves along lines of race. So, while science and religion today uphold the truth that humanity is composed of one race with infinite and beautiful diversity, socially, there are different races. The key point here is that society is a manifestation of the thoughts and beliefs of people, and that thoughts and beliefs are in a constant state of change. So, the more our thoughts and beliefs are aligned with a truer reflection of the spiritual and physical reality, the healthier humanity will be.

"Jazz and gospel music, like many aspects of expressive culture, can serve to heal society and individuals. Since both genres were created through the social interaction of all the diversity that is uniquely American, and since they are most deeply rooted in the music and culture of Africa and its Diaspora and Europe, I believe they have a particularly potent role to play in healing the mind and culture infected with racism. The strongest role that jazz and gospel can play, I believe, is in emphasizing their spiritual roots, which by definition are inclusive rather than exclusive and are expressive of God's all-embracing and ever-present love. Moreover, as a spiritual music, jazz leads one's consciousness toward the transcendent while effecting change in society.

"So, at the level of the spirit, there are no borders or "race," "gender," "nationality," "ethnicity," or anything that is defined by the physical world; but, at the level of society, all of these divisions and more exist and are very real. Jazz and gospel play a unique role by not only illustrating models of unity in musical forms, but by reflecting its spiritual source into society. Education in and through jazz or gospel must also include historical scientific theories and religious views and, more importantly, current knowledge from the physical and social sciences as well as religious and philosophical studies. Musicians can then project into the future the potential of what this music can become as it continues to grow."

Pic.10.36A & B *The mere fact that we work, live, and breathe in close proximity to each other or hear each other's music in the streets and airways of life makes the separation of musical worlds virtually impossible. Here in Los Angeles and San Francisco, California, both the street musicians and those that hear their music will be influenced by the music on a continuum ranging from mild or passive to strong. Over time, the influence may have a lasting impact on one's own creolization process. (Author's note: Yes, fees were paid in both cases).* Photo: Authors.

"O Son of Spirit," by Ben Koen, from the CD: **Reliance,** c. Qing Shan Music, 1997.

Professor Koen writes, *"The melody for this song was inspired one beautiful day while I was walking down a dirt road on the island of Moorea. As I was walking and saying the passage in my heart "O Son of Spirit, My first counsel is this. Possess a pure, kindly, and radiant heart,"* [10.9] *I came upon a smaller dirt road to my right hand side. The scene is still emblazoned in my mind; there were gorgeous green trees lifting up toward the sky and gently bending toward the road. The trees were full of vibrant red flowers with a bit of white gently sketched throughout the petals. What was so attractive to me was that the road was covered with these flowers, which seemed to create a kind mystical path that called me to tread upon it. Without hesitation, I followed that path, which eventually led to the majestic and awe-inspiring ocean. The melody, reminiscent of the spirit of South African jazz (a beautiful blend of local musics, jazz, gospel, and blues), rests upon a rhythm that our drummer, Marvin "Bu-ga-lu" Smith, describes as an Algerian 6/8 rhythm.*

"The meaning of the words is, of course, vast and speaks to each heart in unique ways. For me, one of the things I understand from this is the central importance of that eternal, non-physical aspect of a human's being, the soul; that with a

'pure, kindly, and radiant heart,' the spiritual aspect of being human, that makes each of us beautifully unique and simultaneously at one with each other, gives us a clear vision and all-embracing love that has been described in all world religions, is a sign of the kingdom of God on earth. In its relation to the concept of race, this passage focuses my mind in a special way that while it recognizes the social reality of race, is focused on that spiritual essence that is a reflection of God's view of us, where I believe God looks at the purity of heart, not any transitory aspect of being human, be it color, gender, nationality, social status, job, academic degree, title, or other such temporary labels."

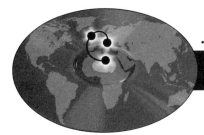

. . . More Global Fusions!
Inside the Musician's World

Dalinda and Hossam Ramzy

The producer of this piece, Hossam Ramzy, is himself a multifaceted master of Egyptian as well as jazz and world percussion. Primarily a studio musician (one who makes a living creating and producing recordings) living in England and having done multiple projects with such artists as Peter Gabriel and a host of other world-music figures, Mr. Ramzy vivifies the creolization process. So too, does the performer of this piece, Dalinda. Mr. Ramzy (and Diz Heller) write, *"How do you define the connection between inspiration and one's origins? How do you pinpoint the artistic background of someone who considers herself a collector of influences from places she has lived in and those she carries within her, rather than belonging to any particular culture of this world?*

"Dalinda, originally Bosnian, was born in Libya on the Saharan fringe of the Mediterranean. From an early age she was exposed to a kaleidoscope of musical influences: Italian canzonnas that she learned from her young friends, the Slavic/Balkan folk music that her father listened to, the soulful sounds of Edith Piaf and Russian gypsy ballads her mother adored, and the Arabian music everywhere around her. Eventually, in Tripoli, an outlet for her expression was missing, and so she left Libya for England in a quest to fuse the music of her childhood with the music in her mind."

"Esh-Hal-Qadni," by Dalinda, Hossam Ramzy & Chalif Hassan, from the CD: **Turquoise,** Arc Music Productions, c. 2002.

As the music begins, the fusion of elements includes the use of modern bass and a blending of rhythms from a variety of Arabic musical styles dating back centuries earlier, as well as the inclusion of the traditional instruments: the haunting sound of the **neh** (Arabic flute), the use of a call-and-response pattern between the voice and violins (pre-dating anything resembling the "orchestra" in Western cultures), and the Qa'nun (plucked zither). What follows, however, is a manifestation of the creolization process now sweeping even the most ancient cultures of the Middle East and North Africa brought on by musicians such as Hossam Ramzy, many of whom are now living throughout Europe and America.

The music picks up its tempo, begins altering its rhythmic pattern, and eventually doubles time (creating a rhythm at twice the speed of the original tempo) in a feel (rhythmic groove) akin to a jazz-fusion-samba over which the guitar with distortion plays a solo that eventually finds its way back to the original tempo. In all respects, this is a fascinating blend of cultures. The lyrics follow a love-lost theme:

Esh-Hal-Qadni	*How will I be patient enough*
Esh-hal-qadni nosboro esh hal?	*How will I be patient to get over your love?*
La'wasalni minek mersaal	*No letters arrived from you*
La tesool, wa la tesaal	*You don't ask about me anymore*
Swawolt aleik el-nai	*I asked the Neh (nay) about you*
Swawolt aleik el-oud	*I begged the Oud to tell me where you are*
Sawolt aleik el-ashiqeen	*I asked about your lovers*
Sawolt el-naas elhaimeen	*I asked the experienced in love about you*
Esh-Hal-Qadni	*How will I be patient to get over your love?*

Inside the Musician's World

Michael Zaporski
with Nikolas Fehr (bandoneon)

Note: When I discussed Mr. Zaporski's compositions with him, one composition that stood out had the unique fusion of jazz with the haunting melody of the accordion-like instrument known as the **bandoneon.** Mr. Zaporski commented:

"The music of jazz is constantly growing, changing, morphing. The interesting thing about music from the creative artist standpoint is that one of the greatest compliments you can give someone is to take something you learned from him or her and use it in your own music and in your own language. I was quite enamored with the bandoneon. It reminded me of my experiences listening to Toots Thielman (jazz harmonica performer) playing with Bill Evans. It was the haunting sound of it, I wasn't thinking of anything French or European per se; it just evolved from the sound of the past.

"Well, he (Nikolas Fehr) turned me on to South American music (the tango, etc.). I suppose what is special is that these musics are also a bit like jazz (creative fu-

sions of multiple elements and cultures). At any rate, this piece wrote itself in about 10 minutes. It's a rather long form, nothing remarkable about the chord structure, but it's influenced by my exposure to Latin jazz, tango, and Chopin etudes. It's just me being enamored with the sound of the instrument. That's what is unique about the spirit of jazz (wherever that occurs): constantly new, refreshing. Sometimes I hate the word 'jazz' – because it doesn't speak about the spirit of creativity that IS jazz.

"Jazz is open to all kinds of different experiences from any culture at any level. The greatest thing I've learned from the old jazz artists is that every culture has a beauty to its music. Every culture has something wonderful to say. The guys that I learned from always held that in high esteem. There is no unimportant culture on this earth. Any true jazz artist will take anything that they hear and respect it."

"A Bientot," by Michael Zaporski with Nicholas Fehr, from the CD: **Insight,** c. Daddy Z Productions, 2003.

Of this unique fusion, the bandoneon artist Mr. Fehr writes: *"The bandoneon is a large relative of the concertina. Although the bandoneon's invention is shrouded in uncertainty, it is clear because of its small size, which allows expression that is impossible on larger instruments, that the first bandoneons were created to fill the role of the pipe organ in small, organless churches in rural Germany. While its presence in churches was short-lived, it achieved some popularity among the German masses and traveled with poor immigrants who left Germany, especially those headed for Argentina. Through various means it became associated with the Buenos Aires underworld, taking residence in the brothels where tango had already begun to develop. The bandoneon has persisted for nearly a century as the focal instrument of Argentine tango music and therefore is an integral symbol of identity for the tango culture of Buenos Aires.*

"Argentine composer and performer Astor Piazzolla (1921-1992) was instrumental in the transformation of the tango from an outdated dance music to an eclectic concert music stemming from its strong Argentine roots. Over the course of his career, he transformed traditional tango into what he called Tango Nuevo (akin to the Bossa Nova of Brazil) and brought both it and the bandoneon

Pic. 10.38A *Nicholas Fehr holding a bandoneon.* Photo: N.Fehr.

to international prominence. Piazzolla and other composers, such as Aldemaro Romero of Venezuela, have written an important body of art music for the bandoneon." In subsequent phases of the creolization process, the music of the Argentine bandoneon also found its way back to European clubs and cabarets, as did ragtime and jazz. In this case, both find their way to back to America and into the composition of Mr. Zaporski.

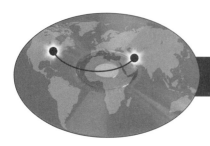

Inside the Musician's World

Arash

Michael's Experience: Among the most enjoyable parts of being an instructor of "creativity" through any medium is the contact with a student or "creative colleague" who has the combination of passion, discipline, and "talent," or an intuitive desire to create. One such student sat in one of my classes nearly an entire semester taking notes fluently, passionately asking questions (usually after class), and finally towards the end of the semester asked humbly: *"Would you be interested in playing one of my CDs?"*

I assumed he meant a CD from his collection until he handed me the CD with his picture on the cover. *"Is this you? Are you a musician?"* (He shrugged.) I asked, "Why didn't you tell me this earlier?" (He smiled and shrugged again.) I then played the selection below. Composed (lyrics and music), sequenced, arranged, and performed vocally by Arash, the song represents the fusion of influences available to all young musicians today. As in the past, musicians will combine the music of their ancestry and the technology or modern devices of their day in the creolization processes of their generation.

I later learned that Arash exuded an important characteristic emphasized in much of Iran (Persia): a sincere and deep sense of humility and respect for elders (and teachers in particular). This quality translated to the role of the student meant: *sit, listen, learn, ask questions, and do not be concerned with demonstrating your prowess.* The trait of being a good listener, however, also requires that the individual have solid self-esteem and a knowledge that, in time, work and effort will lead to his voice also being heard and honored.

CD 4.11

"Doroogh Goo (Dishonest)," by Arash, from the CD: <u>**Doroogh Goo,**</u> c. 2005.

This piece is a fusion of the "ancient" instruments ***dombek*** (dombeki or Arab/Persian hand drum) and ***santour*** (played on a synthesizer), with the formulas of an older style Persian poetry and music (call-and-response patterns and melodic lining of violin and synthesizer with voice). But also included, in part due to mass migrations of Persians to Europe and America before, during, and since the Iranian revolution of 1978-79, is the increased creolization and fusion of numerous elements in Western musical composition and production with ancient formulas.

Beyond the inclusion of a more modern rhythmic structure pasted over the four-beat Western popular music meter and the utilization of modern sequencing and recording production, smooth vocals, and processing (utilization of equalization, reverb, and other signal processing devices to blend and alter sound), you also will hear the inclusion of chords or harmony in the accompaniment. Although harmony was primarily an outgrowth of Western music, acquired over centuries at the expense of more complicated pitch menus (scales or modes) or rhythms, it is now a means for the fortification of emotion in much of today's popular music worldwide.

The lyrics are, however, a reflection of the age-old dilemma of love lost and remain still the descendant of the ancient art of Persian and Arabic metaphors, this time equating the tainted love with the thorn of the rose and the "doroogh goo," or dishonesty, of the other person:

Pic. 10.40 *An ad for a Persian musical concert to be held at the Howard Johnson Plaza hotel illustrates how communities find or create the familiar amongst the unfamiliar (find home away from home). Also, now many members of their new community will have the opportunity to experience the "exotic" or unfamiliar... in their own backyard.* Courtesy of Persian Newsletter: Persian House in Michigan.

Doroogh Goo (Dishonest)

Too many people come and say "I like you ..." dishonestly
They say that love is like a flower in the human heart
Sounds like my part in this love is like the very thorn of the rose

She said that "I love you ..." I trusted her fully
And she cried for me ... and I trusted her tears fully
She sat in front of me and spoke her words of love
Telling me stories of building our life together
But she lied, she lied, I swear to God she lied

Finally she left me and here is my story
A broken heart, tears, and many reminders
Some poetry, some songs, and tears every night
I said to her that I don't have a crystal palace
From all of the riches in the world, I only have you and your love

Inside the Musician's World

Istvan Dely
and the Slovak Philharmonic
Chamber Orchestra

Note: Mr. Istvan Dely (from whom we heard in Unit VIII) writes: *"'In healthy societies,' and I'm quoting Yaya Diallo, a Miniyanka-born musician trained in Mali but who spent much of his adult life in Canada:*

'the musicians are expected to live by high standards of morality and self-restraint. Music is powerful. By their example, the musicians will influence the youth for better or worse. As the youth are the society's future, it is very important that their role models be good ones. The fundamental princi-

ple of traditional African musical training is devotion to music in the service of the cosmos, the environment, and the community.'

"Then, from the ancient Chinese books of Li-Ki and Confucius, respectively: 'Virtue is the principle of human nature and music is the flower of virtue.' 'How could a man devoid of the virtues inherent to man cultivate music?'

Mr. Dely goes on to say: *"To sum up: music is a psycho-biological human need and in order for it to link up the best in past traditions with what is desirable and imperative for our vision of the future, it must fulfill a threefold function:*

- *On the mystical plane, it should confer spiritual knowledge, attract the souls to the beauty of the Creator, and kindle the flame for the Creator's guidance.*

- *On the moral plane, it should express and inspire the noblest sentiments, stimulate the desire for moral excellence and obedience to divine teachings, and be a source of comfort and tranquility to anguished souls.*

- *On the social plane, it should promote the well-being of the community, create harmony, and promote world unity and universal brotherhood.*

"And now I'll quote Fernando Ortiz: 'Should we strip music of its true nature and vital functions, it would become like a tree: uprooted, cut off from the nurturing soil, it would soon wither and die, no matter how lavishly we adorn it with shining globes and sophisticated lights. (Music), as an art form, is potentially socially transcendent. It can lead us to action, not distraction; to emersion, not diversion; it transports us beyond the range of everyday life, recreating life's moments of transcendence. (Especially in the case of music created by oppressed communities)—such music not only speaks to us but moves us to act. It is meant to guide us onto the path of right living, not to derail us from our communal purpose. The role of (such) music is always fundamental, collective, religious, ceremonial, and dramatic.'"

"After three centuries, during which musical creativity shone forth resplendent from Europe, that mighty stream slowly came to an ebb as its sources in European folklore dried up in the wake of the Industrial Revolution when the masses were uprooted from their rural settings and came pouring into urban centers. A change in the musical direction of composers in the late 19th and 20th centuries formally pointed the way out [of mono-culturalism] toward non-European music, hitherto considered primitive and inconsequential.

"Since the beginning of the twentieth century, and in an ever-growing measure, Western music has been receiving the revitalizing infusion of Black music, notably from Afro-American music. The most striking feature of this new musical language is the ever-present predominance of rhythm, which makes it better fitted than music from other parts of the world to express our frenetic pace of life. It is no coincidence that the universalization of Black music has proceeded in successive waves following a pattern of increasing degrees of rhythmic difficulty and complexity, from monorhythm to polyrhythms. To complete the circle, the music of Mother Africa herself, richest in rhythms and vitality, has entered the world scenario alone or in cross-overs with the most avant-garde of Western musicians.

"From the mingling and merging of all these currents, enriched by contributions from all the peoples of the Earth, a new universal cycle of music is beginning to take shape, what may well come to be considered as the classical music of the New Millennium."

"Bachbata," by Istvan Dely/Johann Sebastian Bach, recorded by the Slovak Philharmonic Chamber Orchestra, from the CD: **Embrace,** c. 2002.

Recorded music: Brandenburg Concertos, Concerto Nº 3 in G Major, Allegro) with the Capella Istropolitana (Slovak Philharmonic Chamber Orchestra) and Istvan Dely & Shangó Dely: batá drums (Okónkolo, Itótele, Iyá), tambora, agogó, shékere.

About this work, Mr. Dely writes: *"To some, this piece might sound like outright blasphemy. To me it's my very reverential and loving tribute to two of the major musical influences of my adolescence: European baroque music and African sacred drums. For years they have not only coexisted peacefully within me but strived to embrace each other and become one. Finally I gave birth to this love child of mine, a recording project entitled "Embrace," which is still in its infancy. Hopefully it will grow and develop and help bridge the artificial gap between European and African classical music and their audiences."*

In any instance, this is a fitting conclusion of a text (and specifically a unit) committed to seeing the interconnections and realities of our world's cultures and music.

Pic. 10.41 *Skepticism, resistance, and blatant attacks on initiatives encouraging the integration of cultures and overcoming repression or hierarchical perceptions based upon race, nationality, religion, or gender are common and can be expected. The fear of change to our known ways and entrenched traditions is always challenging. Ultimately, however, rebuilding a respectful perspective on human history will require a complete reformation of both what we learn and how we learn it.*

As you gaze on this beautiful beach, you may not immediately see the correlation between the statement above and what appears to be a peaceful beach—perhaps on someone's private island. Once we learn that this is one of the primary beaches in Normandy upon which one of the largest military assaults in human history was launched, and yet today is a lovely tourist attraction, we are able to get a picture of the potential within human culture to alter the course of events or heal from a long and arduous history of divisiveness. Today, devoid of any scars reflecting the enormous efforts to stop one of the most horrific holocausts in human history, we now may witness the potential of a culture's ability to heal ancestral imbalances and devise new systems of converse, commerce, and education. Photo: Authors.

Unit X Activities

Exercising Our Creativity—The *Art* of Collaboration

Do you say often:

"I'm too busy…," or
"I don't dance, sing, repair cars, cook…," or
"I don't have time to go to the concert, (read a novel, take a walk, etc.)," or
"I have too much to do?"

The fact is that most of us feel we are short on time, and all of us tell ourselves that we are too busy to do many of the things we enjoy or wish to do. Time and energy, or the lack of it, gets blamed for more unexercised passions and uncreated works of human capacity than all other excuses combined. But time, its use and perception, is relevant to each culture and ultimately, individual. Therefore, it is not the abundance of time and energy, or lack thereof, but rather how we choose to spend it—that is really the issue. Those who practice creating, be it music or cooking, frequently say that the act of creating something with passion actually *generates* energy. It also can enhance a person's effectiveness, meaning it takes *less time* to accomplish many tasks when we practice creativity and exercise our passions regularly than when we don't.

In some instances, the act of finding reasons not to exercise our passions may result from a fear of failure, or not being as good as someone else, or perhaps from the fear of being criticized. We might also wish to observe the larger cultural messages under which we've been brought up. That is, what have we been trained to consider as important? What will bring us respect from others (particularly subculture groups such as friends and family)? What do we consider the "practical" utilization of our time and energy (based upon our perceptions of responsibility and accomplishment)? Yet many of us likely feel we have a *song to sing, a poem to write, a picture to paint, if only…* . If we break the "if only" down, we almost always will find that we set our priorities not only according to the real responsibilities of life (family, food, shelter, etc.) but also in response to fears or misaligned material priorities that seldom bring quality to our lives or help strengthen our communities.

Giving Back

Michael Zaporsky commented earlier: *"The interesting thing about music from the creative artist standpoint is that one of the greatest compliments you can give someone is to take something you learned from someone and take it and use it in your own music and in your own language."*

One of the fundamental goals of this text is to assist the reader to acquire the skills and perceptions necessary to become more actively and creatively engaged in life. Like all disciplines, enjoying life and expressing ourselves creatively demands a certain amount of diligence and practice. Prioritizing our time and energy to allow for creative pursuits requires enthusiasm and the motivation to do so, continual reassessment of priorities, and, often, the recognition of the fears and doubts that impede our development.

Here are a few steps that may help you in the pursuit of a more creative lifestyle:

1. If we're human, then we have fears. If we have fears, then among them will always be the fear of failure or criticism. Admitting this very human reality can allow us to systematically begin to face and overcome fear.

2. Every minute we spend in passionately developing (what some call) our gifts or talents (assuming they don't degrade, harm, or restrict others from doing the same) will bring energy with which we can face our responsibilities. We should set aside a few minutes each day or a few hours each week to explore some part of our creativity.

Pic. 10.44 Students in a composition class learn the art of collective creative consultation. It is within the vision of sharing our individual creativity within our community that creolization finds its most effective power in helping us forge a process of collective creativity. From the process comes the "product," and usually one more diverse and creative than any of the individuals could have imagined. Photo: Authors.

3. Because creativity demands exploration, we will need to allow ourselves to fail, to embrace mistakes as "natural," and ultimately to begin to experience the "process" (engaging in creative endeavors which enhance our, and hopefully others', lives) with little or less concern for the ultimate product or "goal" that will result from our efforts.

Stage 1: Individual Preparation
(Learning Our "Instrument")

Many of us raised in so-called "Western" (European/American) cultures are more prone to feeling we *must know or be trained in something,* that we must be trained as specialists or have considerable experience in order to attempt some creative endeavor. To the contrary, a high percentage of individuals in so-called "third world" or "developing" countries are frequently encouraged to participate regardless of training and are also used to *create* much more with, frequently, very much less. From the standpoint of creativity, being willing to try, whether or not you are an "expert," is an advantageous attitude.

To understand the creativity of the artist-musician, we naturally must strive to create art ourselves. That is, to get into the musician's world. This project is designed to assist us to experiment with our own creative skills in much the same way musicians would develop their art. Therefore, we will outline the steps of the creative musician working in a group context … but more importantly, we hope that these suggestions will encourage you to interact creatively with others in your community—or to build a community around your creative interests.

Ingredients

- Find one or more quotes, ideas, or musical selections from this unit on creolization. Write it down and take some time to reflect on its meaning.
  - Pick a creative skill (an instrument) you already feel comfortable with or one which you would like to pursue.
    Your Instrument: All musicians have an instrument by which they convey their thoughts. Most of the artists you enjoy have spent countless hours perfecting the techniques of their instrument, learning new songs or ideas, and working with other musicians with whom they share their experiences and create their art.

If you are a musician reading this, then the process of selecting your instrument (passion) may be simple. But if you are like the majority reading this, you are not a musician. What could be your instrument? It must be something you can "play" reasonably confidently and preferably with considerable pleasure. It may be cooking or a craft, or sports; it may be children, family, or friends. Regardless, all you need to do is find something that is very important to you, that you know well (or desire to know well). Then you design an activity whereby you can explore this passion in a "new," fresh, or exciting manner.

- In what way can you reflect the idea(s) you selected through your instrument?

You will simply need to find a means for demonstrating what you did in front of others (e.g., make a video or Powerpoint presentation of your activity, write a letter or poem, make a collage or a photo-book). Whatever instrument(s) you "play," choose one you love! As artists, we look to find forms, images, sounds, colors, anything that can reflect or symbolize our thoughts and ideas. You may wish to list words, metaphors, images in nature which can *reflect* the importance of the idea. We may also have taken a photograph, have a piece of music, or desire to combine our experience with a drawing or craft or set it to music.

- Practice, prepare, put all of your passion into making your "song" or individual contribution to the group or community. Try hard not to judge or question what you do. Simply (and actually, at first, it may not be so simple) *complete it,* knowing that the accomplishment of creating and reserving space for creativity is–the goal!

Take chances!

Try new ideas continually.

You can always go back; but without risk, you cannot move forward.

It has been years (perhaps centuries) of indoctrination,
that the "end" or goal determines our success in life … when, ironically,
it has always been the process and how we live (in this case—doing our best)
that has really ever mattered.

Creativity is the process of investing ourselves, our thoughts, and our actions into something that we deem valuable. It is the act of fulfilling a portion of our talent or potential. It is also the means by which we become more flexible, open-minded, and non-judgmental in our attitudes toward diverse cultures or music, a process which leads to better relationships with others and a fulfilling life. Creativity is the practice of healthy risk-taking that allows us to develop flexibility and a persistent passion for growth and learning.

Anything that blocks our potential or passionate engagement in the activities of life (and this includes excessive nervousness in front of others, fear of not being accepted or of failing, etc.) can be overcome by keeping a few points in mind:

- We did not choose our talents or innate abilities, nor most of our weaker areas or tests and challenges in life. Therefore, we have nothing to lose in trying our best in all areas.

- Those who judge others often do so in an effort to mask their own fears or insecurities. Even if our results appear less than those of others, through the sincerity of our efforts, others will feel our passion and engagement, the centerpiece of art.

- The author has personally overcome (or taught others to overcome) performance anxiety by finding ways to remove himself from the stigma of being critiqued in presentation or performance, by decreasing self-absorption (which increases fears, expectations, and anxiety), and by learning the art of detachment from any outcome or perception of our performance. Whether we have prepared or not, when presentation time comes around, we must become clear and hollow channels, for whatever we are capable of accomplishing must flow through a clear and unblocked channel.

*A learned elder once said that the goal in life is to fill
whatever your potential to the brim. Some may possess the potential of a gallon,
others a cup... and still others may appear to have only a thimble.*

*But what impresses us more, someone with a lot of talent or resources
but who does not have to try at anything they do,
often taking what they have for granted?*

*Or, someone who may have little apparent potential,
but who exerts EVERY OUNCE of ENERGY to EVERY ACTIVITY they undertake....
no matter how small?* [10.10]

Other advice from elders:

*Believe in the source of our gifts or inspiration as coming from a Higher source,
which channels though "Us," the performer ... the channel ...*

*If we don't own our creation, if it belongs to everyone, if we don't attach ourselves to it,
we can not fear failure or be affected by others' criticism! Prepare passionately, then let go!
"The world is divided into people who do things and people who get the credit.
Try, if you can, to belong to the first class. There is far less competition."*

Dwight Morrow, 1931

Stage 2: Developing a "Creative" Community

As we begin to think about the status of community in our lives, most of us will come to the conclusion that we would like to have more time with others, more opportunities for becoming closer to others, and, in general, more activities and rituals which bring a deeper interaction or establish a deeper bond with others. Because the majority of the world's best music is the result of intense and refined community collaboration, we suggest the following motivations for a creative group activity:

FIRST: The vast majority of the world's music is created in groups. From rock bands, to symphony or gamelan orchestras, to opera or musical casts with as many as one hundred performers, the combination of different talents and skills coming together in sound and motion is what makes much of the world's music so infectious.

SECOND: The vast majority of the world's peoples dance, sing, listen attentively, or interact with the musicians in a community environment. Whether as an event for entertainment or enrichment, or in the context of rituals that mark and enhance the passage of life, few musical expressions are created outside of the context of community.

THIRD: By working in groups, we are able to practice the most important skill of a music appreciator—honest *listening and consultative* habits. Individual projects, papers, and essays are great ways of demonstrating what we know as individuals, but group work allows for exposure to things we don't know or can't assume. Moreover, it is the art of compromise, dialogue, and fusion, as we've already discussed, that is essential to the music creative process. In the final analysis, there are very few things that bring lasting joy and fulfillment in life that are not experienced within the context of community. Even moments of intense personal pleasure usually find their greatest lasting benefit when shared with others. Now try to follow these steps:

1. *Once you have identified* your own method of fulfilling your individual creativity (the practicing of your instrument in preparation for the group activity), identify a group of individuals with whom you would like to experience a creative group interaction. Although you may turn to your workplace, church, or family, you may also create an activity as part of a party, dinner event, or special evening for which you invite individuals you've been meaning to learn more about.

2. *Invite each individual* to bring their own ideas related to the topic or event you've selected as your theme. Ask each individual to bring something that they can use for the creative activity (a pad of paper for the poet, an instrument for the musician, markers and paper for the artist, comfortable shoes for the dancer, etc.). They may prepare ideas in advance or be encouraged to create spontaneously at the gathering.

   If you are in a class or school, it will be up to the instructor to assign a topic (i.e., Unit X) or to determine whether the groups will create presentations for the class, the school, or the community. Our only job is to follow the steps used by musicians all over the world as they prepare to create the music we admire.

3. *Survey each individual* as to their thoughts on the topic as well as what they wish to contribute. Listen carefully, as your group member may be saying one thing but really be desiring to contribute something else. Only careful listening and a desire to assist others fulfill their potential will ultimately create the synergy from which the community creativity will thrive.

4. Once everyone has spoken, the real fun begins. Now we will create a "performance" collage. Begin consultation of what you will do, while keeping the following in mind:

   a) Most of us are trained to focus on goals and outcomes, not processes. Our learned behavior tells us to "solve" the problem, to create a "product," or to establish and work for the end result. This must be countered with the voice of process: *"Let's make sure everyone contributes in a manner that they feel honored—and see what results."* **Caution:** Do not let yourself set a formula; rather, let the formula and product evolve from the process of universal inclusion of all the voices in the group.

   b) As humans, we are always limited by what we know. By now we realize that the only manner in which new knowledge is obtained is by placing ourselves in situations where we don't know or aren't sure. Therefore, as a community we perpetually reassure each other that unfamiliar ground, uncertainty, even conflict are necessary in the acquisition of wisdom and fulfillment of potential.

   c) Make sure the time parameters and availability of equipment or materials are well known in advance. Decide whether the "performance" presentation is made just for ourselves or whether others should know in advance (i.e., no surprises, no personal or hidden agendas that could create anxiety or taint the value of creative collaboration).

   d) Finally, when possible, make sure that whatever you create is offered to someone else. The elderly, children, the disadvantaged or fostering communities or educating in other environments are great places to start.

> *"This is the duty of our generation as we enter the twenty-first century— solidarity with the weak, the persecuted, the lonely, the sick, and those in despair. It is expressed by the desire to give a noble and humanizing meaning to a community in which all members will define themselves not by their own identity but by that of others."* Elie Wiesel

> *"If you were all alone in the universe with no one to talk to, no one with which to share the beauty of the stars, to laugh with, to touch, what would be your purpose in life? It is other life, it is love, which gives your life meaning. This is harmony. We must discover the joy of each other, the joy of challenge, the joy of growth."* Mitsugi Saotome

> *"The individual is not an isolated element, but rather an integral part of the institutions and organizations, which surround him and form his social environment. His capabilities, attitudes, skills, and knowledge must be acquired and formed in the context of his participation in and contributions to the continuing development of the social structures that conduce to the well-being of all. This development of the individual is enhanced when the responsibilities of establishing goals, strategies, and methods are shared with (others)."* Readings on Bahá'í Social and Economic Development, p. 37

A

B

D

C

The pictures here all represent different means or processes by which we change and alter our perceptions of the world through creative exchange with other humans. Can you identify the dynamic of exchange represented by each? [A) British quartet in Prague; B) Chess in Detroit; C) Media broadcast of an outdoor global music festival; D) A Mexican restaurant in Hungary]

In each is a powerful lesson that we CAN and MUST enjoy the diversity of our world, learn how to respect and honor those from whom we "borrow," and acknowledge our "history" with a vision to our collective potentials. "Our Musical World" – as a single creative entity – is merely a reflection of what will likely be manifest as "Humanity comes of age." Photos: Authors.

Unit X: Endnotes

[10.1] We will be using "American" to indicate, as is proper of all the Americas (North, Central, and South). We will use United States or Brazil, for example, to indicate specific cultures. Readers in the United States should attempt to reorient themselves to this delineation, as citizens from other parts of the Americas are generally offended by "American" being synonymous with being from the U.S.A.

[10.2] Slavery lasted only 13 years because the small population and remote location made any hope of prosperity through the development of a viable cotton industry futile. At any rate, the American cotton industry had already cornered the market.

[10.3] One important value of a fully-functional community environment that has a balanced and natural perception of the cycle of life and the generational diversity within the cycle is that the acceptance of change (the tradition of change) is unilateral across the generations. Elders at peace with the nature of youth and their desire to find or create their own voice will respond with encouragement; youth in turn will honor their elders with the incorporation of their wisdom (and expressions) into their "new" concoctions.

[10.4] Although not pleasant to examine, an unbiased look at the history and evolution of American institutions shows clearly perpetual patterns of misappropriation and a taking advantage of African-Americans by European-Americans in all areas of society (termed: white privilege). In music, until "black" businesses and record companies began to flourish (post -"Motown," early 1960s), white-owned record companies, radio stations, and commerce were nearly exclusively responsible for the propagation of "black" music and compensation of African-American musicians.

[10.5] "Ragging" was coined from the "ragged" rhythms and rough or varied sounds that African-American musicians created in comparison to European songs of the time. Like most African-American genres from blues to hip-hop, the music was initially criticized and then later embraced, owing to its uniqueness and vibrant spirit when compared to the other music of its generation.

[10.6] From a paper on Scott Joplin published by the Ragtime Society, Ontario, Canada (Quoted in Music: Black, White, and Blue, 1972, Ortiz Walton, p. 15)

[10.7] ibid. p. 15.

[10.8] At a *rent party*, tenants would hire a musician or band to play and pass the hat to raise money to pay their rent. The rent party played a major role in the development of jazz and rhythm and blues music in larger northern cities.

[10.9] The text is from the "Hidden Words" of Baha'u'llah, the prophet-founder of the Baha'i Faith. The full text is: "O Son of Spirit, possess a pure, kindly and radiant heart, that thine may be a sovereignty ancient, imperishable and everlasting."

[10.10] This is a paraphrase from the Writings of Abdu'l-Baha, the Son of Baha'u'llah.

A Closer Look: Sound and Pitch

Sound Waves—The means by which musical sound, once initiated, travels through the air and is distinguished from other sounds. Pitched instruments will generally have a single frequency (measured in herz, e.g., tuning A= 440 hz. or vibrations per second), but each instrument will sound different according to the shape of the sound waves it generates. Although there are an infinite variety of wave-forms (i.e., each voice is like a snowflake, having its own unique wave form). we categorize sound waves into four primary wave forms:

Sine-

Moves smoothly with rounded form through the air

Approximate Instrument sound: Flute

Triangle-

Moves in a triangular or pyramid shape through the air.

Approx. Instrument sound: Clarinet

Sawtooth-

Moves through the air in jagged sloping and falling manner.

Approx. Instrument sound: Oboe

Pulse or Square-

Moves through the air in square up and down motion. The harshest of wave forms.

Approx. Instrument sound: Distorted Electric Guitar

In reality, except for waves generated by synthesizers, no human-produced sounds have an equally constant or similar wave form. Furthermore, drums, non-pitched instruments, and non-pitched sounds in nature may be composed of a variety of frequencies or simultaneous wave-forms. The primary difference in how we perceive the wave-forms is in the sound "color" or <u>timbre</u>. This is the difference between one singer's voice quality and another's, or the difference between a flute and clarinet playing the same notes.

Wherever we go in the world, the sights, sounds, tastes, and visions of other worlds can very easily become part of our own. This Parisian violinist has been playing the same stretch of alleys in a famous restaurant district for nearly nine years. Each year, he has new technology (wireless amplifiers), newer pieces (popular songs of that year, mixed with popular "classics"), and every tourist that hears him, takes pictures, or talks with him, is subject to adding his influences to their own. This is nothing new; in fact, this sort of exchange has been going on since the very beginning of humanity. However, rather than learn to focus on the manner in which our commonalities express themselves "diversely"—we have, for the most part, been trained to see only the "diversity" itself. For this reason, "multicultural" experiences seem so new—despite being the arguably the most ancient tradition in our planet's history. Photo: Authors.

Appendix

APPENDIX

Further Exploration: Web sites

This is a partial list of web sites that appear to have creditability (are created by knowledgeable sources or from individuals within each culture group) and passion for the topic. To view updated information about each topic, view the non-profit site for the Center for Cultural Healing (CCH).

Units I & II: (or throughout the text)

www.arcmusic.co.uk
General Web site for Arc Music International Catalog
of International Music

larkinthemorning.com
General Web site for World Musical Instruments

www.minculture.gov.ma
Moroccan Government and Culture

www.frafrasound.com
Web site of Fra Fra Sound, Netherlands

www.incason.com or www.ixtlanartists.com
Web sites for Inca Son, also: Harmonia, and Kevin Locke

www.arigradus.com
Web site for Ari Gradus

Unit III: Native American: The Spirit in Symbolism

www.nativeculturelinks.com
Note: click on desired link including
- Information on Individual Native Nations
- Native Organizations and Urban Indian Centers
- Tribal Colleges, Native Studies Programs, and Indian Education
- Languages
- The Mascot Issue
- Native Media – Organizations, Journals and Newspapers, Radio and Television
- Powwows and Festivals
- Native Music and Arts Organizations and Individuals
- Indians in the Military
- Native Businesses
- General Indian-Oriented Home Pages

www.airpi.org
American Indian Policy Center

www.bluecloud.org
> American Indian Culture Research Center

www.afn.ca
> Assembly of First Nations

www.oncampus.richmond.edu
> Association for the Study of Am. Indian Literatures

www.cba.nau.edu
> Center for American Indian Economic Development

www.iaca.com
> Indian Arts and Crafts Association

www.elements.nb.ca
> General Native info/Powwow web site

www.powwows.com
> General Powwow listing and information

www.kevinlocke.com
> Kevin Locke's Web site

www.ecuadormanta.com
> Ecuador Manta's Web site

www.tigertigermusic.com
> Lee Tiger's Web site

www.3rdmesa.com
> Casper's Web site

www.nije.indian.com
> National Indian Justice Center

www.nmai.si.edu
> National Museum of the American Indian

www.nativeweb.org
> Native Web (Resources or News)

www.nativevue.org
> Native film and media connection

Unit IV: Africa–America: Tales and Visions of a Racial Legacy

www.lib.subs.edu
> African-American web sites listing/John B. Cade Library

www.blackquest.com
> African and African-American History, Culture, & Studies

www.straightblack.com
> African-American Resources

www.myblackinfo.com
> African-American web sites list

www.blackrefer.com/music5c.
> African/African-American web sites for music (many varieties)

www.indiana.edu/aaamc
> Archives of African-American Music & Culture/Indiana Univ.

www.africanamericas.com
> Variety of African-American Music links

Spirituals

www.ymbarnwell.com
> Spirituals Web links and Bibliography

Blues

www.thebluehighway.com
> Blues History links

www.sempermediagroup.com
> Joe Reilly's Web site

www.madcatmusic.net
> Contact for Shari Kane and Madcat Ruth

Capoeira

www.planetcapoeira.com
> Capoeira and other African Diaspora information

www.capoeira4all.com
> Links to over 700 Capoeira sites worldwide

www.capoeira.com
> List of Capoeira Resources

Calypso

www.topy5trinidad.com
> "Top" Trinidad and Tobago web sites

www.caribplanet.homestead.com
> Caribbean and Calypso Resources

www.humboldt.edu
> Carnival Culture Resources on Calypso/Carnival

www.calypso.org.uk
> Calypso Organization of the United Kingdom

www.trinisoca.com
> General Web site for Carnival and Trinidad's Musicians

Hip Hop

www.hiphop-directory.com
> Worldwide Hip Hop Resources

www.library.cornell.edu/olinuris
> Hip Hop Bibliography

www.blackrefer.com
> "Black" Music Directory, includes Hip Hop Resources

Unit V: The Middle East (and Southern Asia): Religion and Music

Hindu

www.hindunet.org
Hindu Resource Center

www.hinduwebsite.com
General Hindu listing of resources

www.vedicchantcenter.org
Further information on Vedic chanting

Judaism

www.jewfaq.org
General Information on Judaism

www.jewishnet.net/
Global Jewish Information Network

www.jewish-music.huji.ac.il/jmrc
Jewish Music Research Center

Buddhism

www.sinc.sunysb.edu/clubs/buddhism/web sites

www.buddhanet.net
"Top" Buddhist Web sites

Christian

www.chrisitanwebsites.org
Christian Web site Directory

www.botcw.com
Christian Web site Directory

www.osb.org/gen/topics/chant
Gregorian Chant Bibliography and Web sites

Islam

www.talkislam.com
Islamic Web site and Resource listings

www.islamic-world.net
Text and audio resources on Islam

www.uga.edu/islam
Islamic Art, Music, and Architecture

Bahá'í

www.bcca.org
Directory of Bahá'í Web sites

www.bahai.org
General Information on the Bahá'í Faith

www.bahai-media.org
Listing of Bahá'í related Media and recordings

Arabic/Persian Culture and Music

www.arab-music.com
General link to Arabic/Iranian/Turkish music

www.arabicnights.com
General Arabic Entertainment Directory

www.iranian.ws/music
General Persian Music and Cinema Web site

www.iranmania.com
General Directory of Iranian/Persian Web sites

www.euphrates.ca
Euphrates' Web site (Arab-Canadian Hip-Hop)

Unit VI: Europe: The Influence of Ancestry and Imperialism

European History

www.deremilitari.org/links
General European Evolution/History

www.besthistorysites.net
General European Evolution/History

www.ams-net.org
General European Musicology (all eras)

www.musicasacra.com
General Web site for European Sacred Music

European Musical Evolution

Medieval

www.medieval.org/emfaq/site
General Web site for "Early" Music

www.diamm.ac.uk
Medieval Music Digital Archives

Renaissance

www.geocities.com/vienna/choir
General Web site for Renaissance Music

historymedren.about.com
Web site for Medieval and Renaissance Music

history.hanover.edu/courses
General Reformation Music Web site

Baroque

www.baroquemusic.org
General Web site for Baroque Music

www.oup.com/us/catalog/general
Oxford University's Opera History
(Keyword: opera)

Classical and Romantic

www.carolinaclassical.com
> General Web site for the "Classical" Period

www.classicalmusic.about.com/od/
> General for the "Classical/Romantic" Periods

www.essentialsofmusic.com/eras
> General for the "Classical/Romantic" Periods

Other

music.wayne.edu
> Wayne State Music Department Web site, Detroit, Michigan (to contact: J.Hartway[Units I/VI], D.Tini [Units VI/X], K.Markou & L. Dyament [Unit VII], C.Collins [Unit X])

music.umich.edu
> University of Michigan Music Department Web site, Ann Arbor, Michigan (to contact: J. Borders, W.Malm [Unit IX], J. Becker [Unit IX])

Unit VII: Jewish and Romani: Stories of Creativity and Influence

Jewish (see Unit V)

www.jmwc.org
> Jewish Music Web center

www.jewishmusicgroup.com
> General Web site for Jewish Music

www.geminichildrensmusic.com
> Gemini's Web site

www.avishaimusic.com
> Avishai Cohen's Web site

Jewish/Rom

www.yalestrom.com
> Source for both Klezmer and Jewish/Rom Music

Romany (Rom/Roma)

romani.org
> General Info. Rom Organizations (including: Music & Dance)

romaweb
> Listing of Rom Articles and Information

scn.org/roma
> Listing of Rom Web sites

dzeno.cz
> Czech Republic Romany Radio Web site

idw.idebate.org/roma
> General Articles of Roma International Movement

Flamenco

www.sfflamenco.com
> General Flamenco Information and Listings

deflamenco.com
> Links to Flamenco Web sites

flamencoinc.org
> Personal Recommendations of Flamenco Sources

Guitar

guitarfox.com
> General Listing of Guitar Sources

Greece

www.greekmusic.com
> Popular Greek Music Resource

www.oeaw.ac.at/kal/agm/
> Ancient Greek Music Information

greekcity.com
> Listing of Greek Videos and Music Resources

Unit VIII: Africa and Latin America: Rites, Rituals, and Community Life

Rites, Rituals and the Life Cycle

ritesofpassage.org
> General Web site for Rites of Passage Information

ritesofpassage.net
> Web link to "Rites of Passage" Television Saga

photus.com/religion/india_life-cycle
> Life-cycle Rituals of Various Religions and Sects

Africa – History, Culture and Music

blackquest.com
> Listing of African (and African-American) web sites
> (click: Africa Homepage or Africa Within)

archaeology.about.com/od/africa/
> General Web sites for most African Countries

www.afriqueindex.com/music/african
> General Web sites for a variety of African Music
> (Note: for best results – select individual African cultures/countries "…and music")

www.afropop.org
> Source for "Modern" African Music (1950's to present)

www.mbongivillage.org
  Biza/Tito Sompa's Web site

nigeria-arts.net/music/
  General Nigerian Arts and Music Web site

www.naijajams.com
  Nigerian Music and Samples Web site

www.afromix.org/html/musique/pays/zaire
  Democratic Republic of the Congo Music
  Source

Spanish Colonization of the Americas
  (see: any encyclopedia "… Spanish colonization of the Americas")

Latino Web sites – General History
  (see: most large universities have a "Latino"
  culture studies department; Otherwise: www.
  lib.iastate.edu/commons/hhm/recommended.
  html is a Source for Latino Web sites)

www.public.iastate.edu/~savega/us_latin.
  General Listing of Latino Web sites

www.si.edu/resource/faq/nmah/latino.htm
  Resources of the Smithsonian Institute for
  Latino cultures

Culture and Music of Cuba

www.ibiblio.org/cuba/
  General Listing of Cuban Web sites including
  Music

www.afrocubaweb.com/
  Web site for various Afro-Cuban Resources

www.descarga.com/cgi-bin/db
  Latino Music Web site (for CD's and information)

www.cubanmusic.com/
  Cuban Music Web site

Culture and Music of Puerto Rico

www.musicofpuertorico.com/
  General Web site for Puerto Rican Music and
  Musician Bios

www.topuertorico.org/culture/music.
  General Web site for Puerto Rican Culture and
  Music

www.prfdance.org/perform.htm
  Web site for PRF Puerto Rican Dance Company

www.salsadancedvd.com/Salsa
  General Salsa Dance and Music Web sites

Culture and Music of Mexico

www.mexonline.com/cultart.htm
  General Culture and History Web site of
  Mexico

www.alegria.org/body_lnk_music.html
  General Web site for Mexican Music

www.mariachi.org/
  General Web site for Mariachi Music

Culture and Music of the Dominican (Republic)

www.iasorecords.com/
  General Web site for Bachata and Merengue
  Music

www.bachataradio.com/
  General Web site for Bachata and Merengue
  Music

Unit IX: Asia: Seeking Balance (and Healing) Through Music

Music Therapy/Music and Healing (and Asian Music)

www.musictherapy.org/
  General Web site for the American Music
  Therapy Assoc.

www.helpself.com/directory/music
  Listing of Music Therapy Sites

www.brainconnection.com
  Music and the Brain Web sites

www.amc-music.org/musicmaking/thebrain

www.amc.org.uk/
  General Asian Music Web site (in the UK)

Culture and Music of India

www.gosai.com/
  General Web site for E. Indian Culture and
  Music

www.esamskriti.com/
  General Web site for E. Indian Culture,
  Hinduism, & Music

www.indiasheritage.org/
  General Indian Culture Web site

www.bollywoodworld.com/
  Bollywood Web site

www.musicindiaonline.com/
  General Indian Music Web site (all varieties)

www.indian-music.com/
  General Indian Music Web sites (includes
  teacher/student zone)

Culture and Music of China

www.chinapage.com/china
General Chinese Culture Web site

www.chinese-culture.net/
General Chinese Culture and Current Events
Web site

www.chineseperformingarts.org/
Chinese Music and Performance in USA and
Europe

www.chineseoperainstitute.com.sg/
Chinese Opera Web site

www.beijingpage.com/
General Information on Beijing (including
opera)

Culture and Music of Korea

www.culture-arts.go.kr/english/perform
General Information on Korean Culture and
Music

www.korea.net/Search/Directory/DirList
General Links to Korean Culture Web sites

210.95.200.104/eng/performance/regper
Information on Korean Performances and
Music

www.clickkorea.org/eventsnnews
General Information on Korean Culture,
Music, & Dance

Culture and Music of Japan

www.yookoso.com/
General Japanese Culture and Music Web site

www.japansociety.org/events/
General Japanese Culture Web site

www.sal.tohoku.ac.jp/~gothit/
Listing of Humanities Web sites in Japan

www.japan-zone.com/culture/noh.shtml
General Japanese Culture Web site
(includes Noh & Kabuki)

www.csuohio.edu/history/japan/
General Japanese Culture and Music / Film
Web site

Culture and Music of Indonesia

www.budpar.go.id/
General Indonesian Culture and Arts Web site

www.library.ucla.edu/url/colls/sea/
General Internet Links to Indonesian Culture

www.indonesianmusic.com/faq/7.html
General Internet Links to Indonesian Music
(many varieties)

Unit X: Creolization: Creating Community Beyond Race and Nation
(General: search "creolization" or "creolization and Seychelles" for articles on the phenomenon of creolization in language and culture)

Culture and Music of Seychelles

www.seychelles.seybay.com/index
General Listing of Seychelles Web sites
(click useful links)

www.virtualseychelles.sc/pecu/pecu
Seychelles Music Web site

Jazz and American Creolization in Jazz
(see Unit IV web sites on African-American/
African Diaspora music)

www.indiana.edu/aaamc
Archives of African-American Music &
Culture/Indiana Univ.

www.africanamericas.com
Variety of African-American Music links

Glossary

A

A cappella Music unaccompanied by instruments.

accompaniment Usually musical support for a melody or solo instrument. More frequent focus on harmony and rhythm than on melodic content.

accordion An aerophone with reeds contained within a casing or behind headboards. Air is created with folding bellows, passed over the reeds, and released by keys or buttons to play melodies or chords.

acoustic instrument Any unamplified (not electronically enhanced) instrument

aerophone Instruments that produce vibration by the use of air. This is one of five categories of the Sachs-Hornbostel system of instruments. Aerophones include: trumpets, horns, wood-winds, flutes, pipes, and even the human voice.

affinity A liking or attraction for something. In particular *affinity transfers* occur in our world, when we have an attraction for some quality (in music, food, etc.) and find that "quality" somewhere else – thus attracting us to a previously unknown expression.

African-American music All music created by people of African ancestry living in the Americas (North, Central, and South – and the Caribbean). This includes, also, music of European ancestry in the Americas – as all European American ancestry has been influenced by African-American evolution as well.

African diaspora All dispersed African cultures. This includes all of the Americas, the Caribbean, and much of the rest of the World, especially "hub" cities in Europe (e.g., London, Paris, Amsterdam, etc.) and regions around the world colonized by European cultures.

African music A generic heading for hundreds of different culture groups, linguistic systems, and their music over centuries. Many of the designations by "country" (results of colonization) are irrelevant to the identity of language and culture.

antiphony A *performance practice* that focuses on alternating two or more groups or musicians (as in "call-and-response" style).

appropriation Generally refers to a forceful taking or using of something (without permission). Modern uses of the world simply refer to "taking" something and may imply permission. "Mis-appropriation" is used to indicate there was no permission or respect given in the acquisition.

aria An accompanied "solo" song that serves as an emotional highlight in opera. Arias are usually musically complex and can stand alone as separate musical works in concert.

articulation The manner in which a pitch or sound is begun or completed. Consists of accents and duration as well.

Ashkenazi A reference to Jewish communities that evolved from the Middle East through Russia. Eastern Europe, and into Germany and Western Europe.

Azan (Ad'han) Islamic call to prayer. In Muslim cultures, it will be sounded five times each day.

B

bagpipe An *aerophone* that uses an air bag to store air that is released through one or more drones and a chanter.

Baha'i (the Baha'i Faith) An independent world religion founded by the "Bab" ("Gate") and *Baha'u'llah* (Arabic for the "Glory of God") to unite the world's religions, races, and nations.

Baha'u'llah Prophet or Son (Manifestation) of God and Founder of the Baha'i Faith. Declared his station in 1863 in Iran.

Universal House of Justice The international administrative body of the Baha'i Faith, located in Haifa, Israel.

ballad A general designation for a slower-paced song that focuses generally on human love.

bandoneon A German-invented, free-reed instrument particularly popular in Argentina and for use in the *orquesta tipica* or tango orchestra.

banjo A chordophone of African origin (from the *Akonting* of the Jola group from Senegambia), particularly popular in the United States for bluegrass and country music.

Bar Mitzvah (also B'nai Mitzvah/Bat Mitzvah) (from Hebrew: "one to whom the commandments apply") – a ceremony at the age of maturity (12 or 13), marking the time when boys ("bar") and girls ("bat") become responsible for their own actions and Faith.

Baroque A "period" and designation for music and art dating in Europe from 1600-1750CE.

bass Both a term to define the lower frequencies in the spectrum of pitch, and for instruments or voices that play these lower frequencies. The "bass," when used to describe an instrument in popular music, refers to the string bass or electric bass guitar.

bata Though a drum from both the Yoruba (Nigeria) and Caribbean, there are numerous other occurrences of this term (see encyclopedia: "Bata" for a disambiguation).

beat A pulse in music. Beats are generally organized in groupings (meter) and are the means by which two or more musicians can maintain a structure by which they might play together. In popular music, the "rhythm" of the music is frequently referred to as the "beat" (as in, "I like the beat."). This reference is actually to the texture of rhythms.

bebop General term for past-paced jazz that includes strong focus on improvisation, it became popular after the "big band era" (1950's/60's).

binary form Any two-part form (A section / B section).

bluegrass Scottish/Irish music transplanted to the Appalachian Mountains, mixed with jazz, blues, and extensive improvisation.

blues An evolving genre from West African storytelling in the United States. Blues was predominantly a reflection of the individual's sense of "truth" and has evolved through numerous stages. It is among the most influential musical genres in North American popular music.

bolero Originally a 3-beat dance from Spain, the term is frequently used to define "ballads" or slow songs sung in Spanish.

Bollywood The informal name given to India's (Mubai-based) film industry. Bollywood film-making remains among the most prolific of film industries in the world.

bombe An instrument (similar to the *berimbau* of Brazil) used in the Seychelles Islands to accompany "blues-like" improvisatory story telling.

boogie-woogie A style of piano-based blues and ragtime that emerged prior to the popularity of *traditional jazz.*

bossa nova A slow-beat style of Brazilian music, made popular by Joao Gilberto and Antonio (Tom) Carlos Jobim. It is also popular among North American/European jazz musicians.

bowed lute Any lute-like instrument that is played with a bow.

break dancing An important part of "hip-hop" culture, break dancing likely evolved from the influence of *capoeira* (Brazilian dancers) in South Bronx and Queens, New York.

Buddhism A prolific religion in Asia, it focuses on the teachings of Gautama Buddha, referred to as "the Buddha." One source comments:*"It is a dharmic, non-theistic religion, a way of life, a practical philosophy, and a life-enhancing system of applied psychology."* (Wikipedia.org)

C

cadence In Western music, a point of ending or musical repose at the end of a melodic/harmonic phrase. It can also refer to a rhythmic pattern (marching band) or beat or tempo of poetry.

Cajun Both a term used to describe Acadian exiles to Louisiana and the culture (food, etc.,) of Louisiana that grew from their mixing with Spanish, Caribbean, and other immigrants to the region.

call-and-response A general term for any music that introduces a musical idea and is responded to by another. In African-American music, it is characterized by lining out, and the call and response between a soloist and a choir or ensemble.

calypso A musical genre of Trinidad, popular at Carnival time.

canon Music where one or more melodic lines are imitated through much of the work.

cantata A vocal / instrumental composition that evolved from the *Reformation*, usually based upon religious text. The cantata (of the *Baroque* period) became the basis for many hymns and was generally an hour (or so) in duration.

capitalism (capital) An economic system, dominant in the Western world since the breakup of feudalism, in which most of the means of production are privately owned and production is guided, and income distributed, largely through the operation of markets.

Carnatic (Karnatic) A region of South India (below the Himalayas) that also has unique music and dance styles.

Carnival (carnavale) The Carnival Season is a holiday period (generally) during the two weeks before the traditional Christian fasting of Lent. The origin of the name "Carnival" is unclear. The most common theory is that the name comes from the Italian carne- or carnovale, from Latin carnem (meat) + levare (lighten or raise), literally "to remove the meat." It is especially popular in Italy, the Caribbean, and Brazil.

chamber music Music of the chamber or room. Chamber music originated as "popular music" for the aristocracy of Europe—but also includes, today, any performance of European "art" music in small ensembles.

chant A general term for the "intoning" or pitched recitation of religious text.

Chicago-style blues Also, sometimes called "rhythm and blues." It was the primary force from which R&B emerged – or, the creation of Delta-style blues with electronic instruments and drum set.

chord Any combination of (generally) three or more pitches together. Chords are particularly important in Western music. The most common varieties are major and minor.

chordophone One of the Sachs-Hornbostel classifications of instruments. Any instrument that used as "chord" or string to produce sound. Includes, among others, the guitar, piano, and violin.

chorus A large vocal group, the section of a musical piece where the energy is elevated (from the verse), or an individual musician's turn at improvising through one sequence of piece of music.

Christianity A general term for the religion and influences based on the teachings and life of Jesus Christ. Also a reference to the church and human/cultural and political organizations that evolved from the adherence to Christ's life/teachings.

classical/classical music As or like Ancient Greek or Roman antiquity. Also, any art or music of lasting and defined civilizations or cultures. Also, European "art" music or music extending from Christian institutions.

Classical period A period generally defined as 1750-1825, denoting extensive focus on creating order, organization, and definition in art.

clavé The time line of Pan-Latino music. Stick-like instruments (*idiophones*).

community (community life) A general reference to the solidarity of culture systems with a well-developed and balanced understanding of (respect for) of the life-cycle, ancestry, sacrifice, and communication across the human experience.

concerto A multi-section (movement) work that dialogues a soloist with accompaniment (usually *orchestra*).

conjunto A distinctive style of accordion music of Mexican-Americans.

consonant A term describing any music that sounds pleasing or balanced to the listener. (Highly subjective and based on the listener's experiences). The opposite of consonant is dissonant.

contour (melodic) The general shape (rise and fall) of the melody.

copyright Placing and registering ownership for a work.

countermelody A melody that moves contrary or in juxtaposition to another melody.

country music A generic term given to any music with a predominant connection to European-based folk music styles, to the Southern U.S.A, ranching, farming, or blue-collar workers, or which uses sounds or instrumentation common to the genre (notably: pedal steel guitar, banjo, Southern U.S. accents, etc.).

country dance (contredans/kamtolé) A body of dances that evolved from or through colonization from European cultures, including the reel, waltz, polka, and mazurka, among others.

creativity The capacity to adapt, to enjoy change, to problem-solve, and to manifest personal or community flexibility and capacities in altering existing ideas and expressions.

Creole Of or from the creative fusion of cultures. A specific language or culture group created from the combining of two or more other cultures or languages.

creolization A general term to denote the creative fusion or interaction and exchange between cultures. A perpetual process of ongoing adaptation and fusion.

culture balancing To create a balance or alter the characteristics of a culture for the betterment of that culture system.

culture healing A process of identifying cultural imbalances (traits or characteristics that have a harmful effect upon a culture/community's individuals), and seeking alternative (healing) traits or characteristics from outside the culture system.

cultural economics Referring to any human culture having only so much time, resources, or energy. Wherever a culture places those resources and energy determines their return or gain. Conversely, for every area wherein a culture invests, there are likely other areas that will be neglected.

cultural imperialism A reference to any culture's values or expressions dominating or controlling the perception of benefit or value of another's.

D

darabukkah (dombecki/tombak) A ceramic, hour-glass shaped drum (*membranophone*) used as the primary rhythm instrument for many North African/Middle Eastern genres.

dastgah The Persian (Iranian) modes or scales.

decolonization The consequences and cultural dynamics that have resulted from a colonizer's "granting of independence" to its colonies. Refers also to the *cultural healing* or balancing dynamics now engaged in by those culture systems.

development In music, the expansion of a theme or musical idea over the course of a composition. A specific (middle) section of sonata-allegro form in classical/postclassical period composition.

diaspora Any culture dispersed from their point of origin (e.g., Indian, African, Spanish, Jewish diasporas).

digital music (instruments) Any music which uses computer or digital technology to generate sound or is used in producing textured layers (arrangements/production) of music.

dissonance (consonance) The opposite of consonance. Lacking balance or appeal to the listener. Sharp contrast to music perceived as "appealing." (Note: common in horror films or performance art denoting anger, horror, etc.)

"Dixieland" (see "traditional jazz")

drone The sustaining of a pitch or combination of pitches throughout the performance of a piece. Common in Indian instrumental music.

drum set (trap set) Among the most important and prolific instruments in humanity today. The drum set evolved from early (*traditional* style) jazz.

dualism Involves the existence of two fundamental principles (or concepts), often in opposition to each other (e.g., good vs. evil, black vs. white). A prevalent block to the potential of multiple truths co-existing simultaneously.

E

electrophone Sachs-Hornbostel modern classification for any instrument using electricity to generate sound. Primarily includes the synthesizer.

empirical A central concept in science and the scientific method is that all evidence must be empirical, or empirically based—that is, dependent on evidence or consequences that are observable by the senses or provable by scientific methodology.

encoding The act of altering communication or creating double meaning in an expression, rendering it unperceivable by an external group, based usually upon the disrespect incurred by hierarchical classification. See also *signifying*.

ensemble Any group of artists or musicians. Generally used to refer to larger groups of musicians.

equal temperament A system of tuning evolving from the Baroque period wherein the notes within an octave were divided into twelve equal parts.

erhu A bowed lute common throughout most of China.

ethnic music Music that reflects a particular culture or culture group (remembering: all music is equally ethnic).

ethnomusicology The study of "people's" music. Generally is used to refer to the study of "non-Western" music (though all music is ethnic).

F

fancy dancing A pan-Native American style of competitive dance with bright costumes and strong or wide-sweeping movement.

Farsi The language of Iran or Persian culture.

fiddle Any violin used for American folk music (same instrument as the violin).

field hollers Work songs created by Africans in America during slavery and indentured servitude.

files (mind files) A metaphor for the manner in which we acquire and collect (retain), label, or categorize our experiences from which we build our values and perceptions of "the world."

flag song This is an honor song, wherein the flags of nations and sponsoring communities are honored at pow-wows.

flamenco A fusion music and dance originating in the Andalusian region of Spain, which incorporates North African, Spanish/Mediterranean, Jewish, and especially Romany influences.

folk music Often used to denote music created by oral transmission or from a particular ethnicity from "nonprofessional" musicians. Can also be used to create a hierarchy between musical genres or cultures in contrast to "art music" (as such, can be derogatory or patronizing).

form (in music) The organization or structure of a piece of music. Each piece has a logic or blueprint. The form is the piece's overall succession of sections or organizational logic.

frame drum A membranophone with a skin (or membrane) stretched over a round frame, such as a tambourine.

free rhythm Music without a structured or regular beat.

frequency The number of cycles or vibrations per second of any given pitch. Pitches or frequencies are measured in *hertz* (100hz equals 100 cycles per second).

fusion (cultural) A term to express the result of any two or more cultures coming into contact and the expression which results from their exchange of ideas.

> **fusion (musical)** Though all music can be said to be a "fusion" of two or more cultures and influences, the result of recent decades in the increase in technology and media is accelerating the rate and depth of musical fusions worldwide.

G

Gaelic An adjective means "pertaining to the Gaels," whether to their language or their culture.

As a noun, it may refer to the group of languages (originally) spoken by the Gaels, or to any one of the individual languages.

gamelan The word "gamelan" extends from the Javanese word "gamel," (to strike or hammer). A gamelan is a musical ensemble of Indonesian origin featuring a variety of instruments, such as metallophones, xylophones, drums, and gongs; bamboo flutes, bowed and plucked strings; and, frequently, vocalists.

genre (musical) As in literary terms – a style or classification of music.

ghazal A strophic song sung in Urdu. Ghazals have been influential in the development of Indian film songs.

gong kebyar A type of Balinese *gamelan*.

Gothic period Generally refers to the latter part of the European Medieval period (12th to 15th centuries). Gothic art and music transitioned to the Renaissance.

grand entry The opening entry dance at Native American pow-wows.

grass dance A Native American dance originating from the Plains communities – commonly performed as part of today's pow-wows. Grass dancing may have originated as a means of flattening the grass by dancing to prepare for community rituals. Grass dances (to protect the community) may have been mistaken as "war dances" by American militia.

Gregorian chant (plainsong) A body of traditional chants (songs) used in the liturgies of the Roman Catholic Church. Gregorian chants are named after Pope Gregory I.

griot Also djali or djeli, the griot is a West African praise singer, poet, or wandering musician. The tradition is very important to the evolution of blues and other individual story forms in the Americas.

guitarron Spanish for "large guitar," is a deep-bodied 6-string guitar used to play the bass lines in mariachi music.

Guru A spiritual guide or enlightened teacher. In India, gurus are seen as the way to self-realization and fulfillment.

H

haiku A mode of Japanese poetry based on the older *hokku* formulas.

harmony Two or more pitches sounding at the same time. Most harmony is formulated on three or more pitches (see *chords*). Harmony provides a strong basis for emotion. Although more emphasized in the evolution of Western (European/American) music, harmony is now increasingly found in all forms of popularized music.

> **harmonic progression** A formula of building tension and release. Most pieces start from a home base (tonic chord), and then, through a series of *chords*, move away from the base (increasing tension) and finally hitting a pivot chord which returns to home.

harmonium A general term for pedal-pumped or pressure-bellows free-reed organs, probably originating between the mid 1700's and Alexandre Debain's Parisian version of 1842. All variations of harmoniums are generally more portable than other organs. In India, harmoniums are used to accompany song or chant.

Hasidic (Hasidim) The movement originated in Eastern Europe (Belarus and Ukraine) in the 18th century. Rabbi Israel ben Eliezer (1698–1760), also known as the *Ba'al Shem Tov*, founded Hasidic Judaism, which places a strong emphasis on spirituality and "joy," using music and even dance to connect to God.

head voice Vocal production centered in the "mask," face, or head of the singer.

healing (musical) Utilization of music to produce a balancing effect physically, mentally, emotionally, or spiritually. (See also *music therapy*).

highlife A musical genre that originated in Ghana, Sierra Leone, and Nigeria in the 1920's as a blending of British military band music and West African musical/cultural practices. Highlife later fused big band jazz, and other African, American, and European popular musical formats, spreading to other West African countries.

Hindustani The Northern region of India. Also refers to music and dance of the Northern region and to "Hindi-Urdu," a reference to the interconnection and similarities between these two northern and central Indian languages.

hip-hop A reference to both the musical genre and culture (including dance, graffiti art, dress, and language). Hip-hop is viewed by many as the modern descendant of blues and the West African griot. As a musical form, it has encompassed numerous fusions with Jamaican, Brazilian, African, and other American genres. Today, hip-hop is a genre that finds expression in much of the world.

hymn A hymn is a type of song, usually religious, specifically written for the purpose of praise, adoration, or prayer, and typically addressed to a god or other religiously significant figure.

I

idiophones The Sachs-Hornbostel classification of any instrument whose vibrations or sound is caused by striking solid materials. Includes all bells, gongs, marimbas, shakers, etc.

imperialism Any form of governance by "empire." Imperialism has been, historically, the formula for expansion, conquering others, and governance of one's empire for much of human history. It is, in a cultural sense, also a force contradictory to educational/cultural justice.

improvisation The spontaneous composition of music "at the moment," using formulas and patterns known to the musician as required by the genre being performed.

incidental music Any music that supports a story, play, dance, movie, etc.. Programmatic music is also "incidental."

interval The distance or space between any two pitches.

intuition An understanding without apparent effort. Insight seemingly independent of previous experiences or empirical knowledge.

inter-culture Exchange or interaction between or among cultures.

intra-culture Exchange or interaction within cultures.

iqa'a Meter or beat groupings in Arabic music.

Islam A monotheistic religion based upon the teachings of Muhammad. Islam is the second-largest religion in the world today; adherents of Islam are known as Muslims.

J

jazz A "fusion" musical art form that evolved from around the start of the 20th century in New Orleans, rooted in African American musical styles blended with Western music technique and instrumentation. Jazz music has numerous styles, each of which shares: improvisation and the use of rhythmic "groove" or texture.

Jewish culture/religion Also known as the Jewish nation, or the Children of Israel, an ethno-religious group descended from the ancient Israelites and from converts who joined their religion. Like all religions, there is a close connection between the "culture" and religion of members of the Jewish community.

jhala/jor Two sections of a *raag*.

jig A folk-dance type as well as the accompanying dance-tune type, popular in Ireland. It is sometimes seen in its French or Italian forms, *gigue or giga*.

jingle dance A Native American dance frequently done at pow-wows by women. Metallic "jingles" are attached to the skirts to create the "jingling" effect while dancing.

K

Kabuki A form of traditional Japanese theater. Kabuki theater is different from *Noh* in its use of dancing, acrobatics, elaborate make-up, and modern effects. Kabuki is sometimes translated as "the art of singing and dancing."

kamal ngoni An 8-stringed instrument from West Africa.

karaoke Karaoke has been a popular form of entertainment first in Japan, then the rest of East Asia, since at least the 1980s. It has since spread to other parts of the world. In karaoke, amateur singers sing popular songs to musical soundtracks minus the original vocalists.

kata Detailed patterns of movement in both martial arts and other art forms such as kabuki theater.

Karnatic (see Carnatic)

kayageum Korean zither with movable bridges similar to the koto of Japan and guzheng of China.

key (key center/tonal center) A fundamental pitch that is the basis or center for a musical piece.

klezmer (klezmorim) A musical tradition of Hasidic and Ashkenazic Judaism. Around the 15th century, a tradition of secular (non-liturgical) Jewish music was developed by musicians, called kleyzmorim or kleyzmerim. The repertoire is largely dance songs for weddings and other celebrations. Due to the Ashkenazi lineage of this music, the lyrics, terminology, and song titles are typically in Yiddish (from Wikipedia.org/klezmer).

kreolité "Creole" cultures or their creolization process *kreolité*.

L

Lakota Part of the "Great Sioux Nation," the Lakota are the Westernmost of the three Sioux groups occupying lands in both North and South Dakota.

larger culture (superculture) The larger culture influence of a person or community (e.g., North American, British, Nigerian or West African).

Latino Latino (and *Latina* for females) generally refers to an American of Latin American descent (sometimes referred to as Hispanic American heritage).

libretto From Italian "small book." Librettos are the text or basis for the creation of an opera.

life cycle A general reference to the natural human cycle, encompassing birth, passage to maturity, continuity of family, and evolution to "old age." Also a reference to a healthy understanding of the natural human condition.

liturgy A religious ritual (generally referring to Christianity) for public worship.

lute Any "guitar-like" instrument or chordophone whose strings are stretched along a neck or fingerboard.

M

madh A type of Islamic praise song.

madrigal A free secular and imitative work for voice emerging from the Medieval/Renaissance periods.

major scale (mode) A menu of pitches that, based on the equal tempered diatonic (7-note) scale, would be a combination of whole steps (w) and half steps (h) as follows: w w h w w w h.

Manifestations of God The Prophets of the major world religions. They are seen as being "Manifestations" or Reflections of the Will of God.

maqam (maqamat) Scales or modes for Arabic (Middle Eastern/North African music).

Mardi Gras French for "fat Tuesday," the final day of *carnival* prior to Ash Wednesday.

mariachi A musical ensemble in Mexico, particularly popular in the Northern and Central regions, consisting of violins, trumpets, Spanish guitar, vihuela, and *gitarrón*.

mass A celebration of the Eucharist in the Western liturgical rites of the Roman Catholic Church and in the Anglo-Catholic tradition of Anglicanism. Masses are divided into two groups: the proper and the ordinary.

mbira Also known by numerous other words (including thumb piano, and karimba or kalimba), it consists of staggered metal keys mounted on a wooden or calabash resonator.

measures Groupings of beats. In most Western music, the groups of beats are organized in 2, 3, or 4. A strong pulse extenuates the beginning of each measure.

media (media technology) Any form of electronic or communications media influential in the development or propagation of cultural or music ideas.

medieval The term medieval generally encompasses the period of time from the fall of the Roman Empire (476 AD) to approximately the middle of the fifteenth century.

melody A series of pitches occurring one after another (linear organization).

membranophone Sachs-Hornbostel categorization of all drums (or instruments which use as "skin" or membrane to create sound).

merengue Literally "merengue" as in the egg-white delicacy, it is a polka-based musical form credited to the Dominican Republic.

meter A term describing the organization of beats or pulses into groupings (or *measures*).

microtone Any system of pitches organized in smaller increments than the Western equal tempered scale. Includes Indian *raags* and Arabic *maqamat*.

minimalism A type of music in which a minimum of change or alteration of texture or form occurs.

mis-appropriation Reinforcement of the "appropriation" or the taking of something from one culture without due respect or acknowledgement.

monolithic Unchanging, does not permit variation. A reference to perceptions of cultures of race as unchanging.

monophony Single texture (line or voice) music, such as one person chanting or singing.

motet A sacred composition for voices emerging from the Middle Ages.

motive A musical fragment of any variety that is used as a unifying element of a longer work.

movement A section or larger portion of an instrumental work.

musical (musical comedy/play) An outgrowth of English operettas and centuries of musical plays or theater in Europe, musical comedy evolved in the United States from these influences and the Jewish or Yiddish transplanted genres in New York. Many of the first films in Hollywood history were also musicals.

music therapy A clinical or evidence-based use of music in therapy.

Muslim (see Islam) Those who follow the teachings and laws of Muhammad (Mohammad).

mutia A "tambur" (large tambourine) circle dance from the Seychelles Islands.

N

nationalism Attitudes and actions that stress the importance of "national" identity; can have both positive and negative ramifications. Particularly strong in Europe during the "Romantic" period.

Native American A preferred name for First Nation or the First American peoples.

Noh Classical Japanese musical drama extending from 14th century.

neo-classical Music that is like or as that of "classical" periods. A particular style of 20th century music based on that of late Baroque and Classical periods.

ney A popular end-blown flute used in the Middle East.

non-Western Any cultural trait, art, or music not directly connected to Europe or European influence.

notation (musical) A means of retaining (writing) musical ideas and passing them to other musicians. Many cultures have musical notation methods.

O

octave The spacing or distance between pitches of eighth-notes (either half or twice the frequency).

opus (op.) "Work" in Latin. Usually appearing with a number, it is a means of cataloguing a composer's works.

opera Any form of musical storytelling using theater, music, scenery, and telling most, if not all. the story through vocal or sung setting of the text.

Chinese opera A form of musical storytelling dating back to the early 8th century. There are believed to be over 300 different "forms" of Chinese opera.

German opera *Opera* (see above) sung in German. Usually based upon German folklore. Richard Wagner is most famous for his operas.

Italian opera Likely the first and most known form of Western opera. Italian opera is also closely linked to Italian nationalism.

oral tradition In contrast to written traditions, the conveying of any facet of a culture's history or stories through oral presentation, retention, or performance.

oratorio An opera-like format for telling sacred stories (usually from the Bible), as in Handel's *Messiah*.

orchestra A larger instrumental ensemble. Probably the first orchestras were in North African (Middle Eastern) music. The orchestra evolved from the Renaissance to a formula of standardized instrumentation in 18th-century Europe.

orchestration Taking a song or piece of music and expanding it for a wider assortment of instruments, or orchestra.

overtones The harmonics or vibrations that sound above a fundamental pitch.

P

pans (steel drums) An instrument originating in Trinidad and Tobago after WWII. Steel oil drums were pounded and converted to instruments.

pansori A form of Korean storytelling that usually has only a single singer (female) and a drummer accompaniment.

passion A strong feeling, emotion, or desire to act/achieve. Also refers to the suffering of Jesus leading to the Crucifixion.

pendulum (cultural) A reference to the ebb and flow of trends in culture. From dramatic to reserved, classical to romantic, conservative to liberal, etc.

pentatonic Any five-note scale or mode.

performance The creation of a musical (or other) work in isolation of the flow of life. A form of concert or exaggerated presentation.

phrase A musical segment. Often phrases mirror human languages in duration and flow.

pitch A specific frequency; highness or lowness of a frequency.

plainchant/plainsong "Chant" or song without accompaniment.

polka A 19th-century Bohemian dance that became popular in much of Europe and its colonies.

polymeter Two or more meters or beat systems occurring at the same time.

polyphony Two or more melodies or textural layers occurring at the same time.

counterpoint A type of polyphony (from "contra punctus") where two or more melodies flow and the emphasis is on their movement rather than the harmony.

homophony A line of melody with accompaniment.

polyrhythms Different rhythms occurring simultaneously.

pow-wow (Powwow) An important "pan-Native American" gathering of "drums" (drum circles), dancers, and community. Powwows celebrate Native heritage and community life.

prayer A form of communication to a Higher Power.

production (musical) The enhancement, recording, or arrangement of a piece. Generally refers to the creation of a work for media (audio/video recording) or "live" staged performance.

programmatic music Any music based on or supportive of a program (or story).

pulse The beat in music.

Q

qa'nun A horizontal zither instrument popular in the Middle East and North Africa.

quality (tone quality) Also known as *timbre*, this is the way an instrument or voice sounds. (e.g., raspy, smooth, strong, airy).

Quechua (Quichua) Native American people in the Andes regions. Also the language of the Incas.

Quena An Andes-area bamboo flute.

Qu'ran/Koran The Holy text of Islam.

R

raag (rag/raga) A mode or pitch system for Indian music. Raags also entail numerous other associations and connections frequently to Hindu stories and history.

ragtime (ragging) The practice of improvising in a unique rhythmic system prior to the 20th century. Ragging gave way to a distinctive genre known as "ragtime."

rap A reference to reciting poetic lyrics over a beat without pitch. Both distinct from and related to hip-hop.

rasa A reference to numerous associations and spiritual/cultural qualities and disciplines that attach themselves to Indian raags. Also a metaphor for the fulfillment of music.

rasika One who practices or is knowledgeable of rasa.

Rastafarianism A movement initiated by Marcus Garvey in the late 19th century. It grew to become a movement of "black liberation," based upon passages gleaned from the Bible.

recapitulation The return of an original melody or section of music. In sonata-allegro form, the final section.

recitative A form of chanted/sung text. Especially in opera, it served the purpose of covering the narration or dialogue that would lead to each *aria*.

reed (instrument) Any instrument using a "reed,"or bamboo piece, to create vibration. Includes the clarinet, oboe, bassoon, and many organs.

re-education A term to indicate a need to rethink how we learn or teach.

Reformation A movement extending from the 15th century in Germany that led to the development of the Protestant church and reform of Roman Catholic practices in Christianity.

regalia The specific clothing and symbolic "treasures" of each Native American dancer.

reggae A genre of Jamaican origin that evolved from ska (the first variation) and rocksteady as a fusion with British rock, American R&B, and Jamaican musical genres in the 1960s. It became linked with the Rastafarian movement through Bob Marley and Peter Tosh.

Renaissance Any period of rebirth. Particularly used to classify European culture spanning (roughly) the 14th to the 16th centuries.

requiem A mass for the dead.

rhythm The flow of music over time. Often spoken of as "the beat."

rhythm and blues Otherwise referred to as Chicago-style blues, or R&B. The adding of "rhythm" (a rhythm section) to the blues. It also has an evolution that includes modern artists only remotely linked to the original genre.

rhythm section A formula of drums, bass instrument, and accompaniment instrument (guitar, banjo, or piano) that evolved out of *traditional jazz* of the early 20th century. It is now part of the world's popular music.

rite (rites of passage) Rituals that mark the passage of the life cycle.

ritual Any event that occurs regularly and with significance to a culture.

rock (rock 'n' roll) An outgrowth of the black church. It became linked to rhythm and blues and later evolved through the European American community to have a distinctive sound in each decade. Also linked to counter-culture movements.

romantic Of or possessing great emotion or dramatic elements.

    Romantic period Philosophical movement in European cultures from approximately 1825 to the turn of the 20th century.

Romany (Rom/Roma) Often erroneously referred to as "gypsies" (as from Egypt). Romany are believed to have evolved from India and are among the most prolific contributors to the innovations and development of musical genres in Europe.

rubato Italian term to deviate (or slow and free) the tempo.

rumba An important Afro-Cuban music and dance tradition linked to mating dances and religious dances of West Africa. Provided many of the ingredients for mambos, salsa, and other pan-Latino genres.

S

Shabbat/Sabbath (see Jewish) Originally denoting Saturday, the seventh day of the week, or, more precisely, the time period from Friday sunset to Saturday nightfall as taken from the Bible as the "day of rest."

sacred (music) Any music linked to a religious purpose or used to express the Holy writings or events of a religion.

salsa A "sauce" of rhythms and dances. Salsa emerged out of the fusion of Cuban and Puerto Rican cultures in combination with communities in New York barrios and Spanish Harlem.

samba A Brazilian music and dance genre associated with *carnavale*.

Santeria A merging of Roman Catholic traditions and "sainthood" and West African or indigenous rituals.

santour A multi-string zither with movable bridges, struck with two hammers.

saxophone An invention of Adolphe Sax (circa 1840). It is commonly used in jazz and Western popular music.

scale A menu of pitches used as the basis of a composition.

score The written notation for a composition or orchestrated piece of music. Used by conductors in orchestral conducting.

secular (music) Any music not directly connected to religion or sacred purpose.

Sephardic/Sephardim A "sub-group" of Jewish tradition in the Iberian Peninsula (Spain and Portugal). Also carries strong influences from North African cultures.

Seychelles (Islands) A group of islands in the Indian Ocean (East of Kenya/North of Madagascar).

shamisen A traditional Japanese lute or chordophone.

signifying The tradition of creating or implying meaning that is often encoded.

Silk Road An interconnected series of routes through Southern Asia traversed by caravan and ocean vessel, and connecting Chang'an (today's Xi'an), China, with Antioch, Asia Minor, as well as other points. It extends over 8,000 km (5,000 miles).

sitar A large "lute-like" chordophone with two sets of stings, predominant in Indian classical music (particularly Hindustani). A sympathetic set of strings resonates to create a buzzing sound.

solo Performing alone or in separation from the accompaniment.

sonata A Baroque multi-movement work for solo instrument. Or, a multi-movement work for piano and another instrument.

sonata form A format paralleling European academic traditions: exposition (thesis), development (body) and recapitulation (conclusion).

sonograph A format for taking musical notes (sono-sound/graph-picture).

soul A reference usually associated to African-American music, but one that implies possessing deep and sincere emotion.

spirituals A genre of African-American evolution that mixed work songs and African song structures with Christian hymnody.

steel drums (see pans)

stereotyping The act of creating biased categories.

strophic form A song in which several verses are sung to the identical melody.

superculture (larger culture) The larger or most dominant culture structure.

swing A reference to a specific rhythmic feel or groove used in jazz.

symphony A multi-movement work generally composed for symphonic orchestra.

symphony orchestra (orchestra) A set instrumentation solidified in Manheim, Germany that has a specific formula of string instruments, winds, brass, and percussion.

syncopation (see rhythm) Placing stress or accents in between the beats. Common in music of African/pan-Latino origin, and much of today's popular music throughout the world.

T

tabla Often used to refer to a pair of Indian drums (tubblaa), it also means "drum" in Arabic.

tala Rhythmic meter in Indian music.

tambal A hammer dulcimer or zither; also referred to as a *cymbalum*.

tambura (also tanpura) The four-stringed drone instrument used in Indian classical music. The double-sided drum used in *merengue* from the Dominican Republic.

tango A musical dance genre originating in Argentina with strong connections to *flamenco* and other European musical genres.

taragot A Hungarian reed instrument similar to the saxophone and clarinet.

tempo (see rhythm) The speed or rate of the beat.

tenor The upper male voice. Part of SAT(tenor)B choral formula.

tetrachord A four-note scale or portion of a diatonic (7-note) scale.

texture The density or layering of musical instruments in a piece of music.

theme A melody that is the basis of a longer work.

through-composed A piece of music that has little or no repetition. Usually linked to programmatic music.

Tibetan Buddhist chant (dbyang) A particular style of Buddhist chanting.

timbre The sound or tone color or quality of the sound (linked to sound-wave forms).

time A reference to the manner or way in which music flows. A good sense of rhythm.

tonality (tonal music) Music with a recognizable tonality or tonal formula.

tone color (see timbre)

tone poem A type of programmatic music evolving from the Romantic period. An orchestrated story.

tonic The home-based pitch or key.

traditional A reference to something that changes little. However, the original definition (from *traditionis*) refers to something that gives way to something else (or changes). All traditions change.

traditional jazz Often called "Dixieland," a preferred term is traditional jazz. It was the first jazz tradition.

trance (music/state) An altered state of consciousness. Often a music ritual that is designed to create a hypnotic or ecstatic state.

tuning The alignment of instrumental tunings with a set standard.

U

ud (oud) A most important lute in Arabic music. Likely the precursor to the guitar.

Underground Railroad A network of clandestine routes by which African slaves in the 19th-century United States attempted to escape to free states, or as far north as Canada, with the aid of abolitionists.

UNESCO Acronym for United Nations Educational Scientific and Cultural Organization.

Universal House of Justice The international or governing body of the Baha'i Faith.

unison A matching of pitches of two or more instruments, or the performing in octaves (octave unison)

V

values (cultural) The characteristics or traits honored and cherished by an individual or cultural group.

Vedas Four scriptural texts that are the founding documents of Hinduism.

vernacular A reference to secular or popular culture or music.

vibrato A wavering or quick fluctuation in pitch.

vihuela A small folk guitar (resembling a mandolin) used in *mariachi* music.

violin A descendant of the rabab (rababah), it is the most pronounced instrument in the symphonic orchestra.

vocables Singing "meaning" with syllables that are not part of a language.

voice human voice: Can produce a number of *timbres* or voice qualities, including "head voice" (focused in the mask or nasal center of the face0; "falsetto" (focused in the upper head with little or no throat or chest voice) and "chest voice" (focused deeper in the throat or chest of the singer); voice (in orchestration): an individual instrument or single layer of the texture.

W

Western Anything linked to European and European-dominated or colonized cultures.

Western music A reference to music that has evolved from European heritage.

work songs Any songs that are used to motivate or sustain work. Africans under slavery in the Americas used their ancient practice of singing while working to sustain the burden of injustice and mistreatment.

world music A general reference to the emerging world music scene. A reference to non-Western or non-European-based music.

Y

yang (yin/yang) In ancient Chinese philosophy and metaphysics, describes two primal opposing but complementary forces found in all things in the universe.

yang qin (yang chin) A Chinese hammered dulcimer.

Yiddish A language that mixes Hebrew and German with strong Slavic components.

Yoruba A large cultural group primarily from Nigeria and instrumental in the evolution of new world music/cultural expressions.

Z

zampoña A type of Native American pan-flute from the Andes region.

zapateo Meaning "shoe tapping," a flamenco-derived folkloric tap dance.

zapateado Any style of pan-Hispanic tap-style dancing.

zheng (guzheng) A Chinese zither with moveable strings (see guzheng).

zither Any chordophone wherein the strings are attached in a horizontal fashion (includes the piano, harpsichord, and hammer dulcimer).

zydeco A style of Creole or Cajun music from Louisiana that fuses numerous instruments and genres.

Index

A

accents (*see* rhythm)

accordion

acoustic instruments

Adh'an (Azan)   169, 174–6, 206

aerophone(s)   182, 220, 230, 394, 401

affinity   iv, xvi, xxiv, 27, 40, 46, 55, 105, 131–2, 138, 140, 150, 216–17, 225, 308, 324–5, 336, 345, 352, 354, 357, 359, 360, 367, 451, 453, 472

    affinity base   105

    affinity transfer   55, 324, 367, 451

African-American music   107, 109, 115, 132–3, 137, 444, 448, 481

    blues   iv, viii , xxii, 118, 292

    calypso   iv, 39, 105, 107, 129–30, 133–6, 142, 325, 339, 345, 444

    capoeira   105, 107, 125, 129–33, 144

    Delta blues   117, 141, 491

    (65)gospel   iv, vi, xv

    hip-hop   *see* hip hop

    jazz   *see* jazz

    reggae   80, 84, 86–7, 96, 105, 128, 130, 132, 141–2, 290, 324, 333, 339, 342, 345, 375, 444, 451, 453

    rhythm and blues   125, 127, 142, 291, 325, 327, 336–7, 342, 444, 474, 483, 510

    rural blues   117

    spirituals   iv, 105–6, 108–10, 112–15, 117, 128, 267, 444, 465, 468, 491

    work songs   105–6, 109–10, 113, 116–17, 128, 141, 465

African Diaspora   39, 68, 97-144, 290–1, 308, 325, 450–1, 482–3, 494

Africa(n)

    Benin   332–3, 338, 353

    Congo   x, xi, 318, 322–3, 328–31, 334, 357–8, 462

    Congo, Democratic Republic of   318, 328–30

    Ethiopia   478–80

    history   111, 308, 315

    Igbo   3, 111, 133, 326–7, 365

    jazz   496 *see also* jazz,

    Kenya   306

    Masai   306

    Morocco   viii, xiv, 13, 16–17, 22–4, 154, 177, 179–80

    music   39, 193, 314, 324–5, 328, 333

    North Africa   24, 168–9, 172–3, 181, 216, 258, 261–2, 264, 272, 286, 292, 478, 498

    Congo, Republic of   330

    South Africa   261, 332, 481, 487

    Zaire (former)   318, 328–30

Akioshi, Toshiko   418

alap/alapana   *see* raag

Albenez, Isaac   294

    Asturias (Leyenda)   x, 293–4

Al-Jundi, Zein   184, 202

America(n)

    history   8, 35, 73, 77, 92, 108, 110, 143, 211, 449

    music   xix , 8, 36, 60, 79, 82, 107, 109, 115–16, 132–3, 137, 192, 269, 324–5, 327, 342, 345, 348, 351, 373, 400, 342, 444–5, 447–9, 465, 478, 481, 498, 502

    revolution   254

    Pan-American   129, 133, 443

Andalusia(n) (Al-Andalus/Andalous)   viii, 16–17, 24, 178–80, 184–5, 201–2, 263–4, 278, 291–2, 295

Andes (Andean)   viii, 43–5, 52–3, 55, 78–80

André, David   459

Angelou, Maya   106

appropriation   121, 144, 465

    mis-appropriation   111, 144

Arash   xii, 188, 500

Arc Music International   ix, x, xi, xii, xiii, 265, 276, 287, 345, 350, 354, 388, 399, 407, 482

Argentina xvi, 352, 356, 499

aria 102, 230, 400, 439

Arkatkar, Mrinalin 160–1, 194, 379–84, 386, 389, 403, 439

Armenia(n) 5, 56, 215, 277

Armstrong, Louis 257, 367, 469–70, 475

articulation 125

assimilation iv, 108–112, 116, 129, 142, 269, 491, 494

Austria(n) 4, 38, 211–12, 216, 237, 245, 282, 286

      Vienna 212, 240, 256, 297–98, 392, 401

B

Bach, (Johann Sebastian) xii, 231–2, 503

bachata 338–40

bagpipe 288

Bahá'í (the Bahá'í Faith) ix, xiii, 192–5, 202, 207, 494, 508

      Abdu'l-Bahá ix, 145, 191, 193, 358

      Bab, the ix, 190–2, 207

      Bahá'u'lláh 190–1

      Haifa (Israel) 42, 164, 189–90, 207, 441

      Hidden Words, the ix, 189, 207

      Promise of World Peace, the 191, 441

      Seven Valleys, the 432, 440

      Universal House of Justice, the 190, 207, 441

bandoneon 498–9

bands xv, xvi, 41, 226, 254, 275, 280–1, 287, 304, 466, 469, 471, 474–5, 507

      concert viii, xi, 254, 204

      marching 254, 275, 304

      military 254, 275, 304

      rock n' roll *see* Rock n' Roll

banjo 49, 468, 470

Bar Mitzvah *see* Jewish

Baroque v, 215, 218, 220, 222, 227, 229–31, 234, 236, 255, 317, 393, 503

Bartley, Robert 418, 429, 448

Basho, Matsuo 248, 251, 256

      haiku 247–8, 251, 256

bass 17, 34, 46, 49, 96, 114, 121 123–4, 221, 280-1, 288–9, 304, 327–8, 343, 346, 348–9, 354, 462, 470–1, 474, 483, 486–7, 489, 493, 497

beat *see* rhythm

bebop *see* jazz

Becker, Judith 408, 421–2, 424

Beethoven, (Ludwig von)

      Symphony No. 9 x, 242, Unit VI

berimbau ix, 131–3

Bharata Natyam 195, 378, 383

bias

      human bias(es) 99, 105, 442

binary form 483

bluegrass 465, 480–1

blues *see* African American

bolero 342–3

Bolivia(n) xvi, 45, 79, 352, 354, 365

Bollywood 377, 389

bombe 451

Borders, James 157, 159, 212

bowed lute 398

Brazil (Brazilian) xi, xv, xxii, 125, 131–32, 324, 326, 352–4, 356, 359, 433, 444, 499, 510

break dancing 131

Buddhism 153, 164–5, 206, 369–70, 38, 391–92, 420

      Gautama 370

      Metta Sutta 164

      Siddhartha Guatama 165

      Tibetan 266, 433

      Vatthupama Sutta 369

Burga, Alfonso 80–1, 83, 87

Burning Bush x, 262–4

Byzantine 215, 287, 295

      empire v, 295

C

cadence 221–22, 226, 473

cadenza 13

call-and-response 66, 73, 114, 17, 180, 185, 493, 498

calypso iv, 23, 105, 107, 219–30, 133–6, 142, 325, 339, 345, 444

      calypsonian iv, 133–4

canon 227, 260

cantata ix, 230–1, 233

cantor/cantillation) *see* Jewish

capitalism (capital) 36–7, 47, 51, 63, 105, 148, 250, 307–8, 329–30, 445, 449

Caribbean xv, 41, 56, 98, 128, 131, 133, 143, 306, 335, 342, 347, 355–6, 358–9, 367, 380, 412, 452, 460, 466, 468–69, 471, 482, 494
see also individual countries

Carnatic (Karnatic) 379–80, 383, 385–6

carnival (carnivale/carnavale) 129, 133–4, 136, 144, 337, 353

Casper viii, 84–7, 92, 241

Celtic (Celts) vi, 3, 34, 120, 286–8, 480–3, 486

Center for Cultural Healing, the ii, xxiv, 130, 460

chamber music 260

chant (intonement) v, 157, 161, 172, 175, Unit V

charango 45

chen *see* Zheng

Chicago xiv, 5, 34, 56, 117–18, 123, 157, 165, 333, 381, 466, 469, 474, 492

> Chicago-style blues 117–18

China (Chinese) Unit IX

> Beijing (Peking) 395–97, 399, 402

> Chin 398

> Chinatown 390, 402, 409

> Chou 391, 394

> Han 76, 391–3, 405

> Ming 393, 397

> Mongol 187, 391–2, 394

> new year

> opera ii, vi, 26, 58, 390, 393–95, 398–99, 439
> > *also see* Opera

> Qing xi, xii, 393, 395, 397, 496

> Shang 391

> Sui 246, 392

> Yuan 391–2, 394

chord(s) *see* harmony

chordophone 77, 182

chorus 17, 45, 86, 92, 96, 121, 173, 180, 185–6, 222, 233, 242, 255, 263, 287, 342–3, 346, 351–2, 384, 394, 412, 414, 490

Christianity/Christian xv, 63, 110–13, 143–4, 148–50, 153, 159, 166–9, 171, 176, 178, 180, 184, 195, 210–16, 221, 229–30, 235, 252, 258, 260, 286–7, 291, 297, 303, 308, 339, 406, 439, 465, 491

> Bible 166, 173, 234, 372

> Church 166, 193, 205, 215–16, 218–19, 221, 223, 229, 234, 244, 259, 311, 341, 357

> Crusades 168, 170, 183–4, 187, 213–14, 216, 218, 230, 236, 259

> Gregorian Chant 157–59, 216, 225
> > *also see* chant

> Holy Roman Empire 38, 216, 218–19, 225

> hymns *see* hymn

> Jesus Christ 221, 235

> liturgy 157, 216–17

> Roman Catholic 134, 157, 166, 173, 205, 216, 219, 221, 223, 229, 235–6, 244, 252, 286, 295, 337, 341

> Vatican 158, 205, 223

chromatic (chromaticism) 285

circle *see* Native American

classical

> Ancient Greek 192, 213, 219, 225, 255, 295, 300

> music Unit VI, 167, 233

Classical period 236, 244, 255–6, 392

clavé (clavé rhythm) 327, 337, 345–6, 462

Cohen, Avishai x, 267–8

Collins, Chris xi, 485–8

Columbus, Christopher 210

Coltrane, John 446

community Unit VIII

concert/concretizing viii, xi, 38, 56, 103, 113, 117, 135, 141, 184, 202, 212, 214, 219–20, 230, 239, 240, 249, 254, 256, 266, 268, 282, 293–4, 304, 344, 366, 386, 418, 421, 438, 485, 487, 499, 501, 504

concerto xii, 227, 238, 294, 488, 503

Confucius 391, 397, 502

Congo *see* Africa

conjunto 338

consonant (dissonant) 226

contour 160, 174, 202, 301–2

counter-culture 155–6, 194

country music 26, 55, 98, 103, 147, 195, 324, 348, 356, 465

Creole/creolization vi, xxii, Unit X

Cruz, Celia xvi, 339, 343

Cuba(n) ii.xv, 133, 294, 325–6, 336–8, 340–6, 348, 353, 355–6, 358–9, 365, 368, 412, 491

cumbia vi, xi, 80, 128, 340, 345, 353, 356, 358–9, 368

culture(s)

    culture balancing iv, 75, 77–8, 86, 92

    culture-bearers xix, xxiii, 24, 59, 69, 92, 94, 105, 159, 315, 365, 405, 436

    cultural-centricity 105

    cultural imperialism 218, 308

Cyprus xv, 297–8

Czech Republic 20, 238, 293, 311, 331, 489

    Kutna Hora 208

    Prague 103, 208, 238, 259, 293, 464, 489, 509

D

Dalinda xii, 497

dance (dancer) 67, 71, 178, 277–78, 291–92, 318, 375, 377–78, 384, 459, 508

    African 353, 356

    Kathak 383

    Indian 377–78

    Native American see Native American

darabukkah see dombecki

dastgah 173, 189

Debby, Mohamed 16–17, 180

decolonization 318, 447

DeCoque, Oliver 334

Democratic Republic of the Congo see Africa

Dely, Istvan 356, 358–9, 501–3

    Dely, Leonor xi, 359

Diallo, Yaya 357–8, 501
    see also: African Diaspora

dissonance (consonance) 299

"Dixieland" see "traditional jazz"

djaly see griot

doina 276, 285, 299

dombecki (dombek/darbukkah) 183, 199, 500

Dominican Republic 338–40, 345, 355–6, 359

    Dominican 338–40, 344–5, 355, 56, 359

drone x, 39, 160–1, 317, 385, 403

drum set (trap set) 327, 359, 470

dualism (dualistic) 97, 151–3, 445

dynamics xxii, 13, 117, 132, 143, 150, 162, 184, 189, 199, 214–15, 228, 260–1, 264, 267, 291, 303, 305, 324, 335–6, 348, 352, 360, 362, 381, 394, 400, 439, 444, 446–7, 453, 455, 465–9, 478, 484

E

eagle 63–4, 71, 94–5

Ecuador viii, 45, 79–81, 92, 352, 355

Einstein, Albert 25, 151

Elizer, Rabbi Israel Ben 258, 261

    Hassidic see Jewish

Ellington, "Duke" 3, 464, 470, 475

empirical 97, 375

encoding iv, 107, 109, 112–13, 116, 127–30, 133, 135, 142, 339

ensemble xi, 12, 43, 55, 181, 262, 288, 303, 365, 384, 388, 398, 406–7, 410, 13, 416, 418, 421–2, 424, 427, 440, 467

equal temperament 255

erhu 398, 401–2

Ethiopia 478–80

    Eritrea 332, 478–80

ethnic music 206, 211–12

ethnomusicology ii, xiv, xxi, xxiii, 65, 135, 211, 422–3, 428, 439

Euphrates ix, 196–8, 200

F

Fania All-Stars 343, 368

Farsi (Persian) 192, 207

fiddle 486–7

field hollers see worksongs

files (mind files) iv, xix, xxi, xxii, 51, 75, 84, 92, 146

filtered responses 102

First Nation 65, 84

flamenco (flamenca) v, 278–95, 304–37–38, 343

    compas 292

    zapateado 278, 292, 348

folk music xi, xvi, 48, 109–10, 150, 222, 227, 257, 261, 279, 285, 295, 298, 394, 482, 485, 487, 489, 497

form (musical) xxi, 44, 227

free jazz *see* jazz

frame drum 434

frequency 49, 159, 309, 407, 417, 453, 459, 510

fugue ix, 228, 233–34

fusion

    cultural xiii, 16, 111, 144, 167, 189, 296, 362, 367, 420, 443, 451, 458–9, 467, 478, 480

    musical 179, 275, 469

G

gamelan vi, xi, 408, 410–11, 420–7, 434, 507

genre (music) 215, 324

Gothic period 213

grass dance 67

Gregorian chant (plainsong) *see* Chant

H

harmony Unit VI

head voice 76

Hebrew *see* Jewish culture/religon

hip-hop iv, 2, 61, 84, 86, 102–03, 105, 107, 116, 119–20, 124–27, 131–32, 142, 144, 151, 195–7, 199–200, 249–50, 255, 316, 324, 339, 342, 449, 451, 462, 473, 493, 510

hymn 111, 117, 245–6, 251, 493

I

idiophones 182, 439

improvisation 10, 20, 49, 180, 185, 188, 205, 167, 281, 292, 342, 354, 386, 388–89, 432, 434, 466–7, 470, 473, 477–8, 482–83, 485, 487

incidental music 227

interval 226

Islam v, 153, 168–80, 187, 192, 198–9, 202, 206–7, 258, 262, 420

    Azan (Ad'han) 119, 174–6, 206

    five pillars 171–72, 200

    Qu'ran (Koran) 17, 172, 175, 206

    Mosque 58, 154, 157, 168, 171, 174–8, 201, 291

J

jazz vi, viii, ix, xiv, xv, xvi, xxi, xxii, Unit IV, Unit X

Jewish culture/religion 261, 264, 267

    Ashkenzi 261–65, 267–69, 286, 292

    Bar Mitzvah 260

    cantor (cantillation) ix, 157, 162–4, 194, 215

    Jewish scale 264

    Klezmer 262–5, 267–8, 279–82, 304

    Klezmorim 264, 281

    Rabbi (Rebbe) 162–63, 258, 261, 281

    Sabat (Sabbath) 205

    Sephardic v, x, 183, 261–65, 267–69, 286, 292

    Yiddish x, 261–3, 265, 267–8, 280–1

jig 288, 486

K

karaoke 444

kata 413

key (key center/tonal center) 28, 31, 83, 94, 123, 180, 206, 214, 225–6, 238–40, 249, 251, 258, 262, 267, 485, 487, 494–5

L

larger culture (superculture) 30, 34–8, 40, 46, 51, 100, 167, 257, 299, 361, 468

liturgy 157, 216–17

lute 19, 49, 182–83, 293, 316, 334, 341, 343, 385, 389, 398

M

major scale (mode) 36–7, 89, 117, 185, 215, 226, 264, 267, 284, 293, 295

Mass 46, 86, 114, 143, 147, 157, 159, 205, 220, 239, 273, 291–2, 374, 453, 474–5, 491, 500

measure 117, 121, 128, 142, 249, 265, 288–9, 327, 333, 335, 352, 385, 478, 482, 502

meter *see* rhythm

motive 10, 25, 227

movement x, 6, 13–14, 18, 57, 66, 73, 81, 91, 96, 112, 114, 129, 131, 229–30, 235–7, 242–4, 261, 277, 290, 294, 298, 301, 343, 361–2, 367, 374–6, 394, 417, 438, 440, 447–8, 460, 473–4, 482

Muslim *see* Islam

N

Nationalism 38, 150, 213, 128, 230, 235–36, 243–44, 246, 284, 298, 442, 463

Native American iv, ix, xxi, 57, 60, 62–7, 79, 82–4, 90, 92, 95, 119, 121–2, 191–3, 210, 271, 313, 359, 395, 412, 482

      Lakota 3, 26, 65, 74–77, 87, 93, 95

      Pow-wow viii, 87, 901, 92, 94–5, 121–3, 193

Neo-Classical 236, 255, 295

non-Western 19, 144, 149, 167, 206, 308, 459

O

opus (op.) x, 242, 292, 304

opera 361, 376, 387, 390, 393–400, 403, 406, 414, 429, 439, 488, 507

      Chinese opera ii, v, 26, 58, 390, 393–5, 398–9, 439
        also see China/Chinese

      German opera 150, 393

      Italian opera v, 215, 244–5, 251, 255, 400

oral tradition 287, 315

oratorio 220, 230

orchestra ix, x, xii, xiv, 12, 16–17, 28, 50, 55, 167, 179–81, 188–9, 220, 222, 225, 230, 233, 242–3, 247–9, 255, 290, 294, 297–9, 345, 388, 394, 402, 498, 501, 503

overtones 395, 478

P

phrase 101–2, 117, 142, 186, 201, 206, 215, 222, 234, 270, 414

pitch 226–7, 234, 255, 284, 317, 385, 407, 439, 473, 500, 510

plainchant/plainsong *see* chant

polka 27, 96, 339, 351, 483

polymeter *see* rhythm

polyphony 216, 219–20, 222, 227–8, 255

polyrhythms *see* rhythm

Pow-wow (Powwow) *see* Native American

prayer ix, 68, 83, 95, 158–9, 162, 164–5, 168–69, 171–6, 191–4, 200, 206, 328, 332, 367, 386, 430, 432–3

programmatic music v, 247, 249, 298, 302

pulse 81, 88, 124–6, 185, 276, 285, 289, 290, 511

Q

qa'nun 183, 498

quality (tone quality) 194, 422

Qu'ran/Koran *see* Islam

R

raag (rag/raga) 284, 381, 384–6, 388–9, 403, 439, 467–8, 488

ragtime 466, 468, 471–2, 499, 510

rap 100, 124–5, 451

recapitulation 227

recitative 230, 295, 439

reed 401, 422

reggae 80, 84, 86–7, 96, 105, 128, 130, 132, 141–2, 290, 324, 333, 339, 342, 345, 375, 444, 451, 453

Requiem ix, 239

rhythm 8, 13, 15, 17–18, 33, 39, 45–6, 49–50, 52, 74, 77, 80, 96, 98, 116–18, 121–2, 125, 127, 129, 132, 135, 142, 159, 173–4, 180, 185–6, 222, 227, 267, 276–7, 285, 287, 288–92, 302, 323, 325, 327–9, 336–38, 342–3, 345–6, 351, 353–5, 359–60, 364, 373, 375, 384, 386–87

      accents 39, 54, 66, 73, 146, 173, 269, 277, 290–1, 327–8, 337, 345, 351, 395, 415, 462, 446, 470, 473, 483

      backbeat 486

      meter 17, 19, 77, 121, 158, 173, 186, 269, 288–89, 327, 348, 352, 386, 388, 483, 500

      polymeter 289, 291

      polyrhythm 291

      syncopation 291, 466

      tempo 50, 73, 86, 96, 135, 222, 228–9, 243, 264, 276, 290, 299, 352, 388, 400, 407, 417, 471, 498

rhythm and blues 8, 98, 116–18, 121, 125, 127, 142, 291, 325, 327, 336–7, 342, 444, 474, 483, 510

rite 216, 260, 309–10

ritual xxii, 5, 6, 15, 18, 71, 83–4, 89–90, 112, 2172, 229, 232, 290, 308–10, 313, 317, 324–5, 353–6, 361–2, 365, 367, 374, 421, 465 rock (rock n' roll) xxii, 146, 515–2, 156, 158, 211, 223, 226, 233, 244, 249, 255, 290–1, 293, 324, 327, 337, 339, 343–5, 347, 358–9, 375, 386, 466, 473–4, 507

romantic period 234–47

S

Sabat/Sabbath *see* Jewish

Santeria 336, 342, 356

saxophone 49–50, 193, 486

scale 18, 76, 111, 189, 207, 226–7, 230, 240, 264, 269, 284, 400, 439, 478

score 28–9, 55, 225, 242

secular music 213, 465, 493

Sephardic/Sephardim v, x, 183, 261–5, 267–9, 286, 292

solo xi, 346, 385, 424, 466, 472–3, 488, 498

sonata 220, 227, 231, 260

soul 2, 13, 39, 43, 68, 77, 80, 107, 118, 122, 128, 157, 189, 191–2, 194, 196–7, 239, 249–51, 329, 331, 340, 343, 346, 349, 357–8, 378, 386–7, 414, 429–30, 440, 460, 472, 476, 496

strophic form 185, 227

superculture *see* larger culture

swing 38, 120, 213, 217, 290, 447, 462, 465, 470, 472, 475, 480–81

symphony iii, ix, x, 242–3, 249–50, 289–90, 297, 316, 489, 507

syncopation *see* rhythm

T

tala 289, 385–6

tango 19, 292, 340, 352, 498–9

tempo *see* rhythm

tenor 114, 221, 487

texture 8, 19, 23, 33, 45, 50, 80, 89, 92, 181, 199, 210, 226–28, 230, 233, 235, 247, 252, 287, 289–90, 301–2, 317, 327, 346, 364, 400, 407, 436, 451, 466, 470

theme ix, 127, 135, 193, 219, 227, 240, 244, 250, 351, 353, 356, 393, 400, 436, 439, 498, 508

through-composed 89, 227

timbre 33, 49, 52, 174, 202, 233, 300, 387, 407, 422, 511

tonality (tonal music) 172

tone color *see* timbre

tone poem v, 212, 247–48

tonic 157, 160, 221, 226, 473, 483

traditional music x, xi, 45, 79, 287, 324–5, 396, 406–7, 411, 421, 454–5, 482

tuning 316, 510

ud (oud) 17, 19, 39, 98, 183–6, 271, 275, 293, 295, 316–17, 398, 498

unison 77, 121, 228, 355, 378, 412, 414

V

vernacular 127, 205

vibrato 264, 368, 439

vihuela 271, 293, 349

violin 17, 183, 185, 203, 231, 238, 242, 260, 264, 271, 275–6, 281, 293, 298, 349, 385, 401, 488, 500

vocables 67

voice iv, vi, xix, 12, 33, 45, 50, 74, 113, 118, 120, 124, 126–9, 137, 147, 154–5, 157, 159, 165, 172–4, 180–2, 185–6, 194–6, 221–2, 228, 241–2, 245, 257, 264, 268, 271, 275, 300, 306, 315, 325, 331, 333, 344, 352, 358, 365, 400, 406–7, 409, 411, 415, 417–18, 429, 434, 440, 455, 475, 491, 498, 500, 508, 510–11

W

Western music 17, 45, 148, 157, 160, 166–8, 180, 183, 206, 216, 220–2, 226–7, 255, 257, 260, 262, 290, 299, 325, 385–6, 414, 423, 439, 500, 502

world music ii, xx, 56, 65–6, 184, 274, 356, 422, 486, 497

X

xylophone 327, 368, 440

Y

yang 395, 398–99, 440, 490

Z

zither 17, 183–84, 406, 498

zydeco 481–3